# Foucault's Analysis of
# Modern Governmentality

WITHDRAWN

# Foucault's Analysis of Modern Governmentality

## A Critique of Political Reason

Thomas Lemke

Translated by Erik Butler

VERSO
London • New York

This English-language edition first published by Verso 2019
Originally published in German as *Eine Kritik der politischen Vernunft –
Foucaults Analyse der modernen Gouvernementalität*
© Thomas Lemke 2019
Translation © Erik Butler 2019

This translation of this work was funded by Geisteswissenschaften International –
Translation Funding for Work in the Humanities and Social Sciences from Germany,
a joint initiative of the Fritz Thyssen Foundation, the German Federal Foreign
Office, the collecting society VG WORT and the Börsenverein des Deutschen
Buchhandels (German Publishers & Booksellers Association)

1 3 5 7 9 10 8 6 4 2

**Verso**
UK: 6 Meard Street, London W1F 0EG
US: 20 Jay Street, Suite 1010, Brooklyn, NY 11201
versobooks.com

Verso is the imprint of New Left Books

ISBN-13: 978-1-78663-645-4
ISBN-13: 978-1-78873-251-2 (HBK)
ISBN-13: 978-1-78663-643-0 (UK EBK)
ISBN-13: 978-1-78663-644-7 (US EBK)

**British Library Cataloguing in Publication Data**
A catalogue record for this book is available from the British Library

**Library of Congress Cataloging-in-Publication Data**

Names: Lemke, Thomas, author.
Title: A critique of political reason : Foucault's analysis of modern
  governmentality / Thomas Lemke ; translated by Erik Butler.
Other titles: Kritik der politischen Vernunft. English
Description: London ; Brooklyn, NY : Verso, 2019. | Includes bibliographical
  references.
Identifiers: LCCN 2018032852| ISBN 9781786636454 (paperback) | ISBN
  9781786636447 (us ebook)
Subjects: LCSH: Foucault, Michel, 1926-1984—Political and social views. |
  Political science—Philosophy. | BISAC: POLITICAL SCIENCE / History &
  Theory. | POLITICAL SCIENCE / Political Ideologies / Communism &
  Socialism. | POLITICAL SCIENCE / Political Ideologies / Democracy.
Classification: LCC JC261.F68 L4513 2019 | DDC 320.01—dc23
LC record available at https://lccn.loc.gov/2018032852

Typeset in Minion Pro by MJ&N Gavan, Truro, Cornwall
Printed and bound by CPI Group (UK) Ltd, Croydon, CR0 4YY

*A moral system, with axioms, corollaries, and iron logic, and reliable application to every moral dilemma – that is what is demanded of philosophers. [...] A philosopher who hesitates to make such a profession is all the more energetically required to deliver a general principle. If thought does not simply reaffirm the prevalent rules, it must appear yet more self-assured, universal, and authoritative than if it had merely justified what was already in force. You consider the prevailing power unjust; would you rather have no power at all, but chaos? [...] What people cannot endure is the attempt to evade the either/or, the mistrust of abstract principles, steadfastness without a doctrine.*

      – Horkheimer and Adorno, Dialectics of Enlightenment

*One must pass to the other side – the 'good side' – but in order to extract oneself from these mechanisms which make two sides appear, in order to dissolve the false unity, the illusionary 'nature' of this other side with which we have taken sides.*

        – Foucault, 'Non au sexe roi'

# Contents

# Preface to the English-language Edition

Forty years ago, Michel Foucault coined the neologism 'governmentality' (*gouvernementalité*) in his lectures at the Collège de France of 1978 and 1979. The term is derived from the French adjective *gouvernemental*, meaning 'concerning government'. In the lectures, Foucault mobilizes an older understanding of the term. While the word has a purely political meaning today, he shows that up until well into the eighteenth century the problem of government was placed in a more general context. Government was a term discussed not only in political tracts but also in philosophical, religious, medical and pedagogic texts. In addition to management by the state or administration, government also addressed problems of self-control, guidance for the family and for children, management of the household, and directing the soul. Foucault proposes this broad understanding of government that does not conceive of subjectivation and state formation as two independent and separate processes but analyses them from a single analytical perspective, focusing on the rationalities and technologies of governing human beings. In the 1978 lectures Foucault traces the genealogy of governmentality from classical Greek and Roman days, via early Christian pastoral guidance, up to state reason and police science, while the 1979 lectures focus on the study of liberal and neo-liberal forms of government.

For a long time, what Foucault himself called a 'history of "governmentality"' remained largely unknown. The only relevant material he authorized for publication was the talk of 1 February 1978 and two short summaries of the lectures' findings. The complete lecture series at the Collège de France from 1978 and 1979 were only published in 2004, and appeared in English translation some years later. Despite

this extremely difficult editorial situation, Foucault's work on governmentality received a lot of scholarly attention across a large variety
of disciplines. The publication of the collection *The Foucault Effect:
Studies in Governmentality* in 1991 was a significant event in this
respect. This volume, co-edited by Graham Burchell, Colin Gordon
and Peter Miller, presented translations into English of the already
published 1978 lecture and some other important texts by Foucault. It
also made available articles by researchers directly affiliated with Foucault (Daniel Defert, François Ewald, Jacques Donzelot, Robert Castel,
Pasquale Pasquino and Giovanna Procacci) and by scholars from an
Anglo-Saxon background like Colin Gordon, Graham Burchell and Ian
Hacking. *The Foucault Effect* marked the beginning of a huge interest
in Foucault's concept of governmentality. In the following years, many
studies in Great Britain, Australia, New Zealand, the United States and
Canada took their inspiration from Foucault's work on government to
analyse contemporary social and political transformations.

The growing interest in 'governmentality studies' was grounded
in both theory and politics. From the 1990s onwards, many radical
intellectuals turned to Foucauldian concepts as they had become
increasingly dissatisfied with classical forms of critique and analysis
that too often relied on dogmatic political-economic approaches or
reductionist concepts of ideology as 'false consciousness'. Alongside
such altered intellectual and theoretical constellations, interest in Foucault's concept of governmentality also stemmed from the collective
experience of (welfare) state regulatory models and instruments being
displaced by forms of neoliberal government. Studies of governmentality analyse the social dissemination of market-driven solutions and
entrepreneurial patterns not as a diminishing or reduction of state
sovereignty but as a restructuring of governmental techniques and the
rearticulation of identities and subjectivities. Instead of operating with
dichotomies such as power and subjectivity, state and society, ideas and
practices, they look for the systematic ties between rationalities and
technologies of government. Finally, studies of governmentality have
opened up an epistemological-political field that Foucault defined as
the 'politics of truth', investigating the discursive operations and institutional mechanisms through which truth claims are generated and
distributed – and the power effects tied to these truths.

Soon, 'governmentality studies' became a thriving research perspective. Since the turn of the millennium, the concept of governmentality

has no longer been predominantly discussed in the Anglophone world. In Scandinavia, France, Germany and many other countries scholars have also sought to refine and extend Foucault's work on government as a critical tool for analysing political technologies and rationalities in contemporary societies. Today, studies of governmentality continue to flourish, forming a dynamic research field within the social and political sciences and cultural studies. While they are marked by diverse disciplinary orientations and focus on different empirical objects, they are nevertheless informed by a common analytic perspective. Studies of governmentality investigate mechanisms of the conduct of individual and collective bodies, extending from the surveillance of company employees to control practices in public spaces and governing transnational institutions such as the European Union. However, rather than representing a coherent research programme or homogeneous approach, these studies are being carried out by a loose network of researchers using the concept in various ways and with divergent theoretical interests.

When I started working on my PhD thesis in the early 1990s, the research field of 'governmentality studies' was only in its infancy. What prompted me to work on Foucault and governmentality was anchored in a very different constellation, but one that was far from being disconnected from the rise of neoliberal forms of government and the revision of academic and social critique it engendered. As I was interested in the Critical Theory of the Frankfurt School and Marxist theory, deciding to study political science at the Goethe University in Frankfurt seemed a logical step for me in the second half of the 1980s. Apart from classical Critical Theory, I focused especially on the work of Antonio Gramsci, Nicos Poulantzas and the French regulation school, and regularly attended the seminars of Josef Esser, Joachim Hirsch and Alex Demirović, eminent scholars working on materialist state theory (Alex would later become the supervisor of my PhD thesis, Joachim my co-supervisor). In 1990, I went to Paris for six months to prepare a PhD thesis on the work of the French regulationists and to study the French language. It was there that I first encountered the writings of Michel Foucault (starting with *The Order of Discourse*), which were not part of the curriculum in Frankfurt at all. Reading Foucault, I got more and more drawn into a different intellectual cosmos – while simultaneously pursuing the same political and theoretical interests (at least I thought so). I was attracted by Foucault and his concept of genealogy, but struggled with his understanding of critique and power. Back in Frankfurt, I learned that Foucault had provided a 'genealogy of the modern state' in his still unpublished lectures at the Collège de France of 1978 and 1979. Excited by the prospect of reconciling my lasting interest in materialist state theory with Foucault's genealogy of power, I decided to redefine my PhD project into one that would focus on Foucault's notion of government. In 1993, I was back in Paris and regularly visited the Bibliothèque du Saulchoir where the Fonds Michel Foucault was located (today, it is part of the Institut Mémoires de l'Édition Contemporaine in Caen). For several months, from Monday to Friday I listened to the audio tapes that documented Foucault's lectures, making transcripts and going through the archive material. My ambition was to bring Foucault into dialogue with the tradition of Critical Theory I was familiar with, and the result of this critical encounter was the book that finally came out a few years later.

*Eine Kritik der politischen Vernunft: Foucault und die Analyse der modernen Gouvernementalität* was published in 1997 by Argument, a small left-wing publishing house in Hamburg and Berlin. It was based on my PhD thesis submitted in political science at Goethe University in Frankfurt am Main one year before. I thought that the book might sell around 300 copies, the number of intellectuals and academics I estimated would be interested in this account of Foucault and his notion of government. In the 1980s and well into the 1990s, Foucault was not a reference at all in the German social sciences. His work was only discussed – mostly negatively – in philosophy and history, and was not deemed of any analytic or critical value for sociology, political science or anthropology. Fortunately, my calculation proved to be wrong. The book sold extremely well (it is now in its sixth edition), received a large amount of very favourable reviews in academic journals and newspapers, and soon became a widely cited reference for those interested in Foucault's work. *Eine Kritik der politischen Vernunft* initiated and substantially shaped 'governmentality studies' in Germany, and it has become an indispensable resource for German-speaking scholars interested in Foucault's analytics of power.

The book is now more than twenty years old, and the theoretical and academic debates have shifted profoundly since its first edition. This is particularly the case in regard to the reception and appraisal of Foucault's work, which has attracted an enormous amount of attention across disciplinary boundaries in the past two decades. This interest was significantly spurred by comprehensive editorial projects and posthumous publications. In 1994, the *Dits et Ecrits* came out in French, a collection which assembled all shorter texts written by Foucault. Its publication led to a new phase of reception. Texts that had been dispersed or difficult to find are now part of these four volumes, which have been partly or completely translated into other languages. Starting in 1997, the lectures Foucault gave at the Collège de France from 1970 until his death in 1984 were edited and published in French; most of them are now available in English. Today, Michel Foucault is one of the most cited authors in the social sciences and humanities. Once marginalized in academic discourse (at least in Germany), his writings have become central references, which has led to tendencies to canonize and normalize his work. As it is especially Foucault's analytics of government that has found huge interest in many disciplines and witnessed a dynamic reception in the past decades, the question arises of why it might be of interest to read an English translation of a book on the topic published a long time ago.

One possible answer to this question is that *Foucault's Analysis of Modern Governmentality: A Critique of Political Reason* provides an original account of Foucault's analytics of power from 1970 until his death in 1984 that still stands up to contemporary interpretations. The complete argument is presented in English for the first time here, though some of the material appeared in a widely cited article published in *Economy & Society* in 2001 ('The Birth of Bio-Politics: Michel Foucault's Lecture at the Collège de France on Neo-Liberal Governmentality'). The account of Foucault's concept of government has also informed my books *Biopolitics: An Advanced Introduction* (2011) and *Foucault, Governmentality, and Critique* (2011) and several articles, as well as *Governmentality: Current Issues and Future Challenges* (2011), a collection of articles co-edited with Ulrich Bröckling and Susanne Krasmann. *Foucault's Analysis of Modern Governmentality* shows, using material that has still only partly been translated into English, that Foucault revised and further elaborated the 'genealogy of power' in the second half of the 1970s. At the centre of this theoretical reorientation stood the notion of government that guided his research in the following years, situating the question of power in a broader context. First, governmentality mediates between power and subjectivity and makes it possible to investigate how processes of domination are linked to 'technologies of the self' and how forms of political government are articulated with practices of self-government. Second, the problematic of government accounts for the close relations between power and knowledge and helps to elucidate what Foucault in his earlier work called the nexus of 'knowledge-power'.

Furthermore, the book offers a comprehensive and systematic analysis of Foucault's work on government while simultaneously attending to the many lines of thinking he developed. As one of the first monographs to make use of Foucault's lectures, it provides a clear and well-structured exposition that is both theoretically challenging and also accessible for a wider audience. Thus, the book can be read both as an original examination of Foucault's concept of government and as a general introduction to his 'genealogy of power'. Another strength of the book is that it historically and theoretically contextualizes Foucault's lectures at the Collège de France of 1978 and 1979, and shows how the concept of government was taken up in different lines of research in France before it gave rise to 'governmentality studies' in the Anglophone world. Foucault's work inspired the writings of colleagues and collaborators mentioned above, and in turn was informed by their genealogical investigations of insurance technology, social economy, police science and the government of the family. While this work focused on the transformations of governmental technologies in the nineteenth century, historians like Dominique Séglard, Christian Lazzeri, Dominique Reynie and Michel Senellart used the notion of government to analyse state reason and early modern arts of government. The book situates Foucault's work on government within this wider domain of research, making visible lines of connection and shared theoretical interests while avoiding scientific isolationism or the simple story of a solitary genius.

Finally, the book invites the reader to revisit the question of critique. Observing that the activity of critique is mostly informed by a 'juridico-discursive' style of thought focusing on judging and condemning, negating and rejecting, I argue that Foucault outlines an experimental form of critique which comprises two seemingly contradictory dimensions. He conceives of experience as dominant structure and transformative force, as existing background of practices and transcending event, as the object of theoretical inquiry and the objective of moving beyond historical limits (note the double meaning of *expérience* in French as both 'experiment' and 'experience'). In his work on governmentality and in his later writings in general, Foucault wants to give 'a more positive content' to the concept of critique, seeking to expose normative categories, to put them to the test in order to assess and assist the development of a new normative grammar that might make it possible to spell out alternative social forms and modes of subjectivity beyond the juridical horizon. As I see it, both Foucault's desire to develop a vocabulary of critique that distances itself from judgements and his interest in linking politics and ethics take up and extend some ideas also found in the Frankfurt School of Critical Theory (for a more comprehensive argument see my article 'Critique and Experience in Foucault' published 2011 in *Theory, Culture & Society*).

The original German edition would not have been possible without the advice and comments I received from many different individuals. For their invaluable help in locating important archive material I would like to thank Peter Miller, Paul Rabinow, Isabelle Séruzier, Judith Revel and Yves Roussel. Robert Castel, Daniel Defert and Jacques Donzelot helped me to resolve problems with my interpretation of Foucault's work. I would also like to thank those who read and commented on different versions of the manuscript, among them Stefan Wunderlich, Ronald Noppe, Thomas Sablowski, Hans-Peter Krebs, Guido Felhölter, Karin Waringo, Tomke Boenisch, Matthias Wismar, Karin Lotz, Reiner Hartel, Wilhelm Roskamm and especially Celina Rodriguez-Drescher and Annette Prassel.

This English edition is based on the original version of the manuscript. No literature has been added, nor is the argument modified or amended. It would have been an impossible task to incorporate and engage with the secondary literature published in the past twenty years. However, the book is still up to date in terms of the primary sources. While I enjoyed a privileged knowledge of some material for several years (at least up to 2004 when the French edition of Foucault's lectures at the Collège de France of 1978 and 1979 came out), many texts I draw on have since been published, which makes it easier to check and reassess the claims I make in the book. I have only corrected a few obvious mistakes and anachronistic phrases, especially the references to 'unpublished material'. Also, all passages are omitted that exclusively address a German-speaking readership (thus, the German preface is left out for this edition except for the acknowledgements). As the lectures at the Collège de France are available today, I refer to the page numbers instead of the dates the lectures were given (the bibliographic apparatus is updated and contains all lectures now published in English).

I would like to express my gratitude to those who made this English edition possible, especially Stuart Elden who finally convinced me that the translation of the book even after more than twenty years would still make an important contribution to the international debate on Foucault. He and Matthew Hannah wrote the reader's reports, and I would like to thank them both for their generous remarks and for their essential advice. I would also like to thank Verso for taking the risk of translating the book, and Sebastian Budgen for his editorial support of the project. A first attempt to translate the book with the same publisher in 2002 failed, as we did not get funding for the project. This time we were luckier. *Geisteswissenschaften International*, a translation funding programme for German works in the humanities and social sciences set up by the German Publishers and Booksellers Association, kindly agreed to finance the translation into English. Finally, I would also like to thank Erik Butler for his elegant translation of the book into English, Carolin Mezes who helped me to correct some mistakes and to update the bibliographical apparatus, Paul North for his comments on an earlier version of this preface, and Franziska von Verschuer for her comments on the translation and preface as well as her support in correcting the proofs.

I am extremely grateful for the opportunity to present this book to an Anglophone audience, and I am confident that this edition will find an interested readership among scholars, students and the broader public looking for analytic and critical instruments for engaging with the present. My wish is that this 'untimely' book will foster the engagement with Foucault's concept of government and contribute to the ongoing debate on how to use his famous theoretical 'toolbox' to tackle the political and social issues at stake today.

Frankfurt am Main, 27 February 2018
Thomas Lemke

# Introduction

## Paradoxes, Contradictions, Aporias
### The Order of Discourse as
### the Discourse of Order

Several decades after the philosopher's death, Michel Foucault's work continues to spark controversy. In particular, the 'genealogy', or 'analytics', of power that he elaborated provides the object of scholarly and political discussion; by turns, it meets with hearty endorsement and vehement rejection. Simply noting as much already points to a defining feature of his project: it leaves no one indifferent. The intensity of responses makes it clear that Foucault's books strike a nerve in readers. His works raise questions – or promise answers – that concern everyone, and leave no one unaffected.

This is not just because of the everyday nature of the objects Foucault examines. It is not only about the content of the *History of Madness*, *The Birth of the Clinic*, *The Birth of the Prison* or *The History of Sexuality*. The terms, concepts and methodology that the author employs prove equally significant. The way Foucault handles the material – how he arranges and investigates it – poses a challenge and demands that readers take a position, if not a stand. Perhaps more than any other theorist, Foucault has a polarizing effect. His studies have given rise to unusual, and seemingly irreconcilable, lines of battle.

On one side stand those who hold that Foucault's analysis of power continues and promotes projects of social criticism by dismantling hierarchies and processes of political domination. From this perspective, his books are more than historical studies. They afford insight into how power works. Instead of simply providing a self-sufficient, closed reconstruction of historical objects and past events, they are committed to a 'history of the present' (Foucault) and, as such, offer valuable instruments for political and social confrontations in our own day. Such orientation on concrete praxis is evident not just in

Foucault's description of 'theory as a toolkit', but also in his participation in numerous political groups and social movements. Foucault's political engagement spanned a broad field, ranging from anti-racist initiatives to providing information about the situation in prisons, supporting Vietnamese boat people, and advocacy for the Polish labour union *Solidarność*. At the same time, advocates observe, Foucault contributed to critical (self-)reflection on intellectual labour by stressing the political significance of how knowledge is produced, structured and disseminated. In this regard, the 'genealogy of power' stands close to the tradition of critical theory, which aims to analyse and critique social relations of domination.

Conversely, others contend that a host of unsolved problems bedevils the critical potential and political significance of Foucault's work. They adopt an entirely different viewpoint. Granted, Foucault may have been a political activist, but his theoretical project cannot ground such engagement. His analytics of power raises an array of epistemological and normative questions that it cannot answer satisfactorily. The diagnosis holds that Foucault's theoretical agenda is unsuited to developing a critique of modern power mechanisms; if anything, it suspends the possibility of doing so in substantive fashion. The fault lies in the way Foucault conceives power, which he puts in such comprehensive terms that it proves impossible even to imagine a society free from its workings. Thereby, the argument goes, Foucault runs together two ideas: power as the condition for the existence of society, on the one hand, and power as a matter of social asymmetry, on the other. The unresolved tension between critical intent and a neutral conceptualization of power yields any number of paradoxes, contradictions and aporias that make it impossible for Foucault to deliver on the critical claims he advances.

The situation does not amount to a polarized field, with one side directly facing the other, so much as it involves a dividing line that runs on a diagonal. Often, the same theorists stress the critical merits of Foucault's work and its immanent problems, appreciatively noting empirical substance and clear analysis, on the one hand, while disapproving of his rejection of any normative framework, on the other. Furthermore, the analytical instruments enabling insight into the operations of power are what make the critique of power seem obsolete: Foucault achieves a theoretical view that is both detailed and deep – a 'microphysics of power' – only inasmuch as he suspends judgement.

This remarkable constellation provides the starting point for the work at hand: how are such divergent assessments – contradictory and mutually incompatible, in part – of Foucault's work possible? What underlies the ambivalence and irritation that his books prompted? Foucault's analysis of power informs debates on the ideological bases of social domination, as well as theoretical reflections on racism; likewise, it has been enlisted to expand the scope of Western Marxism and feminist discussions of patriarchy. Yet at the same time, Foucault's contribution to the critique of power relations is precisely what has been dismissed. The more time I devoted to the question, the more urgent it seemed to find an answer. Only later did I realize that the answer would come from 'shifting' the question I had posed.

Initially, debates about the implications of Foucault's analysis of power occurred chiefly in the Anglo-American world.[1] At the beginning of the 1980s, Nancy Fraser drew notice to a singular tension in Foucault's writings and explored its ramifications in a series of essays. On the one hand, she observes, Foucault's analyses demonstrate empirical richness and offer vivid accounts of how modern mechanisms of power operate. His genealogical approach has the merit of identifying the decentred and productive nature of power processes; this theoretical setting makes it possible to examine their microphysical and everyday workings. Foucault elaborates a framework that exposes the limitations

---

1. For an overview of this phase of Anglo-Saxon discussion, see Hackman, 'The Foucault Conference' (1982); Simon, 'Foucault in America' (1986); Gordon, 'Foucault en Angleterre' (1986b); Roth, 'Review Essay of Recent Literature on Foucault' (1988); Schneider, 'Eine Philosophie der Kritik' (1988); see also Reid, 'Foucault en Amérique: biographème et kulturkampf' (1994) for more recent reception in the United States.

The question of the political consequences – and ambivalence – of Foucault's work has received attention in English- and German-speaking countries, above all. Accordingly, French (or Italian, Spanish, etc.) discussions are not treated here. Particular aspects of French debates are addressed in the articles by François Boullant and Yves Sintomer; Boullant, 'Michel Foucault à hue et à dia' (1986a); Boullant, 'Que faire du colloque de la CFDT?' (1986b); Sintomer, 'Zwischen Ruhm und Mumifizierung' (1995); see, also, Schneider, 'Eine Philosophie der Kritik' (1988). For reception in Italy and Spain, see Bomio, 'L'effeto Foucault' (1986a); Horn, 'Conference Notes' (1986); as well as Bomio, 'Michel Foucault' (1986b); for Japan, see Bierich, 'Foucault und Japan' (1994).

The account that follows is somewhat long-winded inasmuch as it proceeds by author, and not systematically. However, this effect is intentional: the aim is to identify the schemes of recurrent objections and similar figures of argument. For a thorough discussion of politico-theoretical critiques of Foucault's work, see Schäfer, *Reflektierte Vernunft* (1995), 103–53.

of explanatory schemes along the lines of ideology, economy or the state. His importance is to have provided the empirical and conceptual basis for treating sexuality, the family, schools, medicine and so on as political phenomena.[2]

But, on the other hand, Fraser notes, Foucault's genealogical histo-riography rests on a preliminary methodological decision that holds consequences, too: suspending the questions that would enable dis-tinction between legitimate and illegitimate forms of power. In other words, the same methodological strategies that enable empirically and politically significant accounts of modern forms of power are bur-dened by normative problems. Accordingly, Fraser faults Foucault for not making clear, anywhere in his writings, just how much he seeks to bracket normative issues. Does he mean simply to question the framework of liberal political theory, or is he breaking with matters of justification and legitimacy (*Begründungsfragen*) altogether? It is never clear whether Foucault is simply rejecting a given normative concept, which is clearly defined, or refusing any and every grounding-effort – which amounts to promoting cultural and ethical relativism.[3]

As Fraser puts it, the central problem is as follows: 'How ... did he get from the suspension of the question of the legitimacy of modern power to this engaged critique of bio-power?'[4] Foucault's ter-minology – 'disciplinary society', 'carceral archipelago', 'domination', 'subjugation' and so on – shows that his analysis of power is anything but neutral and disinterested. Yet, at the same time, he fails to provide an answer to key political questions: 'Why is struggle preferable to submission? Why ought domination to be resisted?'[5]

In order to answer these questions, Fraser affirms, it is impossi-ble not to enlist normative criteria. She takes a further step, too, and declares that social critique must not only afford the criteria for dis-tinguishing between better and worse practices, but also be able to separate acceptable forms of resistance from unacceptable ones. It is not enough to observe that change is possible; one must also indi-cate the form it should assume. Fraser insists that theoretical critique can prove politically effective only against the backdrop of better

---

2. Fraser, 'Foucault on Modern Power' (1981), 279–81.
3. Ibid., 275–6.
4. Ibid., 282.
5. Ibid., 283; Fraser, 'Michel Foucault: A "Young Conservative"?' (1985), 182–3.

alternatives. That is precisely what Foucault's writings lack, however: 'I see no hints as to how concretely to interpret "domination", "subjugation", "subjection", et cetera, in some completely new "postliberal" fashion'.[6] As such, without the prospect of any alternatives, Foucault's critique of biopower leads to a 'paradoxical situation': Foucault can neither explain nor justify the normative, political verdicts he constantly pronounces (for instance, that discipline is 'bad').[7]

Fraser is not alone in making this assessment. Charles Taylor also stresses the 'paradoxical' nature of Foucault's work.[8] On the one hand, Foucault's studies seem to belong to the tradition of Critical Theory, inasmuch they formulate a critique of contemporary social relations. But on the other hand, Foucault rejects the very idea of anything good (or better), which has not yet been achieved or is being repressed; instead, he seeks to 'distance himself from the suggestion which would seem inescapably to follow, that the negation or overcoming of these evils promotes a good'.[9] Taylor grants that Foucault's writings afford important insights into modern politics and factor into contemporary struggles. Still, a problem remains inasmuch as Foucault 'adopts a Nietzschean-derived stance of neutrality between the different historical systems of power, and thus seems to neutralize the evaluations which arise out of his analyses'.[10]

Like Fraser, Taylor considers the normative dimension to be neutralized inasmuch as Foucault conceives power independent of freedom or truth. In his eyes, this approach is unviable: 'the notion of power or domination requires some notion of constraint imposed on someone by a process in some way related to human agency. Otherwise the term loses all meaning'.[11] Power may be discussed meaningfully, Taylor contends, only to the extent that it can be distinguished from the desires, interests and intentions on which it is exercised. Since Foucault's works give up on addressing this repressive nature of power, they give up on critique, too. What is more, critique would also require moving beyond the negation of standing circumstances and opening

---

6. Fraser, 'Foucault on Modern Power' (1981), 283.
7. Fraser, 'Michel Foucault: A "Young Conservative"?' (1985), 172–3; see also Fraser, 'Foucault's Body-Language' (1983).
8. Taylor, 'Foucault on Freedom and Truth' (1986), 94, 99.
9. Ibid., 69.
10. Ibid., 79–80.
11. Ibid., 90.

up positive prospects: unmasking power relations not just to destabilize them, but to disclose new, freer and less repressive social forms.[12]

According to Taylor, such a perspective is closed to Foucault. His Nietzschean orientation entails relativism and 'utterly monolithic analyses'[13] that necessarily confound any and every liberatory claim. Inasmuch as each regime of power produces its own truth, change cannot be cast in terms of a strategy of internal reform; it can only be conceived as passage to another regime. This leaves no room for hope, either. Changing from one regime to another brings no gain in freedom or truth, for they must now be redefined and, as such, admit no comparison. Ultimately, Foucault's position entails absurdity: he would be unable to say whether he would rather live in the Song Dynasty in China, under Hammurabi in ancient Babylon, or in the United States of America in the twentieth century.[14]

Michael Walzer also demonstrates concern about Foucault's 'political epistemology'. Like Fraser and Taylor, he diagnoses 'incoherence':[15] Foucault calls for resistance without explaining how it is to be justified or what form it should assume. The problem stems from the relativism he advocates, which deprives his critique of a foundation: 'Foucault believes that truth is relative to its sanctions and knowledge to the constraints that produce it. There would appear to be no independent standpoint, no possibility for the development of critical principles'.[16] According to Walzer, Foucault's thesis that no neutral standpoint exists from which critique may be elaborated – his assumption that every position is always already tied up in power – leads to a variant of anarchism. Yet, in contrast to anarchists (who contend that abolishing power regimes will renew free and independent subjectivity), Foucault cannot arrive at a utopian perspective. Because he considers men and women the products of codes and disciplines, no possibility for envisioning a free individual exists:

And so Foucault's radical abolitionism … is not anarchist so much as nihilist. For on his own arguments, either there will be nothing left at all, nothing visibly human; or new codes and disciplines will be

12. Ibid., 79–80; Taylor, 'Connolly, Foucault, and Truth' (1985), 378–9.
13. Taylor, 'Foucault on Freedom and Truth' (1986), 94.
14. Ibid., 98; Taylor, 'Connolly, Foucault, and Truth' (1985), 382–3.
15. Walzer, 'The Politics of Michel Foucault' (1986), 64–5.
16. Ibid., 64.

produced, and Foucault gives us no reason to expect that these will be any better than the ones we now live with. Nor, for that matter, does he give us any way of knowing what 'better' might mean.[17]

Walzer draws a parallel to Thomas Hobbes's political theory. Hobbes considered the institution of sovereignty to pose the necessary condition for the existence – indeed, the survival – of society. Likewise, Foucault deems discipline indispensable for modern societies. Yet inasmuch as he rejects discipline in every form, the issue of whether rights exist or not interests him as little as it did Hobbes: totalitarian dictatorship and liberal democracy amount to two different forms of the same disciplinary society. For Walzer, the lack of normatively meaningful criteria represents a 'catastrophic weakness'[18] in Foucault's political theory.

Richard Bernstein's discussion also focuses on the role played, and the form taken, by critique in Foucault's work. In a patient analysis, Bernstein identifies an array of interrelated themes, and he seeks to make the author's critical intentions clearer; simultaneously, he analyses each cluster of topics to bring out fundamental but unresolved ethico-political problems that follow from the questions Foucault poses. But although he declares that his reading is 'more sympathetic' than those offered by Fraser and Taylor, Bernstein concludes that Foucault cannot solve the problems he articulates: his theory runs aground because he provides no normative justification for the positions taken. To be sure, when Foucault outlines the limits of traditional theoretical concepts, he opens up new possibilities for critique, illuminates the complex interactions of power mechanisms, and forces us to abandon notions that have become self-evident and reassuring articles of faith. All the same, the limitations of his project are unmistakeable: 'we are left with hard issues that are not resolved. These all cluster about the question of the ethical-philosophical perspective that informs his critique.'[19]

---

17. Ibid., 61.

18. Ibid., 67; see also Walzer, *The Company of Critics* (1988), 261–86.

19. Bernstein, 'Foucault: Critique as a Philosophical Ethos' (1989), 424. This summary listing of contributions to the debate about the 'paradoxical' relationship between power and critique is anything but exhaustive. A number of similar objections are voiced by, e.g., José-Guilherme Merquior and Derek D. Nikolinakos. See Merquior, *Foucault* (1985), esp. 147; Nikolinakos, 'Foucault's Ethical Quandary' (1990), esp. 125.

The problems Anglo-Saxon readers voice about the normative implications of Foucault's work also set the tone of the sociological and philosophical reception in Germany.[20] Time and again, his critique of power has been faulted for 'groundlessness'.[21] On the one hand, the abundance of detail and vividness Foucault offers has met with appreciation. However, suspicion prevails that diagnostic depth has been purchased at the price of normative judgements. Ultimately, Foucault's approach is said to culminate in the 'monism'[22] or, alternately, 'metaphysics'[23] of power. The 'paradox of a strange combination of right-wing epistemology and left-wing praxis'[24] paralyses Foucault's theoretical undertaking – which results from power relations itself and produces power effects of its own. In consequence, Foucault cannot legitimate subjects of resistance or criteria of critique: his theory proves anti-humanistic and irrational.

The interpretation presented by Jürgen Habermas – in particular, his specific assessment of post-war philosophy in France – has shaped both German and international discussion in decisive fashion. Accordingly, the two chapters of *The Philosophical Discourse of Modernity* devoted to Foucault's analysis of power have exercised enormous influence.[25]

---

20. For an overview of the German reception see Eßbach, 'Michel Foucault und die deutsche Linke' (1984); Hesse, 'RFA: une réception critique' (1986); Schneider, 'Eine Philosophie der Kritik' (1988); Eßbach, 'Zum Eigensinn deutscher Foucault-Rezeption' (1989); Liebmann-Schaub, 'Foucault, Alternative Presses, and Alternative Ideology in West Germany' (1989); Dauk, 'Stille Post: Zum Königsweg der Foucaultrezeption' (1989b); Schneider, 'Foucault in Deutschland' (1991); Dinges, 'The Reception of Michel Foucault's Ideas on Social Discipline, Mental Asylums, Hospitals and the Medical Profession in German Historiography' (1994).

21. Engler, 'Macht, Wissen und Freiheit' (1990), 882.

22. Fink-Eitel, 'Michel Foucaults Analytik der Macht' (1980), 64; Fink-Eitel, 'Zwischen Nietzsche und Heidegger: Michel Foucaults "Sexualität und Wahrheit" im Spiegel neuerer Sekundärliteratur' (1990), 369.

23. Breuer, 'Foucaults Theorie der Disziplinargesellschaft' (1987), 324.

24. Münster, 'Zur Kritik des strukturalistischen Ansatzes in den Humanwissenschaften am Beispiel von Michel Foucaults "Archäologie des Wissens"' (1987), 42.

25. Bernhard J. Dotzler and Ingeborg Villinger, as well as Thomas R. Flynn and Dominique Janicaud, identify points where Habermas misinterprets Foucault's work in *The Philosophical Discourse of Modernity*, and they offer a critical analysis of his strategy of argument. Dotzler and Villinger, 'Zwei Kapitel für sich: Notizen zu Habermas' Foucault-Kritik' (1986); Flynn, 'Foucault and the Politics of Postmodernity' (1989), 187–94; Janicaud, 'Rationality, Force and Power: Foucault and Habermas' (1992). Other assessments of the differences between Habermas and Foucault concerning

Here, Habermas undertakes the ambitious project of reconstructing Foucault's intellectual development from his first book up to *The History of Sexuality*. His central contention is that Foucault's work lacks self-reflection: Foucault does 'not [think] genealogically when it comes to his *own* genealogical historiography'.[26] In particular, Habermas focuses on the 'performative contradiction' that occurs inasmuch as Foucault subjects the human sciences to critique in terms of power yet, at the same time, enlists scientific/scholarly criteria to provide their 'genealogy'; in other words, Foucault cannot avoid using the tools of reason when critiquing reason. His lack of attention to the underpinnings of his own position represents a theoretical deficit in Habermas's eyes: 'presentism', 'relativism' and 'partisanship' result when historiography can neither move beyond the horizon of its initial assumptions nor indicate its normative foundations. Ultimately, Foucault's critical project remains caught in 'relativist self-denial' and winds up amounting to 'unholy subjectivism'.[27]

Foucault's genealogical critique, according to Habermas, cannot respond to the simplest political questions. Given his theoretical point of departure, Foucault fails to tell us why we 'should ... muster any resistance at all against this all-pervasive power circulating in the bloodstream of the body of modern society, instead of just adapting ourselves to it'.[28] Inasmuch as power relations, knowledge production, and modes of subjectivation connect in systematic fashion, Foucault's conception of power expands to an extent that compromises its critical potential: where can an impulse for change be found, if every kind of power just gives rise to another kind of power, and any countervailing instance already lies within the horizon of power? This

the question of critique are offered by John Rajchman and Thomas McCarthy. Rajchman notes that Foucault – in contrast to Habermas – breaks with a professorial form of critique and no longer orients himself on the model of alienation, ideology and repression. McCarthy, on the other hand, insists that the effort to find an alternative to the Enlightenment tradition failed, and that Foucault came closer and closer to the theoretical options articulated by Habermas. Rajchman, *Michel Foucault. The Freedom of Philosophy* (1985), esp. 77–95; McCarthy, 'The Critique of Impure Reason: Foucault and the Frankfurt School' (1990). For an excellent account of the debate and an examination of the politico-theoretical positions underlying it, see Kelly, 'Foucault, Habermas, and the Self-Referentiality of Critique' (1994). The third part of this book explores the relationship between Foucault and Habermas at greater length.

26. Habermas, *The Philosophical Discourse of Modernity* (1990), 269.

27. Ibid., 281, 276.

28. Ibid., 283–4.

'paradoxical linking of a positivist attitude with a critical claim'[29] paralyses Foucault's theoretical undertaking: his 'genealogy' can do without power just as little as the human sciences it indicts. In a word, Foucault becomes ensnared in 'contradiction' when he 'contrasts his critique of power with the "analysis of truth" in such a fashion that the former becomes deprived of the normative yardsticks that it would have to borrow from the latter'.[30]

Habermas does not seek to refute Foucault only on theoretical grounds: the 'aporias' he exposes hold political significance. Finding fault with incoherent positions is not enough for the simple reason that Foucault – as Habermas rightly notes – is 'aware' of aporias; he 'sees this dilemma' and, if nothing else, 'is incorruptible enough to admit these incoherences'.[31] Habermas does not take issue with Foucault because of the aporias themselves so much as with the ways he handles them. Because Foucault 'persists' in his contradictory positions, he disqualifies his own theory; worse still, his claims prove politically dangerous inasmuch as they seek to base social criticism on aesthetic rather than rational criteria; this amounts to 'professing irrationalism'.[32]

Habermas contends that Foucault's liberatory project holds reactionary implications. He assigns him a place, along with figures ranging from Georges Bataille to Jacques Derrida, among French 'young conservatives' – a group supposedly waging war against modern society on the basis of feeling, individual experience and imagination.[33] Foucault's work does not belong to Enlightenment tradition so much as it renews well-known themes of the Counter-Enlightenment; it seeks to discredit modernity as a whole by flattening out complexity and ambiguity through a totalizing conception of power.[34] Habermas traces the exaggerated critique of reason back to the politico-intellectual situation in France after May 1968. In this light, Foucault's theoretical positions represent an immoderate reaction to the disappointing results of the May revolt and post-May movements: 'syndromes of reneging on the left'.[35]

29. Ibid., 270.
30. Habermas, 'Taking Aim at the Heart of the Present' (1986), 108.
31. Habermas, *The Philosophical Discourse of Modernity* (1990), 279, 281, 276.
32. Ibid., 278.
33. Habermas, 'Modernity versus Postmodernity' (1981), 13–14.
34. Habermas, *The Philosophical Discourse of Modernity* (1990), 291, 293.
35. Ibid., 414. This also fits with Habermas's comparison of Foucault's work

*The Critique of Power*, by Axel Honneth, stands as one of the most important works on Foucault's conception of power. The book starts out with the socio-theoretical problems identified by Adorno and Horkheimer's Critical Theory, which analyses the process of civilization along the lines of the philosophy of history, in terms of the progressive mastery of nature. Honneth views Foucault's and Habermas's projects, respectively, as attempts to take up the questions opened by *Dialectic of Enlightenment* and resolve its aporias.[36] Both theoretical undertakings are oriented on the social sphere, but they approach it from opposite standpoints: Foucault appeals to strategic action and enlists the paradigm of struggle, whereas Habermas works with the idea of communicative action and the model of consensus.

For Honneth, these efforts represent competing, but unequal, attempts to continue the tradition of Critical Theory. He examines the positions of Adorno, Foucault and Habermas as steps of progressive elucidation, 'stages of reflection in a critical theory of society'. In a Hegelian fashion, he describes a theoretical process that leads from Adorno to Habermas; in this scheme, Foucault occupies an intermediate station. Whereas Adorno failed to make the social sphere a theoretical object, Foucault remained stuck in an incomplete understanding of society. Only Habermas's *Theory of Communicative Action* 'is no longer deprived of the standards in connection with which a critique of the capitalist model of socialization could be indicated'.[37]

Like Habermas, Honneth diagnoses a 'disquieting contradiction' in Foucault's works: 'Whereas the entire framework of Foucault's historical studies rests on moral convictions for which, to a certain extent, a universal validity must inevitably be claimed, one does not find even a hint of these once the theory is systematically explicated'.[38] For both Habermas and Honneth, Foucault wound up becoming ensnared by the 'aporia of a totalising critique of reason'[39] – as did Adorno. As such, he could not do justice to the ambiguity of modern rationality and rationalization (*der moderne Rationalitätsprozess*), nor could he even

with Arnold Gehlen's conservative social theory, which offers a 'similar theoretical perspective'. Ibid., 293.

36. Horkheimer and Adorno, *Dialectic of Enlightenment* (2002).
37. Honneth, *The Critique of Power* (1997b), 302.
38. Honneth, 'Afterword to the Second German Edition' (1997a), xxvi.
39. Honneth, 'Foucault and Adorno: Two Forms of the Critique of Modernity' (1995b), 128.

be sure of his means of critique: the rational content of theoretical argument. Like Habermas, Honneth concludes that Foucault's political engagement lacks a firm foundation. In contrast to Habermas, he does not view this lack of normativity in terms of relativistic self-contradiction so much as the result of the categorical definition of the social field as a battleground. Inasmuch as the model of strategic action by definition excludes normative agreements (legal standards, moral prescriptions, and so on), Foucault's strategy culminates in 'political decisionism'.[40]

Stefan Breuer does not make a favourable assessment, either. Concentrating on the notion of disciplinary society, he voices agreement with Habermas and Honneth; Foucault's problem lies in a 'metaphysics'[41] that makes power the 'universal key' for all social and intellectual phenomena. Thereby, Breuer observes, Foucault's analysis proves reductionist in multiple ways: it can neither account for the ambivalent nature of modern power mechanisms, nor can it address normative questions meaningfully. Although Foucauldian genealogy claims to be objective, 'in truth [it is] pure subjectivism'.[42]

Remarkably, however, Breuer's verdict does not lead him to dismiss Foucault's analyses or his notion of disciplinary society: 'In fact, the concept should be negated and retained simultaneously'.[43] Breuer acknowledges that Foucault's historical studies possess empirical and descriptive merit – which is to be valued all the more, given that Habermas's concept of the lifeworld proves singularly inert and devoid of content. For Breuer, 'disciplinary society' should not be abandoned so much as reformulated with an eye to working through conceptual bottlenecks, which could be articulated more clearly in the framework of a more systematic social theory.[44]

---

40. Honneth, *The Critique of Power* (1997b), 162. That said, Axel Honneth later took some distance from this interpretation and relativized his critique of Foucault's conception of power: 'now I see a few things more clearly than I did in *The Critique of Power*, for instance … For too long, I wanted to interpret Foucault as a theorist of social power, not of historically transcendental power'. Honneth, 'Eine Ergänzung zur Diskursethik' (1995a), 19. Still, it is not clear what Honneth means in making this distinction – that is, what the object of a 'theory of historically transcendental power' is supposed to be.

41. Breuer, 'Foucaults Theorie der Disziplinargesellschaft' (1987), 324.

42. Ibid., 330.

43. Ibid., 331.

44. Ibid., 336; Breuer, 'Sozialdisziplinierung' (1986), 65. One of the most pointed

Were not Foucault's critics right to fault him for the contradictions immanent in his work? Did they not accurately describe the theoretical incoherence of calling for political resistance on the basis of a neutral conception of power? Was it not necessary to dissolve these aporias, contradictions and paradoxes in one direction or another? It seems Foucault had only two possibilities. According to the first line of reasoning, he overcame the problem and affirmed the validity of his neutral conception of power by giving up on critical ambitions: he came to advocate theoretical relativism, no longer seeking to distinguish between better or worse, greater or lesser freedom, or more or less just forms of power. Alternatively, Foucault made his political motives and normative value judgements clear – that is, he gave up on the neutrality he had professed – so that the critical standards of his theoretical engagement became manifest and available for political mobilization. Either-or.

When I first began working on Foucault, I accepted that his analysis of power lacked (self-)reflection. Yet at the same time, I recognized that many reasons existed to call such a diagnosis into question. My engagement with Foucault's 'paradoxes' followed a course that proved paradoxical in its own right: the more obvious and manifest the

---

critiques of Foucault's conception of power comes from the philosopher Manfred Frank. That said, Frank relies almost exclusively on Foucault's inaugural lecture at the Collège de France. Like other critics, he seeks the 'criterion that allowed Foucault to draw from his theory of power precisely *those* consequences that he in general drew, and whose moral engagement we appreciate [...]. In other words, in whose name – through an appeal to whom or what – can he announce a call to arms against the power that manifests itself in exclusion?'. Frank, *What Is Neostructuralism?* (1989), 183. According to Frank, standing relations admit criticism only when a positive standard holds; critique of a given order and acts of political engagement can occur only in the name of a new, different order – which is still an order. Foucault's supposed appeal to non-order is meaningless inasmuch as it is 'a completely characterless formation, similar to the mythical Tohuwabohu, or chaos'. Ibid., 183–4.

This contradiction, Frank continues, shapes Foucault's work until the end; his analysis of power does not deserve to be called 'critical', since it does not attack a determinate condition of order, but order *per se*. Since every order is a system of exclusion, Foucault is averse to order as order. The political consequence of this bearing turns the point of departure into its opposite: since, in principle, Foucault opposes everything, 'in the final analysis' he numbers among the 'preservers of the state'; his position has great similarity with a 'blind flailing (without principles) or running amok'. Ibid., 184. An impulse that starts out critical of power winds up yielding actionism and fatalism since there is nothing left to oppose the omnipresence of power. Ibid., 186; see also Frank, 'On Foucault's Concept of Discourse' (1992), 111–13.

'problem' became, the more I asked myself whether it really posed a problem. There were at least three reasons for my mounting scepticism.

To start with, it is highly improbable that such manifest contradiction escaped Foucault, a subtle thinker attuned to the political consequences of theory. On the contrary – as Habermas has noted (among others) – Foucault was well aware of the paradoxes, even if he never changed his position with regard to them. The question, then, was why he did not abandon his contradictory outlook in order to resolve the problem in one way or another. Can this bearing really be reduced to 'professing irrationalism',[45] or did Foucault have something else in mind – and if so, what? If we accept that Foucault consciously operated with contradictions, what did he want to achieve?

A second reason, connected to the first, involves the kind of critique levelled at Foucault. On the one hand, I felt that contradictions in his work were identified correctly and accurately, on the other hand, I was left with the impression that seeking them out proves unproductive and negative; doing so follows a rationalistic strategy focused on insufficient theoretical reflection and intellectual misprision. Critics intone lamentations about a lack of self-reflection, then sound a call for a coherent theoretical position to resolve the problem. From this perspective, 'disquieting contradictions' represent the product of 'inconsistency'[46] or, alternately, 'the result of Foucault's deficient reflection on the normative conditions of his own writings'[47] – that is, a mistake or shortcoming of his theoretical work.

The third aspect concerns the apparent randomness of the political positions that Foucault adopted. Even though critics propose similar diagnoses, the assessment of his overall politics does not present a clear picture. Foucault has been labelled a 'young conservative';[48] for others, he represents nihilism or anarchism.[49] Axel Honneth views Foucault as standing close to the positivism of systems theory; in contrast, Mark Poster holds that he continued the tradition of Western Marxism 'by other means'.[50] Notwithstanding comparable accounts of problems,

45. Habermas, *The Philosophical Discourse of Modernity* (1990), 278.
46. Taylor, 'Connolly, Foucault, and Truth' (1985), 381.
47. Honneth, 'Afterword to the Second German Edition' (1997a), xxvi.
48. Habermas, 'Modernity versus Postmodernity' (1981), 13.
49. Marti, *Michel Foucault* (1988), 149; Fink-Eitel, *Foucault zur Einführung* (1989), 120–2.
50. Honneth, *The Critique of Power* (1997b), 195–202; Honneth, 'Foucault and

then, readers have ironically enough not arrived at a uniform classification of Foucault's writings. Quite the opposite. Their status remains
unclear – or, better: contradictory.

In this light, the 'problem' of Foucault shifted, and critique fell back
on his critics. Revisiting their interpretations, I found a host of misunderstandings, misreadings and prejudices. A significant portion of
secondary literature consists of longwinded repetitions and common-
places, imputations made solely for polemical reasons, unproductive
modes of engagement, and countless oversimplifications and caricatures. A core problem of much criticism is that it operates with a
conception of power from which Foucault explicitly sought to distance himself; readers attack him on the basis of what he revealed to
be problematic and wished to leave behind.[51] These critics work with
a negative conception focused on constraint, repression, domination
and so on. Yet Foucault wished to demonstrate the political and historical limitations of this very model. As such, it is not Foucault's works
so much as those of his critics that prove singularly self-referential and
sterile: his putative lack of self-reflection means, in fact, that he did not
share their basic theoretical assumptions. For this reason, I switched to
'defending', 'justifying' and 'legitimating' Foucault's theoretical strategy – and looked for problems elsewhere.

Such an approach ultimately proved unsatisfying, too, for it missed
the novel and interesting aspects of Foucault's work. Switching sides
did nothing to change the 'problematic' as a whole. Two reasons made
this conclusion inevitable. First, it was doubtful what theoretical
advantage the position offered: did not my line of argument prove
just as 'rationalistic' as that of Foucault's critics inasmuch as it situated
problems only in the realm of theories and ideas? Was I not doing the
same thing as the critics I wanted to refute when I tried to show that
Foucault had not, in fact, become entangled in contradictions – that

---

Adorno: Two Forms of the Critique of Modernity' (1995b), 131; Poster, *Foucault,
Marxism and History* (1984), 39–40.

51. This is William E. Connolly's main objection to Taylor's interpretation of
Foucault: 'I contend that those such as Taylor who seek to dismiss fundamental fea-
tures of the project by showing it to be incoherent will find it more difficult to make
that charge stick once they are not allowed to precede their critiques of Foucaultian
genealogy by a translation of it into the very formulations it seeks to interrogate'.
Connolly, 'Taylor, Foucault, and Otherness' (1985), 369; see also Rouse, 'Power/
Knowledge' (1994), 104–5. For Taylor's response, see Taylor, 'Connolly, Foucault, and
Truth' (1985).

they 'actually' resulted from how others interpreted him? In seeking to disprove critics, I implicitly accepted their premises – that is, (a) the idea that theory must be free of contradiction; (b) that Foucault's apparent contradictions held only in terms of thought; and (c) that these contradictions discredited any and all political praxis.

The matter opened on to a second problem, perhaps of even greater magnitude. I had sought to promote a 'true', 'correct' and 'accurate' interpretation against hasty and distorted readings. In so doing, I failed to see how I was playing along in the same 'game of truth' that Fraser, Habermas and others had already rehearsed – that I was acknowledging they were right by accepting their rules and seeking to refute them. Precisely inasmuch as I had been looking for the one and only 'truth' – the 'real Foucault' – I could not do justice to what was actually at stake. To be sure, it was right – and important – to work against inadequate interpretations, and there could be no doubt that misreadings of Foucault's works abound. Still, it was not enough *just* to defend the 'real Foucault' against misguided interpreters. Such a strategy of argument presents two key disadvantages: on the one hand, it focuses on 'securing' a certain theoretical terrain – terms and concepts – and, on the other, it continues to move within the same critical horizon it means to escape. In my effort to remain true to Foucault's intuitions by defending them against critics, I had failed to see that this kind of piety is 'the most touching of treasons'.[52] The path did not lead forward, either: it simply turned the problem upside down.

I had to start again. I had overlooked the most obvious and concrete difficulty: a real problem that I had wanted to eliminate altogether without treating it properly. I had set about seeking out hidden truths and obscure points of reference without taking the real difficulty seriously, searching for what others had *overlooked* or disregarded – mistakes and *oversights* – instead of working with what they had found. My point of departure needed to change. Instead of viewing the difficulties I encountered (which others had met with, too) in terms of an intellectual shortcoming, insufficient familiarity with the texts or temporary incomprehension – as obstacles that would vanish in the course of reaching a 'correct' understanding – I needed to make problems and points of trouble the starting point and vector of my own work. After all, Foucault presents difficulties for others, too. As such,

---

52. Foucault, 1984o, 'The Art of Telling the Truth' [1994], 147.

they possess something like an 'objective' status: if so many authors with different theoretical priorities and political orientations agree on the matter, there really is something in Foucault's writings that provokes or produces problems.[53]

It became clearer and clearer to me that aporias, contradictions and paradoxes do not represent a defect or mistake in Foucault's work – something to be explained away or resolved. On the contrary, they constitute its theoretical significance and define its 'problematic'.

Perhaps the question whether Foucault's critics are right or not is a matter of secondary interest – or simply idle. Whether justified or not, criticism exists. It amounts to a (discursive) fact, and the existence, or positivity, of this fact is where I had to start. Surely, I was 'on the right side': misunderstandings and misreadings of Foucault are legion. However, the point is not to be, or prove oneself, right. Nor is the decisive and *final* question whether Foucault 'really' contradicts himself or not – or whether interpreters have read him 'correctly' or not. The key item is the empirical reality that his works have been *perceived* as contradictory.

Thus, the difficulty of situating Foucault politically does not follow from inept or faulty assessments of his work; instead, it is both the result and the goal of the same.[54] Foucault's critics have also read him

---

53. Régis Debray's observation goes in the same direction: 'Foucault's thinking confronts us with the following question: can there be a Foucauldian politics or not?'. Quoted in Kammler, *Michel Foucault: Eine kritische Analyse seines Werks* (1986), 192. It does not matter that Debray's response – like that of most of Foucault's interpreters – proves negative; whether the answer turns out to be positive or negative, the question itself is more important: even Foucault's most vehement critics must presuppose it and acknowledge that it accompanies his work as a whole.

54. Foucault himself put the matter in a nutshell in response to an interviewer's question about his political stance: 'I think I have in fact been situated in most of the squares on the political checkerboard, one after another and sometimes simultaneously: as anarchist, leftist, ostentatious or disguised Marxist, nihilist, explicit or secret anti-Marxist, technocrat in the service of Gaullism, new liberal, etc. An American professor complained that a crypto-Marxist like me was invited to the U.S.A., and I was denounced by the press in Eastern European countries for being an accomplice of the dissidents. None of these descriptions is important by itself; taken together, on the other hand, they mean something. And I must admit that I rather like what they mean. It's true that I prefer not to identify myself and that I'm amused by the diversity of the ways I've been judged and classified. Something tells me that by now a more or less approximate place should have been found for me, after so many efforts in such various directions; and since I obviously can't suspect the competence of the people who are getting muddled up in their divergent judgments, since it isn't possible

'correctly'. Their objections should not be viewed in terms of truth content so much as 'symptoms' – hence the need for a *symptomatic reading* when approaching them.[55]

I decided to make a detour and approach the problem from another direction. A singular dilemma confronted me. On the one hand, there was no doubting that Foucault's analyses of power up to *Discipline and Punish* and the first volume of *The History of Sexuality*, notwithstanding their merits, entail a number of theoretical ambiguities and methodological difficulties; the 'rational core' of many readers' objections involves pointing them out. Yet Foucault always made sure to offer correctives to earlier studies and the methodological instruments employed. He often changed not just the themes and objects of his investigations, but also their conceptual framework. For all that, Foucault's readers rarely address his revisions of the analytic apparatus; alternatively, they present them alongside early theories without qualifying remarks, in order to buttress the thesis that incoherence and contradiction prevail. And so, I faced the problem of identifying differences between Foucault's earlier and later positions, while stressing the overall continuity of his project.

The critique reconstructed above is legitimate and holds practical consequences. Readings that identify contradictions, paradoxes and aporias generally come along with the claim that a 'theoretical break' occurred in Foucault's work, which is supposed to explain his interest in subjectivity and ethics later on in terms of radically abandoning the problematic of power. Such a view assumes that Foucault left behind the framework of his early studies and moved to another theoretical

---

to challenge their inattention or their prejudices, I have to be convinced that their inability to situate me has something to do with me. And no doubt fundamentally it concerns my way of approaching political questions'. Foucault, 1984g, 'Polemics, Politics and Problematizations: An Interview with Michel Foucault', 383–4.

55. A number of the terms employed here (e.g. 'symptomatic reading', 'displacement', 'problematic') go back to the works of Louis Althusser and his specific appropriation of the French history of science: a 'symptomatic reading' aims to reconstruct a 'problematic', that is, the theoretico-analytical frame of reference in which certain terms, concepts, theories, and so on function, which make it possible to formulate problems and pose questions. This means that a problematic achieves definition through both the presence and absence of problems, since it determines not just the space of the thinkable and sayable but also what is unthinkable and unsayable within its rules. Symptomatic reading aims to uncover this 'unthinkable'. On the concept, see e.g., Althusser et al. 2009, 28–32.

terrain: his work on practices of subjectivation is taken as a caesura in his project, the sign and consequence of failure. Commonly, the diagnosis of a 'theoretical break' provides the basis for periodizing his work in three chronological stages: in the 1960s, Foucault pursued the *Archaeology of Knowledge*; in the 1970s, its shortcomings led him to give it up in favour of the *Genealogy of Power*; finally, the *Theory of the Subject* elaborated during the 1980s represents the culmination of his project.

Viewing Foucault's work in three stages – 'archaeology', 'genealogy' and 'subject theory' – offers a number of advantages. In this light, Foucault's theoretical efforts amount to a process of circular progression; his final works touch on the themes of his first studies: the 'death of man' posited early on leads back to the discovery of subjectivity and freedom. This interpretive model takes up Foucault's interest in discontinuity and applies it to his own writings. It presents a thinker who finally returns to where he started, telling the story of an error corrected in old age – the fruit of a process of intellectual 'maturation'.[56]

Such a view requires just as much explanation as it affords. For Foucault, breaks always represent the point of departure, not the end goal – whereas here, only bare fact is noted: changes in analytical tools, the object and period under investigation, style, and so on (in the last volumes of *The History of Sexuality*). None of that stands open to debate. If each book takes on a different analytical object and develops new conceptual instruments, the real question is whether such transformation points to shifting the theoretical terrain altogether: abandoning the problem of power and turning (or, as the case may be, returning) to something else entirely. Does Foucault's interest in ancient ethics and subjectivity amount to leaving behind the analysis of power, which led to a dead end?

In the book at hand, I would like to advance the opposite thesis: Foucault turned to processes of subjectivation as the result, and due consequence, of his interest in practices of power. The shift does not mean abandoning positions so much as offering a corrective in continuity with earlier studies, which it works out in greater detail and

---

56. Fink-Eitel 1989, 104: 'It would appear that he went from the "objectivistic" extreme, during the second and third phase, to the "subjectivistic" extreme in the final one. However, one can also see the course of his theoretical work – and its presumably unconscious logic of development – as ultimately returning, in circular fashion, to where it started.'

relativizes at one and the same time. The theoretical move bears on the conception of power, above all.

More and more, I submit, Foucault recognized that the model of power as strategy – which he had developed at a critical remove from juridical notions and analysed in terms of struggle, war and conquest – led him to identify a host of problems that proved insoluble within this framework. Two problems struck me, above all.

The first concerns the relationship between subjectivity and power. On the one hand, Foucault develops a critique of the effects of power processes on subjects. On the other, he tends to understand subjects as the products of these same mechanisms, stressing how bodies are shaped and ordered – the ways in which confining, disciplinary institutions produce them. If power is what brings about subjects in the first place, this raises the question of how categories such as 'domination', 'constraint' and 'subjugation' still apply. Although Foucault takes distance from liberal notions that view subjective freedom in opposition to state domination, he winds up replacing autonomy with heteronomy that is subject to anonymous strategies of power. It remains unclear what practices of resistance look like – or whether they exist at all.

The second problem lies at the other end of the spectrum of liberal thought: the nature of state power. *Contra* analyses of social macrophenomena, Foucault offered a 'microphysics of power', concentrating on site-specific practices and particular institutions. Yet here, too, he remained within the problematic that he subjected to critique. It is not enough to focus on micropolitical phenomena and understand the state as the result of social relations of power alone. Rather, the question is how the strategic model of power can serve to explain the persistence of power structures and enduring social domination in the form of the 'state'.

Given the shortcomings of both the 'structure-centred' and 'subject-centred' modes of analysing power, Foucault relativized the paradigm of war for analysis of social relations. He had introduced 'Nietzsche's hypothesis' in order to develop a critique of the juridical conception of power, but the limitations of viewing the social field in terms of war became increasingly clear to him.[57] He had struck the outer point of what the 'analytics of power' permits; a change of conceptual framework proved necessary. This meant expanding the analytical tools for

---

57. Foucault, 1977e, '7 January 1976' [2003], 16.

examining subjectivation processes as they relate to forms of social domination: investigating 'how self-control is integrated into the practice of controlling others'.[58]

The following seeks to show how *government* ('gouvernement') stands at the centre of Foucault's 'theoretical shift'.[59] It does not mean that Foucault gave up the genealogy of power and moved on to subjectivity. Instead, 'government' introduced a new analytical dimension; by this means, Foucault explored power relations in terms of 'conduct' – and he did so in order to create a distance from both the model of legality and that of war. The problematic of government represents an effort to resolve the problems these models pose. As a comprehensive scheme, it avoids the traditional separation between micro and macro levels of analysis: 'political government' as practised by the state represents one form of government among others. At the same time, the new paradigm grasps the relationship between governing others ('gouvernement des autres') and modes of self-government ('gouvernement de soi') in a fuller fashion, thereby enabling a more thorough examination of processes of subjectivation.

The concept of government is central for understanding Foucault's work as a whole. Its innovative strength derives from its function as a 'hinge' between different aspects of the overall project. For one, government represents the point of connection for strategic power relations and conditions of domination; in contrast to his earlier works, Foucault now distinguishes between domination and power. Indeed, the government perspective both enables and demands such a distinction.[60] Second, the concept of government mediates between power and subjectivity, shedding light on how techniques of domination connect with 'technologies of the self'.[61]

Given the importance Foucault attaches to the concept of government, it is remarkable how little attention this corrective to the analysis of power has received. In debates about the theoretical and political dimensions of Foucault's writings, the problematic of government is practically absent. Most readers do not even register the structural

---

58. Foucault, 1984n, 'The Concern for Truth' [1988], 258.

59. Foucault, 1984a, *The Use of Pleasure* [1990], 6.

60. Foucault, 1984s, 'The Ethics of the Concern for the Self as a Practice of Freedom' [1997], 295–6.

61. Foucault, 1988b, 'Technologies of the Self', 27; Foucault, 1981c, 'Sexuality and Solitude' [1997], 178.

changes within the 'genealogy of power'; instead, they view new objects and concepts in terms of a move from 'politics' to 'ethics'. One possible reason for this incomplete picture is that Foucault's *History of Sexuality* starts out by focusing on just one side of the problematic: forms of self-relation – or 'technologies of the self'. Premature death prevented the author from elaborating the concept of government in the narrower, political sense. Another reason, which is surely just as important, is that most of the lectures where Foucault elaborated his conception of government remained unpublished when this book first came out. Accordingly, a significant portion of the work at hand reconstructs relevant lectures at the Collège de France from 1978 ('Sécurité, territoire et population') and 1979 ('Naissance de la biopolitique'). One of this book's central aims is to present to the public, for the first time and in systematic fashion, writings and audio recordings that were long absent from discussion.

Analysing power in light of the government problematic takes us back to the question posed at the outset. This 'theoretical shift' lends concrete form and substance to the categories of critique and resistance in Foucault's work. The relationship between power, truth and subjectivity lies at the heart of his interest in the question of government. Foucault's thesis holds that the defining trait of power in the Western world is to 'lead' individuals in agreement and cooperation with a truth that power itself produces. Foucault identifies government as a specific way of exercising power, which does not function by oppression, constraint or ideological distortion so much as the production of truth. In contrast to other forms of power, government does not call for subordination and obedience on the part of individuals; it demands acts of truth. As such, the central question is 'to see how men govern (themselves and others) by the production of truth'.[62]

If what Foucault calls the 'will to truth' has become a feature of political rationality, then this circumstance holds grave consequences for critique that argues by means of contrast and affirms what is right against the backdrop of social conditions that are false – for instance, by focusing on repression or ideology. Such forms of critique enlist a common strategy: they concentrate on the 'falseness' or 'irrationality' of social relations and denounce power in exclusively negative terms – error, distortion, mystification, oppression, violence, constraint and the

---

62. Foucault, 1980b, 'Questions of Method', 79.

like. But, according to Foucault, the political problem is not the untruth of social relations so much as their truth; irrationality poses less difficulties than rationality: the 'negativity' of power is not as important as its 'positivity'. From this perspective, the conception of truth motivating critique offers no solution; instead, it represents a further aspect of the general problem of a society in which knowledge and power stand closely connected. Accordingly, the question Foucault poses does not concern 'the economy of untruth' but 'the politics of truth'.[63]

In contrast to what many critics assume, this question – which animates Foucault's research project – does not lead to relativism, that is, a position for which all truth claims are equal; nor does it mean that only individualistic or voluntarist strategies are possible. It is not enough to hold the mirror of universalism up to Foucault's work and try to expose its 'contradictions', 'paradoxes' or 'aporias' by making it conform to a 'game of truth' whose problems it is meant to reveal. Foucault sought to cultivate a '*limit-attitude*'[64] that refused the logic of either-or by taking distance both from the absolutism of a single truth and from efforts simply to dissolve it.

But it demanded a high price. Foucault's work, which concerns historically variable forms of distinguishing between true and false, remains open to attack to the same extent that it refuses the 'game' of universality and, as such, must occupy a position outside of 'the true'. In this regard, Foucault shared the fate of Mendel, which he describes in *The Order of Discourse*:

> People have often wondered how the botanists or biologists of the nineteenth century managed not to see that what Mendel was saying was true. But it was because Mendel was speaking of objects, applying methods, and placing himself on a theoretical horizon which were alien to the biology of his time. ... Mendel spoke the truth, but he was not 'within the true' of the biological discourses of his time: it was not according to such rules that biological objects and concepts were formed. It needed a complete change of scale, the deployment of a whole new range of objects in biology for Mendel to enter into the true and for his propositions to appear (in large measure) correct. Mendel was a true monster, which meant that science could not speak of him.[65]

---

63. Foucault, 1977k, 'The End of the Monarchy of Sex' [1996], 220.
64. Foucault, 1984d, 'What Is Enlightenment?', 45.
65. Foucault, 1971a, 'The Order of Discourse' [1981], 60–1.

~

This book is divided into three parts. Part I ('The Microphysics of Power') presents the 'genealogy' of the analytics of power. Whereas Foucault's 'archaeology of knowledge' during the 1960s concentrated on the internal rules of discourse formation and largely bracketed the question of how political, social and economic factors determine them, studies after his inaugural address at the Collège de France took up the problem of the 'order of discourse'. The relationship between power processes and forms of knowledge moved to the fore. But at this early stage Foucault still focused on forms of power he would later describe as 'negative': exclusion, constraint, repression, prohibition and so on. The political and social confrontations of May 1968 (in particular, his involvement in the prison movement) led Foucault to recognize the shortcomings of this analytical orientation. In turn, *Discipline and Punish* – the product of theoretical engagement with the penal system – articulated the 'technological' and 'strategic' character of power relations and replaced a juridico-negative conception with a strategico-positive frame of analysis.

The privileged object for the 'microphysics of power' is the disciplinary formation of the individual body; analytical models include war, struggle, battle, conquest and the like. This approach offered the advantage of exposing the weak points of traditional investigative methods, which assess political matters in terms of rights and the law. All the same, it entailed two grave problems, which ultimately led Foucault to abandon 'Nietzsche's hypothesis'. First, the relationship between the microphysics and macrophysics of power, individual disciplinization and social control, remained obscure. Second, a narrow conception of the relationship between subjectivity and power prevailed: analysing individuals in terms of disciplinary training, above all, made even the possibility of resistance appear doubtful.

Part II ('Governmentality') addresses the concept of government, which Foucault introduced in an effort to resolve the problems named above. If the notion of 'biopower' expanded the field of analysis by adding the dimension of population and its regulation, the government problematic went further still: not only did it broaden the analytical terrain, it also changed the underlying mode of conceptualization by defining power – in contradistinction to juridical and strategic models alike – in terms of 'leading' and 'conduct'. In the process, disciplinary power lost its political and theoretical priority: subordinated to techniques of government, it came to represent just one form of power among others.

The government problematic enabled Foucault to respond to theoretico-political problems by making them the point of departure for subsequent studies. On the one hand, he undertook a 'genealogy of the modern state' concentrating on the evolution of modern political rationality. On the other, he performed the 'genealogy of the modern subject', examining how the 'Western' experience of subjectivity came to be constituted. *The History of Sexuality* pursues the latter objective. The former is the focus of lectures at the Collège de France in 1978 and 1979.

The lectures on the 'genealogy of the modern state' investigate the context in which modern, political rationality emerged: Christian pastorship. Foucault's thesis is that techniques of guidance and conduct within Christianity – which developed in a context of religious division and political concentration – subsequently underwent expansion and secularization. Following this model, 'raison d'état' and 'police' represent concrete responses to the question of government's objectives and goals. The governmental rationality they provide is no longer defined religiously but 'politically', and it aims only for growth of the state's strength. The old form of government – whereby the state was self-justified and self-generated – yields to liberal governmentality: now, political reason depends on the economico-rational action of individuals maximizing utility.

When the 'social question' emerged in the nineteenth century, liberal rationality underwent a series of deep-reaching changes. Studies by Foucault's colleagues and collaborators (among others, Robert Castel, Jacques Donzelot, François Ewald and Giovanna Procacci) show how the liberal programme of social regulation increasingly gave way to 'insurance society', which fleshed out economic reason by adding elements of 'social' rationality. The final chapter examines Foucault's reading of neoliberal authors. Especially in the works of the Chicago School, Foucault sees – in addition to a critique of the welfare state – the effort to develop a new kind of governmental rationality that applies economic form to the social field.

Part III ('Politics and Ethics') examines Foucault's 'genealogy of the modern subject' from the vantage point of government as self-conduct. *The History of Sexuality* analyses differences between modes of subjectivation from Greek antiquity and early Christianity in terms of the moral value attached to sexual experience. Foucault's interest, both methodologically and politically, is not to launch an uncritical appeal for (returning to) ancient notions of self-guidance. Instead, 'ethics' refers to how one conducts oneself (and one's life). The focus of investigation is the relationship between subjectivity and power, on the one hand, and the relation between power and truth, on the other.

The concept of government enables Foucault to define the locus of subjectivity and resistance much more clearly than in earlier works; he introduces new terminology and concepts ('technologies of the self', 'practices of freedom' and so on) and distinguishes between power and domination. Inasmuch as (Christian) techniques of guidance are defined by their connection to the production of 'truth', Foucault's politics takes aim at modern forms of subjectivation relying on sub-jectivity that is supposed to be 'true'. A distanced perspective arises from a 'history of truth' that exposes the historicity (and, with it, the contingency and arbitrariness) of the supposedly universal and neces-sary obligations we are enjoined to obey.

The concluding section of this part discusses Foucault's approach in contradistinction to both universalist and relativistic variants of critique on the basis of his engagement with Kant and the question of Enlightenment. Foucault held that his own project belonged to this tradition. In contrast to an 'analytics of the true' – which asks about the formal conditions of rationality – Foucault defined critique as a response to techniques of government: it is both a struggle for truth and a refusal of modes of leadership and conduct. Such critique is not based on knowledge, which it then legitimates, so much as it embodies an 'attitude' or 'ethos'. Foucault provoked so much 'disquiet' precisely because he conceived of another ('unfounded', 'illegitimate') form of critique – one that does not legitimate itself by appealing to law, rights or truth but is self-generated and without any instance of censorship. Foucault 'problematizes' the way that we practise critique today, for-mulating questions that others think they have already answered. In concrete terms, Foucault's 'aporias', 'contradictions' or 'paradoxes' confront us with what is not 'self-evident' about the 'truths' that sup-posedly provide the basis for performing critique in the first place.

Just a few more words on the purposes of this study and the limits of its scope. First and foremost, my aim is to demonstrate a *theoretical* change in Foucault's power analytics, which has received little attention to date. Necessarily, this emphasis means that the *historical* and *political* conditions underlying his theory enter the equation only in a marginal capacity. Undoubtedly, this represents a shortcoming, especially since Foucault always understood the formulation of theory in terms of the 'history of the present' and changed his objects and methods of investigation in response to concrete historical questions and political challenges. Accordingly, it seems hardly justifiable to write a study of Foucault's analytics of power without reflecting on the political and social situation in France, the state of the French left, encounters with 'real socialism' and Eastern European dissidents, the significance of the *nouveaux philosophes*, the emergence of new social movements, and the like.

All the same, I have not followed such a path. For one, I am not interested in providing the 'genealogy of genealogy' – that is, investigating the historical conditions for the emergence of Foucault's project, or pursuing the discursive circumstances that made it possible. My ambition is far more modest. This book focuses on Foucault's texts, seeking to bring out how they relate to each other; as such, politico-historical 'contexts' are taken up peripherally, at most. My goal is to examine the form of critique and methodology that Foucault put to work, because these two aspects – which are closely interrelated – present the greatest problems. More than anything, Foucault's 'toolkit' interests me in regard to contemporary issues.

Another reason I largely avoid addressing historico-political circumstances is that I do not wish to propose a model of derivation and explore how political conditions somehow 'shaped' Foucault's theory – or, conversely, how he 'applied' it. Nor do I wish to ask how Foucault's theory 'expressed itself' in his political commitments in order, say, to argue for 'parallels' between his radical, left-wing interventions and his writings, or the 'logical' (or 'paradoxical', or 'contradictory', etc.) relationship between them.

The reason follows from the object of study. Challenging the notion of a logical link between theory and practice, for the sake of sketching a form of critique that does not rely on abstract necessity so much as the freedom of a practical bearing – however paradoxical it may seem – represents one of Foucault's most significant *theoretical* achievements.

# Part I

## The Microphysics of Power

# 1

# From the Archaeology of Knowledge to the Problem of Power

From its inception, Foucault presented his project as methodologically distinct from both traditional historiography and social criticism. He gave this new approach the programmatic name of *archaeology*. Thus, *Histoire de la folie à l'âge classique*[1] investigated the history of madness and the institutionalization of psychiatry in terms of an 'archaeology of silence'.[2] In works that followed – Foucault's book on illness and the emergence of clinical medicine, then his study of the life sciences, language and economy – the very titles announced the claim: *Naissance de la clinique: une archéologie du regard médical*,[3] and *Les mots et les choses: une archéologie des sciences humaines*.[4] Finally, in *L'Archéologie du savoir*,[5] Foucault sought to define the theoretical profile of his endeavours and identify the specific terrain of research and conceptual innovations that an 'archaeological method' offers.

A look at these books makes it clear that Foucault's concept of archaeology breaks with what the word traditionally conveys. His project does not dig for first beginnings, nor does it represent a philosophical search for hidden meaning. Archaeology does not attempt to 'interpret' historical material with regard to 'causes' at work 'behind' or 'underneath' it. The task is not to 'discover' the intellectual or material principle underlying social phenomena, either. On the contrary, it means casting doubt on the central hypotheses of history conceived

---

1. Foucault, 1961, *History of Madness* [2006].
2. Ibid., xii.
3. Foucault, 1963, *The Birth of the Clinic* [2003].
4. Foucault, 1966a, *The Order of Things* [1994].
5. Foucault, 1969a, *Archaeology of Knowledge* [2002].

in such a way. Archaeology takes aim at history viewed as a system of homogeneous relations constituting a net of causality, which then sets a pattern of derivation or analogy into motion. It rejects the hypothesis that a unified form of historicity exists, guaranteeing the same modes of transformation for economic structures and mentalities, politics and technology. Finally, archaeology denies the postulate that history breaks down into phases or sequences containing their own, inherent principle of coherence.[6]

Counter to conceptions of 'total history', Foucault presents archaeology as a form of 'general history'. Archaeology no longer refers historical material to a dimension of hermeneutic depth that is supposed to grant it meaning. Instead, it 'describes' historical material in its 'superficiality', or 'positivity'. That said, this change of orientation does not mean to give up on the idea of synthesizing varied forms of history in order to arrive at a 'plurality of histories juxtaposed and independent of each other'; rather, the point is 'to determine what form of relation may be legitimately described between these different series; what vertical system they are capable of forming; what interplay of correlation and dominance exists between them'.[7]

Foucault's twofold refusal – to pluralize histories and renounce any attempt at explanation, on the one hand, or to pursue lines of derivation in order to achieve full and 'saturated' explanation, on the other – gives rise to a problem that also represents the condition for calling things into question in the first place: the problem of power. The 'power question' arises because archaeology does not trace historicity back to a single principle, although it does not renounce analysing causality either. But Foucault's early works treat the matter implicitly; for the most part, it remains subordinate to another problem, which constitutes archaeology's specific object: the problem of knowledge.[8]

6. Ibid., 11; Foucault, 1966b, 'The Order of Things' [1996], 13–14; Foucault, 1969c, 'The Archaeology of Knowledge' [1996], 37–8; Foucault, 1969d, 'The Birth of a World' [1996], 66–7; Foucault, 1978c, 'Dialogue on Power', 8–9.

7. Foucault, 1969a, *Archaeology of Knowledge* [2002], 11.

8. Although Foucault's writings during the 1960s share the label of 'archaeology', they offer marked differences in terms of content and method. The book at hand concentrates, above all, on Foucault's effort to develop an archaeology of knowledge at the end of the decade, when he set out to systematize his previous theoretical efforts. For two excellent accounts of Foucault's early works see Kammler, *Michel Foucault: Eine kritische Analyse seines Werks* (1986), 21–124; and Gutting, *Michel Foucault's Archaeology of Scientific Reason* (1989).

## The Problem of Knowledge

Archaeology does not stand alone in subjecting to critique the field of problems and investigation as articulated in traditional, historico-philosophical terms. It represents part of a complex, theoretical confluence whose contours emerged in confrontation with the traditional aims and methods of history and philosophy. Foucault's project for a 'general history' bears the imprint, first, of efforts by scholars working in the context of the *Annales* journal to reorient historical study; second, anti-empiristical tendencies in the history of science contributed to historiographical approaches focused on identifying problems; finally, critical engagement with the hermeneutic tradition represents a solid component of the structuralism debate. Needless to say, these points of overlap and 'vicinity'[9] are matched by fundamental differences, which ensure the autonomy of Foucault's archaeological project.

Like contributors to *Annales*, Foucault locates his theoretical undertaking between socio-economic history and the history of ideas. His methodological approach also works to counter the separation between material practices and immaterial ideas, which underlies traditional historiography; instead, it seeks to determine the 'materialism of the incorporeal'.[10] At the same time, however, Foucault rejected the concept of mentality that some proponents of the 'new historiography' endorsed.[11] His 'history of madness' and 'history of illness' are not organized in terms of mentalities; instead, archaeology situates the field of investigation in the context of the nascent human sciences, which it analyses in terms of changing social and institutional practices.

9. Foucault, 1969a, *Archaeology of Knowledge* [2002], 18.

10. Foucault, 1971a, 'The Order of Discourse' [1981], 69.

11. Chronicling mentalities represents an important research perspective for *Annales* historiography. The concept of mentality (*mentalité*) was developed in contrast to the history of ideas (or 'spirit'); instead of focusing on rarefied matters, the project involves studying everyday aspects of history and thematizing connections between forms of consciousness and material practices. On the journal's own history, working program, interdisciplinary method and critique of traditional forms of historiography, see Honegger, *Schrift und Materie der Geschichte* (1977); Hutton, 'Die Geschichte der Mentalitäten: Eine andere Landkarte der Kulturgeschichte' (1981); Schöttler, 'Mentalitäten, Ideologien, Diskurse' (1988a); Schöttler, 'Sozialgeschichtliches Paradigma und historische Diskursanalyse' (1988b); Burke, *The French Historical Revolution: The Annales School 1929–89* (1990).

To do justice to this research interest, it is necessary to maintain critical distance from projects of the history of mentalities, which work towards a *psychological* understanding of historical problems.[12]

Foucault had to develop a different conception of his object of inquiry in order to free himself from psychological constrictions and situate collective dispositions and modes of behaviour, as well as changes within them, on a more fundamental level. This level is the knowledge (*savoir*) of a society, which provides the background both for 'material practices' and 'ideological forms'; indeed, it is meant to encompass both poles. Foucault introduces *savoir* in contrast to *connaissance* to set his project apart from a subject-centred conception of knowledge. Unlike *connaissance, savoir* does not simply indicate the relationship between the subject (of cognition) and the (real) object; this relationship is not the precondition and point of departure, but itself the product of historical processes:[13]

> In a society, different bodies of learning, philosophical ideas, everyday opinions, but also institutions, commercial practices and police activities, mores – all refer to a certain implicit knowledge (*savoir*) special to this society. This knowledge is profoundly different from the bodies of learning that one can find in scientific books, philosophical theories, and religious justifications, but it is what makes possible at a given moment the appearance of a theory, an opinion, a practice.[14]

------

12. On the problem of the tendency towards psychologism and 'the fuzziness it allows to settle in between this domain and that of economic and political transformations', Donzelot, *The Policing of Families* (1979), xxv; see Schöttler 1988a, 88–93; on Foucault's distance from the 'concept of mentality', see Foucault, 1969a, *Archaeology of Knowledge* [2002], 177; Foucault, 1977m, 'The Confession of the Flesh' [1980], 194; Foucault, 1984g, 'Polemics, Politics and Problematizations: An Interview with Michel Foucault', 388; Donzelot, *The Policing of Families* (1979), xxiv–xxv; Veyne, 'Comment on écrit Rome' (1983); Burke, *The French Historical Revolution: The Annales School 1929–89* (1990), 101–3.

13. Foucault, 1968c, 'On the Archaeology of the Sciences' [1998], 323–33; Foucault, 1980a, 'La poussière et le nuage', 38–39.

14. Foucault, 1966b, 'The Order of Things' [1996], 13. In developing this concept, Foucault pursues a number of theoretico-strategic objectives. First, he means to show that 'knowledge' cannot be boiled down to ideas; likewise, it is not simply a matter of practical application. Instead, knowledge is what makes it possible for certain understandings, institutions and practices to emerge at all. Second, this allows him to avoid the mistake of assigning priority to theory over practice: practices, institutions and theories occupy the same level of analysis. Third, it means 'knowledge' cannot simply be traced back to a causality that precedes it: knowledge and its transformations do

*French epistemology* is characterized by rejecting the classical problematic for developing a critique of knowledge and an interest in processes of knowledge formation. That said, epistemology and archaeology differ in the questions they pose and how knowledge processes are conceptualized. If archaeology finds the 'point of balance of its analysis in the element of *connaissance*',[15] epistemology stands at the 'threshold of scientificity'[16] and asks how this frontier is crossed: how concepts and metaphors are refined so that they finally achieve scientific status. Whereas Foucault takes as his point of departure a more comprehensive concept of knowledge, aiming to neutralize questions of validity, epistemology concerns 'the opposition of truth and error, the rational and the irrational, the obstacle and fecundity, purity and impurity, the scientific and the non-scientific'.[17]

Archaeology and epistemology do not differ only in terms of the fields addressed; a further distinction concerns the *rationalist* constitution of the 'discontinuity' and 'productivity' of knowledge. In an epistemological framework, discontinuity refers to the break between 'scientific' and 'everyday' knowledge. The productivity of scientific insight is supposed to leave behind the 'errors' and 'illusions' of everyday understanding – 'exterminating' or 'destroying' them, and so on. As such, scientific knowledge proves productive to the extent that it breaks with the negativity of everyday understanding. In contrast, archaeology poses the question whether this line of demarcation between science and non-science can be maintained at all. Archaeology is based on the suspicion that the sharp opposition between science and non-science points to a rationalist position which cannot be taken for granted; instead, such a distinction represents the historical result of scientific developments.[18]

---

not result from causal processes; rather, they are what put the complex play of causality into motion in the first place. Foucault, 1969e, 'Titres et travaux', 844.

15. Foucault, 1969a, *Archaeology of Knowledge* [2002], 202.

16. Ibid., 206.

17. Ibid., 210.

18. Needless to say, this short sketch cannot do justice to the significance that the works of Gaston Bachelard and Georges Canguilhem hold for Foucault's theoretical development. Not only did Foucault study under Canguilhem; he also incorporated insights from the history of science into his own works and expanded them. Foucault, 1980d, *Remarks on Marx* [1991], 60–1. For appreciative reference to Bachelard, see Foucault, 1972f, 'Piéger sa propre culture'; for homage to Canguilhem, see Foucault, 1971a, 'The Order of Discourse' [1981], 60; Foucault, 1978a, 'Introduction by

Foucault does not elaborate the concept of knowledge just to take distance from the psychologism inherent in the notion of mentality and epistemological rationalism. He also sets the concept apart from the 'formalism' of *structuralism*.[19] On the one hand, he shares the critical view of constitutive subjectivity formulated by 'structuralist' semiology, psychoanalysis and ethnology, and he acknowledges that the problem holds 'in terms not unlike those' for the field of history.[20] He also likens his archaeological projects to areas where structural analysis has charted its greatest successes: for instance, the psychoanalytic investigation of 'the unconscious of science'[21] or, alternatively,

---

Michel Foucault' [1991]; Foucault, 1985a, 'La vie: l'expérience et la science'; as well as Canguilhem, 'Mort de l'homme ou épuisement du cogito' (1967). A very good reconstruction of Foucault's relation to French epistemology is found in Gutting 1989, 9–54. See, also, Kammler, *Michel Foucault: Eine kritische Analyse seines Werks* (1986), 111–22; Rajchman, *Michel Foucault. The Freedom of Philosophy* (1985), 50–4; Kusch, *Foucault's Strata and Fields* (1991), 24–40. Another study worth consulting is by Dominique Lecourt, who analyses and subjects to critique the works of Bachelard, Canguilhem and Foucault in terms of their contributions to the materialist theory of society. Lecourt, *Pour une Critique de l'Epistémologie* (1972). In contrast, Walter Privitera's claim of a 'filial relationship' between Bachelard and Foucault is exaggerated, as are his efforts to demonstrate how the 'vagueness of some of Foucault's basic, epistemological assumptions' follows from 'the way he employs Bachelardian concepts'. Privitera, *Stilprobleme: Zur Epistemologie Michel Foucaults* (1990), 11, 15.

19. It is difficult to speak of structuralism (or 'poststructuralism' or 'neostructuralism') as a unified school of thought. As such, 'structuralism' should be understood only as shorthand for the formulation of certain problems, or a 'system of echoes'. Foucault, 1969a, *Archaeology of Knowledge* [2002], 12; Deleuze, 'How Do We Recognize Structuralism?' (1998), 282. The shared reference point of these heterogeneous positions and research projects involved rejecting the existentialist historicism and subjectivism of the post-war period – and welcoming the findings of structural linguistics and semiotics, above all. Levi-Strauss's anthropology, the semiology of Barthes and Kristeva, and Lacanian psychoanalysis, are all oriented on the model of language and 'decentre the subject'. That said, this current was not limited to the realm of the sciences; it overlapped with tendencies in the literary works of Blanchot, Bataille, Klossowski and others. Foucault, 1980d, *Remarks on Marx* [1991], 75–6.

On the label of 'structuralism', see Foucault's remark: 'It's for those who use the label to designate very diverse works to say what makes us "structuralists". You know the joke: what's the difference between Bernard Shaw and Charlie Chaplin? There is no difference since they both have a beard, with the exception of Chaplin of course'. Foucault, 1969d, 'The Birth of a World' [1996], 67. For a comprehensive overview of the history of French structuralism, see Dosse, *History of Structuralism, Volume 1* (1997a); Dosse, *History of Structuralism, Volume 2* (1997b).

20. Foucault, 1983e, 'Critical Theory/Intellectual History' [1988], 23.

21. Foucault, 1968a, 'Foucault Responds to Sartre' [1996], 54.

the 'ethnology ... of our rationality'.[22] On the other hand, however, Foucault stresses that archaeology in no way seeks the 'transfer to the field of history, and more particularly to the history of knowledge ..., a structuralist method'.[23]

Foucault made this distancing gesture for good reason. Towards the end of the 1960s, he grew increasingly aware of the ambivalent status of the structuralist critique of autonomous subjectivity. On the whole, thinkers performing such a critique were not concerned with calling the human sciences into question so much as articulating the implicit and transparent rationality of the same. Even though this meant denouncing humanism as 'ideology', 'dissolving' standing notions of 'man' still served to guarantee the scientificity of the human sciences. On this score, Althusser's[24] rigorous distinction between bourgeois-humanist ideology and Marxist science overlapped with Levi-Strauss's effort to elaborate an anthropology analogous to the natural sciences. Structuralists had no doubt about the role of knowledge or the status of science itself. The latter were conceived 'neutrally' – and therefore exempt from being called into question. This problem, however, is precisely what interested Foucault: the 'birth of the human sciences' and their articulations alongside 'non-scientific' social and institutional practices shaped *Madness and Civilization*, *The Birth of the Clinic* and *The Order of Things*.[25]

Many structuralist works of the period lacked appreciation for this problematic because they conceived of language as a homogeneous and closed system of meanings, which was supposed to be the same for everyone. In consequence, the assumption prevailed that linguistic utterances possess the same significance irrespective of context or

---

22. Foucault, 1969b, 'Who Are You, Professor Foucault?' [1999], 91.

23. Foucault, 1969a, *Archaeology of Knowledge* [2002], 16–17; Foucault, 1966a, *The Order of Things* [1994], 15–16.

24. Foucault was a student and friend of Althusser, and his intellectual journey may hardly be understood without the latter's critique of existentialism and phenomenology – as well as the distance he took from the Hegelian model of history. Like Althusser, Foucault understood his work as a response to theoretical and political problems of Marxist praxis: the 'crisis of Marxism' (Althusser). Accordingly, the theoretical positions of these two thinkers will be treated at multiple points in the study at hand.

On Foucault's relationship with Althusser, see 1966d, 516; 1967, 21; 1971c, 170; 1980d, 56–60; Kammler 1986, 91–7; Schenkel and Vries 1989, esp. 27–45; Eribon 1994a, 313–52. Also, see 'Subjectivation and Subjugation' in Chapter 5.

25. Gordon, 'Other Inquisitions' (1979), 24; Gordon, 'Afterword' (1980), 230–1.

speakers' social positions. Research sought out the general structures underlying languages, myths, systems of kinship and so on. On the one hand, this meant – *contra* subject-centred history and concepts of continuous time and space – foregrounding structural determinants, ahistoricity and patterns that defy change. But, at the same time, on a deeper level, such projects demonstrated agreement with the humanism they combated inasmuch as they assumed the existence of an unchanging human nature and universal laws.[26]

The dualism underlying the separation between a linguistic system and concrete language use (*langue/parole*) – which opposes pure (suprahistorical) possibility to (historical) realization – leads to a deficient notion of historicity. It sets the realm of structure apart from a historical dimension where relations possible in combinatory terms are held in reserve, some of which are then realized in actual fact. In this light, the historical process represents a matter of spelling out an alphabet that is always already at hand, as if the latter were not subject to change, too: structure comes to stand outside of time and assume the role of an 'unmoved mover'; by this logic, the 'event' stands as a particular instantiation of the general system, but the system itself is not analysed in its own unicity. On the basis of such juxtaposition of universal and anonymous linguistic rules, on the one hand, and historical and concrete language use, on the other, the investigative focus falls on general conditions of possibility and formal analysis.[27] Foucault indicates that his position differs from structuralist efforts on this point: 'Unlike those who are labelled "structuralists", I am not really interested in the formal possibilities afforded by a system such as language'; instead, 'language can be analysed in terms of its formal properties only on the condition of taking account of its concrete functioning'.[28]

---

26. Macdonell, *Theories of Discourse: An Introduction* (1986), 11–12.

27. Foucault, 1967, 'The Discourse of History' [1996], 27–8; Foucault, 1968b, 'History, Discourse and Discontinuity' [1972], 233–4.

28. Foucault, 1967, 'The Discourse of History' [1996], 28; Foucault, 1969a, *Archaeology of Knowledge* [2002], 67. That said, such a perspective does not mesh with the charge of 'contempt for history' levelled at structuralism by Marxists, in particular. The criticism voiced by Alfred Schmidt and Urs Jaeggi in Germany, E.P. Thompson and Raymond Williams in Great Britain, and Jean-Paul Sartre and Henri Lefebvre in France did not concern the opposition between abstract structures and concrete historical praxis so much as inadequate 'mediation' between these terms. Indeed, these critics held that structuralism had 'lost sight of the historical dialectic between possibility and reality' inasmuch as it was no longer oriented on an 'objectively reasonable

He introduces the term *discourse* to mark out his specific field of interest, defined as a 'group of statements that belong to a single system of formation'.[29] At the same time – as in the case of 'archaeology' – Foucault changes the 'current usage' of the word entirely and gives it a 'quite different meaning'.[30] The term *discourse* derives from structural linguistics; conventionally, it occupies a position between two poles of analysis, *langue* and *parole*, and plays a mediating role. But Foucault is not concerned with the 'middle ground' between a generative system of rules and instances of concrete application, nor is he interested in an intermediary realm between the social and symbolic spheres. Instead, his understanding of 'discourse' heralds a turn away from the field of linguistic analysis: 'discourse is constituted by the difference at a given epoch between what one could say correctly at one period (according to the rules of grammar and those of logic) and what is actually said'.[31]

Foucault has no interest in determining a system of possible utterances – a 'finite body of rules that authorises an infinite number of performances'.[32] Instead, he devotes his attention to those linguistic sequences that have, in fact, been formulated. In contrast to structuralist

---

state of society'. Schmidt, 'Der strukturalistische Angriff auf die Geschichte' (1969), 204, 202; see also Schmidt, *Geschichte und Struktur* (1971); Jaeggi, *Ordnung und Chaos* (1970). Consequently, structuralism was faulted on the grounds of what it sought to overcome: the dichotomy between structure and action and the problem of objectivity and subjectivity. Sartre expresses this view when he speaks of a 'permanent contradiction between a practico-inert structure and the human being who discovers that he is conditioned by it. Each generation adopts a different stance towards these structures, and such distance is what makes it possible to change the structures themselves. [...] It's always a matter of thinking for or against history'. Sartre, 'Jean-Paul Sartre répond' (1966), 94–5; see Foucault, 1966b, 'The Order of Things' [1996], 14; Foucault, 1968a, 'Foucault Responds to Sartre' [1996], 54–6. For all that, the problem does not concern thinking for or against history so much as it concerns thinking historically. Foucault occupies the same ground as structuralist authors inasmuch as he rejects a humanist conception of history. For him, structuralism does not attack history, but a certain defective conception: 'what is being bewailed with such vehemence is not the disappearance of history, but the eclipse of that form of history that was secretly, but entirely, related to the synthetic activity of the subject'. Foucault, 1969a, *Archaeology of Knowledge* [2002], 15; see also Foucault, 1969c, 'The Archaeology of Knowledge' [1996], 59.

29. Foucault, 1969a, *Archaeology of Knowledge* [2002], 121.

30. Ibid., 121.

31. Foucault, 1968b, 'History, Discourse and Discontinuity' [1972], 238; Kocyba, 'Eine reine Beschreibung diskursiver Ereignisse' (1988), 33; Barrett, *The Politics of Truth* (1991), 126–9.

32. Foucault, 1969a, *Archaeology of Knowledge* [2002], 30.

analysis, archaeology does not explore the general laws governing construction within discourses, but the historical conditions of their actual emergence and existence:

> The question posed by language analysis of some discursive fact or other is always: according to what rules has a particular statement been made, and consequently according to what rules could other similar statements be made? The description of the events of discourse poses a quite different question: how is it that one particular statement appeared rather than another?[33]

In other words, archaeology does not ask about the general conditions that make utterances possible so much as the historical conditions for them to exist at all. *The Archaeology of Knowledge*,[34] which appeared at the end of the 1960s, outlines Foucault's differences with structuralism on the one hand and hermeneutics on the other.

## A General Theory of Discursive Practices

*The Archaeology of Knowledge* announces an ambitious theoretical undertaking: to develop a method of research 'beyond structuralism and hermeneutics'.[35] For all that, Foucault's effort to carve out his own terrain remains stuck at a halfway point inasmuch as the position he articulates still lies within the horizon of linguistic analysis.[36]

---

33. Ibid., 30; see also Foucault, 1969d, 'The Birth of a World' [1996], 66; Foucault, 1979n, 'Discussion at Stanford'.

34. *The Archaeology of Knowledge* seeks to clarify this theoretical question, as do two shorter texts where Foucault seeks to define the specificity of the 'archaeological method'. Foucault, 1968b, 'History, Discourse and Discontinuity' [1972]; Foucault, 1968c, 'On the Archaeology of the Sciences' [1998].

35. Dreyfus and Rabinow, *Michel Foucault: Beyond Structuralism and Hermeneutics* (1983).

36. A host of problems arose in the wake of *The Archaeology of Knowledge* concerning, among other things, the difference between science and ideology, how to account for historical change, the analysis of subjectivity and so on. The study at hand concentrates on one of them (which, moreover, is sketched only in preliminary fashion): the connection between discursive and non-discursive relations. For a thorough account of the theoretico-strategic stakes and methodological aspects of Foucault's archaeological project, see Lecourt, *Pour une Critique de l'Épistémologie* (1972), 77–105; Dreyfus and Rabinow, *Michel Foucault: Beyond Structuralism and*

The problem is evident in the object archaeology assigns itself. The utterance (*énoncé*) stands at the centre of discourse analysis, yet it also points to a social 'context'. Grammatical sentences or logical propositions, as manifestations of *langue* (that is, realizations of a linguistic system), are unlimited in principle. In contrast, Foucault 'sets out to establish a law of rarity': his project 'is based on the principle that *everything* is never said'.[37] Analysing utterances starts with the infinite plenitude of linguistic elements' combinatory possibilities, but it bears on the gap separating 'what is actually said' from statements that are 'theoretically' possible. The objective is to seek out 'the principle of rarefication or at least of non-filling of the field of possible formulations'.[38]

This distinction enables Foucault to focus theory on the problem of determining and defining utterances. The utterance is 'not ... a structure (that is, a group of relations between variable elements ... authorizing a possibly infinite number of concrete models)'[39] – and certainly not the result of a subjective, semantic operation – so much as a 'function'. What is it, then, that conditions utterances and makes them solidify into discourses? The particularity of the utterance is constituted by a twofold demarcation. On the one hand, it represents a discursive event, and, 'like every event', it is 'unique'. On the other hand, the utterance stands open to 'repetition, transformation, and reactivation'.[40] Archaeology seeks to identify the rules of such formation and transformation. Against this background, discourse analysis means to lay hold of 'other forms of regularity, other types of relations'.[41]

In order to define the object of archaeology more precisely and open the way for empirical research, Foucault must concretize the 'equivocal

*Hermeneutics* (1983), 44–100; Kammler, *Michel Foucault: Eine kritische Analyse seines Werks* (1986), 69–124; Kögler, *Michel Foucault* (1994), 60–8.

37. Foucault, 1969a, *Archaeology of Knowledge* [2002], 134.
38. Ibid., 134.
39. Ibid., 97.
40. Ibid., 31.
41. Ibid., 32. Clemens Kammler has formulated this problem of archaeology as follows: 'Taking distance from structuralism (semiology) and hermeneutics holds two consequences for discourse analysis. It must define "rules" that do not constitute a (quasi-) transcendental instance in relation to their manifestations; it must isolate "events" (utterances) that are simultaneously unique, repeatable, and transcendental, but without the conditions of repeatability/transformability being transcendental – without the uniqueness of events resulting from subjective meaning-attribution'. Kammler, *Michel Foucault: Eine kritische Analyse seines Werks* (1986), 80.

meaning'[42] of his conception of discourse; he has to indicate what separates it from non-discourse (and connects these two elements). To this end, he distinguishes between relations that are *discursive* and two other kinds: first, *primary* or *'real'* relations ('which, independently of all discourse or all object of discourse, may be described between institutions, techniques, social forms, etc.'), and, second, *secondary* or *'reflexive'* relations that play out within discourse (i.e. subjects' self-reflective definition of their own behaviour).[43] Foucault makes the distinction in order to avoid equating 'discursive practice' and 'interiority' ('secondary relations', in his parlance), as has traditionally occurred. He seeks to overcome a topical conception that pictures interaction between discourse and non-discourse as a hierarchical opposition concerning, for example, being and consciousness, practice and theory, or material reality and appearance. Instead, Foucault conceives discourse in non-hierarchical terms, whereby it represents one practice among others.[44] He describes a space constituted by primary (real), secondary (reflexive) and discursive practices simultaneously. This, however, only formulates the task for a 'general theory'[45] of discursive practices. 'The problem is to reveal the specificity of these … relations, and their interplay with the other two kinds'.[46] Indeed, *The Archaeology of Knowledge* does not examine the problem in systematic fashion. If anything, Foucault brackets it inasmuch as he presents the field of utterances as 'a practical domain that is autonomous (although dependent), and which can be described at its own level (although it must be articulated on something other than itself)'.[47]

Foucault offers a singular response to the problem of the 'permeability of a discourse' or the *'switch* of events'[48] – that is, how non-discursive factors are 'inscribed' in discourses. He refuses 'to see in discourse the surface of the symbolic projection of events or processes that are situated elsewhere', and, for this reason, he 'suspends … causal

---

42. Foucault, 1969a, *Archaeology of Knowledge* [2002], 120.

43. Ibid., 49; see also Foucault, 1968b, 'History, Discourse and Discontinuity' [1972], 236.

44. Foucault, 1969a, *Archaeology of Knowledge* [2002], 49–50; Foucault, 1966b, 'The Order of Things' [1996], 14.

45. Foucault, 1969a, *Archaeology of Knowledge* [2002], 74, 175.

46. Ibid., 50.

47. Ibid., 137.

48. Ibid., 184; translation modified.

analysis.'[49] Yet at the same time, discursive practices are supposed to depend on non-discursive ones. Foucault's 'solution', then, is to say that discourses achieve priority through the practical organization of primary and secondary relations:

> When one speaks of a system of formation, one does not only mean the juxtaposition, coexistence, or interaction of heterogeneous elements (institutions, techniques, social groups, perceptual organizations, relations between various discourses), but also the relation that is established between them – and in a well determined form – by discursive practice.[50]

Since Foucault wishes to take the 'positivity' of discourse seriously, he cannot appeal to the rules 'behind' discursive facts that permit them to exist. Instead, he must locate their efficacy elsewhere: 'within the dimension of discourse'.[51] Systems of formation do not originate in the realm of ideas or mentalities, nor do they arise from social or economic points of determination. They 'reside in discourse itself'.[52] But, in order to account for both the 'rarity' (or 'poverty')[53] of utterance-events and discursive immanence, Foucault revises the status of discursive rules of formation: he turns descriptive regularity into a set of prescriptive rules. Rejecting both objective laws and subjective ascriptions of meaning, his only way out is to present the regular patterns observed in discourse formations as the conditions for their existence.[54]

---

49. Ibid., 182.

50. Ibid., 80–1; Dreyfus and Rabinow, *Michel Foucault: Beyond Structuralism and Hermeneutics* (1983), 63.

51. Ibid., 85.

52. Ibid., 82.

53. Ibid., 135.

54. Like Dominique Lecourt, Hubert L. Dreyfus and Paul Rabinow have described the '"archaeological" circle': Lecourt, *Pour une Critique de l'Epistémologie* (1972), 122. 'The result is the strange notion of regularities which regulate themselves. Since the regularity of discursive practices seem to be the result of their being governed, determined, and controlled, while they are assumed to be autonomous, the archaeologist must attribute causal efficiency to the very rules which describe these practices' systematicity'. Dreyfus and Rabinow, *Michel Foucault: Beyond Structuralism and Hermeneutics* (1983), 84–5; see also Kammler, *Michel Foucault: Eine kritische Analyse seines Werks* (1986), 155–6; Macdonell, *Theories of Discourse: An Introduction* (1986), 94–6.

This methodological decision holds a fatal consequence. Foucault contends that the regularity of utterances does not derive from extra-discursive practices; rather, it follows from differential positions within discourse, and discourses generate their own principles of determination. As such, he comes close to returning to the primacy of the sign posited by structuralism. In other words, Foucault draws near to the view with regard to which he started out developing a critique.

> But to analyse a discursive formation is to seek the law of that poverty, it is to weight it up, and to determine its specific form. In one sense, therefore, it is to weigh the 'value' of statements. A value that is not defined by their truth, that is not gauged by the presence of a secret content; but which characterizes their place, their capacity for circulation and exchange, their possibility of transformation, not only in the economy of discourse, but, more generally, in the administration of scarce resources.[55]

With that, 'in one sense', Foucault succumbs to the 'formalist illusion' for which he has faulted structuralism: 'that is, … imagining that these laws of construction are at the same time and with full title the conditions of existence'.[56] The archaeological project reaches an impasse. To find a way out from this dead end, it needs a different foundation: to locate determinative principles in a context that does not rely on linguistic analysis. 'The archaeology of the human sciences has to be established through studying the mechanisms of power which have invested human bodies, acts and forms of behaviour'.[57]

In due course, Foucault came to concentrate on a question he formulated in *The Archaeology of Knowledge* but did not work through: 'the question of power'.[58]

---

55. Foucault, 1969a, *Archaeology of Knowledge* [2002], 135–6.
56. Foucault, 1968c, 'On the Archaeology of the Sciences' [1998], 330.
57. Foucault, 1975g, 'Body/Power' [1980], 61.
58. Foucault, 1969a, *Archaeology of Knowledge* [2002], 136. For Foucault's observation that archaeological problems may also 'be taken up later elsewhere, in a different way, at a higher level, or using different methods' see Foucault, 1969a, *Archaeology of Knowledge* [2002], 229.

## Discourse and Power

Foucault's inaugural lecture at the Collège de France, where he received a chair in 1970, is entitled *The Order of Discourse*. It focuses on the relationship between non-discursive procedures, forms of regulation and coercive mechanisms that produce and proliferate discourse. In contrast to works to date, however, Foucault does not emphasize discursive order as such so much as strategies of limitation and restriction that determine and define this order as an order. The point of departure is the hypothesis

> that in every society the production of discourse is at once controlled, selected, organized and redistributed by a certain number of procedures whose role is to ward off its powers and dangers, to gain mastery over its chance events, to evade its ponderous, formidable materiality.[59]

Foucault identifies three basic modalities for regulating discourse in bourgeois societies. The first type operates with the distinction between what is permitted and what is forbidden; hereby, prescriptions, penal norms and taboos circumscribe the realm of possibility. The second instrument of regulation establishes an opposition between what counts as rational and what counts as irrational – the 'mad', on the one hand, and those who move within the space of what qualifies as socially 'reasonable', on the other. The third principle works by way of the difference between true and false, enjoining subjects to produce true discourses and constantly assessing enunciations in terms of truth content.[60]

But even though Foucault incorporates social practices more than he did in his archaeological writings, the lecture proves limited in its innovative potential. The main reason is that he thematizes power only along the lines of external 'exclusion' and inner 'rarefaction'.[61]

---

59. Foucault, 1971a, 'The Order of Discourse' [1981], 52.

60. Ibid., 52–6. Foucault identifies the distinction between true and false – the 'will to truth' – as the central element regulating discourse because it comes to prevail over other procedural forms in the course of history. Ibid., 54–5. Like judgements of reason, prohibitions must appeal to sociological, medical, and psychological knowledge and fit themselves out with the attribute of 'truth'. In thematizing connections between truth and power, the significance of Nietzsche's work is already evident – which will prove central to Foucault's further theoretical evolution.

61. Foucault distinguishes between mechanisms of exclusion that rely on a non-discursive, institutional basis and internal procedures of rarefaction such as

Conceptualizing the relations between power and discourse in this way gives rise to a question that is impossible to answer in the framework chosen. As Foucault proceeds, one can only wonder what is being repressed, rarefied and regulated: to what 'danger' – or, alternately, 'chance events' and 'ponderous and formidable materiality'[62] – does 'discursive "policing"'[63] respond?

The weakness of this line of argument lies in its analytical indecision. On the one hand, Foucault speaks of how 'prohibitions, barriers, thresholds and limits [have] been set up to master, at least partly, the great proliferation of discourse in order to remove from its richness its most dangerous part, and in order to organize its disorder according to figures which dodge what is most uncontrollable about it'.[64] It follows that he must assume the existence of a discourse preceding mechanisms of regulation and ordering. On the other hand, he contests the thesis that, over and beyond systems of rarefaction, 'there reigns a vast unlimited discourse, continuous and silent, which is quelled and repressed by them and which has the task of raising up by restoring the power of speech to it'.[65]

Foucault cannot free himself from the idea of 'wild exteriority'[66] – of which he had previously developed an elegant critique:

> No doubt there is in our society, and, I imagine, in all others, but following a different outline and different rhythms, a profound logophobia, a sort of mute terror against these events, against this mass of things said, against the surging up at all these statements, against all that could be violent, discontinuous, pugnacious, disorderly as well, and perilous about them – against this great incessant and disordered buzzing of discourse.[67]

---

commentary, authorial prerogative and the organization of knowledge in disciplines. Ibid., 56–61. A third modality involves regulating speaking subjects' access to discourse. In this context, he includes 'ritual', which determines the specific qualifications necessary for participation in discourse; 'societies of discourse', where privileged forms of knowledge circulate; 'doctrine'; and, finally, 'social appropriations of discourse', in which the educational system plays a key role. Ibid., 61–4.

62. Ibid., 52.
63. Ibid., 61.
64. Ibid., 66.
65. Ibid., 66.
66. Ibid., 61.
67. Ibid., 66.

The theoretical problem that such a construction poses does not stem from its universal-historical ambition alone. Nor does it derive from the fact that the need for ordering mechanisms is justified on the basis of a quasi-anthropological 'dumb fear' – or that it rests, more or less explicitly, on a vitalism that sets the creative power of discourse in opposition to a regulating and restrictive police force. Rather, the decisive shortcoming is to equate the positivity and productivity of discourses with their 'restrictive and constraining function'.[68] If discourses are not located outside of power processes and do not precede them before being suppressed, repressed, regulated, etc., then – Foucault's preliminary and inadequate answer goes – they are in fact characterized by their coercive character. Since the exclusion (or suppression) of other forms of enunciation represents a condition for the constitution of discourses, the conditions of their organization coincide with their conditions of existence: order per se is power and constraint.[69]

As such, *The Order of Discourse* remains situated within the archaeological programme, even though the emphasis shifts from the pole of discourse to that of power. If *The Archaeology of Knowledge* made its point of departure the 'illusion of autonomous discourse' (Dreyfus and Rabinow) – which realizes non-discursive, determinative rules within discourses themselves – *The Order of Discourse* assimilates discursive formations to non-discursive practices and, in so doing, equates processes of rarefaction and exclusion with the very structure of discourses. In either case, the strategy for solving the problem proves insufficient: the texts simply attach a different prefix to the same operation.[70]

In fact, Foucault quickly abandoned this perspective – which, he

---

68. Ibid., 61.

69. Dreyfus and Rabinow, *Michel Foucault: Beyond Structuralism and Hermeneutics* (1983), 104–5; Kammler, *Michel Foucault: Eine kritische Analyse seines Werks* (1986), 135–7.

70. Thus, it is not surprising that Foucault later deemed the underlying idea inadequate and declared that he would 'gladly throw it overboard': 'I think that in *The Order of Discourse* I conflated two concepts, or rather that for what I take to be a legitimate problem (that of articulating the data of discourse with the mechanisms of power) I provided an inadequate solution. It was a piece I wrote at a moment of transition. Till then, it seems to me, I accepted the traditional conception of power as an essential judicial mechanism, as that which lays down the law, which prohibits, which refuses, and which has a whole range of negative effects: exclusion, rejection, denial, obstruction, occultation, etc. Now I believe that conception to be inadequate'. Foucault, 1977i, 'The History of Sexuality' [1980], 183.

recognized, 'might seem to identify the relations of power to discourse with negative mechanisms of selection'.[71] Thus, *The Order of Discourse* does not sketch a programme to be carried out so much as it represents a transitional text. It stands as Foucault's effort to systematize his studies to date and reorient his focus. It opens up the problematics of power by asking how discourses are to be determined and defined – and then closes the book on them again by conceiving this relation in negative terms. Soon, taking critical distance from the archaeological method, Foucault would elaborate another conception of the relations between knowledge and power, concentrating less on negativity and restriction than on positivity and productivity.

---

71. Ibid., 184.

# 2

## The Genealogy of Power

You are evidently referring to what Genet told me one day about prisons. During the war he was in prison at the Santé and he had to be transferred to the Palais de Justice in order to be sentenced; at that time the custom was to handcuff the prisoners two-by-two to lead them to the Palais de Justice; just as Genet was about to be handcuffed to another prisoner, the latter asked the guard, 'Who is this guy you're handcuffing me to?' and the guard replied: 'It's a thief'. The other prisoner stiffened at that point and said, 'No, I'm a political prisoner, I'm a Communist, I won't be handcuffed with a thief'. And Genet said to me that from that day on, with regard to all forms of political movements and actions that we have known in France, he has had not merely a distrust, but a certain contempt.[1]

Foucault's work during the 1970s shows a pronounced shift of accent with respect to the methodological approach of the 1960s. Archaeology had concentrated on analysing discursive formations by placing the utterance front and centre; for the most part, this meant neglecting its social, economic and political conditions as non-discursive factors. Foucault's critique of simplistic conceptions of causality and his rejection of historico-philosophical modes of explanation led him to treat the problem of determination on a more theoretical level. However,

what was lacking here was this problem of the 'discursive regime', of the effects of power peculiar to the play of statements. I confused this

---

1. Foucault, 1974b, 'Michel Foucault on Attica' [1991], 31.

too much with systematicity, theoretical form, or something like a paradigm. This same central problem of power, which at that time I had not yet properly isolated, emerges in two very different aspects at the point of junction of *Madness and Civilization* and *The Order of Things*.[2]

What archaeology had determined only in negative terms now received its own weight. In addition to analysing the immanent regularity and positivity of discourses, Foucault introduces a method of investigation that explicitly examines their external conditions, restrictions and institutionalization. Borrowing from Nietzsche, he calls this method *genealogy*.[3] Like archaeology, genealogy is 'a form of history which can account for the constitution of knowledges, discourses, domains of objects etc., without having to make reference to a subject'.[4] The difference lies in the perspective: in contrast to archaeology, the point of reference in genealogy 'should not be ... the great model of language and signs, but ... that of war and battle'.[5]

---

2. Foucault, 1977d, 'Truth and Power' [1984], 55; see also Deleuze, *Foucault* (1988), 31.

3. Genealogy is systematically presented in the 1971 essay, 'Nietzsche, Genealogy, History'. Foucault, 1971b, 'Nietzsche, Genealogy, History' [1984]. By way of the concepts of *Herkunft* (descent) and *Entstehung* (emergence), Foucault sets 'effective history' (Nietzsche) in opposition to analysis along the lines of the philosophy of history and vulgar materialism. The essay holds theoretical significance for Foucault's further studies, especially because it defines, for the first time, the body as the object of power practices and the focus of genealogy: 'The body is the inscribed surface of events (traced by language and dissolved by ideas) [...]. Genealogy, as an analysis of descent, is thus situated within the articulation of the body and history. Its task is to expose a body totally imprinted by history and the process of history's destruction of the body'. Ibid., 83. For Foucault, then, genealogy in the Nietzschean sense is not a philosophico-theoretical undertaking, but a kind of medical diagnosis. It bears on conscious acts less than bodily processes. The genealogist resembles a doctor 'who plunges to make a diagnosis and to state its difference'; ibid., 90; the doctor metaphor also occurs in Foucault, 1971b, 'Nietzsche, la généalogie, l'histoire' [1984], 80; Foucault, 1972e, 'I problemi della cultura' [1996], 95. On Nietzsche's 'presence' in Foucault's work, see Foucault, 1971h, 'The Will to Knowledge' [1997], 13–14; Foucault, 1975f, 'Prison Talk' [1980], 53; Foucault, 1972e, 'An Historian of Culture' [1996], 97–8; Foucault, 1973d, 'Le monde est un grand asile', 434; Foucault, 1974c, 'Truth and Juridical Forms' [2000], 5–12; Rippel and Münkler, 'Der Diskurs und die Macht' (1982), 115–24; Dauk, *Denken als Ethos und Methode* (1989a), 93–9; Allen, 'Government in Foucault' (1991), 421–5.

4. Foucault, 1977d, 'Truth and Power' [1984], 59.

5. Ibid., 56. It is no coincidence that this methodological reorientation was attended by a growing disinterest for, or 'weariness' with, literary-theoretical problems. Foucault, 1971e, 'Je perçois l'intolerable', 203. As Judith Revel has shown,

Thereby, the problem of power sets the course for Foucault's work. What proves decisive is not the general, (socio-)philosophical and speculative question concerning the essence, or nature, of power so much as the task of investigating processes at work in the contemporary world, both historically and concretely. This focus follows from Foucault's judgement that he still has not examined power processes' actual mode of functioning or their specific quality adequately. This deficit not only represents a theoretical lack. It also articulates a political problem.

> Isn't this difficulty of finding adequate forms of struggle a result of the fact that we continue to ignore the problem of power? After all, we had to wait until the nineteenth century before we began to understand the nature of exploitation, and to this day, we have yet to fully comprehend the nature of power … The question of power remains a total enigma. Who exercises power? And in what sphere? We now know with reasonable certainty who exploits others, who receives the profits, which people are involved, and we know how these funds are reinvested. But as for power … We know that it is not in the hands of those who govern. But, of course, the idea of the 'ruling class' has never received an adequate formulation.[6]

The central problem, then, is that 'power' does not pose a problem at all. Paradoxically, the question of power as the key concept of the political sphere has fallen 'outside the field of political analysis'.[7] Power

---

Foucault's numerous literary studies throughout the 1960s were hardly 'peripheral' works. They were central to his overall project, and in two ways. For one, literary texts by Roussel, Klossowski, Bataille and others enabled Foucault to free himself from the premises of subject philosophy. Second, they seemed to make it possible to hear voices that had been excluded from the Western 'order of discourse'. As such, Foucault's discussions of literature permitted him to escape the consequences he had drawn elsewhere. *History of Madness* investigates the constitution of modern reason; in contrast, Foucault's literary-theoretical writings offer a form of resistance 'transgressing' the limits of discourse while respecting the rules of language. At the same time, such a 'division of labor' led Foucault to turn away from literary-theoretical lines of inquiry more and more: how can literary praxis be combined with collective praxis, how is it possible to tie this rather 'theoretical' and 'abstract' form of resistance with political movements? Ibid., 203; see also Foucault, 1977j, 'Lives of Infamous Men' [2000]; Revel, 'Scolies de Michel Foucault (1992), esp. 75–87.
   6. Foucault, 1972b, 'Intellectuals and Power' [1977], 212–13.
   7. Foucault, 1977d, 'Truth and Power' [1984], 58.

has not been perceived as a phenomenon in its own right, constituting a distinct field of investigation; instead, it has received attention
with respect to legal legitimacy and economic functionality – in terms
of freedom and sovereignty, or class domination and reproduction.
Consequently, power processes have been derived from more fundamental social structures (whether politico-legal or economic in nature)
without having been investigated in terms of how power operates:

> To put it very simply, psychiatric internment, the mental normalization
> of individuals, and penal institutions have no doubt a fairly limited
> importance if one is only looking for their economic significance. On
> the other hand, they are undoubtedly essential to the general function-
> ing of the wheels of power.[8]

This diagnosis also determines the theoretical standpoint of the *genealogy of power*: Foucault understands his work as a continuation of
the 'critique of political economy' under the conditions of a 'crisis
of Marxism'. Marx made the problem of exploitation 'visible' and
showed – counter to classical economic theory – the political nature
of relations of production that seem to be private.[9] Likewise, Foucault
'discovers' the problem of power by elaborating the 'productivity of
power' *contra* traditional political theory. This 'discovery' did occur in
the wake of a historical event that revealed the inadequacy of standing
analytical instruments and forms of conceptualization, i.e. the essentialist and economistic tendencies of Marxist theories. 'This task could
only begin after 1968, that is to say, on the basis of daily struggles at
the grass-roots level'.[10]

---

8. Ibid., 58.

9. Marx, *Capital: A Critique of Political Economy* (1976).

10. Foucault, 1977d, 'Truth and Power' [1984], 58; see also Donzelot, 'La misère
de la culture politique' (1978). Examining Foucault's work against the backdrop of
the 'limits' of Marxist theory and politics, Barry Smart identifies, besides the waning
appeal of Soviet socialism, three theoretical problems: the premise that economic
factors prove decisive 'in the final instance', insufficient attention to the interrelationship between politics and power and the claim to scientificity. Smart, *Foucault,
Marxism and Critique* (1983), esp. 4–31; see also Laclau, 'Diskurs, Hegemonie und
Politik' (1982); Buci-Glucksmann, 'Formen der Politik und Konzeptionen der Macht'
(1982).

## 'Daily Struggles at the Grass-Roots Level': May 1968

May 1968 marks a crossroad in Foucault's work in many ways.[11] For the first time, universities and educational institutions became the privileged site for political and social struggles; how knowledge is put into circulation came to the fore.[12] In this setting, the political question emerged about the relationship between knowledge and power: the 'economy of knowledge'. 'How does the appropriation and distribution of knowledge occur? How can knowledge take its place in society, develop within it, mobilize its forces, and subordinate itself to an economic system?'.[13]

The key significance of May 1968, then, is to have exposed the organization and distribution of knowledge as a political process. At the same time, another change occurred when (spontaneous) forms of mass protest emerged outside established political institutions on the left – and, in part, against them. Such protest revealed the unexpected vulnerability of the capitalist system in one of the most centralized bourgeois democracies; moreover, participants had the experience of a counter-power that was not organized hierarchically.[14] May events

---

11. Foucault pointed repeatedly to the significance of May 1968 for his work. Foucault, 1975h, 'Talk Show' [1996], 133–4; Foucault, 1977i, 'The History of Sexuality' [1980], 183; Foucault, 1980d, *Remarks on Marx* [1991], 138–40; Foucault, 1983h, 'An Ethics of Pleasure' [1996], 375; Foucault, 1984g, 'Polemics, Politics and Problematizations', 386. In this context, I am less interested in the originality of his position than in situating it in a politico-theoretical context. See Foucault's remarks on the 'question of power': 'I don't think I was the first to pose the question. On the contrary, I'm struck by the difficulty I had in formulating it. When I think back now, I ask myself what else it was that I was talking about, in *Madness and Civilization* [*History of Madness*] or *The Birth of the Clinic*, but power? Yet I'm perfectly aware that I scarcely ever used the word and never had such a field of analysis at my disposal. I can say that this was an incapacity linked undoubtedly with the political situation we found ourselves in'. Foucault, 1977d, 'Truth and Power' [1984], 57.

12. Foucault, 1971f, 'Revolutionary Action: "Until Now"' [1977], 219–21.

13. Foucault, 1970a, 'Le piège de Vincennes', 71. For Foucault, May 1968 exposed how the mediation and transmission of knowledge functions as repression on two scores: excluding some from acquiring knowledge and imposing on others a regime that discounts alternative forms of knowledge. From this perspective, the university and student life do not represent a space of freedom outside of, and in opposition to, economic calculations of utility and political constraints; instead, they form a continuum with other forms of exclusion and instruments of repression. Foucault, 1971d, 'A Conversation with Michel Foucault', 193–6; Foucault, 1971f, 'Revolutionary Action: "Until Now"' [1977], 222–5; Foucault, 1975h, 'Talk Show' [1996], 135–6; Macdonell, *Theories of Discourse: An Introduction* (1986), 12–21.

14. Foucault, 1971f, 'Revolutionary Action: "Until Now"' [1977], 232.

occurred outside the traditional political frame of reference inasmuch as they could not be conceived simply as a matter of class struggle. On the contrary: the coalition formed by students and workers could be broken only through the combined efforts of the Gaullist government and communist union CGT, which enjoined its members to return to their workplaces. In the words of André Glucksmann, many held that the 'restraint exercised by the Communist leadership ... was even more effective than governmental resistance'. Undoubtedly, the role played by the Communist Party (PCF) and the CGT in putting down the May revolt was a kind of revelation for all who associated these organizations with radical and progressive politics. In consequence, critical intellectuals distanced themselves more and more from party communism. The PCF became a 'revolutionary party ... determined not to make a revolution' (Jean-Paul Sartre).[15]

This negative assessment was further compounded in August 1968, when the Prague Spring was put down by violent means and the PCF discredited. Following these experiences, Foucault and other left-wing intellectuals wondered whether the 'conservative influence'[16] of the PCF represented more than a problem of unfavourable circumstances or bad strategy. Many thinkers began to seek out dogmatic elements in Marxist theory. In particular, the emergence of new social subjects and themes of political discussion – equal rights for women, ecological opposition to nuclear power, rights for sexual minorities and so on – posed a problem. Many were dissatisfied by the Marxist tendency to understand such issues in terms of class politics and examine them only along these lines. Because of standing distinctions between the 'primary and secondary contradictions' of capitalism, other 'fronts' received attention in terms of conflict within the sphere of production; they were not evaluated politically and theoretically in their own right.[17]

---

15. The assessments of Glucksmann and Sartre are quoted in Smart 1983, 7, and Kritzman 1988, 10. For an account of the relation between left-wing intellectuals and the French Communist Party (PCF) before and after May 1968, see Descombes, *Le même et l'autre* (1979), 155–9; Schoch, *Marxismus in Frankreich seit 1945* (1980), 128–67; Judt, *Marxism and the French Left* (1986), 169–98; Poster, *Foucault, Marxism and History* (1984), 1–43. For Foucault's own view of the PCF's dominance during the 1960s, see Foucault, 1977d, 'Truth and Power' [1984], 52–3.

16. Foucault, 1971d, 'A Conversation with Michel Foucault', 196.

17. '[O]n the one hand, an effort that was very widely asserted, to ask politics a whole series of questions that were not traditionally a part of its statutory domain

May 1968 marked a break, and not just for Foucault. It became increasingly clear that the ways communist organizations had responded to events and social movements did not result from mistaken strategy alone. They connected with Marxist theory as it stood. In this respect, what happened in the period following 1968 was 'profoundly anti-Marxist'.[18]

At the same time, events offered more than a lesson that resistance must occur on a larger scale than a single organization. Political confrontations also made it plain that power defies centralization. How else could revolutionary efforts have failed, given their breadth and the weakness of the state apparatus? To account for the outcome, it was not enough to analyse the 'repressive state apparatus'; it was equally necessary to examine the extent to which 'ideological state apparatuses' had intervened in order to secure, reproduce or constitute domination.[19] Nor was it possible to continue to separate economic

---

(questions about women, about relations between the sexes, about medicine, about mental illness, about the environment, about minorities, about delinquency); and on the other hand, a desire to rewrite all these problems in the vocabulary of a theory that was derived more or less directly from Marxism'. Foucault, 1984g, 'Polemics, Politics and Problematizations: An Interview with Michel Foucault', 385–6.

18. Foucault, 1975g, 'Body/Power' [1980], 57.

19. The term 'ideological state apparatus' (ISA, in contradistinction to 'repressive state apparatus') stems from Althusser, who develops the concept especially in 'Ideology and Ideological State Apparatuses' (1969). (The overall manuscript from which the essay is taken was published in 1995 as *On the Reproduction of Capitalism*.) Althusser's distinction is analytical: the police and military not only exercise physical repression, but also mediate 'values'; by the same token, school, church, family, and so on may operate by way of physical violence in addition to psychic coercion. For Althusser, the significance of ISAs is that they organize 'voluntary subordination'; in consequence, a direct use of force proves necessary only in exceptional instances. Drawing on Gramsci, Althusser locates the 'material existence of ... ideology' not in ideas and consciousness but in material practices and rituals; accordingly, he defines ideology in terms 'of "constituting" concrete individuals as subjects'. Althusser, 'Ideology and Ideological State Apparatuses (Notes Towards an Investigation)' (2001), 166, 171; Althusser, *On the Reproduction of Capitalism* (2014); see also Schenkel and de Vries, *Umleitung oder: Wie heißt Bruno mit Nachnamen?* (1989), 27–33.

Among other advantages it offers, this conception of ideology breaks with the notion of 'false consciousness' and thematizes the productive role played by ideological processes within social practices of power. In other words, Althusser reformulates the reproduction of relations of production as a question. That said, this conception of ideology poses problems, too. For one, Althusser concentrates on the sites of ideology production (the ISAs) more than the mechanism of production. Second, and in contrast to Gramsci, he approaches the problem of ideology from the side of the state, which is supposed to colonize social power. But these problems

factors, on the one hand, from political and ideological factors, on the other – a distinction founded on the hierarchical and dichotomous model of base and superstructure. After May 1968, a new historical stage came into view, 'where struggles in the factories are linked more than they used to be with struggles outside the factories (concerning housing, the question of the "quality of life", etc.); where it is recognized that the general ideological struggle is an integral part of the political struggle'.[20]

Nor was 1968 just the year of May protests and the Prague Spring. It was also the high-water mark of the Vietnam War and the Chinese Cultural Revolution – which likewise signalled a process of upheaval or 'political opening'.[21] It was now possible, *contra* traditional understandings of politics, to 'politicize' more and more issues and fields of engagement – to challenge the borders between the private and the political, and, ultimately, to call into question the meaning of 'the political' itself. When asked whether the prison movement was really a 'political movement', Foucault replied that the site of politics had shifted:

> isn't that one of the decisive features of all political movements today: the discovery that the most everyday things in life – how one eats, feeds oneself, a worker's relationship to his employer, the way one loves, how sexuality is suppressed, familial coercion, the ban on abortion – that all this is political? Making all of this the object of collective action, that's politics today. And so, the political or nonpolitical nature of an action is no longer determined by its goal, but through the ways and means that objects, problems, fears, and suffering get politicized – everything the nineteenth-century political tradition in Europe had banished as unworthy of political action.[22]

In other words, Foucault defines the political less on the basis of a privileged object (e.g. the sphere of production or the state) than in terms of a certain mode of collective action. It may bear on the productive sphere just as readily as relations between the sexes

---

notwithstanding, Althusser's line of questioning set the course for many courses of investigation – including Foucault's 'genealogy of power'.
20. Foucault, 1974b, 'Michel Foucault on Attica' [1991], 31.
21. Foucault, 1977d, 'Truth and Power' [1984], 53.
22. Foucault, 1973c, 'Prisons et révoltes dans les prisons', 428.

or living conditions; the matter does not concern the aims of collective action so much as its form. It is no accident that the prison movement, which questioned the distinction between 'political' and 'non-political' inmates, brought the issue into focus; naturally, it had proven extremely difficult for prisoners to organize collective action and develop a political praxis. At the intersection of both these problems the Groupe d'Information sur les Prisons, or GIP, organized by Foucault and others, set to work.[23]

## Le Groupe d'Information sur les Prisons

In the social upheaval following the May events, more than a hundred left-wing radicals (for the most part, Maoists) were sentenced to jail terms. At first, demands were voiced along traditional, left-wing lines: in 1970, the Maoist Gauche prolétarienne demanded that their comrades be recognized as 'political prisoners'. Before long, however, the incarcerated Maoists recognized that they had made a 'political mistake' inasmuch as 'the ... elimination of common-law prisoners was part of the system of political elimination of which they were themselves the victims'.[24]

By claiming the status of 'political' prisoners, in contradistinction to 'ordinary' or 'social' ones, they had made their own a category of bourgeois criminal law and, at the same time, accepted a form of jurisprudence that only seems unpolitical. They had failed to recognize that the very distinction they took up represents a solid component of bourgeois relations of domination: 'it is, after all, the bourgeois class that, for political reasons and on a basis of its political power, defined

---

23. On the history of the prison movement and the GIP, see Foucault, 1979l, 'Louis Appert'; Foucault, 1980e, 'Toujours les prisons'; Defert and Donzelot, 'La charnière des prisons' (1976); Deleuze, 'Foucault and the Prison (1986b); Gandal, 'Intellectual Work as a Political Tool: The Example of Michel Foucault' (1986); Perrot, 'La leçon des ténèbres: Michel Foucault et la prison' (1986); Eribon, *Michel Foucault* (1991). The GIP was not the only group pursuing intellectual-critical engagement along these lines. The Groupe d'Information sur la Santé (GIS), founded by Foucault and others, examined power effects in the health sector and the political function of medicine in a bourgeois-capitalist society. See Foucault, 1972i, 'Medicine et lutte des classes'; Foucault, 1973f, 'Summoned to Court' [2000]; Castel, 'Les aventures de la pratique' (1986).

24. Foucault, 1974b, 'Michel Foucault on Attica' [1991], 32.

what is called common law'; in other words: 'It is from the point of view of property that there are thieves and stealing'.[25]

Initially, the struggle against the sentences and conditions of imprisonment took the form of hunger strikes (September 1970 and January–February 1971) and demonstrations. On 9 January 1971, justice minister Pleven set up a commission charged with developing a 'special constitution' (meant to avoid the term 'political constitution') for prisons. That same day – together with Jean-Marie Domenach, the publisher of the journal *Esprit*, and the historian Pierre Vidal-Naquet – Foucault announced the founding of the GIP. Above all, the group included intellectuals (among others, Daniel Defert, Gilles Deleuze, Jacques Donzelot, Robert Castel and Jacques Rancière). Nevertheless, its aims and modes of engagement sharply differed from traditional forms of intellectual activism.

The GIP's principal activities involved the publication of a journal and organizing press conferences and demonstrations. That said, the goal was not simply to 'raise awareness' or 'change minds'. The group sought both to address the social function and institutional forms of punishment and to account for how consciousness is materialized, i.e. 'lived', in concrete practices.

> If it were a question of raising consciousness, we could simply publish newspapers and books, or attempt to win over a radio or television producer. We wish to attack an institution at the point where it culminates and reveals itself in a simple and basic ideology, in the notions of good and evil, innocence and guilt. We wish to change this ideology which is experienced through those dense institutional layers where it has been invested, crystallized, and reproduced. More simply, humanism is based on the desire to change the ideological system without altering institutions; and reformers wish to change the institution without touching the ideological system. Revolutionary action, on the contrary, is defined as the simultaneous agitation of consciousness and institutions.[26]

---

25. Foucault, 1972d, 'On Popular Justice: A Discussion with Maoists' [1980], 36; Foucault, 1974b, 'Michel Foucault on Attica' [1991], 32; see also Defert and Donzelot, 'La charnière des prisons' (1976); Eribon, *Michel Foucault* (1991), 224–8.
26. Foucault, 1971f, 'Revolutionary Action: "Until Now"' [1977], 228.

The GIP did not understand its work as an expression of humanistic concern. Its activities did not focus on the human being 'behind' the condemned, nor did the group seek to develop a reformist perspective in order to promote a 'better' or 'more humane' penal system. Members' intentions were 'quite radically different'.[27] They did not wish to effect partial improvements, but to question the need for prison at all by making the modes and goals of penal practices the object of a political discussion.[28]

In contrast to traditional left-wing activism, the GIP did not seek to advocate on prisoners' behalf or give them a voice. Thus, when the group conducted a survey asking prisoners about their conditions of detention, the point was not to use sociological findings to contrast claims and realities and unmask the repressive nature of incarceration. Members of the group already agreed that prisons – like courts, hospitals, psychiatric institutions, universities and so on – constitute instances of repression. Such a view represented the point of departure more than the point of arrival. Since it was clear that prison serves repressive purposes, the task was to provide an account that would be as full and detailed as possible. Needless to say, one of the prison's key functions is to deprive inmates of means of communication and access to information. The GIP intervened at precisely this juncture, seeking to give prisoners the possibility to speak for themselves – to interact and communicate with each other and the outside world about conditions in detention centres. These efforts were motivated not just by a critique of traditional forms of 'representative', left-wing politics, but also by the ambition to make power relations manifest in their concreteness and everydayness – not to criticize them in the abstract, but to make them visible as they really are.[29]

## Critique and Crisis: The Prison Question

Involvement in the GIP held significant consequences for Foucault's theoretical work. The lectures at the Collège de France in 1971 and

---

27. Foucault, 1974b, 'Michel Foucault on Attica' [1991], 30.

28. Foucault, 1971e, 'Je perçois l'intolerable', 204–5; Foucault, 1984p, 'Interview with Actes' [2000], 394–5.

29. Foucault, 1971g, 'Le discours de Toul', 237–8.

1972, as well as the accompanying seminars, were devoted to studying disciplinary society. Moreover, Foucault took a stand on the problem of penal institutions and practices in an array of interviews, forewords and essays.[30] But for all that, his political engagement in the prison movement did not amount to applying theory to practice. On the contrary: involvement with the GIP is what prompted Foucault to change his theoretical perspective.[31]

Above all, the 'concrete experience'[32] of working with the GIP led Foucault to a new insight that decisively shaped the further course of his theoretical and political engagement: the gap between the legal (or, alternately, theoretical) status of prisons and actual practices within them. Prisoners are not just deprived of freedom for a given period; they are also subjected to a system of forces and constraints that does not form part of the legal apparatus itself: 'prison … largely escapes the control of the judicial apparatus …. It also escapes the control of public opinion, and finally it often escapes the rules of law'.[33]

---

30. The problem of prison and penal practices interested Foucault to the end. This is attested not just by the host of articles, lectures, and interviews on the topic, e.g. 'Préface' (1973a); 'I, Pierre Rivière' (1973h); 'From Torture to Cellblock' (1975c); 'Confinement, Psychiatry, Prison' (1977o); 'Manières de justice' (1979d); 'Il faut tout repenser, la loi et la prison' (1981f); 'What is Called "Punishing"?' (1984j); but also by plans for two research projects on the politics of punishment, which premature death kept him from completing. Gandal, 'Intellectual Work as a Political Tool: The Example of Michel Foucault' (1986), 18 note 26.

31. Gilles Deleuze has described this reciprocal interpenetration of theory and politics in vivid terms: 'Possibly we're in the process of experiencing a new relationship between theory and practice. At one time, practice was considered an application of theory, a consequence; at other times, it had an opposite sense and it was thought to inspire theory, to be indispensable for the creation of future theoretical forms. In any event, their relationship was understood in terms of a process of totalization. For us, however, the question is seen in a different light. The relationships between theory and practice are far more partial and fragmentary. On one side, a theory is always local and related to a limited field, and it is applied in another sphere, more or less distant from it. The relationship which holds in the application of a theory is never one of resemblance. Moreover, from the moment a theory moves into its proper domain, it begins to encounter obstacles, walls, and blockages which require its relay by another type of discourse […]. Practice is a set of relays from one theoretical point to another, and theory is a relay from one practice to another. No theory can develop without eventually encountering a wall, and practice is necessary for piercing this wall'. Deleuze, in Foucault, 1972b, 'Intellectuals and Power' [1977], 205–6.

32. Foucault, 1977i, 'The History of Sexuality' [1980], 184.

33. Foucault, 1984p, 'Interview with Actes' [2000], 394; see, also Deleuze, 'Foucault and the Prison (1986b); Defert and Donzelot, 'La charnière des prisons' (1976).

If this observation holds, doubt arises whether the critique of prisons can be a matter of confronting those in charge and calling for instances of 'aberration' or 'mismanagement' to be rectified. Instead, one should investigate the possibility that such ills possess a systematic quality. It might be that 'shortcomings' belong to the normal functioning of the prison, that a 'surplus' of humiliation forms part of the institutional logic and that a connection holds between claims of resocialization and crime prevention, on the one hand, and the fact that these goals regularly fail to be met, on the other. Is the 'crisis' of the prison not its everyday and usual form of existence? Does prison provide the privileged form of punishment not in spite, but precisely because, of the fact that it is permanently 'in crisis'? If so, this prompts the question of the meaning of 'crisis': if the word refers to an exceptional phenomenon, what rule underlies this 'exception'? Could it be that presupposing an 'ideal' or 'normal' model of functioning independent of, or beyond, crisis already represents a problem? And what consequences does this hold for the critique and the perspectives it can offer?[34]

A 'reversal' of perspective characterizes Foucault's work after *The Order of Discourse*. His involvement in the prison movement prompted him to revise his earlier theses concerning the relationship between discourse and power. By Foucault's own account, work with the GIP led him to recognize a new problem that 'undermined' his previous notions:

Until then I envisioned exclusion from society as a sort of general function, a bit abstract, and I tried to plot that function as in some way constitutive of society, each society being able to function only on condition that a certain number of people are excluded from it. Traditional sociology, sociology of the Durkheim type, presented the problem rather in this way: How can society hold individuals together? What is the form of relationship, of symbolic or affective communication that is established among individuals? What is the organizational

---

34. This investigative angle has shaped many works written in Foucault's wake. Replacing logical categories with concrete, historical instances follows from the suspicion that applying analytical schemes such as 'crisis' and 'contradiction' to social relations in fact promotes the 'emergence of new techniques of regulation'. Donzelot, *The Policing of Families* (1979), 8. This change of perspective shifts attention towards how contradictions are operationalized and unfold as a process.

system that permits society to constitute a totality? I was interested by the somewhat opposite problem, or, if you will, by the opposite response to this problem, which is: Through what system of exclusion, by eliminating whom, by creating what division, through what game of negation and rejection can society begin to function?[35]

This theoretical undertaking had meant taking distance from both the history of ideas and sociological formulations of problems addressed. Foucault sought neither an ideal 'spirit' of a society nor the material principle of its coherence; instead, he examined how processes of coercion and operations of exclusion produce social identity. In keeping with this epistemological interest (*Erkenntnisinteresse*), he subordinated positive conditions and principles of constitution to more fundamental mechanisms of exclusion and repression: a 'repression-suppression system';[36] society takes shape by way of processes of rejection, which in turn provide the material basis for the functioning of 'positive' processes. According to this model, societies differ only in terms of the form that negativity assumes: modes of exclusion, repression, prohibitions, etc.[37]

Now, Foucault came to view such a premise as inadequate. Examination of the workings of prisons revealed the limitations of a perspective stressing negative mechanisms such as exclusion and repression:

> the question that I ask myself now is the reverse: prison is an organization that is too complex to be reduced to purely negative functions of exclusion; its cost, its importance, the care that one takes in administering it, the justifications that one tries to give for it seem to indicate that it possesses positive functions. The problem is, then, to find out what role capitalist society has its penal system play, what is the aim

35. Foucault, 1974b, 'Michel Foucault on Attica' [1991], 27–8; see also Foucault, 1971d, 'A Conversation with Michel Foucault', 193–4; Foucault, 1978d, 'La folie et la société', 478–80.

36. Foucault, 1971d, 'A Conversation with Michel Foucault', 193.

37. With regard to penal practices, for instance, this premise enables Foucault to outline a typology of societies in terms of their negative principles of constitution: 'exiling' societies respond to illegality by shutting out perpetrators; others 'massacre and torture'; while a third kind observes the principle of 'reparation' – they all contrast with 'inclusive' societies, which imprison offenders. Foucault, 1971e, 'Je perçois l'intolerable', 203–4; Foucault, 1972a, 'Die Große Einsperrung', 296–301; Foucault, 1972c, 'Confining Societies' [1996], 85; Foucault, 1973g, 'The Punitive Society' [1997].

that is sought, and what effects are produced by all these procedures for punishment and exclusion?[38]

Foucault was no longer content to denounce the (negative) character of exclusion and repression in prisons. Instead, he asked about the institution's positive effects. The point was not to deny that the prison represents an instrument of repression and performs operations of exclusion. Rather, the point is that these aspects do not tell the whole story. More precisely: the question of why the prison exists should not be put only in functionalist terms; the concept of function itself must be made the object of a theoretical analysis: how does the prison function?

Foucault stands the traditional formulation of the problem on its head. Prison does not try to 'exclude' so much as to 'include'; its goal is not 'correction' so much as 'training'; its importance does not involve incarceration and restricting freedom so much as producing useful and obedient individuals. The question of the prison leads to the problem of discipline.

---

38. Foucault, 1974b, 'Michel Foucault on Attica' [1991], 28.

# 3

# Discipline: The Political Anatomy of the Body

Man is not fitted for society by nature, but by discipline.

Thomas Hobbes, *De Cive*[1]

To sum up our findings so far: Foucault initially approached the problem of power by way of a specific form of discourse analysis. Doing so led to the unsatisfying conclusion that non-discursive rules of formation and determination can only be localized *within* the field of discourse. To remedy the problem, he undertook a change of method and made the *relations* between knowledge and power the centre of investigative interest. Thereby, however, he continued to focus on the negative effects of such relations and examined power chiefly in terms of coercion, rarefaction, exclusion and so on. In turn, *Discipline and Punish* performed a decisive step beyond this 'negative' conception of power and opened a new perspective for analysing power.[2]

*Discipline and Punish*, which appeared in 1975, explicitly connects with the prison revolts of preceding years.[3] In contrast to what the

---

1. Quoted in Gordon, 'Governmental Rationality: An Introduction' (1991), 14.

2. This chapter first sketches Foucault's course of argument; then, in order to identify the book's theoretical demarcations and analytical merits, attention turns to the 'architecture' of the 'micro-physics of power' it operationalizes. Foucault, 1975a, *Discipline and Punish* [1995], 26. Chapter 5 will explore two decisive problems that such an approach entailed – which led Foucault to reorient his genealogy of power along the lines of government.

3. That said, the study is not simply the product of a certain set of political circumstances. Foucault, 1975a, *Discipline and Punish* [1995], 29. It also occupies a theoretical field that extends from Robert Castel's socio-historical works on the 'history of psychiatry' to Gilles Deleuze's philosophical writings. Castel, *Le*

subtitle promises, the 'birth of the prison' does not stand at the centre of the study. Instead, on the basis of historical changes in penal practices at the end of the eighteenth century and the beginning of the nineteenth century, Foucault explores a complex process of social transformation that culminated in entirely new modes of exercising power – which, in his estimation, prevail to this very day and guarantee the enduring role of the prison, critical objections and even crises notwithstanding. For this reason, his 'history of the prison' is simultaneously a 'history of the present'.[4]

This book's point of departure is the question why, during the shift from the eighteenth to the nineteenth century in France, corporal punishment was replaced by seemingly 'incorporeal' imprisonment. The introduction illustrates the break in penal practices by juxtaposing an account of the execution of the regicide Damiens in 1757 with a set of prison rules from 1838. Whereas the former is a public ceremony of utmost physical cruelty, the latter involves a minute and detailed plan for regulating everyday life in prison. Foucault goes on to show how incarceration played at most a marginal role in the traditional, feudal-absolutist regime of punishment; here, its main purpose was to seize and detain individuals.[5] It was not until the start of the nineteenth century that France and other European countries witnessed the 'colonization of the penalty by the prison'.[6] Within a relatively brief span of time, prison sentences came to occupy the principal position in the catalogue of available punishments; notwithstanding numerous disadvantages, obstacles and problems, imprisonment seemed to admit no alternative. Many efforts have been made to explain why physical punishment was replaced by incarceration; they break down into accounts focused on the internal dynamics of an evolving penal system and external factors, respectively.

---

*Psychanalysme* (1973); Deleuze and Guattari, *Anti-Oedipus: Capitalism and Schizophrenia* (1977); see also Foucault, 1975a, *Discipline and Punish* [1995], 309 n. 2. Until the end of the 1970s, theoretical proximity and personal friendship defined relations between Foucault and Deleuze. See Foucault, 1970b, 'Theatrum Philosophicum' [1998]; Foucault, 1972b, 'Intellectuals and Power' [1977]; Foucault, 1977a, 'Preface'; Deleuze, 'Die Geschichte einer Freundschaft' (1986a); on philosophical and methodological differences, see Deleuze, 'Désir et plaisir' (1994).

    4. Foucault, 1975a, *Discipline and Punish* [1995], 31.

    5. Ibid., 117–20; Foucault, 1972a, 'Die Große Einsperrung', 297.

    6. Foucault, 1975a, *Discipline and Punish* [1995], 117.

Analyses of the first kind enlist a mode of historiography that conceives the rupture in penal practices in terms of linear progression, as a quantitative phenomenon: less cruelty and suffering, more compassion and humanity. This amounts to interpreting movement towards imprisonment as a matter of lessening the intensity of punishment within an autonomous system that follows its own internal laws by humanizing the ways penalties are carried out.

The second approach traces the emergence of the prison back to politico-legal and economic changes at the end of the eighteenth century. It would seem that privileging imprisonment derives from egalitarian notions corresponding to the efforts of bourgeois societies to secure a foundation in natural law. Unlike monetary fines, for instance, the prospect of being 'deprived of liberty' affects all members of society equally. Imprisonment also 'makes it possible to quantify the penalty exactly according to the variable of time'.[7] Finally, it represents the 'logical' form of punishment in a commodity-producing society. Hereby, the 'wages-form' lends the prison its 'economic "self-evidence"': imprisonment as a way of paying off debt is as 'natural' in a capitalist society as using time to measure service and remuneration.[8]

Foucault rejects both explanations for being insufficient in different ways. For one, the 'birth of the prison' does not amount to a diminution of the intensity of punishment so much as a change in goals and methods. The inner organization of the penal system cannot account for it; instead, it must be understood in relation to 'general and in a sense external reasons'.[9] But for all that, this transformation does not result solely from external determinants, that is, politico-legal and economic processes. Although Foucault does not deny that such factors play an important role in the triumph of the prison, he insists that they are not enough to explain its success. Indeed, his critique is directed against efforts to reduce the prison to the legal dimension and to explain it on the basis of economic imperatives alone.[10]

7. Ibid., 232.

8. Ibid., 23–4, 232–3.

9. Ibid., 55.

10. Notwithstanding his esteem for their work, this is the basis for Foucault's disagreement with the analysis offered by Georg Rusche and Otto Kirchheimer. Rusche and Kirchheimer, *Punishment and Social Structure* (1939); cf. Foucault, 1975a, *Discipline and Punish* [1995], 24, 54–5; Foucault, 1980b, 'Questions of Method', 74; Lévy and Zander, 'Un grand livre: Peine et structure sociale' (1996).

Foucault offers two arguments against such a view. For one, prison represents more than a *legal* privation of liberty: from the very start, law books affirmed that incarceration should lead to improvement. The prison does not just lock people up and punish them; it also seeks to educate and better them. Underneath – and against – the apparatus of justice, prisons establish a form of 'infra-penality' that not only carries out the sentence but can also revise and modify it (through early release, reformed or relaxed conditions of detention, provisions for granting partial liberties, and so on). Second, the institution of the prison cannot be 'derived' from *economic* forces at work in the capitalist system of production. In terms of strict, economic categories, prisons are 'unprofitable': they offer no immediate gains. More still, they inhibit the mobility of the labour force and constitute a foreign body in the workings of the market.[11]

Foucault maintains that juridico-economic efforts to explain the emergence of the prison must be joined by consideration of technologico-strategic factors. In other words, the economic dimension holds sway both 'more directly' and 'more indirectly'. Even though incarcerated individuals are not incorporated by force into a process that aims to generate surplus value, the operative economy inscribes itself on their bodies in an immediate way. The 'surplus value' of the prison consists of 'manufacturing economical individuals'. The aim of prison labour is not to produce commodities, but to fashion docile and useful subjects; the prison does not represent the application of technology so much as a gigantic apparatus for effecting transformation. Industrial machinery designed to make goods corresponds to prison machinery, which 'fashions' useful individuals. 'If, in the final analysis, the work of the prison has an economic effect, it is by producing individuals mechanized according to the general norms of an industrial society'.[12]

Foucault does not want to explain the institution of the prison on the basis of a developmental dynamic immanent to the penal system; nor

---

11. Foucault, 1975a, *Discipline and Punish* [1995], 242–3; Foucault, 1973e, 'A propos de l'enfermement pénitentiaire'.
12. Ibid., 242; Ewald, 'Anatomie et corps politique' (1975); Raulff, *Das normale Leben* (1977), 86–9. 'Penal labour must be seen as the very machinery that transforms the violent, agitated, unreflective convict into a part that plays its role with perfect regularity. The prison is not a workshop; it is […] a machine'. Foucault, 1975a, *Discipline and Punish* [1995], 242.

does he wish to derive it directly from the forces of capitalist, industrial society. Instead, the emergence of the prison and the generalization of incarceration form part of 'general and essential transformations' that, from the seventeenth century on, restructured the feudal order.[13] Accordingly, Foucault's analysis concentrates on describing a form of power that invests the body, breaks it down into parts, calculates its gestures and manipulates its modes of comportment. It operates through an array of techniques that aim to train bodies in such a way that their forces can be effectively used and optimally controlled. Such techniques, which come to pervade the whole of the 'social body' in the course of the seventeenth and eighteenth centuries, are what he calls *disciplines*.[14]

## The Prison as Technology: Discipline

Viewing changes in penal methods in terms of disciplination means analysing punishment as a 'complex social function' and presupposes a number of heuristic principles.[15] Discipline cannot be equated with institutions or apparatuses. It cannot be traced back to legal or economic foundations; nor is it restricted to repressive or ideological effects. '[I]t is a type of power, a modality for its exercise, comprising a whole set of instruments, techniques, procedures, levels of application, targets; it is a "physics" or an "anatomy" of power, a technology'.[16]

Disciplinary technology takes aim at a body 'that may be subjected, used, transformed and improved';[17] its 'merit' involves a 'recoding of existence' different from both physical repression and ideological manipulation.[18] Discipline does not repress or mask so much as it forms and structures modes of perception and habits. In contrast to traditional kinds of domination such as slavery and serfdom, discipline simultaneously heightens the body's forces for economic use and weakens them for the purpose of political subjugation. That said, discipline does not just combine utility and subjugation. It ties them into

---

13. Ibid., 139.
14. Ibid., 207.
15. Ibid., 23.
16. Ibid., 215.
17. Ibid., 136.
18. Ibid., 236.

a productive and self-amplifying circuit, forging a specific technology of power that enhances the economic utility of the body in proportion to the degree to which it is politically subjugated. This coupling of economic and political imperatives is what defines discipline and its status as a technology:

> The historical moment of the disciplines was the moment when an art of the human body was born, which was directed not only at the growth of its skills, nor at the intensification of its subjection, but at the formation of a relation that in the mechanism itself makes it more obedient as it becomes more useful, and conversely.[19]

---

19. Ibid., 137–8. Foucault finds the technological principle for disciplinary power in the Panopticon, developed by Jeremy Bentham in 1787: a prison with a ring-shaped building on the periphery and a tower at the centre. The outer structure consists of individual cells, each with two windows – one facing inward, towards the tower, and the other facing outward, so that light enters from both sides. By means of this design, prisoners are always visible, yet they can see neither the guards nor other inmates. The Panopticon realizes an optics of power: 'in the peripheric ring, one is totally seen, without ever seeing; in the central tower, one sees everything without ever being seen'. Ibid., 202.
   Its significance lies, first, in its universal applicability. The panoptic principle can be employed not only in prisons, but also in hospitals, schools, factories, etc., for the purpose of monitoring patients, observing pupils or supervising workers. For all that, the Panopticon is not a 'pure form' to be filled with different contents so much as 'a figure of political technology' that may be detached from concrete applications. Ibid., 205. As such, second, it represents an automatized and deindividualized form of exercising power. By engineering a permanent state of visibility for prisoners, it leads from allo-surveillance to auto-surveillance. Because they cannot see the guards, inmates act, at every moment, in keeping with their exposure to a controlling gaze. Indeed, the surveillance tower need not even be manned: 'the perfection of power should tend to render its actual exercise unnecessary; ... this architectural apparatus should be a machine for creating and sustaining a power relation independent of the person who exercises it; in short, ... the inmates should be caught up in a power situation of which they are themselves the bearers'. Ibid., 201. Because the exercise of power is rendered anonymous, a singular shift occurs that makes the compulsory effects of power and its targets collapse into one: 'He who is subjected to a field of visibility, and who knows it, assumes responsibility for the constraints of power; he makes them play spontaneously upon himself; he inscribes in himself the power relation in which he simultaneously plays both roles; he becomes the principle of his own subjection'. Ibid., 202–3. Both these aspects of the Panopticon – its universal applicability and its anonymous and deindividualized mode of exercising power – make it 'a case of "it's easy once you've thought of it" in the political sphere'. Ibid., 206; Foucault, 1973e, 'A propos de l'enfermement pénitentiaire', 437–8; Foucault, 1976c, 'Questions on Geography' [1980], 71–2; Foucault, 1977g, 'The Eye of Power' [2008]; Foucault, 1978c, 'Dialogue on Power' [1975]; Raulff, *Das normale Leben* (1977), 95–8.

## The Power of Economy and the Economy of
## Power: Discipline and Capitalism

The advantage of the method Foucault presents in *Discipline and Punish* is the emphasis it places on the 'relative autonomy' of power relations: articulating their technological specificity in conjunction with economic, politico-legal and scientific factors. Foucault seeks to replace reductionist – that is, essentialist and economistic – models of explanation with social analysis carried out in historically concrete terms.

The disciplines responded to the increased population and augmented productive apparatus of the eighteenth century; they provided techniques for 'aligning' the accumulation of capital and the accumulation of human beings. The task involved moving from feudal power mechanisms, which had functioned by 'skimming off' goods and services, to forms of power oriented on 'value-creation'.[20] Now, demographic and economic imperatives demanded technologies combining a low (economic and political) overhead with increased social efficacy. A new 'economy' emerged; its 'methods for administering the accumulation of men made possible a political take-off in relation to the traditional, ritual, costly, violent forms of power'.[21] These 'economic' mechanisms, which did not obey the principle of violence/deprivation so much as that of production/profit, enabled an '"incorporation" of power' shaping individuals on the level of gestures, attitudes, modes of acting and habits.[22]

The accumulation of capital and the accumulation of human beings do not represent independent phenomena. When Foucault speaks of the 'constraint of a conformity that must be achieved'[23] or the 'pressure to conform'[24] that discipline induces, he does not mean that two external processes are at work. Each presumes the other: the problem of acquiring human beings would have proven insoluble without developing a productive apparatus that made – and kept – these people useful; by the same token, the accumulation of capital was tied to production techniques and forms of labour that succeeded in using a multiplicity of human beings in an economically profitable

20. Foucault, 1975a, *Discipline and Punish* [1995], 183.
21. Ibid., 220–1.
22. Foucault, 1977d, 'Truth and Power' [1984], 66.
23. Foucault, 1975a, *Discipline and Punish* [1995], 183.
24. Ibid., 182.

way. Foucault makes it clear that the 'political colonization of the body' undertaken by the disciplines is tied to economic utility. Effective exploitation does not simply call for forming a productive value. More generally, a labour force can only be constituted within a system that subjugates individuals: 'the body becomes a useful force only if it is both a productive body and a subjected body'.[25] This system of subjugation operated via 'sequestration', which transformed lifespan into manpower. Before manpower can be exploited, time spent living must be transformed into time spent working; individuals must be calibrated with the course of production and subordinated to its cycle: 'the problem of industrial society is to see to it that the individual's time ... can be integrated into the production apparatus in the forms of labour-power'.[26] Accordingly, sequestration does not guarantee a mode of production or represent a factor in its reproduction so much as it constitutes it; it does not belong to the 'superstructure', but functions at the 'base' of society.[27]

Foucault understands this 'political anatomy'[28] as a complement and completion of the Marxist critique of political economy: 'sequestration [is] the correlative, in terms of power, of the accumulation of capital in economic terms'.[29] The question of power stands alongside the problem of exploitation: 'If economic exploitation separates the force and the product of labour, let us say that disciplinary coercion establishes in the body the constricting link between an increased aptitude and an increased domination'.[30] Thus, even though capitalist economy and disciplinary mechanisms 'cannot be separated',[31] Foucault's point of departure is not a logical connection so much as

---

25. Ibid., 26.

26. Foucault, 1973i, '28 March 1973' [2015], 232.

27. Foucault, 1975a, *Discipline and Punish* [1995], 223; Foucault, 1973c, 'Prisons et révoltes dans les prisons', 429–30; Foucault, 1974c, 'Truth and Juridical Forms' [2000], 32–4.

28. Foucault, 1975a, *Discipline and Punish* [1995], 221.

29. Foucault, 1973i, '28 March 1973' [2015], 232.

30. Foucault, 1975a, *Discipline and Punish* [1995], 138. On the specific relation between capitalist exploitation and the disciplination of the working class, see Foucault, 1973g, 'The Punitive Society' [1997], 32–4; Foucault, 1974c, 'Truth and Juridical Forms' [2000], 76–87. Foucault also treated this theme in his lectures at the Collège de France on 21 February and 7 March 1973, as well as 12 March 1975. Foucault, 2013, *The Punitive Society* [2015]; Foucault, 1999, *Abnormal* [2003]; Gros, *Michel Foucault* (1996), 75.

31. Foucault, 1975a, *Discipline and Punish* [1995], 221.

a historical one. When he observes that '[t]he growth of the capitalist economy gave rise to the specific modality of disciplinary power',[32] he is not simply pointing to the significance of economic factors for establishing and generalizing disciplinary mechanisms; in equal measure, he is referring to discipline's specificity and independence, which cannot be reduced to a modality of the political superstructure, capitalist socialization. Despite the close historical relationship between capitalism and discipline, the latter represents a 'political technology that may and must be detached from any specific use'.[33]

## Consensus and Bodies: Discipline and Law

The disciplines cannot be boiled down to constraints exercised by the capitalist economy. Nor do they depend directly on political structures or correspond to the formal principles of law. Still, they are 'not absolutely independent',[34] either. Both formal law and the fiction of contractual partners exercising the same rights are connected with the 'physis' of disciplinary power in a complicated manner:

> The general juridical form … was supported by these tiny, everyday, physical mechanisms, by all those systems of micro-power that are essentially non-egalitarian and asymmetrical that we call the disciplines. And although, in a formal way, the representative régime makes it possible, directly or indirectly, with or without relays, for the will of all to

---

32. Ibid., 221.

33. Ibid., 205. Discipline as a technology of power can be implemented in 'the most diverse political régimes, apparatuses or institutions'. Ibid., 221. Although capitalism and the disciplines emerged simultaneously, a 'logical' connection does not prevail between them (that is, the latter will not necessarily disappear with the end of capitalism). Political technologies such as discipline can be implemented not just within societies organized along capitalist lines; they can also be used in other social formations. Discipline possesses technological materiality and specificity that make it impossible to 'derive' it from economic or social factors. It does not follow, however, that it is 'neutral' and affords a 'pure medium' which is 'open' to any context at all. Political technologies may be 'relatively autonomous' on the whole, yet they always develop in a certain socio-historical context in keeping with economic and political processes; as such, they 'respond' to concrete problems and 'offer' particular solutions in this framework. Accordingly, Foucault observes that Soviet socialism adopted Taylorism from the West, and with it moral and aesthetic forms and disciplinary techniques – which it then intensified. Foucault, 1976f, 'The Politics of Soviet Crime' [1996], 192.

34. Foucault, 1975a, *Discipline and Punish* [1995], 222.

form the fundamental authority of sovereignty, the disciplines provide, at the base, a guarantee of the submission of forces and bodies.[35]

The disciplines constitute the functional complement to rights that are formally equal. The political transition from the monarch's sovereignty to the principles of popular sovereignty made disciplinary mechanisms necessary. Aggregate will presupposes that bodies and modes of conduct be broken down into discrete parts: 'Discipline is the underside of democracy'.[36]

In contrast to bourgeois conceptions of natural law, juridico-political consensus does not fashion the social body. Instead, this occurs through the materiality of power operating on and through individual bodies.[37] 'Society' does not represent the free union of equal individuals; it is produced by discipline as a 'system of ... constraints'.[38] Legal agreement between individuals requires factual agreement: formal equality presupposes material equality. However, it does not follow that bourgeois political theory, with its assumption of discrete legal subjects, is simply false. Although it proves 'ideological' inasmuch as it covers up the constitutive role that processes of discipline play in the formation of 'individuality', it also corresponds to reality inasmuch as it accurately describes the result of these same processes: 'The individual is no doubt the fictitious atom of an "ideological" representation of society; but he is also a reality fabricated by this specific technology of power that I have called "discipline"'.[39]

This does not mean that all disciplinary processes apply in the same measure everywhere – creating an 'egalitarian' society of disciplined individuals, who all stand subject, in the same way, to the operations of an anonymous instance of power. Foucault stresses how disciplines perform a discriminating and selective role. The contract acts as the instrument of property owners to bind themselves to each other; likewise, a system of constraints, doctrines and punishments ties those without material resources to an apparatus that does not belong to

---

35. Ibid., 222.

36. Foucault, 1975d, 'An Interview with Michel Foucault' [1985], 2; Foucault, 1975a, *Discipline and Punish* [1995], 221–4; Foucault, 1977g, 'The Eye of Power' [2008], 11.

37. Foucault, 1975g, 'Body/Power' [1980], 55.

38. Foucault, 1973i, '28 March 1973' [2015], 240.

39. Foucault, 1975a, *Discipline and Punish* [1995], 194.

them. These 'habits' constitute the 'complement of the contract'.[40] Even though the disciplines take the stage as a 'subsystem of the law' that extends the legal order to the sphere of individual lives by applying general and equal principles to everyone, they do not, in fact, represent a continuation of legality so much as a kind of 'counter-law'.[41] Underneath – and counter to – the legal contract between formally equal partners, discipline forges a 'private' bond whose task involves 'introducing insuperable asymmetries and excluding reciprocities'[42] and, simultaneously, masks the 'political' nature of the relationship. Where law draws formal borders to the exercising of power, discipline maintains an everyday and omnipresent machinery, which escapes these restrictions time and again.[43]

The difference between the law of sovereignty and the mechanism of discipline, then, amounts to more than a theoretical contradiction: it forms part of political reality, which is distinguished by competition between different modes of regulation. Discipline may work with rules, like the law. But whereas legal rules result from a sovereign (popular) will, disciplines invoke a 'natural' rule, the *norm*, which escapes politico-voluntaristic legislation. That is, norms are not defined in the context of a system of positive legality. The disciplines have a different theoretical background: they are inseparably tied to the development of the 'human sciences'. The latter, which developed in the eighteenth century, arose when legal organization met up with the mechanism of disciplinary constraints: their 'legislation' is not based on juridical rules, but on the 'natural' norms discovered by medicine, psychiatry, sociology and so on.[44]

---

40. Foucault, 1973i, '28 March 1973' [2015], 239.

41. Foucault, 1975a, *Discipline and Punish* [1995], 223.

42. Ibid., 222.

43. For an effort to demonstrate this position's 'proximity' to Marxist legal theory, see Palmer and Pearce, 'Legal Discourse and State Power: Foucault and the Juridical Relation' (1983); Turkel, 'Michel Foucault: Law, Power, and Knowledge' (1990), esp. 178–87; Moore Jr., 'Law, Normativity, and the Level Playing Field' (1993).

44. Foucault remarks that, over the course of the nineteenth century, the discourse of norms gradually permeated legal discourse. In terms of criminal law, this meant enlisting psychiatric-medical knowledge for juridical processes of determination. For discussion of one of the first instances in criminology, see Foucault's reconstruction of the case of Pierre Rivière. Foucault, 1973h, 'I, Pierre Rivière' [1996]. That said, it is more a matter of tendency than thoroughgoing replacement. Foucault never claims the (sovereign) rights and law were entirely replaced by (disciplinary) norms: 'Is this the new law of modern society? Let us say rather that, since the eighteenth century, it

## The Birth of the Human Sciences

Disciplines do not just 'normalize' law; nor do they simply stand in closer relation to the accumulation of capital and human beings. Equally, they presuppose the accumulation of knowledge about the human being. In order to ensure the economic utility and political subjugation of bodies, disciplines rely on producing the specific knowledge about 'man' that the human sciences provide. The 'technical matrix of the petty, malicious minutiae of the disciplines and their investigations'[45] provides the foundation for the development of these sciences. The historical development of scientific 'disciplines' and the establishment of disciplinary mechanisms amount to correlative processes, each of which builds on the other.

The coordinated interrelation between generating knowledge and exercising power marks discipline as a political instrument. In the course of the eighteenth century, the generalization and fusion of disciplinary procedures reached a level where 'the formation of knowledge and the increase of power regularly reinforce[d] one another in a circular process': the disciplines 'crossed the "technological" threshold'.[46] Disciplines do not just produce useful individuals and subjugate them at the same time. They also generate knowledge about subjugated individuals. By the same token, subjugation presupposes exact knowledge. 'It is a double process, then: an epistemological "thaw" through a refinement of power relations; a multiplication of the effects of power through the formation and accumulation of new forms of knowledge.'[47] Factories, schools, hospitals and the like are not simply 'reordered' by means of discipline, leaving their institutional form untouched.[48] Rather, they undergo a thorough change in terms of goals and modes of functioning. Disciplines transform the institutions where they are implemented; the latter come to be apparatuses that presuppose and produce knowledge simultaneously. The normative knowledge that the human sciences provide is not applied or implemented so much as it enters into the process of exercising power; indeed, it constitutes an integral component of power.

---

has joined other powers'. Foucault, 1975a, *Discipline and Punish* [1995], 184; Foucault, 1977f, '14 January 1976' [2003], 37–40.

    45. Foucault, 1975a, *Discipline and Punish* [1995], 226.

    46. Ibid., 224.

    47. Ibid., 224.

    48. Ibid., 224.

This does not mean that the human sciences may be boiled down to purely disciplinary mechanisms. They are neither the expression nor the product of the disciplines. To be sure, 'one of the conditions of the emergence of the human sciences' was 'the great nineteenth-century effort in discipline and normalisation'.[49] However, if a historical connection holds between disciplination-processes and the way that the individual increasingly came to constitute the object of scientific study in the course of the nineteenth century, this does not mean that the human sciences derive from discipline or are identical with it: 'I am not saying that the human sciences emerged from the prison'.[50] Instead, Foucault's thesis holds that the emergence of the human sciences and the changes they catalysed in the structure of knowledge could only come about because new political and economic developments 'required the involvement of definite relations of knowledge in relations of power'.[51] If the human sciences owe their existence to a regulatory apparatus of control and verification in schools, hospitals, armies and prisons, this fact does not diminish the autonomy of these forms of knowledge or the truths they afford.

The human sciences also occupy a central position in Foucault's analysis of the 'birth of the prison' because they created an important epistemological precondition for changing mechanisms of punishment: the 'discovery' of the soul. Hereby, Foucault does not have an anthropological fact in mind – now, at long last, explored and investigated – so much as a historical product that simultaneously provides the object of new insight and represents the point of departure for modern juridical power. As such, the historical shift from corporal punishment to imprisonment does not lessen the intensity of the penal regime; it changes what receives punishment. Modern penality concentrates more on the prisoner's 'soul' than his body. From the nineteenth century on, punishment has aimed less at a legally determinate action than at the perpetrator 'behind' the deed: his aggressions, weaknesses, unfitness and so on: 'it *is* these shadows lurking behind the case itself that are judged and punished'.[52]

If Foucault is right, then examining penal methods within the

---

49. Foucault, 1975g, 'Body/Power' [1980], 61; see also Foucault, 1975a, *Discipline and Punish* [1995], 183.
50. Foucault, 1975a, *Discipline and Punish* [1995], 305.
51. Ibid., 305.
52. Ibid., 17.

framework of a 'political technology of the body' proves inadequate and contradictory. For all that, Foucault does not view the 'soul' as the counterpart of the body so much as its extension or the 'duplication … of a "non-corporal"'; it is not the Other of the body, but forms the 'present correlative of a certain technology of power over the body'.[53] This does not mean that the soul amounts to an illusion or the product of ideology. It possesses a 'historical reality' or a 'corporal materiality': 'it is produced permanently around, on, within the body by the functioning of a power that is exercised on those punished – and, in a more general way, on those one supervises, trains and corrects, over madmen, children at home and at school, the colonized, over those who are stuck at a machine and supervised for the rest of their lives'.[54]

In this light, the 'soul' is neither a universal substance nor a matter of illusion. It stands as an 'effect and instrument' within a 'political anatomy'. Hereby, determinate power and the object of specific knowledge fuse: 'it is … the machinery by which the power relations give rise to a possible corpus of knowledge, and knowledge extends and reinforces the effects of this power'.[55]

## The Prison as Strategy: Delinquency

Foucault's analysis of discipline as a 'political technology of the body'[56] raises a number of questions. In keeping with traditional modes of explanation, Foucault adduces economic and legal reasons for why incarceration became a universal practice. He also points out that the prison may be viewed only in conjunction with eighteenth- and nineteenth-century developments: the expansion and generalization of the disciplines and the emergence of the human sciences. Does this mean that Foucault was only interested in broadening the scope of

---

53. Ibid., 29.

54. Ibid., 29.

55. Ibid., 29. In this 'political anatomy', Foucault is referring to Ernst Kantorowicz's study of medieval political theology, which distinguished between the monarch's physical frame and the authority the king embodied symbolically. Kantorowicz, *The King's Two Bodies* (1957). In analogous fashion, Foucault distinguishes between the body of the condemned and his 'soul' – which represents a relay, as it were, through which power relations take physical effect. Foucault, 1975a, *Discipline and Punish* [1995], 28–9.

56. Foucault, 1975a, *Discipline and Punish* [1995], 30.

explanation or adding more factors into the equation – completing the economico-legal picture with technological and scientific elements in order to account for the success of the prison? Has the prison come to be a self-evident matter, without any alternative, over the last 200 years because incarceration represents the functional form of punishment in a bourgeois-capitalist society – in keeping with its legal order and forms of knowledge?

The answer is no. Foucault does not mean simply to add another level of study, but to develop an entirely new form of analysis – one intended to break with the notion of 'function' as a whole. Such analysis does not simply seek to demonstrate that the prison is inseparable from a determinate technological development – the disciplination of society. It also elaborates the strategic significance of the disciplinary technology at work by focusing on how imprisonment is deployed in social struggles and confrontations. As such, the emphasis falls less on the technological nature of power than on its strategic dimension. More precisely: only after power has been defined as a technology can the question of its strategic significance be formulated.

Even if the prison corresponds at 'a deep level with the very functioning of society',[57] it has also, and from the inception, been the target for a host of criticisms that fault it, precisely, for not functioning properly.[58] Indeed, measuring the institution in terms of its supposed ability to reduce crime leads to the obvious conclusion that it has failed. This goal has never been achieved. The prison has not diminished crimes; instead, it has generated criminals. It has not lessened criminality so much as encouraged recidivism. But if this is so, then the question arises why the institution, in spite of its abiding 'lack of success', has been retained. If prison has established itself as the universal penal instrument yet cannot fulfil the expectations placed on it, why does it continue to exist? No answer is possible if one contrasts claims and realities – that is, if one poses the question in terms of functionality and meeting declared goals. 'But perhaps one should reverse the problem and ask oneself what is served by the failure of the prison; what is the use of these different phenomena that are continually being criticized?'[59]

57. Ibid., 232.
58. Foucault, 1973g, 'The Punitive Society' [1997], 25.
59. Foucault, 1975a, *Discipline and Punish* [1995], 272.

## Another Penal Politics

In order to answer the question why the prison is 'offered as its own remedy',[60] analysis must pass beyond the narrow borders the penal system itself has drawn. Foucault examines the abandonment of 'gruesome' physical punishment and the emergence of imprisonment during the eighteenth and nineteenth centuries against the backdrop of major social changes. As bourgeois-capitalist society evolved, violent crime increasingly yielded in significance to crimes against property: theft and fraud pushed aside murder and acts of inflicting bodily harm. At the same time, the inner organization of crimes shifted; under the pressure of more efficient prosecution, large bandit organizations dissolved into the activities of individuals or groups of outsiders.[61]

That said, such 'displacement' in the 'economy of illegalities' does not represent a shift within any given structure of delinquency. Rather, it points to a 'circular process',[62] whereby unlawful practices come to be subjected to new modes of evaluation and definition. If legislation against vagabondage intensified, judicial proceedings against theft mounted, and the police apparatus reduced gaps in its operations more and more, this did not occur because attitudes towards crime had changed. Nor did any of this result from an increased number of property offences, or a refocusing of prosecutorial efforts. Instead, Foucault locates the decisive factor for changes in 'another policy with regard to illegalities'.[63] Shifting weight from violent offences to property offences cannot be viewed in isolation; it 'forms part of a whole complex mechanism, embracing the development of production, the increase of wealth, a higher juridical and moral value placed on property relations, stricter methods of surveillance, a tighter partitioning of the population, more efficient techniques of locating and obtaining information'.[64]

Foucault notes 'a remarkable strategic coincidence'[65] between changes in the structure of criminality and the critique of physical punishment advanced by humanist reformers during the second half of the eighteenth century. Those seeking to reform traditional justice

---

60. Ibid., 268.
61. Ibid., 75–6.
62. Ibid., 78.
63. Ibid., 82.
64. Ibid., 77.
65. Ibid., 78.

attacked immoderate use of corporal punishment; that said, they
viewed it as 'an excess that was bound up with an irregularity even
more than with an abuse of the power to punish'.[66] In other words,
these critics held that too little punishment occurred, not too much.
The king's jurisdiction stood divided into independent instances that
were poorly coordinated and cancelled each other out inasmuch as
they did not encompass the whole of society. Nor was criminal justice
riddled with holes just because of the conflicts and competing interests of subordinate officials. An array of common laws and procedural
differences also blocked regular and uniform penal practice – to say
nothing of times when royal power intervened and issued pardons,
reduced punishments, granted exemptions, and so on.[67]

Proposals for reform addressed such scattered and pluralized
authority, above all: 'The criticism of the reformers was directed not
so much at weakness or cruelty ... as at a bad economy of power'.[68]
Accordingly, reform did not aim to establish new criminal law based
on greater justice or more 'humane' principles, but 'to set up a new
"economy" of the power to punish, to assure its better distribution, so
that it should be neither too concentrated at certain privileged points,
nor too divided between opposing authorities; so that it should be
distributed in homogeneous circuits capable of operating everywhere,
in a continuous way, down to the finest grain of the social body'.[69]

'New economy of power' does not refer to applying different means
in order to achieve the same goals, or instrumentalizing available means
to accomplish other objectives. Instead, it names a movement in which
purposes and practices alike underwent a change. Under the *ancien
régime*, non-application was the rule. The condition for society functioning politically and economically often meant disregarding edicts
and decrees. The system afforded privileges to individuals and groups
as institutionalized exceptions and tolerated non-adherence to laws
and regulations on a massive scale. Illegalities were not restricted to a
determinate social group, but pervaded society as a whole. But starting in the mid-eighteenth century – when economic wealth increased
and became more concentrated, and, at the same time, the population

66. Ibid., 78.
67. See Foucault, 1977m, 'The Confession of the Flesh' [1980], 207.
68. Foucault, 1975a, *Discipline and Punish* [1995], 79.
69. Ibid., 80.

grew appreciably – the process moved in the opposite direction. In the transition from a society of legal-political repression to a society based on the economic appropriation of labour and products, the economy of illegalities meshed with the course of general, social development: offences against property became distinct from violations of rights, 'pilfering and theft tended to replace smuggling and the armed struggle against the tax agents'.[70] Whereas the bourgeoisie kept profitable illegalities for itself, the common people could only commit crimes against property. As the structure of illegalities changed, the role of the penal system did, too. It no longer operated as an apparatus for suppressing unlawfulness globally, but served to differentiate between illegal activities.[71]

Foucault's thesis holds that penal reform, with its critique of traditional methods of sanction, 'was born at the point of junction between the struggle against the super-power of the sovereign and [the struggle] against the infra-power of acquired and tolerated illegalities'.[72] A complex net of relations emerged between superordinate and subordinate powers, connecting the absolute authority of the sovereign with relative leeway for subjects: 'By placing on the side of the sovereign the additional burden of a spectacular, unlimited, personal, irregular and discontinuous power, the form of monarchical sovereignty left the subjects free to practise a constant illegality; this illegality was like the correlative of this type of power'.[73]

On the basis of this deep-seated bond between unbounded might, on the one hand, and a factual order of legal transgressions, on the other, critique of the monarch's privileges also aimed at the standing regime of illegality. In other words, plans for reform sought to restrict penal authority and its implementation with respect to lawlessness on the part of the people, too.[74] The humane punishment advocated by

---

70. Ibid., 84.
71. Ibid., 89.
72. Ibid., 87.
73. Ibid., 88.
74. For this reason, the fight against torture received a strategic significance in penal reform: 'it was the form in which, in the most visible way, the unlimited power of the sovereign and the ever-active illegality of the people came together'. Ibid., 89. The public ceremonies of execution and torture were dangerous insofar as the role of the people thereby was 'ambivalent'. On the one hand, the people was necessary to witness the spectacle of sovereign power, but on the other hand the gruesome execution of sentences was often the starting point for uprisings and affirmations of

reformers was not grounded in a new 'sensibility' so much as it followed the demand for a regulation that would fulfil the imperatives
of bourgeois-capitalist society. 'Humaneness' does not represent consideration for the person of the wrongdoer so much as it names a new
'"economic" rationality that must calculate the penalty and prescribe
the appropriate techniques'.[75]

## Class Justice and Delinquency

Criminal justice reform at the end of the eighteenth century started
out by fighting against the system of illegalities underlying feudal-
absolutist society. It devised the idea of public punishment to generalize
penality and simultaneously restrict it by making it a matter of calculation. This goal was pursued by means of a 'semio-technique of
punishments'[76] meant to anchor the prospect of punishment so firmly
in citizens' minds that no violation was likely to occur. However, the
utopia of a 'penal society' – which operated as 'ideological power',[77]
above all – proved inadequate against the backdrop of the social
struggles that prevailed between 1789 and 1848. At the turn from the
eighteenth century to the nineteenth, popular violations of the law
achieved a new dimension that hindered this ideal's thoroughgoing,
political implementation.

The new understanding of violations of the law meant, first, that
they were now situated in a general political horizon. In the context
of revolution, certain unlawful practices (for instance, refusal to pay
taxes or perform military duty) transformed into political movements.
Conversely, certain political movements became attached to violating
the law; for instance, royalists exploited peasant resistance against new
laws about property, religion and military service.

Second, illegal practices came to be associated with social struggles: 'A
whole series of illegalities was inscribed in struggles in which those strug-
gling knew that they were confronting both the law and the class that had
imposed it'.[78] These combats no longer aimed at tax farmers, banks and
agents of the king, but at the new system of private ownership of land and

---

solidarity with the condemned. Ibid., 63–9.
    75. Ibid., 92.
    76. Ibid., 103.
    77. Ibid., 103.
    78. Ibid., 274.

exploitation in workshops and factories: landholders seeking to implement new laws and factory owners who lowered wages, raised working
hours and prohibited the organization of labour.

The third point concerns how violations of the law were structured.
If illegalities had become the affair of outsiders and lone individuals in
the course of the eighteenth century, they took on a different shape as
the nineteenth century dawned. New laws about property and military
service, as well as regulations concerning wages and the employment
regime, gave rise to peasant unlawfulness and labour delinquency
threatening the established order on a massive scale through insur-
rections, acts of violence and theft.[79]

This 'threefold diffusion of popular illegalities' occurred in tandem
with 'their insertion in a general political outlook; their explicit articulation on social struggles; [and] a communication between different
forms and levels of offences'.[80] This historical process was sufficiently
pronounced to 'serve as a support for the "great fear" of a people who
were believed to be criminal and seditious as a whole, for the myth of
a barbaric, immoral and outlaw class'.[81] Under such conditions, the
'failure' of the prison holds politico-strategic significance:

> One [might] suppose that the prison, and no doubt punishment in
> general, is not intended to eliminate offences, but rather to distinguish
> them, to distribute them, to use them; that it is not so much that they
> render docile those who are liable to transgress the law, but that they
> tend to assimilate the transgression of the laws in a general tactics of
> subjection. Penality would then appear to be a way of handling ille-
> galities ... In short, penality does not simply 'check' illegalities; it
> 'differentiates' them, it provides them with a general 'economy'.[82]

---

79. Ibid., 273–6; Foucault, 1973e, 'A propos de l'enfermement pénitentiaire',
435–6; Foucault, 1973g, 'The Punitive Society' [1997], 32–4.

80. Foucault, 1975a, *Discipline and Punish* [1995], 275.

81. Ibid., 275. Foucault considers the expansion of popular illegalities to be the
backdrop for a significant change in penal theory that emerged at the beginning of
the nineteenth century. Whereas eighteenth-century penology proceeded by assuming that breaking the law represents a general disposition – fuelled by interests and
passions common to all mankind – the new view held that violations of the law are
almost entirely the activity of certain social classes. Whereas criminals were found
in all social sectors, now they were sought only in the lowest. Ibid., 275–7. See the
section 'Dangerous Individuals and Dangerous Classes' in Chapter 8.

82. Ibid., 272.

If, in this context, Foucault speaks of 'law ... [serving] the interests of a class',[83] he does not just mean that the laws served certain classes, which instrumentalized them for their own interests. The classification and systematization of illegalities did not simply mirror standing power relations. Instead, it produced and reinforced new mechanisms of domination. The judicial apparatus is not something neutral, which class interests then corrupt. Rather, modes of domination already stand inscribed in its materiality and mode of functioning: 'Legal punishments are to be resituated in an overall strategy of illegalities'.[84]

The 'achievement' of the prison, then, is not to perform an equalizing function – assuring punishment that bears on everyone in equal measure and can be applied to all infractions – but a strategy of discrimination and selection. In its seeming indifference to crimes, it enables a determinate kind of unlawfulness, *delinquency*, to be set apart and emphasized: prison 'isolates, outlines, brings out a form of illegality that seems to sum up symbolically all the others, but which makes it possible to leave in the shade those that one wishes to – or must – tolerate. This form is, strictly speaking, delinquency'.[85]

The organization of a determinate group of illegalities in the form of delinquency, then, defined a political strategy that did not aim to repress legal violations but to distinguish between them. Against this (strategic) background, it is mistaken to speak of the prison's 'failure' or 'lack of success'. On the contrary, the prison succeeded at producing delinquency and the delinquent subject. Yet again, Foucault stresses the distinction between the register of rights and law, on the one hand, and politico-strategic categories, on the other: 'In short, although the juridical opposition is between legality and illegal practice, the strategic opposition is between illegalities and delinquency'.[86]

How is it that the prison gave rise to the very delinquency it was supposed to eliminate? Here, too, Foucault seeks to distinguish this

---

83. Ibid., 272.

84. Ibid., 272; Deleuze, *Foucault* (1988), 31–2.

85. Foucault, 1975a, *Discipline and Punish* [1995], 277.

86. Ibid., 277; Foucault, 1975c, 'From Torture to Cellblock' [1996], 146–9. 'Illegality is not an accident, a more or less unavoidable imperfection. It's an absolutely positive element of social functioning, whose role is allocated in the general strategy of society. Every legislative arrangement has brought about protected and profitable spaces where the law can be violated, others where it can be ignored, and others finally where infractions are sanctioned'. Ibid., 148.

account from a functionalist model of explanation: producing delinquency and a delinquent milieu was not a matter of planning so much as it represented an unintended effect of the prison system. From the 1830s on, a new kind of strategy turned this unintended, negative result to positive ends. It became evident that defining unlawfulness as delinquency afforded a number of political and economic advantages. 'Visible' delinquency distracted from other, 'invisible' illegalities. It offered economic profit inasmuch as its prohibitions gave rise to a field of unlawful activities that proved highly lucrative (trade in arms, prostitution, drugs and so on); finally, a political significance emerged inasmuch as delinquents could be used as decoys and informants, permitting political parties and workers' organizations to be infiltrated. In sum, it can be said to 'represen[t] a diversion of illegality for the illicit circuits of profit and power of the dominant class'.[87]

More still, the stigma of delinquency promoted the splitting of the popular classes and the 'moralization' of the proletariat. Even though delinquents came from marginal social groups especially and were often deployed against the working classes (as police auxiliaries or manpower reserves), the proletariat ultimately made bourgeois conceptions of morality and legality its own – and with that, the condemnation of theft and crime. Against repeated efforts to represent the labour movement as an organization of murderers, thieves and alcoholics – so that its suppression might be justified – workers were forced 'to recreate for themselves a sort of moral puritanism that was for them a necessary condition for survival and a useful instrument in the struggle as well'.[88] Up to the nineteenth century, solidarity with prisoners had represented a constant in all political revolutions. Now, the splits and contradictions between proletariat and 'lumpenproletariat' (or, alternately, *plebs*) became a solid component of the bourgeois strategy of domination.[89]

---

87. Foucault, 1975a, *Discipline and Punish* [1995], 280; Foucault, 1977m, 'The Confession of the Flesh' [1980], 195–6; Raulff, *Das normale Leben* (1977), 132–8.

88. Foucault, 1974b, 'Michel Foucault on Attica' [1991], 32, 34.

89. Foucault, 1972c, 'Confining Societies' [1996], 90–1; Foucault, 1972d, 'On Popular Justice: A Discussion with Maoists' [1980], 22–3; Foucault, 1973c, 'Prisons et révoltes dans les prisons', 426–27; Foucault, 1975f, 'Prison Talk' [1980], 39–48; Defert and Donzelot, 'La charnière des prisons' (1976).

# 4

# Nietzsche's Hypothesis

The history of the army brings out more clearly than anything else the correctness of our conception of the connection between the productive forces and social relations. ... The whole history of the forms of bourgeois society is very strikingly epitomized here. If some day you find time you must work the thing out from this point of view.

Marx[1]

*Discipline and Punish* is subtitled 'The Birth of the Prison'. In fact, the book seeks to explain far more. Its aim is not restricted to reconstructing a past epoch, the history of an institution or changes in penal practices. Instead, the author has chosen the object of investigation because, in this light, power relations can be exposed that have shaped social relations to this day. A critical, diagnostic perspective underlies the 'history of prison', addressing contemporary mechanisms of domination in terms of their historical conditions of emergence.

The prison plays a key role within this genealogical project because its position is both paradigmatic and exceptional. On the one hand, the prison has an *exemplary meaning*, since a technology of power is materialized in it that also pervades many other realms. The prison forms part of a machine running through the whole of society, which all but makes it a prison, too. Conversely, the constitution of society as a 'carceral archipelago'[2] represents the condition for the prison's social acceptability: 'Is it surprising that the cellular prison ... should

---

1. Marx, 'Letter from Marx to Engels on 25 September 1857' (1975), 186.
2. Foucault, 1975a, *Discipline and Punish* [1995], 297.

have become the modern instrument of penality? Is it surprising that prisons resemble factories, schools, barracks, hospitals, which all resemble prisons?'.[3]

On the other hand, the prison occupies a *special position* within the disciplinary continuum. Far more than school or factory, hospital or army, it exercises 'despotic discipline' that pushes 'to their greatest intensity all the procedures to be found in the other disciplinary mechanisms'.[4] The prison's key importance follows from the way it encompasses all facets of disciplinary technology and 'concentrates' different disciplinary methods and models: 'the politico-moral schema of individual isolation and hierarchy; the economic model of force applied to compulsory work; the technico-medical model of cure and normalization. The cell, the workshop, the hospital'.[5] This is why 'the prison is the last figure of this age of disciplines'.[6]

The double position Foucault assigns the prison determines the contours of the 'genealogy of power' – but also poses grave problems. Foucault argues that the prison offers a point of departure for examining, in their technological materiality, the determinative principles of modern processes of power. The example of the prison enables one to study, in clear articulation, the mode of power characteristic of modern societies as a whole. Before discussing the difficulties this thesis entails for explaining power relations today, a few words are in order about the interpretive efforts against which Foucault deploys his theoretical instruments.

## Beyond Repression and Ideology:
## The Concept of Power-Knowledge

Examining power in terms of technology requires a change of perspective, away from institutions and authorities towards conditions of power. In other words, power's relational nature constitutes the focus of analysis. Defining power as technology does not concern the technologies that power implements, but the technology that power *is*.[7]

---

3. Ibid., 227–8; Foucault, 1973e, 'A propos de l'enfermement pénitentiaire', 439–40.
4. Foucault, 1975a, *Discipline and Punish* [1995], 236.
5. Ibid., 248.
6. Foucault, 1975c, 'From Torture to Cellblock' [1996], 147.
7. Much of the confusion and many of the misunderstandings that this theoretical

Accordingly, Foucault is interested less in who holds power, or where it is concentrated, than in the question of how it 'works'.[8]

Traditionally, political theory has offered two (complementary) answers to the question of how power operates. Power is said to work as physical repression and/or ideological manipulation: (initially) as repression and (subsequently) as ideology; it involves violence, constraint, exclusion, obstruction, obfuscation and so on. In contrast, Foucault's 'history of the prison' seeks to expose the selectivity and limits of such categories. He analyses the prison as the materialization of a new practice that differs from two other 'penal styles': physical punishment, on the one hand, and punishment as a 'semio-technique', on the other. In other words, it is impossible to boil the prison down to an institution for oppressing bodies or manipulating ideas; instead, it is situated in a new technology of power – discipline – which aims to produce useful individuals. The goal is for inmates to learn gestures and modes of conduct, develop habits, and make certain conceptions of time and space their own. At the same time, disciplinary technology presupposes the production of knowledge about these individuals, which makes it possible to know them, evaluate the potential and limitations of their capacities, investigate the conditions for changing them, identify their relative 'normality' and so on. It constitutes a

---

perspective has met with – from the very beginning – stem from the fact that Foucault broadens 'technology', which is traditionally reserved for operations bearing on nature, to exercising dominion over human beings. Foucault breaks with the model of technology as a specific form or effect of controlling nature, or natural resources, and enlists it to understand social relations. His conception of political technology rejects the idea of control from without in order to show 'that our thought, our life, our way of being down to the most everyday level are components of the same systematic organization and therefore exhibit the same categories as the scientific and technological world'. Foucault, 1966d, 'Entretien avec Madeleine Chapsal', 518; see also Gordon, 'Afterword' (1980), 238.

8. However, this does not mean that it is unimportant or superfluous to determine those who hold political responsibility. Foucault means to show that this step is not enough: 'I don't believe that this question of "who exercises power?" can be resolved unless that other question "how does it happen?" is resolved at the same time. Of course we have to show who those in charge are, we know that we have to turn, let us say, to deputies, ministers, principal private secretaries, etc., etc. But this is not the important issue, for we know perfectly well that even if we reach the point of designating exactly all those people, all those "decision-makers", we will still not really know why and how the decision was made, how it came to be accepted by everybody'. Foucault, 1984x, 'On Power' [1988], 103–4; see also Foucault, 1977f, '14 January 1976' [2003].

'political anatomy' that cannot be described in negative terms; instead, it must be analysed in 'positive' categories.[9]

Accordingly, the first step of Foucault's theoretical strategy involves taking issue with ideology critique and contesting the notion of repression. The point is not to neutralize or disqualify these perspectives, but, on the contrary, to open up new terrain by demonstrating the limitations and shortcomings (which result from power relations) of the models they employ. Foucault finds fault with critical strategies that rely solely on notions of ideology – or repression – and therefore fail to account for the 'productivity' or 'positivity' of disciplinary technology. Let us take a closer look at the objections Foucault raises.

Many forms of ideology critique operate with a base-superstructure metaphor. Hereby, 'immaterial' ideas, mentalities, conceptions and so on are provisionally detached from 'material' practices – and then 'derived' from them, or held to be 'imparted' by them. This approach gives rise to the problem of their actual relationship (*Adäquanzbeziehung*) and prompts questions about how to recognize the 'real truth'. It is necessary to presuppose the possibility of a 'correct representation' in order for a 'false image' of the world to exist. Ideology critique holds that power exercises effects on consciousness by means of incorrect, distorted or deformed ideas. Foucault takes issue with both underlying assumptions: the notion of a material separation between thought and reality and the methodological focus on conscious processes.

To begin with, conceiving ideology in this fashion presupposes a binary opposition between science and ideology. The latter refers to a set of false or imperfect ideas that do not (or do not yet) fulfil the standards of scientificity. In contrast, Foucault is interested in the 'non-scientificity of science'[10] – that is, how certain discourses achieve the status of being scientific (while this qualification is denied to others), and how the (human) sciences achieve definition within certain institutional and social practices. The problem, then, is not that disciplinary knowledge is 'false', but the fact that it counts as 'right' in a specific historical context.

Second, Foucault takes issue with assigning priority to consciousness. In the framework of disciplinary technology, conscious processes are not the target of power so much as they form the medium and

9. Foucault, 1975a, *Discipline and Punish* [1995], 23, 180.
10. Foucault, 1976g, 'The Social Extension of the Norm' [1996], 198.

switchboard for a 'political anatomy' that seeks to train the body. Power does not operate via 'spiritualization' so much as 'incorporation'.[11] Accordingly, Foucault deems it 'more materialist' to investigate the body and effects on it before bringing up the question of ideology.[12] Conceiving power as a process of masking, or concealment, 'masks' how it actually functions inasmuch as this perspective solidifies and reproduces belief in the primacy of consciousness and the freedom of the will – fictions that represent an integral component of bourgeois-capitalist societies.[13]

If countering prevalent modes of ideology critique proves relatively straightforward, Foucault acknowledges that he has had 'much more trouble'[14] freeing himself the notion of *repression* – which played a role in his studies for much longer. More and more, in the course of the 1970s, he recognized the limitations and problems of addressing power exclusively in these terms.[15] In particular, two points struck him as inadequate.

For one, viewing power as repression proves extremely limited and covers only a small part of the spectrum of possible effects. It reduces highly varied forms of domination, subjugation, obligation and influence to the imperative of obedience, and it does so without analysing the fact of obedience itself. Inasmuch as obedience seems to be 'self-evident', questions concerning its conditions and preconditions no

---

11. Foucault, 1977d, 'Truth and Power' [1984], 66.

12. Foucault, 1975g, 'Body/Power' [1980], 58; Foucault, 1974d, 'White Magic and Black Gown' [1996], 290–1.

13. Foucault engages with the notion of ideology critique at length; Foucault, 1977d, 'Truth and Power' [1984], 60; Foucault, 1977f, '14 January 1976' [2003], 34; Foucault, 1973i, '28 March 1973' [2015], 236–7. Michèle Barrett has read Foucault's entire *oeuvre* as a consequence of, and engagement with, its Marxist variant. Barrett, *The Politics of Truth* (1991). On the differences between Foucault's approach and ideology critique, see the essays by Jürgen Link and Paul Veyne. Link, 'Warum Foucault aufhörte, Symbole zu analysieren' (1985); Veyne, 'L'idéologie selon Marx et selon Nietzsche' (1977).

14. Foucault, 1977d, 'Truth and Power' [1984], 60.

15. 'When I wrote *Madness and Civilization* [*History of Madness*], I made at least an implicit use of this notion of repression. I think, indeed, that I was positing the existence of a sort of living, voluble, and anxious madness which the mechanisms of power and psychiatry were supposed to have come to repress and reduce to silence. But it seems to me now that the notion of repression is quite inadequate for capturing what is precisely the productive aspect of power'. Ibid., 60. The following chapters show how Foucault in fact continued to rely on the conception of repression up to *The History of Sexuality, Volume 1*. See, especially, Chapter 6 in Part II.

longer come up at all; ultimately, power is explained simply through power. For this reason, the concept of repression refers to 'a power that only has the force of the negative on its side, a power to say no; in no condition to produce, capable only of posting limits, it is basically anti-energy. This is the paradox of its effectiveness: it is incapable of doing anything, except to render what it dominates incapable of doing either, except for what this power allows it to do'.[16]

Foucault also rejects the notion of repression for another reason. The idea of 'repression' presupposes a natural and universal body that is 'held down' and forced into silence by processes of power, which vary historically. Resistance to the latter would seek to 'restore' or 'liberate' such a 'natural' body. But the analysis of disciplinary power shows that all bodies are always already 'political': trained, calibrated and fitted to a time-space continuum – part of a 'political anatomy'.

As such, the notion of repression – and the critical goal of 'discovering' the body underneath, or beyond, its effects – mystifies the way power actually works by seeking to locate subversive potential in a 'natural' state; in fact, it can never be anything other than the historically variant product of the techniques of power.

> It is illusory to believe that madness – or delinquency or crime – speak to us from a position of absolute exteriority. Nothing is more interior to our society, nothing is more within the effects of its power, than the affliction of a crazy person or the violence of a criminal. In other words, we are always on the inside. The margin is a myth.[17]

---

16. Foucault, 1976a, *The History of Sexuality, Volume 1: An Introduction* [1978], 85; Foucault, 1975g, 'Body/Power' [1980], 59.

17. Foucault, 1976g, 'The Social Extension of the Norm' [1996], 198; see also Foucault, 1975a, *Discipline and Punish* [1995], 29; Raulff, *Das normale Leben* (1977), 48–51; Deleuze, *Foucault* (1988), 28–9; Rajchman, *Michel Foucault: The Freedom of Philosophy* (1985), 84–93. 'What you call "naturalism" designates two things, I believe. A certain theory, the idea that underneath power with its acts of violence and its artifice we should be able to recuperate things themselves in their primitive vivacity: behind the asylum walls, the spontaneity of madness; through the penal system, the generous fever of delinquence; under the sexual interdiction, the freshness of desire. And also a certain aesthetic and moral choice: power is evil, it's ugly, poor, sterile, monotonous, dead; and what power is exercised upon is right, good, rich'. Foucault, 1977k, 'The End of the Monarchy of Sex' [1996], 221.

That said, Foucault's critical assessment does not mean that he wishes to argue against the reality of ideological obfuscation or physical repression. He considers their existence a matter of historical fact.[18] The point is not to deny that ideology and/or repression exist, but to show that these modalities of power do not cover the whole field of effects. Foucault seeks to expose the blind spots of models that focus on 'negative' effects of power. Yet how is it possible to analyse the 'productive' and 'positive' quality of power relations without making recourse to ideology and repression? Foucault responds by replacing (initial) repression and (subsequent) ideology with a new concept: *power-knowledge* (*pouvoir-savoir*):

> power relations … do not simply play a facilitating or obstructing role with respect to knowledge … power and knowledge are not bound to each other solely through the action of interests and ideologies; so the problem is not just to determine how power subordinates knowledge and makes it serve its ends or how it superimposes itself on it, imposing ideological contents and limitations. No knowledge is formed without a system of communication, registration, accumulation, and displacement that is in itself a form of power, linked in its existence and its functioning to other forms of power. No power, on the other hand, is exercised without the extraction, appropriation, distribution, or restraint of a knowledge. At this level there is not knowledge [*connaissance*] on one side and society on the other, or science and the state, but the basic forms of 'power-knowledge' ['*pouvoir-savoir*'].[19]

---

18. See e.g. Foucault, 1977b, 'Sexualität und Wahrheit', 8; Foucault, 1983h, 'An Ethics of Pleasure' [1996], 375.

19. Foucault, 1972h, 'Penal Theories and Institutions' [1997], 17. The concept of power-knowledge, which Foucault introduced in a lecture at the Collège de France in 1971–2, connects with a series of further methodological changes. The concept of the dispositive (*dispositif*) – otherwise employed chiefly in military, medical and juridical contexts – represents another important theoretical development after *The Archaeology of Knowledge*. Foucault uses it to refer to a heterogeneous ensemble linking discourses, institutions, apparatuses, laws, scientific pronouncements and so on. Although the elements can change their positions or functions within this net, they are subordinated to a shared 'strategic imperative'. Foucault, 1977m, 'The Confession of the Flesh' [1980], 195. As such, the difference from earlier works and terminologies (*epistémé, énoncé, discours*) involves forging a more comprehensive concept that also incorporates non-discursive elements; in turn, analysis follows a new strategic orientation: 'This is what the dispositive consists in: strategies of relations of forces supporting, and supported by, types of knowledge. In seeking in *The Order of Things*

Above all, the 'working hypothesis' – or 'analytical grid' – of power-knowledge holds methodological significance.[20] It does not provide a suprahistorical schema, but has a concrete theoretical-strategic purpose. Its heuristic aim is to undertake a 'systematic reduction of value' in order to avoid the problem of a given insight's truth or legitimacy.[21] To this end, Foucault breaks with the idea of an external relationship between power and knowledge; he relativizes a line of questioning that asks how power practices 'apply' or 'exploit' knowledge – and, conversely, how knowledge processes 'elicit' or 'secure' power.

None of this is to say that posing the problem of truth or legitimacy is unnecessary, superfluous or false. On the contrary, Foucault insists that an instrumental connection between power and knowledge has always held ('Sovereigns were always surrounded by pedagogues; kings were counselled by philosophers, scholars, and wise men'). But power-knowledge examines a new aspect of the relationship, which emerged in tandem with the social division of labour and the systematization, institutionalization and professionalization of the human sciences: 'The nineteenth century brought something new, which is that knowledge must function in society as endowed with a certain quantity of power.'[22]

From this perspective, the discourses of teachers, judges, social workers, doctors and psychiatrists no longer represent external factors to power. They do not offer knowledge, which then comes to be instrumentalized. Instead, such knowledge has a straightforward function: to formulate and define the distinctions between normal and abnormal that prevail in social and institutional practices. A 'normalizing discourse' emerges.[23] Foucault's concept of power-knowledge does not

---

to write a history of the *episteme*, I was still caught in an impasse. What I should like to do now is to try and show that what I call a dispositive is a much more general case of the *episteme*; or rather, that the *episteme* is a specifically *discursive* dispositive, whereas the dispositive in its general form is both discursive and non-discursive, its elements being much more heterogeneous'. Ibid., 196–7, translation modified; see also Dreyfus and Rabinow, *Michel Foucault: Beyond Structuralism and Hermeneutics* (1983), 121; Kammler, *Michel Foucault: Eine kritische Analyse seines Werks* (1986), 157–62; Deleuze, 'What Is a Dispositif?' (1992).

20. Foucault, 1990b, 'What Is Critique?' [2007], 60.
21. Ibid., 60.
22. Foucault, 1973i, '28 March 1973' [2015], 235.
23. Ibid., 241; Foucault, 1974c, 'Truth and Juridical Forms' [2000], 78–9.

stand above history or hold in general terms – an abstract scheme for application on particular, concrete societies. Rather, it represents a historically specific phenomenon tied to the constitution of the human sciences.[24]

Foucault's hypothesis shifts the point of emphasis and breaks with a critical tradition that sets power and knowledge in opposition to each other: power does not function as a limitation or obstacle to knowledge, nor does knowledge serve to mask, or manifest, power. Power does not prevent or repress the formation of knowledge; instead, it stimulates and produces it. Foucault not only rejects thinking about power and knowledge in external terms; he also seeks to critique the hierarchical idea of subordination and superordination, as well as the notion of historical deduction. Power processes do not simply apply, or exploit, forms of knowledge; nor can constellations of power be boiled down, or traced back, to modes of organizing knowledge. Foucault rejects both these schemes as monocausal for affirming the priority of knowledge or that of power exclusively. Instead, he posits a 'rule of immanence':[25] fields of knowledge are constituted on the basis of power relations that 'install' potential objects; conversely, they can

---

24. Foucault, 1990b, 'What Is Critique?' [2007], 60. A slight change to the concept of power-knowledge occurs as Foucault proceeds. *Discipline and Punish* affirms not only parallels between power and knowledge, but also their immanence: 'Perhaps, too, we should abandon a whole tradition that allows us to imagine that knowledge can exist only where the power relations are suspended and that knowledge can develop only outside its injunctions, its demands and its interests ... We should admit rather that power produces knowledge (and not simply by encouraging because it serves power or by applying it because it is useful); that power and knowledge directly imply one another; that there is no power relation without the correlative constitution of a field of knowledge, nor any knowledge that does not presupposed and constitute at the same time power relations'. Foucault, 1975a, *Discipline and Punish* [1995], 27.

For an excellent theoretico-historical account of how Foucault developed the concept of power and its significance for critiquing the notion of 'epistemological sovereignty', see Keenan 1987 esp. 12–19 and Rouse 1994. Foucault distinguishes three historical types of connection between power and knowledge: *measure* (in Greek antiquity, where knowledge of mathematics and the physical world followed the same procedures as law and monetary exchange), *inquiry* (during the late Middle Ages, when the natural sciences formed out of methods of forensic investigation), and *examination*, which emerged with the human sciences and joined hierarchical surveillance with normalizing sanctions. Foucault, 1972h, 'Penal Theories and Institutions' [1997], 17–19; Foucault, 1975a, *Discipline and Punish* [1995], 184–94, 225–8; Raulff, *Das normale Leben* (1977), 64–8, 28–30.

25. Foucault, 1976a, *The History of Sexuality, Volume 1: An Introduction* [1978], 98.

become the target of power processes because they have already been produced cognitively.[26]

Foucault's view has met with grave misunderstanding. It would seem that the concept of power-knowledge gives up on systematic distinctions between its two components. Does not questioning the traditional opposition between power and knowledge mean collapsing the border that separates one term from the other – declaring knowledge power, and power knowledge? Indeed, many of Foucault's readers have understood Foucault's 'rule of immanence' as a 'rule of identity' and – in keeping with their own theoretical perspective – faulted or defended him for doing so.[27]

In fact, making such an equation yields nothing in analytical terms. On the contrary: the problematic that is supposed to be subjected to critique remains intact, if in reversed form. Foucault does not reject the opposition between power and knowledge so they may stand as the same thing, but in order to break with the whole problematic of exteriority and interiority: 'Between techniques of knowledge and strategies of power, there is no exteriority, even if they have specific roles and are linked together on the basis of their difference [qu'elles s'articulent l'une sur l'autre]'.[28]

When Foucault insists on the inner connection between power and knowledge *and* the difference between them, the methodological point is to contest views that opt for strict identity or opposition.

26. Foucault, 1975f, 'Prison Talk' [1980], 51–2.

27. Positing the unity of power and knowledge stands opposed to the genealogical conception of history for at least two reasons. First, it presumes that the historical process had to unfold exactly as it did – and therefore makes it impossible to be reconstructed and described concretely. Second, it cannot account for the stability of power forms and patterns of behaviour, for if power and knowledge were identical, then every change of knowledge would directly lead to a change of power forms. Equating knowledge and power dissolves the specificity of the processes the latter undergoes, which are distinct from the forms the former assumes; in consequence, neither the epistemological effects of knowledge nor the constraining effects of power admit analysis. For the relation between power and knowledge to pose a question at all, a moment of 'underdetermination' (Kusch) proves necessary: 'If I had said, or meant, that knowledge was power, I would have said so, and, having said so, I would have had nothing more to say, since, having made them identical, I don't see why I would have taken the trouble to show the different relations between them'. Foucault, 1984n, 'The Concern for Truth' [1988], 264; Foucault, 1983e, 'Critical Theory/Intellectual History' [1988], 38–9; see also Ewald, 'Foucault, une pensée sans aveu' (1977); Kusch, *Foucault's Strata and Fields* (1991), 152–4.

28. Foucault, 1976a, *The History of Sexuality, Volume 1: An Introduction* [1978], 98.

The compulsion to come down on one side or the other constitutes the object of analysis. Accordingly, Foucault's 'genealogy of power' achieves definition by developing a critique of a conception of power that thematizes only its negative effects: 'it seems to me that this analytics can be constituted only if it frees itself completely from a certain representation of power that I would term ... "juridico-discursive".[29]

## The King's Head: The Juridical Conception of Power

Juridical conception of power refers, for Foucault, to a scheme of analysis and evaluation that interprets power in legal terms, above all: laws, prohibitions, censorship, constraints and so on. Such a representation is dominated, on the one hand, by the idea of free individuals, and, on the other, by the notion of political sovereignty. In this framework, power involves a (social) contract, whereby (legal) subjects surrender their freedom to a higher, autonomous instance. Power is constituted following the 'model of Leviathan':[30] arising from multiple individuals and volitions, political sovereignty emerges as a unified will and body. Hereby, the contract becomes the matrix for political power. Power constituted in this manner yields constraint only when it spills over and abandons the limitations legally set by the contract. In such a case, the exercise of power splits into legitimate and illegitimate uses – one in keeping with rights and law and the other abusing them. The conception rests on the idea of the limitation and binary nature of the legal code. Three postulates define it, in particular:

1. The Postulate of *Ownership*. Power is conceived exclusively in terms of appropriation: it represents a good, or a substance, which can be possessed, sold or traded. It follows that some social groups or classes 'own' power, whereas others are excluded from it.

2. The Postulate of *Localization*. Power processes run from top to bottom; starting at a centralized instance, they pervade society and exercise effects on individuals. It follows that power is equated with political authority and concentrated in state apparatuses.

---

29. Ibid., 82.
30. Foucault, 1977f, '14 January 1976' [2003], 34.

3. The Postulate of *Subordination*. Power processes serve to reproduce the social order and have a primarily functional character; their
modality involves prohibitions, constraints, acts of exclusion and so
on. This means that power serves to maintain and continue social
relations – e.g. standing modes of production or patriarchal rule –
which remain external to it.[31]

According to Foucault, the juridical conception proves theoretically
lacking inasmuch as it cannot grasp the complexity of power relations. That said, the problem is not just theoretical in nature, nor is
it simply a matter of picturing power incorrectly. Foucault seeks to
demonstrate the concrete, historical reasons for such 'failure'. In historical perspective, the juridical conception of power derives from the
'juridical-political theory of sovereignty',[32] which provided the foundation and justification for feudal monarchy. As Foucault observes, the
renewal of Roman law during the late Middle Ages represented one of
the 'technical' preconditions for building vast territorial empires and
their administrative and military apparatuses. Law played a double
role in this context. If, on the one hand, it served as an instrument of
constraint and a means of domination, it also guaranteed a certain

---

31. Foucault, 1973i, '28 March 1973' [2015], 228–33; Foucault, 1977f, '14 January
1976' [2003], 24–34; Deleuze, *Foucault* (1988), 25–7; Sawicki, *Disciplining Foucault*
(1991), 20–4. Needless to say, this account is very abbreviated and extremely schematic and fails to do justice to most political theories. Pasquale Pasquino, for instance,
has cautioned against simply equating Thomas Hobbes's *Leviathan* and the juridical
conception of power. Pasquino, 'Political Theory of War and Peace: Foucault and the
History of Modern Political Theory' (1993), 79–84. This reservation is certainly war-
ranted. All the same – even if it is right to point out an insufficient nuance or the lack
of sources and evidence – Foucault's theoretical interest does not bear on differences
so much as on points in common between various political discourses.

Barry Hindess addresses the 'juridical conception of power' at length. Taking
up Foucault's observations, he persuasively demonstrates that, for the tradition of
'Western' political thinking after Hobbes, power has counted not just as the capacity
for action but also, and especially, as a right; hereby, the ability to act and the right to
do so are based on the consensus of those over whom power is exercised. With much
greater attention to detail, Hindess demonstrates how power is conceived in terms of
contrafactual conditions, above all: power in the hands of some prevents others from
doing what they would otherwise do. The chief effects of political power are evident
in relation to parties who, at least in principle, act autonomously. By the same token,
power counts as legitimate inasmuch as it seems to rest on the actual or implicit consensus of 'autonomous' subjects. Hindess, *Discourses of Power* (1996).

32. Foucault, 1990a, *'Society Must Be Defended'* [2003], 34.

mode of functioning, ensured security, and provided the basis for legitimacy. Accordingly, law was not 'simply a weapon skillfully wielded by
monarchs; it was the monarchic system's mode of manifestation and
the form of its acceptability'.[33]

An important consequence of this historical alignment of law and
sovereignty was that not just defenders and advocates of monarchy,
but also anti-monarchical forces, appealed to the law. Whether reinforcing or restricting monarchical power was at issue, the central item
of contention always involved 'natural' or 'correct' laws/rights. Indeed,
the critique of absolutism that Rousseau and other eighteenth-century
proponents of enlightenment formulated did not take aim at the
monarchical-juridical system as such; instead it was directed against
a monarchy that, counter to what it claimed, had offended the law
time and again and placed itself above legality by acting in an arbitrary fashion. Such a critique of absolutist despotism 'only' shifted
the accent from the prince's sovereignty to 'popular sovereignty'; it
did not touch on the systematic structure of the law and its function
in organizing domination: 'Political criticism availed itself ... of all
the juridical thinking that had accompanied the development of the
monarchy, in order to condemn the latter; but it did not challenge the
principle which held that law had to be the very form of power, and
that power always had to be exercised in the form of law'.[34]

Foucault's thesis holds that the juridical conception of power is
historically tied to feudal-absolutist society. It proves dysfunctional
– or at least in need of completion – inasmuch as bourgeois-capitalist
society witnessed the rise of a new type of power, which no longer
traversed social relations from top to bottom. If, under the *ancien
régime*, power functioned as the right to acquire goods and services,

---

33. Foucault, 1976a, *The History of Sexuality, Volume 1: An Introduction* [1978],
87; Foucault, 1977f, '14 January 1976' [2003], 25–6. Franz Neumann has shown the
double nature of law and rights and its connection to the contradictions of bourgeois-
capitalist socialization. As he analyses them, autonomy and coercion, violence and
law, sovereignty and freedom, and subjective and objective rights constitute the two
poles of the 'rule of law' that, with varying points of emphasis, has characterized
European legal traditions and political theory since the Middle Ages. Neumann, 'Der
Funktionswandel des Gesetzes im Recht der bürgerlichen Gesellschaft' (1986b), esp.
31–6.

34. Foucault, 1976a, *The History of Sexuality, Volume 1: An Introduction* [1978],
88; see also Dreyfus and Rabinow, *Michel Foucault: Beyond Structuralism and Hermeneutics* (1983), 130–1; Plumpe and Kammler, 'Wissen ist Macht' (1980), 210–11.

bourgeois society 'invented' a 'new mechanism of power which had very specific procedures, completely new instruments, and very different equipment': disciplinary power, which provided 'one of the basic tools for the establishment of industrial capitalism and the corresponding type of society'.[35]

Against this backdrop, the 'genealogy of power' seeks to do theoretical justice to the historical change in power mechanisms and to trace power's actual mode of operation conceptually. According to Foucault, political analysis should free itself from the idea of sovereignty, legal codes and the central figure of the king in order to examine the productive aspect of power processes defining capitalist societies:

> At bottom, despite the differences in epochs and objectives, the representation of power has remained under the spell of monarchy. In political thought and analysis, we still have not cut off the head of the king.[36]

This assessment proves surprising in light of extensive Marxist writings on the institution of law and bourgeois constitutionality. But, according to Foucault, the juridical conception of power does not 'belong' to liberal or conservative political theories; it persists within the tradition of Marxism. Despite differences of political theory, liberalism shares with 'a certain contemporary conception that passes for ... Marxist ... "economism" in the theory of power'.[37]

---

35. Foucault, 1977f, '14 January 1976' [2003], 36; Foucault, 1975a, *Discipline and Punish* [1995], 138; Foucault, 1976g, 'The Social Extension of the Norm' [1996], 197–9.

36. Foucault, 1976a, *The History of Sexuality, Volume 1: An Introduction* [1978], 88–9.

37. Foucault, 1977e, '7 January 1976' [2003], 13. It is clear, then, that Foucault's critique does not concern Marxist theory as a whole, but only its economistic variants. Indeed, Foucault's productive engagement with Marx is extremely important for evaluating his theoretical work. It has rightly – and often – been observed that Foucault fails to do justice to the complexity of Marxism (an objection that also applies to his initial assessment of liberalism; see the second part of this study for how he later revised his position) and substitutes summary judgements and caricatures for nuanced discussion. Poulantzas, *State, Power, Socialism* (2000), 36, 146–7. That said, one should note that his critique does not bear on theoretically sophisticated forms of Marxism so much as the versions that have produced the greatest political effects; in other words, it does not concern Marx's work but dogmatic Marxism – 'I mean scholastic Marxism, that traditional corpus of knowledge and texts'. Foucault, 1975d, 'An Interview with Michel Foucault' [1985], 3; Foucault, 1977d, 'Truth and Power' [1984], 58–9. Etienne Balibar has stressed that 'the whole of Foucault's work

Foucault contends that the economism of many Marxist analyses represents a variant of the juridical conception of power. Specifically, they fuse legal and economic categories, tying together contract and exchange; in other words, they equate power and goods. If, at times, power receives attention as a right modelled on the commodity – something that can be possessed, exchanged or transferred – at others, power relations are viewed only in terms of economic functionality and the potential they hold for social reproduction. In the latter case, power is thought to have the task of preserving relations of production and class domination simultaneously. As such, this version of Marxism remains stuck in the juridical model of power as much as their counterpart: 'we have ... in one case a political power which finds its formal model in the process of exchange, in the economy of the circulation of goods; and in the other case, political power finds its historical raison d'être, the principle of its concrete form and of its actual workings, in the economy'.[38]

However, in objecting to '"economism" in the theory of power',[39] Foucault does not mean to deny the significance of economic factors when analysing social power relations. Instead, the point is that 'power relations and economic relations always constitute a sort of network or loop'.[40] Foucault's concern is *not* to separate power and economy. Quite the opposite: he wants to ask how they are connected. In order to formulate this question in the first place, one must take leave of modes of analysis that restrict the relationship to a matter of correspondence or derivation.

'Economistic' analysis distorts concrete relations more than it illuminates them. It means presupposing that the economy is all important and elaborating a causal chain that works with dependencies,

---

can be seen in terms of a genuine struggle with Marx, and ... this can be viewed as one of the driving forces of his productiveness'. Balibar, 'Foucault and Marx: The Question of Nominalism' (1992), 39. For Foucault's appreciation of Marx, see, e.g., Foucault, 1975f, 'Prison Talk' [1980], 52–3; Foucault, 1977e, '7 January 1976' [2003], 5–6; for evaluation of Foucault's work from a Marxist perspective, see Lecourt, *Pour une Critique de l'Epistémologie* (1972); Minston, 'Strategies for Socialists? Foucault's Conception of Power' (1980); Poster, *Foucault, Marxism and History* (1984); Balibar, 'Foucault and Marx: The Question of Nominalism' (1992); Maler, 'Foucault et Marx: une confrontation inactuelle?' (1994); on the reception of Foucault by the German left, see Eßbach, 'Michel Foucault und die deutsche Linke' (1984).

38. Foucault, 1977e, '7 January 1976' [2003], 14.
39. Ibid., 13.
40. Ibid., 14.

adequations, determinations and so on. The 'genealogy of power' rejects this view of the economy as a self-regulating sphere, which takes care of things automatically and only requires 'external' safeguards. Foucault's point is that power relations always already inhabit the conditions that supposedly underlie them: the legal relations they legitimate and the economic relations they secure. Power relations are not external to other types of relations, but immanent within them.[41]

The problem Foucault identifies can be addressed only after making a strategic decision. If the 'indissociability of the economy and politics' is not limited to formal isomorphism or functional subordination – neither to adequation nor to determination – then, and only then, can one pose the question of 'a different order, ... precisely that order that we have to isolate'.[42]

## War and Struggle: The Strategic Conception of Power

Foucault provides a preliminary answer to the question of how to analyse power in non-juridical and non-economic terms when he proposes a theoretical perspective representing 'precisely the

41. As we have seen, this means that they are *not* identical with those types of relations. If relations of economy, knowledge and sexuality also represent relations of power, it is not because they are the same thing; instead, they are interwoven in complex fashion: power relations 'are the immediate effects of the divisions, inequalities, and disequilibriums which occur in the latter, and conversely they are the internal conditions of these differentiations'. Foucault, 1976a, *The History of Sexuality, Volume 1: An Introduction* [1978], 94; see also Foucault, 1982b, 'The Subject and Power', 223; Kocyba, 'Eine reine Beschreibung diskursiver Ereignisse' (1988), 36.

To be sure, this idea is not new – it already occurs in the writings of Marx, Gramsci, and Althusser. The critique of economism and determinism is as old as Marxism itself. What Gramsci seeks to describe in terms of hegemony corresponds to Althusser's notion of overdetermination and the 'relative autonomy' of superstructures. In this context, Foucault's originality involves pursuing what Althusser anticipated but did not execute in full inasmuch as he still held to an unhistorical conception of capitalist production: 'We must carry this through to its conclusion and say that this overdetermination does not just refer to apparently unique and aberrant historical situations [...], but is *universal*; the economic dialectic is never active *in the pure state*; in History, these instances, the superstructures, etc. – are never seen to step respectfully aside when their work is done ... From the first moment to the last, the lonely hour of the "last instance" never comes'. Althusser, *For Marx* (2006), 113; see also Balibar, 'Foucault and Marx: The Question of Nominalism' (1992), 51; Schenkel and de Vries, *Umleitung oder: Wie heißt Bruno mit Nachnamen?* (1989), 40–3.

42. Foucault, 1977e, '7 January 1976' [2003], 14.

opposite'[43] of a negative and juridical viewpoint: the *strategic-positive conception*. According to this model, the basis for power relations does not lie in juridico-economic factors, but in politico-military conflicts. It follows 'Nietzsche's hypothesis':[44] power relations should not be viewed in terms of exclusion, distortion and prohibition, but along the lines of war, confrontation and struggle.[45]

Responding point for point to the juridical conception, this perspective seeks 'to invert the general direction of the analysis'.[46] As regards the first postulate, Foucault emphasizes that power is not a possession; instead, it names a connection that only exists *in actu*. Power cannot be appropriated, exchanged or transferred because it is not a substance but a relation.[47] Second, this feature means that power cannot be centralized in a group or class that wields it, with others remaining wholly excluded. Third, power processes do not express 'deeper' reality, which they somehow mirror, secure or reproduce. State apparatuses represent a 'concentrated form', the intensified effect, of power relations much broader in scope; consequently, neither controlling nor destroying such apparatuses will make certain forms of power disappear.[48]

This model disqualifies the juridical conception of power and provides a new analytical grid. 'The strategical model, rather than the model based on law'[49] should be employed – and for concrete, historical reasons. The evolution of bourgeois-capitalist societies at once enables and demands as much. Just as the juridical form of analysis was tied to feudal social formations, the strategic model is tied to

43. Foucault, 1977f, '14 January 1976' [2003], 28.

44. Foucault, 1977e, '7 January 1976' [2003], 16.

45. Ulrich Raulff has pointed out three further aspects of the concept of strategy in the 'microphysics of power'. First, the concept of strategy improves our understanding of power relations without invoking a constitutive subject; second, it offers a higher level of abstraction, allowing the juridical conception to be analysed as one model, or form, of power among others; third, it stresses the productivity of power relations, their integration into social production (economy, education, morality, etc.). Raulff, *Das normale Leben* (1977), 82–3.

46. Foucault, 1977f, '14 January 1976' [2003], 26.

47. 'In fact, power is not possessed [...]. Power is exercised [...] over the whole surface of the social field, according to a whole system of relays, connections, points of support, of things as tenuous as the family, sexual relationships, housing, and so on. However finely we penetrated the social network, we find power [...] as something that takes place, is effectuated, exercised'. Foucault, 1973i, '28 March 1973' [2015], 228.

48. Ibid., 229, see also 229–31.

49. Foucault, 1976a, *The History of Sexuality, Volume 1: An Introduction* [1978], 102.

bourgeois societies. On the level of theory, changing the framework of explanation corresponds to historical transformations in the order of power mechanisms.[50]

In contrast to sovereign power, disciplinary power does not amount to a legal code so much as it observes a military mode of operation. Discipline 'transfers' methods and techniques that were initially applied in the army to other social realms such as the factory: 'the massive projection of military methods onto industrial organization was an example of this modelling of the division of labour following the model laid down by the schemata of power'.[51]

At the same time, the matter goes beyond transferring military methods to other institutional spheres: the disciplines implement procedures and provide technology and knowledge with a martial character.[52] The military develops forms of organization and procedural rules that find application in other realms, which become detached from their point of origin; now, the universalization and interconnection between disciplines makes them into a political technology. The thoroughgoing disciplination of society comes to provide the precondition for politics, creating the concrete basis for an abstract aggregation of wills: 'While jurists or philosophers were seeking in the pact a primal model for the construction or reconstruction of the social body, the soldiers and with them the technicians of discipline were elaborating procedures for the individual and collective coercion of bodies'.[53]

Foucault reverses Clausewitz's well-known dictum. Not only is war politics pursued by other means – politics is war pursued by other means:

50. Plumpe and Kammler, 'Wissen ist Macht' (1980), 210.

51. Foucault, 1975a, *Discipline and Punish* [1995], 221. Clemens Kammler rightly sees a parallel to Marx's analysis of capital. Kammler, *Michel Foucault: Eine kritische Analyse seines Werks* (1986), 149–50. Like Foucault, Marx points to an 'elective affinity' between industrial and military forms of organization: 'The technical subordination of the workman to the uniform motion of the instruments of labour, and the peculiar composition of the body of workpeople, consisting as it does of individuals of both sexes and of all ages, gives rise to a barrack discipline, which is elaborated into a complete system in the factory, and which fully develops the before mentioned labour of overseeing, thereby dividing the workers into operatives and overseers, into the private soldiers and sergeants of an industrial army'. Marx, *Capital: A Critique of Political Economy* (1976), 426–7; cf. Foucault, 1975a, *Discipline and Punish* [1995], 221. For an explicit reference by Foucault to Marx's analysis of capital as the 'methodological principle' for his own investigations, see Foucault, 1981e, 'The Meshes of Power' [2007], 156–8.

52. Foucault, 1975a, *Discipline and Punish* [1995], 157–9.

53. Ibid., 169.

It may be that war as strategy is a continuation of politics. But it must not be forgotten that 'politics' has been conceived as a continuation, if not exactly and directly of war, at least of the military model as a fundamental means of preventing civil disorder. ... In the great eighteenth-century states, the army guaranteed civil peace no doubt because it was a real force, an ever-threatening sword, but also because it was a technique and a body of knowledge that could project their schema over the social body.[54]

Viewing power relations from the perspective of struggle, war and confrontation holds immediate consequences for Foucault's own theoretical position. The strategic conception of power occupies a politico-epistemological field that is 'dominated' by the juridical model of power. As such, confrontation with, and rejection of, the juridical conception does not represent a theoretical undertaking alone; it also affords the precondition for, and a component of, political struggle. Theoretical understandings of power prove inseparable from developing practical modes of engagement and articulating political choices. The juridical conception can only thematize power relations distinguished by a negative mode of operation. This means that 'positive' power effects remain beyond the scope of analysis: the disciplination of individuals, the moralization of the working class, the production of 'delinquency' and so on cannot be understood or subjected to critique as operations of power. In contrast, Foucault's strategic analysis exposes the power effects of juridical analysis and its blindness with respect to the 'productivity of power', and ultimately assigns the whole perspective a place in the field of power relations to be deciphered.

Foucault progressively inverted the direction of analysis in works from *The Order of Discourse* to *Discipline and Punish*. By doing so, he could expose problems of political analysis oriented on the model of law. However, the approach presented a significant theoretical problem of its own. Inasmuch as the strategic model pursues 'precisely the opposite' of juridical analysis, it remains within the same problematic without really offering a way out. Instead of 'cut[ting] off the king's head',[55] Foucault reverses what he criticized and substitutes war and struggle for law and contract.

---

54. Ibid., 168; Foucault, 1975b, 'La politique est la continuation de la guerre par d'autres moyens', 704; Foucault, 1977e, '7 January 1976' [2003], 14–16.
55. Foucault, 1977d, 'Truth and Power' [1984], 63.

In rejecting the matrix of the legal code when analysing power relations, Foucault's 'discourse of struggle'[56] has the tendency to abandon
all reference to law and to dissolve power into war: 'It is not possessed
because it is in play, it is risked. At the heart of power is a warlike relation ..., and not a relation of appropriation'.[57] War and law trade places:
'the study of this micro-physics presupposes that the power exercised
on the body is conceived not as a property, but as a strategy ... ; that
one should take as its model a perpetual battle rather than a contract
regulating a transaction or the conquest of a territory'.[58] *Discipline and
Punish*, which begins with a critique of the juridical conception of
power, ends with 'rumbling from the midst of the battle-field'.[59]

All the while, Foucault practices the same kind of analysis for which
he faults the juridical conception: above all, he discusses its negativity
and shortcomings. His debate with the linguist and political activist
Noam Chomsky put the limitations of this mode of engagement into
relief. Whereas Chomsky called for envisioning a just society on the
basis of humanistic theory,[60] Foucault rejected politics that addresses
social conditions in these terms. For him, such a conception represents part of the society it should serve to subject to critique:

> it seems to me that the idea of justice in itself is an idea which in
> effect has been invented and put to work in different types of societies
> as an instrument of a certain political and economic power or as a
> weapon against that power. ... And contrary to what you think, you
> can't prevent me from believing that these notions of human nature, of
> justice, of the realisation of the essence of human beings, are all notions
> and concepts which have been formed within our civilisation, within
> our type of knowledge and our form of philosophy, and that as a result
> form part of our class system; and one can't, however regrettable it
> may be, put forward these notions to describe or justify a fight which
> should – and shall in principle – overthrow the very fundaments of
> our society.[61]

---

56. Foucault, 1972b, 'Intellectuals and Power' [1977], 214.
57. Foucault, 1973i, '28 March 1973' [2015], 228.
58. Foucault, 1975a, *Discipline and Punish* [1995], 26.
59. Ibid., 290.
60. Foucault, 1974a, 'Human Nature: Justice versus Power', 172–5.
61. Ibid., 187. The debate between Chomsky and Foucault also represents the
collision of two different conceptions of the intellectual. In contrast to Chomsky,
Foucault does not see the intellectual's role in terms of designing the utopia of a just

Yet in advancing such an argument, Foucault violates his own 'rule of immanence'.[62] From the (correct) insight that law and justice form integral components of bourgeois-capitalist socialization, he draws the (false) conclusion that one can only attack power in the name of war – and not with the aim of attaining a higher, or at least a different, kind of justice.

> It is true that in all social struggles, there is a question of 'justice'. … But if justice is at stake in a struggle, then it is as an instrument of power; it is not in the hope that finally one day, in this or another society, people will be rewarded according to their merits, or punished according to their faults. Rather than thinking of the social struggle in terms of 'justice', one has to emphasise justice in terms of the social struggle.[63]

With that, a central problem of 'Nietzsche's hypothesis' is made plain. As right – and important – as it may be to question the humanist variant of critique, it is not enough to reject it simply by inverting the problem. Foucault's martial conception of power leads back to

---

society; instead, the intellectual should provide 'a topological and geological survey of the battlefield' – or write books that function as 'bombs' or 'Molotov cocktails'. Foucault, 1975g, 'Body/Power' [1980], 62; Foucault, 1978c, 'Dialogue on Power' [1975], 21–2; and Foucault, 1975d, 'An Interview with Michel Foucault' [1985], 14.

62. Foucault, 1976a, *The History of Sexuality, Volume 1: An Introduction* [1978], 98.

63. Foucault, 1974a, 'Human Nature: Justice versus Power', 180; Foucault, 1972b, 'Intellectuals and Power' [1977], 212. This is also why, in an exchange with Maoists, Foucault objected to instituting 'people's courts'. The latter do not represent a revolutionary gain at all, but simply extend traditional forms of organization and domination. Setting apart the judicial apparatus and presuming its neutrality is – like the very idea of justice – an integral part of bourgeois domination that facilitates splitting the *plebs* from the proletariat. Here, too, Foucault speaks in terms of combat and rejects the idea of a 'better' legal order: 'When we talk about courts we're talking about a place where the struggle between the contending forces is willy-nilly suspended: where in every case the decision arrived at is not the outcome of this struggle but of the intervention of an authority which is in a position of neutrality between them and consequently can and must in every case decide which party to the dispute has justice on its side. The court implies, therefore, that there are categories which are common to the parties present […] and that the parties present to the dispute agree to submit to them. Now, it is all this that the bourgeoisie wants to have believed in relation to justice, to its justice. This is why I find the idea of a people's court difficult to accept'. Foucault, 1972d, 'On Popular Justice: A Discussion with Maoists' [1980], 27.

the same mode of analysis it intends to surpass. 'Nietzsche's hypothesis' still adheres to the thesis of repression, which ultimately gives
it its meaning and stability: 'The two hypotheses are not irreconcilable; on the contrary, there seems to be a fairly logical connection
between the two. After all, isn't repression the political outcome of
war ... ?'[64]

---

64. Foucault, 1977e, '7 January 1976' [2003], 16.

# 5
# The 'Disciplination' of Power Analysis

The 'genealogy of power' performs two distancing gestures that make it possible to investigate the defining traits of power relations and their bearing on social practices. The approach moves beyond methodologies that view power relations only in terms of physical repression and ideological manipulation by stressing the technologico-productive nature of the processes at work. Simultaneously, genealogy sets itself apart from juridical and economistic models of analysis by emphasizing the strategic and combative aspects of power relations. In this framework, Foucault exposes the shortcomings and problems of many theories of power and broadens the scope of investigation: inasmuch as the variety and depth of power processes become clear, critical reflection can occur.

But for all that, the 'microphysics of power' that Foucault proposes does not simply afford theoretical gains for examining the concrete operations of power. It entails two analytical problems, which threaten to obscure the many advantages that the technologico-strategic perspective provides.

The first problem is that Foucault views practices of power and knowledge only from a technological angle, while examining processes of subjectivation in terms of subjugation, above all. Subjects are 'formed' or 'produced' in power processes; inasmuch as they are 'disciplined' or 'trained', they constitute the object of the 'human sciences'. In restricting the scope of investigation to technologies of power and knowledge, Foucauldian genealogy adheres to a monocausal scheme of explanation. It cannot account for the double nature of subjectivation processes, which involve subjugation and self-constitution alike.

The second problem arises from Foucault's tendency to boil processes of collective will-formation and modes of consensus down to military-strategic confrontation. Inasmuch as he reserves the concept of strategy for warlike encounters, he offers an inadequate analysis of the state – even though he presents his approach as a theoretical achievement. Although he is right to observe that the state does not constitute the centre of power, it is not enough to treat it as merely the effect of power relations. The state plays a 'strategic' role in power relations as they emerge historically – thus, its nature cannot be fully grasped in terms of war, struggle and conquest.

Ultimately, the weakness of Foucauldian power analytics derives from its theoretical focus on disciplinary processes. Foucault understands power as disciplination, above all, and the operating mode of discipline structures his analysis of power. At its centre stands the individual body, the target and object of training and shaping. Inasmuch as power and discipline run together, a strange picture results: the 'genealogy of power' constantly mobilizes the productivity of power relations in order to illustrate them in reference to a technology that itself remains curiously limited and 'negative': discipline.

As such, Foucault's writings up to *Discipline and Punishment* are doubly marked by a 'disciplination of power analysis'. In the first place, genealogy remains focused on disciplinary processes; hereby, discipline affords the model of power *par excellence*, and genealogy proceeds as the 'microphysics of power', above all. Second, as a consequence of this theoretical limitation, a 'disciplination effect' sets in inasmuch as critical perspectives bearing on the strategic and technological analysis of power are pushed aside.[1]

## Subjectivity and Resistance

Foucault succeeded in exposing the problems that follow from positing original, or natural, freedom in order to denounce the oppression

---

1. Foucault's theoretical focus on disciplinary mechanisms followed from his political assessment that this form of exercising power had remained dominant into the 1970s. As he puts it, 'the techniques employed up to 1940 relied primarily on the policy of imperialism (the army/the colonies), whereas those employed since then are closer to a fascist model (police, internal surveillance, confinement)'. Foucault, 1972d, 'On Popular Justice: A Discussion with Maoists' [1980], 18.

of individuals. In comprehensive and convincing fashion, he laid bare the philosophical foundations of a way of thinking that relies on the idea of sovereign and constitutive subjectivity. In a next step, however, he simply reversed the position he had subjected to critique, claiming that 'bodies ... are constituted as *subjects* by power-effects'.[2] In consequence, he presented subjectivity as a matter of moulding, or shaping, and tended to view freedom as an 'illusion'.

Such 'subjugated subjectivity' held immediate consequences for assessing potential resistance. Even though Foucault affirmed the importance of practices of resistance over and over, the analysis he offered in *Discipline and Punish* proved minimal. This 'gap' was no coincidence. Given the significance and scope of disciplinary processes, the very possibility of alternatives remained unclear. In proportion to the depth and detail that the genealogy of 'mechanisms' and 'technologies' of power provided, questions arose about where space for practices of resistance might be found. The circumstance proved especially vexing inasmuch as Foucault meant for his work to contribute to contemporary struggles. Now, it seemed that his analysis had shown them to be pointless.

## Subjectivation and Subjugation

Foucault's genealogy has often been faulted for theoretical reductionism, that is, failing to address processes of subjectivation accurately. The rational basis for many critiques of his work lies here. According to Axel Honneth, the problem is that Foucault 'supposes that the psychic characteristics of the subject, that is to say, its personality structure, are in general products of particular kinds of bodily discipline'; to this extent, the subject amounts to a field of manipulation for technologies of power, and individuals represent 'formless and conditionable creatures'.[3] A 'theoretical dilemma'[4] ensues: on the one hand, Foucault develops a critique of modern power mechanisms and their effects, but on the other hand, he understands subjects as products of these same mechanisms. '[A]lthough everything in his critique of

---

2. Foucault, 1977f, '14 January 1976' [2003], 29; emphasis in original.

3. Honneth, 'Foucault and Adorno: Two Forms of the Critique of Modernity' (1995b), 129; Honneth, *The Critique of Power* (1997b), 199.

4. Honneth, 'Foucault and Adorno: Two Forms of the Critique of Modernity' (1995b), 131.

the modern age appears concentrated on the suffering of the human body under the disciplinary action of the modern apparatus of power, there is nothing *in* his theory which could articulate this suffering *as* suffering.'[5]

Michel Pêcheux – whose discourse theory takes up and continues Foucault's work – puts things in similar terms. Foucault's accounts of processes of subjugation, normalization and individualization contribute to current struggles against power, yet time and again 'he covers up what he discovers by rendering the points of resistance and the bases of revolt by the dominated classes essentially ungraspable'.[6] Because Foucault rejects both Marxism and psychoanalysis, it proves impossible for him 'to establish a coherent and consistent distinction between the material process of the subjection of human individuals and the procedures of animal domestication'; as a result, he succumbs to 'biologism ... of Bakunian inspiration'.[7]

---

5. Ibid., 131. That said, it is completely exaggerated to claim that Foucault's lacking conception of the subject amounts to a 'very crude version of behaviorism' in order to situate his work in proximity to systems theory and equate it with the 'positivistic indifference' of a Niklas Luhmann: 'Thus, a systems theory one-sidedly restricted to steering processes is exposed as the juncture at which Foucault's theoretical convictions come together like threads'. Honneth, *The Critique of Power* (1997b), 189, 195; see also Honneth, 'Foucault and Adorno: Two Forms of the Critique of Modernity' (1995b), 131. In Honneth's estimation, this question is also where the difference between Foucault and Adorno lies. Although their critiques of modernity have many points in common, Foucault – unlike Adorno – pursues a 'deconstruction of the subject' ultimately seeking to demonstrate that 'the modern individual is nothing but a violently produced fiction'. Honneth, 'Foucault and Adorno: Two Forms of the Critique of Modernity' (1995b), 129–30.

6. Pêcheux, 'Dare to Think and Dare to Rebel! Ideology, Marxism, Resistance, Class Struggle' (2014), 21.

7. Ibid., 21; see also McNay, *Foucault and Feminism* (1992), 40–7; McNay, *Foucault. A Critical Introduction* (1994), 100–4; Barrett, *The Politics of Truth* (1991), 145–55; Kögler, 'Der hermeneutische Mangel der Machttheorie' (1995), 14–15. A pupil of Althusser, Pêcheux elaborated his own form of discourse analysis to concretize his teacher's thesis of 'ideological interpellation'. Pêcheux's critique of Althusserian ideological state apparatuses largely overlaps with his objections to Foucault's conception of the subject. Correctly, he points out that Althusser concentrates on instances of ideological production more than the mechanism, or materiality, of ideology; accordingly, Althusser views subjectivation as the functional subjugation of a pre-constituted subject that always already stands facing ISAs – and leaves the process of subject-constitution itself in the dark. Pêcheux, 'Ideology: Fortress or Paradoxical Space' (1983), 33; Žižek, 'The Subject before Subjectivation' (1988).

Inasmuch as he provides a historical account of disciplinary technology, Foucault proceeds in much greater detail; but just like Althusser, he is at pains to explain the

Such critique is exaggerated.[8] Foucault did not view subjectivity as simply the product of power technologies. Indeed, affirming as much would run counter to the principles of genealogy, which does not consider power a one-sided determination, but a relationship.[9] That said, it is correct that Foucault never provides a concrete account of how subjugation and self-constitution work together as a 'double-entry system';[10] lopsided emphasis falls on subjugation processes. Inasmuch as Foucault speaks of discipline 'making'[11] individuals and the 'carceral texture of society'[12] – or a system 'of constraints'[13] and an 'individualized instrument of coercion'[14] – it is easy to think that his writings offer a variant of the same, functionalist conception of power they are supposed to expose. None of this can be explained as mere rhetoric to political ends; grave difficulties surround the categories Foucault employs, and points of theoretical ambivalence persist.[15]

---

'materiality of the ideological': how the individual 'makes[s] the gestures and actions of his subjection "all by himself"'. Althusser, 'Ideology and Ideological State Apparatuses (Notes Towards an Investigation)' (2001), 182. Clemens Kammler and Warren Montag have also remarked on the parallels between the ways Althusser and Foucault conceive of subjectivation processes. Kammler, *Michel Foucault: Eine kritische Analyse seines Werks* (1986), 188–90; Montag, '"The Soul Is the Prison of the Body": Althusser and Foucault, 1970–1975' (1995); see also Althusser, 'Spinoza – Machiavel' (1993), 75.

8. If I speak of a 'rational core' of criticism, this assessment should be qualified in two respects. First, many commentators systematically eliminate points of ambivalence in Foucault's works in favour of readings that seek to show the untenability of the author's position. In contrast, I am interested in presenting the advantages of this form of analysis as well as its problems – so that points of ambivalence stand front and centre. Second, such criticism (although it often appeared after Foucault's death) chiefly concerns *Discipline and Punish* and *The History of Sexuality, Volume 1* and takes the conception of power here as the paradigm governing Foucault's works as a whole. The study at hand seeks to show that Foucault's conception of power and subjectivity changed at precisely this juncture.

9. See for instance, 1977f, 29: 'Power is exercised through networks, and individuals do not simply circulate in those networks; they are in a position to both submit to and exercise this power. They are never the inert or consenting targets of power; they are always its relays.'

10. Foucault, 1975a, *Discipline and Punish* [1995], 214.

11. Ibid., 170.

12. Ibid., 304.

13. Foucault, 1973i, '28 March 1973' [2015], 240.

14. Foucault, 1975d, 'An Interview with Michel Foucault' [1985], 3.

15. Michael Kelly has observed that the first problem already lies in the scope of explanation proposed by *Discipline and Punish*. Does Foucault intend simply to afford a historical investigation of the French penal system in the eighteenth and early nineteenth centuries (by analysing the birth of the prison in relation to other social

The key problem is how Foucault tries to lay hold of the 'materiality of power'. Discipline employs mechanisms that do not operate directly on the body, or indirectly via consciousness. Instead, it works via the 'soul': rehearsing gestures, learning modes of behaviour, forming habits, and so on. *Discipline and Punish* does not claim to be just a book on the 'birth of the prison' or an analysis of disciplinary society; it also means to offer a 'genealogy of the modern "soul"'.[16] Foucault wants to pursue the physicality of power relations on all levels, including that of psychic materiality. Like the body, the 'soul' does not represent an anthropological constant that, at most, varies with time and circumstance. Like physical processes, psychic processes must be situated in historical context. They do not provide methodological points of departure that can be presumed not to change so much as they represent 'the effect and instrument of a political anatomy':[17] contingent forms of constitution. In contrast to what Honneth assumes, the Foucauldian 'soul' is neither an ideological moment nor an illusionary concept; it possesses material reality. The trouble, then, concerns Foucault's reductive view of psychic processes: he thematizes them only as 'relays' of power aimed at the body; the soul exists,

> it has a reality, it is produced permanently around, on, within the body by the functioning of a power that is exercised on those punished – and, in a more general way, on those one supervises, trains and corrects, over madmen, children at home and at school, the colonized, over those who are stuck at a machine and supervised for the rest of their lives.[18]

---

practices and institutions), or does he view modern society as a whole as a disciplinary arrangement that functions as a prison? Either reading is possible and admits textual evidence. Kelly, 'Foucault, Habermas, and the Self-Referentiality of Critique' (1994), 368. Cf., e.g., Foucault, 1975a, *Discipline and Punish* [1995], 309 n. 3 in contrast to Foucault, 1975a, *Discipline and Punish* [1995], 308.

16. Foucault, 1975a, *Discipline and Punish* [1995], 29.

17. Ibid., 30, 290

18. Ibid., 29. One of the reasons why Foucault boils psychic processes down to corporeality may lie in his aversion to explanatory efforts along psychological lines. Whereas his early works still moved on psychological terrain, in the 1970s he equated interest in psychic processes with 'technology of the "soul"' that creates the infrastructural preconditions for the interventions of social work, pedagogy, psychotherapy and so on. Stressing corporeality provides a point of contrast to analyses that view power processes in terms of manipulating and steering consciousness, and turns against a rigid separation between body and mind. Foucault, 1954a, *Mental Illness and Psychology* [1987]; Foucault, 1954b, 'Dream, Imagination, and Existence' [1986]; Foucault, 1961, *History of Madness* [2006]; Foucault, 1975a, *Discipline and Punish* [1995], 30.

This version of a 'genealogy of the modern "soul"' goes both too far and not far enough. It goes too far inasmuch as it pictures subjectivity as the appendix and complement of (disciplinary) power, without any reality *sui generis*; disciplinary technology 'regards individuals both as objects and as instruments of [the] exercise [of power]'.[19] The theoretical perspective falls short inasmuch as Foucault cannot fulfil his promise to examine the 'materiality of the immaterial'. Instead of examining the specificity and 'physicality' of subjectivation processes, he describes their materiality as mere 'duplication' of physical training procedures.[20] As such, he cannot explore what, precisely, defines subjectivation: at every turn, subjectivity emerges as the result of power technologies. 'The individual and the knowledge that may be gained of him belong to this production'.[21]

If the analytical instrument of 'power-knowledge' permits Foucault to show both that knowledge cannot simply be traced back to power, and that power is not just a product of knowledge – that the one cannot be derived from the other, but they are always closely tied, simultaneously autonomous and dependent – he still presents the picture of heteronomous subjectivity, stripped down to an 'effect/instrument' of power technologies. What is more, the two elements reinforce each other reciprocally in the 'microphysics of power'. Inasmuch as he starts from an anti-essentialist and anti-naturalist position when elaborating the scope and significance of power processes and knowledge-forms, he arrives at a view of subjectivity surrounded on all sides by mechanisms of power-knowledge and circulating as a passive element within a scheme of universal domination.[22]

And so, the Foucauldian project of the 'genealogy of power' remains

---

19. Ibid., 170, 303.

20. Ibid., 29.

21. Ibid., 194. A striking example for such reductionism occurs in Foucault's assessment of rape, which is limited to the bodily aspect of the crime: 'And when one punishes rape one should be punishing physical violence and nothing but that. And to say that it is nothing more than an act of aggression: that there is no difference, in principle, between sticking one's fist into someone's face or one's penis into their sex'. Foucault, 1977o, 'Confinement, Psychiatry, Prison' [1988], 200. A few years later, Foucault distanced himself from this view and characterized it as 'misleading'. He had merely intended to point out a problem: on the one hand, sex can expect nothing from penal law; on the other, rape, which always has a sexual component, must always be punished. Foucault, 1980j, 'Discussion with Philosophers'.

22. Minston, 'Strategies for Socialists? Foucault's Conception of Power' (1980), 13–14; Dean, *Critical and Effective Histories* (1994), 166–7.

stuck at the halfway point. Subjectivity is produced in order to be oppressed: it amounts to 'shap[ing] an obedient subject'.[23] Foucault is right to take issue with a tradition of theory that builds on notions of constitutive and transcendental subjectivity – lopsidedly privileging conscious processes and making the subject and its freedom the point of both departure and arrival – only to ask how such freedom is restricted and how the subject comes to be repressed by an external power. In contrast, his genealogy seeks to demonstrate that subjectivity is not a universal substance so much as a historical form; it points to the manifold practices in which and through which subjectivity is 'produced' or 'fabricated' in the first place. But for all that, his project still remains within the horizon of constitutive subjectivity, albeit unwillingly. Even in rejecting it, Foucault continues to refer to a problematic he would like to discard in its entirety. Inasmuch as he stresses the subject's heteronomy, instead of its autonomy, he emphasizes the other side of the picture, instead of changing the overall field. Because of such 'counter-identification',[24] Foucault proves just as unable as proponents of constitutive subjectivity to investigate processes of subjectivation in concrete terms: if the latter simply make them their point of departure, they are always already completed for Foucault inasmuch as they are (over)determined by power processes.[25]

Like the genesis of modern subjectivity described in *Dialectic of Enlightenment*, the 'genealogy of the modern "soul"' in *Discipline and Punish* proves hermetically sealed as a system; although there is no way out, it sounds a political call presupposing that an exit actually exists.

---

23. Foucault, 1975a, *Discipline and Punish* [1995], 129.

24. Pêcheux, 'Dare to Think and Dare to Rebel! Ideology, Marxism, Resistance, Class Struggle' (2014), 9.

25. Comparing the different materialisms of Marx and Foucault, Etienne Balibar also offers critique that goes in this direction. Whereas 'historical materialism' remains stuck within the logic of the philosophy of history, Foucault's 'bodily materialism' must answer the question of what 'leads to its immediate proximity to vitalism, or indeed biologism'. Balibar assumes the voice of a fictive Marx to expose the 'ambiguities' of Foucauldian materialism: 'I agree with you entirely that historical *individuals* are *bodies* subjected to disciplines, but I put forward the idea that these "bodies" themselves, in the particular situation of their class (and why not sex, knowledge, or culture), must themselves be thought of *in relational terms*'. Balibar, 'Foucault and Marx: The Question of Nominalism' (1992), 55–6; see also Certeau, *The Practice of Everyday Life* (1984); Kammler, *Michel Foucault: Eine kritische Analyse seines Werks* (1986), 188.

Foucauldian 'resistance' echoes Adorno and Horkheimer's 'message in a bottle'.[26]

## Power and Resistance

Foucault's ambivalent understanding of how subjectivity and power relate holds consequences for his conception of resistance. His detailed account of highly effective (disciplinary) power that brings forth obedient and docile individuals is supposed to expose mechanisms and techniques in order to contribute to subjects' struggle against this same power. And yet, by elaborating the scope and efficacy of power technologies, Foucauldian genealogy would seem to declare that no practices of resistance are even possible at all.

Nicos Poulantzas has offered one of the most important critiques of Foucault's concept of resistance. He shares the view that power is not a substance, but a relation. Like Foucault, he rejects the claim that political and social struggles are external to power relations. However, Poulantzas criticizes Foucault for the idea that resistance is always already encompassed by power relations it cannot transcend. From this perspective, genealogy remains indexed on power, albeit in negative fashion. As such, it amounts to reaction more than action. In the worst case, it serves as a dynamic instance – a catalyst – for refining and improving the mechanisms of power. '[I]f power is always already there, if every power situation is immanent in itself, *why should there ever be resistance?*'.[27]

The central problem Poulantzas identifies is Foucault's failure to adhere to his own relational approach. Consequently, his conception

---

26. Jacques Donzelot contends that the public success of *Discipline and Punish* and the relative failure to open up another basis for penal practices follow from a 'fundamental ambiguity' in the book. On the one hand, Foucault's study forcefully discredited repressive and preventative measures in penal politics, yet in simply showing their untenability, it did not so much as hint at a way out from the dilemma. On the contrary, the coherence of the book's argument derives from its hermetic quality: 'The critique would be as follows: if discipline and punishment are linked together in an infinite process, then showing how the former feeds on the latter's failure and hollows out its foundations – and doing so to open up a new way of thinking about punishment – doesn't all this mean running the risk of winding up caught in a vicious circle, where even a partial solution to the mechanism described would occur at the expense of the theory as a whole?'. Donzelot, 'Les mésaventures de la théorie' (1986), 60. For an assessment of the book's impact, see Lenoir, *Sociétés and Représentations* (1996).

27. Poulantzas, *State, Power, Socialism* (2000), 149.

of power is constantly shifting: 'It designates at one moment a *relation* (the power relation), at another, and often simultaneously, *one pole* of the power-resistances relation'.[28] Ultimately, such theoretical ambiguity leads to second-order essentialism: power is defined as relation and not a substance, on the one hand; on the other, it represents a pole 'facing' the resistance it precedes and structures.[29]

As such, assuming the co-originality of power and resistance yields only obscurity.[30] Again and again, Foucault breaks with his microphysical conception of power and turns to the 'interstices of power' available to those subject to domination.[31] But by abstractly juxtaposing power and resistance in this manner, he strays from his promise to understand power in 'strictly relational'[32] terms: 'We are never trapped by power: we can always modify its grip in determinate conditions and according to a precise strategy'.[33]

If, on the one hand, Foucault conceives power relationally, affirming that 'no absolute outside' exists,[34] on the other hand, he still tries

28. Ibid., 150.
29. Ibid., 146–53; Macdonell, *Theories of Discourse: An Introduction* (1986), 118–24. To a great extent, Poulantzas's *State, Power, Socialism* grapples with Foucault's work – and determines points in common and differences between the author's own effort to analyse the state in Marxist terms and the 'microphysics of power'. Yet if Poulantzas keenly uncovers analytical weaknesses in Foucault, he still proves unable to make use of the relational conception of the state as a 'condensation of a class relationship of forces' in a consistent fashion. Although he rejects Althusser's distinction between ideological and repressive apparatuses as 'economistic' and 'idealist' (ibid., 170–4), he still adheres to his course of argument on essential points. Like Althusser, Poulantzas locates power chiefly in apparatuses and the relations that hold between them; he also makes the state the point of departure for analysing social relations, and restricts its role to ensuring cohesion. Because of such generalization, it remains unclear what it is that makes the state specifically capitalist, and how bourgeois interests are inscribed in it.
On parallels and differences between how Foucault and Poulantzas conceive of power, see Jessop, *Nicos Poulantzas: Marxist Theory and Political Strategy* (1985), 313–36, esp. 318–20; Jessop, 'Poulantzas and Foucault on Power and Strategy' (1990). In comparing these two theorists as 'defenders of the rule of structures', Nikolaos Tsiros is content to rehash old prejudices. Tsiros, *Die politische Theorie der Postmoderne* (1993), 71, 61–73.
30. 'Where there is power, there is resistance'; Foucault, 1976a, *The History of Sexuality, Volume 1: An Introduction* [1978], 95.
31. Foucault, 1977m, 'The Confession of the Flesh' [1980], 202.
32. Foucault, 1976a, *The History of Sexuality, Volume 1: An Introduction* [1978], 95.
33. Foucault, 1977k, 'The End of the Monarchy of Sex' [1996], 224.
34. Foucault, 1976a, *The History of Sexuality, Volume 1: An Introduction* [1978], 95.

to find something beyond power relations. At one point, he calls this 'something' *plebs*.[35] In earlier writings and interviews, Foucault had defined the plebs as a social group different from the proletariat.[36] Now, the term acquires a new meaning. *Plebs* does not define a socio-logical reality or social class, 'but a centrifugal movement, an inverse energy, a discharge'.[37] Even if Foucault means to abstain from sub-stantializing gestures – preferring to speak of 'something "plebeian"' instead of *plebs* per se – it remains unclear what, exactly, it represents: 'there is indeed always something in the social body, in classes, in groups and individuals themselves which in some sense escapes rela-tions of power'.[38] But what is this something supposed to be, if we always already stand enmeshed in power relations? Foucault's guarded language ('still always', 'something', 'in a certain sense') indicates that he recognized the problems this entailed for his initial assumptions. He fails to provide an answer about what constitutes this 'plebeian' element, which is found 'in the bodies and souls' of individuals; it forms 'not so much what stands outside relations of power as their limit, their underside, their counterstroke', and 'it responds to every advance of power by a movement of disengagement'.[39]

The core problem, then, is that Foucault does not follow through on his own call for immanence and relationality. He rightly assumes that strug-gles are not external to power relations, but he draws the false conclusion in assimilating struggles to power. The real theoretical challenge would involve preserving the tension between power and resistance and asking how resistance is generated within power relations. But, in the frame-work Foucault has adopted, the success or failure of political strategies cannot be addressed. Resistance seems to be predetermined through and through – the ferment of power that cannot be attacked, because its very definition is that it productively incorporates and reintegrates struggles. In consequence, resistance remains cast in negative terms and proves fun-damentally abstract: an 'underside'.[40]

35. Foucault, 1977w, 'Power and Strategies' [1980], 137–8.
36. Foucault, 1972d, 'On Popular Justice: A Discussion with Maoists' [1980]; Foucault, 1975a, *Discipline and Punish* [1995].
37. Foucault, 1977w, 'Power and Strategies' [1980], 138.
38. Ibid., 138.
39. Ibid., 138; see also Kammler, *Michel Foucault: Eine kritische Analyse seines Werks* (1986), 153–5.
40. Foucault, 1976a, *The History of Sexuality, Volume 1: An Introduction* [1978],

## The Microphysics and Macrophysics of Power

A second set of problems compounds the ambiguity of Foucault's treatment of subjectivity and resistance: conceiving subjectivity along the lines of power-technology must occur in conjunction with examining the state from the perspective of power strategies. But the 'microphysics of power', while concentrating on processes and methods for training individuals, neglects the problematic of the state.

Yet again, there are valid reasons to take distance from the state as the primary reference point in political theory.[41] Foucault draws a line of separation between his project and the tradition that boils the problem of power down to the state and its apparatuses – that is, analysis in terms of law and sovereignty.[42] Counter to approaches privileging the state, he affirms 'the value of an analysis which follow[s] a different course'.[43] Instead of proceeding from the top down, microphysical analysis works from the bottom up:

> Between every point of a social body, between a man and a woman, between the members of a family, between a master and his pupil, between everyone who knows and everyone who does not, there exist relations of power which are not purely and simply a projection of the sovereign's great power over the individual; they are rather the

96; Minston, 'Strategies for Socialists? Foucault's Conception of Power' (1980), 9, 23; Wickham, 'Power and Power Analysis: Beyond Foucault?' (1983), 484.

41. Taking theoretical distance in this way also signifies Foucault's political critique of revolutionary Marxist movements that target the state apparatus exclusively. Foucault points to three consequences of such an orientation. The first problem involves the revolutionary movement constituting itself as a party that is internally constructed as if it were a state apparatus itself – functioning in terms of the same hierarchies and disciplines as what it seeks to combat. Foucault, 1978m, 'Méthodologie pour la connaissance du monde', 616–8. Second, this strategy does not involve destroying the state apparatus so much as using it – at least for a period of transition – to serve the 'dictatorship of the proletariat'. Foucault, 1972d, 'On Popular Justice: A Discussion with Maoists' [1980], 8–9. Third, any new political order to emerge will continue to depend on the specialists and technicians of the former regime. Foucault attributes the failure of the Soviet model to, among other things, neglecting power relations that operate outside, underneath, or alongside state apparatuses. Foucault, 1975g, 'Body/Power' [1980], 59–60; Foucault, 1976i, 'Sorcery and Madness' [1996], 202.

42. Foucault, 1977d, 'Truth and Power' [1984], 63–4; Foucault, 1977i, 'The History of Sexuality' [1980], 187–8.

43. Ibid., 187.

concrete, changing soil in which the sovereign's power is grounded, the conditions which make it possible for it to function. The family, even now, is not simply a reflection or extension of the power of the State; it does not act as the representative of the State in relation to children, just as the male does not act as its representative with respect to the female. For the State to function in the way that it does, there must be, between male and female or adult and child, quite specific relations of domination which have their own configuration and relative autonomy.[44]

The state neither covers the whole spectrum of social power relations, nor does it constitute their foundation.[45] Foucault faces a problem, however, inasmuch as microphysical analysis cannot address how the state factors into the organization of power relations, since this approach shrinks its specificity down to the point of vanishing altogether.

Within the 'microphysics of power', the state has two meanings. For one, it does not occupy the central position that political analysis commonly assigns it; instead, it operates on the basis of more fundamental power relations, which precede it and define its contours and mode of functioning. 'The State is superstructural in relation to a whole series of power networks.'[46] Second, the state is not just *superstructure* with respect to an infrastructure of power technologies; it is also an *instance of codification*. 'I would say that the state consists in the codification of a whole number of power relations which render its functioning possible.'[47] Both aspects of the state – a superstructure-phenomenon and a codification-instance – define each other reciprocally: the state represents a superstructure because it 'only' codifies what has already arisen from microphysical relations of power. That is, it fixes those power arrangements to which it owes its own emergence, without constituting them itself. Only on such a theoretical basis is it possible to say that 'mechanisms of power ... have been and are invested, colonized, used, inflected, transformed, extended ... by ... forms of overall domination.'[48]

---

44. Ibid., 187–8; Foucault, 1976a, *The History of Sexuality, Volume 1: An Introduction* [1978], 94–5.

45. Foucault, 1977d, 'Truth and Power' [1984], 64.

46. Ibid., 64; Foucault, 1976c, 'Questions on Geography' [1980], 71–3.

47. Foucault, 1977d, 'Truth and Power' [1984], 64.

48. Foucault, 1977f, '14 January 1976' [2003], 30; see also Lloyd, 'The (F)utility of a Feminist Turn to Foucault' (1993), 438–45; Dean, *Critical and Effective Histories* (1994), 156–7.

The problem, first, is that such metaphors and descriptive terminology suggest an external relationship between the state and
micropowers, instead of locating the state itself in a microphysical net
of relations. Then, there is the question whether it is enough to restrict
the state's role in constituting power relations to codifying them – in
other words, treating it as a superstructural phenomenon. In fact,
Foucault remains within the juridical conception he has criticized. Just
as juridical theory views power in terms of legal categories, Foucault
analyses the state in terms of law and rights: as a legal-political structure with a codifying function. The 'microphysics of power' is haunted
by a strange identification with the legal-institutional system, which
takes up and reproduces the premises of the juridical conception.[49]

Only in reducing the state to a legal structure can disciplinary technology receive the comprehensive meaning Foucault grants it. The
disciplines represent a kind of 'counter-law'[50] that not only expands
the forms of law on the micro level, but undermines its borders. This
is why Foucault considers discipline, not law, to be the basis of power
relations. More still, selective reference to the state (of law) means that
Foucault understands legal structures as an instance of domination: an
instrument of rule and its legitimation, the machinery of constraint.
With that, he simply pushes a central question aside: the problem of
collective will-formation.[51]

---

49. Poulantzas identifies this problem clearly and shows how Foucault, in
restricting the state to the public sphere, remains 'surprisingly' beholden to a 'narrow,
juridical definition'. Poulantzas, *State, Power, Socialism* (2000), 36.

50. Foucault, 1975a, *Discipline and Punish* [1995], 223.

51. Foucault, 1975c, 'From Torture to Cellblock' [1996], 148; Foucault, 1975d,
'An Interview with Michel Foucault' [1985], 3. Alan Hunt and Gary Wickham have
pointed out further ambiguities and problems. Even if their account is occasionally
one-sided, the central contention is valid: Foucault systematically underestimates the
significance of modern law in the 'economy of power'. As they observe, his theory
focuses on penal law (and thereby neglects other legal spheres), fails to distinguish
between premodern and modern jurisprudence, and sets discipline and legal form
in abstract opposition to each other. In consequence, Foucault presents law as a
second-order and inefficient mechanism that opposes – or lags behind – social developments. In doing so, he fails to note that the law is also a social relation; the form it
assumes does not stand firm once and for all, but is constantly subject to historical
change. As such, Foucault's thesis about the negativity law amounts to a straw man in
his critique of traditional political thought: 'The equation of law with negative pro-
scription involves the acceptance of an ideological conception that came to form the
conventional view of the monolithic unity of state and law; a view that, paradoxically,
Foucault is prepared to accept in launching his own critique of the presumption of a

All this follows from the way Foucault rejects the problematic of *Leviathan*. To be sure, microphysical analysis reveals the problems and limitations of a conception of power that conceives it from the standpoint of an organizing centre and localizes it in the state. But also on this score, Foucault simply inverses the traditional problematic. The dictum that 'power comes from below'[52] still operates with the topology of 'above' and 'below'. Foucault means to call this matrix of political space into question as a whole – to replace it with a model of power that does not work with the idea of a 'basis' and 'superstructure' so much as a network. Yet he does not entirely succeed. Foucault does not conceive of political macrostructures as the sum of particular, sectoral relations of force; instead, he starts out – at least as a rule – from reciprocal effects, or 'double conditioning'.[53] For all that, he never investigates, in systematic fashion, the role the state plays in this arrangement – or how, conversely, social relations of force are 'embodied in the state apparatus, in the formulation of the law, in the various social hegemonies'.[54]

To be sure, 'cut[ting] off the king's head' is necessary to pursue political analysis.[55] Yet this only represents a first step. In turn, one

---

monolithic state power'. Hunt and Wickham, *Foucault and Law* (1994), 60–1.

In an earlier study, Wickham draws attention to 'variation' in Foucault's understanding of the relationship between law and power. Wickham, 'Power and Power Analysis: Beyond Foucault?' (1983), 472; his analysis wavers between rejecting determinism and affirming it. On the one hand, Foucault rejects an instrumental connection between power and law and claims that 'law (*droit*) [...] has always served as a mask for power'; Foucault, 1977w, 'Power and Strategies' [1980], 140; on the other hand, he declares that law has 'concealed' the actual functioning of disciplinary mechanisms. Foucault, 1977f, '14 January 1976' [2003], 37.

52. Foucault, 1976a, *The History of Sexuality, Volume 1: An Introduction* [1978], 94.

53. Cf. Foucault, 1976a, *The History of Sexuality, Volume 1: An Introduction* [1978], 100; Foucault, 1977d, 'Truth and Power' [1984], 64; Foucault, 1977w, 'Power and Strategies' [1980], 142.

54. Foucault, 1976a, *The History of Sexuality, Volume 1: An Introduction* [1978], 93. As Gerhard Plumpe and Clemens Kammler observe, it proves 'difficult' for Foucault to abandon the concept of social totality: 'Bracketing relations of social interdependence, which admit no description in factual terms without a concept of social synthesis, has the effect, for discourse theory, that the structure of the interdiscursive field hardly proves visible at all. This underlies the vagueness of Foucault's formulations. What representation-theory monocausally reduces to a "vertical" dimension, Foucault dissolves into "horizontal" dispersion'. Plumpe and Kammler, 'Wissen ist Macht' (1980), 216.

55. Foucault, 1977d, 'Truth and Power' [1984], 63.

must account for why the headless body acts as if it still had a head.[56] If the state's sole task is to codify power relations, the question of the rules and laws now to be followed remains open. What comes to stand as the object of legislation and what does not? What form do rights and laws assume, and via what institutional divisions do they operate? In brief: what defines the conditions of codification, if they no longer count as self-grounding?

Foucault has an answer – albeit an inadequate one. Strategies guarantee the coherence of power relations. Foucault advances the concept of strategy to close the 'gap' between the micro and macro levels. It possesses a double function. On the one hand, strategies bundle manifold, heterogeneous and local power relations into 'general conditions of domination'; out of the plurality of micropowers, 'a more-or-less coherent and unitary strategic form', or 'general principle',[57] takes shape. On the other hand, inverse movement also occurs – from top to bottom. In this context, strategies generalize, reinforce, transform or renew scattered power relations inasmuch as they ensure 'concatenation' that 'rests on [these mobilities] and seeks in turn to arrest their movement'.[58]

Given the theoretical framework, however, the concept of strategy does not explain anything. Indeed, it requires an explanation in its own right. Foucault's recourse to strategies as 'mediators' between the micro and macro level proves problematic. For one, doing so occurs on the basis of a *repressive thesis* – which presupposes what is supposed to be explained. Foucault starts with 'global strategies', i.e. relations of domination already in place, in order to investigate how the 'micropowers' fit into, or are embodied in, them. In fact, the real task for genealogical analysis would be to show how 'macrostructures' more or less systematically (re)produce 'micropractices'. 'Micro' and 'macro' do not refer to separate levels of a social ontology or name universal essences, whose relationship or interaction is to be investigated; rather, they are produced within the immanence of a historical field that operates with gradations along the social spectrum ranging from local to global.[59]

---

56. Dean, *Critical and Effective Histories* (1994), 156.

57. Foucault, 1977w, 'Power and Strategies' [1980], 142; Foucault, 1975a, *Discipline and Punish: The Birth of the Prison* [1995], 81.

58. Foucault, 1976a, *The History of Sexuality, Volume 1: An Introduction* [1978], 93; see also Dean, *Critical and Effective Histories* (1994), 157.

59. Wickham, 'Power and Power Analysis: Beyond Foucault?' (1983), 481.

Second, the *war hypothesis* represents a problematic context for viewing strategic operations. 'Nietzsche's hypothesis' does not make it clear how power relations achieve systematization, reproduce themselves, and achieve permanence. The question is whether power relations may be analysed in terms of war, conquest and struggle alone, or whether their stability does not in some way rest on the 'acceptance' or 'consensus' of subjects – a consensus not necessarily produced by violence or constraint. Foucault does not address this question because he has already 'gotten rid of' the problem: consensus is automatically – technologically – ensured by the disciplination of subjects; the question of acceptance no longer arises, because the subjects themselves have been produced in keeping with social specifications and 'norms'.[60]

Foucault was right to criticize the 'great fantasy ... of a social body constituted by the universality of wills',[61] yet he succumbed to the error of simply inverting the juridical perspective. In so doing, he dissolved the problem of will-formation into the materiality of power over the body. Before long, he recognized this shortcoming and the need to flesh out the microphysical approach:

> It is now necessary to pose the problem of will. ... [O]ne cannot confront this problem, sticking closely to the theme of power without, of course, at some point, getting to the question of human will. It was so obvious I could have realized it earlier.[62]

---

60. 'In the omnifunctional position assigned to them by Foucault, the techniques of power absorb not only the question of physical violence but also that of consent. The latter thereby becomes a non-problem which is either given no theoretical elucidation at all or else is collapsed into the "internalized repression" type of analysis. But over and above the disciplines of normalization, there must be other "reasons" that explain consent. For if those disciplines were enough to account for submission, *how could they admit the existence of struggles?*'. Poulantzas, *State, Power, Socialism* (2000), 79.

61. Foucault, 1975g, 'Body/Power' [1980], 55.

62. Foucault, 1990b, 'What Is Critique?' [2007], 76. In 1978, talking with the Japanese literary historian Rumei Yoshimoto, Foucault acknowledged the question of conditions for collective will-formation: 'I consider the problem of how individual wills relate to other levels of will in revolution and struggle to be an important, unresolved question [...]. To be honest, I haven't examined this question enough in my works'. Foucault, 1978m, 'Méthodologie pour la connaissance du monde', 615.

# Part II
## Governmentality

# 6

# From Discipline to Government

After *Discipline and Punish*, Foucault's works display two aspects that seem to lie worlds apart. On the one hand, lectures, talks, articles and interviews explore political rationalities and the 'genealogy of the state'. On the other hand, the *History of Sexuality* book project examines ethical questions and the genealogy of the (desiring) subject. This double change of focus occurred in reaction to the problems and objections occasioned by earlier works. That said, Foucault was not pursuing separate theoretical objectives. Addressing macropolitical questions in explicit fashion called for verifying the analytical framework employed – just as the overall conceptual shift required that the field of investigation be expanded. In this light, the following describes two complementary steps, which intersect in the concept of government: critical interrogation of the hypotheses of repression and war, and the 'discovery' of biopower.[1]

---

1. See also the assessment of Pasquale Pasquino, who collaborated closely with Foucault: 'It became clear during our discussions of the second half of the 1970s that the discourse on disciplines had reached an impasse and could go no further. That it threatened above all to lead to an extremist denunciation of power – envisioned according to a *repressive* model – that left both of us dissatisfied from the theoretical point of view. If a close analysis of disciplines opposed the Marxist thesis of economic exploitation as a principle for understanding the mechanisms of power, this analysis by itself was not enough and required the investigation of global problems of the regulation and ordering of society as well as the modalities of conceptualizing the problem. Hence the question of *government* – a term that Foucault gradually substituted for what he began to see as the more ambiguous word, "power"'. Pasquino, 'Political Theory of War and Peace: Foucault and the History of Modern Political Theory' (1993) 79; Pasquino, 'La problématique du "gouvernement" et de la

First, let us look at how Foucault checked his methodological instruments. Following *Discipline and Punish*, he diagnosed a series of 'difficulties' characterizing recent works:

> Lines of research that were very closely interrelated but that never added up to a coherent body of work, that had no continuity. Fragments of research, none of which was completed, and none of which was followed through; bits and pieces of research, and at the same time it was getting very repetitive, always falling into the same rut, the same themes, the same concepts. ... We are making no progress, and it's all leading nowhere. It's all repetitive, and it doesn't add up. Basically, we keep saying the same thing, and there again, perhaps we're not saying anything at all.[2]

The fragmentary or repetitive nature of his studies is not what strikes Foucault as problematic. Instead, he determines that he has offered an inadequate response to the juridical theory of power. Two alternative modes of analysis are available for understanding power along non-juridical lines. The first views power as repression, and the second in terms of war. Foucault considers his works following *The Order of Discourse* to continue these two forms of analysis – and then distances himself from this tradition:

> It is obvious that everything I have said to you in previous years is inscribed within the struggle-repression schema. That is indeed the schema I was trying to apply. Now, as I tried to apply it, I was eventually forced to reconsider it; both because, in many respects, it is still insufficiently elaborated – I would even go so far as to say that it is not elaborated at all – and also because I think that the twin notions of 'repression' and 'war' have to be considerably modified and ultimately, perhaps, abandoned. At all events, we have to look very closely at these two notions of 'repression' and 'war'; if you like, we have to look a little

"véridiction"' (1986a); Deleuze, *Foucault* (1988), 75–7; Deleuze, 'Life as Work of Art' (1995c), 112–13; Deleuze, 'A Portrait of Foucault' (1995a), 108–10.

    Many authors signal an 'impasse' in power analytics and claim that Foucault experienced an intellectual crisis during the mid-1970s. Ibid., 109; Blanchot, 'Michel Foucault as I Imagine Him' (1986), 84–6; Eribon, *Michel Foucault* (1991), 276; Ewald, 'Foucault verdauen' (1989), 56.

    2. Foucault, 1977e, '7 January 1976' [2003], 3–4.

more closely at the hypothesis that the mechanisms of power are essentially mechanisms of repression, and at the alternative hypothesis that what is rumbling away and what is at work beneath political power is essentially and above all a warlike relation.[3]

Behind these guarded statements lies the suspicion that the concepts employed to date – 'repression' and 'war' – still belong to the juridical tradition they are meant to criticize. If so, then breaking with this idea of power requires revising the modes of conceptualization. That said, Foucault was still at the initial stage of reworking his position vis-à-vis early works. Although he spoke of a 'rupture'[4] that occurred around 1975–6, it would take time before he wholly separated himself from the model of discipline and abandoned the hypotheses of repression and war.

## The Repressive Hypothesis

One year after *Discipline and Punish*, *The History of Sexuality, Volume 1* appeared. The book was meant as the introduction to several projected volumes comprising the 'history of sexuality' and presented the methodological framework for further research. Its centrepiece is a critical engagement with the assumption that prohibitions, taboos and acts of exclusion shape modern sexuality. The 'repressive hypothesis' – which Foucault also calls 'Reich's hypothesis'[5] – proves untenable for both theoretical and political reasons, since it fails to explain the relationship between sexuality and power.[6]

Foucault does not contest the fact that sex (*le sexe*) has been misrecognized, prohibited and negated since the classical age. But for him, negative phenomena represent 'component parts that have a local and tactical role to play in a transformation into discourse';[7] they operate within a power strategy that cannot be boiled down to repression alone. Indeed, during the period in question, an extraordinary

---

3. Foucault, 1977e, '7 January 1976' [2003], 17.
4. Foucault, 1984q, 'The Return of Morality' [1988], 242.
5. Foucault, 1977e, '7 January 1976' [2003], 16.
6. Foucault, 1976a, *The History of Sexuality, Volume 1: An Introduction* [1978], 12–13; Foucault, 1976i, 'Sorcery and Madness' [1996], 201.
7. Foucault, 1976a, *The History of Sexuality, Volume 1: An Introduction* [1978], 12.

increase occurred in the political and social significance attached to sexuality. Sexuality became a central factor in the framework of newly organized power. Hereby, it was not repressed so much as 'produced': 'one had to speak of [sex] as of a thing to be not simply condemned or tolerated but managed, inserted into systems of utility, regulated for the greater good of all, made to function according to an optimum.'[8]

The vehemence and intensity of his engagement with *repression* also indicate how difficult it was for Foucault to free himself from this notion. Repression had played an important role in developing a non-juridical and non-economic method for analysing power. It belonged to a strategic programme that sought 'to reveal the problem of domination and subjugation instead of sovereignty and obedience'[9] by joining the hypotheses of Reich and Nietzsche. Now, Foucault recognized that this approach did not help him account for the productivity or immanence of power relations.[10]

---

8. Ibid., 24; Foucault, 1976l, 'The West and the Truth of Sex' [1978], 6–7; see also Foucault, 1977k, 'The End of the Monarchy of Sex' [1996]. *The History of Sexuality, Volume 1* contests the repressive hypothesis in two ways. Foucault rejects not just the idea of originary, individual sexuality, which came to be stifled and must now be emancipated, but also the notion that the dispositive of sexuality primarily serves class oppression. Instead, he claims that 'sexuality' is a bourgeois invention, a means of self-affirmation that constitutes its '"class" body'. Only in a secondary sense and later on (in the course of the nineteenth century) did the dispositive come to apply to the social body as a whole, where, as a hegemonic instance, 'in its successive shifts and transpositions, it induces specific class effects'. Ibid., 127, see also ibid., 152–9; Foucault, 1977f, '14 January 1976' [2003], 31–4.

9. Ibid., 27.

10. Pierre Macherey has helped to clarify the problem by showing how Foucault rejects not only the (Freudo-Marxist) *hypothesis of repression/oppression*, but also the (psychoanalytic) *thesis of production*; this represents an important reason for his critical engagement with psychoanalysis. See Foucault, 1976a, *The History of Sexuality, Volume 1: An Introduction* [1978], 151–3. Indeed, psychoanalytic efforts positing a 'productive' relationship between power and sexuality have long sought to contest the illusion of sexual 'emancipation': 'one should not think that desire is repressed, for the simple reason that the law is what constitutes both desire and the lack on which it is predicated. Where there is desire, the power relation is already present: an illusion, then, to denounce this relation for a repression exerted after the event; but vanity as well, to go questing after a desire that is beyond the reach of power'. Ibid., 81–2.

Foucault takes a further step by refusing a conception of the relationship between power and sexuality that simply mirrors emancipatory discourse. Both the repressive hypothesis and the thesis of production form part of the juridical conception of power. This (illusory) alternative is what Foucault leaves behind by making the *thesis of immanence* the basis for investigation power relations: 'What distinguishes the analysis made in terms of the repression of instincts from that made in terms of the

Changing his theoretical approach, Foucault no longer presents the repressive hypothesis as an alternative to the juridical conception of power. Instead, he views it as its logical continuation: 'In defining the effects of power as repression, one adopts a purely juridical conception of such power'.[11] This amounts to discrediting repression on two scores. For one, it no longer stands opposed to the juridical conception of power, but functions as a juridical term itself, presupposing the sovereignty of the individual and his or her rights. There needs to have been an original freedom or subjectivity preceding power mechanisms for repression to occur. Second, 'repression' represents a 'disciplinary' term conceived and elaborated in the human sciences; it relies on an array of psychological themes and points of reference that serve normalizing purposes. Because of this twofold (juridical and disciplinary) provenance of 'repression', its 'critical use … is tainted, spoiled, and rotten from the outset'.[12]

*The History of Sexuality, Volume 1* treats the repressive hypothesis as an integral and inseparable part of the juridical conception of power. At the same time, Foucault discusses both the juridical model and the notion of repression as aspects of a strategy reaching deep into, and structuring, the forms that the analysis and critique of power assume. As paradoxical as it seems, picturing power's mode of functioning only in negative terms represents a precondition for a positive conception: power 'masks itself by producing a discourse, seemingly opposed to it but really part of a larger deployment of modern power'.[13] As such, the negative conception belongs to the productivity of power: a condition

---

law of desire is clearly the way in which they each conceive of the nature and dynamics of the drives, not in the way in which they conceive of power. They both rely on a common representation of power which, depending on the use made of it and the position it is accorded with respect to desire, leads to two contrary results: either to the promise of a "liberation", if the power is seen as having only an external hold on desire, or, if it is constitutive of desire itself, to the affirmation: you are always-already trapped'. Ibid., 82–3; Macherey, 'Towards a Natural History of Norms' (1992), 183–4. On Foucault's engagement with psychoanalysis, see Raulff, *Das normale Leben* (1977), 138–43; Miller, 'Michel Foucault and Psychoanalysis' (1992); Marques, *Foucault und die Psychoanalyse* (1990).

11. Foucault, 1977d, 'Truth and Power' [1984], 60; Foucault, 1976a, *The History of Sexuality, Volume 1: An Introduction* [1978], 82.

12. Foucault, 1977f, '14 January 1976' [2003], 40.

13. Dreyfus and Rabinow, *Michel Foucault: Beyond Structuralism and Hermeneutics* (1983), 130; see also Foucault, 1976a, *The History of Sexuality, Volume 1: An Introduction* [1978], 44–5.

for its acceptance. Both the repressive thesis and the idea of an external relationship between power and freedom are part of the dispositive Foucault means to critique: 'Power as a pure limit set on freedom is, at least in our society, the general form of its acceptability'.[14]

Foucault's diagnosis is clear. What remains less clear, however, are the theoretical consequences he draws from assigning the repressive hypothesis such political significance. Indeed, the analysis of the relationship between sexuality and power sketched in the first volume of *The History of Sexuality* remains stuck within the juridical conception – a mechanism Foucault otherwise exposes so well. *The History of Sexuality, Volume 1* cannot free itself from a 'central difficulty'.[15] Even though Foucault lays bare the repressive hypothesis's shortcomings, his critique still implies a difference between sex and sexuality. Accordingly, it retains the notion of distortion, prohibition or repression:

> I had begun to write it as a history of the way in which sex was obscured and travestied by this strange life-form, this strange growth which was to become sexuality. Now, I believe, setting up this opposition between sex and sexuality leads back to the positing of power as law and prohibition, the idea that power created sexuality as a device to say no to sex.[16]

This is precisely the theoretical position so convincingly subjected to critique in the same study. As such, *The History of Sexuality, Volume 1* – like *The Order of Discourse* – represents a transition; its line of argument remains ambivalent. If, on the one hand, Foucault has rejected the juridical conception of power, on the other hand, he cannot escape it: 'My analysis was still held captive by the juridical conception of power. I had to make a complete reversal of direction'.[17]

---

14. Foucault, 1976a, *The History of Sexuality, Volume 1* [1978], 86.
15. Foucault, 1977i, 'The History of Sexuality' [1980], 190.
16. Ibid., 190.
17. Ibid., 190. *The History of Sexuality, Volume 1* poses a further difficulty. Though less important for the book's overall theoretical architecture than the opposition between sex and sexuality, it makes it clear where the weakness of the 'thesis of immanence' lies. Specifically, Foucault counterposes an Eastern *ars erotica* to Western *scientia sexualis* as a different mode of organizing pleasure, instead of developing the possibilities of another 'economy of pleasures' immanent to Western sexuality. 'One of the numerous points where I was wrong in that book was what I said about this *ars erotica*. I should have opposed our science of sex to a contrasting practice in our own

## The War Hypothesis

Foucault does not restrict his critical review of his own methodology to the repressive hypothesis and related notions. He also questions 'Nietzsche's hypothesis', that is, war as the framework for investigating social power relations. If the problem of repression stands at the centre of *The History of Sexuality, Volume 1*, the 1976 lectures at the Collège de France address whether war can serve as a model for power relations:[18]

> We might also ask whether notions derived from what was known in the eighteenth century and even the nineteenth century as the art of war ... constitute in themselves a valid and adequate instrument for the analysis of power relations.[19]

At first glance, nothing seems unusual about this question – nothing that would signal a break with earlier works. But in fact, the very formulation represents a departure: it introduces a distancing movement. In order to 'completely reverse direction', Foucault does not replace

culture'. Foucault, 1983b, 'On the Genealogy of Ethics: An Overview of Work in Progress', 234; see also Foucault, 1976a, *The History of Sexuality, Volume 1: An Introduction* [1978], 65–91, esp. 70–1, 90–1.

18. A translation of the 1976 lectures at the Collège de France has appeared in 1990 in Italian under the title, *Difendere la società. Dalla guerra delle razze al razzismo di stato*. Foucault, 1990a, *'Society Must Be Defended'* [2003]. In 1997, a revised and redacted version appeared in France, edited by the Centre Michel Foucault. Foucault, 1997, *'Society Must Be Defended'* [2003]. Early talks from the 1976 lectures (7 January 1976 and 14 January 1976) were published during Foucault's lifetime. Foucault, 1977e, '7 January 1976' [2003], 1–21; and Foucault, 1977f, '14 January 1976' [2003], 23–41. The following instalments of the series (21 and 28 January 1976) appeared after his death, as well as the year's final lecture (17 March 1976). Foucault, 1986, '21 January 1976' and '28 January 1976' [2003], 43–85; and Foucault, 1991, *'Society Must Be Defended'* [2003], 239–64. A brief synopsis – by Foucault himself – is found in Foucault, 1976m, 'Course Summary' [2003]. For analysis of the 1976 lectures from the perspective of the philosophy of history and political theory, see Napoli, 'Michel Foucault et les passions de l'histoire' (1993); and Pasquino, 'Political Theory of War and Peace: Foucault and the History of Modern Political Theory' (1993).

19. Foucault, 1986, '21 January 1976' and '28 January 1976' [2003], 47. Foucault breaks the question into parts: Do military institutions and practices constitute the core of political institutions? Is war a fundamental condition, and phenomena of domination, differentiation and social hierarchy secondary? Are struggles and antagonisms between individuals, groups and classes ultimately to be traced back to bellicose processes? Can power processes be analysed in terms of strategy and tactics? Foucault, 1976m, 'Course Summary' [2003], 266–7.

the juridical model with that of war; instead, he questions the basic investigative schema he has employed to date, thereby undertaking a genealogy of his own (genealogical) approach. No longer – as still occurs in *Discipline and Punish* – does he start with the hypothesis that power relations may be understood in terms of war, struggle and confrontation; now, he asks how the war discourse emerged in relation to juridical discourse. Foucault assigns the war model a historical place of its own: 'How, when, and why was it noticed or imagined that what is going on beneath and in power relations is a war?'.[20]

Foucault dates the emergence of war as the analytic grid for viewing the course of history and the reality of power relations to the seventeenth century. In a seeming paradox, this new kind of discourse arose at the moment when power relations centralized more and more and 'the emergence of a State ... perpetually traversed by relations of war'[21] occurred. Private feuds and battles faded, and a state equipped with a military apparatus – which professionalized and monopolized war – took the place of everyday and omnipresent fighting. In parallel to the 'pacification of society', a discourse emerged that discovered war under the surface of social order; the view is not based on an opposition between society and war so much as continuity between them. This 'historico-political discourse'[22] – which arose in confrontation with, and critique of, the power of sovereignty – set itself the same task that Foucault has assigned his work: 'This is, basically, a discourse that cuts off the king's head'.[23]

For politico-martial discourse, negative reference to juridico-political notions is key. Just as the juridical conception of power rests on a binary legal code, the martial framework sees a 'binary structure'[24]

---

20. Foucault, 1986, '21 January 1976' and '28 January 1976' [2003], 47; see also Foucault, 1976m, 'Course Summary' [2003], 266–7. Alessandro Fontana and Mauro Bertani rightly speak of how the 1975–6 lecture series marks a 'turning point' in Foucault's research. Fontana and Bertani, 'Situating the Lectures' (2003), 273-93.

21. Foucault, 1986, '21 January 1976' and '28 January 1976' [2003], 49.

22. Ibid., 59.

23. Ibid., 59. Foucault speaks of how 'this discourse was born twice. On the one hand, we see it emerging roughly in the 1630s, and in the context of the popular or petit bourgeois demands that were being put forward in pre-revolutionary and revolutionary England. It is the discourse of the Puritans, the discourse of the Levellers. And then fifty years later, in France at the end of the reign of Louis XIV, you find it on the opposite side, but it is still the discourse of a struggle against the king, a discourse of aristocratic bitterness'. Ibid., 59. On the sources Foucault may have employed, see Foucault, 1990a, *'Society Must Be Defended'* [2003], 281–3.

24. Foucault, 1986, '21 January 1976' and '28 January 1976' [2003], 51.

that pervades society, dividing it into two camps and lines of battle. In contrast to the view of a philosophical or juridical subject occupying a universal and neutral position, historico-political discourse holds that the subject must necessarily stand on one side or the other; a 'perspectival discourse'[25] emerges. If the historiography of old played the political role of describing and reinforcing sovereign glory, 'this new type of discourse and historical practice'[26] tells a story running in an 'absolutely opposite' direction. As a 'counterhistory',[27] it dissolves the identificatory continuity between the monarch and his people by breaking with the postulate that the history of the great encompasses that of the small, too.

Foucault argues that, in the course of the nineteenth century, politico-martial discourse transformed into medico-biological discourse.[28] The shift occurred in the framework of a general change in the mechanisms of power. It did not simply herald – as Foucault still claimed in *Discipline and Punish* – the transition from the order of sovereignty to the order of discipline. Foucault addresses the transition in his final lecture of 1976 and the concluding chapter of *The History of Sexuality, Volume 1* – which, by his own assessment, presents the motivating factor underlying the book as a whole. From this point on, he acknowledges the need to expand and nuance the analysis of power by developing a new conceptual instrumentarium.

## The Problematic of Biopower

Now, in addition to sovereign law and disciplinary mechanisms, Foucault identifies a third technology of power, which seeks to *regulate population*. It involves more than adding another feature to, or discovering a further dimension of, the analysis of modern power mechanisms. The perspective of regulation permits Foucault both to re-evaluate the concept of discipline and to view sovereignty in a new light.

---

25. Ibid., 52.
26. Ibid., 69.
27. Ibid., 69.
28. I will not discuss the concrete contents of lectures here – Foucault's historico-political theses and their significance for analysing racism – since methodological changes provide the point of interest. However, the matter is treated in the section 'From the War of the Races to State Racism' in Chapter 8.

In earlier works, discipline occupied the foreground as a specific technology. Individual disciplination served as a foil for the critique of the juridical conception of power; analysis bore on specific institutions and avoided global analyses of the state. But if Foucault started out contrasting the productivity of disciplinary mechanisms with the negativity of sovereign power, he came to assign discipline a place in a more comprehensive political technology – one that aims not just at training the body but also at controlling the population. The perspective of regulation enables him to relativize the significance of, and oppositions between, the other two forms of power and understand them from a more general vantage point: that of biopower.

## Discipline and Biopower

The concluding portion of *The History of Sexuality, Volume 1* takes theoretical distance from the concept of sovereign power – as occurs in previous studies, too. But Foucault no longer defines this distance by way of a specific mechanism (law vs. discipline); instead, he does so in terms of a radically changed goal. Sovereignty had been defined as power organized in the form of 'deduction' (*soustraction*): laying claim to goods, products, services and so on. In a limit case, it had the potential to do as it wished with the lives of subjects. Even though, in factual terms, the sovereign 'right of life and death' held only with restrictions and extreme checks, it symbolized the utmost form of power commanding the right to intervene and expropriate.[29]

By Foucault's account, a new form of power was progressively superimposed over such 'power of death' from the seventeenth century on; it aimed to administrate, secure, cultivate and manage life. Power mechanisms changed along the lines of a new objective:

> 'Deduction' ... tended to be no longer the major form of power but merely one element among others, working to incite, reinforce, control, monitor, optimize, and organize the forces under it: a power bent on generating forces, making them grow, and ordering them, rather than one dedicated to impeding them, making them submit, or destroying them.[30]

---

29. Foucault, 1976a, *The History of Sexuality, Volume 1: An Introduction* [1978], 135; Foucault, 1991, *'Society Must Be Defended'* [2003], 241.

30. Foucault, 1976a, *The History of Sexuality, Volume 1: An Introduction* [1978],

In contrast to sovereign might, which either put to death or let live, the new power let die and granted life. Power over death transformed into power over life – biopower – which did not bear on legal subjects so much as living beings. Foucault identifies 'two basic forms' along which the entire political technology of life evolved. Instead of being 'antithetical', they 'constituted … two poles of development linked together by a whole intermediary cluster of relations': on the one hand, the *disciplination' of the individual body* and, on the other, the *regulation of the population*.[31]

Foucault elaborated the first technology of power in previous studies. Now, he introduces a new aspect of analysis with the mechanism of regulation, which involves more than changing the scope or expanding the field of investigation. The regulation of population does not transfer disciplinary processes to macropolitical terrain so much as it marks a new object and modality for the exercise of power. Disciplination and regulation arise at different points in time, have separate objectives, implement different means to achieve goals and, finally, occupy different sites:

1. *Point in time.* In keeping with the analysis offered in *Discipline and Punish*, Foucault dates the emergence of discipline as a specific technology to the seventeenth century. This *'anatomo-politics'*[32] concerns the individual body. It views the human being as a complex machine and seeks to enhance the man-machine's abilities and potentials while integrating them into systems of economic production and systems of political rule. Then, in the second half of the eighteenth century, another technology of power emerges, which 'does not exclude [disciplinary technology] but … dovetail[s] into it, integrate[s] it, modif[ies] it to some extent, and above all, uses it by sort of infiltrating

136; see also Foucault, 1991, *'Society Must Be Defended'* [2003], 241.

31. Foucault, 1976a, *The History of Sexuality, Volume 1: An Introduction* [1978], 139, 138–73; Foucault, 1991, *'Society Must Be Defended'* [2003], 242. The mounting significance of biopower in Foucault's work may be illustrated on the basis of the weight it receives in two texts. Whereas the final 1976 lecture still presents discipline and biopower as separate technologies, whose reciprocal effects admit study, in *The History of Sexuality, Volume 1* – which appeared not long thereafter – they constitute two aspects of a more comprehensive conception encompassing both individual disciplination and collective regulation. See also Donnelly, 'On Foucault's Uses of the Notion "Biopower"' (1992); Marchetti, 'La naissance de la biopolitique' (1997).

32. Foucault, 1976a, *The History of Sexuality, Volume 1: An Introduction* [1978], 139.

it.[33] Disciplinary power is not replaced or pushed aside; instead, this political technology comes to operate at another level. Unlike discipline, it does not aim at the individual body so much as the social body – which is not conceived in legal terms, as the sum of (contract-making) individuals, but as an autonomous (biological) entity. An entirely new 'body' joins individual and society: the population.

2. *Objectives and means.* Population is defined by intrinsic processes and phenomena such as birth and mortality rates, health levels, life expectancy, wealth production and circulation, and so forth. Such '*bio-politics of the population*'[34] does not focus on the individual, but on varied expressions of life on a vast scale. Attention falls on what happens to masses of people: conditions of variation, controlling matters of probability and modifying effects in order to avert or balance out the dangers that result from communal existence conceived as a biological whole. This change of objective signals a change of the tools that power enlists. Not training and surveillance, but regulation and control are the main instruments of biopolitics. Instead of disciplining, this 'technology of security' 'aims to establish a sort of homeostasis'; it does so 'not by training individuals, but by achieving an overall equilibrium that protects the security of the whole from internal dangers'.[35]

3. *Sites.* The two technologies of power do not differ only in terms of objective, instruments or time of emergence. They also differ in terms of spatial situation – or political localization. The disciplines had developed at the beginning of the seventeenth century in the framework of particular institutions (army, school, hospital, workshops and so on). The regulation of populations started towards the middle of the eighteenth century, in the context of state centralization. As such, they represent distinct arrangements: 'the body-organism-discipline-institutions series and the population-biological processes-regulatory mechanisms-State'.[36]

Foucault's purpose in identifying two strands within the concept of biopower is primarily heuristic. The distinction cannot be rigorously maintained – and for both analytical and historical reasons. It proves

33. Foucault, 1991, '*Society Must Be Defended*' [2003], 242.
34. Foucault, 1976a, *The History of Sexuality, Volume 1: An Introduction* [1978], 139.
35. Foucault, 1991, '*Society Must Be Defended*' [2003], 249.
36. Ibid., 250; Foucault, 1976a, *The History of Sexuality, Volume 1: An Introduction* [1978], 139.

*analytically* untenable inasmuch as disciplination and regulation form 'two poles of development linked together by a whole intermediary cluster of relations'.[37] They cannot be viewed in isolation; rather, they constitute a political field and define each other reciprocally. Discipline is not a form of individualization exercised on given particulars; it presupposes that a multiplicity already exists. By the same token, population is the aggregation of individualized existences into a new political form. As such, 'individual' and 'mass' do not represent opposites so much as two sides of a single political rationality aiming to control life both on the individual scale and on the level of the population as a whole.[38]

Second, there are *historical* reasons not to split the two political technologies. Discussing the eighteenth century, Foucault still posits a relatively clear line of separation, but he observes that the police, for instance, already constituted a disciplinary and state apparatus during this period; by the same token, nineteenth-century regulation on the part of the state relied on an array of infrastate institutions (insurance, relief funds, charitable organizations, medico-hygienic institutions and so on). Ultimately – Foucault contends – the two types of power became linked over the course of the 1800s and yielded concrete dispositives; sexuality was one of the most important.[39]

---

37. Ibid., 139.

38. Lecture, 11 January 1978, Foucault, 2004a, *Security, Territory, Population* [2007], 7–12.

39. Foucault, 1991, *'Society Must Be Defended'* [2003], 250. This is where the project of *The History of Sexuality* starts: the specific political significance of sexuality stems from its 'pivot' position between both forms of power. Foucault, 1976a, *The History of Sexuality, Volume 1: An Introduction* [1978], 145. On the one hand, it represents a physical conduct accessible to disciplinary measures and, on the other – through its effects in terms of reproduction – it participates in biological population-processes. 'Sexuality exists at the point where body and population meet. And so it is a matter for discipline, but also a matter for regularization'. Foucault, 1991, *'Society Must Be Defended'* [2003], 251–2. Sexuality occupies a privileged position since its effects are situated both on the micro level of the body and on the macro level of the population. It comes to provide an interpretive scheme for personality and a 'cipher of individuality': sexual motivations are sought 'behind' modes of behaviour, 'under' words and 'in' dreams. Conversely, it becomes 'the theme of political operations, economic interventions, … and ideological campaigns for raising standards of morality and responsibility; it [is] put forward as the index of a society's strength, revealing of both its political energy and its biological vigor'. Foucault, 1976a, *The History of Sexuality, Volume 1: An Introduction* [1978], 146.

In the nineteenth century, this pivot position of sex led to the valorization of medico-hygienic knowledge and its implementation as a 'political

In this context, the concept of *norm* plays a key role. Whereas 'power over life and death' had operated on the basis of a binary legal code, laws yield to norms more and more now. The absolute law decreed by the sovereign comes to be replaced by the relational logic of weighing, measuring and comparing. Society defined along the lines of (natural) law gives way to 'normalizing society',[40] which is no longer populated by legal subjects so much as living organisms.[41]

Still, it is impossible not to see a far-reaching shift in the meaning Foucault attaches to 'norm' and 'normalizing society'. He continues to define norms at a remove from legal frameworks, but he no longer situates them in the context of 'disciplinary society'. He declares that the equation between 'normalizing society' and 'disciplinary society' amounted to a 'first and inadequate interpretation',[42] which he now abandons. Henceforth, the norm is the term connecting individual disciplination and social regulation. Foucault defines it as the

> element that will circulate between the disciplinary and the regulatory, which will also be applied to body and population alike, which will make it possible to control both the disciplinary order of the body and the aleatory events that occur in the biological multiplicity.[43]

---

intervention-technique'. Foucault, 1991, *'Society Must Be Defended'* [2003], 252. Whereas Foucault previously viewed such expansion of medicine as 'a sort of arbitrating discourse' that makes the heterogenous levels of disciplinary mechanisms and legal principles compatible with each other, he now understands it as the convergence of discipline and regulation. Foucault, 1977f, '14 January 1976' [2003], 39. Medicine no longer simply concentrates on investigating the individual body; meeting up with the 'theory of degeneration', it combines the question of individual health with the life of the species. In this framework, irregular sexuality does not involve just problems of individual pathology resulting from debauchery, perversion, masturbation and so on; it also holds reproductive consequences and bears on progeny. The theorem of degeneration permits medicine to expand its sphere of competence and simultaneously modifies its structure of operation, formulating knowledge that treats social problems in medico-technical terms; a connection is forged between the scientific understanding of biological-organic processes and the implementation of this knowledge in concrete practices of power. Medicine becomes a 'power-knowledge that can be applied to both the body and the population ..., and it will therefore have both disciplinary effects and regulatory effects'. Foucault, 1991, *'Society Must be Defended'* [2003], 252; see the section 'Social Medicine' in Chapter 8.

40. Foucault, 1976a, *The History of Sexuality, Volume 1: An Introduction* [1978], 144.

41. On the concept of the norm in Foucault, see Macherey, 'Towards a Natural History of Norms' (1992); Ewald, 'Michel Foucault et la norme' (1992); Canguilhem, *The Normal and the Pathological* (1989).

42. Foucault, 1991, *'Society Must Be Defended'* [2003], 253.

43. Ibid., 252.

Initially, Foucault had defined normalizing society on the basis of mechanisms of disciplination 'increasingly colonizing the procedures of law',[44] whereby the law faded more and more vis-à-vis the norm. Now, his definition is 'a society in which the norm of discipline and the norm of regulation intersect along an orthogonal articulation'.[45] That said, it was not long before Foucault modified this perspective, too; instead of focusing on standard normativity, he distinguished between various norms and explored the problematic of biopower in different context (see section 'Sovereignty – Discipline – Security' in Chapter 7).

## Biopower and the War Paradigm

Ultimately, the genealogy of historico-political discourse led Foucault to discern a new technology of power. The concept of biopower means giving up the tendency to equate power and discipline. Disciplinary procedures come to represent one mode of exercising power among others. Biopower integrates and subsumes disciplinary processes, which become an element within a more comprehensive scheme encompassing individual disciplination and the regulation of the population.[46]

However, this initial step did not go far enough, inasmuch as no conceptual reorientation accompanied the expanded field of analysis. Even after introducing the problematic of biopower, Foucault continued to understand processes of power primarily in terms of domination and subjugation. He employed the same analytical instruments he had applied to disciplinary institutions, only now he sought to examine a technology of power distinct from disciplinary techniques, working with other means and following different aims. In consequence, he recognized that he had to offer a second corrective. The relativized

---

44. Foucault, 1977f, '14 January 1976' [2003], 38–9.

45. Foucault, 1991, 'Society Must Be Defended' [2003], 253; Foucault, 1976a, The History of Sexuality, Volume 1: An Introduction [1978], 144.

46. 'Power of the disciplinary type such as the one that is exercised [...] in a certain number of institutions [...] is absolutely localized, it's a formula invented at a given moment [...]. [B]ut it is clear that it does not adequately represent all power relations and all possibilities of power relations. Power is not discipline; discipline is a possible procedure of power'. Foucault, 1984f, 'Politics and Ethics: An Interview', 380; cf. Foucault, 1981c, 'Sexuality and Solitude' [1997], 178. Thus, it is incorrect to assume – as Stefan Breuer does (like many others) – that Foucault developed a 'theory of disciplinary society' until the end. Breuer, 'Foucaults Theorie der Disziplinargesellschaft' (1987), 319.

perspective on disciplinary processes also required revising the war model that had provided the basis for investigating power relations until this point. The two steps did not occur independently: the 'emergence' of biopower required checks and changes in the conceptional framework; likewise, the increasingly apparent shortcomings of the war model are what prompted the 'discovery' of biopolitics in the first place.

A close relationship holds between Foucault's interest in the thematics of biopower and the distance he took from the war paradigm as the framework for analysing power relations. If it was true that the politico-martial discourse transformed into a biological discourse during the nineteenth century, he needed to account for this historical shift in theoretical terms. It was not enough to start by positing the existence of two external, mutually antagonistic groups. Foucault set out to examine the genealogy of a historical process within which politico-military 'contradictions' and conflicts were 'translated' into a biologico-medical field of problems. Inasmuch as 'State control of the biological'[47] really did occur in the course of the nineteenth century, the state could not be conceived as the expression of social relations of force or the instrument of political struggles. Rather, the state itself represent a 'stake' (*Einsatz*) in relations of force inasmuch as it formulates their objectives and means of functioning – 'condensing' and 'displacing' them simultaneously. The paradigm of struggle holds only limited significance in an 'economy of power' that assigns the state the key role in organizing social relations.[48]

---

47. Foucault, 1991, '*Society Must Be Defended*' [2003], 240.

48. Nicos Poulantzas, in particular, has sought to develop a conception of the state as the 'condensation' of power relations, instead of picturing it in terms of outward confrontations. Hereby, social struggles are immanent to the state: 'popular struggles are inscribed in the State not because they are exhaustively included in a totalizing Moloch-State, but because the State itself bathes in struggles that constantly submerge it. All the same it should be made clear that even struggles that go beyond the State (and not only class struggles do this) are not thereby "extraneous to power": they are always inscribed in power apparatuses which concretize them and which also condense a relationship of forces (factories or companies, to some extent the family, and so on)'. Poulantzas, *State, Power, Socialism* (2000), 141. Antonio Gramsci had already described this political transition as the 'shift from war of maneuver to war of position'. Gramsci, *Prison Notebooks* (2007), 161. In contrast to Poulantzas (and Althusser), Gramsci starts with 'civil society' (*società civile*) in order to determine how it was possible for 'bourgeois hegemony' to emerge, which largely avoids directly physical mechanisms of violence. Gramsci's thesis holds that bourgeois domination

Foucault's 'discovery' of biopower coincided with his questioning of the war hypothesis. For all that, mounting distance from 'Nietzsche's hypothesis' did not lead him back to the juridical conception of power; instead, it extended the scope of critique. If Foucault had faulted the juridical conception for conceiving power only in negative terms, now he came to realize that conceiving power as a martial relation could not account for the productivity and positivity of biopower, either.

Disqualification of the war model, which a careful formula in *The History of Sexuality, Volume 1* already announced,[49] became a defining theme immediately following the publication of this book. Foucault recognized that this conception of power raised a 'whole range of problems':

> Who wages war against whom? Is it between two classes, or more? Is it a war of all against all? What is the role of the army and military institutions in this civil society where permanent war is waged? What is the relevance of concepts of tactics and strategy for analysing structures and political processes? What is the essence and mode of transformation of power relations?[50]

Foucault laments that talk of class struggle, relations of force and strategies often occurs without clarification of the terms employed.

---

and the institutionalization of the state can only come about once a certain way of living has been systematically organized and mechanisms have been set up that permit the subjugated to be led: 'The state was just a forward trench; behind it stood a succession of sturdy fortresses and emplacements'. Ibid., 169, 117, 161–3, 569.

Chapter 7 explores how Foucault seeks to understand both these views as poles within the analysis of government. Foucault examines the problem Gramsci defines in terms of hegemony as a process of simultaneous subjectification and 'statification'. See his frequent reference to 'hegemony' in *The History of Sexuality, Volume 1*. E.g. Foucault, 1976a, *The History of Sexuality, Volume 1* [1978], 93, 94, 123, 125, 141. For a comparison of how Gramsci and Foucault employ the term, see Smart, 'The Politics of Truth' (1986).

49. 'If we still wish to maintain a separation between war and politics, perhaps we should postulate rather that this multiplicity of force relations can be coded – in part but never totally – either in the form of "war" or in the form of "politics"; this would imply two different strategies (but the one always liable to switch into the other) for integrating these unbalanced, heterogeneous, unstable and tense force relations'. Foucault, 1976a, *The History of Sexuality, Volume 1: An Introduction* [1978], 93.

50. Foucault, 1977d, 'Truth and Power' [1984], 65; Foucault, 1976j, 'Some Questions from Michel Foucault to *Hérodote*' [2007]; Foucault, 1977g, 'The Eye of Power' [2008], 15.

Marxism deserves credit for identifying class struggle as the motor of history, yet it proves inadequate inasmuch as it concentrates more on the constitution of class and less on the particularities of struggle. Marxism 'especially ... [defines] this class, where it is situated, who it encompasses, but never concretely [addresses] ... the nature of the struggle'.[51]

The military-strategic analysis of power that Foucault formulates poses 'two difficulties',[52] above all. First, it is impossible to write the 'history of the vanquished' because, by definition, they are deprived of speech and must use a language imposed on them. Second, there is the question whether 'domination processes are not much more complex and ambiguous than war'.[53] To illustrate this point, Foucault points to the *lettres de cachet*, petitions to the absolutist king in pre-revolutionary France seeking the incarceration of certain individuals:

---

51. Foucault, 1977k, 'The End of the Monarchy of Sex' [1996], 225; see also Foucault, 1977m, 'The Confession of the Flesh' [1980], 208; Foucault, 1978m, 'Méthodologie pour la connaissance du monde', 606. An important specification is necessary at this point. Foucault's theoretical problems do not stem from the fact *that* he understands social relations to be conflictual and violent so much as the way that he conceives the genesis and structure of such conflicts. A comparison with Marx's conception of class struggle makes as much plain. Etienne Balibar draws attention to a key difference that emerges on the basis of a matter of agreement. Both Marx and Foucault view social relations as relations of force, and neither one analyses power as a substance. 'But these arguments are *not understood in the same way*. One could say that Foucault understands them simply *as having an external nature*, which means at the same time that "the opposing aims" in a strategic conflict destroy, neutralise, mutually reinforce or modify one another, but do not form a superior unity or individuality. On the contrary, for Marx, the condition for the development of a conflict is the *interiorisation of the relationship* itself, in such a way that the antagonistic terms become the functions or the bearers of the relationship.' For this reason, Balibar continues, Marx 'conceive[s] of class relations as being internally irreconcilable, as relations from which the dominated can escape only by destroying the subjugating relationship itself, and thereby transforming themselves into different individuals from those who "constituted" that relationship'. Balibar, 'Foucault and Marx: The Question of Nominalism' (1992), 52. Balibar's assessment holds for Foucault's position up to *The History of Sexuality, Volume 1*, and his essay concentrates on this text, above all. In contrast, my argument here is that, by means of the problematic of government, Foucault develops his conception of social conflicts in the direction indicated by Marx, that is, towards an 'interiorization of the relationship itself'.

52. Foucault, 1977u, 'La torture, c'est la raison', 390.

53. Ibid., 390–1.

There, one sees that detention and internment are not authoritarian measures from above – not measures that struck people out of the blue, that were imposed on them. In reality, people themselves perceived it as necessary – among themselves, even in the poorest families, and especially in the most destitute groups. Internment is imposed as a kind of necessity for solving the problems that people have with each other. Grave problems in families, including the poorest, could not be solved without the police, without internment. Thus, a whole literature results, where people tell the authorities how unfaithful a husband has been, how much a wife deceived her spouse, how unbearable the children are. They demanded the internment of the accused themselves, in the language of the reigning power.[54]

The *lettres de cachet* show that internment is not to be understood solely as the result of overreaching, absolutist (state) power. Incarceration was also sought 'from below', by family members and neighbours. Consequently, the metaphor of war and the analytical tools accompanying it prove inadequate for understanding certain 'enigmatic' phenomena: 'In any case, there exists a gigantic demand aimed at the state'; the state is not simply an instrument of domination for subjugating the vanquished; instead, 'something like a completely incomprehensible will' confronts it. Foucault recognizes that he 'cannot avoid this question'.[55] It provides the focus of his 1978 lectures at the Collège de France and changes the problematic of power as a whole. The concept of government occupies the foreground.

## The Concept of Government

The 1978 lectures centre on the 'genealogy of the modern state'.[56] Although the series of talks was announced under the working title

---

54. Ibid., 391; see also Foucault, 1982q, *Disorderly Families* [2016], 242–50.
55. Foucault, 1978m, 'Méthodologie pour la connaissance du monde', 618.
56. Lecture, 5 April 1978, Foucault, 2004a, *Security, Territory, Population* [2007], 354. For a long time the 1978 and 1979 lectures at the Collège de France have remained largely unknown. The only documents concerning these lectures that Foucault authorized for publication were the lecture on 1 February 1978 and course synopses. Foucault, 1978o, 'Governmentality' [2000]; Foucault, 1978z, 'Course Summary' [2007]; Foucault, 1979m, 'Course Summary' [2008]. The lecture on 31 January 1979 had been transcribed in part, and the lecture on 25 January 1978 in full. Foucault,

*Sécurité, territoire et population*, Foucault came to recognize the key role played by the concept of government. It provides the 'guideline'[57] of analysis. Accordingly, in the fourth lecture of the series, Foucault decided to change the original rubric and adopt a new one ('histoire de la gouvernementalité').

Governmentality encompasses three aspects:

1. The ensemble formed by institutions, procedures, analyses and reflections, the calculations and tactics that allow the exercise of this very specific albeit complex form of power, which has as its target population, as its principal form of knowledge, political economy, and as its essential technical means dispositives of security.

2. The tendency that, over a long period and throughout the West, has steadily led towards the pre-eminence over all other forms (sovereignty, discipline and so on) of this type of power – which may be termed 'government' – resulting, on the one hand, in the formation of a whole series of specific governmental apparatuses, and, on the other, in the development of a whole complex of knowledges [*savoirs*].

3. The process or, rather, the result of the process through which the state of justice of the Middle Ages transformed into the administrative state during the fifteenth and sixteenth centuries and gradually becomes 'governmentalized'.[58]

The concept of government receives a distinct profile through the complex interplay of rupture and continuity. On the one hand, Foucault takes distance from earlier versions of his conception of power; on the other, he pursues central intuitions of the 'microphysics

1984w, 'La phobie d'État' [2008]; Foucault, 1992, 'La population' [1978]. Finally, an (incomplete) translation of the 1978 lecture series existed in German. Foucault, 1982k, *Security, Territory, Population* [2004]. At the time of this book's writing, Seuil (France) had published both introductory talks for the lecture series from 1978 and 1979 on audio cassette, under the title *De la gouvernementalité*. The complete lecture series at the Collège de France from 1978 and 1979 was only published in 2004 and appeared in English translation some years later (2007 and 2008). Given the difficulty of access to materials at the time of writing this book, I had to rely mainly on my own transcripts of recordings held at the time at the Fonds Michel Foucault in Paris (documents C 64, 2–12, and C 67, 1–12).
57. Foucault, 1978z, 'Course Summary' [2007], 363.
58. Foucault, 1978o, 'Governmentality' [2000], 219–20; translation modified.

of power'. The break involves elaborating a conception of power that differs from both the model of law and the model of war:

> Basically power is less a confrontation between two adversaries or the linking of one to the other [...]. The relationship proper to power would not therefore be sought on the side of violence or of struggle, nor on that of voluntary linking ..., but rather in the area of the singular mode of action, *neither warlike nor juridical*, which is government.[59]

In other words, Foucault does not take distance from the juridical conception of power alone. He also breaks with his conception of power in terms of war. Still, this does not mean that 'government' heralds the pacification of politico-historical discourse. On the contrary: the concept points to plural struggles beyond any revolutionary teleology that aims at a unified goal organized around a central contradiction: 'Rather than speaking of an essential freedom, it would be better to speak of an "agonism" – of a relationship which is at the same time reciprocal incitation and struggle; less of a face-to-face confrontation which paralyses both sides than a permanent provocation'.[60]

The significance of government is evident both in contrast to Foucault's earlier conceptions and in points of continuity. Foucault means for the methodological principles that shaped previous works to hold.[61] He assigns the concept of government the same role, for

---

59. Foucault, 1982b, 'The Subject and Power', 221; emphasis added.

60. Ibid., 222. Michel Senellart has discussed this double negation of the concept of government extremely well. Senellart, 'Michel Foucault: "gouvernementalité" et raison d'Etat' (1993), 287–8. See, also, Foucault's observation: 'To think the social bond, "bourgeois" eighteenth-century thinking adopted the *juridical form of the contract*. In order to think struggle, "revolutionary" thought of the nineteenth-century adopted the *logical form of contradiction*: the latter, no doubt, is no more valid than the former'. Foucault, 1977w, 'Power and Strategies' [1980], 143–4. On the emergence of the term *government* in Foucault's work and the stages in which it was introduced, see Keenan, 'Foucault on Government' (1982).

61. Three theoretical shifts had defined the *microphysics of power*. The first involved taking distance from a mode of analysing institutions that concentrates on internal power relations or how they are reproduced, in order to uncover the *technologies of power* 'behind' or 'underneath' them. Second, instead of identifying functions and assessing their 'performance' or 'adequation', it looked for *strategies*, resituating operations on a historical field of competing forces. Third, instead of accepting standing objects and seeking to identify what relations ordered and 'reconciled' them, it sought out the conditions for their *constitution* and the immanent practices of knowledge and power that 'produce' objects in the first place. Foucault declares his intention

examining the state, that the concept of discipline plays for analysing specific institutions. As such, his lectures focus on the question whether government represents a general technology of power that encompasses the state as discipline does the prison – i.e. whether government, for the state, is what the techniques of incarceration, separation and so on are for hospitals, prisons and other institutions.[62]

In contrast to his microphysical studies, Foucault undertakes a significant clarification of the object under investigation. Instead of analysing government only as a technology of power, he concentrates on its *political rationality*.[63] This involves examining the technology of

---

to bring the same theoretical operations (technology, strategy and constitution – not institution, function and object) that shaped the 'genealogy of the prison' to bear on the 'genealogy of the state'. Lecture, 8 February 1978, Foucault, 2004a, *Security, Territory, Population* [2007], 116–120.

62. Lecture, 8 February 1978, ibid., 119; Foucault, 1982b, 'The Subject and Power', 222–3; Séglard, 'Foucault et le problème du gouvernement' (1992), 124–5.

63. Governmentality is a neologism derived from the French word *gouvernemental*, meaning 'concerning government'. Senellart, 'Course Context' (2007), 399–400. The word was known even before it figured as a central term in Foucault's work. Roland Barthes had already used the 'barbarous but unavoidable neologism' in the 1950s, to denote an ideological mechanism that presents the government as the origin of social relations. For Barthes, governmentality refers to 'the Government presented by the national press as the Essence of efficacy'. Barthes, *Mythologies* (1989), 130. Foucault takes up this 'ugly word', but detaches it from the semiological context. Lecture, 8 February 1978, Foucault, 2004a, *Security, Territory, Population* [2007], 115. Governmentality no longer refers to a mythological symbolic practice that depoliticizes social relations, but represents the 'rationalization of governmental practice in the exercise of political sovereignty'. Lecture, 10 January 1979, Foucault, 2004b, *The Birth of Biopolitics* [2008], 2.

Here as elsewhere, the concept of (political) rationality does not imply a normative assessment. Its significance is relational: 'rational' refers to the agreement of rules, procedures, forms of thought and so on with the totality of conditions under which it is possible to treat certain problems at a given point in time. As such, 'rationality' does not refer to Reason, writ large, so much as the historical practices that provide the context for generating strategies of perception and judgement:

I think one must restrict one's use of this word to an instrumental and relative meaning. The ceremony of public torture isn't in itself more irrational than imprisonment in a cell; but it's irrational in terms of a type of penal practice which involves new ways of envisaging the effects to be produced by the penality imposed, new ways of calculating its utility, justifying it, graduating it, etc. One isn't assessing things in terms of an absolute against which they could be evaluated as constituting more or less perfect forms of rationality, but rather examining how forms of rationality inscribe themselves in practices or systems of practices, and what role they play within them, because it's true that 'practices' don't exist without a certain regime of rationality. But, rather than measuring this regime against a value-of-reason, I

government especially as a *programme*: 'government' designates a discursive field within which the exercise of power is 'rationalized'. The process involves working out terms and concepts, identifying objects and limitations, affording arguments and justifications, and so on. In other words, political rationality permits a problem to be articulated and offers certain strategies for solving or managing it. What interests Foucault in the discourses he discusses – economics, moral philosophy, theories of policing, philanthropy and so on – are the rationales and programmes formulated. These programmes not only express wishes and intentions, but define an implicit knowledge:

> Every programme also either articulates or presupposes a *knowledge* of the field of reality upon which it is to intervene and/or which it is calculated to bring into being. The common axiom of programmes is that an effective power is and must be a power which *knows* the objects upon which it is exercised. Further, the condition that programmatic knowledge must satisfy is that it renders reality in the form of an object which is *programmable*. This operation is reminiscent of the function Kant attributes in the *Critique of Pure Reason* to the concept of the schema which, as Deleuze puts it, 'does not answer the question, how are phenomena made subject to the understanding, but the question, how does the understanding apply itself to the phenomena which are subject to it?'[64]

A programme is not pure knowledge, which then comes to be implemented and instrumentalized. Rather, it always already represents an intellectual transformation of reality, which political technologies take up in turn. The latter include apparatuses, procedures, institutions, legal forms and so on, which are supposed to make it possible to rule subjects in keeping with a political rationality. That said, the relationship between political rationalities and political technologies does not

---

would prefer to analyse it according to two axes: on the one hand, that of codification/prescription (how it forms an ensemble of rules, procedures, means to an end, etc.), and on the other, that of true or false formulation (how it determines a domain of objects about which it is possible to articulate true or false propositions). Foucault, 1980b, 'Questions of Method', 79; see also Ewald, *Histoire De L'Etat Providence* (1986a), 61–2; Procacci, 'Governing Poverty: Sources of the Social Question in Nineteenth-Century France' (1994), 209.
    64. Gordon, 'Afterword' (1980), 248.

represent a perfect correspondence between the world of discourse and that of practice. Points of incongruity are precisely what open the space for historical analysis. History does not amount to a plan going into fulfilment. Instead, it involves what lies 'between' the two levels Foucault has identified; thus, the 'failure' of the prison programme produces delinquency as an 'unintended effect'. Foucault's 'history of the prison' is located in the 'gap' between programme and 'reality'.[65]

By restricting analysis to political rationalities, Foucault exhibits less interest for 'history as it really happened' (after all, a programme is not identical with what occurs) than in disclosing a new field of historical research focused on the relationship between 'programme' and 'real' history:

> You say to me: nothing happens as laid down in these 'programmes'; they are no more than dreams, utopias, a sort of imaginary production that you aren't entitled to substitute for reality. Bentham's *Panopticon* isn't a very good description of 'real life' in nineteenth-century prisons.
>
> To this I would reply: If I had wanted to describe 'real life' in the prisons, I wouldn't indeed have gone to Bentham. But the fact that this real life isn't the same thing as the theoreticians' schemas doesn't entail that these schemas are therefore utopian, imaginary, etc. One could only think that if one had a very impoverished notion of the real. For one thing, the elaboration of these schemas corresponds to a whole series of diverse practices and strategies: the search for effective, measured, unified penal mechanisms is unquestionably a response to the inadequation of the institutions of judicial power to the new economic forms, urbanization, etc. ... For another thing, these pro-grammes induce a whole series of effects in the real (which isn't of course the same as saying that they take the place of the real): they crystallize into institutions, they inform individual behaviour, they act as grids for the perception and evaluation of things. It is absolutely true that criminals stubbornly resisted the new disciplinary mechanism in the prison; it is absolutely correct that the actual functioning of the prisons, in the inherited buildings where they were established and with the governors and guards who administered them, was a witches' brew compared to the beautiful Benthamite machine. But if the prisons

---

65. Foucault, 1984j, 'What Is Called "Punishing"?' [2000], 385–6; Gordon, 'After-word' (1980), 246–50.

were seen to have failed, if criminals were perceived as incorrigible, and a whole new criminal 'race' emerged into the field of vision of public opinion and 'justice', if the resistance of the prisoners and the pattern of recidivism took the forms we know they did, it's precisely because this type of programming didn't just remain a utopia in the heads of a few projectors.[66]

But what *is* government? Foucault starts out with a broad and 'vague'[67] conception, distinguishing 'political government' from the 'problem of government in general'.[68] However, he does not do so for want of analytical precision; rather, he means to assign government a historical place. By way of a brief history of the term, Foucault demonstrates that the seemingly self-evident concept of government we have today – the equation of government and political government, as well as our focus on state institutions – represents a restriction of the original semantic field, which set in relatively late.

Until the eighteenth century, the problem of government was posed in significantly wider terms. Whereas the word now has an exclusively political sense (the government of a state, a party, an apparatus, and so on), it displayed a broader array of meanings between the fifteenth and eighteenth centuries. Then, 'government' referred to a number of highly varied phenomena. Among other things, it signified: moving oneself or an object (in space), securing (material) well-being, leading someone (morally), prescribing something (medically) and, finally, a (verbal, authoritative, sexual, etc.) relationship between individuals. As many and as varied as these fields and forms of activity may be, it is striking that none of the meanings concern administrating a political

---

66. Foucault, 1980b, 'Questions of Method', 81; see also Foucault, 1981a, "'Omnes et Singulatim'", 227. That said, the simple fact that many of Foucault's readers deem his analysis of programs a matter of actual, concrete historical (*realgeschichtlich*) investigation may stand as proof of their force and impact (*Realitätsmächtigkeit*). On the problem of points of divergence between programs, technologies and actual historical effects, see Hirschman, *The Passions and the Interests* (1977), esp. 115–36. On Foucault's reception by historians, see Megill, 'The Reception of Foucault by Historians' (1987); Perrot, *L'Impossible Prison* (1980); Goldstein, *Foucault and the Writing of History* (1994); Le Goff, 'Foucault et la "nouvelle histoire"' (1997).

67. Lecture, 8 February 1978, Foucault, 2004a, *Security, Territory, Population* [2007], 116.

68. Foucault, 1978o, 'Governmentality' [2000], 201; Foucault, 2004a, *Security, Territory, Population* [2007], 89.

structure or territory. On the contrary, it seems that the 'political' definition of government, which now seems so common and obvious, was
entirely unknown before the sixteenth century.[69]

But, if the various meanings of 'govern' do not derive from the
sphere of political semantics, they still have a point in common. As
Foucault observes, problems of self-control, directing one's family and
children, managing a household and guiding souls indicate that *government* has always referred to 'conducting human beings', whether
individually or as a collective.[70]

Accordingly, Foucault defines government as *conduct*, a continuum extending from 'government of the self' (*gouvernement de soi*) to
'government of others' (*gouvernement des autres*); hereby, the understanding of government as political leadership, which prevails today,
represents a special instance of governing others. Against this backdrop, Foucault asks why, at a certain point in time, the conception
of government came to be restricted and to possess a purely political
significance. The 1978 lectures investigate the matter; from this point
on, government represents the 'key term'[71] within Foucault's analytics
of power.

---

69. Lecture, 8 February 1978, Foucault, 2004a, *Security, Territory, Population*
[2007], 122; Senellart, *Les arts de gouverner* (1995), 24–5.

70. Lecture, 8 February 1978, Foucault, 2004a, *Security, Territory, Population*
[2007], 120–2.

71. Allen, 'Government in Foucault' (1991), 431; see also Neuenhaus, *Max Weber
und Michel Foucault* (1993), 67; Keenan, 'Foucault on Government' (1982), 36.

# 7

# The Genealogy of the Modern State

Furthermore, I do not hesitate to say that in nearly all Christian nations today, ... religion is in danger of falling into the hands of the government. Not that sovereigns are terribly keen to establish dogma themselves, but they are increasingly usurping the will of those who explain dogma: they are depriving the clergy of its property and putting clergymen on salary, and they are using the priests' influence and turning it to their own exclusive profit. They are turning clergy-men into functionaries and, often, servants, and they are using the clergy to reach the deepest recesses of the individual soul.

Alexis de Tocqueville[1]

The concept of government is Foucault's response to two complexes of problems – 'state' and 'subjectivity' – articulated in previous studies. Inasmuch as it failed to take sufficient distance from juridical notions, the 'microphysics of power' ultimately led to difficulties resembling the theoretical problems it was meant to subject to critique. In turn, the question arose about a centralized instance of power strong enough to discipline and fashion subjects. Foucault repeatedly denied the existence of anything producing such cohesion, leaving it open how microstrategies achieve coordination and come together into the comprehensive technology of domination he implicitly assumed.

In order to do justice to this twofold problem, Foucault enlists a conception of government that does not view subjectivation and state formation as separate processes, but investigates them from a single

1. Tocqueville, *Democracy in America* (2004), 805.

analytical perspective.[2] His methodological concern is to examine politico-legal forms of institutionalization as they bear on historical modes of subjectivation, without reducing the one to the other. In this framework, the state is not simply a legal structure. Instead, its defining trait, in modern times, is that it represents 'both an individualizing and a totalizing form of power'.[3] The 'freedom' of subjects and the 'power' of the state are not external to each other, but constitutively related. Accordingly, Foucault's 'genealogy of the modern state' is also 'a history of the subject'.[4]

Putting the task in these terms, Foucault's 1978 lecture advances a historical argument: the modern (Western) state is the result of a complex combination of 'political' and 'pastoral' power. Whereas the

---

2. This conception also represents a theoretical advantage vis-à-vis the definition of the state that Poulantzas offers. For him, '[t]he individual-private sphere is created by the State concomitantly with its relative separation from the public space of society'. Poulantzas, *State, Power, Socialism* (2000), 70, 69–76. In contrast, Foucault understands the state itself as a form of governing. As we will see in the further course of argument, this position also marks a point of difference with Gramsci, who concentrates on 'civil society'. By analysing government, Foucault intends to make the interplay between interiority and exteriority, state and society, the object of analysis: 'it is possible to suppose that if the state is what it is today, it is so precisely thanks to this governmentality, which is at once internal and external to the state – since it is the tactics of government that make possible the continual definition and redefinition of what it is within the competence of the state and what is and is not, the public versus the private and so on. Thus the state can only be understood in its survival and its limits on the basis of the general tactics of governmentality'. Foucault, 1978o, 'Governmentality' [2000], 221.

3. Foucault, 1982b, 'The Subject and Power', 213.

4. Lecture, 22 February 1978, Foucault, 2004a, *Security, Territory, Population* [2007], 184. This double genealogy pursues a double aim. First, Foucault seeks to prove that the 'macrophysics of the state' can be analysed on the basis of the same methodological principles as the 'microphysics of power', but without incurring the latter's points of theoretical ambiguity. Second, he wants to show that it is possible to examine the genesis of subjectivity without enlisting a humanistic frame of reference. Lecture, 5 April 1978, Foucault, 2004a, *Security, Territory, Population* [2007], 355–8; Dean, *Critical and Effective Histories* (1994), 175.

For organizational reasons, this section focuses on the 'genealogy of the modern state', that is, the development of political rationalities. The other aspect of Foucault's project – the 'genealogy of the modern subject' – will be discussed in Part III. The following seeks to collate and systematize Foucault's scattered interviews, articles, talks and lectures on this theme. As such, it is a matter of reporting Foucault's theses (and not presenting my own). To be sure, this approach is not unproblematic. However, inasmuch as this side of Foucault's work remained largely unknown at the time of writing of this book, theoretical discussion of the concept of government is reserved for the next section.

former stems from the ancient *polis* and is organized in terms of rights and laws, universality, the civil sphere and so on, the latter represents a Christian conception, at the centre of which stands the comprehensive guidance of individual lives. If this premise is correct, then analysis of the modern state requires the examination of – over and above 'political' practices and forms of institutionalization – seemingly 'private' techniques elaborated within pastoral modes of guidance. Foucault argues that the idea of government as the leading of human beings, which prevailed up into the eighteenth century, goes back to the relationship, originating with Christianity, between a spiritual leader and his flock: *pastoral power*.[5]

## The Government of Souls: The Christian Pastorate

Christian pastoral power possesses an array of qualities that set it apart from both Greco-Roman and Hebrew forms of government. As such, it is necessary not just to distinguish between government and other modes of exercising power – domination, exploitation and so on – but also to elaborate the difference between various conceptions of leadership and specifically Christian techniques of government.

In ancient Greek and Roman tradition, 'government' does not refer to leading human beings, but to ruling the city to which people belong. It involves steering a community – and not directly leading the human beings who belong to it. The prevailing image in ancient political theory is the 'ship metaphor', whereas the 'shepherd metaphor' proves only marginally significant. In classical political thought, leadership is symbolized by the captain steering the ship (i.e. the *polis*), not the sailors.[6]

---

5. I have already presented some elements of Foucault's understanding of pastoral power elsewhere. Lemke, "'Der Eisberg der Politik'': Foucault und das Problem der Regierung' (1995).

6. Lecture, 8 February 1978, Foucault, 2004a, *Security, Territory, Population* [2007], 119–24; Foucault, 1978k, 'Sexuality and Power' [1999], 121. To illustrate this conception of government, Foucault mentions Plato's *Statesman* – which explicitly discusses, and rejects, the pastoral theme. For Plato, the concept of the shepherd is only fitting for those happy times when no politics existed yet – because there was no need. Then, the herd of humankind was guided by divine hand, received nourishment from nature's bounty, inhabited a mild climate and so on. Now that this paradisiacal state is gone and the gods have withdrawn from the world, the statesman is required.

The idea of government as the guidance of human beings was initially unknown to the Greeks and Romans. It first emerged in Egypt and Mesopotamia and was subsequently elaborated among Hebrew tribes. Foucault emphasizes aspects of the Hebrew pastorate that contrast sharply with Greek techniques of government:

1. The *Object* of Government. The shepherd does not exercise power over a territory or a city, but a flock, a mobile mass of human beings. According to the Greek conception, the gods possess the land. The Hebrew pastor-god promises his flock a land that will one day belong to them. At the centre of Greek political thinking stands the idea of the commonwealth (*Gemeinwesen*). In the Hebrew conception, a pastor steers a herd of scattered individuals that exists only in and through his presence and action; without him, the flock would be lost and dissolve altogether.

2. The *Purpose* of Government. The pastor-god's task is the salvation of his flock. Whereas assistance was sought from the Greek gods in times of danger, seeking help from the Hebrew shepherd does not represent an exception. In keeping with the scope of the idea of salvation, enduring, individualized and goal-oriented protection is necessary – comprehensive supervision of the entire flock and each one of its sheep ('omnes et singulatim').

3. The *'Foundation'* of Government. The Hebrew pastorate rests on the principle that exercising power is a duty. Greek leaders were also supposed to make decisions in the interests of everyone and serve the community; the reward for fulfilling obligations was living on in the remembrance of the living. In contrast, the watchfulness of the shepherd stood closer to 'devotion' and 'sacrifice'; it required that the leader give up his own interests and direct all attention to the weal of the flock.[7]

However, the statesman does not stand above others, directing them and their fate. He is not a shepherd but a weaver, bringing together the various elements of society: 'The royal art of ruling consisted in gathering lives together "into a community based upon concord and friendship", and so he wove "the finest of fabrics". The entire population, "slaves and free men alike, were mantled in its folds". Foucault, 1981a, "'Omnes et Singulatim'", 234; see also lecture, 8 February 1978, Foucault, 2004a, *Security, Territory, Population* [2007], 128–30.

7. Lecture, 8 February 1978, Foucault, 2004a, *Security, Territory, Population* [2007], 123–5; see also Foucault, 1978k, 'Sexuality and Power' [1999], 121–3; Foucault, 1981a, "'Omnes et Singulatim'", 233.

In turn, the *Christian* pastorate introduced a number of changes modifying the figures of Greco-Roman and Hebrew government. Above all, it
arranged – or rearranged – certain elements (Salvation, Law and Truth):

1. *Salvation.* The Greek polis and the Hebrew flock presume the shared
fate of the leader and those he leads. The Christian pastorate also has
the idea of mutual obligation, but the relationship proves more paradoxical and complex. The Christian pastor does not work with a stable
community of determinate human beings so much as within a subtle
economy of sins and merits subordinate to the imperative of salvation.
On the one hand, salvation is an individual affair; on the other, it does
not represent a matter of free choice. Indeed, it is impossible to refuse
salvation, or the path to it. Pastoral authority means forcing people, if
need be, to do what is necessary to achieve salvation.

2. *Law.* The second change concerns obedience. Whereas Hebrews and
Greeks allowed themselves to be led only by laws – or, alternatively,
by persuasion/conviction – Christian pastorship introduces pure or
generalized compliance: obedience for obedience's sake. A means to an
end becomes an end in itself: obedience no longer represents an instrument for attaining certain virtues, but becomes a virtue in itself: one
obeys in order to achieve the state of obedience. Stripped of reference
to anything outside itself, it receives the status of a fundamental virtue
providing the precondition for attaining all other virtues.

At the same time, the Christian pastorate established, alongside
the legal-political authority of tradition, a new way for analysing and
judging conduct, at once more flexible and more finely woven than
what preceded it. Another form of culpabilization arises, no longer
functioning in a partial and temporary manner, but in enduring
fashion and, in principle, without end. This strategy for assessing and
evaluating human lives abstracts from concrete, individual actions
and moves thoughts, volitions, wishes, desires and so on to the fore in
order to provide correction and guidance. Constraint involving (moral
and legal) laws is joined by the authority of a pastor whose constant
supervision and spiritual custodianship alone guarantee the path to
salvation.

3. *Truth.* For the Greeks, guidance was a matter of free will within
temporal boundaries; it served the purpose of self-control. In contrast, Christian practice involves continual and compulsory guidance;

self-examination and conscience do not serve to promote autonomy but to anchor dependency. Accordingly, exercising this form of power demands not just knowledge of what the flock – i.e. each of its members – does, but also knowledge about what individuals think and feel: insight into the conscience and the ability to steer it.

Christian pastorship developed an array of techniques and methods bearing on truth and its production. Knowing the inner truth of individuals represents the indispensable technical precondition for the 'government of souls'. The pastor needs to have analytical methods – techniques of reflection and guidance – for securing such knowledge. Accordingly, the Christian pastorate works with a historically unique practice unknown elsewhere: comprehensive and thoroughgoing *confession*. As an institution, confession enables the examination of consciences: knowing inner secrets is indispensable for guiding souls. At the same time, it amounts to more than secrets being revealed; confession means not only taking stock of facts, but also producing truth. As such, it establishes a hierarchical distinction between secrets that have been disclosed, qualifying certain 'truths' as 'hidden'. These truths make it possible to forge an enduring bond between the pastor, his flock, and each one of its members.[8]

The 'genealogy of pastoral power' proceeds in two steps. Initially, Foucault observes, aspects of Hebrew pastorship were taken up and changed. By this means, Christian pastorship forged techniques of guidance that later achieved a 'political' dimension extending far beyond their religious roots.

We can say that Christian pastorship has introduced a game that neither the Greeks nor the Hebrews imagined. A strange game whose elements are life, death, truth, obedience, individuals, self-identity; a

---

8. Lecture, 8 February 1978, Foucault, 2004a, *Security, Territory, Population* [2007], 123–30; Foucault, 1978k, 'Sexuality and Power' [1999], 124–5; Foucault, 1981a, '"Omnes et Singulatim"', 234–42; Foucault, 1982b, 'The Subject and Power', 213; Bernauer, *Michel Foucault's Force of Flight: Toward an Ethics for Thought* (1990), 162–5. The Christian pastorate will receive more attention in Part III of this book, since its articulation of salvation, obedience and truth corresponds to three levels constituting Christian subjectivity: analytical individuation (through the interplay of sins and merits), subordination (operating in terms of a network of servitude and dependencies) and subjectivation (producing a secret and inner truth). Lecture, 22 February 1978, Foucault, 2004a, *Security, Territory, Population* [2007], 163–90.

game which seems to have nothing to do with the game of the city surviving through the sacrifice of the citizens.[9]

Yet appearances are deceiving. The form of power that Christian pastorship developed is not 'political' inasmuch as it aims for spiritual salvation in another world. Still, Foucault views pastoral power less in terms of its religious content than as a specific technology of power enabling human beings to be led. The path leading from the 'government of souls' to political government has passed, inasmuch as pastoral technology has been integrated into political form, to the modern state: 'Our societies proved to be really demonic since they happened to combine those two games – the city-citizen game and the shepherd-flock game – in what we call the modern states'.[10]

## The Government of Human Beings

Foucault's analytics of government is based on the premise that pastoral techniques of guidance elaborated forms of subjectivation on which the modern state and capitalist society subsequently built. However, this does not mean that the modern state is the necessary consequence of the Christian pastorate, nor that capitalism logically derives from the tendencies towards individualization that it inaugurated. Instead, Foucault's point is that social and political upheavals in modernity should be viewed in terms of concurrent processes of totalization and individualization. The modern state is at once a legal-political structure and 'a new distribution, a new organization of this kind of individualizing power' – that is, 'a modern matrix of individualization, or a new form of pastoral power'.[11]

Foucault locates the historical transition from 'governing souls' to 'governing human beings' in the political and religious confrontations of the fifteenth and sixteenth centuries. Reformation and Counter-Reformation movements did not make the pastoral office disappear or cause church power to be transferred to the state. The

---

9. Foucault, 1981a, '"Omnes et Singulatim"', 239.
10. Ibid., 239; see also Foucault, 1978j, 'La philosophie analytique de la politique', 550–1; Foucault, 1982b, 'The Subject and Power', 213.
11. Ibid., 214–15; see also Foucault, 1978j, 'La philosophie analytique de la politique', 550; Foucault, 1981a, '"Omnes et Singulatim"', 225.

opposite occurred: the pastorate was extended and generalized, gradually becoming detached from its religious origins. In addition, questions emerged outside, or 'underneath', the purview of church authority concerning people's everyday lives, raising children, the institution of marriage, professional activity and so on. Philosophy – which had practically vanished during the Middle Ages, when it was subordinated to theology – underwent a renaissance, now offering answers to questions of proper conduct and how to live in an orderly fashion. In a word: the problem of government 'exploded' in a host of different forms; governing the state represented only one aspect.[12]

Foucault situates this development at the point of intersection between two historical processes that proved decisive for the problematic of government. On the one hand, feudal-estate structures had long been in decline, as states came to be centred in vast territorial and colonial empires. On the other hand, the Reformation and Counter-Reformation represent movements that called into question, time and again, how people are to be shown the path to salvation.[13]

The simultaneous concentration of state power and religious dispersion gave rise to an array of new problems concerning political sovereignty. Two questions in particular came to the fore: the scope and object of government, and the type of rationality to be employed for governing. In this context, when Foucault speaks of the 'art of government' or uses the neologism 'governmentality', he is referring to a shift of the politico-epistemological field that made this line of questioning both possible and necessary. In historical perspective, debate about the aim and rationality of government could arise only when government itself no longer counted as something 'self-evident'. Only inasmuch as government represented a problem could 'governmentality' – that is, reflection on the conditions of government – emerge as an item of contention. In turn, 'art of government' points to the artificial nature of guidance that has left behind the theologico-cosmological continuum, where the 'natural state' of

12. Lecture, 8 March 1978, Foucault, 2004a, *Security, Territory, Population* [2007], 231–2; Dauk, *Denken als Ethos und Methode* (1989a), 107–12; Bernauer, *Michel Foucault's Force of Flight: Toward an Ethics for Thought* (1990), 161–2.
13. Foucault, 1978o, 'Governmentality' [2000], 202; lecture, 1 February 1978, Foucault, 2004a, *Security, Territory, Population* [2007], 89.

things does not require any such reflection – or, more precisely, makes it utterly inconceivable.[14]

## Reason of State

Foucault sees the first attempt to answer the question concerning an 'art' of government in *reason of state*, which emerged in the sixteenth century and simultaneously inaugurated a new object of political action and a distinct form of rationality.[15] Reason of state represents the 'point of formation, of crystallization'[16] of the art of government and, it turns out, an obstacle to its further development. When it emerged, it defined 'a rationality specific to the art of governing states'[17] vastly exceeding the limited scope and negative meaning it came to possess later on. Initially, reason of state counted as something new, innovative and scandalous: 'raison d'état' was 'raison diabolique'. Inasmuch as its calculations followed 'political reason' alone – which

---

14. To avoid misunderstanding, it merits repeating that Foucault's coining of terms such as *governmentality* does not refer to the ways that subjects are actually ruled – that is, concrete, historical practices of government (as opposed to conceptions, ideas and intentions). Instead, governmentality refers to knowledge underlying governmental practices and forms of rationality, which guides and justifies political action. The issue is the rationalization of governmental practice when exercising political sovereignty. Lecture, 10 January 1979, Foucault, 2004b, *The Birth of Biopolitics* [2008], 1–4.

The texts examined (politico-theoretical works, theological treatises, police regulations, legal writings, analyses of criminality and so on) represent 'programs' (Foucault) or 'diagrams' (Deleuze). They are neither identical with reality nor can they be directly 'applied' or 'implemented'; rather, they form part of history itself. As such, they hold interest for our purposes inasmuch as they open up a new field for historical work, which focuses on the instrumental and technological nature of discourses enabling elements and categories to be combined for governing subjects.

15. Foucault's discussion of reason of state rests on the work of Friedrich Meinecke (*Die Idee der Staatsraison in der neueren Geschichte*, Berlin 1924). Nevertheless, his interpretation differs on key points. The differences concern – in addition to methodology (Foucault's rejection of historicism) – the weight assigned to historical facts. Unlike Meinecke, Foucault investigates the development of an individualizing power: 'Whereas Meinecke's analysis runs along the axis of life-expansion-power [*puissance*], Foucault's runs along the axis of government-regulation-subjectivity'. Senellart, 'Michel Foucault: "gouvernementalité" et raison d'Etat' (1993), 293. On the question of historicism and the historico-theoretical premises of Foucault's work, see Chapter 13.

16. Foucault, 2004a, *Security, Territory, Population* [2007], 165.

17. Foucault, 1981a, '"Omnes et Singulatim"', 243.

discards theological considerations – 'political sectarians' were thought to be atheists or polytheists.[18] Foucault illustrates the striking break that *ratio status* represented vis-à-vis *ratio pastoralis* through the example of *De regno*, by Thomas Aquinas. This medieval work presents the king's rule over his people by way of three analogies: God, nature and the father of a family. The sovereign can govern only to the extent that he forms part of a theologico-cosmological continuum that extends from God down to human beings, via nature. Just as God directs Creation, the soul the body, and the father the family, the king must, like a shepherd, lead human beings to their destiny (spiritual salvation in another world). As such, this form of government possesses nothing specific about it; it is neither conceptionally nor practically autonomous: 'Saint Thomas's model for rational government is not at all a political one'.[19]

This continuum is precisely what fell apart during the sixteenth century: Copernican astronomy, Galileo's physics and the grammar of Port-Royal all sought to demonstrate that God governs the world through general and universal laws that are intelligible and can be explained by the rules of logic, mathematics and grammar. Nature – which formerly consisted of miracles, analogies and signs – turned into something calculable. The cosmos, following simple laws held to be universal and rational, no longer belonged to a shepherd leading his flock to salvation, but to a lawgiver, or sovereign.[20]

The discovery of general regularities in nature and language occurred in parallel to the emergence of a special status for politics. The new idea held that the sovereign's relationship to his subjects does not continue the divine continuum on earth: it differs from the relationship between God and nature, the father and his children, and the shepherd and his flock. In this unprecedented, *political* framework, the sovereign no longer has the task of leading people to salvation. Instead, he should direct them within an autonomous field: the state and reason of state constitute the elements of a new 'art', which has no model as yet.[21]

---

18. Lecture, 8 March 1978, Foucault, 2004a, *Security, Territory, Population* [2007], 241–2.

19. Foucault, 1981a, '"Omnes et Singulatim"', 244; see also lecture, 8 March 1978, Foucault, 2004a, *Security, Territory, Population* [2007], 232–4; Foucault, 1988c, 'The Political Technology of Individuals', 149–50.

20. Lecture, 8 March 1978, Foucault, 2004a, *Security, Territory, Population* [2007], 232–4.

21. That said, the art of government does not define itself only in contrast to

Reason of state broke with Christian tradition, yet it did not accept the answer proposed in *The Prince* concerning government's foundations and goals. Between 1580 and 1650, Machiavelli stood at the centre of political debates about the art of government. Not just opponents of reason of state, but also its adherents rejected the 'solution' he had offered. Even though Machiavelli presented a rational form of government that no longer made recourse to natural or divine law, his conception proved limited insofar as it was oriented entirely on the person of the prince and served the latter's passions and interests: 'Machiavelli's entire analysis is aimed at defining what keeps up or reinforces the link between prince and state, whereas the problem posed by reason of state is that of the very existence and nature of the state itself'.[22]

Like Machiavelli, theorists of *raison d'état* sought to take distance from an art of government based on religious schemes of justification. However, they also wanted to elaborate a new type of governmental rationality that would not be subordinate to rules. Reason of state looks for a form of rationality free from external determinants: 'the art of government eschews theological and cosmological foundations and avoids recourse to the person of the prince; instead, it defines a sphere of autonomous rationality that must find its principles within itself'.[23]

---

efforts to secure a religious foundation. In addition to discarding theological references, it does away with the legal-moral tradition that deems government to be just by nature. Previously, when human laws stood in a continuum with natural and divine law, the idea of justice was inscribed in governmental praxis. Thus, when the cosmologico-theological continuum of the medieval state vanished, so did the juridico-moral foundation for justice and law. The rationality that sixteenth-century reason of state follows is neither theological nor legal. Foucault, 1981a, '"Omnes et Singulatim"', 240; Séglard, 'Foucault et le problème du gouvernement' (1992), 127–8.

In his excellent study of 'arts of government', Michel Senellart concretizes Foucault's theses, outlining the path from the Church Fathers' early medieval conceptions of government to sixteenth-century political theory. Senellart describes the break with the circular (or 'specular') relationship between politics and ethics, which still defined medieval manuals for the training of future rulers in terms of religious ideals [*'mirror of princes'*]; here, good government presupposes a virtuous prince. Senellart, *Les arts de gouverner* (1995), esp. 45–59.

22. Foucault, 1981a, '"Omnes et Singulatim"', 244.

23. Foucault, 2004a, *Security, Territory, Population* [2007] 232–7; Foucault, 1988c, 'The Political Technology of Individuals', 150. Senellart points to an important change in Foucault's view of Machiavelli. Senellart, 'Michel Foucault: "gouvernmentalité" et raison d'Etat' (1993). In *The History of Sexuality, Volume 1*,

Sixteenth- and seventeenth-century political theory defines reason of state as a specific art (or technology) corresponding to certain rules that, instead of representing custom or tradition, belong to the realm of rational knowledge.[24] Two key aspects distinguish such 'political reason'.

First, it makes no reference to human, divine or natural laws. The state, and the state alone, stands as the object and measure of such rationality: 'the state is governed according to rational principles that are intrinsic to it and cannot be derived solely from natural or divine laws or the principles of wisdom and prudence. The state, like nature, has its own proper form of rationality, albeit of a different sort'.[25] Just as *principiae naturae* must be sought in nature, the principles of the state must be sought in the state itself. In this respect, the new rationality proves 'reflective and perfectly aware of its specificity'.[26]

Second, reason of state breaks with the idea of external finality and secularizes formerly religious goals: happiness, salvation, prosperity and so on can only be achieved within the state, inasmuch as one subordinates oneself to it and obeys its institutions. According to Foucault, the defining trait of reason of state is to have taken up the themes of Christian pastorship (salvation, obedience and truth) and resituated them in a 'political' problematic of directing human beings.[27]

---

he declares that Machiavelli 'was among the few ... who conceived the power of the Prince in terms of force relationships'; accordingly, it is enough to 'do without the persona of the prince, and decipher power mechanisms on the basis of a strategy that is immanent in force relationships'. Foucault, 1976a, *The History of Sexuality, Volume 1: An Introduction* [1978], 97. In the 1978 lectures, however, Foucault proposes an entirely new view of Machiavelli, who now represents the end of an age more than a new beginning.

24. Foucault's discussion refers to G. A. Palazzo, *Discorso del governo e della ragione vera di stato*, Venice (1606); B. P. von Chemnitz, *Dissertatio de ratione Status in imperio nostro romano-germanico*, Geneva (1647); G. Botero, *Della ragione di Stata dieci libri*, Rome (1590).

25. Foucault, 1978o, 'Governmentality' [2000], 213.

26. Foucault, 1981a, '"Omnes et Singulatim"', 242.

27. Lecture, 8 March 1978, Foucault, 2004a, *Security, Territory, Population* [2007], 236–8. As a reflection on the nature of the state and its specific rationality, reason of state is not purely theoretical, nor does its abandonment of theologico-moral logic mean that it incorporates an irrational element into the political order. To the latter point: reason of state sets itself apart from juridico-moral conceptions, but in so doing it follows a coherent logic, even in 'exceptional cases'. Foucault demonstrates the rationality at work with the example of the 'theory of the coup d'État'.

Inasmuch as reason of state derives from neither divine wisdom nor the interests of the prince, but is based on rationality belonging to the state alone, a new relationship emerges between politics-as-practice and politics-as-knowledge. Reason of state calls for knowledge that differs in essence from traditional forms. It is no longer enough for kings to be judges, philosophers or clerics. Instead, the leader of others must be a 'politician': in the position to enlist specific, political expertise distinct from moral, juridical or theological authority. Inasmuch as the state constitutes a natural entity existing in its own right (that is, it holds no obligations vis-à-vis human or divine laws, nor does it derive from them), governing the state requires specialized knowledge of its specific properties and workings.[28]

The notion of strength (*force*) stands at the centre of this epistemological shift. In the framework of reason of state, government is possible only when the strength of the state and the means to increase it are clear (as well as the strengths and weaknesses of other states). It is no longer possible to invoke general principles (divine wisdom, human reason, natural law and so on). Concrete, measurable knowledge is required; instead of being determined in reference to transcendental principles, it achieves definition in terms of immanent relations of force. As such, reason of state means developing a historically unprecedented complex of analyses and techniques of measurement: organizing practical knowledge centred on the state

---

In this framework, the issue does not concern power changing hands or being usurped, but the suspension of law and legality, period. Reason of state is not based on a system of legality and legitimacy; it is not a matter of ruling in keeping with the law, but, if need be, ruling the law. As such, the coup does not represent a break with reason of state; it represents one of its forms of action. Reason of state accepts laws to the extent that they can be implemented as elements of its own game. If and when the moment comes that it can no longer make use of laws, it sets itself above them in the name of saving the state. Thus, no opposition holds between this reason and violence; rather, state violence is the manifestation of its intrinsic reason. Lecture, 15 March 1978, ibid., 261–7.

By the same token, the art of government is not simply a matter of political theory. Historically, reflection on the state's autonomous rationality proved immensely 'practical' inasmuch as it bore on two tasks: instituting an administrative apparatus in territorial monarchies and developing a specific type of knowledge, with new objects and investigative methods. Although it detached itself from religious-moral moorings, such knowledge was subordinate to the conditions of a 'state reason'.

28. Foucault, 1988c, 'The Political Technology of Individuals', 151.

and its strength, the elements composing it, its resources and so on. Such knowledge is afforded by 'statistics' – the science of the state – mercantilism and cameralism.[29]

This shift in the regime of knowledge corresponds to a changed aim of government. The concept of strength establishes an unprecedented kind of 'politics' with the objective of calculating and using the state's forces. The central idea is no longer quantitative expansion of territory and legal borders; instead, focus falls on concentrating and enhancing resources in order to increase might. The 'physics of the state' replaces the rightful rule of the sovereign. Accordingly, the art of governing can no longer be limited to preserving the status quo and securing what already stands. It aims for continual fortification of the state: simply preserving the given order, when one is surrounded by enemies, would lead to ruin. Only by maintaining and expanding might can the state live and survive in competition with other states. As such, *raison d'état* means rational government 'in accordance with the state's strength'.[30]

A wholly transformed model of history underlies this reorientation. The state no longer has any goal outside itself. Religiously motivated and absolute eschatology, tying history to its fulfilment, yields to unlimited time and space; now, individual states fight for survival. In other words, a constantly imperilled eschatology of 'universal peace' nourished by the relativity of forces emerges. Such a peace does not derive from the unity of the church or empire – with rival territories vanishing in light of a 'kingdom of heaven'. On the contrary, it presumes a multiplicity of independent and autonomous states, none of which is strong enough to dominate the others.[31]

At the same time, such a political order does not achieve definition through a permanent state of war; instead, it aims for a certain balance of power. The corollary of strengthening the state is arriving at a point of equilibrium: a 'static' dimension complements and completes political dynamics. The new political perspective requires the implementation of two arrangements representing both the condition for such dynamics and their direct consequence. One concerns

---

29. Foucault, 1978o, 'Governmentality' [2000], 212.

30. Foucault, 1981a, '"Omnes et Singulatim"', 246.

31. Lecture, 22 March 1978, Foucault, 2004a, *Security, Territory, Population* [2007], 285–310; Foucault, 1978z, 'Course Summary' [2007], 363–5; Foucault, 1988c, 'The Political Technology of Individuals', 148–50.

the relationship between states, and the other functions within the individual state.

Maintaining order externally requires two apparatuses that complement and secure each other: abiding military potential and diplomacy.[32] Inasmuch as the goal of the military-diplomatic dispositive is to maintain an external balance between states – each of which seeks to increase its forces – it entails the problem of cultivating strength as much as possible without endangering order within. 'Police' is the name for efforts to resolve the matter.

## Police

The meaning of 'police' that emerged in the seventeenth and eighteenth centuries, especially in Germany and France, does not have much in common with the narrow and largely negative set of tasks to which the term now refers (foiling crime, averting danger and so on).[33] At the time,

---

32. The military-diplomatic dispositive changes the traditional principles of warfare and negotiating in important ways. First, the goal of *warfare*: during the Middle Ages, continuity between war and the law prevailed. War had no *ratio* of its own that distinguished it from theologico-juridical logic. Waging war concerned (contested) rights, and it occurred in order to restore rights – or to right a wrong. Moreover, war itself was a juridical procedure, and the result – victory or defeat – signified divine judgement. In contrast, the new political reason makes it possible to go to war without appealing to law or rights at all: its only aim is to restore balance. This shift of goal presupposes the institution of a permanent military apparatus and developing a specific kind of knowledge centred on strategies and tactics on the field.

In similar fashion, with the Treaty of Westphalia at the end of the Thirty Years War, diplomacy shifts from following juridical principles to physical ones. Now, its basis is the idea of preserving a balance of power: states, like individual human beings, constitute a society, and their relations to each other and coexistence must be determined accordingly. Lecture, 22 March 1978, Foucault, 2004a, *Security, Territory, Population* [2007], 296–306; Foucault, 1978z, 'Course Summary' [2007], 365; Séglard, 'Foucault et le problème du gouvernement' (1992), 131–2.

33. For an excellent account of German police science, see Maier, *Die ältere deutsche Staats- und Verwaltungslehre* (1986). See Stolleis 1996 for corresponding traditions throughout Europe; Tribe, 'Cameralism and the Science of Government' (1984) on the relationship between policing and cameralism; Pasquino, 'Theatrum Politicum' (1991b) for the conception of the police state as a 'welfare state'; and Foucault, 1976b, 'La politique de la santé au XVIIIème siècle' [2000] and Foucault, 1979b, 'La politique de la santé du XVIIIème siècle' [2014] for an analysis of 'medical police'. Foucault refers to German and French police literature above all and distinguishes it from the tradition in England. Foucault, 1988c, 'The Political Technology of Individuals', 153–4; Foucault, 1982c, 'Space, Knowledge and Power' [1984], 241–2; Senellart, 'Michel Foucault: "gouvernementalité" et raison d'Etat' (1993), 294–5.

*police* designated a specific sphere of activity with its own, particular methods. It did not refer to 'an institution or mechanism functioning within the state, but [to] a governmental technology.'[34] The goal was to preserve – or, if possible, improve – the state's position on the overall field of competition and secure peace within by ensuring individuals' 'welfare'. That said, the two objectives were not equal in status, nor did they exist independently. Rather, the two aims were interconnected: 'police' was understood as a general 'technology of state forces'.[35]

The particularity of police technology lies in the way the relationship between the state and individuals is conceived, as well as the reversal that such rationality implies. Individual happiness and prosperity no longer stand as the goal of a good government, but represent the necessary precondition for the state's strength and survival. That is, consequence and result turn into an instrument and a condition. The central paradox of this kind of 'welfare state' involves 'develop[ing] those elements constitutive of individuals' lives in such a way that their development also fosters the strength of the state'.[36]

The idea of happiness, or prosperity, provides the principle for identifying state and subjects. In this context, 'police' – in contrast to religious or moral government – does not directly address individual life, death, labour or morality; rather, it views the latter elements indirectly, in terms of their positive or negative contribution to the state's well-being. Police represents 'a kind of political marginalism, since what is in question here is only political utility'.[37] At the same time, however, the police's sphere of activity does not stop at the individual and his or her pursuits. It does not constitute a border so much as, in fact, it suspends all abstract borders and multiplies possible spheres and modes of intervention.

Contemporary regulations and theoretical treatises make it plain that the realm of policing tends towards infinity.[38] The sphere of poten-

---

34. Foucault, 1981a, '"Omnes et Singulatim"', 246; Foucault, 1982c, 'Space, Knowledge and Power' [1984], 241–2.

35. Foucault, 1978z, 'Course Summary' [2007], 367; Gordon, 'Governmental Rationality: An Introduction' (1991), 10.

36. Foucault, 1981a, '"Omnes et Singulatim"', 252.

37. Foucault, 1988c, 'The Political Technology of Individuals', 152.

38. Foucault uses the following works for his analysis: L. Turquet de Mayerne, *La Monarchie aristo-démocratique, ou le gouvernement composé des trois formes de légitimes républiques*, Paris (1611); N. Delamare, *Traité de la police*, Paris (1705); P. C. W. von Hohenthal, *Liber de Politia*, Leipzig (1776); J. H. von Justi, *Grundsätze der*

tial police intervention 'branches out into all of the people's conditions, everything they do or undertake. Its field comprises justice, finance, and the army'; '[t]he police's true object is man' (Turquet de Mayerne). 'The police sees to everything regulating "*society*" (social relations) carried on between men'; it seeks 'to lead man to the utmost happiness to be enjoyed in this life' (Delamare). The writings of von Hohenthal and Willeband describe the vast array of problematic realms in need of regulation, ranging from religion, morality, security and healthcare to city planning and the manual trades. Von Justi elaborates the difference between politics and policing. The former, in his eyes, is basically a negative undertaking that involves the state's fight against inner and outer enemies, whereas the latter represents a positive task: promoting the life of citizens and the polity's robustness.[39]

That said, the domain of police intervention remains strangely undefined. The multiplicity of, and variation between, its objects leaves it unclear where, precisely, policing makes its contribution or what, exactly, this contribution is. At the same time, the significance of policing lies in this same generality and indeterminacy: in principle, it regulates all forms of human life in community. Possible objects and potential spheres of intervention are not that important; people and property do not occupy the foreground so much as the relations between them and the quality of these relations. 'Policing' focuses on communal life in a single space, property relations, production, exchange and so on – in particular, the human being as a working and industrious creature, a living being (*Lebewesen*). As such, its sphere of intervention cannot be limited to 'public' matters. Indeed, the distinction between public and private spheres (and therefore the restricted, largely negative meaning of *police*) emerged only in the context of eighteenth-century bourgeois society, marking the transition from the 'police state' to the liberal state.[40]

The police state is closely tied to the notion of the strength of the

---

*Polizey-Wissenschaft*, Göttingen (1756). This selection corresponds to his periodization of police technology: utopia (Turquet de Mayerne), applied practice (Delamare) and an autonomous academic discipline (von Justi). Foucault, 1988c, 'The Political Technology of Individuals', 154–60.

39. Quotes in Foucault, 1981a, '"Omnes et Singulatim": Towards a Criticism of Political Reason' [1981], 248–50; see, also, lecture, 29 March 1978, 2004a, *Security, Territory, Population* [2007], 311–32.

40. Foucault, 1981a, '"Omnes et Singulatim"', 248–52.

polity. It pursues a specific goal: proper policing assures that people are able to exist, and in as great a number as possible, that they have a livelihood and do not die at an excessive rate, and so on. At the same time, ensuring life is not just a matter of material subsistence: 'The role of the police is to supply [the state] with a little extra strength. This is done by controlling "communication", i.e. the common activities of individuals (work, production, exchange, accommodation)'.[41] 'Police' means that all the technologies guaranteeing 'better living' also preserve and heighten the state's resources. As such, it may be understood as a secularized form of pastoral power, looking after everything and everyone and leading subjects to an (economically) sensible life: in other words, economic pastorship.[42]

The new governmental technology of police emerged in tandem with a new epistemological object, as well as a new 'political personage': *population*.[43] On the one hand, population constituted the object of scientific analysis and political intervention; on the other, it represented the condition for the polity's wealth and, as such, a privileged element in state politics. According to theorists of police, policing and policy, it had to be integrated into a regulatory apparatus to ensure that it would work productively. Conversely, productivity was guaranteed only inasmuch as the population came to be trained, stabilized and regulated. This meant, for example, fixing salaries, preventing

41. Ibid., 248.

42. Lecture, 29 March 1978, Foucault, 2004a, *Security, Territory, Population* [2007], 311–32; see also Gordon, 'Governmental Rationality: An Introduction' (1991), 12. This definition of the tasks of the police calls for breaking with traditional forms of intervention. Feudalism had been characterized by the relationship between legal subjects, whose rights and duties derived from birth and estate. In contrast, the human being is at the heart of the police state: a living being bound up in relations of work and exchange. Foucault, 1988c, 'The Political Technology of Individuals, 154–5. Policing relies on laws, decrees and regulations; however, it establishes a mode of intervention that differs radically from that of the law. Police measures represent neither an application nor an extension of justice: the king does not act via laws bearing on subjects in mediated fashion; rather, he intervenes directly in the lives of his inferiors. Therefore Foucault speaks of a 'permanent *coup d'état*' that eludes all legal justification and finds its principle in the demands of police practice itself. Lecture, 5 April 1978, Foucault, 2004a, *Security, Territory, Population* [2007], 339. The police state establishes a form of power that uses traditional (legal) instruments, but it implements them in a way opposed to the original, juridical context of application. Barrett-Kriegel, 'Michel Foucault and the Police State' (1992).

43. Lecture, 25 January 1978, Foucault, 2004a, *Security, Territory, Population* [2007], 67–79; Foucault, 1992, 'La population', 33–58.

immigration, reducing infant mortality or averting epidemics – all of which entailed developing certain forms of knowledge such as medicine, demography, hygienic regimes and so on. The world of the police was a world of comprehensive regulation and individual disciplination, and it called for permanent supervision and surveillance in order to ensure the public weal.

However, the 'population' – as subject and object in one – is what exposed the limits of reason of state and led to a 'blockade' of the art of government in the seventeenth century. Alongside 'massive and elementary historical causes'[44] such as the Thirty Years War, urban and peasant revolts, and financial crisis, two internal problems brought this form of government to an end.

The first was the *right of sovereignty*. The police cannot be separated from a theory and practice of government that provided a certain economic technology by calculating the relative strength of competing European states: mercantilism. Although mercantilism represents the 'first rationalization of exercise of power as a practice of government'[45] inasmuch as it tied the state's prosperity to individual welfare, it was less interested in the land's well-being *per se* than in augmenting the sovereign's wealth and power.

Mercantilism sought to reconcile the art of government and sovereignty. Specifically, it aimed to derive principles of government from a reinvigorated theory of sovereignty. Conceptions of contractuality and natural law that had emerged in the seventeenth century were supposed to create the basis for a new form of government within an old institutional framework by forging mutual obligations between the sovereign and his subjects. This model of compromise was destined for failure inasmuch as governing the population required forms of regulation and modes of intervention tending to exceed the operating potential of absolutism.

The second problem was the *household economy*. Mercantilism remained indebted not just to a legal framework conceived in terms of sovereignty, but also to the economic model of the household. It sought to establish a kind of 'economic sovereignty', whereby the economy would possess its own rationality, even if it was not (yet) autonomous. The couple formed by prosperity and population did

---

44. Foucault, 1978o, 'Governmentality' [2000], 213.
45. Ibid., 214.

not take the stage as a self-sufficient machine that government could simply employ for its purposes; instead, the interrelationship had to be reworked again and again, and constantly monitored and maintained. Mercantilism set up an economic scheme that remained indebted to the old frameworks of *oikos* and domestic governance. Here, the economy did not constitute an autonomous reality with laws of its own and built-in regulatory mechanisms. On the contrary, the sovereign was its 'owner' and 'landlord'.[46]

Thus, notwithstanding the epistemologico-political breaks that reason of state effected, the art of government remained caught between two models: 'On the one hand, there was this framework of sovereignty, which was too large, too abstract, and too rigid; and, on the other, the theory of government suffered from its reliance on a model that was too thin, too weak, and too insubstantial, that of the family'.[47] Mercantilism, as a means of increasing wealth, relied on the classical tools of sovereignty – just like the police: even if its interventions no longer appealed to juridical logic, it enlisted procedures and instruments borrowed from the juridical world: laws, decrees and commands. Only with the rise of new phenomena specific to the population did it become possible to focus the concept of economy on something other than the family and expose the inadequacy of these models for regulatory intervention.

## *Physiocratic Critique*

At the start of the seventeenth century, the 'political sect' emerged and formulated a new form of political rationality: reason of state. A hundred years later, new heretics appeared and took issue with the instruments of the police state: the *economists*. Physiocrats and cameralists did not invoke political reason; instead, they appealed to a specifically 'economic' reason. For all that, the new form of governmentality did not make a complete break with tradition; instead it modified, or reorganized, reason of state and the disciplines.[48]

46. Ibid., 212–15; Gordon, 'Governmental Rationality: An Introduction' (1991), 11–12; Séglard, 'Foucault et le problème du gouvernement' (1992), 133–4; Dean, *Critical and Effective Histories* (1994), 184–5.

47. Foucault, 1978o, 'Governmentality' [2000], 214–15; Foucault, 2004a, *Security, Territory, Population* [2007], 103.

48. Foucault, 1978o, 'Governmentality' [2000], 218–20.

Foucault illustrates the course taken by the police state's critics on the example of famine. For *mercantilists,* famine could be predicted but not prevented inasmuch as it remained caught up in juridico-moral categories. According to this view, scarcity was God's punishment and stemmed from the evil nature of humankind. Accordingly, a juridico-disciplinary system was established to counter the shortage of foodstuffs: price regulations, laws about storage, transport and so on. These practices aimed to produce as much inexpensive grain as possible and sell it abroad in order to import gold, which the sovereign would then have at his disposal. The system miscarried, however: peasants regularly went to ruin by generating a surplus of grain; they were forced to plant less, leading to a lack of food the following year.[49]

The *physiocrats* reacted to this failure by making decisive changes to the inherited juridico-moral system. Their point of departure was the 'nature of things', not the (evil) nature of man. From this perspective, famine counted as a natural phenomenon, and combating it meant taking the fact of varying crops and resources as the point of departure. In contrast to mercantilists, physiocrats claimed that grain must command a good price in order to avert famine: if this happens and prices climb, they will not do so forever; at a certain point, they reach a 'natural' price (as opposed to the 'just' price of the Middle Ages).

Whereas mercantilists, making innumerable prescriptions and laws, had assumed that matters prove infinitely flexible and admit regulation at will, physiocrats held that an autonomous, 'natural' law exists – 'physis', which cannot be changed. Any intervention in the course of nature disturbs, indeed worsens, things. From this perspective, policing is not only impossible, it is unnecessary: matters regulate themselves on their own. Physiocrats sought to replace a (juridical) regime with (natural) regulation. They faulted mercantilism for not offering a solution so much as a problem: instead of preventing famines, the juridico-disciplinary system produced them by disregarding the 'nature of things'. In order to act in conformity with nature, regulation and fixed prices are not called for – on the contrary, free prices, trade and export are required.[50]

The key difference between mercantilists and physiocrats lies in

---

49. Lecture, 18 January 1978, Foucault, 2004a, *Security, Territory, Population* [2007], 31–4.

50. Lecture, 18 January 1978, ibid., 31–49.

their opposing perspectives on that singular subject-object, population. Whereas mercantilists located the population on the axis of
ruler/ruled and viewed it as a legal subject, physiocrats viewed the
population as a sum of natural processes – accordingly, it must be
treated on a natural basis. Whereas mercantilists thought there could
never be enough population, physiocrats did not consider population
to be an absolute value so much as a relative quantity: there is need for
a suitably large labour force, but it should not be *too* large, since this
would mean decline in income. The 'right' balance cannot be set once
and for all; fortunately, it is also unnecessary to do so, since matters
'sort themselves out' on their own. This 'naturalness' of the population,
which the physiocrats 'discovered', has several dimensions:

1. The 'natural' quality of the population lies in its relative diversity.
For the physiocrats, population is not a given, fixed quantity – raw
social material – so much as a dependent variable admitting change
in keeping with conditions (e.g. climate, geography, trade, laws and
habits). Consequently, the relationship between the sovereign and his
subjects cannot be a matter of obedience/revolt; rather, 'population' has
the tendency to escape the will of the sovereign inasmuch as its natural
facticity dictates the conditions and limits for any possible intervention.

2. Accordingly, any action must take this feature as the point of departure. But even though the exact behaviour of individuals cannot be
determined in advance, a driving force remains constant, which can be
counted on and provides the basis for intervention: desire ('le désir').
The natural quality of desire defines the population and renders it
'permeable' to technologies of power. Governing the population on the
basis of its natural desire represents the exact opposite of the juridico-
moral programme of sovereignty. If, formerly, the sovereign had the
task of negating desire and imposing limits, the physiocrats identified
the problem of affirming it: what can stimulate, push forward and mul-
tiply popular desire?

3. Population is also natural because of its regularity: the abiding proportion of men and women, consistent mortality rates, accidents, cases
of illness and so on. In this framework, statistics discarded the inherited
'science of the state' and investigated the new reality of 'population' by
way of 'natural properties'. The latter display a distinct kind of materiality; they are more than the sum of individual parts and cannot be boiled

down to the familial model. In this context, human life became the object of an entirely new knowledge-formation: the human sciences, which seek to determine the abiding, regular features of 'man'.[51]

However, when physiocrats invoked 'naturalness', they were not appealing to a remainder of tradition, or a premodern relic. The call signalled a new epoch of history. During the Middle Ages, proper government had belonged to the 'natural' order foreseen by God. Such a conception of nature, which tied political thinking into a cosmological continuum, was discarded by early modern theorists of reason of state, who, in replacing it with an artificial 'Leviathan', garnered opprobrium for putative atheism. In turn, the economists reintroduced 'naturalness'. But now, *nature* referred to something different, which had nothing more to do with the divine plan for Creation. Instead of the divinely ordained cosmos, a natural world stood at issue – which had not existed previously and was now 'discovered' and set in opposition to *police* ('If prices rise, they'll level off again on their own'). Just as the police state had followed a prescription to secure order it had authored itself, the new governmentality had to bring forth naturalness by artificial means. To this end, it looked to human life in community – labour, trade and so on: the naturalness of emergent 'society'. Not the paradigm of law or discipline so much as the model of the market and freely circulating people and commodities provided the point of orientation.

But for all that, the physiocratic art of government remained within the horizon of sovereignty; the natural quality of social processes continued to have an index in the ruler. From the mid-eighteenth century on, liberal critiques time and again exposed the limits of physiocratic technology, which equated the sovereign's knowledge and the freedom of (economic) subjects in an effort to preserve the appearance of harmony between politics and economy. In turn, a new, 'liberal' art of government assigned singular significance to 'political economy': a form of rationality providing the basis for a new governmentality – and, at the same time, the principle restricting its scope.[52]

---

51. Lecture, 25 January 1978, ibid., 67–79; Foucault, 1992, 'La population', 41–9; Séglard, 'Foucault et le problème du gouvernement' (1992), 137–9; Burchell, 'Peculiar Interests: Civil Society and "Governing the System of Natural Liberty"' (1991), 126–7.

52. Lecture, 10 January 1979, Foucault, 2004b, *The Birth of Biopolitics* [2008], 1–25; Gordon, 'Governmental Rationality: An Introduction' (1991), 17. Foucault had

## The Liberal Art of Government

In the mid-eighteenth century, transformations led to a new stage of governmental thinking: *liberalism*, which called for individual 'freedom'. That said, its premise was not personal freedom so much as a principle of governmentality seeking to produce what it described as already being in existence. Liberalism did not take stock of actual facts so much as it represented a body of knowledge, or programme, for designing a new scheme of relations between rulers and those they ruled.

The defining feature of liberalism is that individuals count as the object of governmental practice and, simultaneously, its necessary (and voluntary) partners – 'accomplices'. In this framework, governmental activity is tied to actions on the part of the individuals governed. In other words, the government's rational activities must accord with individual actions, which are rational and motivated by self-interest, because the (economic) rationality of private parties is what enables the market to function in keeping with its true nature. Ultimately, such rationality ensures the welfare of the state: when the market functions naturally, it functions in the best possible way, and when it functions in the best possible way, it promotes the state's strength. Accordingly, liberal government breaks with the simple application of technologies of domination that had defined reason of state and the police state. The external opposition between power and subjectivity yields to an inner bond: this principle of government demands the 'freedom' of the ruled, and rational use of freedom represents the condition for 'economic' government. The art of liberal government consists of replacing outward, legal restriction with internal regulation: *political economy*.

Political economy no longer analyses governmental practices from the standpoint of the law, but looks to their actual effects. (It is not a matter of whether the sovereign is justified in raising taxes, or whether it is legitimate to do so, but what happens when taxes are raised – in general, for a certain group, and so on.) In contrast to the physiocratic

---

already analysed the shift from the classical 'analysis of wealth' to political economy in *The Order of Things*. Foucault, 1966a, *The Order of Things* [1994], 166–215. However, in this context, epistemologico-conceptional changes stand at the centre, whereas the change of political rationalities and technologies is treated only implicitly.

position, nature no longer represents an autonomous realm where, in principle, no intervention should occur. Rather, 'nature' itself depends on governmental action; it is not a material substrate, where governmental practices find application, but their correlate and reverse. Political economy replaces reflection on the inner laws of nature with thought bearing on the nature of governmental practices'.[53]

As for reason of state, police, mercantilism and so on, Foucault does not understand liberalism as an economic theory, political ideology or social utopia so much as a thought-through practice: 'Liberalism ... is to be analysed as a principle and method of the rationalization of the exercise of government'.[54]

Liberalism did not simply 'invent' an inner principle of governmental action. Rather, it defined this principle with regard to a projected, outer goal. In contrast to reason of state, the point of departure is not the fact that states exist and grow; the premise that the state has an immanent goal and seeks to strengthen itself no longer holds. Unlike the regime of police, liberal governmentality does not fear that 'too little government' is in place (say, because countless social spheres lack rules and prescriptions, provisions are not sufficiently detailed or the administrative apparatus is not elaborate enough). Instead, it inverts the perspective: liberalism affirms that 'there is too much government' and asks why the state exists – and what aims it serves. For theorists of reason of state, the state already had criteria for determining what is good and right (e.g. strengthening itself and optimizing available instruments of rule). Liberalism effected a shift rich in consequences. It introduced, for the first time, a 'critical' principle that went far beyond assessing optimization efforts. Under liberal governmentality, practices are not examined only in terms of the best available means, or lowest costs, for achieving goals, but also in terms of the possibility and legitimacy of the procedures used to achieve these aims – and whether these aims are themselves legitimate.

This orientation signals a complete change in the problematic of government. The question 'Why is it necessary to govern?' can only arise inasmuch as the putative unity between the state and the art of government has dissolved. The question would make no sense in the

---

53. Lecture, 10 January 1979, Foucault, 2004b, *The Birth of Biopolitics* [2008], 13–25.

54. Foucault, 1979m, 'Course Summary' [2008], 318.

context of reason of state or police science. It means that the art of government now aims at something other than itself – it no longer possesses internal justification or counts as 'self-evident', but must find validity with respect to something else. As such, the liberal art of government cannot be separated from a new problematic that emerged during the eighteenth century: *society*. In the name of this new, epistemologico-political object, liberal thinking examined practices of government to determine whether they were necessary and useful or, on the contrary, superfluous – if not harmful. Whereas reason of state had pursued political optimization by maximizing the state, liberalism worked with society – and not the state. It meant asking, 'What makes government necessary, and what ends must it pursue with regard to society in order to justify its own existence?'[55]

Foucault approaches the question by way of three thematic complexes that define the liberal art of government: knowledge, subjectivity and power.

## Adam Smith: The Invisible Hand

The premise of political economy is that the practices of government have their own nature, which they must respect. In other words, governmental action should harmonize with the laws of a nature that it produces. Hereby, the principle shifts from being oriented on outward congruency to focusing on inner regulation: it is no longer legitimacy or illegitimacy but success or failure that form the coordinates of governmental action; the centre of reflection no longer bears on human presumption or misuse of power, but inadequate knowledge of how it works. With that, political economy introduces to the art of government, and for the first time, the question of truth and the demand for self-limitation as fundamental principles. The problem no longer concerns how the prince should rule in keeping with divine, natural, and/or moral laws; nor is the question the same one that reason of state had posed – about maximizing the state's powers. Instead, the point is to understand the 'nature of things', which simultaneously determines the possibilities and limits of governmental activity.[56]

---

55. Ibid., 319.
56. Lecture, 10 January 1979, Foucault, 2004b, *The Birth of Biopolitics* [2008], 16–19.

Thus, Foucault does not view political economy as a theory of governmental action so much as a 'mechanism of truth-formation'; in this context, it is the market that produces such truth. Whereas, until the mid-eighteenth century, the market represented a 'site of jurisdiction' subject to legal and moral categories (e.g. 'fair prices'), it now becomes a 'site of veridiction'. The market is supposed to obey 'natural' mechanisms that enable a 'natural' price to emerge, expressing a certain relationship between the costs of production and the expectations of demand. The market turns into a site where the truth reveals itself, and 'good' government must act according to this truth. The criteria for the rightness or falseness of practices are oriented on the market, which functions as the site where government action is verified or proven false. Until this point, the market was tied into a moral-juridical continuum assigning it an epistemologico-political station; now it represents an instance for judging and evaluating government.[57]

Liberal government implies permanent reference to truth. That said, such truth no longer means external conformity to divine law or an originary, natural order. Instead, its index lies in the reality of human behaviour (in other words, reality that is historical and mutable). Foucault identifies two stages of this transformation. The first stage was marked by the immediate proximity between reason of state and police science. The latter displayed a pragmatic orientation and was a matter of application; lacking epistemological autonomy, it followed the calculations of the state and served to increase its forces. In principle, a seamless police apparatus monitored society and regulated every aspect of life. The second stage, according to Foucault, followed the physiocratic thesis, elaborated in contradistinction to the idea of an artificial 'Leviathan', that human society constitutes a kind of second nature. Accordingly, physiocrats demanded that society be ruled only in keeping with 'natural' laws, whose autonomy any and all forms of government must respect; in this framework, the principle of *laissez-faire* serves to counter an all-inclusive apparatus of surveillance and regulation.

And yet, physiocratic critique did not surpass reason of state inasmuch as it, too, was defined by the theoretical accordance of knowledge and government: if the sovereign grants his subjects liberties, he can afford to do so because he already knows everything that is happening

---

57. Lecture, 17 January 1979, ibid., 27–50.

at a given moment. The appeal to *laissez-faire* was made in the context of despotic sovereignty that was no longer bound by divine laws, traditions and customs – only by the knowledge it shared with economic agents. If Quesnay's *tableau* had enabled the sovereign to supervise the entirety of economic processes within the state, then Adam Smith's thesis of the 'invisible hand' represented a radical critique of this way of conceiving the connection between economic freedom and despotic sovereignty; it demonstrated the impossibility of the physiocratic idea of 'economic sovereignty'.[58]

Smith's 'invisible hand' is neither a symbol of optimism nor a theological relic. In a seeming paradox, it combines public welfare with private egoism and posits a productive relationship between the prosperity of all and the pursuit of private interests. According to Foucault, however, the innovative force of Smith's image does not lie in the idea of the 'hand' (that is, a coordinating instance directing the multiplicity of individuals to ensure the public weal) so much as that of 'invisibility'. In other words, the hand's invisibility does not stand for a shortcoming; rather, it constitutes a necessary and indispensable condition for bringing about public welfare. The 'invisible hand' can achieve its goals only inasmuch as, and because, it is invisible: not being seen is the condition for its success. The public weal is ensured only when individual actors do not seek it out as a way of measuring what they do, but follow egoistic interests. For Smith, economic rationality is not hampered by the impossibility of taking the totality of the economic process into account; on the contrary, such ignorance founds economic rationality in the first place, since the economic world is by nature opaque.

The key point is that the effectiveness of the 'invisible hand' does not extend to economic actors alone; it also establishes a mechanism enabling it to act as a paradigm of the social order in general. In this framework, society may be conceived as a totality independent of the state. Not just individual economic actors, but political rule will necessarily fail if it tries to realize the national weal directly. Such incapacity on the part of the state stems from the impossibility of keeping watch over the totality of economic processes. The limitation of state power

---

58. Lecture, 28 March 1979, ibid., 283; Gordon, 'Governmental Rationality: An Introduction' (1991), 15–16.

follows directly from its limited knowledge: if it is already impossible for the state to watch over economic processes, how is it supposed to be able to steer them?[59]

*The Wealth of Nations*, then, is also a 'critical' undertaking in the Kantian sense: a 'critique of state reason'. Just as *Critique of Pure Reason* exposes the limits of human knowledge with regard to the cosmos, Smith's work demonstrates the state's inability to grasp the totality of economic processes. But like Kant, Smith does not stop at a (negative) determination. If Kant's insight into the unattainability of the *Ding an sich* leads him to explore the possibilities of human knowledge, for Smith the impossibility of economic sovereignty defines the condition of the state's existence and assigns it its principle of legitimacy. In liberalism, the state does not have the task of directing and surveilling the economic sphere, but regulating it in keeping with the rules that prevail here. The state no longer dictates the law for the economy, but governs according to economic law.[60]

And with that, the immediate, pragmatic unity of knowledge and

---

59. Lecture, 28 March 1979, Foucault, 2004b, *The Birth of Biopolitics* [2008], 267–86; Burchell, 'Peculiar Interests: Civil Society and "Governing the System of Natural Liberty"' (1991), 132–4; Gordon, 'Governmental Rationality: An Introduction' (1991), 15–16.

60. Lecture, 28 March 1979, Foucault, 2004b, *The Birth of Biopolitics* [2008], 276–86. This aspect is central to Foucault's understanding of liberalism, which he derives from neither economy nor the law. Instead, it represents a critical principle for governmental action: 'So, rather than a more or less coherent doctrine or a politics pursuing some more or less precise aims, I would be inclined to see in liberalism a form of critical reflection on governmental practice.' This form of critique is not necessarily tied to the institution of the market or the form of law, but rather 'may be based on this or that economic theory or refer to this or that legal system without any necessary and one-to-one connection'. Foucault, 1979m, 'Course Summary' [2008], 321; see also lecture, 28 March 1979, Foucault, 2004b, *The Birth of Biopolitics* [2008], 283–6; Gordon, 'Governmental Rationality: An Introduction' (1991), 18–19; Burchell, 'Liberal Government and Techniques of the Self' (1993), 269; Rose, 'Government, Authority and Expertise in Advanced Liberalism' (1993), 292.

In a similar way, Denis Meuret's 'political genealogy of political economy' examines the political significance of Smith's work and the epistemological break of 'political economy' with the economic doctrines of absolutism: 'Our hypothesis is that Smith, in providing a new representation of the economy, also offered a new definition of the state's legitimacy, its role, and its relations to the citizenry – in short, a new definition of the political system; this representation occurred at precisely the right moment to be welcomed by three interested parties – citizens of the state, the state itself, and capitalism – as the principle organizing their coexistence'. Meuret, 'A Political Genealogy of Political Economy' (1988), 231.

government – which defined reason of state and police science – falls apart and makes room for a complex relationship between (autonomous) scientific knowledge and an art of government that is wholly separate in principle. Political economy offers a body of knowledge that governmental practices must incorporate, if they are to prove successful. Conversely, it does not develop any detailed programmes for guiding governmental practices or directing how they are carried out. Political economy defines a form of knowledge closely tied to the art of government (*tête-à-tête*), but it cannot constitute the latter.[61]

Still, political economy does not demonstrate 'objectivity' because it adopts a standpoint independent of politics in principle, but because it affords a new form for objectivating the reality of ruling, which situates governmental action in a new politico-epistemological configuration: the space of (civil) society, on the one hand, and a new form of subjectivity, on the other.

### David Hume: Subjectivity and Interest

Albert O. Hirschman's *The Passions and the Interests* describes how, in the post-feudal world, the manifest failure of moral enjoinders and religious commandments led to various ideas for implementing comparatively harmless forms of behaviour in order to neutralize other, more dangerous ones. In this context, the term 'interest' was coined for impulses deemed to possess an equilibrating or regulating function. In the course of the eighteenth century, the idea came to prevail that 'one set of passions, hitherto known variously as greed, avarice, or love of lucre, could be usefully employed to oppose and bridle such other passions as ambition, lust for power, or sexual lust'.[62]

In similar fashion, Foucault works out the relationship between the concept of interest and a new form of subjectivity that emerged in eighteenth-century British empiricism – one defined neither by free will, nor by the opposition between body and soul, but by inherent 'interests'. In this framework, the subject appears as the bearer of

---

61. Lecture, 5 April 1978, Foucault, 2004a, *Security, Territory, Population* [2007], 333–61; Rose, 'Government, Authority and Expertise in Advanced Liberalism' (1993), 290–2.

62. Hirschman, *The Passions and the Interests* (1977), 41.

individual preferences, which prove just as irreducible as they are untransferable; personal choice does not admit being traced back to more fundamental principles, nor can it be replaced or restricted. The new concept of interest refers to a form of will that is immediate and subjective at one and the same time. It cannot be derived from juridical will; indeed, it differs radically from it.

On the basis of the writings of David Hume and Jeremy Bentham, Foucault demonstrates the irreducibility of interest and the difference between the interest-subject and the legal subject, whose points of reference are the market and the contract, respectively. Whereas the theory of social contract holds that individuals renounce their original and natural rights in an act of transfer, Hume argues that such a regulation can be accepted only inasmuch as it counts as temporary and may be revoked at any time. As he observes in his *Treatise of Human Nature*, the basis for such a contract cannot be the contract itself, nor can it lie in the capacity to bind or modes of obligation. Instead, it is interest that makes concluding a contract advantageous and useful at a given moment. However, the self-same interest will dissolve the contract when such conditions no longer hold and the contract presents an obstacle to pursuing one's own wishes. Accordingly, the interest-subject permanently transcends the self-imposed limitations of the legal subject.[63]

---

63. Lecture, 28 March 1979, Foucault, 2004b, *The Birth of Biopolitics* [2008], 272–4; Burchell, 'Peculiar Interests: Civil Society and "Governing the System of Natural Liberty"' (1991), 127–32; Gordon, 'Governmental Rationality: An Introduction' (1991), 21. Foucault's discussion of 'interest' concentrates on the break it effects vis-à-vis the idea of complementarity between economy and law. The politico-juridical problematic developed in the eighteenth century – which focused on an individual legal subject – did not entail a complementary economic problematic. On the contrary, the economic problematic followed a rationality of another order altogether. 'Economic' criteria were not added to, or integrated into, politico-legal calculations, so much as a radical dissociation occurred between the politico-juridical and economic spheres. The heterogeneity and incompatibility between *homo economicus* and *homo legalis* points to fundamentally different relationships with political power. Whereas the problematic of *homo legalis* means limiting the exercise of sovereign power up to a certain point ('You aren't allowed to do that, because you have no right to do so'), the problematic of *homo economicus* invalidates sovereignty's pretension of commanding the totality of economic processes ('You aren't allowed to do that, because you don't – and can't – know what you're doing'). The former grounds the necessity for political sovereignty by marking out limits; the latter puts the very idea of sovereignty into question. Lecture, 28 March 1979, Foucault, 2004b, *The Birth of Biopolitics* [2008], 267–83; Burchell, 'Peculiar Interests: Civil Society and "Governing

Thus, the liberal art of government faces the problem of defining a political space for sovereignty and determining its object, given the structural heterogeneity between legal and economic subjectivity. Theoretically, there are two solutions that would 'harmonize' both these principles:

1. *Reducing the extent of regulation.* One solution would be to restrict regulatory efforts and leave the structure of government intact. If the totality of economic processes eludes sovereignty, then exercising such sovereignty might be limited spatially, as it were: it would be valid everywhere, except in the sphere of the market.

2. *Moving from political activity to theoretical passivity.* Another possibility (and this was the physiocrats' position) would be to change the form of government itself. The sovereign would adopt a bearing vis-à-vis the market analogous to a geometer's view with respect to geometrical realities. On the one hand, the sovereign acknowledges the market and its immanent laws, but on the other he assumes a position granting him abiding and complete control of processes here.[64]

That said, against the backdrop of the manifest incompatibility of the principles of sovereignty and the market – as well as the question of how to rule individuals who live as both legal and economic subjects – such efforts to strike a 'balance' between *homo legalis* and *homo œconomicus* prove unsatisfactory. In the one case, the sovereign is reduced to being an organ for carrying out economic science. In the other, the art of government is divided in two: an economic art of government and a juridical art of government. In contrast to both these perspectives, liberalism tries to construct a space of governmentality in which economic and politico-legal subjectivity represent, in equal measure, relative components of a more comprehensive arrangement. In order to preserve a unified art of government, the general validity of its principles for the entirety of the sovereign's realm, and the specificity and autonomy of the laws

---

the System of Natural Liberty'" (1991), 137.
    64. Lecture, 4 April 1979, Foucault, 2004b, *The Birth of Biopolitics* [2008], 293–4; Burchell, 'Peculiar Interests: Civil Society and "Governing the System of Natural Liberty'" (1991), 137–8.

of political economy, it is necessary to assign a new object and a new sphere to the art of government, where its power might be exercised: civil society. Civil society provides the answer to the question of how to rule, in keeping with the law, a space of sovereignty inhabited by economic subjects.[65]

## Adam Ferguson: Civil Society

In the course of the eighteenth century, the concept of civil society received an entirely new meaning. Whereas, until mid-century (e.g. in the writings of Locke), it counted as a juridico-political structure, above all, a significant change now occurred: the equation between civil society and political society collapsed. Foucault illustrates the concept's new dimension on the basis of Adam Ferguson's *Essay on the History of Civil Society* (1783).

First, Ferguson's conception of (civil) society starts with a historico-natural constant: human beings have always existed in groups, thus it is meaningless to look at isolated loners or think in terms of a pre-societal war of all against all. The transition from nature to history, from non-society to society, never occurred. Human nature is historical 'by nature', and the 'natural state' of humankind is a social one.

The 'naturalness' of society cannot be boiled down to its legal or economic aspects. It represents far more than a mechanism for exchanging natural rights, or a space inhabited by economic subjects. The bonds between individuals that it establishes differ radically from legal obligations; at the same time, the sympathies and antipathies that find expression here derive from the egoistic pursuit of economic self-interest. These are the specifically 'social' relations (in contrast to politico-legal and economic ones) that form the basis for, and define the particularity of, civil society.

Second, Ferguson assigns an ambivalent position to economic ties

---

65. Lecture, 4 April 1979, Foucault, 2004b, *The Birth of Biopolitics* [2008], 294–5; Gordon, 'Governmental Rationality: An Introduction' (1991), 21–2. As Graham Burchell has observed, the dilemma of eighteenth-century thinking that Foucault identifies has also been explored by Albert O. Hirschman, John Pocock, Gerhard Oestreich and Norbert Elias. Burchell focuses on the parallels between Foucault and Pocock's analysis, above all. Burchell, 'Peculiar Interests: Civil Society and "Governing the System of Natural Liberty"' (1991), 120–5. For a comparison of Foucault, Elias and Oestreich, see Burkitt 1993 and Kim 1995, as well as the section 'The Culture of the Self: Hellenistic-Roman Ethics' in Chapter 11.

as they bear on social bonds. On the one hand, economic exchange promotes relationships between individuals. On the other, economic links represent a constant source of danger. Time and again, individual, egoistic interests threaten to destroy the same civil society bonds they have fostered. Such 'dissociative association' also constitutes the vectors of a historical dynamic. Economic interplay and the self-serving pursuit of private interest introduce a historical dimension to the natural state of civil society: the same mechanisms that found it threaten it, maintain it and alter it. The historical process unfolds as the permanent formation and reformation of the social net along the lines of new economic structures and forms of government.

Third, in light of civil society's immanent historicity, Ferguson posits the thesis that an 'organic' relationship holds between social bonds and political relations of power. Not only do the natural differences pervading civil society lead to new divisions of labour in the sphere of production; they do the same in the political realm. Even though the decisions made here represent group will as a whole, they do not represent each and every member; some people arrive at different conclusions. The quasi-natural existence of such relations of power, founded in varying personal qualities and individual aptitudes, precedes the institutionalized law that they then legitimate, limit or reinforce. In other words: before power is juridically established, it already exists in the form of spontaneous hierarchies and natural authorities. In Ferguson's works, the problem of grounding or restricting power dissolves into the immanent historicity of civil society.[66]

At the same time, Ferguson's conception of civil society occupies a site of historico-political intersection, which goes back to early liberal confrontation with an all-powerful state and its regulatory claims. The early eighteenth century witnessed the problem of how the centrifugal forces and non-totalizable diversity of economic subjects could be made to conform with the totalized unity of a legal-political realm of sovereignty. The liberal answer was to 'invent' a new politico-epistemological object and problematic, in whose sphere juridical and economic subjectivity could be situated:

---

66. Lecture, 4 April 1979, Foucault, 2004b, *The Birth of Biopolitics* [2008], 298–307; Burchell, 'Peculiar Interests: Civil Society and "Governing the System of Natural Liberty"' (1991), 134–7; Gordon, 'Foucault en Angleterre' (1986b), 830.

civil society. Civil society opened an autonomous realm of spontaneous regulation between economic interests and sovereign rights.
Far more than a territory inhabited by a certain number of subjects,
it constitutes a complex and independent reality with its own mechanisms and dependencies, which any and every legal order must take
into account and accommodate.[67]

As such, civil society does not represent the counterpart of the
state; it does not take form against the state, or in contrast to it, such
that it is constantly threatened by state intervention or encroach-
ment. Instead, it represents the correlative of the liberal technology
of government. However, this does not mean that it lacks historical substance. For Foucault, civil society forms a 'transactional
reality';[68] it arises where different historical practices intersect. As
such, the opposition between society and state does not represent a
political universal, but a historical polarization on the basis of which
liberalism functions. The strict polarity between state and society
corresponds to the historical reality of the eighteenth century, and
much of the nineteenth – as does the political role of the state as the
centre for organizing power. For all that, this same line of division
came to be abandoned time and again over the course of the nineteenth century.[69]

## Dispositives of Security

Before addressing nineteenth-century changes to governmentality, a
few remarks are in order about the inner systematics and theoretical

---

67. Lecture, 4 April 1979, Foucault, 2004b, *The Birth of Biopolitics* [2008], 307–13;
Foucault, 1979m, 'Course Summary' [2008], 319; Foucault, 1982c, 'Space, Knowledge
and Power' [1984], 243; Procacci, 'Notes on the Government of the Social' (1987),
12–13; Procacci, *Gouverner la misère* (1993), 19. Accordingly, it is more a matter of
reciprocal constitution than creating a 'space' for already existing economic subjects:
'*Homo economicus* is, so to speak, the abstract, ideal, purely economic point which
populates the real density, fullness and complexity of civil society; or, alternatively,
civil society is the concrete ensemble within which these abstract points, economic
men, need to be positioned in order to be made adequately manageable'. Lecture, 4
April 1979, Foucault, 2004b, *The Birth of Biopolitics* [2008], 296, quoted in Gordon,
'Governmental Rationality: An Introduction' (1991), 23.
68. Lecture, 4 April 1979, Foucault, 2004b, *The Birth of Biopolitics* [2008], 297.
69. Foucault, 1979m, 'Course Summary' [2008], 319; Foucault, 1983a, 'The Risks
of Security' [2000], 374–5; Neumann, 'Der Diskurs der Regierung' (1988), 67.

role of the material presented until now. Two items in particular are
of consequence for the further course of argument: first, the complex
relationship between freedom and security established by the liberal
art of government, and, second, its delimitation with respect to
earlier technologies of power.

In contrast to reason of state, the new art of government that
started to emerge at the mid-eighteenth century did not aim only
to maximize the state's forces; rather, it pursued 'economic government'. However, this historical shift did not reduce state power right
away. A 'natural' limit was posited for state intervention, which had
to count on the naturalness of social phenomena. This limit was
not negative. Instead, the very naturalness of phenomena opened a
sphere for possible interventions unknown until this point, which
did not necessarily assume a regulatory form: 'laissez-faire', 'stimulating' and 'promoting' came to be more important than regulation,
making decrees and ruling.[70]

The principle of 'less government', then, is not a quantitative
phenomenon. Rather, it indicates a fundamental change in power
mechanisms. The emergence of the liberal art of government implies
establishing new forms of power, which differ from both sovereign
right and disciplinary technologies. Their task is to frame 'natural'
mechanisms in such a way that they may play out their naturalness without incurring damage. The institution of liberal freedoms
cannot be separated from *dispositives of security* (*dispositifs de sécurité*) meant to ensure a certain use of liberty.[71]

## Freedom and Security

Individuals and individual rights occupy the centre of liberal reflection, and the liberal art of government functions only inasmuch
as it guarantees freedom. Yet freedom does not simply amount to
the (negative) individual right to oppose power. Instead, law – or
juridical institutions and mechanisms (such as 'the rule of law'
and parliamentarism) – are historical instruments with the task of
restricting the regulating claims of the absolutist state and securing

70. Lecture, 17 January 1979, Foucault, 2004b, *The Birth of Biopolitics* [2008],
27–47.

71. Foucault, 1978o, 'Governmentality' [2000], 220–1.

a general procedural framework. As such, freedom is not identical with rights and the law; rather, they represent a vehicle of liberal government for consolidating liberty.[72]

It does not follow, however, that freedom represents an absolute value in the liberal art of government. Rather, it provides an instrument for the art of government inasmuch as it forms an indispensable component of governmentality and the (positive) basis for governmental action. In other words, liberalism does not reserve more pockets of freedom than other governmental practices; it does not limit itself to respecting one kind of liberty or another so much as it 'consumes' freedom. Freedom provides the crucial precondition for 'economic' government; it is the medium and instrument of governmental action – such that contempt for it not only violates the law but also signals fundamental ignorance about the purpose of governing in general.[73]

Accordingly, liberalism differs from earlier forms of government with respect to its mode of exercising power. It does not seek to dominate subjects directly or subjugate them, since their activity and freedom constitute the indispensable precondition for the liberal form of government and structure the concrete forms that exercising power assumes. Unlike earlier technologies of government, liberalism does not enlist constraint and violence so much as it presumes individual freedom. In other words, the freedom of individuals does not stand opposed to liberal governmentality but represents its necessary condition and central component.[74]

However, liberal interest in individual freedom does not correspond to lack of interest in coordination and regulation. On the contrary, the element of freedom heightens the need for balance and steering. In order for individual actions to be used for the purposes of government, it is necessary to lend the freedom of subjects

---

72. Foucault does not view the connection between law and liberalism as a matter of nature or logic; instead, it represents a historical relation. Democracy and the rule of law are not necessarily liberal – just as liberalism need not be democratic or assure rights. Legality and participation in government prove to be 'economic'. Foucault, 1979m, 'Course Summary' [2008], 321.

73. Lecture, 24 January 1979, Foucault, 2004b, *The Birth of Biopolitics* [2008], 51–73; Gordon, 'Governmental Rationality: An Introduction' (1991), 20.

74. Lecture, 17 January 1979, Foucault, 2004b, *The Birth of Biopolitics* [2008], 27–50.

a certain form. Liberalism can operationalize freedom only to the extent that it is able to determine a clearly delimited use for it. But to assert freedom in this form, it cannot make recourse to coercion and violence and must renounce implementing centralized power mechanisms of the state.

Liberal government concerns more than a simple legal guarantee of liberties existing independently of governmental practice. Liberalism organizes the conditions under which individuals are able to be free. In this context, freedom is not a given – instead, liberalism 'fabricates' or 'produces' freedom. But in the process of producing freedom, liberalism also imperils the very thing it creates. A problematic (and paradoxical) relationship emerges between freedom and its permanent endangerment: precisely because liberalism brings forth freedom 'artificially', it constantly risks restricting, or even destroying it. The liberal art of government enacts freedom that is fragile and constantly at risk – which therefore provides the basis for new interventions time and again.[75]

The problem for liberalism, then, concerns the extent to which the free pursuit of private interests threatens the general interest: how high are freedom's 'production costs'? Freedom cannot prevail without restriction, but must be subjected to a principle of calculation: *security*. So that the mechanics of interests and the dynamic of desire do not come to pose a danger for individuals and the collective, it is necessary to establish 'mechanisms of security'. The latter represent the flipside of, and condition for, liberalism. Whether, like Bentham, one views freedom as a branch of security or does the opposite (deeming security a condition for freedom), freedom and security stand as the two poles of liberal governmentality:

> the setting in place of mechanisms of security ... mechanisms or modes of state intervention whose function is to assure the security of those natural phenomena, economic processes and the intrinsic processes of the population: this is what becomes the basic objective

---

75. Lecture, 24 January 1979, ibid., 51–73; Senellart, 'Michel Foucault: "gouvernementalité" et raison d'Etat' (1993), 297. Foucault illustrates this problem with the example of competition and monopolization: free trade can occur only to the extent that an array of measures is taken preventing the predominance of one party over another. Lecture, 24 January 1979, Foucault, 2004b, *The Birth of Biopolitics* [2008], 51–65.

of governmental relationality. Hence liberty is registered not only as the right of individuals legitimately to oppose the power, the abuses and usurpations of the sovereign, but also now as an indispensable element of governmental rationality itself.[76]

Formerly, a vast array of legal and economic conditions existed, which obligated the sovereign to protect his subjects. But with liberalism it is no longer a matter of securing external protection for the individual; instead, the production of liberties and the pursuit of private interests are supposed to ensure that individuals and the collective stand exposed to as few dangers as possible. The inward relationship between freedom and security also sets liberal government apart from the police state, where security also holds a key position. In the latter case, however, the aim of the police is to establish safety by surveilling and steering processes of communication and exchange; the preferred instruments are disciplining individuals and tying them to the productive apparatus. According to Foucault, liberalism opts for another path, which takes distance from the universe of police: instead of trying to order all the processes that occur in the population, it seeks to take account of the population's autonomous and necessarily opaque character.[77] Such autonomy no longer represents something natural (as for the physiocrats), which regulates and stabilizes itself on its own; rather, it is something artificial – exposed to risk time and again and requiring security mechanisms in order to play out fully.[78]

76. Lecture, 5 April 1978, quoted in Gordon, 'Governmental Rationality: An Introduction' (1991), 19–20.

77. As Colin Gordon observes, the liberal conception of 'economic government' makes it possible to take over elements of the police state because and insofar as they are 'economic'. Liberalism does not find fault with the police state for its goal of producing a 'good order', but because of the means it uses to pursue this aim: comprehensive regulation and surveillance. The critique is not moral and political, but technical and economic. Liberalism acknowledges the same goal, but it enlists different means, transferring regulation from the state to individual subjects. As such, liberalism does not negate claims to security in favour of a regime of freedom so much as it seeks a 'recoding of the politics of order'. Ibid., 26, 25–7; see also Foucault, 1978o, 'Governmentality' [2000], 218–20.

78. Lecture, 24 January 1979, Foucault, 2004b, *The Birth of Biopolitics* [2008], 51–70; Gordon, 'Governmental Rationality: An Introduction' (1991), 20. Indeed, the relationship between freedom and security is even more complicated. Liberalism enacts freedom that is constantly imperilled – and therefore requires security mechanisms. It is not the case that freedom exists beforehand, which then is threatened. Instead, threats represent the precondition for, and a fundamental component of, freedom. Liberalism knows only freedom that is permanently at risk; insecurity is

Foucault's discussion of security mechanisms provides one of his most important theoretical projects after *Discipline and Punish*; as such, it calls for re-evaluating the results of earlier studies. Two points warrant emphasis in particular. First, 'security mechanisms' concern a modality of power that differs from both sovereign power and disciplinary power. Second, 'dispositives of security' do not simply join the other mechanisms of power, nor do they relativize their meaning or take their place. Instead, the interest Foucault shows for 'security mechanisms' displaces the value attached to other forms of power, which entails a change in his assessment of disciplinary processes.

## Sovereignty – Discipline – Security

What is it that distinguishes security mechanisms from juridical mechanisms, on the one hand, and disciplinary mechanisms, on the other? For one, the *objects* are different: whereas the aim of sovereignty is to extend territorial space, and discipline focuses on the individual body, government takes aim at 'population in general'.[79] That said, the differences between these mechanisms only become clear in their different *modes of operation*, as Foucault illustrates on the basis of ways epidemics were treated from the Middle Ages to the eighteenth century.[80]

Historically, variant reactions to leprosy, plague and smallpox point to significant changes in perception and therapy. During the Middle Ages, sovereign power banished lepers from cities and operated through the binary division leprous/not-leprous. From the sixteenth to the eighteenth century, disciplinary power opted for another form of action towards plague: the sick were not banished;

---

not the price of freedom, but its foundation. Accordingly, danger must be cultivated: it forms part of the naturalness of society. Transience, instability and uncertainty define the liberal world, and they represent the other side of free, human existence. It follows, however, that liberalism requires security it can never ensure: the search for security and imperilled freedom are the building blocks of liberal governmentality. Lecture, 24 January 1979, ibid., 65–70.

79. Lecture, 11 January 1978, Foucault, 2004a, *Security, Territory, Population* [2007], 10.

80. In the lectures on 11 January 1978 and 18 January 1978, Foucault examines the various forms of intervention associated with sovereignty, discipline and security mechanisms with respect to urban planning and famines. Ibid., 1–27, 29–53.

instead, affected urban quarters were quarantined in order to contain the affliction through police measures. Finally, eighteenth-century security technology met smallpox by way of concrete knowledge concerning the number and sites of infection, the age of people affected, mortality rates and so on.[81]

The example of smallpox permits Foucault to stress the difference between disciplinary mechanisms and security measures. Practices of inoculation developed to counter smallpox (fighting illness by controlled exposure to pathogens) heralded a break with received medical knowledge and required that entirely new concepts be elaborated. Illness no longer received treatment in moral-juridical terms, but as a natural fact distributed in the population as so many 'cases' admitting statistical analysis. Whereas disciplinary mechanisms had focused on illness itself and parties infected, security dispositives not only separate the healthy from the sick but treat the population as a whole, accepting a 'normal' rate of infection, mortality and so on.[82]

Like famine, illness is no longer understood in legal or disciplinary categories – and then met with 'medical police' – so much as it receives attention as an empirical fact. Accordingly, security mechanisms do not implement regulatory measures in order to prevent famine or disease. On the contrary: for eighteenth-century economists and physicians, reality is no longer what must be negated, but what cannot be prevented – and since it cannot be prevented, it must be reckoned with and calculated, in order to minimize its negative effects. In a seeming paradox, then, the shortage of foodstuffs gives rise to free markets and sickness leads to inoculating the population with pathogens.[83]

The different reactions to illness on the part of sovereignty, discipline and security point to varying concepts of the *norm* and the 'normal'. Legal norms operated through laws that established and codified standards. Foucault's works on discipline and his critique

---

81. *Discipline and Punish* already contrasts responses to leprosy and plague in order to define juridical and disciplinary mechanisms and their differences. Security mechanisms do not yet receive consideration. Foucault, 1975a, *Discipline and Punish* [1995], 195–200.

82. Lecture, 11 January 1978, Foucault, 2004a, *Security, Territory, Population* [2007], 10; lecture, 25 January 1978, Foucault, 2004a, *Security, Territory, Population* [2007], 57–63; Foucault, 1992, 'La population', 14–25.

83. Ibid., 17.

of the juridical model of power demonstrate how disciplinary technology exploited gaps in the legal mechanisms and 'colonized' the
law.[84] Discipline introduced a hierarchy distinguishing between the
unsuitable and the suitable, the normal and the abnormal, and so
on. Disciplinary technology worked by projecting an optimal model
and then operationalizing it – that is, it implemented procedures
for evaluating individuals on a standard and fitting them to it. The
norm occupied the foreground; on this basis the normal was separated from the abnormal.[85]

Security technology represents the exact opposite of the disciplinary system. Whereas the latter starts with the norm, the
security system starts with the (empirically) normal, which sets
the standard enabling further distinctions to be made. Instead of
evaluating reality in terms of a predefined norm, security technology makes reality itself the norm: statistical frequency, average
rates of illness, birth and death, and so on. Discipline tends to
regulate everything, and it must constantly intervene in order to
change reality. In contrast, 'dispositives of security' make given
reality the point of departure and try to work within its parame-
ters. They do not draw absolute lines of separation between what
is permitted and what is forbidden, but specify an optimal middle
ground within a spectrum.[86]

The analytical distinction between the different modes of operation of sovereignty, discipline and security prompts Foucault to
change his overall picture. In contrast to earlier studies, which
opposed disciplinary normalization to the legal norm, he now
reserves the term normalization for designating mechanisms of
security. He recognizes that law and discipline have the same
premise: neither one starts out with what is normal in descriptive terms; instead, they both operate prescriptively. Accordingly,
Foucault places, alongside the legal *norm*, disciplinary *normation*,
which he in turn distinguishes from the *normalization* performed
by security technology:

---

84. Foucault, 1977f, '14 January 1976' [2003], 38–9.
85. Lecture, 25 January 1978, Foucault, 2004a, *Security, Territory, Population*
[2007], 56–7; Foucault, 1992, 'La population', 9–13.
86. Lecture, 25 January 1978, Foucault, 2004a, *Security, Territory, Population*
[2007], 57–66; Foucault, 1992, 'La population', 14–25.

> Due to the primacy of the norm in relation to the normal, to the
> fact that disciplinary normalization goes from the norm to the final
> division between the normal and the abnormal, I would rather say
> that what is involved in disciplinary techniques is a normation (*nor-
> mation*) rather than normalization.[87]

Discussing 'dispositives of security', Foucault observes that critique
of the juridical conception of power also applies to the disciplinary
mechanisms he once used to demonstrate the 'productivity of power'.
Inasmuch as it makes the norm the point of departure, disciplinary
technology shares the negative code of law, whose limitations for
analysing social power now are evident. Foucault concludes that
modern societies' tendency towards normalization is not restricted
to training individuals and orienting them on a single model. Now,
compared to 'dispositives of security', he finds discipline to be a singularly 'uneconomical' and 'archaic'[88] form of power. As such, his
power analytics no longer assigns disciplinary regulation a position
opposite to the juridical principle; instead, the line of demarcation
runs between (positive) security mechanisms and the (negative)
'juridical-disciplinary system'.[89]

Foucault adds a historical and a political thesis to his analytical distinction between various power mechanisms. The
*political* thesis consists of relativizing the significance of disciplinary processes in contemporary, liberal-capitalist societies.
In the early 1970s, Foucault still stressed the increasing disciplination of society; now, he declares that, in the 'general
economy of power', the dominance of juridical mechanisms
has shifted, via disciplinary mechanisms, to security mechanisms. By this assessment, we are not living in a state of law
or a disciplinary society so much as in what one might call a
'security society': juridical and disciplinary mechanisms are
increasingly subordinated to 'dispositives of security'.[90]

---

87. Ibid., 13; see also lecture, 25 January 1978, Foucault, 2004a, *Security, Territory,
Population* [2007], 57.

88. Foucault, 1992, 'La population', 32.

89. Lecture, 18 January 1978, Foucault, 2004a, *Security, Territory, Population*
[2007], 36.

90. Lecture, 18 January 1978, ibid., 34, translation modified. Foucault's 1978 and
1979 lectures occurred at the high point of extremist, left-wing violence in Europe

However, this *historical* process of transformation does not mean dismantling power mechanisms, nor is it simply a matter of new technologies of power being added on. Rather, modification occurs affecting power mechanisms and their relation to each other. Instead of making them superfluous, the government problematic intensifies questions concerning the conditions of sovereignty and drives the disciplines forward. In the first place, the end of traditional schemes of justification motivated by religion or natural law exacerbates questions about the limits and foundations of political sovereignty. Second, governing the population demands detailed, comprehensive and fundamental leadership; this makes discipline more necessary

---

(RAF, Brigadi Rossi, Action Directe, etc.). State efforts to confront so-called terrorism illustrated, albeit unintentionally, his theses on security mechanisms. In this context, one case proved particularly significant. Klaus Croissant, the attorney for the Red Army Faction, was charged with supporting a criminal organization in Germany; in autumn 1977, he fled to France and appealed for political asylum. In turn, German authorities sought his extradition; even though he was, in fact, granted asylum, this is what ultimately occurred. For an account of events, see Eribon, *Michel Foucault* (1991), 259–61; Macey, *The Lives of Michel Foucault* (1993), 392–6.

Foucault commented on the 'Croissant Case' in several interviews and articles. Although he sided with Croissant and objected to extradition, he took issue with other left-wing intellectuals' characterization of the West German state as 'fascistic'. In Foucault's eyes, this description was historically and politically inappropriate. Foucault did not consider the Federal Republic of Germany a new version of fascism (or another kind of totalitarianism) controlling society from the top down, but a 'security society' distinguished by a considerably subtler mode of exercising power – one that accepts a broader range of actions, within limits, but seeks to minimize risks (accidents, unemployment, illness and so on). Foucault, 1977s, 'La sécurité et l'Etat', 386.

For Foucault, the decision to extradite Croissant demonstrated the other side of this society. In his estimation, we do not live under the rule of law so much as in a 'security state' that carries out measures outside of, and in contradiction to, legal provisions. The basis for such politics is not a social contract but a 'security pact'. Foucault, 1977t, 'Letter to Certain Leaders of the Left' [2000], 427–8. Hereby, no legal limits are set for state intervention; in order to guarantee safety, the state must be able to operate outside, and counter to, the law. Abuses and irregularities do not represent abnormalities or the failure of reality to measure up to an ideal; instead, they are the basis and guarantee for the 'rule of law' and the 'constitutional state'. Insecurity, threats and so on constitute an everyday level of apprehension. Accordingly, the 'state of fear' represents the other side of the 'state of law'. Foucault, 1977c, 'Préface', 139–40; Foucault, 1977q, 'Désormais la sécurité est au-dessus des lois', 366–7; Foucault, 1977p, 'Va-t-on extrader Klaus Croissant?'; Foucault, 1979a, 'Préface de Michel Foucault'; for a parallel in Marxist discussions of 'authoritarian statism', see Poulantzas, *State, Power, Socialism* (2000), 203–47; Hirsch, *Der Sicherheitsstaat* (1980); Neumann, 'Angst und Politik' (1986a).

than ever, inasmuch as they are supposed to function as the counterpart, and completion, of newly won liberties. And so, 'security
society' does not represent the end point of a historical development
– whereby a society of sovereignty yields to disciplinary society,
which in turn gives way to a society of governmentality. Instead, it
amounts to a 'triangle, sovereignty-discipline-government, which
has as its primary target the population and as its essential mechanism the apparatuses of security'.[91]

Yet the schematic distinction between three technologies of
power poses a problem inasmuch as it suggests that we are still living
under the conditions of eighteenth-century, liberal governmentality
– which have remained unchanged for some 200 years.[92] Foucault
demonstrates in concrete, historical terms, that liberal rationality
changed decisively in the course of the nineteenth century, and he
points to substantial differences between early liberal thinking of the
eighteenth century and neoliberal ideas of the twentieth. These transformations of liberal governmentality form the object of chapters
8 and 9.[93]

---

91. Foucault, 1978o, 'Governmentality' [2000], 219; see also lecture, 11 January
1978, Foucault, 2004a, *Security, Territory, Population* [2007], 107–8. Gilles Deleuze
took up this distinction between three technologies of power and developed it in a
few short texts and interviews. Like Foucault, he distinguishes between sovereignty
and disciplinary societies, but he uses another name for the new form of society that
has been on the rise since the Second World War: society of control. Its defining
trait is that it does not work so much 'by confining people but through continuous
control and instant communication'. Deleuze, 'Control and Becoming' (1995b), 174.
The ongoing crisis of closed institutions in fact represents the creeping, scattered
emergence of a new regime of domination, which installs new forms of sanction and
control mechanisms. This mutation can be observed in a number of contexts: within
the penal system, replacement solutions involve electronic bracelets that restrict
the movement of convicts; in education, life-long learning processes are replacing
schools, tests and so on. Ibid., 174–5; Deleuze, 'Postscript on the Societies of Control'
(2008). That said, Deleuze offers only a sketch, largely bracketing the connection
between power technologies and political and economic changes.

92. Foucault, 1978o, 'Governmentality' [2000], 219.

93. Despite Foucault's vivid accounts, a problem with opposing the mechanisms
of sovereignty, disciplinary and security is that doing so lacks historical concreteness.
For instance, 'dispositives of security' seem to represent an integral component of
liberal security politics; at the same time, they enlist elements – as we will see in
Chapter 8 – that are formulated as a reaction to, and critique of, early liberal notions.
Accordingly, it is important not to overestimate nominal distinctions, which simply
open a new dimension of analysis.

In theoretical terms, it is better not to start with the postulate of three different power technologies (which are already constituted and admit variation at best), but to begin with different forms of government with separate aims and means at their disposal (which, moreover, may be more than three in number). From this perspective, police technology represents a form of government among others; in principle, it does not stand opposed to them (e.g. liberal government). In such a framework – which makes Foucault's approach appear more consistent as a whole – 'government' is a comprehensive term encompassing other categories. Another point warrants clarification: Foucault speaks of governmentality in two ways. In general, the word refers to the rise of an autonomous art of government concerning 'right' or 'appropriate' rule, which begins with the reason of state. However, he also discusses governmentality in a more narrow sense. It defines an art of government specific to the context of liberalism and the emergence of a discrete object of government: society.

# 8

# The Government of Society:
# The Invention of the Social

---

Liberal institutions stop being liberal as soon as they have been attained: after that, nothing damages freedom more terribly or more thoroughly than liberal institutions. Of course people know *what* these institutions do: they undermine the will to power, they set to work levelling mountains and valleys and call this morality, they make things small, cowardly, and enjoyable – they represent the continual triumph of herd animals. Liberalism: *herd animalization*, in other words.

Nietzsche[1]

Eighteenth century liberalism constituted itself in opposition to the authoritarian (police) state and its regulatory ambitions. It shifted responsibility and authority to the economic subject and civil society. But, during the second half of the nineteenth century, an important transformation of governmental techniques occurred, in which the state acquired an entirely new meaning: no longer partisan and potentially despotic, it came to signify neutrality, standing above and outside of society and its conflicts. In this light, governmentality meant that the state does not produce political inequality, nor does it preserve outdated social structures. Instead, it represents an indispensable element in resolving political antagonism and guaranteeing social progress. By the end of the century, the state no longer faces society as a foreign body; it becomes the state of society: the *social state*.[2]

---

1. Nietzsche, 'Twilight of the Idols, or How to Philosophize with a Hammer' (2005), 213. I owe reference to the Nietzsche quote to Barry Hindess. Hindess, 'Liberalism, Socialism and Democracy' (1993), 300.

2. Foucault discusses contemporary neoliberal authors in conjunction with

This historical transformation has been examined from numerous standpoints: in terms of the increasing juridification of social relations, as the product of contradiction between political equality and economic inequality, and as the victory of the working class and its organizations. The theoretical peculiarity of the works discussed in the following is that they set aside these models of explanation in favour of a 'genealogy of the welfare state' that focuses on analysing 'political rationalities'.[3] Their common point of departure is the assumption that historical changes to the state cannot be separated from an epistemologico-political shift in the objectivation of society, which took material form during the nineteenth century and differs markedly from the early liberal idea of 'civil society'.

Liberal thinkers had conceived society as the (voluntary) association of individuals, which ultimately derives from the economic and political interests of particulars. For liberal governmentality, the central point of reference is not society, but individuals. In this conception, civil society is identical with the sum of its parts and social phenomena do not constitute a reality *sui generis* – that is, one different from the reality of political and economic subjects. Society and subjects occupy the same plane; they do not belong to separate realms. Society is not a subject, but an object produced by a multiplicity of economic individual interests and political preferences.[4]

But, beginning in the second half of the nineteenth century, 'society' acquired a density of its own, making it impossible to trace it back to the aggregation of individual wills. Seemingly an independent and self-sufficient subject, it now represents something other than the sum of individual subjects; it can no longer be derived from its parts. Henceforth, 'society' names an autonomous sphere of relations

---

early liberalism in his 1978 and 1979 lectures. Because he treats nineteenth-century governmentality only rarely, the following relies on works by his students and collaborators. Foucault, 1978z, 'Course Summary' [2007], 367; Foucault, 1979m, 'Course Summary' [2008], 322–4. The account here draws, in particular, on studies by Robert Castel, Daniel Defert, Jacques Donzelot, François Ewald and Giovanna Procacci. Although these research projects stand on their own, they share the Foucauldian perspective and diagnose deep-reaching changes in nineteenth-century liberal governmentality. As such, they attest to the scope of governmental analysis, which offers any number of points of concentration and interest.

   3. Donzelot, *L'invention du social* (1984), 125; Ewald, 'Risk, Insurance, Society' (1987), 6.

   4. Ewald, *Histoire De L'Etat Providence* (1986a), 64–70.

with specific regularities and objects distinct from both economic and political relations. A 'specific organizational form of society',[5] or a 'new political positivity',[6] emerges: the *social*.

For the authors discussed here – who were Foucault's colleagues and collaborators – the most important reason for this shift followed from the complete rearrangement of liberal politics towards a new system of security in which the state played a central role. The simultaneous emergence of mass poverty and an organized labour movement exposed the insufficiency of liberal security mechanisms, which centred on the individual and his or her civil liberties. In addition, the separation liberalism had effected between politics and economy posed more and more of a problem in terms of economic inequality and political equality. The nineteenth century faced a dilemma for which the liberal security system had no answer, which was neither economic nor political: the *social question*.[7]

## The Government of Poverty: The Social Question

In *History of Madness*, Foucault describes the establishment of the 'Hôpital Général', where the ill, those in need of medical care, the insane and the unemployed all were held. More and more, over the course of

---

5. Donzelot, *L'invention du social* (1984), 72.

6. Ewald, 'Risk, Insurance, Society' (1987), 6.

7. As a rule, the analyses presented here bear on the (social) history of nineteenth-century France, but the problem itself is more general in nature. Under the heading of *The Great Transformation*, economic historian Karl Polanyi has described the co-emergence of the problematic of poverty and the 'discovery of society' in Great Britain: 'The figure of the pauper, almost forgotten since, dominated a discussion the imprint of which was as powerful as that of the most spectacular events in history. If the French Revolution was indebted to the thought of Voltaire and Diderot, Quesnay and Rousseau, the Poor Law discussion formed the minds of Bentham and Burke, Godwin and Malthus, Ricardo and Marx, Robert Owen and John Stuart Mill, Darwin and Spencer, who shared with the French Revolution the spiritual parentage of nineteenth-century civilization. [...] [T]he revolution which ... the Poor Law Reform eventually freed shifted the vision of men toward their own collective being as if they had overlooked its presence before. A world was uncovered the very existence of which had not been suspected, that of the laws governing a complex society. Although the emergence of society in this new and distinctive sense happened in the economic field, its reference was universal'. Polanyi, *The Great Transformation* (2001), 87–8, 81–140. For a brief sketch of the relationship between the 'social question' and the development of the social state in Germany, see Grimm 1987, esp. 138–61.

the eighteenth century, this generalized practice of confinement came to be viewed as irrational. Poverty came to stand as a category of its own, as a matter requiring a specific mode of treatment. Its specificity implied that economic infirmity should be set apart from other forms of destitution. Gradually, the mixed and polyvalent forms of support that had defined care for the poor up into the eighteenth century were abandoned.

They were replaced by a (liberal) rationality that faulted traditional forms of charity and welfare for economic wastefulness and technical inefficiency. This twofold disqualification bore on the sizeable sums that flowed into general pauper relief. Not only did this mean that the poor remained outside the realm of production and found no 'economic' use; more still, such efforts, reasoning held, do not get rid of poverty – they prolong it indefinitely. Liberal rationality tried to break through this negative mechanism by formulating a (positive) relation between poverty and labour and fragmenting the spectrum: the figure of the 'sick poor' vanished and gave way to an array of distinctions between good and bad paupers: those who were simply lazy and those who sought work, people capable of working and those who were not, and so on. By reorganizing the problem around the pole of work, the operation sought to break down poverty in order to separate the 'real' poor from the impostors and freeloaders.[8]

Studies by Giovanna Procacci have stressed that liberal government did not replace one perception of the problem with another, nor did it inaugurate a change of perspective. What is more, traditional practices of welfare and charity did not yield to more efficient or 'more economical' approaches, and no new treatment for the old problem of poverty was proposed. Liberal thinking did not focus on how the problem should be viewed or remedied, but on the problem itself. In various forms and with different degrees of intensity, poverty has always existed. There may have been different ways to look at it or treat it, but in the context of liberal government – which meant a free labour market and the guarantee of equal rights for all – poverty changed status. With the abolition of feudal and estate barriers, the institution of free markets, and the postulate of legal equality, poverty could no longer be approached by traditional means such as paternalism and/or

---

8. Foucault, 1976b, 'The Politics of Health in the Eighteenth Century' [2000], 92–3.

repressive exclusion. On the contrary: the poor became equals among equals. Only within the framework of government practice linking market forces and the statute of general, legal equality – thereby staging a charged relationship between economic liberty and political sovereignty – did being poor turn into a problem.[9]

## Law and Morality

According to François Ewald's analysis of legal politics, the problem of social inequality did not represent a 'blind spot' of liberal thinking. On the contrary, examining the reasons for, and consequences of, inequality in a society of equals stood at centre stage. As such, what is remarkable about liberalism is not the absence of the theme of poverty, or lack of interest in it, but the attention and effort given to treating it. It was impossible for liberal thought to be blind to the fact of social inequality, for it performs an important social function. In other words, inequality does not represent a foreign body so much as an integral component of the social world of liberalism. Inequalities constitute civil society, which defines itself through social differences, and they provide the index for the naturalness of social phenomena and the possibility of society in general. Social inequalities are not the result of a defective society, but a necessary and indispensable element of its everyday functioning:

> Inequalities are natural, inevitable, and irreducible: they constitute a
> component of the order of creation, which is an order of variety and
> diversity; as rewards and punishments for the merits and shortcomings

9. Procacci, 'Notes on the Government of the Social' (1987), 13; Procacci, *Gouverner la misère* (1993), 20–1; Procacci, 'Governing Poverty: Sources of the Social Question in Nineteenth-Century France' (1994), 208–9. 'During the nineteenth century – at least in Europe – the great problem [...] was poverty and destitution. For most of the thinkers and philosophers at the beginning of the nineteenth century the great problem was: How was it possible for this production of wealth – whose spectacular effects were starting to appear throughout the West as a whole – should be accompanied by the absolute or relative (that's another question) impoverishment of the very people producing it?'. Foucault, 1978j, 'La philosophie analytique de la politique', 536. To put things somewhat schematically, François Ewald examines this problem in terms of the change of 'juridical reason'; Giovanna Procacci is more interested in intellectual currents within political economy (and its critique by social economists); and Jacques Donzelot concentrates on its politico-constitutional dimensions.

of particulars, they are necessary for social progress; finally, they are
part of providence: as wellsprings of social cohesion, they stand at the
origin of the existence of societies. Thus, not only can they not be prevented – one should not seek to make them disappear … The existence
of inequalities underlies both the possibility and necessity of a liberal
art of government.[10]

This conception of civil society as the sum of individual interactions
allowed liberal rationality to dismiss any idea of a social system that
went beyond the will of particulars. Liberalism's political 'achievement' is to have rejected the very thought of social causality: between
the wealth of the ones and the poverty of the others, there is no social
connection organizing relations according to a necessary principle.
The reason and cause for inequality does not follow from a generative
system, but derives from the different ways that individuals use their
freedom. Liberalism replaces any thought of antagonism pervading
society with the postulate of continuous, equal liberties. As such, the
freedom of individual will and the principle of responsibility occupy
the centre of liberal thinking. The problem does not involve rectifying
social injustice, but coordinating wills and ensuring the coexistence
of liberties.

As Ewald presents matters, liberals consider the social world to
be simultaneously natural and just. No distinction, no difference of
level, exists between natural and social justice that would require
corrective measures; no basis exists for society intervening in nature.
Accordingly, any step towards righting social relations not only runs
counter to the natural self-regulation of social mechanisms, but also
contradicts the principle of justice. Only in one instance is intervention in the natural course of social relations possible (and necessary):
when their naturalness itself is at stake. If 'freedom' names the universal principle defining the naturalness of society, any liberty that
restricts other liberties is unjust. Thus, the coexistence of liberties
constitutes the measure and the limit of rights and the law. From the
perspective of liberalism, the law does not constrain; on the contrary,
it serves to critique constraint. Necessarily, law has negative character,
because it derives from freedom and is oriented on it: it is impossible
to force people to do anything; one can only prevent them from acting

---

10. Ewald, *Histoire De L'Etat Providence* (1986a), 70–1.

improperly. Constraint is legal in nature when it foils something that unjustly obstructs liberty: the law solders and fixes, but it does not correct.[11]

Liberalism regulates social relations not by way of the law but through morality. Inasmuch as the social world is a just world characterized by coexisting liberties, any instance of inequality must derive from a (false) use of freedom. General freedom of the will has its counterpart in constant moral evaluation that subjects all actions to critical judgement. The liberal world knows perpetrators, but no victims. The reasons for poverty lie in moral failing; it results from individual wills and subjective dispositions. This perspective does not merely define a certain way of understanding the causality of events; at the same time, it formulates a positive programme: if poverty does not arise from the (defective) structure of society, but instead stems from a faulty personality structure, then poverty may be abolished only by heightening moralization, transforming personal will and changing behaviour. As such, moral evaluation functions both as an instrument for diagnosis and a mode of therapy, naming the problem and the course to follow in order to solve it.

According to Ewald, the concept of individual *responsibility* plays a key role in the liberal strategy of moralization.[12] It affords a principle of objectivation as well as a standard of judgement: everyone is responsible for his or her own life. Assuring seamless communication between the law and morality, it provides a unified mode of culpabilization and brackets any idea of social causality that extends beyond personal

---

11. Ibid., 57–63. 'Kant's formulation must not be understood to mean that the law dissolves into the exercise of power; rather, in Kant's terms, it plays the role of critiquing its capacity to do so. One cannot be forced to do anything by legal means; one can only be prevented from doing something. Coercion is legal in nature only when it blocks something that unjustly impedes a liberty – that is, something that violates the principle of coexisting liberties. [...] Legal constraint is never primary or immediate, but as it were reflexive; it belongs to the order of reaction, not action; it is legitimate defense'. Ibid., 62.

12. 'The principle of responsibility enables a view of social life following the model of harmony. [...] The liberal notion of harmony is that morality accords with law, and law with economy – that the guiding principles of each of these fields, instead of standing in opposition, refer to each other and reinforce each other reciprocally. The concept of fault has the purpose of securing such harmony. Its value is universal: economic, juridical, political, and moral. It is a mediating mechanism making it possible for economic behavior to be moral, as well, and for legal sanction to coincide with pangs of conscience'. Ibid., 65.

misconduct. Liberal rationality does not view poverty as a social ill based in economic operations organized along capitalist lines, but as a moral disposition and an individual form of conduct. Thus, efforts to combat it cannot concentrate on reorganizing social mechanisms; rather, they must focus on the individual will (or unwillingness), to which this condition owes its existence; without a transformation of the will, it will come back again and again. Poverty is not the result of an objective reality, but the product and sign of a subjective volition (or its absence). Responsibility for this condition lies ultimately with the poor themselves; it is a matter of individual, not social, responsibility, and as a social responsibility it is strictly an individual matter.[13]

The moralizing imperative does not concern only those without property; it also applies to those with property. The corollary of assigning personal responsibility for poverty is the principle of moral responsibility on the part of the wealthy. Indeed, liberalism is notable for many and varied practices of welfare and charity, which form an integral component of its politics of social security. As such, it does not reject the idea of the social obligation of the rich towards the poor, nor does it contest the need for charitable works. However, it envisions a different form for such social duties: they must be a matter of voluntary, moral decision, not legal, binding obligation. Liberalism does not reject practices of aid and support so much as the idea of a 'right to support' that affirms the rights of the poor with respect to the social obligations of the wealthy.[14]

Although seemingly insignificant, this distinction proves decisive because it results from a strict separation between law and morality that defines liberalism and is indispensable for its functioning. For liberals, civil society precedes political society, and the two are not the same. Positive law only confirms the principles of natural law and lends them binding force. The law is not the artificial work of human hands, but retraces the foundations of natural morality, giving it explicit and codified form. There is no law without morality; instead, morality underwrites the law. Nor does liberalism limit social obligations to those subject to legal sanction. Because the law has the sole function of securing the coexistence of liberties, liberal reason makes only one social obligation the object of legal sanction: not to curtail

---

13. Ibid., 64–70.
14. Ibid., 70–9.

the freedom of others. All other obligations are banished from the negativity of the law to the positive terrain of morality: 'In the liberal perspective, the right to support represents a contradiction *in terms*'.[15]

The 'liberal delimitation'[16] that draws a line between law and morality replaces a confrontational legal claim – with rights on the one hand and corresponding obligations on the other – with a voluntary moral bond that unifies the very people whom economic interests hold apart. Liberal practices of charity, then, do not derive from legal duty, but from a moral imperative that fulfils a politically indispensable function of socialization. Charitable practices create a social tie between rich and poor, givers and takers, and replace an antagonistic relationship with a reciprocal bond. The lack of a legal anchor possesses further significance, too: if poverty is a moral disposition, then charitable practice must not be institutionally fixed; charity contains the principle of its own suspension: it must not guarantee services but should make itself unnecessary. In other words, charity must not be a right – otherwise, the poor cannot become full legal subjects again.[17]

### Work and Poverty

The liberal objectivation of behaviour in terms of responsibility rests on an important epistemological precondition: establishing a strict, practical connection between work and poverty. Assigning poverty to the individual is closely tied to an economic doctrine that assimilates poverty to work: if individual misconduct alone leads to being poor, then, conversely, wanting to work must necessarily represent the way out. The strategy of moralization can only function inasmuch as it forges a negative bond between poverty and work.

Studies by Giovanna Procacci and Jacques Donzelot point to the historical failure of such a conception. A central paradox defines the liberal treatment of poverty: liberalism must presuppose poverty in the same measure that it claims to wish to abolish it. Poverty simultaneously serves as the basis of, and motor for, moral and economic progress that pretends to aim at making it disappear.[18]

---

15. Ibid., 57.
16. Ibid., 57.
17. Ibid., 70–9.
18. Procacci, 'Social Economy and the Government of Poverty' (1991), 154–5. François Ewald points out a second paradox. On the one hand, liberalism recognizes

From the liberal perspective, poverty results from a lack of willingness to work. As such, it cannot find a basis for any right to support. Indeed, any social policy seeking to elevate the standard of living for poor segments of the population proves unthinkable, since this would mean keeping the poor from doing what would eliminate their poverty: working. Moreover, legislating social policy is not only wrong in economic terms; it is also immoral, since it leaves the poor in a state of dependency instead of eliminating poverty itself.

At the same time, poverty must not simply disappear, since it performs a key function within liberal governmentality and possesses economic and moral significance.

Poverty is *economically* necessary. Instead of representing a space beyond economic calculation, it is built into the metabolism of production. The variously adumbrated distinctions between 'real' and 'false' poverty make it possible to integrate the poor who are fit for work into the labour market and thereby ensure a cheap workforce. And poverty is economical in a direct sense, too: it provides the counterpart of, and basis for, the 'wealth of nations' – the precondition and vector of economic prosperity. Poverty names unsatisfied – indeed, as yet unknown – needs, and it symbolizes a market without frontiers.

Poverty is also *morally* indispensable: its role is to serve the 'pedagogy of freedom' and constantly illustrate what the wrong use of liberty entails. As the stigma of moral error, poverty must remain present in order to mobilize people's better qualities. As such, it performs an important economic function and, at the same time, serves to encourage moral perfection.[19]

Thus, the view of poverty is not to be separated from the strategic significance of work within the overall problematic of liberalism. Not only does it have a negative connection to poverty, it also has a constitutive relationship with wealth, functioning as a hinge between them. Work represents the magic key for solving the problem of poverty.

---

the absolute necessity of support practices and makes them an important component of its politics of security. On the other hand, it must refrain from fixing these practices (legally), organizing them instead around the principle of voluntariness and subordinating them to the ultimate goal of suspending them altogether. 'The practical paradox of liberalism is that, because of its objectivation of freedom, it deprives itself of the instruments that it needs most for its own self-preservation'. Ewald, *Histoire De L'Etat Providence* (1986a), 79.

19. Procacci, *Gouverner la misère* (1993), 41–64.

Work and wealth form a progressive circle; each one points to the other, and they reinforce each other mutually. In this light, the solution to the problem of poverty involves eliminating all obstacles preventing access to a free labour market, such that the impoverished population may be integrated into the cycle of production and all members of society come to be property owners.[20]

That said, nineteenth-century events showed that such trust in the wonders of work was unwarranted. Liberalism's promise to dissolve poverty into work did not go into fulfilment. Not only did industrial capitalism and the free market not absorb old forms of poverty, they created new, hitherto unknown forms of impoverishment, different in intensity, scope and distribution. 'Pauperism' – mass poverty – took the place of poverty as an individual destiny. Working proved unable to realize the hopes placed in it; it did not function as a general principle of order, but became a factor of disorder. Instead of solving the question of poverty, the liberal coupling of poverty and work itself turned into a problem.[21]

This problem was not just a matter of the gap between formal equality and material inequality, that is, the difference between legal and social reality. The difficulty did not follow from the inequality of the poor so much as their equality. The economic and political rules of the liberal regime turned the poor into a new kind of subject – one that could not be dealt with through old-fashioned paternalism or exclusion from society. These morally and legally autonomous subjects could not be managed by either patriarchal or repressive means: although poor, they were equals among equals. This combination of politico-legal equality and economic inequality could only function so long as the latter could still be viewed as the result of individual behaviour and on the basis of theoretical equality.[22]

---

20. Ibid., 117–31.

21. Grimm, *Recht und Staat in der bürgerlichen Gesellschaft* (1987), 142: 'Counter to the premises of liberalism, this misery could not be blamed on individuals, but in part represented the predictable consequence of political decisions, in part the result of unpredictable social developments and, as such, proved relevant to matters of political and constitutional law.' Hegel is a particularly astute analyst of this problem and the meaning it holds for the dynamics of bourgeois societies: 'Against nature man can claim no right, but once society is established, poverty immediately takes the form of a wrong done to one class by another. The important question of how poverty is to be abolished is one of the most disturbing problems which agitate modern society.' Hegel, *Hegel's Philosophy of Right* (1967), 277–8.

22. Procacci, *Gouverner la misère* (1993), 65–101; Procacci, 'Governing Poverty: Sources of the Social Question in Nineteenth-Century France' (1994), 210–11.

Mass impoverishment led such an equation to fall apart more and more. If the close connection between poverty and work was constitutive for liberal thinking, yet the free labour market proved incapable of eliminating poverty – and, indeed, brought forth more of it – then a problem already held on the level of formal equality: inasmuch as work serves as a mechanism for absorbing poverty, what is more self-evident than calling for a right to work in order to get rid of poverty once and for all? Yet such a right contradicts the right to ownership (of the means of production). It demands, for its material implementation, that the state intervene. In other words, it brings forth the very danger that liberalism means to counter in the first place.[23]

In the course of the nineteenth century, the close bond between poverty and work, which once had defined the liberal art of government, underwent relativization again and again. To counter revolutionary demands that society be radically reorganized, it was urgent to separate the question of poverty from legal demands for work and to view things in a manner that avoided reference to politics and economy. The original, economico-legal interpretation of the connection between poverty and work was modified by working

---

23. Donzelot, *L'invention du social* (1984), 33–49. 'The difficulty came less from the inequality of the poor so blatantly showed than from their *being equal* to everyone else, despite their destitution. Already at the formal level of equality the impossibility of excluding the poor was contradicting the universal character of liberalism's egalitarian foundations. Moreover, a free labor market proved incapable of actually reabsorbing poverty and hence was no solution. On the one hand, a duty of assistance accomplished through the provision of employment would have called upon the state to intervene in the labor market as an economic agent, contrary to the liberal aversion to any political interference with economic processes. On the other hand, to acknowledge a subjective right to work would have put the state in the position of being considered responsible for the material means of livelihood, reinforcing its political dependence upon popular consent. The link between poverty and labor, self-evident for liberal theory, actually heightened the political intensity of the social question'. Procacci, 'Governing Poverty: Sources of the Social Question in Nineteenth-Century France' (1994), 211.

Jacques Donzelot illustrates the problem on the basis of historical confrontations concerning the right to work and the institution of 'national workshops' after the 1848 revolution. In 1789, the Third Estate had stood allied with the propertyless Fourth Estate in seeking limits on state interventions. But now, the latter called for reviving state services at the expense of civil liberties. Following the introduction of universal suffrage, the problem mounted, since the conflict between nominal equality and economic subjugation was more evident than ever. Donzelot, *L'invention du social* (1984), 33–49; see also Marx's analysis in 'The Eighteenth Brumaire of Louis Bonaparte' (1979), 99–197.

new elements into the equation: on the one hand, by intensifying and reformulating moral categories, and, on the other, by taking up medico-hygienic considerations. This theoretical elaboration made it possible to steer mass poverty away from the economic system. Indeed: the new line of interpretation finally managed to transform the potential for disorder and destabilization into a means of achieving order.[24]

## Social Economy and Paternalism

Liberal security politics remained indebted to the calculus of responsibility until the end of the 1800s, but political rationality about managing poverty had already changed during the first half of the nineteenth century. The studies by Foucault's associates discussed in the following concentrate on two elements that signalled a corrective and complement to the strategy of classic liberalism: social economy and paternalism.[25]

The emergence of mass poverty following broad-scale migration from the countryside and industrialization gave rise to *social economy*, in contradistinction to political economy. During the early nineteenth century, Malthus in Great Britain and Sismondi in France had already responded to political economy's manifest failure to explain how

---

24. Donzelot, *The Policing of Families* (1979), 53–8; Procacci, *Gouverner la misère* (1993), 201–6; Procacci, 'Governing Poverty: Sources of the Social Question in Nineteenth-Century France' (1994), 211. Much as Giovanna Procacci has done apropos of the 'social question' in France, Mitchell Dean has analysed the government of poverty in Great Britain along Foucauldian lines. Dean, *The Constitution of Poverty* (1991); for a synopsis, see Dean, 'A Genealogy of the Government of Poverty' (1992).

25. Jacques Donzelot also examines philanthropy as a liberal strategy that counters calls for the right to work or state support with even tougher moralization. It sets up a 'calculated distance' between state functions and welfare services, thereby 'turning the question of political right into a question of economic morality: since there is no legally constituted social hierarchy, since the state is no longer the apex of a pyramid of feudal oppressions, and since we are all formally equal where it is concerned, you cannot rightfully demand that it take charge of your welfare, but neither do you have any grounds for refusing our advice, for it is different from the orders you once obeyed. Rather than a right to assistance from the state, whose increased role would disturb the workings of a society freed from its shackles – the main impediment being the state itself – we will give you the means to be self-sufficient by teaching you the virtues of saving; and for our part, we are at least entitled to a disapproving scrutiny of the demands for aid that you might still put forward, since they would constitute a flagrant indication of a breach of morality'. Donzelot, *The Policing of Families* (1979), 55–6.

poverty and free markets could exist simultaneously. Social economy expanded the moral analysis of poverty's causes with a further dimension: 'milieu'. Social economy's achievement, in operative terms, is to distinguish between reasons for, and conditions of, poverty. It continues to fault the carelessness of workers, but this general disposition can meet with more or less favourable conditions; it can be augmented or lessened.[26]

That said, it was not just a matter of making additions to standing analyses. The discourse of social economy also presented a new view of the poor's recklessness: a matter of variable disposition admitting correction came to represent an immutable trait. From now on, (self-) neglect defined workers' social identity. Individual pedagogics gave way to 'social pathology'.

This shift in the objectivation of workers meant changing social security practices. If a lack of circumspection and responsibility characterizes workers in general, then charity cannot occur in passing; it must be instituted for good. At the same time, it must be assured that the institution not stand subject to political regulation or legal fixation; it should remain a 'private' matter. The liberal response to the problem is 'patronage'. Its significance lies in the break it introduces in the continuum extending from formal equality, on the one hand, to actual inequality, on the other. A symmetrical conception of rights yields to an asymmetrical order: assigning comprehensive obligations to the employer – the 'patron' – and denying the possibility of free will to employees. Radicalizing the principle of responsibility, on one end of the spectrum, corresponds to dismantling it, at the other end.

Inasmuch as they counted as 'irresponsible', workers were not equal to their employers, nor could they be. On the contrary, they required guardianship and surveillance on the part of a 'patron', whose economic potency also represented a moral value. In order to fulfil the need for security in the political sphere while meeting the call for private regulation, employers became public figures functioning as 'mainstays of authority' in the general framework of 'paternalism': bearers of a public mission that unfolds optimally when political government promotes private initiatives. In consequence, legislative and

26. Procacci, 'Social Economy and the Government of Poverty' (1991); Ewald, *Histoire De L'Etat Providence* (1986a), 90–3; on 'milieu', see lecture, 11 January 1978, Foucault, 2004a, *Security, Territory, Population* [2007], 22–3.

juridical authority shifted, blurring the traditional liberal distinction between the social-private and the state-public spheres. The dividing line between public and private interest vanished. Under paternalism, economy and politics fused; as a result, the politics of social security met up with the core problem of economics: production.[27]

According to François Ewald, patronage's 'politics of production' managed human beings on the industrial model.[28] Such practices displayed two complementary aspects. First, the insecure position of employees was exploited to ensure their dependency (through workers' colonies, childcare, savings banks, and so on). Second, it was not enough for workers to be tied to the company: they had to be made productive (through education, discipline, instilling good habits, and so on). In other words, the institution of patronage combined the demands of the economy and political domination in a technology that made both terms reinforce each other. Its politics of security aimed at exploitation and subjugation simultaneously. The task was to transform an abstract wage-relation into a concrete, individualized form that would reinforce the standing political and economic order.[29]

The patronage economy points to a philosophy of social distinction and hierarchy miles apart from classical liberalism. The employer must ensure the reproduction of the workforce as a race – instead of promoting workers' emancipation through savings and property (however modest). This heralds a change in the programme of security politics, too. It is no longer an individual matter, but the duty of one class towards another. Class division becomes an elementary component of liberal government. Charity, which once obeyed the law of

---

27. Donzelot, *L'invention du social* (1984), 157–77; Ewald, *Histoire De L'Etat Providence* (1986a), 109–21; Gordon, 'Governmental Rationality: An Introduction' (1991), 25–7.

28. Ewald formulates the central problem as follows: 'How is it possible to develop industry without revolutionary consequences? Patronage must grapple with the difficulty of turning industry against itself, in a sense, and stabilizing a mobile element'. Ewald, *Histoire De L'Etat Providence* (1986a), 129; see also Foucault, 1977g, 'The Eye of Power' [2008], 9–10; Foucault, 1977m, 'The Confession of the Flesh' [1980], 202–3.

29. Ewald, *Histoire De L'Etat Providence* (1986a), 150–70. For this reason, relations between 'patron' and workers elude the regulatory mode of law: 'The idea of reciprocal rights between *patron* and employee is replaced by the notion of a moral bond, which is defined by a relationship of dependency, subordination, and guardianship'. Ibid., 161.

brotherhood, now follows a logic of interdependence; in the process, the formation of classes becomes an important part of liberalism's strategy for security. If the events of 1848 and 1871 exposed the danger of the undisciplined and pauperized urban classes, then integrating the working class into the political body and the emergence of a 'proletariat' represented an essential element of class struggle on the part of the bourgeoisie.[30]

Constituting class in this way required a central line of division within the spectrum of those without property, separating an economically determined proletariat from a socially determined *plebs*. According to Giovanna Procacci, social economy 'invented' a new social figure: the 'pauper'. In this discursive context, pauperism is not defined by economic categories; it does not refer to a certain level or intensity of poverty so much as a form of destitution that poses a social danger. Pauperism names the spectrum of the mob, a collective and mainly urban phenomenon: an element of the population threatening it from within – calling forth a sense of fluidity, indeterminacy and so on. In this manner, social economy managed to distinguish between pauperism and poverty. The separation enabled the elimination of the former to be the corollary of preserving the latter.

From this perspective, poverty represents a social fact of capitalist, industrial society, whereas pauperism represents a hyper-natural form of life that is ultimately primitive. The logic may be summed up as follows:

> On the basis of an analysis of the instinctive antisocial tendencies of the individual, society comes to be presented as inevitable restraint: freedom and equality, innate tendencies which can find expression in their pure state only in 'savage' society, and there encounter only natural limits and obstacles, are unavoidably frustrated and repressed in civilized society. … Thus, if it is true that humanity is spontaneously social, this means that it tends instinctively towards an uncivilized society based on natural appetites.[31]

---

30. Donzelot, *The Policing of Families* (1979), 58–70; Defert, '"Popular Life" and Insurance Technology' (1991).

31. Procacci, 'Social Economy and the Government of Poverty' (1991), 159–60.

For social economy, the ever-present danger that the social bond will dissolve and lead back to the state of nature is especially present in classes where poverty, ignorance and isolation prevail. All the same, poverty must not disappear: inborn tendencies should not be repressed, for they are the precondition for producing wealth; instead, they should be channelled and pacified by means of a 'social regime'. The concept of pauperism does not aim at eliminating inequality, but at eliminating difference. Pauperism is 'dangerous' because it represents ways of living that do not fit into the project of socialization. The centrepiece of this strategy involves creating a subject different from the productive and economic subject: a subject aware of his or her duties and responsibilities, a civil (*bürgerliches*) and political subject. It does not mean combating poverty – which bears the stigma of inequality – but pauperism: a complex of behavioural characteristics underscoring social differences.[32]

In the discourse of social economy, pauperism does not arise from an economic structure, but a moral disposition. The strategy is to define poverty as 'the fault of the poor', which makes it possible to moralize society as a whole by means of techniques for managing poverty. In consequence, the problem of inequality in a society of equals is depoliticized: inequality no longer results from a different use of liberty; instead, it represents a difference in sociability. This strategy aims to depoliticize conflict by establishing a 'normal' relationship between wealth and poverty.[33]

---

32. Procacci, *Gouverner la misère* (1993), 161–99; Procacci, 'Social Economy and the Government of Poverty' (1991), 156–64.

33. Procacci, *Gouverner la misère* (1993), 207–25; Procacci, 'Governing Poverty: Sources of the Social Question in Nineteenth-Century France' (1994), 212. Although Robert Castel came to focus on the 'metamorphoses of the social question' from the Middle Ages to the present (see Castel, *From Manual Workers to Wage Laborers* (2003)) his earlier works addressed the 'government of madness' more than the government of poverty. At any rate, both perspectives are closely connected: Castel shows how, in a 'contractual society' predicated on individuals' rational use of freedom, the 'unreasonable subject' poses a problem that must be managed and administrated. The 'solution', by his account, involves a specific body of knowledge – psychiatry – which amounts to a medico-juridico system for treating the 'mad' and guaranteeing that the 'normal' are, in fact, normal. Castel, *The Regulation of Madness: The Origins of Incarceration in France* (1988), esp. 157–80.

## The Birth of Security Society

When early liberalism sought to define the category of responsibility, the strict separation between law and morality played a role that was just as important as the principle of regulating social processes. Although paternalism made far-reaching changes to classically liberal designs and introduced a central asymmetry to the relationship between employers and employees, it still rested on the principle of responsibility and the distinction between law and morality. In the second half of the nineteenth century, a development occurred that broke fundamentally with such preconditions.

Over the course of the nineteenth century, liberalism's constitutive distinction between law and morality was abandoned time and again. Hereby, the nature of the law and rights also changed. Law became normative: it no longer made prohibitions, but prescribed what should be done. It incorporated more and more ideas that had been developed in the context of the human sciences; conversely, the norms of the human sciences acquired a legal character.[34] Law was no longer limited to averting danger and providing protection in order to coordinate and secure individual liberties; it became social in nature, suspending the notion of individual responsibility and legal accountability – which now were replaced with 'social responsibility'. Legal claims and moral determinations of guilt came to be voiced less against individuals than directed towards 'society as a whole'. The mode of regulation switched from the principle of individual responsibility to that of social risk.

At the beginning of the nineteenth century, 'accountability' and 'guilt' had formed the central elements of a well-ordered and harmonious society. In turn, the rise of industrial capitalism and its economic and social consequences challenged the idea of collective regulation via the principle of individual responsibility. The renunciation of classically liberal theory seemed to imply that a socialist-revolutionary solution was a viable option – or at least that state intervention in economic processes should occur. Such a course was precisely what bourgeois-conservative forces wanted to avoid.[35]

---

34. Foucault, 1977f, '14 January 1976' [2003], 37–40; for the change in penal law, see Foucault, 1975a, *Discipline and Punish* [1995], 17–23.

35. Donzelot, *L'invention du social* (1984), 67–72.

The way out of this dilemma – as François Ewald and Daniel Defert have shown – involved applying a technology, initially developed and tested in the private sector, to the regulation of society: *insurance technology*. Breaking with both the legal category and the principle of responsibility, it opened a path beyond the dead end of antagonism between individual and state. The insurance system replaced the confrontational, legal claims of particulars with a social bond tying everyone together. It did not address determinate social classes, but the continuum of a population varying in levels of risk according to age, sex, profession and the like. Such risks do not constitute class borders so much as they overlap with them. Instead of placing labour and capital in opposition, insurance protects both groups. As such, insurance technology does not represent the first step towards socialism so much as it guards against it: 'Social insurance is also an insurance against revolutions'.[36]

## The Politics of Accidents

In light of the problem posed by industrial accidents, François Ewald has examined how the dispositive of responsibility was rearranged along lines of social risk. The accident has a function similar to poverty for liberal rationality. Both represent natural misfortunes that form an indispensable component of the liberal universe. Like poverty, the accident – which is possible anywhere and at any time – symbolizes the principle of equality. Inasmuch as it necessitates preventive measures, it serves as a motor for individual perfection and moral progress. According to liberal logic, accidents justify claims for support just as

---

36. Ewald, 'Insurance and Risk' (1991a), 209; Defert, '"Popular Life" and Insurance Technology' (1991); Ewald, *Histoire De L'Etat Providence* (1986a), 171–219. In his 'genealogy of the insurance system', Daniel Defert shows how insurance represents a political technology with two key strategic functions. First, it serves the accumulation of wealth by integrating uncertainty and chance into capitalist circulation as items of value. Second, it makes it possible to replace traditional forms of worker solidarity with an anonymous mechanism that binds workers to society (not each other): 'Between the alternatives of arbitrary private benevolent patronage and obligatory state responsibility, insurance offers a space of regulated freedom. In this sense it offers a gain for the rich who insure their life and goods [...]. For the less fortunate, however, insurance is long able only to offer insurance of their health, hence achieving the *tour de force* of driving them to work and save in order to insure against the loss of a health they do not even possess'. Defert, '"Popular Life" and Insurance Technology' (1991), 231–2.

little as poverty does; instead, they represent a possibility that must always be taken into account, against which provisions are to be made. As an event, the accident cannot be blamed on anyone; thus, damages may be demanded only in the case of manifest guilt. From this perspective, accidents and poverty are matters of individual fate and not social phenomena.[37]

That said, this mechanism for evaluating and assigning guilt proved problematic when a certain type of accident occurred. The reality of industrial accidents made the limitations of individual responsibility clearer than ever. Liberal thinking had been certain that guilty action represents the exception; in contrafactual terms, accidents do not happen when individual, rational actions occur. As industrialization proceeded, however, it became clear that industrial societies cause accidents as a rule: harm results from everyday operations, not just from instances of malfunction. This circumstance led to a problem within liberal law: social misfortunes justifiably called for financial damages, yet no one could be blamed, strictly speaking. Individual accountability was the precondition of, and basis for, liability, since no material compensation could be made without individual fault. But industrial accidents are not defined by a subjective quality; on the contrary, they display a particular 'objectivity' in two respects:

1. The first lies in the *regular nature of modern accidents*. Industrial accidents are not exceptional events so much as normal occurrences, and they follow statistical patterns. They are defined not by being unusual, but by their empirical regularity.

2. The other trait of industrial accidents is that they are a *product of life in community* – more the result of human interdependency than the consequence of interactions between people and machines. Industrial accidents are the 'price of progress': what regularly happens in activities that ultimately redound to universal benefit.[38]

In light of the 'objective quality' of industrial accidents, subjective accountability increasingly came to count as inadequate. The interdependency of actions escaping individual volition moved to the fore. Whereas liberal logic had been based on personal liability – for better

37. Ewald, *Histoire De L'Etat Providence* (1986a), 23–4.
38. Ibid., 16–18, 89–90.

or worse – the second half of the nineteenth century witnessed the rise of a perspective that invalidated this position by focusing on social distribution. Society and its obligations – and not the individual and personal responsibility – became the point of reference. The matter concerned the distribution of goods and ills following a distinct mode of rationality that derived neither from human misconduct nor from natural coincidence (or divine providence).

This social logic meant completely rearranging the liberal conception of justice – which held that natural distribution is just *per se*. The liberal idea of natural justice is closely tied to the principle of individual responsibility; as such, there is no need for socio-legal correctives. But inasmuch as individual responsibility is suspended, natural justice proves obsolete. In the liberal world, inequalities admitted justification – if only to the extent that the wealthy had acquired their possessions individually and the poor bore personal responsibility for their condition. But when the distribution of ills came to be viewed in relative independence from the good or bad behaviour of particulars and now appeared to follow social patterns, the liberal principle of justice posed a problem:

> At the beginning of the nineteenth century, nature had still served as the point of reference for the question of justice: the 'natural' arrangement of goods and ills counted as just. There was nothing to correct, except in a case that counted as unusual: namely, when misfortune suffered by one person was occasioned by the fault of another. But now, justice does not appeal to nature so much as society: it is objectivated as a fact; as the totality of collective goods, it provides the basis for distributing these same goods among individuals. Law becomes social and corrective: the task is to reestablish balances that have been troubled, to reduce inequalities in the distribution of social burdens. The concept of *risk* – which expresses the singular reality of an ill prevailing independent of individual conduct, in keeping with 'the way things are' – and, more generally, the technology of *insurance* makes it possible to conceive and organize this new challenge in juridical terms.[39]

---

39. Ibid., 19; see also Ewald, 'Insurance and Risk' (1991a).

## Insurance Technology

Insurance technology proceeds by devaluating the principle of individual responsibility and transforming the law at a profound level. As Ewald shows, legal mechanisms are increasingly 'colonized' by a calculus of risk that works with other criteria of regulation and evaluation; as such, it implements a different mode of individualization.

'Juridical reason' starts with the reality of accidents and seeks, in turn, to determine their cause. It aims to uncover (potentially) guilty conduct – which provides the sole basis for compensating damages. Calculus based on the notion of responsibility necessarily presumes that no accident would have happened without culpable behaviour. Juridical reason proceeds in keeping with a moral view of the world that represents the other side of the liberal model of harmony: the judge assumes there would not have been an accident, if those involved had not acted as they did – that the world would be orderly, if only human beings acted as they should.

In contrast, 'insurantial reason' adopts an entirely different outlook based on determination, and nothing else. Instead of starting out with a contrafactual assumption, it considers the facticity of events. The index is not subjective will, but objective probability: whatever we might wish, a precisely calculable number of workplace injuries, traffic accidents, deaths and illnesses occur annually, and these figures are repeated with remarkable regularity year on year. For juridical reason, the accident represents the exception in a world that counts as fundamentally harmonious. Insurance shows that the exception obeys a fixed rule and identifies empirical patterns.

By the same token, the difference between law and insurance is evident in the different forms of individualization they advance. The juridical scheme of responsibility sets the accident at a remove and separates victims from perpetrators. The accident involves two persons: it is a matter of one party's fault vis-à-vis another. Insurance works with a wholly different scheme – one that does not involve confrontation with another individual but reciprocity in a collective. Members of an insurance society represent risk factors for each other: they pose dangers for others and, at the same time, stand exposed to the dangers that others pose. But for all that, the general principle of risk does not mean that every person is exposed to – or poses – the same risk. Disregarding concrete persons, insurance individualizes risk. It is no longer oriented on an abstract norm, but on the whole of the population: average individuality, on the basis of which concrete individual risks admit calculation. The contract of sovereignty, which is legally defined, stands opposed to the contract of insurance, which replaces legal categories with an index of social interdependency.[40]

The precondition for setting aside the law and discovering society as a specific object with its own, distinct rules was the emergence of a new form of knowledge: *sociology*.

## Sociological Knowledge

Sociology objectivates society on the basis of principles fundamentally different from liberal ideas. Whereas liberals understood society as a (voluntary) association of individuals – with the whole comprising the sum of its parts, to which it can always be boiled down – society now comes to represent a reality 'independent' of its components. Sociological objectivation inverts the liberal relationship between sum and parts: society is not the association of individual subjects, but a subject itself. It is characterized by its own laws and patterns that impose themselves on individuals as a matter of alien and external fact.

The sociological objectivation of society provides two decisive elements to insurance technology: the constancy of probabilities and the concept of solidarity.[41]

## The Constancy of Probabilities

Ewald reconstructs an important epistemological break that occurred in the human sciences during the nineteenth century. In the early 1800s, the idea still prevailed that human affairs follow universal laws.

---

40. Ewald, *Histoire De L'Etat Providence* (1986a), 175–9.

41. François Ewald's study of insurance technology explores the significance of probability calculations and their role in sociology, which tends to invalidate legal codes. In contrast, Jacques Donzelot's work focuses on the difference between sovereignty and solidarity, especially how conflicts come to be 'depoliticized' as the axis shifts from political rights to social duties. In either case, however, the underlying premise is that sociological knowledge plays a strategic role in the development of such concepts and technologies. In addition, both authors consider that probability calculus and the notion of solidarity serve to defuse conflicts between politics and economy, individual and state, by establishing a 'neutral' space that Donzelot calls 'the social' and Ewald 'insurance society'. Donzelot, *L'invention du social* (1984), 72; Ewald, *Histoire De L'Etat Providence* (1986a), 23; Ewald, 'Bio-Power' (1986b).

Irregularities in the social cosmos counted as exceptions to a general rule, the result of disruptions. Newtonian physics provided the model for the human sciences, and investigations of human phenomena employed methods borrowed from the natural sciences.

Adolphe Quetelet established his 'social physics' to demonstrate continuity between nature and society. He did so by linking statistics with *probability calculation*. Statistics had defined the population as a sum of individuals – a passive complex possessing no traits as such. Against this backdrop, probability permitted an entirely new conception of the relations between the whole and its parts, offering a way out from the dead end of the state and individual by means of a new logic different from both political rights and economic interests.[42]

Ewald enlists Quetelet's studies to trace the emergence of a new method of investigation. Although the object of 'social physics' is still the human being, an epistemological shift occurs in order to examine the individual, now approached by way of a 'detour'. For Quetelet, the individual comes into view only in light of the mass: one must understand people in vast numbers in order to know them individually. The art of probability calculus plays out non-knowledge against itself, thereby making it the basis for analysis. In this framework, 'law' and 'cause' no longer designate objective or effective laws in the Newtonian sense; instead, they stand for empirical regularity: probabilities, tendencies and inclinations.[43]

Probabilistic logic breaks with all notions of substance. Quetelet posits an 'average human being', but no corresponding individual

---

42. Ian Hacking has offered a historical account of the universal application of statistics and probability calculus over the course of the nineteenth century, discussing broad-scale surveys, the beginning of quantitative analysis and so on. That said, the issue does not concern only internal changes within systems of knowledge but also the emergence of a new form of power-knowledge: 'One name for statistics, especially in France, had been "moral science": the science of deviancy, of criminals' court convictions, suicides, prostitution, divorce'. Hacking, 'How Should We Do the History of Statistics?' (1991), 182. Hacking's thesis – and herein lies its relevance for examining liberal government – is that the new conception of science based on calculating probability meant breaking with the old model of causation: 'Although determinism had been eroded, it was not by creating some new place for freedom, indeed we might say that the central fact is the *taming of chance*; where in 1800 chance had been nothing real, at the end of the century it was something "real" precisely because one had found the form of laws that were to govern chance'. Ibid., 185; also, Hacking, *The Taming of Chance* (1990).

43. Ewald, *Histoire De L'Etat Providence* (1986a), 147–61.

actually exists; instead, the term refers to the type of person encountered in society. 'He' is not a model – the original – whose more or less exact copies are actual human beings, but the latters' shared point of reference. Quetelet offers an objectivating scheme that does away with all metaphysical references to abiding human nature; instead, his definition proceeds from the immanence of 'man's' social existence. This mode of analysis does not start from individual specimens, but from the group to which they belong. Sociology is an instrument for understanding a given population in terms of intrinsic features instead of external factors.[44]

The sociological mode of objectivation means that 'human being' no longer counts as a universal; instead of looking for a totality of qualities to be found in everyone, its definition holds in terms of social existence. The theory of the average human being offers a way to understand the register of identities and inequalities on the basis of real differences. At the same time, it shows how a collective identity is possible despite – indeed, through – these same differences. Sociology extracts a principle of cohesion from social divisions by replacing the antagonistic language of law with the homogeneous discourse of statistics.[45]

## Sovereignty and Solidarity

As Jacques Donzelot has shown, the incorporation of statistics and probability into examinations of social realities was not the only blow dealt to the sovereignty of the law. A second front opened, too. By the end of the nineteenth century, the concept of *solidarity* had spread far and wide. Especially thanks to the works of Émile Durkheim, its foremost theorist, it implicitly subjected to critique the validity of legal categories for analysing social phenomena.

In the course of the nineteenth century, the juridico-political conception of (popular) sovereignty – once thought to offer the key to solving political and social ills – came to pose more and more of a problem. Questions arose about the declared sovereignty of citizens at the polls and their factual subjugation in the factories. The idea of sovereignty did not constitute a factor of order, or a principle of

---

44. Ibid., 152–8.
45. Ibid., 166–9; Donzelot, 'The Mobilization of Society' (1982), 173.

coherence, so much as it produced division. On the one hand, the matter involved fears of despotism no longer based on a monarch's whims but on those of the people – a tyranny of the majority. On the other, the notion of sovereignty extended an invitation to reclaim a form of rule that the 'bourgeois' republic had betrayed by excluding the economic sphere from processes of political will-formation. Under these conditions, the decisive question was the principle for steering governmental activity: what the state's contribution should be, and where its borders lie.[46]

According to Donzelot, the 'theory of solidarity' provided an answer. He situates it in a field of tension with a liberal-conservative pole at one end and a revolutionary-Marxist pole at the other. Steering clear of rival alternatives – revolutionary fraternity or liberal charity – the 'theory of solidarity' that Durkheim presents in *La Division du travail social* points to a third way; in this framework, the individual is neither the starting point for society nor positioned against it. This theory offers the strategic 'advantage' of substituting 'mute' social constraint for 'talkative' political voluntarism. As such, society neither represents the product of free will, nor is it constituted by originary and natural associations. Society is not an institution serving the interest of particulars, nor can it be. Instead, society is a material state, where the prevailing patterns and rules always already exceed individual horizons inasmuch as they concern the lives of all its members.

For Durkheim, society defies instrumentalization because it follows its own laws. From the inception, its elementary forms have developed to yield increasingly ramified divisions of labour and complex modes of action. But in the process, social cohesion does not diminish; it switches from one form of solidarity to another. Underneath – if not counter to – legal contracts, mutual dependence grows as society evolves. Accordingly, 'organic solidarity' proves something more basic than formal arrangements between members of society; the law represents a derivative category. In brief: the fundamental law of society is not legal in nature; not sovereignty, but solidarity constitutes the social.[47]

The concept of solidarity made it possible to replace calls for sovereignty with belief in progress; indeed, sovereignty is not only dangerous,

---

46. Donzelot, *L'invention du social* (1984), 49–76.
47. Ibid., 76–86.

but illusory inasmuch as it fails to account for the many-layered reality of social relations. As such, the sphere where sovereignty applies and intervenes had to be restricted. To preserve society from the dead end of sovereign whims, choosing rulers must be separated from governmental practices. Political sovereignty was redefined strictly in terms of selecting those who would hold power; concrete governance turned into a technical affair limited to questions about the means for achieving social advances.[48]

Simultaneously, the notion of solidarity has the merit of specifying the need for, and limits of, the state. It provides criteria that are compatible with a democratic definition of the state and, at the same time, resolves the grievous ambiguities of the sovereignty concept on which both liberal and socialist solutions rely. On the one hand, solidarity founds the social role of the state; on the other, it imposes limits on intervention by obligating it to respect individual liberties and initiatives, which are necessary for overall social progress. As such, solidarity is not the first step towards socialism, but the best means to avoid the subversive reorganization of society.[49]

---

48. Accordingly, Donzelot treats the concept of solidarity not as a 'scientific discovery' but as a 'strategic invention'. Ibid., 77. In his reading, Durkheim's work provides scientific justification for republicanism, formulates its legitimate political goals, and defines the role of the state: 'This analysis introduces an art of government in terms of "neither too much nor too little" and advocates regulating the social bond instead of clinging rigidly to social structures or changing them arbitrarily'. Ibid., 84–5.

49. Ibid., 12–14, 125–34; Donzelot, 'The Mobilization of Society' (1982), 169–74. Donzelot explores the further evolution of solidarity in Maurice Haurious's 'institutional doctrine', Léon Duguit's notion of *service public* and Léon Bourgeois's theory of *solidarism*. The importance of these developments involves a principle of articulation connecting rights and obligations, the state's authority, and its subordination to the demands of society. 'Solidarism' does not take rights as its point of departure, but duties. From the inception, human beings are debtors vis-à-vis society. The latter is defined by the division of labour; if members accept the advantages it provides, they must also accept the duties it imposes. Indeed, duties precede rights. Social obligations constitute society; defining the limits of particular interests, they replace law as the basis for life in community. As opposed to laws, duties express belonging and interdependency. They do not separate people from each other, but tie individuals to each other and invalidate abstract oppositions between subjects and the state. This changes the rules of the game: society is no longer based on the rights of particulars, but is constituted through mutual responsibilities. Donzelot, *L'invention du social* (1984), 86–120; see also Procacci, 'Notes on the Government of the Social' (1987), 15; Procacci, 'Governing Poverty: Sources of the Social Question in Nineteenth-Century France' (1994), 215–16.

## The Defence of Society

Studies of 'insurance society' make the theoretical profile of an ala-
lytics of government clear. The social is not to be viewed only in legal
or military categories. Contractual relations do not constitute it, nor
does it represent the fragile and constantly imperilled result of warlike
confrontations. Rather, the 'invention of the social' goes along with
the emergence of new regulatory techniques. According to the works
discussed here, modes of analysis limited to taking note of 'crises' and
'contradictions' and/or viewing the social state in terms of expanded
rights do not go far enough.

First, whether the establishment of social rights represents a crisis
of classic liberal governmentality or stands in opposition to it, 'society'
constitutes itself in spite – if not, in fact, by way – of such crisis and
contradiction. On the one hand, one may rightly speak of the social
state as the 'victory' of the working class. Still, it is not enough to view
social measures and their legal consolidation simply as the result of
political *struggles*, for the former also change the conditions and stakes
of the latter:

> The point is not to deny any connection between these measures and
> political struggles, but to detect what there is about them that cannot
> simply be traced back to the simple logic of collision, victory or defeat
> – to find out what, specifically, these measures introduce to the field
> of social relations.[50]

---

50. Donzelot, 'La misère de la culture politique' (1978), 580; see also Donzelot,
*The Policing of Families* (1979), 8; Ewald, *Histoire De L'Etat Providence* (1986a), 31–2;
Ewald, 'Risk, Insurance, Society' (1987), 6. Accordingly, Donzelot presents the social
as an 'effective fiction' related to two other fictions: the individual and class struggle.
Donzelot, *L'invention du social* (1984), 77. Ibid., 151: 'social legislation undermined
the military form of power that the employer had enlisted in the name of full and absolute responsibility within his own realm. But would this inevitably lead to his ruin by
eliminating, along with his discretionary might, the sources of liberal economy, as the
paternalist school prophesied? One might rather say that it liberated him by affording
the possibility of instituting a different way of managing labor, freeing him from the
constant demands of supervising and punishing the refractory working class; now,
he could enter a contract with this class, which was less poisonous and defined by
increasing productivity, instead.' Likewise, Giovanna Procacci points out that it is not
a matter of veiling the political character of events, but of showing – counter to sociological and historical functionalism – that the political does not consist of conflictual
oppositions (state–individual, proletariat–bourgeoisie and so on); instead, the task

The social state represents the result of social struggles, yet its strategic significance extends in the opposite direction: an active 'politics of depoliticization' which is supposed to make these very struggles unnecessary. The social does not stand as the product or instrument of the political so much as it entails a complete change of this sphere. In historical terms, the emergence of the social proceeded as the gradual subsumption of the political, silencing the struggles here – rubrics such as 'victory' or 'defeat' came to seem increasingly inadequate.

Second, by the same token, social insurance does not concern a simple, quantitative increase of *rights* – adding new (social) rights to old (liberal) rights. François Ewald, in particular, has demonstrated that the order of social rights changed the very nature of the law:

> Liberal rationality objectivated the legal subject as freedom: the famous principle of free will. In the order of social rights, the subject becomes juridically competent by the simple fact of *being alive*. If social rights are indeterminate in principle, they can never be anything but so many expressions of a fundamental *right to life*. ... The liberal state should secure the possibility of exercising civil rights; it is supposed to demand nothing more of citizens than what is necessary for the common interest. If one can demand social rights from society, in turn society can impose forms of conduct it deems socially appropriate.[51]

Indeed, the 'government of the social' operates by institutionalizing two steps that seem incompatible yet stand in a complementary relation. The corollary of protecting the individual from society is 'defend[ing] society'[52] from the individual who threatens it. At its core, the social draws a dividing line between two forms of population and two ways of treating them: the normal on the one hand, and the abnormal on the other. Its invention cannot be separated from discovering 'perverse', 'degenerate' and 'extremist' elements whose

is to reconstruct the practices that have made such oppositions historically possible. Procacci, *Gouverner la misère* (1993), 24–30; Procacci, 'Governing Poverty: Sources of the Social Question in Nineteenth-Century France' (1994), 216–19.

51. Ewald, *Histoire De L'Etat Providence* (1986a), 24–5; see also Donzelot, *L'invention du social* (1984), 155–8.

52. Foucault, 1986, '21 January 1976' and '28 January 1976' [2003], 61.

existence depends on a norm that defines them and a rule to which they provide the exception.[53]

The 'defence of society' represents the flipside of 'insurance society', the result of a changed scheme of objectivation. Inasmuch as society no longer emerges from the lives of individuals, but stands at their source, it is a subject that must defend itself. The means for doing so is a particular kind of anthropology, which simultaneously offers a symptomatology, pathology and therapeutic method. Such 'social anthropology' no longer takes the individual subject as its reference, but society; subjects are no longer measured with regard to human nature, but by their degree of sociability – their 'second nature'. Inadequately socialized individuals not only count as unreliable and unpredictable loners, but pose a danger to the continued existence of society.[54]

## From the War of the Races to State Racism

In his 1976 lecture series, Foucault examines how politico-military discourse got transformed into a racist-biological discourse.[55] From the seventeenth century on, the model of war provided the matrix for describing the course of history and the reality of power relations. It did not take long for the expression 'race' to surface in this 'politico-historical discourse'. That said, the term did not have a fixed, biologico-social meaning yet; initially, it designated a historico-political division: the idea that society splits into warring camps: two antagonistic social groups exist and live alongside each other without having mixed, since they differ through geographical provenance,

---

53. Donzelot, 'Wiederkehr des Sozialen' (1995), 54–5.
54. Pasquino, 'Criminology: The Birth of a Special Knowledge' (1991a), 246–7. The following considers not only Foucault's works on 'defending society', but also, and especially, studies by Pasquale Pasquino and Robert Castel. Three aspects receive attention in particular: the notion of 'dangerousness', its application to individuals and social groups and the increasing significance of 'social medicine' in the nineteenth century.
55. For a reconstruction of the lectures in terms of the analysis of racism, see Magiros, *Foucaults Beitrag zur Rassismustheorie* (1995), 15–29 and Stoler, *Race and the Education of Desire* (1995), 55–94. On the problem of race and racism in Foucault's theoretical works, see Foucault, 1976a, *The History of Sexuality, Volume 1: An Introduction* [1978], 119, 149–50; Foucault, 1976k, 'Bio-history and Bio-politics' [2014]; Foucault, 1977m, 'The Confession of the Flesh' [1980], 222–6; Foucault, 1978e, 'Eugène Sue que j'aime'.

language and/or religious customs (see the section 'The War Hypothesis' in Chapter 6).

The particularity of such 'racist discourse' is to view political relations in military-martial terms alone. Accordingly, the political bond tying the two groups to each other is arbitrary; their connection is not a matter of social contract and rational encounters, but the result of military force. War – victories won or defeats suffered – structures this political unit. They constitute a whole 'because of the differences, dissymmetries, and barriers created by privileges, customs and rights, the distribution of wealth, or the way in which power is exercised'.[56] As such, this discourse of racial war must always start from a plurality of races, not a single one: one race is defined in opposition to another; antagonism constitutes it. Race theory is relational, then; the point of departure is not given biologically or socially; it represents a power relationship that provides the basis for biological or social distinctions in the first place.[57]

In the course of the nineteenth century, Foucault contends, two important 'transcriptions'[58] of 'race' and 'racism' occurred, changing a semantic field that was initially political. First, talk of the 'war of races' underwent an 'openly biological transcription'[59] that, even before Darwin, based its claims on materialist anatomy and physiology. This historico-biological race theory coded social conflicts as 'struggles for survival' and analysed them along the lines of an evolutionary scheme. The second (social) transformation was to understand the 'clash between two races' as class struggle and analyse it as a dialectic. The beginning of the nineteenth century witnessed the emergence of revolutionary speech that increasingly replaced the race defined in political terms with the theme of economico-social classes.[60]

Foucault's thesis holds that these 'reformulations' of the problematic of racial struggle – which was originally political – factored into an evolving biologico-social discourse from the end of the nineteenth century on. Such *racism* (the first time the word held the meaning it has today) enlisted elements of its biological version to formulate a response to the challenge of social revolution. What was historically

56. Foucault, 1986, '21 January 1976' and '28 January 1976' [2003], 77.
57. Ibid., 60–1, 78–80.
58. Ibid., 60.
59. Ibid., 60.
60. Ibid., 60, 78–81.

novel and theoretically innovative about such biologico-social discourse is that it turned the original idea of social war against itself:

> What we see as a polarity, as a binary rift within society, is not a clash between two distinct races. It is the splitting of a single race into a superrace and a subrace. To put it a different way, it is the reappearance, within a single race, of the past of that race. In a word, the obverse and the underside of the race reappears within it.
>
> ... The discourse of race struggle – which ... was essentially an instrument used in the struggles waged by decentred camps – will be recentred and will become the discourse of power itself. It will become the discourse of a battle that has to be waged not between races, but by a race that is portrayed as the one true race, the race that holds power and is entitled to define the norm, and against those who deviate from that norm, against those who pose a threat to the biological heritage.[61]

The problem of a plurality of races shifts to the singular of race – which is no longer threatened from without, but from within. The notion of a binary society divided into two races yields to the idea of a monistic, biological entity menaced by heterogeneous elements. At the same time, this heterogeneity no longer structures a basic line of separation running through society. Instead, it establishes distinctions that are matters of accident more than substance: 'foreigners', 'deviants', 'others' – i.e. the (side-)products of society itself – are what threaten it. Society brings forth, from within, the dangers that constantly imperil it. The process gives rise to 'a racism that society will direct against itself, against its own elements and its own products'.[62]

As the old theme of racial war evolved, it tended towards 'biologicization of the political'.[63] The historico-political theme of war – with its battles, victories and defeats – gave way to an evolutionary-biological model of the struggle for survival. It was no longer a matter of struggle

---

61. Ibid., 61.

62. Ibid., 62.

63. 'For the first time in history, no doubt, biological existence was reflected in political existence [...]. But what might be called a society's "threshold of modernity" has been reached when the life of the species is wagered on its own political strategies. For millennia, man remained what he was for Aristotle: a living animal with the additional capacity for a political existence, modern man is an animal whose politics places his existence as a living being in question'. Foucault, 1976a, *The History of Sexuality, Volume 1: An Introduction* [1978], 142–3.

in a political sense; the problematic of struggle assumed an exclusively biological meaning: the differentiation of species, survival of the fittest, preservation through adaptation, the danger of degeneration and so on.[64]

On this basis, Foucault concludes that the racism that emerged at the end of the nineteenth century did not form part of a more comprehensive strategy of domination, which might then be implemented and instrumentalized, so much as it afforded a new 'technology of power':[65]

> It is no longer: 'We have to defend ourselves against society', but 'We have to defend society against all the biological threats posed by the other race, the subrace, the counterrace that we are, despite ourselves, bringing into existence'. At this point, the racist thematic is no longer a moment in the struggle between one social group and another; it will promote the global strategy of social conservatisms.[66]

---

64. Foucault, 1986, '21 January 1976' and '28 January 1976' [2003], 61–2. Foucault considers this shift from a plurality of races to a single race to be a response to the revolutionary variant of the theme of race war. However, that does not mean that racism amounts to an ideological construct or coincidental aspect of anti-revolutionary strategy.

For one, the matter does not concern 'translating' political concepts into biological terms – veiling political discourse under scientific cover or, conversely, (re)discovering the true political dimension beneath the biologically tinged, ideological superstructure of actual social conditions. Instead, it involves constituting a certain rationality that enables a new articulation of social problems – bringing up certain themes in the first place, while making others seem inconceivable and vanish. Accordingly, the political is not simply absent in biologico-social discourse; it is itself a certain political rationality that structures fields of social action and guides political practices. Thus, Foucault does not view racism as an ideological factor, which should be handled in terms of false consciousness or mentality. Foucault, 1991, 'Society Must Be Defended' [2003], 256.

For all that, second, racism does not represent a chance element of anti-revolutionary strategy – one response among others to the revolutionary challenge. Biologico-social theory constitutes a counter-design for countering counter-history: it formulates the same goals and takes on the same forms as revolutionary discourse, except that it reverses them entirely. The project of emancipation turns into concern about the purity of the race; the prophetic-revolutionary promise turns into adherence to norms; the struggle against society and its impositions turns into 'defense of society' against biological menaces; discourse against power turns into a 'discourse of power': 'Racism is, quite literally, revolutionary discourse in an inverted form'. Foucault, 1986, '21 January 1976' and '28 January 1976' [2003], 81.

65. Foucault, 1991, 'Society Must Be Defended' [2003], 242.

66. Foucault, 1986, '21 January 1976' and '28 January 1976' [2003], 61–2.

In other words, Foucault views racism as a form of 'government of the social' – a distinct technology of government enabling a biological entity to be steered by seemingly neutral means, beyond politico-legal and economic criteria. Racism defines a political strategy of depo-liticizing and dedramatizing social conflicts by pinning them to the natural world – i.e. the laws and constraints that prevail there. Just as living in nature demands respect for certain exigencies and acknowl-edging that radical change is pointless, so too does life in society: who would presume to change the laws of nature and not come to realize that doing so leads to self-destruction?

To be sure, none of this means that a political element is missing from the analysis. However, the politics that follow abandon rigid adherence to received structures and voluntaristic impulses for seeking change. Conceiving society as a biological whole presupposes the institution of a centralized instance to steer, lead and guide it in order to guaran-tee its 'purity' – one strong enough to counter 'hostile elements' from within and without: the modern state. For Foucault, racism guides the rationality of state actions, materializes in its apparatuses and con-crete policies, and finds articulation as 'State racism'.[67] Not only does racism form a central, functional element within power relations; it comes to be the principle organizing the state. The historico-political discourse of races had concerned the state and its apparatuses, which it denounced as instruments one group used to dominate others, and the state's laws, whose partisan nature it unmasked. In contrast, the discourse of race represents a weapon in the hands of state sovereignty – which once had been the target of this same weapon:

> The theme of the counterhistory of races was … that the State was necessarily unjust. It is now inverted into its opposite: the State is no longer an instrument that one race uses against another: the State is, and must be, the protector of the integrity, the superiority, and the purity of the race. The idea of racial purity, with all its monistic, Statist, and biological implications: … racism is born at the point when the theme of racial purity replaces that of race struggle.[68]

---

67. Ibid., 62; Foucault, 1991, *'Society Must Be Defended'* [2003], 239; Foucault, 1976a, *The History of Sexuality, Volume 1: An Introduction* [1978], 54.

68. Foucault, 1986, 'Lecture 21 January 1976' and 'Lecture 28 January 1976' [2003], 81. As Etienne Balibar has observed, racism plays a 'considerable' role in Foucault's analysis of power. Balibar, 'Foucault and Marx: The Question of Nominalism' (1992),

## Dangerous Individuals and Dangerous Classes

The reorientation in civil law away from the liberal principle of responsibility towards the concept of social risk corresponds to a radical transformation of penal law. Foucault's 'hypothesis'[69] is that the insurance model for social relations gave rise to the idea of punishment, serving to 'defend society' and preserve it from the inevitable risks attending life in community. In the framework of the new penal rationality, sentencing received a new meaning. It no longer sought to punish a legal subject who had broken the law as a matter of personal initiative or to reintegrate this party into the law-abiding community; instead, it aimed at reducing, as much as possible, the risk of criminality that the individual posed and, if need be, 'neutralizing' him.[70]

Such a goal presupposes another mode of objectivating the lawbreaker. In this framework, the lawbreaker is not a universal legal subject of the law, but a human being – albeit a particular kind of human being defined by inhumanity: a 'criminal'. The criminal is not a rational entity whose life follows a course determined by free will, but a person whose psychic and moral constitution is abnormal. And because the 'criminal' is not normal, it makes no sense to look for his motives, interests or intentions. The reason for lawbreaking does not stem from (mis)calculation on the part of the perpetrator; it follows from

---

42. Nevertheless, few authors have systematically investigated this aspect of his work. Angelika Magiros examines Foucault's archaeological and genealogical studies in light of their bearing on current debates on racism (especially *The Order of Things*, the 1976 lectures and *The History of Sexuality, Volume 1*). Magiros, *Foucaults Beitrag zur Rassismustheorie* (1995). Ann L. Stoler's *Race and the Education of Desire* offers an account of the strengths and weaknesses of Foucault's analysis of racism; it also provides an excellent investigation of the complex relations between racism, sexism, nationalism and colonialism in the framework of post-colonial studies. Stoler, *Race and the Education of Desire* (1995).

69. Foucault, 1978b, 'About the Concept of the "Dangerous Individual" in 19th Century Legal Psychiatry', 15.

70. Foucault, 1978b, 'About the Concept of the "Dangerous Individual" in 19th Century Legal Psychiatry', 15–16. The correlative of insurance against 'dangerous classes' through changes in civil law and setting up 'social legislation' is transforming penal law, which now seeks to safeguard against 'dangerous individuals': 'By eliminating the element of fault within the system of liability, the civil legislators introduced into law the notion of causal probability and of risk, and they brought forward the idea of a sanction whose function would be to defend, to protect, to exert pressure on inevitable risks'. Foucault, 1978b, 'About the Concept of the "Dangerous Individual" in 19th Century Legal Psychiatry', 16.

a pathological and defective personality. *Homo criminalis* represents a new type, wholly different from the *homo penalis* of classical criminal justice.[71]

Changing the way the lawbreaker is objectivated presupposes a new organization of knowledge. Pasquale Pasquino has reconstructed this scheme by juxtaposing liberal legal theory and 'social legal theory'. Liberal penology is based on the principle of free will – a trait possessed by every legal subject. As such, it cannot constitute the object of specific knowledge ('criminology'). 'General anthropology' accounts for the deeds of *homo penalis*: 'he' is no different from *homo œconomicus* inasmuch as the actions of both follow rational calculations. Anyone can commit a crime – the postulate of freedom includes freedom to break the law, too. According to the penal rationality of liberalism, *homo penalis* dwells within all of us as a latent potential; violations of the law represent 'his' realization. Because human action is rationally motivated and follows calculations of pleasure and pain, punishment must aim at the will of potential perpetrators. It operates by exercising an effect on the mind, calibrating crime and punishment; calculating the punishment risked deters the subject from carrying out the misdeed. Finding the appropriate sanction for a given violation involves identifying a disadvantage that will strip misconduct of its appeal once and for all. This theory of punishment is dynamic; it works with the principle of balance to neutralize interest in breaking the law.[72]

In the latter half of the nineteenth century, this form of penal rationality garnered more and more criticism. For both practical and theoretical reasons, the 'school of social law' declared that cancelling out criminal volition was outdated. Pasquino sums up the argument:

> Beccaria's theory of punishment as an instrument *ad deterrendum* counterweighting the interest in the committing of crimes is false, both theoretically and practically: practically, because the statistics of crimes and criminals simply continue to rise; theoretically, because the criminal does not think like a normal and honest person such as Beccaria – indeed, we may say that he or she does not think at all. The criminal cannot be a *homo penalis* because he is not a Man.[73]

---

71. Ibid., 1–11.

72. Pasquino, 'Criminology: The Birth of a Special Knowledge' (1991a), 235–40; Foucault, 1975a, *Discipline and Punish* [1995], 104–31.

73. Pasquino, 'Criminology: The Birth of a Special Knowledge' (1991a), 240.

According to the line of reasoning of the 'school of social law', the actions of 'criminals' do not result from the general nature of human beings (who are prone to miscalculation), but express a specific kind of evil. The 'criminal' does not qualify as *homo penalis* precisely because he is not a rational human being. The figure of *homo criminalis* takes the stage, shifting penal rationality towards 'social defence'; here, the axis of culpabilization no longer involves right or wrong calculations, but conformity or non-conformity with regard to social life. The new legal theory is not based on lawbreaking as an anthropological or psychological fact, but on understanding the lawbreaker as part of a separate species and 'social race'.[74]

Pasquino shows how the invention of this new 'juridical figure' changed the justificatory principle of punishment and the nature of the law:

1. *Nature of the law.* In the new framework, law no longer precedes society (defined as the direct expression of members' free wills). It becomes a variable, secondary category. The law does not constitute the rules of communal life; it simply codifies them. The theory of the social contract as the legal foundation of society is inverted: henceforth, law displays a derivative quality – as one manifestation, among others, of a historically mutable society. It is impossible to found society on law, because every human group in history brings forth its own rules; society is not the result of, but the basis for, the law.

---

Hereby, Pasquino relies on arguments presented the Italian jurist Enrico Ferri (*La teoria dell'imputibilitá e la negazione del libero arbitrio*, Florenz 1878) against Beccaria's liberal legal theory. To illustrate the move from deterring criminals to making them harmless, he also compares the works of Jeremy Bentham and Anselm Feuerbach with the penological justifications presented by Adolphe Prins and Franz von Liszt. On changes in the politics of punishment, see Robert Musil's characterization of the 'social school': 'The social view tells us that the criminally "degenerate" person cannot at all be considered from a moral aspect, but only according to the degree in which he is dangerous to society as a whole. What follows from this is that the more dangerous he is the more he is responsible for his actions. And what follows again from this, with compelling logic, is that the criminals who are apparently least guilty, that is to say, those who are insane or of defective morality, who by virtue of their nature are least susceptible to the corrective influence of punishment, must be threatened with the harshest penalties'. Quoted in Pasquino, 'Criminology: The Birth of a Special Knowledge' (1991a), 236.

74. Foucault, 1978b, 'About the Concept of the "Dangerous Individual" in 19th Century Legal Psychiatry', 11–15; Pasquino, 'Criminology: The Birth of a Special Knowledge' (1991a), 240–1.

2. *Justificatory principle of punishment.* Punishment's basis and point of reference shift from the rights of subjects to the norms of society. Inasmuch as law must adjust to evolutionary dictates, society provides the sole instance for legitimating punishment. Penal laws represent mutable codifications of a given society's vital interests. The principle of immanence prevails. Law and rights are no longer measured by some standard of natural justice – so that the positivity of their rules will conform to its prescriptions. Instead, the point is to correct the injustices of nature. Law becomes interventionistic and serves as a social corrective; in contrast, nature offers a negative point of reference.

When 'defending society' stands at issue, the operative principles are self-referential; society provides not only the source of the law, but of the lawbreaker, as well. Criminal law and criminals stand locked together in circular fashion. Penal law, which serves society, reacts to a threat that emerges from society itself: society is constantly producing the same antisocial tendencies that threaten its existence and demand corrective intervention. Just as each society brings forth its own, historically specific culture, it brings forth its own kind of criminals – and the law corresponding to them.[75]

For all that, nature does not simply vanish. If anything, society absorbs and incorporates nature. Simultaneously, the 'society' that law is implemented to defend displays its own, 'social naturalness' differing markedly from 'natural naturalness'. Pasquino remarks the central paradox of the school of social law: 'if it is claimed that criminality is a phenomenon with a social aetiology, how is it possible to say that the criminal has an asocial nature?'.[76]

For Foucault, modern racism offers a response to this very question; it dissolves the paradox of the social origin of antisocial conduct. The 'solution' that racism represents entails, first, making divisions within the social sphere as a biological continuum (that is, a given

---

75. Ibid., 241–4; Gordon, 'Governmental Rationality: An Introduction' (1991), 38–9. Foucault tried to concretize the different aspects of the concept of social defence through a case study. In 1981, at the University of Louvain, he directed an interdisciplinary seminar on the 'genealogy of social defense in Belgium'. The results were published in an edited volume after his death. Tulkens, *Généalogie de la défense sociale en Belgique (1880–1914)* (1988); for a synopsis, see Tulkens, 'Généalogie de la défense sociale en Belgique (1880–1914)' (1986).

76. Pasquino, 'Criminology: The Birth of a Special Knowledge' (1991a), 242.

population, or the human species as a whole) enabling underclasses to be distinguished and arranged in a hierarchy along racial lines. This fragmentation of the biological field enables qualifications of good and bad, higher and lower, and ascendant and descending races; at the same time, a line of division 'between what must live and what must die'[77] is established. The splitting and differentiation of the biological sphere serves to define the general realm of operation for 'biopolitics' and structure the modes of its concrete interventions.[78]

Still, racism is not content to draw a line separating two sides; it also provides a new principle of articulation between these realms. The point of departure is a further reformulation of the traditional theme of racial war. Racism abandons the old, negative relation between the life of some and the death of others ('If you want to live, the other must die') and makes the terms function in an unprecedented manner. The core of this relation is no longer either-or; instead, racism produces a positive and productive relationship between a 'more' and a 'less' ('The more you kill, the more death you cause, the more you will live in turn').[79]

And with that, racism makes it possible to establish a relationship between the life of some and the death of others that is not military-political, but biologico-medical. It establishes an organic connection between the fact of 'degeneration' and the health of the species: to

---

77. Foucault, 1991, 'Society Must Be Defended' [2003], 254.

78. For Foucault, this specifies 'one of the central antinomies of our political reason'. Foucault, 1988c, 'The Political Technology of Individuals', 147. It belongs to a more comprehensive problem he describes by juxtaposing power over death and power over life: the simultaneity of mass destruction and social insurance when justifying modern wars in terms of the life (and survival) of peoples. 'Wars are no longer waged in the name of a sovereign who must be defended; they are waged on behalf of the existence of everyone; entire populations are mobilized for the purposes of wholesale slaughter in the name of life necessity: massacres have become vital'. Foucault, 1976a, The History of Sexuality, Volume 1: An Introduction [1978], 137. Modern racism is of 'vital importance' insofar as it affords a technology that secures the function of killing under the conditions of biopower: 'How can a power such as this kill, if it is true that its basic function is to improve life, to prolong its duration, to improve its changes, to avoid accidents, and to compensate for failings? [...] It is, I think, at this point that racism intervenes'. Foucault, 1991, 'Society Must Be Defended' [2003], 254.

79. It warrants mention that Foucault understands 'death' in a broad sense, encompassing not just direct, physical annihilation but also social and political forms of 'indirect murder: the fact of exposing someone to death, increasing the risk of death for some people. Or quite simply, political death, expulsion, rejection, and so on'. Ibid., 256.

the extent that inferior races vanish and abnormal individuals are eliminated, their share of the species as a whole diminishes and, in consequence, the population/species becomes stronger, more vigorous, more alive and so on:

> This is not, then, a military, warlike, or political relationship, but a biological relationship. And the reason this mechanism can come into play is that the enemies who have to be done away with are not adversaries in the political sense of the term; they are threats, either external or internal, to the population and for the population. In the biopower system, in other words, killing or the imperative to kill is acceptable only if it results not in a victory over political adversaries, but in the elimination of the biological threat to and the improvement of the species or race.[80]

For Foucault, the strategic achievement of racism is threefold: first, it enables breaks within a (biological) continuum; second, it formulates a positive relationship between death and life; third, it lays the foundation for constituting individuals and classes in terms of a specific race. Identifying a collective subject of 'criminals' presupposes that the individual is not a single case, but part of a social collectivity, a group of persons with the same traits. Racism 'normalizes' violations of the law by constructing lawbreakers as an abnormal component of society and bringing this component back into the social body as its internal border. In this framework, the lawbreaker no longer counts as a monster or creature standing outside of society, but an unnatural element of social nature.[81]

## Social Medicine

For penal law that prevailed into the nineteenth century, the central problem was whether an individual qualified as mad or a delinquent. Liberal law, based on the principle of a free will, set up an elementary division: a mentally ill person was not a delinquent; his deed was no

---

80. Ibid., 255–6.
81. Foucault treats the history of the lawbreaker as a 'monster' in his lectures at the Collège de France of 22 and 29 January 1975. Foucault, 2003, *Psychiatric Power* [2006], 91, 75–108; Gros, *Michel Foucault* (1996), 72.

crime, but the symptom of an illness. Condemning violations of the law presupposed legal subjects with a free will.

During the second half of the nineteenth century, this border became increasingly porous and the categories started to mix. Now, the delinquent individual was not only a lawbreaker, but also – and above all – a criminal characterized by a certain psychologico-moral disposition. More and more, lawbreakers came to count as mentally ill, and medico-psychiatric categories replaced the notion of free will:

> So then, the old dichotomy in the Civil Code, which defined the subject being either delinquent or mad, is eliminated. As a result there remain two possibilities, being slightly sick and really delinquent, or being somewhat delinquent but really sick. The delinquent is unable to escape his pathology. … Pathology has become a general form of social regulation. There is no longer anything outside medicine.[82]

This change in penal law towards 'defending society' was made possible by way of a concept corresponding to the notion of risk in civil law: *danger*. The idea of liability without fault corresponds to that of accountability without freedom. The concept of danger displays immense flexibility. 'Dangerousness' is a paradoxical notion, since it simultaneously designates an abstract possibility and a concrete, psychic capacity: on the one hand, it affirms a certain quality particular to an individual; on the other, it symbolizes uncertainty, since proof of dangerousness can only be provided after the fact. It represents a hypothesis concerning the greater or lesser probability of connection between symptoms in the present and future action. As such, it is universally applicable: everything potentially poses a danger or a risk.[83]

---

82. Foucault, 1976d, 'The Crisis of Medicine or the Crisis of Antimedicine?' [2004], 15–16; see also Foucault, 1974d, 'White Magic and Black Gown' [1996], 287. Foucault examines the introduction of medico-psychiatric categories to legal discourse on the example of the 'Pierre Rivière case'. Foucault, 1973h, 'I, Pierre Rivière' [1996].

83. Foucault, 1974c, 'Truth and Juridical Forms' [2000], 57; Foucault, 1977o, 'Confinement, Psychiatry, Prison' [1988], 188–91; Foucault, 1978b, 'About the Concept of the "Dangerous Individual" in 19th Century Legal Psychiatry', 17–18; Foucault, 1978f, 'Attention: danger', 507–8. At the end of the nineteenth century, risk and danger are still synonyms. Only in the twentieth century does the term of risk become conceptionally autonomous from that of danger. On this dissociation, as well as further developments and changes to politics of prevention, see Castel, 'From Dangerousness to Risk' (1991).

And so, the category of danger could apply, beyond the category of criminals, to other marginal groups as well. What tied together material need, vagabondage, criminality, perversion and so on was the danger they represent for society. This concept served as a unified analytical instrument for various social problems and, at the same time, made it possible to treat dangerous individuals differently, in keeping with the intensity and nature of the menace they represented. Danger provided not only the instrument for diagnosing 'antisocial tendencies', but also the key to solving them, and opened an array of treatments: psychiatric therapy, medico-hygienic intervention, charitable or preventative detention and so on.[84]

The notion of dangerousness implies that society is constituted as a body with inherent dangers and maladies. The social significance of this medical complex derives from objectivating human life in community as a biological entity. The 'normalization' of society presupposes its permanent pathologization, making medicine into a 'political intervention-technique'[85] that serves the interests of control and regulation: 'Modern medicine is a *social medicine* whose basis is a certain technology of the social body'.[86]

The eighteenth century had already witnessed a liberal 'health politics' ('noso-politique') of the population, which concerned the well-being of the social body in general and took distance from the 'medical police' of old. Health became the duty of the individual and the goal of intervention on the part of the state. An economic imperative stood behind the commandment to be healthy: physical health was important inasmuch as it furnished labour power, and state interest turned to the conditions for reproducing this resource. The capitalist economy relied on establishing a certain politics of the body to ensure that it remained productive. The biological data of the population came to represent an indispensable element for 'economic regulation' that necessitated, over and above the subjugation of bodies, the permanent improvement of their utility.[87]

---

84. Donzelot, 'Wiederkehr des Sozialen' (1995), 54–5.

85. Foucault, 1991, *'Society Must Be Defended'* [2003], 252.

86. Foucault, 1977h, 'The Birth of Social Medicine' [2000], 136; emphasis added; see also Foucault, 1977m, 'The Confession of the Flesh' [1980], 204–7.

87. Foucault, 1976b, 'The Politics of Health in the Eighteenth Century' [2000], 92–5; Foucault, 1976d, 'The Crisis of Medicine or the Crisis of Antimedicine?' [2004], 14–19; Foucault, 1977h, 'The Birth of Social Medicine' [2000], 137–42.

The precondition for such liberal politics of health involved shifting the problematic of health with respect to other techniques of social support. Foucault's thesis is that autonomizing poverty in economic terms corresponds to the development of a medico-administrative body of knowledge, at the centre of which stands the health of the individual and the welfare of the population. This medico-administrative complex has various aspects:

1. The family represents a decisive switching point for the medicalization of individuals. 'Noso-politics' produces the family–children complex, ordering the relationship between parents and their offspring in a new fashion. It is no longer enough to ensure a certain number of progeny; the children must be guided and supervised – they must have a certain physical constitution and demonstrate certain abilities. In this context, childhood comes to represent an independent period of life, separate from the world of adults and oriented towards an end goal. Raising children becomes an important goal of new policies, and the family the focus of medical and moral campaigns. As the hinge between the general goal of a healthy social body and care for individuals, it gives rise to a 'private' ethics of good health as a relationship of mutual obligation between parents and children.[88]

2. The second element of this 'noso-politics' is the privilege granted to hygiene – that is, the way medicine serves the purposes of 'social hygiene'. Inasmuch as medicine elaborates certain prescriptions, it

---

88. Foucault, 1976b, 'The Politics of Health in the Eighteenth Century' [2000], 96–8. Jacques Donzelot's *The Policing of Families* explores how the bourgeois nuclear family, the intimization of familial relations and the expansion of instances of social education and moralization connect with the 'government of the social'. His thesis is that the 'crisis of the family' (like the 'crisis of the prison') in fact represents its successful institutionalization as a relay point of social control; since the nineteenth century, the family has no longer functioned 'against' or 'outside' society and its constraints at all: 'The first object, the family, will thus be seen to fade into the background, overshadowed by another, the social, in relation to which the family is both queen and prisoner. By and large, the procedures of transformation of the family are also those which implant the forms of modern integration that give our societies their particularly well-policed character. And the celebrated crisis of the family, setting the stage for its liberation, would appear then not so much inherently contrary to the present social order as a condition of possibility of that order's emergence'. Donzelot, *The Policing of Families* (1979), 7–8; on the relationship between education, knowledge and power, see Ball, *Foucault and Education* (1990).

institutes rules for individuals to follow in order to ensure their own
welfare; at the same time, this means creating the basis for medical
intervention in social sectors where the rules are not respected. As
such, medicine comes to play a more and more important role within
a politics that seeks to investigate and improve the social body in order
to keep it 'healthy'. Foucault assumes that the development of medico-
administrative knowledge, which 'treats' society in terms of health and
sickness, represents the germinal condition for the emergence of sociology in the nineteenth century.[89]

Modern medicine constitutes a 'biopolitical strategy'.[90] Its operations
are not limited to identifying and healing illness; above all, they aim at
prophylaxis and prevention. Everything qualifies as a potential object
of medicine insofar as anything may promote or imperil collective
health. The field of medical intervention extends from water quality
to nutrition, city planning and sexual practices – no longer restricted
to the ill or illnesses, it is situated on the plane of 'life' itself. Medicine
becomes an instrument of universal diagnosis and therapy; it proves
indispensable to the extent that the ills it 'treats' constitute integral
components of the naturalness of the social body – ills that can be
combated only through improved, more precise and more 'holistic'
medical knowledge:

> What is diabolical about the present situation is that whenever we want
> to refer to a realm outside of medicine we find that it has already been
> medicalized. And when one wishes to object to medicine's deficiencies,
> its drawbacks and its harmful effects, this is done in the name of a more
> complete, more refined and widespread medical knowledge.[91]

---

89. Foucault, 1976b, 'The Politics of Health in the Eighteenth Century' [2000],
99–100; Foucault, 1977h, 'The Birth of Social Medicine' [2000], 151–5. The role of
medicine as an instance of social control is the focus of Robert Castel's *The Regulation
of Madness*, especially the integration of 'mental illness' into the social body. On the
question of hygiene as political technology, see, especially, Castel, *The Regulation of
Madness: The Origins of Incarceration in France* (1988), 112–23. For a more recent
study inspired by Foucault on the relationship between medicine, health and government, see Petersen and Bunton, *Foucault, Health and Medicine* (1997).
90. Foucault, 1977h, 'The Birth of Social Medicine' [2000], 137.
91. Foucault, 1976d, 'The Crisis of Medicine or the Crisis of Antimedicine?'
[2004], 14.

# 9
# The Government of Individuals: Neoliberalism

Classic liberal rationality deemed the individual alone responsible for personal fortune and misfortune, and it prohibited corrective intervention that did not bear on individual error. But in light of the realities of capitalistic societies, this form of regulating social relations proved increasingly impracticable, and the socialization of risk replaced the principle of individual responsibility. Insurance technology distributed, between all members of society, the costs arising from mistakes and problems in people's lives in their communities – from which certain individuals and groups suffer, in particular. At the same time, the dispositive of risk sounded an imperative to 'defend society' against dangers within.

Foucault contends that this conception of the social has been in a state of crisis since at least the 1970s.[1] This situation stems from problems of accumulation and the Fordist regulation of the capitalist

---

1. This does not mean, however, that no significant changes in governmentality occurred between the nineteenth and twentieth centuries. They are charted especially in studies by Jacques Donzelot – e.g. Keynesian efforts to configures social and economic relations. Donzelot, *L'invention du social* (1984), 157–77; see, also, Donzelot, *The Policing of Families* (1979), 217–34. The end of the chapter returns to this point.

Foucault himself did not examine these transformations. (As we have noted, the lectures presented here skip from classic liberalism to neoliberalism.) That said, he intended to rectify this omission after completing *The History of Sexuality*. A seminar at the University of California, Berkeley, was planned on the 'welfare state' and early twentieth-century governmentality. For a summary of the preparatory discussions and research, see Gandal and Kotkin, 'Governing Work and Social Life in the USA and the USSR' (1985). Foucault also intended to set up a research centre for studying modern ideas about government. Pasquino, 'Political Theory of War and Peace' (1993), 74. His premature death prevented him from doing so.

economy, which are manifest in decreasing growth rates and mounting social expenses, new management strategies and globalization tendencies. The crisis is not just economic, but political and social as well. Since the 1960s, the Keynesian model and the social state have met with an array of critiques formulated, with different points of emphasis, on both the left and the right. Whereas one side laments an increasing sense of 'entitlement' and the corrosive effect of the 'welfare state' on traditional values and social orientations, the other side points to the consolidation of standing social inequalities, which amount to political domination. The object of criticism is not just the lack of state sovereignty – dependency on special interests and mounting bureaucracy – but also the absence of autonomy, the perpetuation of patriarchal-authoritarian social structures, and the combination of security and dependency.[2] In this light, Foucault deems the economic crisis to be inseparable from processes of political disintegration and the emergence of new social movements:

> Indeed, it seems to me that through the current economic crisis and the great oppositions and conflicts that are marked out between 'rich' and 'poor' nations ..., it may be clearly seen how in the more developed nations a crisis of 'government' has begun. And by 'government' I mean the set of institutions and practices by which people are 'led', from administration to education, etc. It is this set of procedures, techniques, and methods that guarantee the 'government' of people, which seems to me to be in crisis today. ... We are, I believe, at the beginning of a huge crisis of a wide-ranging reevaluation of the problem of 'government'.[3]

For Foucault, the rise of neoliberal politics represents a response to this 'crisis of the general apparatus (*dispositif*) of governmentality'[4] and the search for a new one.[5] Its relative success is based on taking

2. For a discussion of the system of social security in terms of its 'negative effects', see Foucault, 1983a, 'The Risks of Security' [2000], esp. 365–7; Foucault, 1976d, 'The Crisis of Medicine or the Crisis of Antimedicine?' [2004], 16–19.

3. Foucault, 1980d, *Remarks on Marx* [1991], 175–7; see also Donzelot, *L'invention du social* (1984), 179–224.

4. Lecture, 24 January 1979, Foucault, 2004b, *The Birth of Biopolitics* [2008], 70; see also Foucault, 1979d, 'Manières de justice', 758.

5. It is important to bear in mind that Foucault delivered these lectures before the victories of Thatcher and Reagan. Although Foucault only discusses neoliberal

elements from right-wing and left-wing critiques of the social state and rearranging them within a programme that aims for an 'auton-omization of the social'.[6] That said, Foucault does not think that the neoliberal project heralds a return to early liberal positions; rather, it involves re-elaborating, on a fundamental level, the positions of clas-sical liberalism. This difference has two main aspects:

1. The first point concerns redefining the *relationship between the state and the economy*. Neoliberalism inverts the classical liberal con-figuration, which, historically, was shaped by the experience of an all-powerful, absolutist state. In contrast to the rationality of classical liberalism, the state no longer supervises market freedom; instead, the market represents the principle for organizing and regulating the state. In this framework, it is more a matter of the state being controlled by the market than a market under state supervision. Neoliberalism replaces a restrictive, external principle with a regulatory, inner prin-ciple: the market form serves as the organizational principle for the state and society.

2. The second point involves a *difference of the basis of governing*. In early liberalism, the principle of rational, governmental action was tied to the rationality of the individuals ruled. Liberal government was

---

theories here, he takes up the question of *socialist governmentality* elsewhere. His point of departure is that real socialism has incorporated elements of liberal gov-ernmentality without developing its own form of government. The perpetual call for 'real' socialism illustrates the problem vividly: demanding truth of socialism shows, above all, that it possesses no governmentality of its own. (No one calls for 'real liber-alism'.) In Foucault's estimation, actual socialist governments replace the problem of rationality with adherence to (and agreement with) a text. But doing so only covers up the decisive issue: readings are proposed to justify socialism, instead of socialism itself defining the terms and operations of government. The role assigned to written works reveals that no independent, socialist governmentality exists. In this light, the ques-tion should not be whether the right books are being read, whether they are being read properly, and so on. In a word: socialist governmentality cannot be derived from texts; one must 'invent' it. Lecture, 31 January 1979, Foucault, 2004b, *The Birth of Biopolitics* [2008], 92–4.
   Foucault saw prospects for a form of governmentality different from the neoliberal model in Mitterand's election and the shared program of socialists and communists – 'what might be called a "logic of the Left"'. Foucault, 1981d, 'So Is It Important to Think?' [2000], 454. Before long, however, it became clear that such hopes were premature.
   6. Donzelot, *L'invention du social* (1984), 224–51.

bound to the interest-motivated and free market activities of trading individuals because their rationality is what makes the market function optimally – ensuring the welfare of all and a robust state. In this conception, individual freedom represents the technical condition for rational government, and the government cannot impose restrictions without imperilling its own foundations. Neoliberalism also ties the rationality of government to the rational action of individuals; however, its reference point is no longer putative human nature, but a mode of behaviour produced by artificial means. Neoliberalism no longer seeks the rational principle for regulating and limiting government in natural freedom, which must be respected, but finds it in an artificially arranged freedom: the entrepreneurial and competitive behaviour of economically rational individuals.[7]

Foucault investigates two forms of neoliberalism in particular: German post-war neoliberalism from 1948 to 1962 and the American liberalism of the Chicago School, which builds on and radicalizes the positions of its predecessor.[8]

## 'Inequality Is Equal for All': Ordoliberalism and the German Model

The theory of German post-war liberalism was formulated – and translated into practical politics, in part – by jurists and economists who had belonged, or stood close, to the 'Freiburg School' in 1928–30 and later published their findings in the journal *Ordo*: Wilhelm Röpke, Walter Eucken, Franz Böhm, Alexander Rüstow and Alfred Müller-Armack, among others. These *ordoliberals* played a decisive role in developing the 'social market economy' and laying the foundational policies for the first years of the German Federal Republic.[9]

---

7. Lecture, 31 January 1979, Foucault, 2004b, *The Birth of Biopolitics* [2008], 75–100; lecture, 7 February 1979, Foucault, 2004b, *The Birth of Biopolitics* [2008], 101–28; Burchell, 'Liberal Government and Techniques of the Self' (1993), 271; Hindess, 'Liberalism, Socialism and Democracy' (1993), 307–10; Rose, 'Governing "Advanced" Liberal Democracies' (1996), 50–62.

8. Part of the lecture on 7 March 1979 addresses French neoliberalism and politics under Giscard's presidency. Foucault, 2004b, *The Birth of Biopolitics* [2008], 194–207.

9. Foucault, 1979m, 'Course Summary' [2008], 322–4.

Foucault draws attention to an array of questions and experiences that the 'Freiburg School' had in common with the 'Frankfurt School'. Not only did both groups emerge at the same time during the mid-1920s and share the fate of exile; equally, they participated in a political problematic dominating the German university in the early twentieth century – one associated with Max Weber, above all. The importance of Weber's contributions is to have shifted the Marxian problem of capital's contradictory logic towards analysis of capitalist society's irrational rationality. This problem represents the point of departure for both the Freiburg and the Frankfurt Schools, although they formulate their lines of questioning in wholly different terms. The Frankfurt School looks for a new form of social rationality that would cancel out and overcome the irrationality of the capitalist economy. The Freiburg School steers the opposite course: it seeks to redefine economic (capitalist) rationality in order to prevent the social irrationality of capitalism.[10]

Foucault sees a further parallel between the two schools in the importance they attach to reflecting on the rise of National Socialism. But here, too, a shared description of the problem meets with diametrically opposed answers. Adorno, Horkheimer and other Critical Theorists insisted on a causal relationship between capitalism and fascism. However, the neoliberals did not view National Socialism as the product of liberalism – on the contrary, it followed from its absence. The collapse of democracy in Germany did not result from a functioning market economy, but occurred because a functional market economy was lacking. From the ordoliberal perspective, National Socialism represents the direct result of anti-liberal policies. In contrast to the Frankfurt School, the Freiburg School does not see a fundamental alternative between capitalism and socialism, but between liberalism and the various forms of state interventionism (Soviet socialism, National Socialism, Keynesianism), which have the common feature – albeit to varying degrees – of threatening freedom.[11]

The theoretical basis for the ordoliberal position, according to Foucault, lies in a radically anti-naturalistic way of conceiving the

---

10. Lecture, 7 February 1979, Foucault, 2004b, *The Birth of Biopolitics* [2008], 101–21.

11. Lecture, 7 February 1979, Foucault, 2008, *The Government of Self and Others* [2010], 101–28; Burchell, 'Liberal Government and Techniques of the Self' (1993), 270.

market and the principle of competition. For ordoliberal thought, the market does not represent a natural, economic reality with laws of its own that the art of government must observe and respect. On the contrary, the market's very constitution and existence depend on political interventions in the first place. By the same token, competition does not represent a natural fact that has always already held in the economic sphere; instead, this fundamental economic mechanism can only function when a number of conditions are assured, which legal measures must constantly work to guarantee. Pure competition is neither something 'naturally' given, nor is it anything that will ever be achieved completely; rather, it underlies a projected goal, which makes constant and active policies necessary. This also signifies the obsolescence of any conception distinguishing between a restricted sphere of freedom and a legitimate realm for state intervention. Counter to such a negative conception of the state – which was the hallmark of eighteenth- and nineteenth-century liberalism – the ordoliberal position holds that market mechanisms and effects of competition can only arise if governmental practices produce them. According to this conception, the state and market economy do not stand opposed to each other; each one presupposes the other.[12]

Foucault identifies three important strategic functions of ordoliberal anti-naturalism:

1. In *theoretical* terms, it means that a strict separation between an economic base and a politico-legal superstructure cannot hold. The dichotomy proves untenable because the economy does not represent a sphere of automatic or natural mechanisms so much as it defines a social field of regulated practices.

2. The *historical* significance of this position involves rejecting a conception of history that seeks to derive socio-political changes from the economic processes of transformation under capitalism. For ordoliberals, the history of capitalism is economico-institutional; the matter does not involve a one-sided causal relation structuring the sequence of events so much as incessant reciprocity: capitalism represents a 'historical figure' through which economic processes and economic

---

12. Lecture, 7 February 1979, Foucault, 2004b, *The Birth of Biopolitics* [2008], 101–21.

'frameworks' are joined, refer to each other and lend each other mutual support.

3. *Politically*, the position aims for the survival of capitalism. For ordo-liberals, capitalism does not really exist inasmuch as there is no logic of capital. What is called capitalism is not the product of a purely economic process, and capitalism as a historical phenomenon does not derive from a distinct logical system. Instead of a clearly delineated and defined formation ('the' capitalism, whose end may be predicted on the basis of its internal contradictions), we stand before a historical singularity ('a' capitalism among others) open to a certain number of economic and institutional variables and operating within a field of possibilities: in other words, a capitalist system. In this light, the constructed nature of capitalism moves to the fore: inasmuch as it represents an economico-institutional totality, it must be possible to intervene in this ensemble – and in such a way that, at one and the same time, one capitalism undergoes modification and another capitalism is 'invented' ('intervenir'/'inventir'). That is, we do not follow the regime of capitalism as it stands so much as we design new ones. Ordoliberals replace the notion of economy as a realm of autonomous rules and laws with the concept of 'economic order' (*Wirtschaftsordnung*), where social interventions and political regulation occur.[13]

---

13. Lecture, 21 February 1979, ibid., 159–79. This line of argument is also evident in discussion of two positions contesting capitalism's capacity for innovation on the basis of its internal laws. On the one hand, ordoliberals take issue with Schumpeter's pessimistic view that capitalism necessarily tends towards monopolization. They agree with him that concentration development does not derive from the economic process itself; instead, its basis lies in the social consequences of competition. For both Schumpeter and ordoliberals, monopolistic organization represents a social phenomenon, not an economic one. However, ordoliberals draw a different conclusion: precisely because monopolization is a social phenomenon, it is not irreversible or necessary; social intervention and creating a proper institutional framework can prevent it. Monopolization does not follow from fate, but the result of a failed political strategy and inadequate institutions.

On the other hand, ordoliberals reject Sombart's thesis that the modern economy harbours an irreversible tendency towards 'mass society', where human relations grow impoverished and anonymous social relations replace the experience of community. Here, too, ordoliberals steer the opposite course: capitalism is not responsible for the problems revealed by Sombart and others; the fault lies with planning methods and bureaucratic apparatuses that enemies of the market system have set up. From this perspective, the neoliberal art of government does not lead to uniformity, but represents a new orientation that will lead away from the homogenizing tendencies

By Foucault's account, ordoliberal theory tried to show, after the experience of National Socialism, that the irrational aspects and dysfunctions
of capitalist society may be overcome through politico-institutional
'inventions', since such problems are not natural, but historical and
contingent. Accordingly, the ordoliberals undertook a change of perspective and replaced a naturalistic conception of economy with an
institutional one. Under such circumstances, it no longer makes any
sense to speak of the destructive 'logic of capital', since doing so presupposes the existence of an autonomous economic sphere with its
own laws and limits. Following ordoliberal reasoning, the survival of
the 'capitalist system' depends on the political capacity to formulate
innovative responses to structural constraints and obstacles that, while
part of the system, ultimately prove more or less coincidental. In a
word, ordoliberals want to demonstrate that there is not just one capitalism with a specific logic, dead ends and contradictions; rather, an
economico-institutional whole exists, which is historically open and
politically changeable.

Conceiving the economic sphere along these lines also means
developing a 'policy of society' (*Gesellschaftspolitik*) that is not limited
to transferring services, but actively produces the historical and social
conditions of the market. From the ordoliberal standpoint, a 'policy
of society' does not provide a negative and compensatory function,
nor is its task to balance out the destructive effects of economic
freedom. Instead of attenuating the antisocial consequences of competition, it should prevent socially produced mechanisms that impede
competition. Such social politics has two aspects: universalizing entrepreneurship and redefining law and rights:

> 1. The first aspect of ordoliberal 'policy for society' involves constitut-
> ing a social framework based on *entrepreneurship*, in keeping with the
> principle that 'inequality ... is the same for all'.[14] The goal of this polit-
> ical strategy is to multiply and expand forms of entrepreneurship in
> the social body. Such generalization serves, on the one hand, to make
> the economic mechanisms of supply and demand, competition, and so

---

of 'mass society'. Lecture, 7 February 1979, ibid., 113–14; Gordon, 'Question, Ethos,
Event: Foucault on Kant' (1986a), 80–1.

14. Lecture, 14 February 1979, Foucault, 2004b, *The Birth of Biopolitics* [2008],
143.

on into a model for social relations as a whole. On the other hand, it effects a 'vital politics' ('*Vitalpolitik*') (Rüstow) that aims to restore and reactivate moral and cultural values that encourage economic activity.[15]

2. The other aspect of ordoliberal 'policy for society' complements and completes the first: *redefining the form of law* and juridical institutions. In order to anchor entrepreneurship at the core of society, social interventions are necessary on a massive scale. Whereas, in the eighteenth century, minimal political interventions represented the precondition for the economy functioning as it should, ordoliberals no longer view law as part of the superstructure; instead, it represents an essential component of the (economico-institutional) base and provides an indispensable instrument for stimulating entrepreneurial activity at the heart of society.[16]

---

15. Lecture, 14 February 1979, ibid., 148, 129–57; lecture, 21 March 1979, Foucault, 2004b, *The Birth of Biopolitics* [2008], 239–65; Gordon, 'The Soul of the Citizen' (1987), 314–15.

16. Lecture, 21 February 1979, Foucault, 2004b, *The Birth of Biopolitics* [2008], 159–84. Foucault points out that the constructivist and anti-naturalist accent of ordoliberals cannot be separated from the historical situation of post-war Germany. The conception of an open economic space, guaranteed only by constant social intervention, provided the political legitimation of the second German republic. In contrast to liberals of the classic stripe, ordoliberals did not face the problem of how a free market could be established within the state as it stood; instead, the question they posed was how to create a state on the basis of economic freedom, which would provide the principle for both the state's legitimacy and its self-limitation. Economic freedom legitimates sovereignty which is restricted to guaranteeing economic activity. In the eighteenth century, liberals had confronted the problem of limiting a state that already existed and setting up economic freedom within it. In post-1945 Germany, the opposite problem held: how a state that did not exist yet could exist on the basis of a realm of economic freedom that did not belong to the state. Max Weber's *Protestant Ethic and the Spirit of Capitalism* argued that individual wealth had counted as a sign of divine election in sixteenth-century Germany. Now, in the newly founded, post-war German state, collective wealth was assigned a similar status. After the experience of National Socialism and the disaster of world war, economic prosperity created a new political order out of national destruction – and the legitimacy of this order. Collective wealth produced social consensus for a state no longer defined in terms of a historical mission, but justified in terms of economic growth. Prosperity palpably and directly signifies the legitimacy of a state that eschews all transcendental schemes and only guarantees the rules of the economic game. A new conception of time arises, organized not in historical but in economic categories; instead of historical progress, economic growth provides its index – and its side-effect is oblivion and annulment of the recent past. Lecture, 31 January 1979, Foucault, 2004b, *The Birth of Biopolitics* [2008], 75–100; Gordon, 'Governmental Rationality: An Introduction' (1991), 41–2.

## The Social as a Form of the Economic: The Chicago School

Like German ordoliberalism, the neoliberalism of the Chicago School takes aim at state interventionism and dirigisme. In the name of economic freedom, it criticizes the uncontrolled growth of bureaucratic apparatuses and the endangerment of individual rights. For all that, the two versions of neoliberalism display profound differences with regard to the conception of society and the political solutions they propose.

Ordoliberals started out from the idea of a 'social market economy', that is, the idea of a market that must constantly be supported by political regulations and framed by social interventions (housing policy, unemployment assistance, health insurance and so on). This conception of social politics is still based on the difference between the economy and the social, which is to be bridged by way of enterprise. Coding social existence as a matter of entrepreneurship simultaneously represents a politics for economizing the social field and a 'vital politics' meant to intercept the negative effects of economic events by political measures. As such, the 'entrepreneurial society' of the ordoliberals is marked by a central 'ambiguity' – which is precisely where North American neoliberals start their reflections.[17]

Foucault's thesis is that the approach taken by the Chicago School duly extends the economic form to the social field in general, such that the difference between the economy and the social vanishes altogether. Hereby, economic schemes of analysis and criteria for decisions are transferred to realms that are not (entirely) economic – or even ones standing at odds with economic rationality. Whereas West German ordoliberals pursue the idea of governing society in the name of economic considerations, North American neoliberals redefine the social sphere as a form of the economic realm. The model of rational, economic action grounds and restricts governmental action. Hereby, government itself turns into a kind of enterprise, whose task is to universalize competition and invent systems of action in market form for individuals, groups and institutions.[18]

---

17. Lecture, 21 March 1979, Foucault, 2004b, *The Birth of Biopolitics* [2008], 239–65; Gordon, 'Governmental Rationality: An Introduction' (1991), 42.

18. Foucault, 1979m, 'Course Summary' [2008], 323; Burchell, 'Liberal Government and Techniques of the Self' (1993), 274.

The precondition for this strategic operation is an epistemological shift that expands the economic field of objects systematically and comprehensively. Now, the economy no longer represents one social sphere among others with a rationality, laws and instruments of its own. Instead, the economic realm encompasses human action in its entirety, insofar as it is characterized by allocating limited resources for competing purposes. Neoliberal thinking bears on the calculations prompting individuals to employ their limited resources for one purpose, and not another. The focus is no longer reconstructing a (mechanical) logic, but analysing human action that is defined by a certain (economic) rationality of its own. In this framework, the economic realm is not a clearly defined, restricted part of human existence; in principle, it encompasses all forms of human conduct and behaviour.[19]

Generalizing the economic form has two ends. First, it functions as a principle of analysis inasmuch as it investigates non-economic realms and modes of action by means of economic categories. Social relations and individual behaviour are deciphered in economic terms, against the horizon of their economic intelligibility. Second, the economic grid amounts to a programme inasmuch as it makes it possible to evaluate governmental practices on the basis of market concepts. Policies can be tested, waste and misuse identified, and the whole filtered according to the scheme of supply and demand. Whereas classical liberalism would insist that the government respect the market, now the market no longer represents a principle of self-restriction on the part of the government but a principle turned against government: 'a sort of permanent economic tribunal'.[20]

Foucault illustrates the connection between the analytical and programmatic aspects of neoliberalism through two examples: the theory of human capital and the analysis of criminality.[21]

First, the point of departure in the theory of *human capital* is how the problem of labour has been handled by economic theory. According to political economy of the classic variety, the production of goods

19. Lecture, 14 March 1979, Foucault, 2004b, *The Birth of Biopolitics* [2008], 215–33; Gordon, 'Governmental Rationality: An Introduction' (1991), 43.

20. Lecture, 21 March 1979, Foucault, 2004b, *The Birth of Biopolitics* [2008], 247, 239–60.

21. Although Foucault mentions other proponents of North American neoliberalism, he primarily discusses the works of Gary Becker in the lectures.

depends on three factors: land, capital and labour. The neoliberal critique holds that only land and capital have received thorough treatment to date, whereas labour has simply been assigned the role of a 'passive' factor in production: it has been neutralized inasmuch as it has been viewed only in quantitative or temporal terms.

Ironically, neoliberals share the Marxian critique of political economy: the charge that it has forgotten labour. That said, their point of orientation is not Marx. Whereas the latter viewed the separation between concrete and abstract labour as the historical product of capitalist socialization, neoliberals view it as a contingent outcome of economic theory. From this perspective, the separation is not a structural problem of the capitalist economy so much as political economy's conceptual shortcoming with regard to the capitalist process: a problem of representation. As such, critique should not start with the economy itself, but focus on ways of thinking about the economic process. It is less a matter of a different economy than a different way of picturing the economy. If classical political economists failed to see labour in its particular modulations and qualitative aspects, this occurred because analysing the economic process, for them, was limited to production, trade relations and consumption in keeping with the mechanics of a given social structure. In a word: for neoliberals, abstract labour does not represent the consequence of the capitalist mode of production so much as the incapacity of political economy to offer a concrete analysis of labour.

Neoliberalism achieves such concretization by way of its theory of human capital. The starting point is not objective-mechanical laws, but subjective-voluntaristic calculations of utility: how do workers employ the means at their disposal? To answer this question and examine the meaning of work, neoliberalism assumes the subjective standpoint of the worker. Workers do not view their wages as the price for selling their manpower. Instead, wages represent income from a particular kind of capital. This capital is not a form among others: ability, skill and knowledge cannot be separated from the person commanding them. As such, 'human capital' consists of two components: innate, physico-genetic makeup and the whole of acquired capacities, which result from appropriate 'investments' – diet, upbringing, education, as well as love, attention and so on. In this framework, workers no longer count as dependent employees of an enterprise so much as autonomous entrepreneurs making independent decisions about where to invest and seeking to generate surplus value: entrepreneurs of themselves.[22]

Second, orientation on market criteria also shapes the Chicago School's analyses of *criminality* and criminal justice. Neoliberal rationality makes a break with the *homo criminalis* of the nineteenth century and steps back from schemes of psychological, biological and anthropological explanation. For neoliberals, the lawbreaker is not psychologically defective or biologically degenerate, but a human being like others. He is a rational-economic individual who invests, hopes for a certain profit and risks losses. From this economic perspective, no fundamental difference exists between murder and a traffic violation. The task of the penal system is to react to the supply of crimes; punishment offers a means to limit the negative, external aspects of certain actions.

To be sure, this objectivation of the lawbreaker as an economically rational individual does not represent a return to early liberal penal philosophy. Eighteenth- and nineteenth-century reformers followed an imperative of moralization and dreamed of eliminating violations of the law altogether. Now, in contrast, breaking the law no longer occupies a position outside the market, but represents a market like others. Neoliberal penology limits itself to intervention meant to restrict the supply of crime by means of negative demand, whereby the costs of the latter should not exceed those of the former. Accordingly, the point is not to eradicate crime once and for all so much as to achieve a temporary and fragile balance between a positive supply curve of infractions and a negative demand curve of penalties.

Thus, as pathological as an individual may in fact be, neoliberals contend that he or she is always rational up to a certain point – open to considering changes in an overall balance. Neoliberal penal policy seeks to influence the interplay of profits and loss, starting with calculations of cost and utility. It does not focus on the players so much as the rules of the game: not the (internal) subjugation of individuals, but fixing and steering their (outer) environment. The neoliberal programme does not seek to establish a disciplinary or normalizing society, but rather a society defined by the cultivation and optimization of distinctive differences. As such, it is neither necessary nor desirable

---

22. Lecture, 14 March 1979, Foucault, 2004b, *The Birth of Biopolitics* [2008], 215–37; Gordon, 'Governmental Rationality: An Introduction' (1991), 44.

for members of society to display unlimited conformity. Society can live with a certain crime rate, which is not a sign of social dysfunction; instead, it manifests the best possible mode of functioning, inasmuch as even violations of the law find rational distribution.[23]

In conclusion, Foucault once again underlines the distance separating the Chicago School from classical liberalism. Neoliberalism has a central point of reference and support: *homo œconomicus*. Coding the social as a form of the economic makes it possible to apply cost–benefit calculations and market criteria to decision-making processes in the family, marriage, professional world and so on. But the economically rational, calculating individual of neoliberal theory differs from eighteenth-century *homo œconomicus*. Whereas the latter represents both an outer limit and the untouchable core for governmental action, the neoliberal thinking of the Chicago School makes this figure subject to behaviouristic manipulation and the correlate of a governmentality that systematically changes the variables of milieu and counts on 'rational choice'.[24]

## Autonomy and Self-Government

Foucault's lectures on the 'genealogy of the modern state' examine a historical field extending from antiquity to the present day; the objects of theoretical reflection encompass Christian confessional practices and neoliberal theories of criminality. Up to this point, I have largely followed Foucault's own exposition. My account has been oriented on two points in particular. First, inasmuch as the lectures' content remains largely unknown, my concern has been more a matter of documentation than commentary.[25] Second, in order to show that a comprehensive research programme stands at issue, I have presented some works that examine the constitution of the social in the

---

23. Lecture, 21 March 1979, Foucault, 2004b, *The Birth of Biopolitics* [2008], 239–60.

24. Lecture, 28 March 1979, ibid., 267–89; Gordon, 'Governmental Rationality: An Introduction' (1991), 43; Dean, *Critical and Effective Histories* (1994), 192–3.

25. To date, only Colin Gordon has presented the lectures' contents. Gordon, 'Governmental Rationality: An Introduction' (1991). But in contrast to the book at hand, he does not seek to reconstruct them with reference to sources; rather, his text is an introduction to a volume of essays inspired by Foucault's analysis of government, offering an excellent discussion of his theses along theoretical lines. See note 26.

nineteenth century by starting with the concept of governmentality.[26] In concluding this section, I would like to sum up findings, sketch a few related perspectives for investigating neoliberal government and, finally, indicate points of connection with the next section.

In schematic terms: Foucault examines the emergence of a new form of power in the Christian pastorate, which is distinct from Greco-Roman technologies of power and defined by 'conducting', or 'steering', human beings. In secular form, he contends, this form of power represents one of the conditions that constitute the modern state. Debates about the 'art of government' in early modernity attest to an 'autonomization of the political' with regard to legitimation and goals that were formerly cast in theologico-religious terms. Accordingly, Foucault interprets reason of state as an effort to detach the state from all forms of transcendence: to found the state in the state alone. Even if he discusses reason of state as the first 'crystallization' of governmentality – inasmuch as the problem of the rationality of governing arose for the first time in this context – one can only speak of governmentality in the modern sense under conditions of liberalism. Here, government does not aim for salvation in the hereafter or even the welfare of the state; rather, liberal government fastens the rationality of government to an external object: civil society; additionally, it makes the freedom of individuals the critical measure of, and limit for, governmental activity.

The liberal programme seeks 'autonomization of the economic', radical separation between economy and politics. At the same time, inasmuch as it still relies on the guarantees afforded by a certain politico-legal framework, classical liberal government of the nineteenth century generated a series of problems that manifested themselves as conflicts – between freedom and equality, formal rights and material subjugation, and so on – which led to a revolutionary threat to the bourgeois-capitalist model of society. The 'solution' to these problems was the 'invention' of an 'intermediary instance': the social. The social neutralized political conflicts by making it possible to redefine political questions as (socio-)

---

26. Especially in an Anglo-Saxon context, the problematic of government has been receiving more and more attention; see Burchell, Gordon and Miller, *The Foucault Effect: Studies in Governmentality* (1991); Gane and Johnson, *Foucault's New Domains* (1993); Barry, Osborne and Rose, *Foucault and Political Reason: Liberalism, Neo-liberalism and Rationalities of Government* (1996); as well as *Economy & Society* (special issue 'Liberalism, Neo-Liberalism and Governmentality' 22/3, August 1993) and *Dansk Sociologi* (October 1995, special issue 'Det sociale og velfærdsstaten').

technical matters and subordinate them to the 'rules' of liberal-capitalist socialization. However, the counterpart of subsuming the political to the social in this manner was the tension that followed from affirming the social in opposition to the economic. The constitution of an 'insurance society' presupposes its integration into an order that (re)produces the economy. Donzelot characterizes Keynesian 'general theory' as a technique for binding together the economy and the social sphere in circular fashion; hereby, the economy provides the means for social redistribution, which in turn is employed to stimulate the economy.[27] That said, the Keynesian model of reciprocal economic and social amplification has, for some time now, been in a state of crisis; consequently, neoliberal critique has gained ground, insisting on an 'economization of the social' in view of decreasing economic growth and mounting social expenditures.

The importance of neoliberalism (especially the North American variant Foucault discusses) lies in its effort to do away with tension between the social and economic realms. The former is no longer mobilized by (and against) the latter; instead, the two are joined together. A relation of necessary complementarity replaces the Keynesian goal of achieving a cyclical balance. Donzelot rightly observes that erasing the borderline between the social and the economic realms does not signal the end of the social so much as it yields another topography. Integrating economic constraint into the social sphere combines greater efficiency with lower costs and promotes the 'autonomization of the social'. The crisis of Keynesianism and the dismantling of the 'welfare state' do not mean returning to early liberal modes of politics, but recoding security politics to facilitate the development of interventionistic technologies, which lead and induce individuals without being responsible for them. Neoliberalism encourages individuals to give their lives entrepreneurial form. It reacts to increased 'demand' for self-fashioning and autonomy by extending an 'offer' to individuals and collectives: they should actively participate in solving matters and problems which, until this point, had been the responsibility of specialized and appointed state apparatuses. The 'price' is that they themselves must take on responsibility for such participation – and their own failure.[28]

---

27. Donzelot, *L'invention du social* (1984), 157–77.

28. Donzelot, 'Wiederkehr des Sozialen' (1995); Burchell, 'Liberal Government and Techniques of the Self' (1993), 275–6.

Donzelot shows how this 'economization of the social' changed the conception of social risk for good. Focus on the problematic of risk shifted from the principle of collective responsibility for ills resulting from life in society towards attaching greater significance to the civic duties of particulars to diminish the burden they impose on society. The political aim is to break open subjects' legal-statutory position by way of moral-economic autonomization. If, under the security contract of old, the fact of illness had implied the right to treatment, today's 'medical crisis' represents a liquidation of this same right; the double mechanism of prevention and self-conduct induces the subject to assume responsibility for his or her own health. Illness, then, is evaluated in terms of expense – and especially with regard to possible abuses of patients' rights and excessive intervention on the part of physicians:

> The crucial factor is not so much a shifting of the frontiers between the normal and the pathological, as the making of these frontiers into items negotiable within society in terms of a pervasive reality-principle which weighs the meaning of life against its cost, in the presence of a state which proposes henceforth only to chair and animate the debate.[29]

Neoliberalism introduces new liberties by handing over everything, at least in principle, to processes of social transaction. It is permitted to speak about anything – on the condition that negotiations occur in terms of cost and utility. Robert Castel has stressed that inasmuch as matters are restricted to what counts as 'realistic', neoliberal 'freedoms' enable new forms of control that avoid both authoritarian repression and the welfare state. Whereas the former include as many citizens as possible by mobilizing coherent apparatuses and bureaucratic instruments, now, new methods emerge that seek to maximize utility. Such technologies no longer separate or eliminate undesired elements from the social body, nor do they reintegrate them with corrective or therapeutic interventions; instead, the point is to assign individuals different social destinies in keeping with their ability to stand up to the demands of competition and profit.[30]

---

29. Donzelot, 'Pleasure in Work' (1991), 280; see also Donzelot, 'L'avenir du social' (1996), 67–81; Foucault, 1976d, 'The Crisis of Medicine or the Crisis of Anti-medicine?' [2004], 16–19.

30. Castel, 'From Dangerousness to Risk' (1991), esp. 293–6. Two technological

In conjunction with Foucault's concept of governmentality, Peter Miller and Nikolas Rose have examined neoliberal conceptions from the perspective of 'governing the autonomous self'. They demonstrate that neoliberal technologies seek to influence individuals' and groups' capacity for self-regulation so they may be combined strategies for maximizing profit and achieving socio-political goals:

> Political authorities no longer seek to govern by instructing individuals in all spheres of their existence, from the most intimate to the most public. Individuals themselves, as workers, managers and members of families, can be mobilized in alliance with political objectives, in order to deliver economic growth, successful enterprise and optimum personal happiness.[31]

According to neoliberal rationality, economic prosperity and personal well-being are closely linked. Work and free time no longer stand opposed to each other; instead, they are complementary: work should admit 'free' shaping, just as freedom ought to be used 'economically'. The 'personal dimension' no longer represents a stumbling block for increasing productivity, but its vehicle. The 'autonomous' subjectivity of productive individuals no longer stands in the way of economic success; instead, it represents its foundation. 'Self-determination' counts as a key economic resource and factor in production. From the perspective of enterprise, this means that fewer and fewer efforts are needed to restrict individual freedom, since working represents an essential component of 'self-realization'. The harmony foreseen by neoliberalism admits no separation between the economic, psychological

---

innovations in particular make it possible to do so: establishing risk profiles through data gathering and data processing and prognostic medicine, which allows an 'ideal' way of living to be specified on the basis of identifying and mapping genes. Castel, 'From Dangerousness to Risk' (1991); Gaudillière, 'Sequenzieren, Zählen und Vorhersehen – Praktiken einer Gen-Verwaltung' (1995); Feyerabend, 'Gentests im Vorsorgestaat' (1997). Pat O'Malley has discussed the morally responsible and rationally calculating individual as two complementary elements of the neoliberal conception of risk. In his estimation, the strategic goal of neoliberalism is to affirm the 'duty of wellness' in relation to 'irrationalities of irresponsibility'. O'Malley, 'Risk and Responsibility' (1996), 201.

31. Miller and Rose, 'Governing Economic Life' (1990), 28. Miller and Rose enlist, besides Foucault's analysis of government, Bruno Latour's socio-constructivist studies. For details of their research strategy, see Rose and Miller, 'Political Power Beyond the State' (1992).

and social realms. Flexible working hours, self-determining cohorts of workers, incentives to achieve and so on, not only aim to transform the organization of production; they also concern the relationship between individuals and the labour they perform. Or, more precisely: it is possible to transform structures of production only inasmuch as individuals 'optimize' their relationship to themselves and their work.[32]

If this premise is correct and neoliberal strategy seeks to replace outdated, rigid regulatory mechanisms with techniques of self-regulation, then it is necessary to investigate the self-steering capacities of the 'autonomous individual' and how they connect with forms of political domination and economic exploitation. The political 'stakes' of Foucault's later studies on the 'genealogy of the modern subject' concern precisely this shift of governmental techniques. Because neo-liberalism not only 'discovers' a new form of the social but also finds a new ('autonomous') form of subjectivity – which it fits out with political imperatives – the problem of 'resistant subjectivity' arises: subjectivity that rejects these same demands and impositions. Foucault addresses the matter by changing the course of his *History of Sexuality*.

---

32. Miller and Rose, 'Governing Economic Life' (1990), 15–31; Donzelot, 'Pleasure in Work' (1991).

# Part III

## Politics and Ethics

# 10

# From the History of Sexuality to the Genealogy of Ethics

Parallel to lecturing on governmentality and analysing liberal and neo-liberal technologies of government, Foucault continued working on the project of the 'history of sexuality'. However, these two courses of study were not independent of each other; rather, the problematic of government led him to give up the book project as planned and start from a new angle – and with considerable temporal delay. If Foucault had started by localizing the constitution of 'sexuality' in practices of power-knowledge, he subsequently shifted the investigative focus to the genealogy of the modern subject as the continuation and completion of the genealogy of the modern state. As such, *The History of Sexuality* does not take sexuality as its object; instead, sexuality provides the point of departure for examining the defining principles of a certain form of subjectivity in which the problem of sexual pleasure and desire plays a sizeable role.

The first volume of *The History of Sexuality* appeared in 1976 under the title *The History of Sexuality, Volume 1*. The back cover of this edition announced five volumes that would comprise the overall project.[1] In

---

1. As projected, the second volume (*La chair et le corps*) would treat the prehistory of our modern experience of sexuality and concentrate on the experience of pleasure in early Christianity. The objects of volumes 3–5 were to be elements of sexual problematization that proved increasingly significant over the course of the eighteenth and nineteenth centuries. Volume 3 (*La croisade des enfants*) would analyse the problem of childhood sexuality; volume 4 (*La femme, la mère et l'hystérique*) the sexualization of the female body; and volume 5 (*Les pervers*) the figure of the pervert. In Foucault's initial design, the final volume (*Population et races*) would explore the themes of population and race in the historical context of 'bio-politics'. Davidson, 'Ethics as Ascetics: Foucault, the History of Ethics, and Ancient Thought' (1994), 65.

1984 – years after the anticipated publication date – *The Use of Pleasure* and *The Care of the Self* appeared as the second and third parts. A look at the contents attests to a considerable revision of the original plan. The changes bear on all levels of investigation. First, Foucault turns his focus to an entirely new historical epoch. The objects of studies to date had been situated in the period extending from the seventeenth to the nineteenth century. Now, Foucault turns his attention to Greco-Roman antiquity. Likewise, the mode of presentation has changed. The style is considerably easier to read and less polemical than in earlier works. But differences do not concern only the period under examination or the form of presentation. The introduction to the second volume sets forth an array of new concepts and another research goal: in the second and third volumes of *The History of Sexuality*, neither knowledge formations nor technologies of power occupy centre stage; instead, the books focus on processes of subjectivation and ethical questions.[2]

Many commentators took Foucault's new-found interest in subjectivity and the ancient 'art of living' as evidence that he had abandoned the theme of power explored in earlier works. Accordingly, after the 'failure' of the genealogy of power, Foucault is supposed to have made a 'turn',[3] or a 'surprising return' that resulted in taking up subject-theoretical considerations again.[4] *The Use of Pleasure* and *The Care of the Self* count as Foucault's 'return'[5] to his earliest interests, which were shaped by existentialist concerns. Foucault is said to have travelled from a 'philosophy of free subjectivity oriented on Heidegger', via detours through the archaeology of knowledge and the genealogy of power, back to a 'philosophy of existence' focused on 'sovereign, individual relations to the self'.[6] In brief, 'much to the chagrin of many of his supporters', he is supposed to have 'virtually abandoned the question of power'[7] in his final works.[8]

---

2. Foucault, 1983k, 'On the Genealogy of Ethics: an Overview of Work in Progress', 5; Foucault, 1983l, 'Discussion with Michel Foucault', 1–4; Kammler and Plumpe, 'Antikes Ethos und postmoderne Lebenskunst' (1987), 186–9; Rüb, 'Von der Macht zur Lebenskunst' (1988), 97–104. On the publication history and rearrangement of the overall project, see Eribon, *Michel Foucault* (1991), 317–24.

3. Visker, *Michel Foucault: Genealogie als Kritik* (1991), 104.

4. Honneth, 'Afterword to the Second German Edition' (1997a), xix.

5. Fink-Eitel, *Foucault zur Einführung* (1989), 99.

6. Ibid., 103.

7. O'Farrell, *Foucault: Historian or Philosopher?* (1989), 119–20.

8. Wilhelm Schmid provided one of the first and most detailed examinations of

In keeping with readers' political positions, this change meets with regret or welcome. In either case, interpreters assume that Foucault broke with the problematic of his earlier works and changed the theoretical field of analysis. It counts as a given that his engagement with practices of subjectivation has nothing to do with his previous interest in power processes – that the late works represent a caesura in his theoretical project.

In fact, however, the follow-up volumes in *The History of Sexuality* do not represent the abandonment of the analysis of power. On the contrary, by developing it and offering correctives, they stand in continuity with early works – adding nuance and relativizing them all the while. If, in *Discipline and Punish*, Foucault still thematized subjectivity in terms of 'docile bodies' and examined their 'production' through disciplinary technology, now, by enlisting the concept of government, he explores historical forms of 'relations to the self' and the ways they connect with power processes and knowledge-forms. In

---

Foucault's final books in the German language. Schmid, *Auf der Suche nach einer neuen Lebenskunst* (1991). The author's intention is to make volumes 2 and 3 of *The History of Sexuality* bear fruit for a 'new founding of ethics' in order to affirm an 'art of living' or 'aesthetics of existence' counter to the laws of normalization society. That said, this theoretical project gives rise to at least two grave problems.

First, there is the question whether the 'art of living' that Schmid sketches is not simply an 'inversion' of the universalist, Enlightenment morality he criticizes. One suspects that replacing the perspective of general rules with individual self-fashioning simply amounts to changing the position of the norm. Inasmuch as the art of living serves a 'new founding' of *Ethics*, writ large, it plays a role with regard to other conceptions of ethics that is just as prescriptive as universalist morality – and like the latter, it reduces the multiplicity of perspectives of valuation to a single maxim, even if it casts matters in terms of styling existence along individual lines.

The second problem follows from the first. Although Schmid denies the frequent objection that Foucault's interest in subjectivity and ethics implies turning from the political to the private, the nature of his study prevents him from systematically addressing the question of how ethical questions are tied to social and political practices. Indeed, Schmid elides the question of how the 'art of living' achieves intersubjective validity and – against his declared attention – comes to advocate an individualist ethics that fits quite well with universalist morality: 'The essential feature of the art of living is not some moral bindingness, but self-responsible work on the forms in which existence is to be shaped, the experiment of thinking and living otherwise'. Ibid., 39–40.

The following attempts to show that Foucault's conception of politics and ethics – counter to Schmid's interpretation, and notwithstanding points of theoretical ambivalence of its own – is not limited to declaring a 'new art of living'. Instead, it voices a political will: not to be governed.

other words, Foucault does not change the theoretical terrain so much
as he recognizes that he has failed to do justice to the analytical categories of his 'genealogy of power'. *The Use of Pleasure* and *The Care of
the Self* approach the problem of the productivity of power from a new
theoretical perspective with different concepts: namely, by opening an
additional dimension for genealogical analysis. The questions remain
posed 'within the framework of [the] general problem of power
relations'.[9]

The concept of government stands at the centre of this 'theoretical shift'.[10] Foucault's analysis of modern governmentality has yielded
evidence that government represents a historical form of power that
operates via subjects and their freedom. Accordingly, subjectivity does
not mark the outer limit of power relations, nor does it designate a
field of application for them. Modern power mechanisms function 'by
means of' specific forms of subjectivation. If this premise is correct,
then Foucault needs to investigate the forms of subjectivity that government presupposes. The 'genealogy of the modern subject' cannot
be detached from investigating modern power mechanisms inasmuch
as analysing government means working out the relationship between
forms of governing the self and forms of governing others: 'the point

---

9. Ewald, 'Foucault verdauen' (1989), 56; see also Pasquino, 'Michel Foucault
(1926–84): The Will to Knowledge' (1986b), 104; Smart, 'On the Subjects of Sexuality,
Ethics, and Politics in the Work of Foucault' (1991), 203–4; Adorno, *Le style du philosophe: Foucault et le dire-vrai* (1996), 80–7. 'I don't think there is a great difference
between these books and the earlier ones. When you write books like these, you want
very much to change what you think entirely and to find yourself at the end of it
quite different from what you were at the beginning. Then you come to see that really
you've changed relatively little. You may have changed your point of view, you've gone
round and round the problem, which is still the same'. Foucault, 1984t, 'An Aesthetics
of Existence' [1988], 48; Foucault, 1984a, *The Use of Pleasure* [1990], 11–12.

Luc Ferry and Alain Renaut also claim that continuity prevails between Foucault's
early analytics of power and his later studies. Ferry and Renaut, *French Philosophy of
the Sixties: An Essay on Antihumanism* (1990), 68–121. For them, however, Foucault's
work exemplifies a theoretical convergence that 'philosophically legitimizes the heterogeneity that emptied the fluid Ego of substance'. Ibid., 65. By their account, the
final volumes of *The History of Sexuality* attest to a philosophical bearing that puts
the subject on 'trial'. Ibid., 105. That said, an all-encompassing charge of hostility to
the subject takes the place of detailed analysis: not only do Ferry and Renault rely on
a substantialist conception of subjectivity; they also run together highly different theoretical works into a homogeneous mass, ultimately presenting a caricature of what
they call '68 philosophy'.

10. Foucault, 1984a, *The Use of Pleasure* [1990], 6.

was to reintroduce the problem of the subject which I had more or less left aside in my first studies'.[11]

As such, it was not enough for a 'history of sexuality' to identify the productivity of power-knowledge complexes in order to critique the repressive hypothesis. Foucault had already freed himself from an analytical scheme that views sexuality as an ontological constant and traces its concrete, historical forms to mechanisms of repression and denial. But he had not gone far enough by simply remarking the inadequacy of this tradition of thinking. He still needed to be able to reach beyond the repressive model and show, in positive terms, how subjects come to recognize a specific 'use of pleasures' as 'sexual' subjects or 'subjects of desire'. If 'sexuality' is not a universal-historical phenomenon, but a historical singularity, and if it does not represent the product of a process of repression, Foucault had to go beyond concentrating on power mechanisms and knowledge formations. It proved necessary to expand the analytical instrumentarium in order to investigate 'the forms within which individuals are able, are obliged, to recognize themselves as subjects of this sexuality'.[12] Previous works had lacked this perspective, and so 'a lot of things which were implicit could not be rendered explicit due to the manner in which I posed the problems'.[13]

In this uncharted space within analysis of power, Foucault introduces two key concepts: *technologies of the self* and *experience*.

---

11. Foucault, 1984q, 'The Return of Morality' [1988], 253; Foucault, 1984i, '"Foucault" by Maurice Florence' [1998], 463. 'I am saying that "governmentality" implies the relationship of the self to itself, and I intend this concept of "governmentality" to cover the whole range of practices that constitute, define, organize, and instrumentalize the strategies that individuals in their freedom can use in dealing with each other'. Foucault, 1984s, 'The Ethics of the Concern for the Self as a Practice of Freedom' [1997], 300.

12. Foucault, 1984a, *The Use of Pleasure* [1990], 4.

13. Foucault, 1984q, 'The Return of Morality' [1988], 243. Matthias Rüb has pointed to many formulations in the introduction to *The Use of Pleasure* that suggest that Foucault ran into a problem in the analysis of power that made its further development necessary: 'I had to', 'was not sufficient', 'seemed necessary', etc. Rüb, 'Von der Macht zur Lebenskunst' (1988), 100; see also Foucault, 1984a, *The Use of Pleasure* [1990], 4–6.

## Technologies of the Self

Foucault develops his new theoretical perspective by consciously taking a distance from earlier works by means of an 'auto-critique'.[14] In so doing, he takes up a distinction that was fundamental for Jürgen Habermas's works during the 1960s and 1970s. Foucault distinguishes three technologies that may serve as analytical grids for all societies:

> the techniques that permit one to produce, to transform, to manipulate things; the techniques that permit one to use sign systems; and finally, the techniques that permit one to determine the conduct of individuals, to impose certain ends or objectives.[15]

That said, Foucault does not simply take over a predefined typology; he adds a fourth analytical dimension. To the techniques of production, sign systems and conduct, he adds 'technologies of the self'. The latter are defined by the way they 'permit individuals to effect, by their own means, a certain number of operations on their own bodies, their own souls, their own thoughts, their own conduct, and this in a manner so

---

14. Foucault, 1981c, 'Sexuality and Solitude' [1997], 177; Foucault, 1993, 'About the Beginning of the Hermeneutics of the Self' [1980], 203.

15. Foucault, 1981c, 'Sexuality and Solitude' [1997], 177. This typology resurfaces almost word for word in Foucault, 1993, 'About the Beginning of the Hermeneutics of the Self' [1980], 203; and in modified form in Foucault, 1988b, 'Technologies of the Self' [1982], 18 and Foucault, 1982b, 'The Subject and Power', 216–19. Habermas develops this distinction in *Knowledge and Human Interests* and 'Technology and Science as "Ideology"'. Habermas, 'Technology and Science as "Ideology"' (2014), esp. 88–93. On Foucault's productively critical view of Habermas, see, also, 1984s, 298: 'I am quite interested in his work, although I know he completely disagrees with my views. While I, for my part, tend to be a little more in agreement with what he says, I have always had a problem insofar as he gives communicative relations this place which is so important and, above all, a function that I would call "utopian"'.
    Didier Eribon offers an excellent account of relations between Foucault and Habermas, including their meeting in 1983, Habermas's erroneous assessment of French philosophy (especially Foucault's work), and Foucault's reservations about a 'theory of communicative action'. All the same, Eribon systematically underestimates the theoretico-political significance that Foucault assigned to Habermas – despite, or precisely because of, their numerous points of disagreement. In many works, Foucault refers directly to questions that Habermas has raised. Accordingly, it is inaccurate to claim that the 'Foucault-Habermas debate' is something 'artificial … fabricated by US-American intellectual circumstances'. Eribon, *Michel Foucault et ses contemporains* (1994a), 309, 289–311; Kelly, 'Foucault, Habermas, and the Self-Referentiality of Critique' (1994).

as to transform themselves, modify themselves, and to attain a certain state of perfection, happiness, purity, supernatural power'.[16]

The concept of technologies of the self moves individuals' relation to themselves to the centre of attention. For all that, this emphasis does not amount to rehashing subject-philosophy. It extends in 'another direction',[17] opening a completely new realm of historicity that replaces the philosophy of the subject with the history of subjectivities. In other words, Foucault takes a further step away from subject-philosophy. In early works, he had presupposed the subject negatively, as it were, inasmuch as he conceived it as a function of power-knowledge complexes. Now, however, theoretical reflection bears on the self-constitution of subjectivity.[18]

The various technologies in question do not belong to separate spheres that are closed off from each other. Instead, they influence and condition each other reciprocally. In particular, Foucault's interest bears on the relationship between technologies of domination and technologies of the self; the way they are configured defines the field

---

16. Foucault, 1981c, 'Sexuality and Solitude' [1997], 177; see also Foucault, 1981h, 'Subjectivity and Truth' [1997], 87–8; Foucault, 1984a, *The Use of Pleasure* [1990], 10–11; Foucault, 1988b, 'Technologies of the Self' [1982], 18. That said, the changes must also be viewed in light of the different objects under examination: 'I thought that the techniques of domination were the most important, without any exclusion of the rest. But, analyzing the experience of sexuality, I became more and more aware that there is in all societies, I think, in all societies whatever they are, another type of techniques'. Foucault, 1993, 'About the Beginning of the Hermeneutics of the Self' [1980], 203.

17. Foucault, 1981c, 'Sexuality and Solitude' [1997], 176.

18. Wilhelm Schmid points out that this expanded scope of analysis occurs 'along Heideggerian lines'. Schmid, *Auf der Suche nach einer neuen Lebenskunst* (1991), 216. If Heidegger showed how technology creates objects, Foucault examines how it makes individuals into subjects: 'For Heidegger, it was through an increasing obsession with *techné* as the only way to arrive at an understanding of objects that the West lost touch with Being. Let's turn the question around and ask which techniques and practices form the Western concept of the subject, giving it its characteristic split of truth and error, freedom and constraint'. Foucault, quoted in Schmid, *Auf der Suche nach einer neuen Lebenskunst* (1991), 216. Schmid identifies points of similarity and difference between Heidegger and Foucault with commendable precision. Ibid., 200–18. Hubert L. Dreyfus and Paul Rabinow point to a series of theoretical parallels, as does Rainer Forst. Dreyfus and Rabinow, *Michel Foucault: Beyond Structuralism and Hermeneutics* (1983); Forst, 'Endlichkeit Freiheit Individualität: Die Sorge um das Selbst bei Heidegger und Foucault' (1990). For Foucault's own account of Heidegger's significance for his work, see Foucault, 1984q, 'The Return of Morality' [1988], 250; Foucault, 1988a, 'Truth, Power, Self', 12–13.

of power relations. In this new theoretical orientation, then, power relations encompass both technologies of domination and technologies of the self. In contrast to earlier works, where technologies of domination occupied the foreground, Foucault now concentrates on subjectivation processes in order to 'study power relations starting from the techniques of the self'.[19]

By expanding the field of analysis in this way, Foucault offers a corrective to possible interpretations of the 'genealogy of power' along deterministic lines. The concept of technologies of the self leads him to reassess the meaning of processes of subjectivation. Whereas earlier works displayed the tendency to equate self-constitution and subjugation, introducing the notion of technologies of the self loosens up the relationship between allo- and auto-constitution. In immediate terms, this 'methodological precaution' means that technologies of domination do not simply determine technologies of the self. What is more, the impossibility of deriving the one from the other implies that their relations do not necessarily exhibit harmony or reinforce each other reciprocally. Technologies of the self do not always amount to an appendix or supplement to technologies of power, that is, their reflection or expression.[20]

However, Foucault's rejection of monocausal determinism between power processes and forms of subjectivation does not mean that their relationship is arbitrary or does not follow a pattern. Although no 'analytical or necessary link'[21] holds between relations to the self and social, economic or political structures, this does not mean that there are no connections at all. Foucault relaxes the bond between technologies of the self and technologies of domination, but he does not give up on examining their relationship. On the contrary, doing so is what opens the possibility for analysing them in the first place: the 'relative autonomy' of technologies of the self, not their determinate nature, constitutes them as an independent object of investigation with a specific historicity.

Foucault enlists the concept of government to elucidate what it means to replace a general and necessary causality with historical and

---

19. Foucault, 1981c, 'Sexuality and Solitude' [1997], 177; Foucault, 1988b, 'Technologies of the Self' [1982], 19.
20. Burchell, 'Liberal Government and Techniques of the Self' (1993), 268–9.
21. Foucault, 1983b, 'On the Genealogy of Ethics: An Overview of Work in Progress', 236.

contingent connections when describing the relationship between technologies of the self and technologies of domination:

> If one wants to analyse the genealogy of the subject in Western civilization, he has to take into account not only techniques of domination but also techniques of the self. Let's say: he has to take into account the interaction between those two types of techniques – techniques of domination and techniques of the self. He has to take into account the points where the technologies of domination of individuals over one another have recourse to the processes by which the individual acts upon himself. And conversely, he has to take into account the points where the techniques of the self are integrated into structures of coercion or domination. The contact point, where the individuals are driven by others is tied to the way they conduct themselves, is what we can call, I think, government. Governing people, in the broad meaning of the word, governing people is not a way to force people to do what the governor wants; it is always a versatile equilibrium, with complementarity and conflicts between techniques which assure coercion and processes through which the self is constructed or modified by himself.[22]

In this light, technologies of the self do not represent a departure from the problematic of power; it is a matter of 'tak[ing] up the question of governmentality from a different angle'.[23] Foucault's theoretical interest in the 1980s focuses on government of the self as it relates to other forms of government. He does not stop asking about power; instead, he 'change[s] direction'.[24] To this end, he introduces a second concept,

---

22. Foucault, 1993, 'About the Beginning of the Hermeneutics of the Self' [1980], 203–4. See the nearly identical formulation in the Howison Lecture at Berkeley in 1980, which Tom Keenan quotes. Keenan, 'Foucault on Government' (1982), 38.

23. Foucault, 1981h, 'Subjectivity and Truth' [1997], 88.

24. Foucault, 1984n, 'The Concern for Truth' [1988], 258. It amounts to a complete misunderstanding of Foucault's theoretical and political interests to claim, as Arpád Szakolczai does, that he 'gave up' analysing strategies of power and the concept of governmentality in order to pursue the genealogy of subjectivity. Szakolczai appeals to the very opposition between power and subjectivity that Foucault wanted to undermine with the concept of government, and he depicts Foucault's studies of the 1970s as a kind of theoretical 'cage' that kept him from exploring the problem that really interested him: the relationship between subjectivity and truth. Apart from the problematic representation of Foucault as a searcher who finally – after getting off track a few times – 'discovered' his 'actual' problems, it is simply false to claim that

which, like the concept of government, is arranged in comprehensive terms: in *The Use of Pleasure* and *The Care of the Self*, the point is to show 'how ... an "experience" [is] formed in which the relationship to oneself and the relationship to others are linked together'.[25]

## Subjectivity and Experience

The concept of experience had already played a key role in *History of Madness*. Here, Foucault contrasted the formation of the modern, rational subject with an originary experience of madness, forever external to processes of rationalization. Later on, he faulted himself for advancing an ahistorical conception of experience that relied on the idea of a 'wild outside' and, for this reason, failed to explain how one and the same historical process brings forth the rational subject and its reverse, the mad subject. When Foucault incorporates the concept of experience into the framework of *The History of Sexuality*, it would appear to point to a continuity when, in fact, a new definition of the term is at work.[26]

Adding the dimension of technologies of the self shifts the focus of *The History of Sexuality* from objective power-knowledge complexes to the subjectivation of the subject, expanding the field of analysis with 'practices of the self'.[27] That said, the category of experience does not mean that interest now bears on the 'subjective factor' – the inner world of the individual as a subjective-personal dimension opposed to the objective-material sphere of power and knowledge. Instead, *experience* refers to what produces the integral connection between analytically distinct realms:

> What I planned, therefore, was a history of the experience of sexual-
> ity, where experience is understood as the correlation between fields of
> knowledge, types of normativity, and forms of subjectivity in a particular
> culture.[28]

---

power is 'not his problem, and it never was'. Szakolczai, 'From Governmentality to the Genealogy of Subjectivity's Path in the 1980s' (1993), 14 and 6.

25. Foucault, 1984n, 'The Concern for Truth' [1988], 258.

26. Foucault, 1969a, *Archaeology of Knowledge* [2002], 17–18; Foucault, 1984e, 'Preface to the History of Sexuality, Vol. II'; Foucault, 1980d, *Remarks on Marx* [1991], 25–42.

27. Foucault, 1984s, 'The Ethics of the Concern for the Self as a Practice of Freedom' [1997], 291.

28. Foucault, 1984a, *The Use of Pleasure* [1990], 4; Foucault, 1984e, 'Preface to the

Foucault's reference to 'experience', then, does not mean that he is limiting the investigation to how events are felt on a personal level. Instead, he wants to look at *seemingly* personal and subjective matters in relation to forms of knowledge and processes of power. The whole of these relations is what defines experience. Knowledge, power and subjectivity each constitute a dimension of experience; instead of being examined discretely, they must be viewed in terms of their interrelationship. In turn, this means that one can no longer start out from an originary and immediate experience and then compare and contrast it with types of knowledge and forms of power. In the framework Foucault now sets up, experience does not mark a point of departure so much as it results from the practices that constitute it.[29] And so, the condition that makes experience possible does not lie in a subject anterior to experience; rather, '[i]t is experience which is the rationalization of a process, itself provisional, which results in a subject, or rather, in subjects. I will call subjectivization the procedure by which one obtains the constitution of a subject, or more precisely, of a subjectivity which is of course only one of the given possibilities of organization of a self-consciousness.'[30]

By historicizing processes of subjectivation, Foucault breaks with the idea of sovereign and constitutive subjectivity. Instead of positing an essential subject, he views subjectivity in terms of a process of becoming. This methodological step entails a 'decentring of the subject'. The condition enabling experience in general represents one possible experience among others. The subject does not stand as the sole form of human existence, nor is it the source of all experience: because the subject is a form and not a substance, there is no 'universal form of subject to be found everywhere'.[31]

---

History of Sexuality, Vol. II'.

29. Foucault, 1984q, 'The Return of Morality' [1988], 243.

30. Ibid., 253. 'The experience we have of ourselves undoubtedly seems to us to be the most immediate and originary, yet in fact it involves schemes and historically constituted practices'. Foucault, quoted in Schmid, *Auf der Suche nach einer neuen Lebenskunst* (1991), 259.

31. Foucault, 1984t, 'An Aesthetics of Existence' [1988], 50; see also Foucault, 1984s, 'The Ethics of the Concern for the Self as a Practice of Freedom' [1997], 291. In this context, Gilles Deleuze remarked 'a sort of neo-Kantianism unique to Foucault'. Like Kant, Foucault is interested in the conditions of possibility of experience – if only to pose an entirely different question: 'the conditions are those of real experience (statements, for example, assume a limited corpus); they are on the side of the

Defining experience in this way offers a host of analytical advantages. First of all, it means viewing subjectivity as a *concretely historical construction*, not as an abstractly natural constant. Defining the subject as a form does not mean that it can now be filled with variable historical contents; as a historical phenomenon, it is the product of specific ways of organizing subjectivity. Taking this methodological approach makes it possible to pose the question of experience outside, or beyond, the subjective realm.[32] Foucault's historicizing definition points to the limits of any given experience and, as such, connects his theory with the notion of 'limit-experience' developed in literary texts by Pierre Klossowski, Maurice Blanchot and Georges Bataille. In this context, the accent does not fall on grounding the subject, but dissolving it: experience is what prevents subjects from remaining self-identical inasmuch as they are constantly changing; in the process, the field of experience changes, too.[33]

Second, this potential for transformation points to another important aspect of experience: its connection to *collective praxis*. Although experiences occur individually, they belong to a social space defined by certain forms of knowledge, power practices and technologies of the self. Accordingly, individual experiences have an index in the collective practices that make them possible – just as, conversely, changes in 'subjective' factors provide the point of departure for social changes:

> starting from experience, it is necessary to clear the way for a transformation, a metamorphosis which isn't simply individual but which has a character accessible to others: that is, this experience must be linkable, to a certain extent, to a collective practice and to a way of thinking. That is how it happened, for example, for such movements as antipsychiatry, or the prisoners' movement in France.[34]

---

"object" and historical formation, not a universal subject (the *a priori* itself is historical); all are forms of exteriority'. Deleuze, *Foucault* (1988), 60; see also Foucault, 1984i, '"Foucault" by Maurice Florence' [1998], 459.

32. 'Can't there be experiences in which the subject, in its constitutive relations, in its self-identity, isn't given any more? And thus wouldn't experiences be given in which the subject could dissociate itself, break its relationship with itself, lose its identity?'. Foucault, 1980d, *Remarks on Marx* [1991], 49.

33. Ibid., 29–30; Foucault, 1984i, '"Foucault" by Maurice Florence' [1998], 462.

34. Ibid., 38–9; see also Foucault, 1984g, 'Polemics, Politics and Problematizations: An Interview with Michel Foucault', 385–6. *Expérience* means in French both 'experience' and 'experiment'; the term incorporates the dimension of the future into

Third, another feature of Foucault's conception of experience involves *basic devaluation*. Inasmuch as subjectivity is a form and experiences involve complex interplay between technologies of power, types of knowledge and subjective modes, truth and experience no longer admit direct comparison. Categories such as 'real', 'authentic' or 'right' – that is, terms bearing on (in)accuracy – no longer apply. Instead, the truth occupies a field of immanence; it is only generated in experiences and does not stand outside of them. Experience, as Foucault understands it, is not so much something true as something real: a historical fact located 'beyond true and false':

> an experience is neither true nor false: it is always a fiction, something constructed, which exists only after it has been made, not before; it isn't something that is 'true', but it has been a reality. To summarize, then: the difficult relation with truth is entirely at stake in the way in which truth is found used inside an experience, not fastened to it, and which, within certain limits, destroys it.[35]

This conception of experience defines the methodological specificity of Foucault's *History of Sexuality*. The project does not chart sexual conduct, nor does it catalogue ideas about sexuality. Instead, it sets out to analyse sexuality as a historical experience. Sexuality is viewed as an ensemble comprising three concurrent dimensions: a field of knowledge defined by means of terminology, concepts, theories, scientific disciplines and so on; a body of rules separating what is permitted from the forbidden, the natural from the monstrous, the normal from the pathological and so on; and finally, the individual's relation to him or herself, which makes it possible to recognize oneself as a sexual subject among others.[36]

---

the present: changing, trying out, experimenting, etc. In this sense, Foucault calls himself 'more an experimenter than a theorist'. Ibid., 27.

35. Ibid., 36.

36. Foucault, 1984e, 'Preface to the History of Sexuality, Vol. II', 333–4; Foucault, 1984n, 'The Concern for Truth' [1988], 257. These three analytically distinct levels also define the axes of genealogy. Instead of concentrating on complexes of power and knowledge (as in earlier works), Foucault now expands the field of investigation and explicitly identifies three independent aspects: knowledge, power and subjectivity. Foucault, 1983b, 'On the Genealogy of Ethics: An Overview of Work in Progress', 238–9; Foucault, 1984a, *The Use of Pleasure* [1990], 4–7; Foucault, 1984e, 'Preface to

Defined in this manner, Foucault's concept of experience articulates the intrinsic connection between the 'history of sexuality' and the topic of government: 'It is a matter of analysing "sexuality" as a historically singular mode of experience in which the subject is objectified for himself and for others through certain specific procedures of "government".'[37] Whereas, in *The History of Sexuality, Volume 1*, Foucault seeks to locate the historical construction of sexuality chiefly in practices of power/knowledge – and hardly takes practices of the self into account – further work leads to a problem that calls the project, as initially conceived, into question: 'while I was doing this project, I noticed that it was not working out. An important problem remained: why had we made sexuality into a *moral* experience?'.[38]

## Morality and Ethics

*The Use of Pleasure* and *The Care of the Self* have as much to do with sexuality as *Discipline and Punish* does with the prison. Just as the latter makes changes in penal institutions and practices the point of departure for examining discipline as a new technology of power, *The History of Sexuality* examines changes in technologies of the self on the basis of moral reflection on sexuality. The analytical goal in *Discipline and Punish* is to challenge the prison's 'normality' – the fact that it appears to be the sole, universal form of punishment – by reconstructing the historical conditions of its rise and considering other penal models. Similarly, *The Use of Pleasure* and *The Care of the Self* take aim at the 'naturalness' of the (desiring) subject by drawing the genealogy of this form and examining other modes of self-relation. In either case, the point of departure and precondition involves breaking with what counts as self-evident – posing a question, a problem.

In *The History of Sexuality*, the question concerns the seemingly natural connection between sexuality and moral concern. Why are sexual acts and pleasures the object of moral worry and disquiet? Why does such moral attention occur, and where does the immense interest

---

the History of Sexuality, Vol. II', 335–8; Foucault, 1984q, 'The Return of Morality' [1988], 243.

37. Foucault, 1984i, '"Foucault" by Maurice Florence' [1998], 463.

38. Foucault, 1984q, 'The Return of Morality' [1988], 252, emphasis added.

bearing on sexuality come from? The question may be formulated from the opposite perspective, too: why are other realms of individual or collective existence less morally charged than sexual behaviour? Why do, say, childhood education or diet represent matters of less moral concern? What is the basis for sexuality's exceptional status as a source of moral unease? This question – or, more accurately, this complex of questions – animates Foucault's investigations: 'It seemed to me, therefore, that the question that ought to guide my inquiry was the following: how, why, and in what forms was sexuality constituted as a moral domain?'.[39]

To be able to pose the question about the relations between sexuality and morality at all, Foucault takes issue with the perspective according to which moral concerns underlie prohibitions and tie them to mechanisms of sanction. Such a view holds that sexual activities pose a moral problem because they are subject to more or less codified prescriptions permitting certain modes of conduct and forbidding others. Foucault has two objections to this 'juridical' conception of the problem of morality. For one, the explanation is circular inasmuch as it cannot say why sexuality needs to be regulated by prohibitions in the first place. The latter do not explain moral concern so much as they require explanation themselves. Second, Foucault points out that moral disquiet is not always or exclusively the result of demands on conduct deriving from a system of prohibitions; indeed, moral worry may be especially pronounced when there are no explicit imperatives for action or codified schemes.[40]

The difference between the law and subjectivity prompts Foucault to make the central distinction between morality and ethics. Hereby, the *moral* sphere divides into three aspects:

1. The real behaviour of individuals in relation to the rules and values recommended to them: 'morality of behaviors';

2. The rules and values that define the positive or negative content of such behaviour: 'moral code';

3. Ways of 'conduct[ing] oneself', the relation individuals entertain with themselves: 'moral subjectivity'.[41]

---

39. Foucault, 1984a, *The Use of Pleasure* [1990], 10.
40. Ibid., 10, 22–3.
41. Ibid., 25–6; Foucault, 1983b, 'On the Genealogy of Ethics: An Overview of

Every moral experience is defined through the interplay of these three factors. On the one hand, they display relative independence. Neither does actual conduct mirror a given moral code, nor does self-relation represent the interiorization of a moral prescription. On the other hand, differences do exist in terms of the relative autonomy of elements. Code and behaviour only bear on each other in the sense of agreement or deviation, but relations between self-conduct and a given code may vary. Any fixed, moral prescription admits different modes of self-relation. The latter constitute what Foucault calls *ethics*: 'the elaboration of a form of relation to self that enables an individual to fashion himself into a subject of ethical conduct'.[42]

Inasmuch as all 'morality', understood broadly, involves both rules of conduct and forms of subjectivation, it is possible to distinguish moral experiences that place greater emphasis on the code from those that stress 'ethics'. In the first case, the systematicity and density-regulation of the code – separations between the forbidden and the permitted, instances of authority and penalty, and so on – prove decisive; conversely, subjectivation occurs 'in a quasi-juridical form'[43] inasmuch as moral subjects recognize laws and prescriptions to which they must subordinate themselves. But it is also possible to conceive forms of morality in which subjects make the moral focus their relation to self insofar as it is tested, tried out and transformed; in this case, the system of codes and regulations of conduct proves relatively insignificant. Following this typology, two axes of moral experience may be distinguished: one oriented on codes, and the other on ethics.[44]

This distinction between morality (in the narrower sense) and ethics stands in continuity with Foucault's critique of the juridical conception of power. The problem that the juridical conception of power poses involves the tendency to equate morality and ethics and subsume self-relations to codifications of behaviour. In making the analytical distinction between morality and ethics, Foucault sets out in a new investigative direction. The separation of ethics from morality shifts primacy from the moral law to forms of self-constitution.

Work in Progress', 238.
    42. Foucault, 1984a, *The Use of Pleasure* [1990], 251.
    43. Ibid., 29.
    44. Ibid., 29, translation modified; Foucault, 1984n, 'The Concern for Truth' [1988], 259; Deleuze, 'Life as Work of Art' (1995c), 100–1.

It is not just that relations to self are *not* the result of codifications of behaviour and imperatives to act in certain ways; more still, only the context of ethics discloses the significance of moral laws in the first place. Moral laws do not simply confront the moral subject from without; they cannot simply be imposed. Instead – however rudimentary a form they take – they must be willed and accepted, known and lived. The moral code must also be a form of self-relation so that the ethical subject can become a subject of the law. Instead of starting from the fact of the law, Foucault is interested in showing how morality takes on prohibitions and systems of obligation.[45]

Yet Foucault's critique does not proceed simply by rejecting the juridical conception or denouncing its flaws; rather, he exposes its 'falsehood' by situating it on a historical field and showing the contingent conditions that made it and its claims to universal validity count as 'right'. The centrepiece of this 'genealogy of morality'[46] is not the philosophical problem of how the moral code determines the behaviour of subjects in various ways, throughout a range of different intensities. Instead, Foucault dynamizes the field of questioning by placing it in a historical problematic. How was it possible for moral laws, prohibitions, laws and so on to play the roles they have played? How did moral experience come to be juridified, and why does the question of the law dominate ethics? In order to take on this problem, it is necessary to expand the analytical instruments that distinguish between morality and ethics. Only under such conditions can one understand how code-elements and forms of subjectivation have been equated – that is, view their connection as the result of a historical process, and not make it the starting point for theoretical analysis. Only when morality and ethics do not constitute an analytical unit can one examine the various forms their relations have assumed; drawing a distinction between them as separate categories enables one to reconstruct why, historically, they have counted as one and the same.

---

45. Pierre Macherey describes this difference in the line of questioning and the primacy of ethics with respect to moral law: '[O]ne must understand how the law, to the extent that it assumes the juridical form of prohibition, is itself only a particular and derived effect, whose production occurs in a more fundamental process which is not strictly speaking one of morality, in relation to certain systems of obligation and bodes, but of ethics'. Macherey, 'Foucault: Ethics and Subjectivity' (1998), 96.

46. Foucault, 1984t, 'An Aesthetics of Existence' [1988], 48–9; Foucault, 1983b, 'On the Genealogy of Ethics: An Overview of Work in Progress', 237.

This 'genealogy of ethics' introduces the question of subjective con-stitution in a comprehensive sense. In this light, the ethical subject does not represent a pre-existing substance; it is the result of practices of power, knowledge and self, whose interplay defines it. For Foucault, no essential subjectivity exists that may be set apart from its contin-gent features; there is no subject *per se* different from the historical circumstances of its realization. Foucault counters the traditional dichotomies operative in the social sciences and philosophy – which picture historical phenomena as a confrontation between two planes – with a radically historical approach defined by immanence. Hereby, the historical counts neither as a context, nor as an environment, for subjectivity; instead, subjectivity assumes a historically contingent and singular form, which no longer admits reference to, or relativization in terms of, generalized abstractions.[47]

This methodological decision also means changing the reality-index of subjectivation processes. They no longer derive from more fundamental practices to which they continue to refer, or on which they depend. They do not represent the 'interiorization' or 'expression' of political, economic or social reality. Instead, they constitute a reality *sui generis* and an independent field of history. Inasmuch as ethics shifts the focus from subjective essence to subjective form, historical modes of subjectivation provide the key to a reality that is no longer defined as the particular instantiation of something more general;

---

47. Viewing subjectivity as a historical form also enables Foucault to break through the *a priori* identity of subject and individual and distinguish different mean-ings of 'individualism': '(1) the individualistic attitude, characterized by the absolute value attributed to the individual in his singularity and by the degree of independence conceded to him vis-à-vis the group to which he belongs and the institutions to which he is answerable; (2) the positive valuation of private life ... (3) the intensity of the relations to self, that is, of the forms in which one is called upon to take oneself as an object of knowledge and a field of action, so as to transform, correct, and purify oneself, and find salvation. These attitudes can be interconnected, no doubt ... But these connections are neither constant nor necessary'. Foucault, 1984b, *The Care of the Self* [1986], 42. Thus, for example, a strong emphasis on the individual, his deeds and personal worth may be accompanied by a neglect of private life; conversely, a strong estimation of the private sphere may be attended by weak self-relation.

This methodological distinction permits Foucault to conceptualize the subject differently than classical-liberal theory by showing that possessive individualism does not represent a universal constant of human existence, just one possible form of sub-jectivation among others. Pizzorno, 'Foucault and the Liberal View of the Individual' (1992); for a comparison with the work of C. B. Macpherson, see Foucault, 1983n, 'A propos de Nietzsche, Habermas, Arendt, McPherson', 9–13.

instead, it stands apart in its singularity. At the same time, however, this singularity does not occupy a position opposed to universality – rather, it encompasses universality inasmuch as it reveals it to be a singular form, too. As such, the 'genealogy of ethics' is simultaneously a 'genealogy of the subject'.[48]

---

48. Foucault, 1984e, 'Preface to the History of Sexuality, Vol. II', 334–5; Macherey, 'Foucault: Ethics and Subjectivity' (1998), 97–100. For Foucault, Kant's particular merit is to view 'the self […] not merely [as] given but […] constituted in relationship to itself as subject'. However, he deems it problematic that Kant joins this insight to the politico-moral call to design a self-relation satisfying general categories: the construction of universal subjectivity. Foucault, 1983b, 'On the Genealogy of Ethics: An Overview of Work in Progress', 252. See Chapter 14.

# 11

# The Genealogy of the Modern Subject

---

*Subject*: that is the terminology of our belief in a *unity* among all the diverse elements of the highest feeling of reality: we regard this belief as the *effect* of one cause – we believe in our belief to such an extent that for its sake we imagine 'truth', 'reality', 'substantiality' in general.

'Subject' is the fiction that many *like* states in us are the effects of one substratum: yet it was *we* who created the 'likeness' of these conditions in the first place; the *fact* is our *likening* these and *making* them fit, *not* the likeness itself (which, rather, must be *denied*).

Nietzsche[1]

At its core, *The History of Sexuality, Volume 1* confronts, and rejects, the hypothesis that sexuality is prohibited and repressed. *The Use of Pleasure* and *The Care of the Self* also critique a line of thinking that represents an extension of the repressive hypothesis: the view that Christianity inaugurated a strict regime of prohibitions and constraints where free sexual morality had once prevailed, such that the tolerance and liberty of ancient Greece were replaced, in both quantitative and qualitative terms, by increased prohibitions and an intensified moral code. From this perspective, Christianity is supposed to have established a sharp line of division between previously unregulated sexuality and its repression, which holds to this very day.[2]

---

1. Nietzsche, 'Notebook 10, autumn 1887' (2003), 179.
2. The following reconstruction of *The History of Sexuality* pursues a double goal. In the framework of investigating sexual ethics, the point is, first, to analyse the historical conditions of existence for a 'universal moral subject' in order to show how governmental technology provides its 'infrastructure'; second, to demonstrate that Foucault's investigation of pre-Christian ethics seeks to identify the contours of

Foucault rejects this version of the repressive hypothesis, too. He demonstrates that, in fact, moral prescriptions hardly differed among the Greeks and early Christians. The medical and (moral) philosophical works of the first centuries of the Common Era feature an array of themes and concerns already found in classical Greek antiquity. They concern, in particular, four realms of moral interest: the sexual act's capacity to produce destructive effects on individual health; fidelity in marriage as an expression of inner strength and outward proof of self-control; same-sex practices between men as a source of moral apprehension; and the deep-seated connection between abstinence and achieving wisdom and truth.[3]

The enduring consistency of themes, worries and demands connecting the classical, Greek, Hellenistic-Roman and Christian worlds does not mean that Christian sexual morality was directly shaped by ancient thinking. Instead, the similarity of objects of moral concern

---

'another subjectivity' in order to find potentials for resisting modern forms of government. I will treat these aspects in sequence: Foucault's analysis of the emergence of the Christian subject of desire here, and the consequences that the 'genealogy of the modern subject' holds for analysing power in Chapter 12.

3. Foucault, 1984a, *The Use of Pleasure* [1990], 15–20. With its accentuation of continuity, this historical perspective implicitly critiques the Nietzschean opposition between Judeo-Christian slave morality and the master morality of the pagan Greeks. Ibid., 250–1. Foucault's reconstruction of ancient and early Christian sexuality and ethics concentrates on philosophical, medical and theological texts; it extends from Plato, Aristotle and Xenophon, onward to Roman Stoicism (Seneca, Marcus Aurelius, Epictetus) and, finally, to Cassian and Augustine. Analysis draws on historical studies by John Boswell, Kenneth J. Dover and Pierre Hadot, Foucault, 1982d, 'History and Homosexuality' [1996]; Foucault, 1982g, 'Des caresses d'hommes considérées comme un art'; Dover, *Greek Homosexuality* (1978); Boswell, *Christianity, Social Tolerance, and Homosexuality* (1980); Hadot, *Exercices spirituels et philosophie antique* (1981); as well as the works of Peter Brown and Paul Veyne. Foucault, 1984a, *The Use of Pleasure* [1990], 8–9; Foucault, 1984q, 'The Return of Morality' [1988], 244; Veyne, 'La Planète Foucault' (1984).

Francisco G. Ortega provides a thorough comparison of historical studies (especially those by Pierre Hadot and Peter Brown) on ancient subjectivity and Foucault's project. Although I do not share the opinion that Foucault's interest in ancient forms of subjectivity 'culminates' in an ethics of friendship, Ortega's study is an extraordinarily erudite and detailed analysis of Foucault's final works, which rightly stresses the meaning of the government problematic for analysing subjectivity: '*without the shift in the realm of power that leads to the question of governing, it would have been impossible for Foucault to move on to the other axis, that of the subject*'. Ortega, *Freie Formen von Sozietät als Problem einer Ethik der ästhetischen Selbstkonstitution in Foucaults historischer Anthropologie des Subjekts* (1995), 105, emphasis in original.

points to a '"quadri-thematics" of sexual austerity'[4] that displays a
certain durability from one age to the next, despite the reworkings it
undergoes. By the same token, but conversely, it follows that Christianity did not enact a rigid, normative regimen where freedom formerly
held; rather, it took up numerous moral commandments that had been
formulated long before Christian religion developed.[5]

The relative continuity of moral themes is not the upshot of analysis, but the point of departure. Foucault is not content to disprove the
thesis that sexual actions became subject to more and more repression
over history. His references to the long tradition of moral concern do
not mean that no changes occurred in the realm of moral experience:
'It would be a mistake to infer that the sexual morality of Christianity
and that of paganism form a continuity. Several themes, principles, or
notions may be found in the one and the other alike, true; but for all
that, they do not have the same place or the same value within them'.[6]
In other words, elaborating the consistency of moral themes in Greek
antiquity and early Christianity does not show that the latter amounts
to a variation, or modulated version, of the former. Positing a limited
continuity is meant to make the real lines of difference appear more
clearly.

Foucault contends that the break between antiquity and Christianity lies at a level other than that of moral prescriptions and rules. The
changes in moral experience that occurred 'are not in the code, but are
in what I call the "ethics", which is the relation to oneself'.[7] The difference between Greeks and Romans, on the one hand, and Christians, on
the other, does not involve the themes of moral concern but their significance within different frameworks of subjectivation. Christianity

---

4. Foucault, 1984a, *The Use of Pleasure* [1990], 21.
5. Foucault, 1983b, 'On the Genealogy of Ethics: An Overview of Work in Progress', 240; Foucault, 1982d, 'History and Homosexuality' [1996], 366–7. Here, too,
it should be emphasized that volumes 2 and 3 of *The History of Sexuality* are not
meant to provide an account of 'what really happened' (*Realgeschichte*) or to offer
a social history (indeed, the medical or philosophical texts are mostly aimed at a
small, privileged minority); instead, Foucault means to present 'a history of the way
in which pleasures, desires, and sexual behavior were problematized, reflected upon,
and conceived in Antiquity in relation to a certain art of living'. Foucault, 1984n,
'The Concern for Truth' [1988], 256; see also Foucault, 1984b, *The Care of the Self*
[1986], 80.
6. Foucault, 1984a, *The Use of Pleasure* [1990], 21–2.
7. Foucault, 1983b, 'On the Genealogy of Ethics: An Overview of Work in Progress', 240.

did not replace a tolerant Greco-Roman lifestyle with strict moral customs defined by the principles of renunciation, disallowance and interdiction; instead, Christians took over many of the austere prescriptions already worked out by the Greeks and Romans – albeit on the basis of an entirely different ethics.[8]

Still, the persistence of the moral code conceals a deep-reaching change of self-relations. Despite the constancy of the objects of moral concern (relations to the body, one's spouse, boys, the truth), pre-Christian ethics proves particular inasmuch as explicit commandments and prohibitions are absent and a space of relative freedom exists; in contrast, Christian moral experience is characterized by codifications of conduct and rules. As such, the main difference between these two kinds of ethics concerns the degree of autonomy the moral system admits. In Christianity, demands of sexual austerity are universal and compulsory, whereas neither Greek nor Roman thinking outline a unified catalogue of comportment: calls for self-control counted as suggestions and recommendations, and their observation was not assured through mechanisms of sanction so much as it represented an indispensable element within a form of subjectivation that gave wide berth to the 'stylization' or 'modelling' of individual existence. Among the Greeks and Romans, technologies of the self yielded distinct practices Foucault calls 'arts of existence': 'What I mean by the phrase are those intentional and voluntary actions by which men not only set themselves rules of conduct, but also seek to transform themselves, to change themselves in their singular being, and to make their life into an *oeuvre* that carries certain aesthetic values and meets certain stylistic criteria'.[9]

In this context, ethics does not refer to a moral law so much as it means constituting oneself as a moral subject. It is defined less by a set of universal rules than by way of practices seeking 'to give ... the most graceful and accomplished form'[10] to individual existence. In order to examine the historical changes that occurred in the shift from classical, Greek ethics to Christian, pastoral ethics, Foucault introduces a set of distinctions dividing the field into four main points, which correspond to four aspects of self-relation:

---

8. Ibid., 244–5.
9. Foucault, 1984a, *The Use of Pleasure* [1990], 10–11.
10. Ibid., 250–1.

1. *Ethical substance*, or ontology: that part of our self, or our behaviour, providing the field for moral judgement – the material that ethics treats. ('At what are moral judgements directed: actions, feelings, intentions or desires?')

2. *Mode of subjugation*, or deontology: 'the way in which people are invited or incited to recognize their moral obligations. Is it, for instance divine law ..., natural law, a cosmological order, ... a rational rule?'

3. *Self-formative activity*, or *askesis*: the means we use in order to constitute ourselves as ethical subjects. ('In what way must we work on ourselves in order to achieve certain aims?')

4. *The goal of moral action*, or teleology. 'Which is the kind of being to which we aspire in a moral way? For instance, shall we become pure, or immortal, or free, or masters of ourselves, etc.?').[11]

According to Foucault, close relations hold between these four aspects of ethics, but 'a certain kind of independence'[12] exists, as well. The relative autonomy of the different ethical dimensions means that certain elements may change without the others necessarily doing the same. The second and third volumes of *The History of Sexuality* examine the relations, dependencies and independencies between these four aspects in Greek and Roman society in order to offer a genealogy of the Christian subject of desire.

## Aesthetics of Existence: The Art of Living in Classical Greece

*The Use of Pleasure* opens with an astonishing observation: sexuality did not occupy the centre of Greek moral reflection. The Greeks viewed sexual relations and actions as part of a more comprehensive reality extending to questions of diet and 'pleasures of the flesh' in a broader sense: *aphrodisia*. The difference between *aphrodisia* and

---

11. Foucault, 1983b, 'On the Genealogy of Ethics: An Overview of Work in Progress', 238–40; see also Foucault, 1984a, *The Use of Pleasure* [1990], 26–8; Hacking, *Historical Ontology* (1984); Davidson, 'Archaeology, Genealogy, Ethics' (1986), 228–9; Kammler and Plumpe, 'Antikes Ethos und postmoderne Lebenskunst' (1987), 192.

12. Foucault, 1983b, 'On the Genealogy of Ethics: An Overview of Work in Progress', 240.

sexuality does not designate a quantitatively different field of conception or a problem of translation; instead, *aphrodisia* defines a type of reality wholly different than what 'sexuality' means for us.[13]

In classical Greece, the source of moral concern did not involve the various modalities of sexual acts, object choices or the orientation of desire so much as the form of relation tying these three elements together. Actions, pleasures and desires formed a dynamic unit, and Greek moral experience constituted itself by way of this ensemble. Accordingly, the focus of ethical interest did not involve determining the nature of sexual actions – which would yield information about them and their components – so much as their immanent force. Foucault stresses two angles from which Greek moral thinking viewed this dynamic: the *intensity of practices* and *actors' mode of behaviour*.

The first variable ('intensity of practices') for evaluating the use of pleasure draws a line of separation between a 'more' and a 'less': the principle of moderation and the problem of excess. To arrive at a moral characterization, neither the choice of objects for erotic activity nor the form they assume proves decisive; instead, the intensity of activities is what matters. By the same token, cause for moral disapproval does not lie in the nature of acts so much as exaggerated indulgence in them.

The second variable ('actors' mode of behaviour') concerns roles. The Greeks did not differentiate between masculine sexuality, on the one hand, and feminine sexuality, on the other – or, for that matter, homosexual and heterosexual dispositions. Instead, the field of *aphrodisia* was structured in terms of two distinct poles and functions: activity and passivity. Greek sexual morality concerned active parties, the subjects of sexual acts, and passive ones, the 'objects' on and with whom sexual acts are performed. Differences between masculine and feminine sexuality are not a biological, natural given so much as they correspond to a fundamental line of social division and relation of domination. The 'active' role of the free man stands opposed to the 'passive' role of women, boys and slaves.[14]

Two polarities, moderation/excess and activity/passivity, provided

13. Foucault, 1984a, *The Use of Pleasure* [1990], 35–6.

14. Ibid., 41–7; Foucault, 1982d, 'History and Homosexuality' [1996], 363; Foucault, 1982g, 'Des caresses d'hommes considérées comme un art', 317; Foucault, 1984n, 'The Concern for Truth' [1988], 260–1.

the framework for Greek moral reflection.[15] Inasmuch as activity and moderation held sway, actions displayed a moral quality; conversely, a lack of either or both represented a potential source of immorality: 'For a man, excess and passivity were the two main forms of immorality in the practice of the *aphrodisia*'.[16] That said, such concern did not entail condemnation of the sexual act. The Greeks did not view sex as an ill or a sign that human nature is bad; it counted as an integral component of human nature. Thus, if Greek moral thinking called for restraint and self-control, it was not because the sexual act is unnatural or wicked in general, but because, by its very nature, it demands to be checked. Two features defined sexual pleasure: in the first place, inasmuch as it is common to human beings and animals, sexual activity possesses a low ontological quality; at the same time, though base and low-ranking, such pleasure is very intense. The interplay of these two factors gives rise to the main problem: the intensity of pleasure causes sexual activity to pass beyond the limits posed by nature and assume undue significance: 'Because of this intensity, people were induced to overturn the hierarchy, placing these appetites and their satisfaction uppermost, and giving them absolute power over the soul'.[17]

In other words, sexual activity did not occasion moral concern because it counted as inherently bad, but because it involves the play of forces that are instituted by nature but constantly threaten to spill out beyond due measure. Greek ethics constituted itself as a technology for mastering and steering such forces in order to avert the ever-present danger of immoderation. This counterforce occupies the axes of struggle and resistance. That said, the struggle did not involve exterminating and driving out lusts – which are part of human nature – but controlling and dominating them. Permanent effort and the formation of a 'polemical' relation to oneself are required. The point is to cultivate a power relationship 'against' oneself to assign pleasure and desire a fitting place.[18]

If Foucault's reconstruction of Greek moral reflection is accurate,

---

15. The addressee of such morality was, admittedly, only the free adult man; in this system, neither women, boys nor slaves could exhibit an immoderate use of freedom.

16. Foucault, 1984a, *The Use of Pleasure* [1990], 47.

17. Ibid., 49.

18. Ibid., 48–50, 63–77.

then the task of ethics did not mean fixing a systematic code separating permitted actions from prohibited ones. Greek 'sexual morality' was not based on a morphology of acts so much as a dynamic of practices defining the conditions for the correct *use of pleasure* (*chresis aphrodision*). This did not occur in terms of vertical agreement with standing laws, but in horizontal relation to other realms of subjective action:

> The main question appears to bear much less on the acts' conformity with a natural structure or with a positive regulation, than on what might be called the subject's 'style of activity' and on the relation he establishes between sexual activity and the other aspects of his familial, social, and economic existence. The movement of analysis and the procedures of valuation do not go from the act to a domain such as sexuality or the flesh, a domain whose divine, civil, or natural laws would delineate the permitted forms; they go from the subject as a sexual actor to the other areas of life in which he pursues his activity. And it is in the relationship between these different forms of activity that the principles of evaluation of a sexual behavior are essentially, but not exclusively, situated.[19]

Foucault examines the emphasis placed on a 'style of activity' along the lines of four 'axes of everyday experience'[20] structuring Greek moral pragmatics: relation to one's own body (dietetics), conduct in marriage and the household (economics), love for boys (erotics) and the relation to truth (philosophy).

*Dietetics* does not present a binding regiment of moral laws. It names a catalogue of principles, suggestions, recommendations and so on that follow the rules of an art of living. Care for one's own body, like assuring and tending to one's progeny, demands that certain patterns be observed in terms of dietary habits and sexual conduct. Household concerns and relations with one's wife – *economics* – call for granting privilege to one's lawful spouse. However, this demand did not follow from a symmetrical relationship that granted the same rights and duties for both partners; on the contrary, it meant cultivating radical asymmetry. Women had to be faithful because their social status was inferior and they stood under the control of their husbands.

---

19. Foucault, 1984b, *The Care of the Self* [1986], 35–6.
20. Foucault, 1984a, *The Use of Pleasure* [1990], 24.

Men, on the other hand, were to be faithful in order to demonstrate self-mastery. The recommendation that the husband demonstrate moderation was not based on a prescribed codex of duties or personal obligation to his wife; rather, it followed the imperative of a 'political regulation':[21] in demonstrating mastery over himself, the man showed that he was capable of ruling others, too. The call to privilege the lawful spouse followed from the social position of being a husband; it was not inherent in the spousal relationship itself. 'Oikos' and 'polis' formed a continuum: the free man respected his wife as he did his fellow citizens.[22]

In contrast to the spheres of dietetics and economics, where the husband was supposed to exercise control vis-à-vis himself, *erotics*, which concerned sexual relations between men, held that the beloved should also exercise moderation: both partners ought to observe the imperative of restraint.[23] This mutual self-restraint introduced an element of unease into relationships between men inasmuch as it undid the central distinction between active and passive roles, dependency and freedom. Love between men constantly raised the question about inequality between equals; as such, it also posed the question of future leaders: on the one hand, the boy was a legitimate object of desire, but on the other hand, since he would come to be a free man and the bearer of political power, he could not accept this role and identify with the position he now occupied.[24]

---

21. Ibid., 167.

22. Ibid., 97–184. With that, mastery of oneself becomes a key precondition for political mastery, since it regulates and modulates the use of power: 'the prince's moderation [...] serves as the basis of a sort of compact between the ruler and the ruled: the latter can obey him, seeing that he is a master of himself [...]. The prince's relationship with himself and the manner in which he forms himself as an ethical subject are an important component of the political structure [...]'. Foucault, 1984a, *The Use of Pleasure* [1990], 174. For the constitutive relation between dominion over others and the imperative of self-control, see Claudine Haroche's essay on guidebooks for raising rulers from the late Middle Ages until the French Revolution. Haroche, 'Le gouvernement des conduites' (1994).

23. 'In economics and dietetics, the voluntary moderation of the man was based mainly on his relation to himself; in erotics, the game was more complicated; it implied self-mastery on the part of the lover; it also implied an ability on the part of the beloved to establish a relation of dominion over himself; and lastly, it implied a relationship between their two moderations, expressed in their deliberate choice of one another'. Foucault, 1984a, *The Use of Pleasure* [1990], 203.

24. Ibid., 187–225; Foucault, 1982d, 'History and Homosexuality' [1996], 363–4.

According to Foucault, this 'antinomy of the boy'[25] became the central problem of Greek sexual-ethical thinking because it brought two incompatible elements together that imperilled the foundations of political order. Increasingly, the view held that pederasty could not be honourable if it did not include something that would transform it into a social valuable relation. As such, pederasty remained a source of moral concern until Socrates and Plato took up the matter and thematized it in a new way. The Platonic conception of eros responds to the difficulties posed by relations between men and boys by shifting the question from the beloved to the nature of love itself and, in so doing, presenting erotic love as a relationship to the truth: that is, as philosophy.

This coupling of eros and truth displaced the inherited problematic in numerous ways. For one, a shift occurred from the deontological question about the right use of pleasure to the ontological question about the nature and origin of love. In consequence, the problem of erotic comportment assumed a position subordinate to the search for the essence of love. In this way, Platonic erotics left behind worries about the boy's honour and moved on to the problem of love for the truth. Finally, distance to received ideas emerged with regard to the subject and object of pleasure/desire. Inasmuch as eroticism is reformulated as a relationship to the truth, the beloved cannot simply occupy the position of object. Instead, lovers can only unite in true love if the same force lays hold of both of them – which means that the beloved is also a subject in the relationship. Love as convergence takes the place of asymmetry between partners. Being the lover means mastery of the truth, and seeking to earn the master's love takes the place of worrying about the boy's honour. By assimilating ethics to the question of truth, a process of transformation started that later – under different political and social conditions – led to the Christian conception of a desiring soul and the need to decipher its secrets.[26]

In sum: on all axes of experience, the Greek use of pleasure observed the principle of self-control (*enkrateia*). Concern for the body's health and taking care of one's progeny called for moderation in diet and sexuality, just as the household's reputation demanded that the lawful spouse receive privileged treatment. Love for boys presupposed respect

25. Foucault, 1984a, *The Use of Pleasure* [1990], 221.
26. Ibid., 229–46.

for their (masculine) subject position and already implied the ideal of renouncing physical contact entirely. The Socratic-Platonic tradition took on this problem and defused it by tying access to the truth to the renunciation of pleasure.[27]

That said, Greek ethics had another dimension, as well. Congruity between ethical and aesthetic dimensions shaped an *aesthetics of existence*; in this context, moral value represents a truth value, as well. The 'aesthetics of existence' refers to a way of living

> whose moral value did not depend either on one's being in conformity
> with a code of behavior, or on an effort of purification, but on certain
> formal principles in the use of pleasures, in the way one distributed
> them, in the limits one observed, in the hierarchy one respected.
> Through the *logos*, through reason and the relation to truth that
> governed it, such a life was committed to the maintenance and repro-
> duction of an ontological order; moreover, it took on the brilliance of a
> beauty that was revealed to those able to behold it or keep its memory
> present in mind.[28]

The political significance of the 'aesthetics of existence' lies here: through 'beauty', a harmonious balance is achieved between self and society, since the principle of self-control enables the (male) subject of pleasure and desire to experience himself as a citizen of the polis, too. The Greek art of existence is distinguished by a technique that escapes oppositional schemes of public/private or ethical/aesthetic. The 'art' of Greek ethics, then, is to conceive a natural connection between the individual and the world, within which there is no room to constitute the self reflexively, as a 'subject'.[29]

---

27. Ibid., 251–2; Foucault, 1984n, 'The Concern for Truth' [1988], 260; Kammler and Plumpe, 'Antikes Ethos und postmoderne Lebenskunst' (1987), 190.

28. Foucault, 1984a, *The Use of Pleasure* [1990], 89; Foucault, 1983b, 'On the Genealogy of Ethics: An Overview of Work in Progress', 240.

29. 'I do not believe that an experience of the subject should be reconstituted where it did not find formulation. [...] And because no Greek thinker ever found a definition of the subject and never searched for one, I would simply say that there is no subject. Which does not mean that the Greeks did not strive to define the condi-tions in which an experience would take place – an experience not of the subject but of the individual, to the extent that the individual wants to constitute itself as its own master. What was missing in classical antiquity was the problematization of the con-stitution of the self as subject. Beginning with Christianity we have the opposite: an

## The Culture of the Self: Hellenistic-Roman Ethics

Imperial Roman civilization witnessed the rise of a form of moral reflection that differed in key respects from the Greek 'aesthetics of existence'. For the latter, desires and pleasures had counted as forces to be reined in; as such, they posed a constant challenge to male citizens of the polis – who tested and demonstrated their fitness for rule by controlling and mastering them. Now, however, they came to appear more and more foreign and threatening: forces that inhibit and harm the psychic balance and bodily integrity of individuals. The counterpart of mounting mistrust with regard to sexual pleasures was the heightened value attached to spiritual enjoyment, and modelling an aesthetic existence on the individual scale diminished in significance as universal rules of conduct came to hold sway.

That said, this process of transformation did not involve trading in the ethical problematic of old so much as varying and modulating the art of living. During the first two centuries of the Common Era, pleasure/desire still represented a force with which one struggled, and individual relation to pleasures continued to follow an ethics of self-control and mastery. But in this play of forces, which was defined by struggle and the permanent menace of excess, the emphasis fell more and more on individual weakness – human susceptibility and vulnerability – and the need for protection. Sexual morality continued to follow the demands of an art of living lending definition to the aesthetic and ethical criteria of existence, 'but this art refers more and

---

appropriation of morality by the theory of the subject'. Foucault, 1984q, 'The Return of Morality' [1988], 253; Foucault, 1980j, 'Discussion with Philosophers'.

Gerhard Plumpe expresses this elision of the subject as follows: 'The decisive point is that the ethos of the polis founds the connection between I and others, self and sociability, as something primordial, so to speak. There is no need for reflective theories to problematize "I as I"'. Plumpe, 'Postmoderne Lebenskunst' (1986), 14; Pasquino, 'Michel Foucault (1926–84): The Will to Knowledge' (1986b), 105. Plumpe also points to an interesting parallel in Hegel's description of the Greek polis: '[T]he central thing here is beauty, which in terms of the political aspect leads to the Greek constitution and sets the Greek world apart. This world is beautiful, but the true [is] always higher. Beauty is not yet truth. This beautiful center of the ethical and the just [is what] is grasped and sought by the free individual, by free individuality – not yet in the specific quality of morality but instead as custom, as the objective aspect of willing. The will has not yet been intensified into the ideality of being-for-self, has not yet arrived at the interiority of the latter'. Hegel, *Lectures on the Philosophy of World History* (2011), 400.

more to universal principles of nature or reason, which everyone must observe in the same way'.[30]

The innumerable precepts of austerity and calls for abstention of the period did not achieve coherence through politically dictated efforts at moralization or a more pronounced tendency towards individualization so much as by way of a shift within the art of living. The emphasis of ethics moved away from an 'aesthetics of existence' to a *culture of the self*, which aimed to intensify and valorize certain practices on the part of individuals: the *care of the self*. 'This "cultivation of the self" can be briefly characterized by the fact that in this case the art of existence ... is dominated by the principle that says one must "take care of oneself"'.[31]

The imperative to care for the self constitutes the background for a series of important changes to the classical, Greek arts of existence that restructured the axes of moral concern. The thematics of *health* confronted inherited medical questions with intensified, moral reflection; it did not discount the body so much as it took the form of mounting unease. Ethical concern no longer bore on unwilled forces or reckless expenditure as the immanent dangers of sexual intercourse; rather, the problem of the general fragility of the human body and its susceptibility to disturbances of function came to the fore. Natural lust, to which one assumes a combative bearing, is replaced by generalized distrust; the focus falls on sexual practices' potentially damaging effects for body and soul. The imperial age witnessed the first signs of sex becoming pathologized – a process that would undergo further elaboration under Christianity. Such pathologization was different from the Greek art of living in two respects: first, the cause for worry no longer involved excess alone, but also stemmed from sex itself; second, (male) sexual pursuits no longer counted as a sign of activity, but as a sign of passivity that overwhelms the subject.[32]

Relation to one's own body was not the only thing to change. So did the status of *marriage* and the meaning of *pederasty*. Over the course of the first two centuries of the Common Era, the accent shifted from marriage as a legal-political institution – asymmetrically conceived in terms of transferring a name, combining resources, child-rearing

---

30. Foucault, 1984b, *The Care of the Self* [1986], 67.
31. Ibid., 43.
32. Ibid., 99–144.

and so on – to a personal relationship between partners who were, in principle, equals. Especially in writings by the Stoics, wedlock came to be conceived as more and more 'conjugal'. Its foundation does not lie in concerns of economic utility, nor does it serve a political objective; instead, it refers to a way of living in agreement with the demands of nature. Marriage concerns the alignment of interests less and less and describes the continuum of a natural relationship that counts as the only appropriate form for human existence: the pairing of man and woman. The universalization of marriage held two consequences, which are closely related. On the one hand, stressing wedlock as a natural state entailed the obligation to marry and granted heightened value to spousal love: marriage and sexual activity should overlap. The institution of marriage was meant to provide the exclusive site for sexual desire and pleasure. On the other hand, as the result of the successful intimization of wedlock and the valorization of marriage duties, pederasty ceased to provide the central point of ethical reflection and aesthetic reference.[33]

According to Foucault, in the transition from city states to a sprawling empire, the basis for exercising power transformed and, with it, the demands placed on the art of living. The demise of the polis also heralded the disintegration of the 'natural' unity between the individual and the world, which had defined classical Greece. The complex dimensions and anonymous structures of the Roman Empire made it impossible to locate the self directly in a political and social field of action. Now, the immanent relation between private and public had to be 'artificially' manufactured, as it were. Under such conditions of crisis, the 'culture of the self' responded to key social and political problems. That said, the ethical problematic it entailed was neither the cultural expression nor the logical consequence of historical changes. 'Culture of the self' did not mirror reality, nor did it result directly from it. Instead, it constituted a reality in its own right: 'Hence the cultivation of the self would not be the necessary "consequence" of these social modifications; it would not be their expression in the sphere of ideology; rather, it would constitute an original response to them, in the form of a new stylistics of existence.'[34]

33. Ibid., 147–232.
34. Ibid., 71; cf also Kammler and Plumpe, 'Antikes Ethos und postmoderne Lebenskunst' (1987), 190–1.

The core feature of 'culture of the self' does not involve retreating into the interiority of private life, nor does it signify moral decline. In fact, the imperative to care for the self does not concern individual bearing so much as it means programming a social practice (albeit one restricted to cultural and political elites). The aim is to define a new relationship to oneself and one's social position, functions and duties. Changes in the conditions for exercising power in a vast, imperial expanse make new forms of subjectivity necessary; the intimization and concentration that it entails are the corollary of processes of anonymization and centrifugal social forces.[35]

The ethics of the polis had required a close tie between exercising power over oneself and wielding power over others, aiming for an 'aesthetic of existence' that would ensure a harmonious relationship between political duties and private interests. Likewise, late Roman 'culture of the self' affirmed the connection between power over oneself and others – but for wholly different reasons, inasmuch as the basis for moral action and the conditions for wielding power had changed:

1. *The basis for moral action.* Whereas, in the polis, the virtuous conduct of rulers expressed the harmony of the whole, the ruler in the imperial age was supposed to adhere to his personal reason, 'logos'. When the political and social structures of the Greek city state vanished, so did the 'natural' connection between the self and sociability. Conversely, the ethical problematic intensified in keeping with the expansion of political space in the Roman empire. The identity of private and political existence went missing; in its place, a self-reflective ethics was elaborated: a self-evident social position with equally self-evident

---

35. Gerhard Oestreich has studied the significance of neo-Stoicism in bureaucracy and the army during the seventeenth and eighteenth centuries for constructing an orderly chain of command. Especially in Prussia, the transition from notions of military deterrence to an 'educational' conception of discipline – which replaced outer constraints with 'self-coercion' (*Zwang zum Selbstzwang*) (Elias) and declared duty, obedience and affect-regulation the fundamental virtues of a new ethics of rank – represented essential preconditions for the efficiency of the military and administrative apparatus: 'Thus, it seems to me that the "innerworldly asceticism" of Calvinism, whose effect on the capitalist spirit Max Weber has determined, has a certain political correlative, namely the influence of an innerworldly, neo-Stoic ascetism and combat-morality on the bearers of the modern state [*Machtstaat*], the army and officialdom'. Oestreich, *Geist und Gestalt des frühmodernen Staates* (1969), 64; for a comparison between Oestreich, Weber and Foucault in terms of 'social disciplination', see Breuer, 'Foucaults Theorie der Disziplinargesellschaft' (1987).

obligations and tasks gave way to a 'culture of the self' that sought to provide explicit reasons for conscious decision-making.

2. *Conditions for wielding power.* The transition from the polis to impe-rial administration made a service aristocracy necessary – which was not the point of origin for power so much as its conduit. Social elites were no longer bound up in the continuum of domination extending from mastery of the self and one's wife to ruling over others. Instead, within this network of power, they occupied a 'hinge' position: with the exception of the emperor, all were simultaneously rulers and ruled.[36]

And with that, the 'political game' became much more complex. Old forms of superiority and dominion had to incorporate elements of equality and reciprocity in order to fulfil the conditions of exercising power. The close relationship between power over oneself and power over others needed to be split open and realigned in terms of 'per-sonal' ethics. Forms of activity grew detached from social position and became, more and more, functions attended by imperatives of duty that did not result from rank so much as reason, or 'logos'. The model for political work no longer followed the catalogue of obligations inherent in an estate; instead it arose from 'retreating into oneself' in order to seek out the laws and rules underlying responsibilities and obligations:

> In a political space where the political structure of the city and the laws with which it is endowed have unquestionably lost some of their importance, although they have not ceased to exist for all that, and

---

36. Foucault, 1984b, *The Care of the Self* [1986], 81–8; Foucault, 1981c, 'Sexual-ity and Solitude' [1997], 179–80; Foucault, 1983b, 'On the Genealogy of Ethics: An Overview of Work in Progress', 241–2. In classical Greece, self-control was tied to asymmetrical relations: being master of oneself meant that one was in the position to rule over others. This connection between mastery of oneself and others tends to fade in Roman ethics: 'you have to be master of yourself not only in order to rule others, as it was in the case of Alcibiades or Nicocles, but you have to be master of yourself because you are a rational being. And in this mastery of yourself, you are related to other people, who are also masters of themselves. And this new kind of relation to the other is much less nonreciprocal than before'. Ibid., 242.

The transformation of care of the self and its 'dissociation from concern for others' in Roman-Hellenistic society provides the object of Foucault's lectures on 27 January and 3, 10 and 17 February 1982. Foucault, 1985c, *The Hermeneutics of the Subject* [2005].

where the decisive elements reside more and more in men, in their decisions, in the manner in which they bring their authority to bear, in the wisdom they manifest in the interplay of equilibria and transactions, it appears that the art of governing oneself becomes a crucial political factor.[37]

As such, the 'culture of the self' assigned a central role to an art of self-knowledge, operating by way of precise prescriptions, tests and exercises in order to uncover the fundamental principles of nature or reason defining binding rules of conduct for all. That said, the aim of procedures for knowing oneself did not (yet) mean posing questions about the origin or merit of such ideas; the issue was evaluating their relationship to one's conduct in terms of universal patterns. With that, however, the question of truth – as a mode of separating correct action from false action – became the core issue in moral self-constitution.[38]

## The Hermeneutics of Desire: Morality and Ethics in Christianity

Early Christian ethics enacted a fateful break with the ancient art of living.[39] It replaced the tradition of an 'aesthetics of existence' – defined in terms of cultivating an aesthetico-political bearing in the world here and now – with a *hermeneutic of desire* that aimed for purity and

---

37. Foucault, 1984b, *The Care of the Self* [1986], 89; see also Foucault, 1983b, 'On the Genealogy of Ethics: An Overview of Work in Progress', 245–6.

38. Foucault, 1984b, *The Care of the Self* [1986], 67–8. 'In the Platonic current of thought [...] the problem for the subject or the individual soul is to turn its gaze upon itself, to recognize itself in what it is and, recognizing itself in what it is, to recall the truths that issue from it and that it has been able to contemplate; on the other hand, in the current of thinking we can broadly call Stoicism, the problem is to learn through the teaching of a number of truths and doctrines, some of which are fundamental principles while others are rules of conduct. You must proceed in such a way that these principles tell you in each situation and, as it were, spontaneously, how to conduct yourself'. Foucault, 1984s, 'The Ethics of the Concern for the Self as a Practice of Freedom' [1997], 285–6.

39. Early Christian ethics provides the focus of volume 4 of *The History of Sexuality* (*The Confession of the Flesh*) which Foucault completed but did not publish during his lifetime. It also seems that he was working on at least one more book, about late medieval sexual ethics. Foucault, 1983b, 'On the Genealogy of Ethics: An Overview of Work in Progress', 230–1.

immortality in another one. Along with the goal, all four dimensions of ethical conduct changed:

> In the Christian morality of sexual behavior, the ethical substance was to be defined not by the *aphrodisia*, but by a domain of desires that lie hidden among the mysteries of the heart, and by a set of acts that are carefully specified as to their form and their conditions. Subjection was to take the form not of a *savoir-faire*, but of a recognition of the law and an obedience to pastoral authority. Hence the ethical subject was to be characterized not so much by the perfect rule of the self by the self in the exercise of a virile type of activity, as by self-renunciation and a purity whose model was to be sought in virginity.[40]

The ethical task shifted away from mastering pleasures – the question of where and when to indulge in them – towards diagnosing truth and illusion. Christian ethics focuses less on controlling sexual activity than on controlling sexual thoughts, wishes and desires. In this framework, self-evaluation and self-control mean deciphering the soul and plumbing the depths of conscience: the commandment of moderation and the maxims of using pleasure correctly yield to unconditional obedience of pastoral authorities and the imperatives of divine law.[41]

In consequence, the accent shifted from ethics as an art of living to a moral code. Inasmuch as sexual activity took on a negative value in Christianity, the actions, qualities and intentions at play increasingly fell subject to 'juridico-moral codification'.[42] Observing and respecting moral rules and codes came to define the conditions for the legitimate use of sexuality – the only way to take away its sinful nature. Greek and Roman ethics had been defined less in terms of universal rules and explicit commandments and prohibitions than by voluntary obligations that yielded a 'stylized existence'. Christianity, in contrast, transformed the ethical problematic into a catalogue of moral laws demanding strict observation: 'From antiquity to Christianity, we pass

---

40. Foucault, 1984a, *The Use of Pleasure* [1990], 92; see also Foucault, 1983b, 'On the Genealogy of Ethics: An Overview of Work in Progress', 247–8.

41. Foucault, 1981c, 'Sexuality and Solitude' [1997], 182–3; Foucault, 1983b, 'On the Genealogy of Ethics: An Overview of Work in Progress', 242–3; Foucault, 1984b, *The Care of the Self* [1986], 239–40.

42. Foucault, 1984a, *The Use of Pleasure* [1990], 138.

from a morality that was essentially the search for a personal ethics to a morality as obedience to a system of rules'.[43]

All the same, codification did not mean that Christianity simply replaced ethics with morality, or free will with obedience. Rather, Christian ethics incorporated ancient technologies of the self into the exercise of pastoral power. The defining trait of Christianity, then, is not replacing ethics with morality so much as inventing morality as ethics: voluntary obedience. Christianity took distance from the technologies of the self of classical antiquity in order to develop a new form of subjectivation that made subordination and obedience the goal of freedom, the sign of its proper use.[44]

Christian subjectivation results from two seemingly contradictory processes. On the one hand, it posits the self as a hermeneutic reality. Christianity assumes that the subject harbours a truth, and that the soul is where this truth lies concealed. The Christian self represents a riddling text that demands constant interpretation by means of ever-subtler practices of observation, decipherment and verbalization. On the other hand – and paradoxically – unyielding attention and efforts at self-decryption aim to abandon the self, to renounce and turn away from the world. Christianity develops a mode of subjectivation that operates by means of objectivation, with the goal of the symbolic death of the subject under investigation: 'Christian culture has developed the idea that if you want to take care of yourself in the right way you have to sacrifice yourself'.[45]

---

43. Foucault, 1984t, 'An Aesthetics of Existence' [1988], 49.

44. Foucault, 1984a, *The Use of Pleasure* [1990], 11; Foucault, 1980j, 'Discussion with Philosophers'; Foucault, 1983b, 'On the Genealogy of Ethics: An Overview of Work in Progress', 250–1; Dreyfus and Rabinow, *Michel Foucault: Beyond Structuralism and Hermeneutics* (1983), 254–5. See also Schmid, *Auf der Suche nach einer neuen Lebenskunst* (1991), 375: 'The axis and hub, for Foucault, is the question of "government": exercising power along Christian-pastoral lines, then those of the secular state, aimed to deprive individuals of conducting (governing) their own lives and replace care of the self with spiritual care.'

45. Foucault, quoted in Bernauer, *Michel Foucault's Force of Flight: Toward an Ethics for Thought* (1990), 180; see also Foucault, 1984s, 'The Ethics of the Concern for the Self as a Practice of Freedom' [1997], 284–5; Bernauer, *Michel Foucault's Force of Flight: Toward an Ethics for Thought* (1990), 164–5. 'The problem of ethics as an aesthetics of existence is covered over by the problem of purification. This new Christian self had to be constantly examined because in this self were lodged concupiscence and desires of the flesh. From that moment on, the self was no longer something to be made but something to be renounced and deciphered'. Foucault, 1983b,

According to Foucault, the reason for Christianity's paradoxical combination of self-affirmation and self-renunciation lies in a complex connection between subjectivation and the search for truth. Inasmuch as technologies of the self bring forth an array of obligations-to-the-truth, the problem of the truth is strategically significant. For one, Christianity stresses the need for 'confession' cultivating a broad range of truth demands: specific theses and dogmas, as well as certain books and figures of authority, must be accepted as the source of truth. There is another kind of truth-obligation, too: Christians must examine who they are as individuals, the stirrings in their bodies and minds, the errors they have committed, the temptations to which they are exposed, and so on. Both truth-imperatives are closely linked: self-examination presupposes belief just as much as grasping the truth demands the soul's purification.[46]

This process of seeking the truth does not aim to reveal the self as an illusion. Rather, the point is to find out the reality of the self; the substance of such reality is what demands unyielding self-examination and self-purification. In contrast to Buddhism, for instance, Christianity is not content to expose that the self is a falsehood; indeed, the self is defined by a dangerous materiality, which demands constant supervision so that it may be analysed precisely and, ultimately, neutralized. As opposed to Greek thought, moral concern does not bear on the intensity of practices or the passivity of participants; these are simply the expression, or consequence, of a more basic fact: the 'bad' nature of the self.

The core of Christian technologies of the self is constituted by a never-ending spiral alternating between formulating the truth and renouncing reality. The Christian discovery of the self opens up

a task that cannot be anything else but undefined. This task has two objectives. First, there is the task of clearing up all the illusions, temptations, and seductions that can occur in the mind, and of discovering the reality of what is going on within ourselves. Second, one must get free from any attachment to this self, not because the self is an illusion but because the self is much too real. The more we discover the truth about ourselves, the more we must renounce ourselves; and the more

---

'On the Genealogy of Ethics: An Overview of Work in Progress', 248.
  46. Foucault, 1981c, 'Sexuality and Solitude' [1997], 178.

we want to renounce ourselves, the more we need to bring to light the reality of ourselves.[47]

In this process of seeking out the truth and taking distance from reality, analysing sexual impulses plays a key role. Christianity sets up a form of sexuality that represents a hinge between deciphering the soul and self-renunciation: 'sexuality, subjectivity, and truth [are] strongly linked together.'[48] The ontological precondition for this connection is shifting the axis of ethical unease away from relations to others, towards one's relation to oneself. The focus moves from actual actions to 'subjectivation': not the acts themselves so much as intentions, desires, thoughts and the like – which are conceived in terms of seeking inner truth. The process does not simply mean passing from viewing sexual pleasures as a kind of social activity to viewing them along the lines of individual passivity; rather, Christian subjectivation amounts to objectivation, too: incorporating the other into the self.[49]

Foucault shows how 'subjectivation as the search for truth' occurs in and through relations to others. First, the process means waging a constant battle in order to break the hold of the other lying beneath

---

47. Ibid., 178.
48. Ibid., 183.
49. Foucault, 1984i, '"Foucault" by Maurice Florence' [1998], 461–2. Foucault illustrates the difference between late Roman and early Christian ethics by comparing texts by Artemidorus (*Oneirocritica*) and Augustine (*The City of God*). Male sexuality predominates in either case, but whereas Artemidorus views the sexual act as a sign of activity, Augustine sees it as an indication of passivity. In the third century CE, Artemidorus's reflection on sexual ethics focuses on penetration, because it corresponds to the social role of a man in communal life. In contrast, Augustine's attention bears on the problem of the erection: he does not view the ethical significance of sexuality in terms of relations to others so much as self-relation. For the Church Father, the erection is the result of, and symbol for, the fallen nature of mankind inasmuch as it permanently attests to disobedience: a 'foreign body' in one's own flesh. In this light, sexual desires do not represent wishes but the negation of will, human sinfulness. Accordingly, the struggle against sexual lust can no longer be a matter of moderating or mastering a 'natural force': 'the spiritual struggle consists, on the contrary, in turning our eyes continuously downward or inward in order to decipher, among the movements of the soul, which ones come from the libido. The task is at first indefinite, since libido and will can never be substantially dissociated from one another. And this task is not only an issue of mastership but also a question of the diagnosis of truth and illusion. It requires a permanent hermeneutics of oneself'. Foucault, 1981c, 'Sexuality and Solitude' [1997], 182; Foucault, 1983b, 'On the Genealogy of Ethics: An Overview of Work in Progress', 233–4; for an extensive analysis of Artemidorus's book, see Foucault, 1984b, *The Care of the Self* [1986], 4–36.

the hull of one's own self – that is, to purify oneself by conquering the foreign element within. Second, for victory to occur, it is necessary to confess one's temptations and errors in this struggle to the proper authorities – to subject oneself to their counsel and follow their instructions. Unconditional obedience to ecclesiastical leadership is not just the precondition for the struggle; it represents a preliminary but unmistakeable sign of victory over the enemy within.[50]

The defining quality of Christianity involves the coupling of subjectivity and power, which functions through confession and voicing the truth. Truth is the bond that ties Christian subjects to their pastor. Not only do pastoral authorities command the proper means of analysis, forms of reflection, procedures of decipherment and so on; the Christian subject submits to the obligation to 'confess' the truth of the soul and its innermost secrets.[51] This double relation to truth and power determines the meaning of 'subject' as a particular, historical mode of organizing the self: the product of Christian experience: 'There are two meanings of the word *subject*: subject to someone else by control and dependence, and tied to his own identity by a conscience or self-knowledge'.[52]

The conclusion Foucault draws from the 'genealogy of the modern subject' holds: Christianity did not introduce a new morality or new prohibitions; rather, it invented a new configuration of subjectivity – and a new form of power. Suspending and transforming ancient

---

50. Foucault, 1982e, 'The Battle for Chastity' [1997], 195.

51. *The History of Sexuality, Volume 1* already devotes sizeable space to analysing the 'confession ritual'. Its significance derives from its universal applicability (outside of a religious-pastoral context, too) and its central function in truth-production. Foucault considers that the secularization and operationalization of confession in a broad array of social spheres represent an important component of modern power mechanisms: 'The truthful confession was inscribed at the heart of the procedures of individualization by power. [...] The confession has spread its effects far and wide. It plays a part in justice, medicine, education, family relationships, and love relations, in the most ordinary affairs of everyday life, and in the most solemn rites; one confesses one's crimes, one's sins, one's thoughts and desires [...]. Western man has become a confessing animal'. Foucault, 1976a, *The History of Sexuality, Volume 1: An Introduction* [1978], 58–9; see also Foucault, 1977m, 'The Confession of the Flesh' [1980], 214–17; Foucault, 1980i, 'Course Summary' [2014]; Foucault, 1988b, 'Technologies of the Self' [1982], 39–49; Dreyfus and Rabinow, *Michel Foucault: Beyond Structuralism and Hermeneutics* (1983), 173–8.

52. Foucault, 1982b, 'The Subject and Power', 212; Foucault, 1978k, 'Sexuality and Power' [1999], 125–6.

technologies of the self, it integrated them into the exercise of pastoral power; in turn, they detached from the institutional context of the Church and achieved universality. The specific feature of this power is not just to force individuals to act in a certain way, but to demand acts of truth. That is, it induces them to (re)cognize and discover acts of truth and to structure selfhood in relation to them. The fundamental trait of pastoral power is a necessary relation to oneself in terms of the truth; its technology of government 'conducts'[53] subjects by means of the truth.[54]

---

53. Foucault, 1978j, 'La philosophie analytique de la politique', 548–9; Foucault, 1980i, 'Course Summary' [2014], 321.

54. Foucault's analysis of the various ethics of sexuality stops with early Christianity. At the same time, he assumes that today's conception of 'sexuality' differs from the Christian notion of 'flesh'. Sexuality does not involve subordination to divine law so much as conformity to medico-psychological norms, with the goal of 'freeing' sexual desire and pleasure. Foucault, 1983b, 'On the Genealogy of Ethics: An Overview of Work in Progress', 243.

# 12

# Subjectivity and Power

The first problem is therefore once again to recognize the *distinctive characteristics [Eigenart]* of Western rationalism, and, within this, of modern Western rationalism, and to explain how it came into being. In light of the fundamental significance of the economy, each such attempt must above all give due consideration to the economic conditions. But equally the reverse side of the causal connection must not be forgotten. For just as economic rationalism is dependent on rational technology and rational law, so also it is dependent on the ability and disposition of people [*Menschen*] in favor of certain kinds of practical, rational *conduct of life [Lebensführung]*.

Max Weber[1]

A host of objections has been raised against the analysis presented in *The Use of Pleasure* and *The Care of the Self*.[2] Most readers agree that the way Foucault conceptualizes ancient ethics and subjectivity represents a step backward – away from the position he took in earlier works. The second and third volumes of *The History of Sexuality* have been interpreted as the '*credo* of a new – and yet well-worn – privatism',[3] the expression of a conservative turn. Foucault is supposed to have given up investigating power-knowledge complexes by installing

1. Weber, *The Protestant Ethic and the 'Spirit' of Capitalism* (2002), 365–6.
2. For an overview of discussions prompted by these volumes, see Rüb, 'Von der Macht zur Lebenskunst' (1988); Fink-Eitel, 'Zwischen Nietzsche und Heidegger: Michel Foucaults "Sexualität und Wahrheit" im Spiegel neuerer Sekundärliteratur' (1990).
3. Kammler, *Michel Foucault: Eine kritische Analyse seines Werks* (1986), 203.

an 'autarchic "self"'[4] beyond power but within discourse: to have abandoned political analysis in favour of a private frame of reference.[5]

Above all, Foucault's interest in the 'aesthetic' dimension of existence counts as an appeal for (political) 'aestheticism'. According to
this view, his final works herald 'radical liberalism',[6] whereby private
parties arrive at ethical decisions without recourse to intersubjective
obligations – on the basis of aesthetic criteria alone. The consequence
of such 'aestheticization of the political' is, first, 'extreme subjectivism
… which blocks out the problematic of socialization'[7] inasmuch as it
subscribes to the goal of individual self-realization unconditionally.
Second, Foucault is said to endorse 'aesthetic decisionism':[8] giving
up standards of rationality that go beyond individual preferences
in favour of an aesthetic choice that reduces normative problems to
matters of taste.

Foucault's conception of ethics, the argument goes, amounts to
amoral aestheticism or social elitism: a 'project for privileged minorities, liberated from all functions in the material reproduction of
society'.[9] From this standpoint, *The History of Sexuality* represents
Foucault's wholesale reversal of the theoretical perspective he had
previously adopted; now, subjectivity no longer stands as a dependent

---

4. Schlesier, 'Humaniora: Eine Kolumne' (1984), 818.

5. See also Vegetti, 'Foucault et les anciens' (1986); Daraki, 'Le voyage en Grèce
de Michel Foucault' (1985); Macdonell, *Theories of Discourse: An Introduction* (1986),
127–8; Cohen and Saller, 'Foucault on Sexuality in Greco-Roman Antiquity' (1994).
Pierre Hadot, who points out gaps and difficulties in Foucault's interpretation of
Roman practices of the self, offers a significantly more nuanced and 'immanent'
critique. Hadot, 'Reflections on the Idea of the "Cultivation of the Self"' (1995);
Davidson, 'Ethics as Ascetics: Foucault, the History of Ethics, and Ancient Thought'
(1994). An array of feminist studies has faulted Foucault for androcentrism: legitimating standing forms of sexual domination by doubling it in theoretical terms, or,
alternately, privileging 'pagan-virile' morality over 'Christian-feminine' morality and
assigning women a passive role as objects of lust. Buker, 'Hidden Desires and Missing
Persons: A Feminist Deconstruction of Foucault' (1990). Schlesier, 'Humaniora: Eine
Kolumne' (1984). On the critical yet productive relationship between feminist theory
and Foucault, see Martin 1982; Treusch-Dieter 1985; Diamond and Quinby 1988;
Phelan 1990; Sawicki 1991; McNay 1992; see Kögler 1994, 192–200 and Sawicki 1997
for an account of feminist discussions of Foucault in the United States.

6. Kögler, 'Fröhliche Subjektivität' (1990), 222.

7. Privitera, *Stilprobleme: Zur Epistemologie Michel Foucaults* (1990), 120.

8. Wolin, 'Foucault's Aesthetic Decisionism' (1986).

9. Rochlitz, 'The Aesthetics of Existence: Post-Conventional Morality and the
Theory of Power in Michel Foucault' (1992), 255.

variable so much as an independent fact.[10] If so, then an originally critical impulse has yielded to pure affirmation: the point is no longer to call the facticity of power relations into question, but to assume a comfortable position within the standing order and renounce all liberatory claims.

## Unholy Subjectivism?

The charge made time and again of shifting 'from the political realm of social confrontations to the life plans of individuals'[11] – or, alternatively, of endorsing 'unholy subjectivism'[12] – is inaccurate for a number of reasons. Undoubtedly, the central problem with such criticism is that it operates on the basis of the same dichotomies that *The History of Sexuality* calls into question. Foucault does not seek to separate the 'ethical' from the 'political', or to move the focus to forms of subjectivation when investigating power relations. Instead, he is examining the historical process that led these two poles to diverge and a specific subjectivity to emerge: the private and the public, the personal and the political, the aesthetic and the ethical do not represent discrete and opposing realms that must be reconciled with each other so much as elements of a single ethico-political problematic tying the 'genealogy of the modern subject' to the 'genealogy of the modern state':

> Such a project is at the intersection of two themes treated previously: a history of subjectivity and an analysis of the forms of 'governmentality'. The history of subjectivity was begun by studying the social divisions brought about in the name of madness, illness, and delinquency, along with their effects on the constitution of a rational and normal subject. It was also begun by attempting to identify the modes of objectification of the subject in knowledge disciplines [*dans ses savoirs*] such as those dealing with language, labor, and life. As for the study of 'governmentality', it answered a dual purpose: doing the necessary critique of the common conceptions of 'power' (more or less confusedly conceived as a unitary system organized around a center that is at the same time

---

10. Merquior, *Foucault* (1985), 138.
11. Privitera, *Stilprobleme: Zur Epistemologie Michel Foucaults* (1990), 120.
12. Habermas, *The Philosophical Discourse of Modernity* (1990), 276.

its source, a system that is driven by its internal dynamic always to expand); analyse it rather as a domain of strategic relations focusing on the behavior of the other or others, and employing various procedures and techniques according to the case, the institutional frameworks, social groups, and historical periods in which they develop.[13]

*The Use of Pleasure* and *The Care of the Self*, then, broaden the field of analysis opened by earlier works and add a third dimension to the 'history of subjectivity' that considers its constitution not only in terms of practices of power and forms of knowledge, but also in terms of self-relation. As such, investigation is not based on two different levels, but follows a single analytical strategy, which situates relations to the self and politico-social structures on the same plane: technologies of government. '[I]n this way one could take up the question of governmentality from a different angle: the government of the self by oneself in its articulation with relations with others'.[14]

The political significance of *The History of Sexuality* consists in working out this third dimension of analysis. The project is anything but a reflection of current debates about lifestyle and personal self-realization.[15] Instead, it reaches back to Foucault's experience, during the 1970s, of social movements pursuing the project of social emancipation. Hereby, Foucault refers to the manifold connections between Marxism and psychoanalysis positing necessary connections between

---

13. Foucault, 1981h, 'Subjectivity and Truth' [1997], 88.

14. Ibid., 88. Ian Hacking points out the innovative aspects of *The History of Sexuality* in comparison to Foucault's previous works: 'The knowledge/power story has been elaborately illustrated in Foucault's books, but those are outer-directed narratives – what we say about others, say to others, have said to ourselves by others, do to others or have done to ourselves. They leave out the inner monologue, what I say to myself. Thus they omit the permanent heartland of subjectivity. It is seldom force that keeps us on the straight and narrow; it is conscience. [...] To say this is not to return to subjectivity. There is nothing private about this use of acquired words and practical techniques. The cunning of conscience and self-knowledge is to make it *feel* private'. Hacking, *Historical Ontology* (1984), 116.

15. See Foucault's answer to the question whether ancient models of ethics anticipate modern self-obsession: 'In the California cult of the self, one is supposed to discover one's true self, to separate it from that which might obscure or alienate it, to decipher its truth thanks to psychological or psychoanalytic science, which is supposed to be able to tell you what your true self is. Therefore, not only do I not identify the ancient culture of the self with what you might call the Californian cult of the self, I think they are diametrically opposed'. Foucault, 1983b, 'On the Genealogy of Ethics: An Overview of Work in Progress', 245.

economic exploitation and sexual prohibition. According to this view, sexual repression forms an indispensable component of universal social oppression; conversely, loosening sexual interdictions and taboos is necessarily the precondition for, and an element of, social emancipation. Paradoxically, such theoretical valorization of sexuality lent it a secondary, political quality: sexual repression was supposed to 'express' more comprehensive repression ultimately anchored in economic relations of production. Inasmuch as it represented a derivative phenomenon, serving to reproduce more thoroughgoing domination, it could be eliminated only to the extent that a more fundamental kind of repression vanished. In other words, sexuality did not constitute a problem in its own right; it pointed to another problem, to which it was indissolubly tied.

Foucault advances two arguments against this way of conceiving the relations between power, knowledge, and subjectivity. First, his critique takes aim at a *monocausal relation of determination between power and sexuality*. Foucault counters such a view by making the historical observation that the dissolution of rigid sexual codes and taboos from the 1960s on has proven much less problematic than might have been expected. Permissive sexual morality did not shake the bourgeois-capitalist order at its core; on the contrary, one might ask whether it has not, in fact, been strengthened. If so, then no necessary relation holds between sexuality and economico-political conditions (or, more precisely, a monocausal determination does not prevail between them). As such, analysis should not focus on codes; instead, it must incorporate the forms of subjectivation through which they operate.[16]

Foucault's other objection concerns the *scientific justification of protest*. The central problem, in his eyes, is that such an approach boils ethico-political problems down to theoretico-scientific questions. By

---

16. 'For a long time many people imagined that the strictness of the sexual codes [...] was indispensable to so-called "capitalist" societies. Yet the lifting of the codes and the dislocation of prohibitions have probably been carried out more easily than people thought they would (which certainly seems to indicate that their purpose was not what it was believed to be); and the problem of an ethics as a form to be given to one's behavior and life has arisen once more. In sum, people were wrong when they believed that all morality resided in prohibition and that the listing of these prohibitions in itself solved the question of ethics'. Foucault, 1984n, 'The Concern for Truth' [1988], 262–3.

combining psychoanalysis and Marxism, 'liberation movements' rely on a 'theory of desire' that places individual impulse in opposition to social law in order to stage a play of drives and renunciation. Foucault deems such a conception problematic because its historical roots lie in Christian pastoral power. Consequently, the danger arises that actors in social movements – inasmuch as their action depends on scientific legitimation – will ultimately embrace what they seek to free themselves from. They face the dilemma of trying to pose the ethical question of other forms of subjectivity, but, at the same time, they cannot find the means to do so: they base the ethical dimension on scientific knowledge that has produced a certain, 'true' subjectivity – with effects that now provide the starting point for their protest.[17]

In this respect, the 'aesthetics of existence' runs counter to a 'science of life'. *The Use of Pleasure* and *The Care of the Self* sketch an 'art of living' opposed to a 'science of life'. Whereas the latter seeks to assimilate life to a natural state of being, Foucault conceives of human existence as a 'work of art'[18] in order to free it from the universal validity claims of the human sciences. His aim is to liberate 'man' from the obligation of deciphering 'himself' as a system of atemporal functions and anthropological constants – with all the norms and demands on conduct that this entails. *The History of Sexuality* breaks with such a reduction of subjectivity to sexuality, and the reduction of sexuality to (timeless) nature. Speaking of life as a work of art points to the 'artificiality' of existence and the fact that no 'true' subjectivity corresponds to any given, biologico-natural disposition. Instead, subjectivity is an artificial/technical construction, the object of a certain kind of technology: technology of the self.[19]

---

17. Foucault, 1983b, 'On the Genealogy of Ethics: An Overview of Work in Progress', 231; Foucault, 1983k, 'On the Genealogy of Ethics: An Overview of Work in Progress', 21.

18. Ibid., 237.

19. Bernauer, 'Beyond Life and Death: On Foucault's Post-Auschwitz Ethic' (1992); Bernauer, *Michel Foucault's Force of Flight: Toward an Ethics for Thought* (1990), 182. 'What strikes me is the fact that in our society, art has become something which is related only to objects and not to individuals, or to life. That art is something which is specialized or which is done by experts who are artists. But couldn't everyone's life become a work of art? [...] From the idea that the self is not given to us, I think that there is only one practical consequence: we have to create ourselves as a work of art'. Foucault, 1983b, 'On the Genealogy of Ethics: An Overview of Work in Progress', 236–7; see also Foucault, 1984d, 'What Is Enlightenment?', 41–2. Lois McNay and Thomas Seibert therefore see in Foucault's interest for an 'aesthetics of

Opening the ethical problematic, then, implies a critique of universalist conceptions (of morality) and requires taking distance in two respects: there is no need to refer ethical problems to scientific knowledge, nor is it possible to derive them from economic and political structures. This twofold distancing with respect to knowledge and power is what defines Greco-Roman technologies of the self and founds their potential relevance for contemporary ethico-political questions.[20] In contrast to code-based moralities, the 'aesthetics of existence' does not represent a material ethics defined in terms of agreement with a catalogue of rules; instead, it is a form of subjectivation that follows the principle of freedom and understands existence as ongoing work on the self. The defining trait of such ethics is not reference to a moral law, but the freedom of practices of the self. At the same time, however, such 'art of living' is not free in the sense of utter arbitrariness or the lack of evaluative criteria. Instead, work on

---

existence' the renewal of the critical and utopian impulses granted to the category of the aesthetic in radical social designs and social philosophies, or subversive artistic avant-garde moments of the twentieth century. McNay, *Foucault. A Critical Introduction* (1994), 146–9; Seibert, 'Das Subjekt der Revolten' (1995).

20. It does not follow, however, that solutions developed in antiquity represent an attractive or practicable alternative now. Foucault does not advocate taking up Greek technologies of self uncritically. The matter does not concern identical solutions so much as a 'similarity of problems'. Foucault, 1983b, 'On the Genealogy of Ethics: An Overview of Work in Progress', 231. There are at least two reasons why ancient technologies of self cannot provide an answer to questions today. First, in historico-methodological terms, Foucault does not consider antiquity to offer a model – and considers appealing to models to be unhistorical. The Greek polis is different from modern, liberal-capitalist societies and does not provide a model or alternative: 'I am not looking for an alternative; you can't find the solution of a problem in the solution of another problem raised at another moment by other people'. Ibid., 231; see Foucault, 1983l, 'Discussion with Michel Foucault', 6. He also rejects any idea of a 'Greek solution' on politico-ethical grounds. In the Greek world, social asymmetry and exclusionary practices were constitutive for ethics. Foucault is well aware that he is discussing a male system of morality, where women count only as passive objects of lust or, at most, partners to be supervised and educated. He makes a point of observing that classical antiquity does not represent the 'age before the Fall' in his eyes. Schlesier, 'Humaniora: Eine Kolumne' (1984), 819. Indeed, Greek ethics are tied to a specific social infrastructure: 'The Greek ethics were linked to a purely virile society with slaves, in which the women were underdogs whose pleasure had no importance'. Foucault, 1984q, 'The Return of Morality' [1988], 344. At the same time, however, rejecting the exemplary status of ancient technologies of the self does not mean that they should simply be disregarded. See Foucault, 1983b, 'On the Genealogy of Ethics: An Overview of Work in Progress', 236; Foucault, 1983k, 'On the Genealogy of Ethics: An Overview of Work in Progress', 25.

the self should achieve a 'beautiful' and 'successful' existence – whose concrete shape is determined collectively and, as such, admits change. For this reason, the 'aesthetics of existence' need not correspond to the Greco-Roman art of life or its social asymmetries.[21]

The Greek solution holds interest because it represents a form of self-commitment that is neither arbitrary nor in need of a universal law. Instead, it follows the principles of 'internal regulation' by tying power over others to the conditions for exercising power over oneself. The maxims of 'self-control' allowed free men of the polis to restrain themselves in the exercise of power inasmuch as they took on, for themselves, the imperative of moderation as an ethical principle.[22] What interests Foucault is this position between subjective

---

21. That said, Foucault's reflections on the possible bearing of ancient notions of subjectivity on current debates are provisional and not elaborated at length. His suggestion to privilege 'aesthetic' criteria over 'juridical' ones prompts a whole array of political problems centred on questions of coordination and regulating conflict: 'assuming a quasi-natural balance, a predetermined harmony in the social field, for such forms of existence is naïve and counter to all experience: multiple arts of living require complex provisions for coordinating them alongside each other. It takes a minimum of universalizable norms for displaying difference to prove possible or meaningful'. Plumpe, 'Postmoderne Lebenskunst' (1986), 15.

Foucault's works offer no answer to this question. As such, efforts to discern the 'germ of a new political thinking' are exaggerated. See Foucault's own remark: 'I admit that I have not got very far in this direction.' Foucault, 1984s, 'The Ethics of the Concern for the Self as a Practice of Freedom' [1997], 294. Thus, the purpose here is not to provide a 'new founding of ethics' (Schmid), but to outline the components of a specific model of critique, which the following chapters analyse in greater detail.

22. 'In order not to be excessive, not to do violence, in order to avoid the trap of tyrannical authority (over others) coupled with a soul tyrannized by desires, the exercise of political power required, as its own principle of internal regulation, power over oneself. Moderation, understood as an aspect of dominion over the self, was on an equal footing with justice, courage, or prudence; that is, it was a virtue that qualified a man to exercise his mastery over others'. Foucault, 1984a, The Use of Pleasure [1990], 80–1; Foucault, 1984s, 'The Ethics of the Concern for the Self as a Practice of Freedom' [1997], 289. Gilles Deleuze also points to the Greek 'invention' of subjectivity independent of forms of knowledge and enabling 'folds' within power: 'the great novelty of the Greeks [...] ultimately emerges thanks to a double unhooking or "differentiation" [décrochage]: when the "exercises that enabled one to govern oneself" become detached both from power as a relation between forces, and from knowledge as a stratified form, or "code" of virtue. On the one hand there is a "relation to oneself" that consciously derives from one's relation with others; on the other there is equally a "self-constitution" that consciously derives from the moral code as a rule for knowledge. This derivative or differentiation must be understood in the sense in which the relation to oneself assumes an independent status. It is as if the relations of the outside folded back to create a doubling, allow a relation to oneself to emerge, and constitute

discretion and objective constraint: 'if I was interested in antiquity it was because, for a whole series of reasons, the idea of a morality as obedience to a code of rules is now disappearing, has already disappeared. And to this absence of morality corresponds, must correspond, the search for an aesthetics of existence'.[23]

## Power as 'Conducting Conducts'

Foucault's concept of ethics does not point to individual self-designs, but to a collective way of living. His 'genealogy of the modern subject' seeks to avoid the alternative between subjectivism and objectivism; upon closer inspection, the 'unholy subjectivism' that is supposed to adhere to this enterprise emerges as political interest in subjectivity situated beyond Christian pastoral power. What interests Foucault in the ethical problematic is the 'idea also that ethics can be a very strong structure of existence, without any relation with the juridical per se, with an authoritarian system, with a disciplinary structure'.[24]

Foucault's theoretical valorization of ethics and his analysis in terms of 'conduct' (*conduite*) lend his concept of power greater precision.[25] As we have seen, Foucault defines the field of power relations

---

an inside which is hollowed out and develops its own unique dimension'. Deleuze, *Foucault* (1988), 100.

23. Foucault, 1984t, 'An Aesthetics of Existence' [1988], 49; see also Veyne, 'The Final Foucault and His Ethics' (1993), 7–8. The relative independence of the question of self-conduct with regard to religious orientation and juridico-institutional schemes of legitimation potentially offers a parallel to contemporary issues: 'I wonder if our problem nowadays is not, in a way, similar to this one, since most of us no longer believe that ethics is founded in religion, nor do we want a legal system to intervene in our personal, private life. Recent liberation movements suffer from the fact that they cannot find any principle on which to base the elaboration of a new ethics. They need an ethics, but they cannot find any other ethics than an ethics founded on so-called scientific knowledge of what the self is, what desire is, what the unconscious is, and so on. I am struck by this similarity of problems'. Foucault, 1983b, 'On the Genealogy of Ethics: An Overview of Work in Progress', 231.

24. Ibid., 235.

25. Colin Gordon and Pasquale Pasquino have pointed out that Foucault's definition of ethics as 'conduct' parallels Max Weber's concept of *Lebensführung*. Gordon, 'Question, Ethos, Event: Foucault on Kant' (1986a), 83–5; Gordon, 'The Soul of the Citizen' (1987); Pasquino, 'Michel Foucault (1926–84): The Will to Knowledge' (1986b), 99–100. Indeed, the works of these theorists admit comparison in many ways. Addressing forms of domination and power effects, they both analyse social relations in terms

as the interplay between technologies of the self and technologies of
domination; hereby, factual capacities, on the one hand, are distinct
from relations of communication, on the other. Likewise, his conception of power takes critical distance from both juridical and 'warlike'
notions, which view power in terms of force. According to Foucault,
neither model does justice to the 'specific nature'[26] of governmental
technology:

> Perhaps the equivocal nature of the term *conduct* is one of the best
> aids for coming to terms with the specificity of power relations. For to
> 'conduct' is at the same time to 'lead' others (according to mechanisms
> of coercion which are, to varying degrees, strict) and a way of behaving
> within a more or less open field of possibilities. The exercise of power
> consists in guiding the possibility of conduct and putting in order the
> possible outcome.[27]

That said, it does not follow from this definition of power as 'conducting conducts' that techniques of government exclude the use of

---

of struggle; likewise, they share an interest in disciplinary processes as they bear on the
evolution of Western rationality; finally, in taking on questions of methodology and
intellectual ethics, they owe a debt to Nietzsche. Foucault – especially at the end of his
life – referred more and more to Weber's writings on the sociology of religion; differences notwithstanding, their projects unfolded 'along the same lines'. Foucault, 1984s,
'The Ethics of the Concern for the Self as a Practice of Freedom' [1997], 282; Foucault,
1984k, 'Le souci de la vérité', 647–8; Foucault, 1988b, 'Technologies of the Self' [1982],
17.
      The secondary literature makes the comparison in terms of rationality and ration-
alization, above all. Hubert L. Dreyfus and Paul Rabinow understand Foucauldian
genealogy to continue the Weberian project of grasping the connections between
power and rationality; hereby, it is Foucault's merit to have concentrated on concrete
historical practices and undertaken a 'finer grained analysis'. Dreyfus and Rabinow,
*Michel Foucault: Beyond Structuralism and Hermeneutics* (1983), 133, 165–7. Barry
Smart also sees a feature shared by Foucault and Weber in the theme, but there is an
important difference: whereas Weber takes rationalization as a global and universal
process, Foucault aims to analyse varying rationalities in different social realms (Smart,
*Foucault, Marxism and Critique*, 125–6). For a comparison of these theorists' concep-
tions of power and domination, see Steven Lukes and Petra Neuenhaus; Lukes, 'Macht
und Herrschaft bei Weber, Marx, Foucault' (1983); Neuenhaus, *Max Weber und Michel
Foucault* (1993). For discussion of the problem of social disciplination in Foucault and
Weber, see Stefan Breuer and Bryan S. Turner. Breuer, 'Sozialdisziplinierung' (1986);
Turner, 'The Rationalization of the Body' (1987), 231–41.
      26. Foucault, 1982b, 'The Subject and Power', 219.
      27. Ibid., 220–1.

force; nor does it mean that consent does not prevail. The distinction is more analytical than empirical. Indeed, power relations may involve legal or factual agreement, just as they may proceed by means of force or constraint. The key point is that such elements do not constitute a power relation. They can be effects or instruments of power relations, but not their foundation or principle:

1. *Consent*. A power relation may be attended by initial or ongoing assent. However, such agreement cannot be used to explain it; it requires explanation in its own right. What motivates consensus, and what techniques ensure that power relations are accepted? It is not enough to take acceptance as a given. Instead, it is necessary to reveal 'conditions of acceptability'.[28]

2. *Force*. Violence/force occurs directly and affects bodies. Power is indirect and bears on subjects. Force operates by excluding leeway for possible actions; here, the activity of some stands opposed to the passivity of others. In contrast, a power relation obtains inasmuch as there is no direct influence on subjects; their own actions sustain it. Under these conditions, power relations possess a distinct form: it is not a matter of a static relationship between persons; rather, they take the form action on actions. This moment of relationality and reflexivity sets power relations apart from a relationship defined by agreement or violence. 'In itself', a power relation is not violence; nor is it a consent which, implicitly, is renewable. It is a total structure of actions brought to bear upon possible actions; it incites, it induces, it seduces, it makes easier or more difficult; in the extreme it constrains or forbids absolutely; it is nevertheless always a way of acting upon an acting subject or acting subjects by virtue of their acting or being capable of action. 'A set of actions upon other actions.'[29]

---

28. Ibid., 219; Foucault, 1984x, 'On Power' [1988], 103; Foucault, 1990b, 'What Is Critique?' [2007], 61.

29. Foucault, 1982b, 'The Subject and Power', 220. Conceptualizing power as 'action on actions' enables Foucault to correct the theoretical orientation of his earlier works, where the anonymity of relations of force and strategies occupied the foreground. However, this does not mean that structural power relations dissolve into subjective actions. The point is to understand structures 'not [as] the product, but rather the effect'. Foucault, 1990b, 'What Is Critique?' [2007], 64. Relations of force do not constitute a structure external to subjects so much as a net of relations that is (re)produced by their actions: 'in terms of relationships which are, if not totally, at least predominantly, relationships of interactions between individuals or groups. In other words, these

Under such conditions, a power relation presupposes both acting subjects as well as the existence of a 'field of possibilities' admitting an array of different answers, reactions, modes of conduct and so on. This means that power relations are distinguished by 'calculating' what subjects do: taking influence and determining actions, forming and steering wills, and the like. It is not determination in a strict sense so much as openness and incompleteness that characterize relations of power: 'The characteristic feature of power is that some men can more or less entirely determine other men's conduct – but never exhaustively or coercively'.[30]

For both these reasons, *freedom* represents a central element within relations of power. In Foucault's analysis of government, power and freedom do not form opposites that mutually exclude each other. Instead, and in multiple ways, 'freedom' becomes the existential condition for power: it provides the *ontological precondition* for a relation of power inasmuch as the exercise of power, as action on possible or actual actions, requires subjective freedom; additionally, it becomes the *material carrier* of a power relation since, without 'freedom', the power relation itself would vanish and yield to simple violence. This means that 'freedom' and power not only do *not* exclude each other, but that they in fact include each other – with the result that 'freedom' constitutes a characteristic element within power relations. 'Power is exercised only over free subjects, and only insofar as they are free'.[31]

That said, freedom does not just provide an existential condition for power; it is also what stands opposed to it and resists it. Precisely because freedom forms an indispensable element of power relations, there is no power relation without the possibility of resistance. Since power and freedom include each other, every power relation implies – 'perforce' – possibilities of resistance that do not occur from outside, in opposition, but operate from within and determine its form: 'This means that in power relations there is necessarily the possibility of resistance because if there were no possibility of resistance ... there would be no power relations at all'.[32]

---

relationships involve subjects, types of behavior, decisions and choices'. Ibid., 64.

30. Foucault, 1981a, '"Omnes et Singulatim"', 253; Foucault, 1990b, 'What Is Critique?' [2007], 66.

31. Foucault, 1982b, 'The Subject and Power', 221; Foucault, 1988d, 'Power, Moral Values, and the Intellectual' [1980], 2.

32. Foucault, 1984s, 'The Ethics of the Concern for the Self as a Practice of

The emphasis placed on freedom as an integral element of power relations holds two important analytical consequences. First, this conceptual shift makes it possible to overcome the negative definition of resistance that marked Foucault's earlier works by lending substance to his thesis that power and resistance originate in tandem. Second, it presupposes a distinction that does not occur in previous studies, which now assumes great significance: the difference between power and domination.

## Power and Domination

In the framework of the 'microphysics of power', Foucault had declined, for a number of reasons, to distinguish between power and domination. First, such refusal was meant to avoid the question of the moral-juridical legitimacy of power. Situated on a level of description, Foucault's microphysical studies sought to steer clear of value judgements and distinctions between 'good' and 'bad' forms of power. Second, reference to the 'omnipresence of power relations' served to bracket the idea of a 'future beyond power', that is, a realm free from domination. Time and again, Foucault pointed out that (left-wing) political utopias cannot lay claim to a site outside of power relations, nor can the intellectuals who advance them. Third, inasmuch as no distinction was made between power and domination, attention was supposed to shift from state-institutional apparatuses to material practices – which, in concentrated and interlocking form, are what produce phenomena of domination in the first place. Foucault did not theorize domination because he sought to 'invert' the perspective of traditional socio-analytical approaches: he wanted to analyse power not from 'above', but from 'below'.[33]

The microphysical method of investigating power also led to the problem, sketched above, of underestimating the roles of both state and subjectivity. That said, the reason did not lie in the absence of a concept of domination so much as the form of its ongoing presence.

In fact, Foucault had not freed himself from the logic of domination at all. He merely reformulated it: instead of approaching the problem

---

Freedom' [1997], 292; Foucault, 1984u, 'Sex, Power, and the Politics of Identity' [1997], 168; Foucault, 1981a, '"Omnes et Singulatim"', 253.

33. Foucault, 1976a, *The History of Sexuality, Volume 1: An Introduction* [1978], 94–6; Foucault, 1990b, 'What Is Critique?' [2007], 60.

of domination in juridical terms, he employed a martial framework for analysis. As in the juridical conception of power, 'domination' stood as a political fact and provided the point of departure for analysis; the difference involved substituting war, conquest and force for agreement, law and contracts. In either case, the reproduction of domination occupied the foreground, not the question of its constitution.

Foucault now confronts this problem by means of the concept of government, which implies a distinction between power and domination. If power is characterized by 'conduct', and 'freedom' represents an integral component of power strategies, then it is necessary to distinguish between 'free' forms of power and those that shut down possible (re) actions. Foucault's term for the former is *relations of power* (*relations de pouvoir*) or *strategic games*.[34] Relations of power are not external to society. Instead of a parasitic, foreign body that takes hold – which, accordingly, one might isolate and remove – they 'are rooted deep in the social nexus'.[35] Conceived in these broad terms, relations of power do not stand opposed to society so much as they form the very condition of its possibility: 'In any case, to live in society is to live in such a way that action upon other actions is possible – and in fact ongoing. A society without power relations can only be an abstraction'.[36]

It does not follow from this definition, however, that all social relations amount to relations of power. Nor is it the case that a single principle of power pervades the whole of society – or that forms, or technologies, of power cannot change. Instead, Foucault means to draw attention to the elemental level of society where power relations are anchored; they are not limited to the political sphere or concentrated in specific institutions. Inasmuch as every aspect of society involves manifold forms of inequality, competing objectives, institutional and organizational complexes, and so on, there is no such thing as a society without relations of power. In this sense, power is a 'social game' intimately tied to the way human communities function.[37]

---

34. That said, in the context of the government problematic, the term 'strategy' no longer designates a 'warlike relation' exclusively; in a more general way, it points to all possible forms for determining the actions of others; hereby, war, struggle, and so on represent options among others.

35. Foucault, 1982b, 'The Subject and Power', 222.

36. Ibid., 222–3.

37. Ibid., 224–5; Foucault, 1983m, 'Discussion with Michel Foucault', 25. It merits emphasis that for Foucault 'society' always represents a historically determined form

In this context, Foucault identifies an abiding mode of exercising power that is institutionalized by economic, political or military means: 'This is where we must introduce the concept of domination'.[38] He distinguishes between strategic games of power, which are changeable and reversible in principle, and *states of domination*, where conditions are rigid, immobile and unyielding. Unlike relations of power, states of domination admit no practices of freedom (or they do so only for some, and in restricted form); they are defined by the fact that an individual or social group has managed to block relations of power and establish enduring asymmetry.[39]

The theoretical distinction between power and domination pinpoints a new problem: if relations of power are 'free' and 'open' in principle, whereas states of dominations are 'rigid' and 'blocked', then what makes the former solidify into the latter? The concept of government plays a key role in the answer Foucault formulates. Instead of simply placing power and domination in opposition to each other, he introduces government as an 'intermediate term':

> We must distinguish between power relations understood as strategic games between liberties ... and the states of domination that people ordinarily call 'power'. And between the two, between games of power and states of domination, you have technologies of government – understood, of course, in a very broad sense that includes not only the way institutions are governed but also the way one governs one's wife

of organization and points to a totalizing tendency that is anything but 'neutral' or 'universal': 'I believe, on the contrary, that this particular idea of the "whole of society" derives from a utopian context. This idea arose in the Western world, within this highly individualized historical development that culminates in capitalism. To speak of the "whole of society" apart from the only form it has ever taken is to transform our past into a dream. We readily believe that the least we can expect of experiences, actions, and strategies is that they take into account the "whole of society". This seems absolutely essential for their existence. But I believe that this is asking a great deal, that it means imposing impossible conditions on our actions because this notion functions in a manner that prohibits the actualization, success, and perpetuation of these projects. "The whole of society" is precisely that which should not be considered except as something to be destroyed. And then, we can only hope that it will never exist again'. Foucault, 1971f, 'Revolutionary Action: "Until Now"' [1977], 232–3.

38. Foucault, 1984s, 'The Ethics of the Concern for the Self as a Practice of Freedom' [1997], 283.

39. Foucault, 1982b, 'The Subject and Power', 225–6; Foucault, 1984s, 'The Ethics of the Concern for the Self as a Practice of Freedom' [1997], 283; Foucault, 1988d, 'Power, Moral Values, and the Intellectual' [1980], 11.

and children. The analysis of these techniques is necessary because it is very often through such techniques that states of domination are established and maintained. There are three levels of my analysis of power: strategic relations, techniques of government, and states of domination.[40]

In other words, the concept of government represents a hinge between strategic games and states of domination, enabling Foucault to retain the analytical insights of the 'microphysics of power' and, at the same time, to free himself from the oversimplifications it has entailed. As a mediating instance, it does justice to a research interest that examines how conditions of domination are constituted and the possibility of resistance. Consequently, Foucault's 'rule of immanence'[41] in analysing power relations does not lead to summary condemnation or moral censure; instead, it means critical inquiry into their potential or actual 'effects of domination'.[42]

As such, it does not follow from Foucault's claim that power is a social fact that all relations of power should be evaluated in the same manner, or that there is no way to judge them. On the contrary, the theoretical distinction between power and domination holds political significance. Only on the basis of this distinction is it possible to formulate a critique of conditions of domination – and strategies to overturn them – without invoking some idea of a realm 'beyond power'. In this way, Foucault retains the premise of 'omnipresent power' in social relations while providing a criterion for distinguishing 'freer' and 'less free' forms of power:

> I do not think that a society can exist without power relations, if by that one means the strategies by which individuals try to direct and control

40. Foucault, 1984s, 'The Ethics of the Concern for the Self as a Practice of Freedom' [1997], 299.

41. Foucault, 1976a, *The History of Sexuality, Volume 1: An Introduction* [1978], 98.

42. Foucault, 1984s, 'The Ethics of the Concern for the Self as a Practice of Freedom' [1997], 295; see also Foucault, 1984f, 'Politics and Ethics: An Interview', 378. 'My point is not that everything is bad, but that everything is dangerous, which is not exactly the same as bad. If everything is dangerous, then we always have something to do. So my position leads not to apathy but to a hyper- and pessimistic activism'. Foucault, 1983b, 'On the Genealogy of Ethics: An Overview of Work in Progress', 231–2.

the conduct of others. The problem, then, is not to try to dissolve them in the utopia of completely transparent communication but to acquire the rules of law, the management techniques, and also the morality, the *ēthos*, the practice of the self, that will allow us to play these games of power with as little domination as possible.[43]

That said, a problem persists inasmuch as Foucault does not always observe the three levels of analysis he proposes and sometimes equates government and 'strategic games'. At some points, government counts as a historically specific, well-defined technology of power; at others, it refers to power *per se*. Such theoretical confusion proves significant because it shapes political options in a decisive manner and restricts the critical potential afforded by the concept of government. If government represented a fundamental fact of human society and determined the outer limits of what is possible, then all changes would have to play out within the political framework of governmental technology; there would be no possibility for passing beyond them and criticizing them as such:

I do not think that the will not to be governed at all is something that one could consider an originary aspiration. I think that, in fact, the will not to be governed is always the will not to be governed thusly, like that, by these people, at this price. As for the expression of not being governed at all, I believe it is the philosophical and theoretical paroxysm of something that would be this will not to be relatively governed.[44]

This position is both theoretically weak and politically unsatisfying, and it can hardly be maintained simply through reference to the 'immanence of power relations'. As we will see in Chapter 14, such a line of argument is not consistent with Foucault's genealogical effort as a whole.[45]

---

43. Foucault, 1984s, 'The Ethics of the Concern for the Self as a Practice of Freedom' [1997], 298.

44. Foucault, 1990b, 'What Is Critique?' [2007], 75; see also the reference to 'rational techniques of government' in Foucault, 1984s, 'The Ethics of the Concern for the Self as a Practice of Freedom' [1997], 299.

45. Barry Hindess has formulated a similar critique, drawing attention to passages where Foucault seems to suggest that he views domination as a universal historical phenomenon, so that only the question of limiting or minimizing it arises. Hindess, *Discourses of Power* (1996), 152–6.

## Practices of Freedom and Forms of Resistance

The emphasis placed on freedom within the problematic of government leads not only to the distinction between power and domination, but also to the connection between power and subjectivity. Freedom is not simply the precondition for relations of power; it also provides the basis for ethics. As a relation to the self, ethics simultaneously involves shaping and modelling freedom. Although ethics and freedom are not the same, no ethics can exist without freedom, for then there would be no foundation or material where ethical work could begin: 'Freedom is the ontological condition of ethics. But ethics is the considered form that freedom takes when it is informed by reflection'.[46]

Just as power exists only *in actu*, as 'acting on actions', freedom is not a means to an end so much as a practice of self-definition. Power systems cannot fully exclude the possibility of resistance, opposition, disobedience and so on. By the same token, there cannot be systems that guarantee freedom. This is not the case because of the fundamental ambiguity of institutions or the corruptibility of the people within them so much as because of the fact that freedom is not a state; it always involves a practice, which achieves definition only in the course of being performed: 'The liberty of men is never assured by the institutions and laws that we intended to guarantee them. ... I think that it can never be inherent in the structure of things to guarantee the exercise of freedom. The guarantee of freedom is freedom'.[47]

In contrast to earlier works, Foucault recognizes that simply rejecting the humanist idea of a sovereign subject is not enough to escape its sphere of influence.[48] Nor is it enough – *contra* the assumption of

---

46. Foucault, 1984s, 'The Ethics of the Concern for the Self as a Practice of Freedom' [1997], 284.

47. Foucault, 1982c, 'Space, Knowledge and Power' [1984], 245.

48. Accordingly, Foucault revises and qualifies what he said about 'the death of man' in *The Order of Things*. Whereas, in the latter work, his point of departure was a historical development in the course of unfolding, now he recognizes that such a perspective means understanding history as a process external to subjects. See, e.g., Foucault, 1966a, *The Order of Things* [1994], 386–7. In a late interview, he admits to having mixed two points together. The first is the thesis that the human sciences do not concern 'human being' in a primordial sense; although they claim to have uncovered human nature and its laws, in fact, they forge a new form of subjectivity by equating 'man' and subjective knowledge. 'The second aspect that I mixed up and confused with the first is that in the course of their history, men have never ceased constructing themselves, that is, to shift continuously the level of their subjectivity, to

free and autonomous subjectivity – to demonstrate how complexes of power/knowledge produce such a view. Rather, one must take the double nature of subjectivation processes into account and analyse the 'interaction'[49] of autonomy and domination in order to see how subjects 'are governed': the ways they govern themselves and others, and how they are subjugated and form themselves at one and the same time. That is, there are two aspects of subjective constitution inasmuch as 'the subject is constituted through practices of subjection, or, in a more autonomous way, through practices of liberation, of liberty'.[50]

'Practices of subjection' and 'practices of liberty' do not refer to matters that are different in substance: passivity on the one hand and activity on the other. Instead, subjectivation processes possess a double determination in either case. Subjectivation is not simply the result of compulsion and constraint; it takes place within a strategic field that necessarily includes possibility for resistance, as well. Thus, the constitution of the 'mad subject' was undoubtedly the result of a system of compulsion; nevertheless, the madman is not unfree inasmuch as he is constituted 'in relation to and over against the one who declares him mad'.[51] Similarly, the construction of a 'homosexual subject' represents a means of oppression, yet it also offers a potential for resistance. On the one hand, the classification serves as a social stigma, but it also – if on a modest scale – may be claimed in order to protect those it brands: inasmuch as homosexuality is conceived as an illness, it proves difficult to condemn those affected by it, or to hold them responsible

---

constitute themselves in an infinite and multiple series of different subjectivities that would never reach an end and would never place us in the presence of something that would be "man". [...] By speaking of the "death of man" in a way that was confused, simplifying, and a bit prophetic, I wanted in substance to say these things'. Foucault, 1980d, *Remarks on Marx* [1991], 123–4.

49. Foucault, 1981c, 'Sexuality and Solitude' [1997], 177.

50. Foucault, 1984t, 'An Aesthetics of Existence' [1988], 50. The distinction between 'practices of freedom' and 'practices of liberation' follows from differentiating between power relations and conditions of domination. Under conditions of domination, the possibility of practices of freedom is slight (after all, diminished leeway for free actions is what defines domination); accordingly, liberation from domination represents the political and historical precondition for practices of freedom. However, this precondition (e.g. a colonized people's struggle for independence) is merely necessary – and incapable of generating, from within, practices of freedom that might attain political and social bindingness. Foucault, 1984s, 'The Ethics of the Concern for the Self as a Practice of Freedom' [1997], 282–3.

51. Ibid., 291.

for their conduct. As such, 'homosexuality' – originally a medical term and an instrument of repression – was able to provide the starting point for an affirmative strategy and resistance.[52]

Accordingly, subjectivation practices do not represent a field apart. They are always tied into economic, political and social processes. It

---

52. Foucault, 1976a, *The History of Sexuality, Volume 1: An Introduction* [1978], 144–5; Foucault, 1977k, 'The End of the Monarchy of Sex' [1996], 217–19; Foucault, 1984u, 'Sex, Power, and the Politics of Identity' [1997], 170–1. An important sign of how Foucault changed his thinking – from a conception that still implied an external relationship between power and resistance to one that viewed them in terms of immanence – is his reassessment of dialectics. Early texts vehemently rejected a dialectical conception of history as a 'logic of contradiction' that fails to do justice to historical struggles: 'I don't accept this word dialectical. No, no! Let me make this very clear. As soon as you say dialectical you begin to accept, even if you don't say it, the Hegelian schema of thesis/antithesis and a kind of logic that I think is inadequate for making a real concrete description of those problems. A reciprocal relation is not a dialectical one'. Foucault, 1978c, 'Dialogue on Power' [1975], 13; Foucault, 1970b, 'Theatrum Philosophicum' [1998], 358; Foucault, 1977d, 'Truth and Power' [1984], 56; Foucault, 1986, '21 January 1976' and '28 January 1976' [2003], 58–9.

However, in later interviews, Foucault implicitly invokes dialectics – and precisely in the context of describing struggles in concrete manner. For example, apropos of homosexuality: 'These categories were used, it is true, to pathologize homosexuality, but they were equally categories of defense, in the name of which one could claim rights. The problem is still very current: between the affirmation "I am homosexual" and the refusal to say it, lies a very ambiguous dialectic. It's a necessary affirmation since it is the affirmation of a right, but at the same time it's a cage and a trap'. Foucault, 1982d, 'History and Homosexuality' [1996], 369; Foucault, 1984u, 'Sex, Power, and the Politics of Identity' [1997], 167.

Foucault clearly recognized how incorporating a 'dialectical dimension' changed his conception of power – as well as the questions this raised for his previous positions: 'On many points – I am thinking especially of the relations between dialectics, genealogy and strategy – I am still working and don't yet know whether I am going to get anywhere'. Foucault, 1980b, 'Questions of Method', 74. A similar understanding of (class) struggles underlies Michel Pêcheux's discourse analysis. Pêcheux conceives ideological domination not as an opposition between ruling and ruled, but as a 'paradoxical space' in which outward confrontation 'is manifested in the very internal organization of the dominated ideology': 'This means simultaneously that the historical process by which the dominated ideology tends to be organized "on its own basis" as proletarian ideology remains paradoxically in contact with bourgeois ideology, precisely to the extent that it attempts to realize the latter's destruction. [...] The double character of ideological processes ... allows us to understand how ideological formations refer to *both identical and different* "objects" (like Freedom, God, Justice, etc.), i.e., whose unity is submitted to a division: the characteristic of the ideological class struggle is to take place in *one* world that never quite *divides into two*'. Pêcheux, 'Dare to Think and Dare to Rebel! Ideology, Marxism, Resistance, Class Struggle' (2014), 7–8; Pêcheux, 'Ideology: Fortress or Paradoxical Space' (1983).

is impossible to investigate the constitution of forms of subjectivity without considering these mechanisms. At the same time, however, this does not mean that such relations may be boiled down to a simple matter of determination, with concrete subjectivity at the end of a causal chain that starts with a socio-economic structure: 'It is certain that the mechanisms of subjection cannot be studied outside their relation to the mechanisms of exploitation and domination. But they do not merely constitute the "terminal" of more fundamental mechanisms. They entertain complex and circular relations with other forms.'[53]

Inasmuch as forms of subjectivation constitute an independent field – which does not derive from other factors so much as it determines, and is determined by, them – it is not enough to limit oneself to combating political, social and religious domination or economic exploitation. Instead, one must develop a form of struggle that takes a further step and aims at forms of subjectivation. Just as forms of subjectivation cannot be reduced to an underlying social structure, resistance to them cannot be limited to struggles against forms of political domination or economic exploitation.

In historical perspective, Foucault contends that this form of struggle has grown more and more important since the 1960s. Manifold social confrontations between men and women, about definitions of health and illness, reason and madness – as well as ecological and peace movements, and activism on the part of sexual minorities – attest to a 'crisis of government', whereby traditional forms of subjectivation are losing their binding force. The defining trait of such struggles is to call the status of the individual into question. A paradoxical approach prevails inasmuch as it does not take a stand for or against the individual, but turns against a technology that makes individuals into subjects: the 'government of individualization'.[54]

That said, resistance does not operate solely by rejecting certain forms of subjectivation. More still, it involves making an important,

---

53. Foucault, 1982b, 'The Subject and Power', 213.
54. Ibid., 212; Foucault, 1978j, 'La philosophie analytique de la politique', 543–6. 'On the one hand, they assert the right to be different and they underline everything which makes individuals truly individual. On the other hand, they attack everything which separates the individual, breaks his links with others, splits up community life, forces the individual back on himself and ties him to his own identity in a constraining way'. Foucault, 1982b, 'The Subject and Power', 211–12.

328 Politics and Ethics

second step: 'promot[ing] new forms of subjectivity'.[55] These two aspects are not independent, because struggle against traditional forms has a performative dimension: the 'invention' of new forms of subjectivity. In and through resistance to established power mechanisms, another form of subjectivity appears, which is unwilling to accept certain constraints and impositions. As such, resistance to standing forms of subjectivation is not just reactive and the means to a (future) end; it represents an end in itself and a self-grounding praxis:

> People do revolt; that is a fact. And that is how subjectivity (not that of great men, but that of anyone) is brought into history, breathing life into it. A convict risks his life to protest unjust punishments; a madman can no longer bear being confined and humiliated; a people refuses the regime that oppresses it.[56]

The concept of freedom, then, does not simply mark a break with the opposition between power and resistance and move beyond the latter's (negative) relation to the former. It also plays a positive role in the formation of subjectivity. Inasmuch as government gives a certain form to the freedom of subjects in order to control and steer them, the self-relation it entails affords potential for resistance inasmuch as it can be used against governmental technologies. Thus, Foucault's interest bears on 'the way in which individuals, in their struggles, in their confrontations, in their projects, freely constitute themselves as subjects of their practices or, on the contrary, reject the practices in which they are expected to participate'.[57] For this reason, the elaboration of an 'ethics' is not something that lies outside of, or beyond, the political sphere; it is already part of resistance to historical subjectivation forms: 'politics as ethics'.[58]

---

55. Ibid., 216; Foucault, 1976a, *The History of Sexuality, Volume 1: An Introduction* [1978], 159.

56. Foucault, 1979i, 'Useless to Revolt?' [2000], 452.

57. Foucault, 1984p, 'Interview with *Actes*' [2000], 399; Foucault, 1988a, 'Truth, Power, Self', 14.

58. Foucault, 1984f, 'Politics and Ethics: An Interview', 377; Olivier, 'Michel Foucault, éthique et politique' (1996). In this sense, Foucault calls Deleuze and Guattari's *Anti-Oedipus* 'a book of ethics', or an 'introduction to a new art of living', not only directed against historical fascism but also against the 'fascism in us all, in our heads and in our everyday behavior, the fascism that causes us to love power, to desire the very thing that dominates and exploits us'. Foucault, 1977a, 'Preface', xiv–xv.

Expanding the field of analysis through the dimension of ethics, then, does not mean abandoning the problematic of power. Instead, it provides a necessary amendment. If power takes effect on subjects by way of their actions, then investigating it demands critical distance from a juridical conception of subjectivity, which fails to grasp the 'specific nature' of power processes:

> If we take the question of power, of political power, situating it in the more general question of governmentality, … then I do not think that reflection on this notion of governmentality can avoid passing through, theoretically and practically, the element of a subject defined by the relation of self to self. Although the theory of political power as an institution usually refers to a juridical conception of the subject of right, it seems to me that the analysis of governmentality – that is to say, of power as a set of reversible relationships – must refer to an ethics of the subject defined by the relationship of self to self. Quite simply, this means that in the type of analysis I have been trying to advance for some time you can see that power relations, governmentality, the government of the self and of others, and the relationship of self to self constitute a chain, a thread, and I think it is around these notions that we should be able to connect together the question of politics and the question of ethics.[59]

To illustrate this very general and theoretical account of the relationship between subjectivity and power, we now turn, in concluding this chapter, to a concrete example that connects questions of resistance and domination, on the one hand, and the problem of another political rationality on the other: the Iranian Revolution.

## Excursus: The Iranian Revolution

Foucault's preparations for his 1979 lectures at the Collège de France on liberal and neoliberal governmentality coincided with a news item of great significance: the Iranian Revolution. At the invitation of the Italian newspaper *Corriere della Sera*, Foucault visited Iran several

---

59. Foucault, 1985c, *The Hermeneutics of the Subject* [2005], 252; Foucault, 1984s, 'The Ethics of the Concern for the Self as a Practice of Freedom' [1997], 300.

times in late 1978 and early 1979, reporting on political events that
ultimately led to the fall of the shah and the return of Khomeini. He
published his analysis of the situation both in the *Corriere della Sera*
and the French journal *Le Nouvel Observateur*.[60]

The articles prompted vehement reactions. Many readers took
them as an expression of thoughtless agreement with a doctrinaire,
religious order of domination that was no less cruel than the auto-
cratic and corrupt regime it had replaced. Some commentators held
that Foucault's reports manifested a bearing that opted for revolt for
its own sake, without any concern for disastrous political effects. For
Foucault, critics held, power is bad *per se*; thus, every form of resistance is justified, no matter the means employed or the aims pursued.
According to this view, the analysis Foucault presented remained stuck
on a moral plane and failed to do justice to the complexities of the
political situation in Iran.[61]

Two aspects of this critique should be distinguished. To be sure, it is
correct that Foucault underestimated the role of clerics in the *historical*
changes that occurred. His reports from Iran attest to deep sympathy
for the masses in revolt – and, in equal measure, his deep fascination

---

60. Didier Eribon and David Macey provide accounts of Foucault's time in Iran.
Eribon, *Michel Foucault* (1991), 281–92; Macey, *The Lives of Michel Foucault* (1993),
406–11. An excellent analysis of the politico-theoretical implications of Foucault's
articles is offered by Lawrence Olivier and Sylvain Labbé, as well as Georg Stauth.
Olivier and Labbé, 'Foucault et l'Iran: A propos du désir de révolution' (1991);
Stauth, 'Revolution in Spiritless Times' (1991). Hervé Malagola analyses the philosophical bearing and terminology in evidence. Malagola, 'Foucault en Iran' (1994).
These reports were embedded in a broader context. In mid-1978, together with other
intellectuals, Foucault founded a working group with the aim of developing a new
form of journalism. Such 'reportage of ideas' (*reportage des idées*) would affirm the
significance of everyday notions. In addition to portraying the opinions, beliefs and
thoughts of 'simple people' – and calling attention to 'overlooked' ideas – the project
sought to investigate matters in social context and in relation to historical events.
The point was to examine how ideas orient and motivate actions: 'It's not ideas that
rule the world. But precisely because the world has ideas (and because it's always
producing lots of them), it isn't passively ruled by those who want to lead – or those
who want to say how to think, once and for all. That's the significance we'd like these
reports to have: combining analysis of what's being thought with analysis of what's
happening. Intellectuals will work together with journalists where ideas and events
intersect'. Foucault, 1978w, '"Les reportages" des idées', 707.

61. Along these lines, see the articles in *Le Nouvel Observateur* 730 (6 November
1978): 'Une Irannienne écrit' and *Le Matin* 24 (24 March 1979): 'A quoi rêvent les
philosophes?' by Claudie and Jacques Broyelle.

with Khomeini's person. Only in a marginal sense do Foucault's reports deal with the question of what kind of rule will replace the shah's. That said, Foucault shared the hope for a democratic development and dislike for the current regime with many observers. Like them, he was mistaken about the mullahs' resolve to build an 'Islamic republic'.

Foucault's articles involve a far weightier problem than making the proper assessment of historical process at work: the *political* significance of his analysis of power is put to the test. Critical commentary on the journalistic texts has pointed to potential, theoretical weaknesses or normative problems. The question arises whether there are 'systematic' reasons for the way Foucault examines political changes: does he support the project of 'Islamic government' and legitimate a regime that has substituted one kind of terror for another? Why does he endorse the revolt? What moral attitude underlies his writings?

In the following – albeit very briefly and in provisional form – I would like to take up these questions in order, first, to study Foucault's analysis of power and his conception of history in light of a concrete example, and, second, to draw attention to the close relationship between subjectivity and power elaborated in his articles. Foucault's newspaper reports, I submit, are based on a question posed by his theoretical works, too: how does power function and how is resistance possible?[62]

### Islamic Government

Counter to what most commentators assume, Foucault's articles on the Iranian revolution do not seek to side with a movement or political programme. Instead, the focus falls on the historical conditions for revolt against the shah. How could such a broad movement arise? What are its preconditions and goals? The numerous interviews and inquiries providing the material for the articles orbit around the motives for revolt. '"What do you want?" During my entire stay in

---

62. The former Iranian prime minister Bani Sadr – whom Foucault got to know while conducting his research – observed the same: 'He wanted to understand how this revolution was able to be produced, developing with no reference to any foreign power, and stirring up an entire nation, despite the distance between towns and the difficulties of communication. He wanted to reflect on the notion of power'. Quoted in Eribon, *Michel Foucault* (1991), 286.

Iran, I did not hear even once the word "revolution", but four out of five times, someone would answer, "An Islamic government".[63]

Yet what did the idea of 'Islamic government' mean for Iranians in 1978? According to Foucault, it involved two different things. For some, it was a *utopia*. For others, an *ideal*. The call for 'Islamic government' ties a lost past to a future hope: it harks back to ancient, religious traditions and connects them with the promise of new, political freedoms. For his part, Foucault does not seem to identify at all with the politico-religious goals that his interlocutors advance. On the contrary, his view of the ideal of an 'Islamic government' takes critical distance: 'It is often said that the definitions of an Islamic government are imprecise. On the contrary, they seemed to me to have a familiar but, I must say, not too reassuring clarity. "These are basic formulas for democracy, whether bourgeois or revolutionary", I said. "Since the eighteenth century now, we have not ceased to repeat them, and you know where they have led".[64]

Indeed, an attentive reading of the articles makes it clear that Foucault does not opt for the idea of 'Islamic government'. On the contrary, he states that such talk does 'not' make him 'feel comfortable'.[65] In no way does he take a stand in favour of the programme elaborated by religious authorities and political parties, which reminds him of the problems articulated under capitalism and state socialism. Foucault leaves no room for doubt that a 'mullah government' does not seem desirable to him, and he evinces scepticism about the political practices likely under an 'Islamic government'.[66]

If, all the same, Foucault shows interest in the idea of an 'Islamic government', it is not because of political or religious rhetoric. Instead, what commands his notice is its practical, everyday significance and its power to motivate a great mass of human beings. Accordingly, Foucault examines 'Islamic government' from two vantage points in particular: first, in terms of *collective will* enabling a multiplicity of different interests to achieve definition, and second, in terms of *political spirituality* permitting the integration of ethics and politics:

---

63. Foucault, 1978t, 'What Are the Iranians Dreaming About?' [2005], 205.
64. Ibid., 206, 205–7.
65. Ibid., 208.
66. Ibid., 205; Foucault, 1979g, 'Open Letter to Mehdi Bazargan' [2000]; Foucault, 1979i, 'Useless to Revolt?' [2000], 452.

When Iranians speak of Islamic government; when, under the threat of bullets, they transform it into a slogan of the streets; when they reject in its name, perhaps at the risk of a bloodbath, deals arranged by parties and politicians, they have other things on their minds than these formulas from everywhere and nowhere. They also have other things in their hearts. I believe that they are thinking about a reality that is very near to them, since they themselves are its active agents. It is first and foremost about a movement that aims to give a permanent role in political life to the traditional structures of Islamic society. An Islamic government is what will allow the continuing activity of the thousands of political centers that have been spawned in mosques and religious communities in order to resist the shah's regime. ...

But one dreams [*songe*] also of another movement, which is the inverse and the converse of the first. This is one that would allow the introduction of a spiritual dimension into political life, in order that it would not be, as always, the obstacle to spirituality, but rather its receptacle, its opportunity, and its ferment.[67]

## Collective Will

A recurrent theme in Foucault's reports is the power of human beings who – largely without military or institutional support – are fighting against a highly armed state apparatus. The Iranian Revolution is a revolution without a backing organization, party, vanguard, or historical precedent. The defining trait of revolutionary events and the condition for their success (the elimination of the regime of the shah) is to constitute a collective will that proves effective beyond party borders and social fragmentation, based on rejecting the regime of domination until now:

Among the things that characterize this revolutionary event, there is the fact that it has brought out – and few peoples in history have had this – an absolutely collective will. The collective will is a political myth with which jurists and philosophers try to analyse or to justify

---

67. Foucault, 1978t, 'What Are the Iranians Dreaming About?' [2005], 207; Foucault, 1978x, 'Foucault's Response to Atoussa H.' [2005], 210; Olivier and Labbé, 'Foucault et l'Iran: A propos du désir de révolution' (1991), 222–3; Stauth, 'Revolution in Spiritless Times' (1991), 267–8.

institutions, etc. It's a theoretical tool: nobody has ever seen the 'collective will' and, personally, I thought that the collective will was like God, like the soul, something one would never encounter. I don't know whether you agree with me, but we met, in Tehran and throughout Iran, the collective will of a people.[68]

Foucault's examination of collective will displays some particularities. For one, the fact that a collective will exists does not necessarily mean that it is something good, just or moral. On the contrary: Foucault points out that in this instance, the constitution of a unified will has been accompanied by antisemitism and xenophobia.[69] Second, the matter has nothing to do with a *volonté générale* distinct from the empirical will of those involved; instead, it refers to the 'will of all' (*volonté de tous*),[70] which is precisely what Rousseau sought to discredit. Finally, collective will does not represent possibility, as opposed to realization; it does not belong to the realm of ideas and imagination, as opposed to that of material practices. Rather, Foucault is interested in this 'will' inasmuch as it produces real effects and takes the stage as a structuring force within political conflict.

Foucault's premise is that Islamic religion has played a key role in the constitution of this collective will. Not only did the religious element enable the politicization of broad swathes of Iranian society; it also made it possible for human beings to build a new relation to themselves and others. Foucault saw people's enthusiasm and the call for 'Islamic government' as something far greater than the effort to change political regime. Transition to another political order was part of a comprehensive movement aiming for a new relation to oneself

---

68. Foucault, 1979c, 'Iran: The Spirit of a World without Spirit' [1988], 215. For Foucault, three paradoxes define the Iranian Revolution. First, it is the revolt of an 'unarmed people'; 'with bare hands', they are fighting against one of the best armed armies of the world and a brutal police apparatus. Second, the protest encompasses broad swathes of the population, multiple social and political groups; for all that, no serious conflicts or contradictions have arisen between them. Third, the absence of a long-term political goal does not represent a weakness; indeed, the fact that there is no concrete program for government, but simply a political strike against domination as a whole, is a source of strength. Foucault, 1978v, 'A Revolt with Bare Hands' [2005], 210–11; Stauth, 'Revolution in Spiritless Times' (1991), 271–3.
69. Foucault, 1979c, 'Iran: The Spirit of a World without Spirit' [1988], 222; Foucault, 1979i, 'Useless to Revolt?' [2000], 451–2.
70. Foucault, 1978v, 'A Revolt with Bare Hands' [2005], 213.

and others. In revolting, people did not want simply to replace one kind of domination with another; they were demonstrating for a new organization of social relations and a new form of subjectivity – and religion was to guarantee this radical transformation. 'For the people who inhabit this land, what is the point of searching, even at the cost of their own lives, for this thing whose possibility we have forgotten since the Renaissance and the great crisis of Christianity, a *political spirituality?*'.[71]

## Political Spirituality

The idea of 'Islamic government', then, does not imply reorienting politics along the lines of religious law or subordinating state violence to religious authority. Instead, it means a new form of government and another regime of truth:

> [I]sn't the most general of political problems the problem of truth? How can one analyse the connection between ways of distinguishing true and false and ways of governing oneself and others? The search for a new foundation for each of these practices, in itself and relative to the other, the will to discover a different way of governing oneself through a different way of dividing up true and false – this is what I would call 'political *spiritualité*.[72]

'Political spirituality' does not mean a return to archaic values for Foucault. Instead, it signifies the articulation of a new political rationality. In this conflict, religion does not play the role of an ideology that masks contradictions or makes different interests compatible. Islam does not express more fundamental antagonisms. On the contrary, it is the 'vocabulary' in which conflict is carried out and lived. In this context, religion is not just a means of struggle; the spiritual dimension itself forms an integral component of struggle: 'the very way of experiencing revolts'.[73]

---

71. Foucault, 1978t, 'What Are the Iranians Dreaming About?' [2005], 209; see also Olivier and Labbé, 'Foucault et l'Iran: A propos du désir de révolution' (1991), 223–4. On the concept of spirituality in Foucault, see Jambet, 'The Constitution of the Subject and Spiritual Practice' (1992); Schmid, *Auf der Suche nach einer neuen Lebenskunst* (1991), 366–72.

72. Foucault, 1980b, 'Questions of Method', 82.

73. Foucault, 1979i, 'Useless to Revolt?' [2000], 450; Foucault, 1979c, 'Iran: The

As such, the idea of 'Islamic government' represents the possibility 'to use religious structures not only as centres of resistance, but also as sources for political creation'.[74] Religion does not interest Foucault only as a negative force opposing a regime and mounting resistance so much as a positive element in the formation of new political subjectivities and new political rationality. It represents the decisive factor for understanding not just the dynamic of historical processes, but also the character and specificity of revolutionary events. Accordingly, Islam does not represent a religious force so much as a political one – or, more precisely, a combination of politics and religion (ethics), which aims less for life in the beyond than changing conditions in this world.[75]

In this conflict, Islam holds strategic significance because it inspires change in the way life is conducted and makes it possible to understand political revolt as part of a fundamental transformation of society. Accordingly, simply changing political structures is not enough:

'But, above all, we have to change ourselves. Our way of being, our relationship with others, with things, with eternity, with God, etc., must be completely changed and there will only be a true revolution if this radical change in our experience takes place.' I believe that it is here that Islam played a role. It may be that one or other of its obligations, one or other of its codes exerted a certain fascination. But, above all,

---

Spirit of a World without Spirit' [1988], 214. Gerhard Stauth overlooks this key aspect when he claims that Foucault's articles discuss religion as a 'medium', or 'representation', of collective will. Stauth, 'Revolution in Spiritless Times' (1991), 274.

74. Foucault, 1978t, 'What Are the Iranians Dreaming About?' [2005], 207.

75. Foucault, 1978y, 'The Mythical Leader of the Iranian Revolt' [2005], 222–3. In an open letter to Iranian prime minister Mehdi Bazargan after the institution of an 'Islamic Republic' – and the beginning of political trials and public executions – Foucault declared that he had wrongly assumed that the spiritual dimension uniting people against the shah would prevent a 'mullah government'. He was also deceived by hope that Islam would secure human rights in a way that capitalism and state socialism had failed to do. Foucault, 1979g, 'Open Letter to Mehdi Bazargan' [2000]; on the question of human rights, see Foucault, 1984r, 'Confronting Governments: Human Rights' [2000]. See also Foucault's response to those who faulted him for incorrectly assessing political developments in Iran and called on him to revise the positions he had taken: 'To be sure, there is no shame in changing one's opinion; but there is no reason to say one has changed it when today one is against severed hands, having yesterday been against the tortures of the Savak [secret police, T.L.]'. Foucault, 1979i, 'Useless to Revolt?' [2000], 452.

in relation to the way of life that was theirs, religion for them was like the promise and guarantee of finding something that would radically change their subjectivity. … People always quote Marx and the opium of the people. The sentence that immediately preceded that statement and which is never quoted says that religion is the spirit of a world without spirit. Let's say, then, that Islam, in that year of 1978, was not the opium of the people precisely because it was the spirit of a world without a spirit.[76]

## Revolution in a 'World without a Spirit'

For Foucault, the Iranian Revolution is not a revolution in the received sense because it cannot be projected on to a standing system of political coordinates. Something new is being manifested, which eludes all traditional schemes of classification. This revolution is revolutionary because it overturns our traditional understanding of what 'revolution' means:

It is a phenomenon that may be called revolutionary in the very broad sense of the term, since it concerns the uprising of a whole nation against a power that oppresses it. Now we recognize a revolution when we can observe two dynamics: one is that of the contradictions in that society, that of the class struggle or of social confrontations. Then there is a political dynamics, that is to say, the presence of a vanguard, class, party, or political ideology, in short, a spearhead that carries the whole nation with it. Now it seems to me that, in what is happening in Iran, one can recognize neither of those two dynamics that are for us distinctive signs and explicit marks of a revolutionary phenomenon. What, for us, is a revolutionary movement in which one cannot situate the internal contradictions of a society, and in which one cannot point out a vanguard either?[77]

Indeed, in the context of the uprising against the shah, Foucault almost never speaks of a revolution; instead, he prefers 'revolt'. He does so because characterizing events as a revolution does not describe them

---

76. Foucault, 1979c, 'Iran: The Spirit of a World without Spirit' [1988], 217–18.
77. Ibid., 212–13; see also Foucault, 1978y, 'The Mythical Leader of the Iranian Revolt' [2005], 222–3.

so much as it lends them a 'meaning' – that is, it classifies, system-
atizes and evaluates them on the basis of an external scheme. What
Foucault rejects in the qualification of 'revolution' is the historico-
philosophical perspective characteristic of political thinking since
the eighteenth century: that revolution refers to what is desirable and
coming – and, as such, what makes the present tolerable. From this
vantage point, revolution has its own rules, 'good' and 'bad' forms,
just aims, and legitimate means for achieving them. 'Revolutionary
discourse' involves stripping events of their uniqueness and particularity – in a word, their *eventfulness* – in order to 'fit revolt to a rational,
controllable history'.[78]

The 'revolutionary perspective' gives events a form and content in
order to fit them to a scheme of historical logic that is relatively independent from the desires and actions of actual human beings. Such
rationality – with the coercive effects it entails – is what gives rise to
the wish for a revolution. Accordingly, Foucault asks whether revolutionary 'hope had been borne, since the end of the eighteenth century,
by a whole rationalism of which we are entitled to ask what part it may
have played in the effects of despotism where that hope got lost'.[79]

This critical interrogation of the power effects of 'revolutionary discourse' does not amount to negating 'radical' breaks and changes. On
the contrary, Foucault means to avoid the distortion that would result
from imposing an external scheme on events. Any revolutionary perspective worthy of the name cannot situate political upheaval along
the lines of a system of moral categories and then verify the legitimacy
of means employed or aims envisioned. Foucault's theoretical strategy
does not focus on evaluating revolution so much as examining it as an
'event' that breaks with existing forms of thought and practice.[80]

Foucault elucidates his intellectual bearing by discussing Kant's
engagement with the French Revolution (in the *Contest of Faculties*).

---

78. Foucault, 1979i, 'Useless to Revolt?' [2000], 791.
79. Foucault, 1985a, 'Life: Experience and Science' [1998], 469; Foucault, 1977k,
'The End of the Monarchy of Sex' [1996], 222–3; Foucault, 1979h, 'For an Ethics of
Discomfort' [2000]. The second part of the article by Lawrence Olivier and Sylvain
Labbé presents an excellent analysis of how Foucault distanced himself, in terms
of the theory of history and politics, from a 'will to revolution'. Olivier and Labbé,
'Foucault et l'Iran: A propos du désir de révolution' (1991), 227–36. The following is
largely based on the arguments they put forward.
80. Foucault, 1979c, 'Iran: The Spirit of a World without Spirit' [1988].

Kant did not see the key feature of the French Revolution in political and social breaks so much as the moral disposition they expressed. What is important, then, is not revolution itself – its success or failure – but the meaning it holds for people, especially those who do not pursue it actively. For Kant, political and social upheaval does not represent progress but only a 'sign of progress':

> What is important in the Revolution is not the Revolution itself, but what takes place in the heads of those who do not make it or, in any case, who are not its principal actors .... The enthusiasm for the Revolution is a sign, according to Kant, of a moral disposition in mankind. The disposition is permanently manifested in two ways: firstly, in the right possessed by all peoples to give themselves the political constitution that suits them and, secondly, in the principle, in accordance with law and morality, of a political constitution.[81]

The distinction between progress itself and the 'sign' of progress is important because it affirms the uncertain, eventful nature of history. For Foucault (and, if one follows his reading, for Kant), revolt does not represent a step along a predetermined course so much as it points to a 'will': the will of individual and collective subjects to give themselves a political constitution suited to them. In this sense, every revolt suggests progress – but it is not progress itself. Revolt represents movement forward only inasmuch as it attests to the fundamental disposition to give political order an autonomously determined form and offer resistance to standing systems of domination. Progress lies in the manifestation of this will, not in the consequences (whether 'good' or 'bad') of revolt.

In this light, it is possible to respond to the charge that Foucault took sides in the Iranian conflict and replaced political analysis with moral judgement. At least two arguments counter such a view.

First, Foucault examines the Iranian Revolution as a historical event that he does not seek to evaluate so much as understand. Given this perspective, it would be absurd to condemn an uprising because it yields another form of government. There is nothing surprising about a revolution failing or not leading to the results intended; what is important is the fact that it opposes power and enables an experience

---

81. Foucault, 1984o, 'The Art of Telling the Truth' [1994], 145.

of resistance that extends into the future: 'the Revolution will always run the risk of falling back into the old rut, but as an event whose very content is unimportant, its existence attests to a permanent potentiality that cannot be forgotten'.[82]

Second, Foucault does not take sides in a concrete conflict so much as he seeks to make the pressure to do so the object of analysis. Foucault has no interest in replacing politics with morality; he wants to call into question a certain political practice based on universalist morality, which, although contingent and singular itself, forces us to take positions in a predetermined system of political coordinates. The articles on the Iranian Revolution only observe the separation between politics and morality in order to ask what stands behind them – and, ultimately, contest them. Foucault does not view religion in Iran as the means for expressing determinate political demands or the form in which revolutionary politics manifests itself so much as the guarantee of a fundamental change of social conditions and the 'substance' of revolts. Religion does not stand opposed to the field of 'actual' politics. It possesses a political dimension of its own to the extent that it 'introduces' a 'spiritual' aspect and connects the possibility for a new politics with the problem of a new subjectivity. As such, the articles raise a question that cannot be answered in moral or juridical terms: 'Is one right to revolt, or not? Let us leave the question open. People do revolt; that is a fact'.[83]

---

82. Ibid., 146.
83. Foucault, 1979i, 'Useless to Revolt?' [2000], 452.

# 13

## The Problem of Truth

This is indeed a problem. After all, why truth? Why are we concerned with truth, and more so than with the care of the self? And why must the care of the self occur only through the concern for truth? I think we are touching on a fundamental question here, what I would call *the* question for the West: How did it come about that all of Western culture began to revolve around this obligation of truth which has taken a lot of different forms?

Foucault[1]

This chapter explores, in fuller detail, a problem of central importance for the theoretical and political status of Foucault's work: the problem of truth. Even if it has been addressed at various points in the preceding, it is necessary to take up the relationship between truth, power and subjectivity in systematic fashion. Doing so will make it possible to elaborate the specific contours of Foucauldian critique in the final portion of the book. Hereby, two points are particularly significant: first, to show differences with Foucault's early efforts at conceptualization along microphysical lines; second, to demonstrate the 'specific nature' of a theoretical undertaking that is different from both 'universalistic' and 'relativist' epistemologico-normative positions.

The problem of truth features in all of Foucault's writings. That said, earlier studies examine 'truth' as the effect of a discursive order or the product of power/knowledge complexes. The government problematic

---

1. Foucault, 1984s, 'The Ethics of the Concern for the Self as a Practice of Freedom' [1997], 295.

permits Foucault to integrate, in systematic fashion, processes of subjectivation into the analysis of relations between knowledge and power: government is not just a form of power bearing on the actions of subjects in a general manner; it links the formation of subjectivity to the production of truth and aims to produce 'true subjectivity'. Its mode of operation 'categorizes the individual, marks him by his own individuality, attaches him to his own identity, [and] imposes a law of truth on him which he must recognize and which others have to recognize in him. It is a form of power which makes individuals subjects'.[2]

The defining feature of government involves establishing a form of power that, instead of directly subjugating or dominating individuals, guides and leads them by producing 'truth'. The more it disappears behind the lawfulness of such truths and the necessity of their imperatives, the more force it exercises. Its arbitrary nature proves harder to discern the more it lays claim to the forms of conduct or goals that agree with these truths. 'How is it that in Western Christian culture, the government of men requires of those who are directed, in addition to acts of obedience and submission, "truth acts" that have the distinctive characteristic of requiring not only that the subject tell the truth, but that he tell the truth about himself … ?'.[3]

Answering the question presupposes the explication and clarification of methodological and theoretical problems that Foucault does not treat in sufficient detail in early works. In consequence, an array of difficulties emerges affecting the epistemological or 'truth content' of his studies, as well as the political effects they entail: 'The problem of the truth of what I say is very difficult for me, and it's also the central problem. It's essentially the question which up to now I have never answered'.[4]

## The Politics of Truth

Connections between truth and power are not unique to 'Western' societies. Foucault holds that every society is marked by its own 'order of the true', or a '"general politics" of truth'.[5] Such a 'truth-regime' possesses several dimensions: qualifying certain discourses as true;

---

2. Foucault, 1982b, 'The Subject and Power', 212.
3. Foucault, 1980i, 'Course Summary' [2014], 321.
4. Foucault, 1980d, *Remarks on Marx* [1991], 32.
5. Foucault, 1977d, 'Truth and Power' [1984], 73.

developing mechanisms and techniques that enable true utterances to be distinguished from false ones; constructing organs and modes of sanction that support these distinctions; authorizing persons and instances responsible for deciding about the truth; and so on.[6] On the basis of this general, socio-theoretical premise, Foucault defines the historical specificity of the "'political economy" of truth'[7] in 'Western' societies, which can be characterized by a number of features:

> 'Truth' is centered on the form of scientific discourse and the institutions which produce it; it is subject to constant economic and political incitement (the demand for truth, as much for economic production as for political power); it is the object, under diverse forms, of immense diffusion and consumption (circulating through apparatuses of education and information whose extent is relatively broad in the social body, notwithstanding certain strict limitations); it is produced and transmitted under the control, dominant if not exclusive, of a few great political and economic apparatuses (university, army, writing, media); lastly, it is the issue of a whole political debate and social confrontation ('ideological' struggles).[8]

The 'order of the true' in Western societies, then, is marked by the fact that the truth is organized in the form of scientific discourses and subject to a permanent economic and politic 'demand'; conversely, economic and political mechanisms cannot function without truth-imperatives. This means that not just the production of truth, but also its circulation and consumption are closely tied to mechanisms of social power. But, at the same time, the truth – precisely because it is bound to economico-political imperatives – stands as the object of social and political struggles and provides the point of departure for strategies of resistance that, on the basis of a 'politics of truth',[9] contest 'dominant truths'.

Foucault's politicized mode of reading the close relations between truth and power in Western societies seems to stand in the tradition of critical projects denouncing 'selective' or 'instrumental' aspects of

---

6. Ibid., 72–3.
7. Ibid., 73.
8. Ibid., 73.
9. Foucault, 1977k, 'The End of the Monarchy of Sex' [1996], 220.

reason. Such critique bears on rationality that presents itself as general and universal, but in fact has only particularized and partial access to the truth – and therefore conceals central power relations in society. This kind of analysis, like the approach that Foucault proposes, lays bare the truth's debt to power; it demonstrates how the truth preserves (bourgeois, patriarchal, racist, etc.) domination by pointing out systematic discrimination and social exclusion.

However, Foucault's project of a 'politics of the true' proves different in a key respect. Most theorists wish to resolve the problem of 'distorted' or 'divided' reason by proposing 'less distorted' or 'more comprehensive' rationality. They pursue a theoretical strategy whose maxims consist of separating truth and power so that the former may function without the latter. In contrast, Foucault does not seek to separate truth and power, and his goal is not to find the 'true truth' – i.e. transparent and 'universal' knowledge. He deems such a project illusory. According to Foucault, it is impossible for truth to function without power because truth is not something external to social conditions; it does not exist independently and then come into conflict with them, but is itself generated within social formations.

Under these conditions, the task can no longer mean uncovering old errors and replacing them with new truths. The struggle does not concern only ideology and lies, but also – and especially – the truth; it is a 'battle about the status of truth and the economic and political role it plays'.[10] What proves decisive, then, is not just the question of how true knowledge may be separated from false knowledge (i.e. what has been contaminated by power relations); rather, and more still, the fundamental problem involves 'how effects of truth are produced within discourses which in themselves are neither true nor false'.[11]

This entails a shift in the coordinates of political critique. The goal is less to separate science and ideology and correct (false) consciousness than it means 'changing ... the political, economic, institutional regime of the production of truth'.[12] The problem no longer involves finding access to the (distorted) truth; the question concerns 'what kind' of truth is produced and how it functions in our society – that is, the distinctions between true and false that prevail, the limits this

10. Foucault, 1977d, 'Truth and Power' [1984], 74.
11. Ibid., 60.
12. Ibid., 74.

entails, the pressures produced, the effects of exclusion and invalida-
tion implied, and so on. 'At what price can subjects speak the truth
about themselves ... ?'[13]

---

13. Foucault, 1983e, 'Critical Theory/Intellectual History' [1988], 30. This question also stands at the core of reflections offered by Critical Theory. Especially in later
writings, Foucault stressed the parallels between his own work and the project of the
Frankfurt School. The main point in common is analysing 'a reason whose structural
autonomy carries the history of dogmatisms and despotisms along with it – a reason
[...] that has a liberating effect only provided it manages to liberate itself'. Foucault,
1985a, 'Life: Experience and Science' [1998], 469; Foucault, 1980d, *Remarks on Marx*
[1991], 115–29; Foucault, 1983e, 'Critical Theory/Intellectual History' [1988], 26–7;
Foucault, 1984x, 'On Power' [1988], 104.
At the same time, 'a clear incompatibility' exists between the approaches inasmuch
as they rely on different conceptions of subjectivity and rationality. Foucault, 1980d,
*Remarks on Marx* [1991], 124. Foucault distances himself from Critical Theory on
two points. First, he observes that many representatives of the Frankfurt School work
with the assumption that a global and uniform process of rationalization prevails in
different social spheres; in contrast, he bases his analysis on examinations of specific experiences such as sexuality, madness, criminality and so on. Foucault, 1981a,
'"Omnes et Singulatim"', 225; Foucault, 1982b, 'The Subject and Power', 209–10.
Second, he faults members of the Frankfurt School for employing a traditional philosophical conception of the subject and then subjecting its alienation or oppression to
critique against the backdrop of 'human essence', or 'nature'. Foucault, 1980d, *Remarks
on Marx* [1991], 123. That said, the critique Foucault offers is based on a summary
view that fails to do justice to the work of Max Horkheimer and Theodor W. Adorno,
in particular. On the whole, it seems that Foucault's objections bear on *Dialectic of
Enlightenment* (which does, in fact, offer a reductive view of the subject and present
an all-inclusive account of the rationalization process).
It is legitimate to accentuate the differences between Adorno and Horkheimer's critique of rationality and power, on the one hand, and Foucault's conception
of a 'politics of truth', on the other. This has occurred both to discredit Foucault's
approach and, conversely, to demonstrate the obsolescence of Adorno and Horkheimer's theses. Honneth, 'Foucault and Adorno: Two Forms of the Critique of
Modernity' (1995b); McCarthy, 'The Critique of Impure Reason: Foucault and the
Frankfurt School' (1990); Miller, *Domination and Power* (1987); Schäfer, 'Aufklärung
und Kritik' (1990); Schäfer, *Reflektierte Vernunft* (1995), 154–98. Yet doing so means
transforming blurry boundaries into rigid opposites. It strikes me as more productive to stress the articulation of problems that Foucault and Critical Theory share,
notwithstanding their different theoretical responses. Certainly it is possible to
extract elements of 'traditional theory' from Critical Theory that does not reduce
the parallels to 'superficial similarities'. Schäfer, *Reflektierte Vernunft* (1995), 188.
By the same token, Foucault's theory might benefit from the insights the Frankfurt
School offers concerning the 'dialectic of Enlightenment'. For Foucault's appreciation
of the 'old' Frankfurt School – as opposed to Habermas's 'continuation' of its project
– see Eribon, *Michel Foucault et ses contemporains* (1994a), esp. 289–303; see also
Demirović, 'Wahrheitspolitik: Zum Problem der Geschichte der Philosophie' (1995)
and Chapter 14 in this volume.

Within such a logic, the point is not to 'discover' *the truth*, but to examine *how* truth is 'invented' – that is, how it is produced and circulates within social relations. As such, the political problem does not lie in the 'untruth' of social relations so much as it bears on the fact of their 'truth':

> It's not a matter of emancipating truth from every system of power … but of detaching the power of truth from the forms of hegemony, social, economic, and cultural, within which it operates at the present time. The political question, to sum up, is not error, illusion, alienated consciousness or ideology; it is truth itself.[14]

Foucault's thesis 'provokes' the questions presented at the beginning of the book at hand. If truth always harbours a relationship to power, then what makes one truth different, in epistemological terms, from another? Does not a position like this culminate in political relativism inasmuch as truth proves self-referential and conditional? Does not this 'politics of the true' ultimately eliminate any claim to truth – and, in so doing, disprove itself? What is the point of a critique oriented on the criteria of a more just, or better, society, if the terms have been generated in a standing framework and, as such, defy all comparison outside the concrete, historical conditions of their existence?

These questions indicate the 'critical point' of genealogy. Foucault did not become aware that he needed to clarify it until late in his career, when he recognized the dimensions of the problem. 'My problem is the politics of truth. I have taken a lot of time in realizing it.'[15]

## A History of Truth: Historical Nominalism

It seems that locating truth within a 'politics of the true' is inscribed in a philosophico-historical problematic defined by the poles of 'universalism' and 'relativism'. As such, the 'genealogy' of governmentality appears to culminate in a relativistic position that, inasmuch as it

---

14. Foucault, 1977d, 'Truth and Power' [1984], 74–5; see also Ewald, 'Foucault, une pensée sans aveu' (1977); Lloyd, 'The (F)utility of a Feminist Turn to Foucault' (1993), 450–1.

15. Foucault, 1977k, 'The End of the Monarchy of Sex' [1996], 220.

refers to the close tie between power and knowledge, contests claims to universal validity and proclaims that all truths are equal. In fact, however, the theoretical and political significance of Foucault's work is to focus on such pressure to opt 'for' or 'against' the truth: 'I would like in short to resituate the production of true and false at the heart of historical analysis and political critique'.[16]

Foucault's 'solution' to the dilemma is to provide historical responses to the philosophical question of the truth by writing a *history of truth*. In contrast to what many readers believe, Foucault's books are neither historical in the classic academic sense, nor are they traditional philosophical studies. Their objects are not those of *scientific history*, for the question does not concern how 'sexuality' or 'madness' changed over the course of time. Nor does his investigative method concern a *philosophical ontology* – what madness 'truly' is or what the 'essence' of sexuality might be, once all historical accidents have been removed. Instead, the project pursues 'historical ontology':[17] seeking out historical discontinuities and breaks in the 'order of the true'.

The 'history of truth' does not bear on what things are *per se*, or how they change over time. Instead, it asks how they exist at a given point: the 'thing in itself' is always already a 'thing for us'. This 'historico-practical test'[18] does not look for 'actual' origins or the 'real' basis of history, which it then contrasts with 'false' ideas or 'illusory' notions. Instead, it seeks out a mobile system of relations and syntheses offering both the conditions of existence for a certain order of things and knowledge about them: forms of subjectivation and objectivation.

Foucault introduces the concept of the *game of truth* in order to analyse this double movement. Its theoretico-strategic significance lies in a changed conceptualization of subjectivity and objectivity.[19] The concept of the truth-game breaks with the framework of epistemology by opening the relationship between subject and object to the different

---

16. Foucault, 1980b, 'Questions of Method', 79.

17. Foucault, 1984d, 'What Is Enlightenment?', 45.

18. Foucault, 1990b, 'What Is Critique?' [2007], 115.

19. A further clarification is necessary at this juncture: Foucault's interest does not bear on all 'games of truth' – only those in which the subject is also constituted as the object of knowledge: the human sciences and the 'mad', 'delinquent' or 'sick' subject. It follows that his attention falls primarily on 'games of power' that function by linking knowledge and subjectivity. Foucault, 1984i, '"Foucault" by Maurice Florence' [1998], 460; Foucault, 1978j, 'La philosophie analytique de la politique', 542; Foucault, 1984a, *The Use of Pleasure* [1990], 6–7.

forms that they can assume in isolation and conjunction. With that, the process of questioning undergoes dynamization. At the centre no longer stand questions concerning the subjective conditions for accurate knowledge about objects, but the problem of how subjects are subjectivized and, at the same time, objects are objectivated: 'the way in which, linking a certain type of object to certain modalities of the subject, it constituted the historical *a priori* of a possible experience for a period of time, an area and for given individuals'.[20]

By this means, Foucault seeks to avoid two mistakes that occur together. The first error involves viewing the formation of objects by taking the subject as the point of departure; the second starts out with objects in order to examine subjective constitution. The theory of the game of truth approaches the problem in a different way – or, more precisely, it shifts the problem as a whole. Rejecting constitutive subjectivity does not mean privileging structural causality and then explaining historical subjects as its consequence or function:

> Refusing the political recourse to a constituent subject does not amount to acting as if the subject did not exist, making an abstraction of it on behalf of a pure objectivity. This refusal has the aim of eliciting the processes that are peculiar to an experience in which the subject and the objected 'are formed and transformed' in relation to and in terms of one another. The discourses of mental illness, delinquency, or sexuality say what the subject is only in a certain, quite particular game of truth; but these games are not imposed on the subject from the outside according to a necessary causality or structural determination. They open up a field of experience in which the subject and the object are both constituted only under certain simultaneous conditions, but in

---

20. Foucault, 1984i, '"Foucault" by Maurice Florence' [1998], 460. 'It is not a matter of defining the formal conditions of a relationship to the object; nor is it a matter of isolating the empirical conditions that may, at a given moment, have enabled the subject in general to become acquainted with an object already given in reality. The problem is to determine what the subject must be, to what condition he is subject, what status he must have, what position he must occupy in reality or in the imaginary, in order to become a legitimate subject of this or that type of knowledge [*connaissance*]. [...]. But it is also and at the same time a question of determining under what conditions something can become an object for a possible knowledge [*connaissance*], how it may have been problematized as an object to be known, to what selective procedure [*procédure de découpage*] it may have been subjected, the part of it that is regarded as pertinent'. Ibid., 459–60.

which they are also constantly modified in relation to each other, and so they modify this field of experience itself.[21]

Because its principle is to call into question the traditional problematic of subjectivity and objectivity, the notion of 'game of truth' has given rise to number of misunderstandings:

1. One misinterpretation involves understanding truth as a 'game' that is unregulated and completely open, and that can be changed at will. In fact, Foucault stresses the regularity and orderly nature of operations; games of truth stand closely related to games of power: 'when I say "game", I mean a set of rules by which truth is produced. It is not a game in the sense of an amusement; it is a set of procedures that lead to a certain result, which, on the basis of its principles and rules of procedure, may be considered valid or invalid, winning or losing'.[22]

2. Another misunderstanding stems from equating games of truth with discursive practices and assimilating them to ideas, mentalities or ideologies. But as Foucault conceives it, truth does not result from discursive practices; instead, it is produced in a field that encompasses both discursive and non-discursive activities. The formation of subjects and objects does not occur simply on the level of ideals within discourses; it includes complex interaction between discourses, practices of power and practices of self. As such, games of truth are not forms of speaking and thinking so much as forms of experience and being.[23]

3. Yet another problem stems from assuming that the concept of the game means giving up claims to truth. Although it establishes a multiplicity of possible truths, this pluralization effect does not relativize the dimension of truth. There is a decisive difference between granting that historically contingent truths exist and claiming that no truth exists. Many of Foucault's critics adopt the polemical strategy of equating the one with the other and declaring that affirming the historicity of truth amounts to rejecting truth altogether. Yet such assimilation

---

21. Ibid., 462.

22. Foucault, 1984s, 'The Ethics of the Concern for the Self as a Practice of Freedom' [1997], 297.

23. Larrauri, 'Vérité et mensonge des jeux de vérité' (1994), 36–9.

presupposes a specific model of truth that claims to be universal and functions within the very 'game of truth' that Foucault critiques. 'I believe too much in truth not to suppose that there are different truths and different ways of speaking the truth'.[24]

The 'history of truth' seeks neither to reconstruct universal patterns nor to abandon the claim of historical explanation. It does not treat the problem of a 'true essence behind appearances', and it does not advance the thesis that no truth exists. Foucault's scepticism about universals does not result from relativism. On the contrary, he insists that the 'history of truth' differs radically from relativistic undertakings. His approach may be illustrated by way of an example.

Foucault starts from the hypothesis that 'madness' does not exist as an anthropological constant or universal of history. The 'mad' have not existed at all times, only to be perceived and treated differently depending on circumstances. Positing that madness, writ large, did not always exist, Foucault takes a second step and asks how different factors and practices made it possible for something like madness to possess historical reality: if there is no madness as a universal, then what forms of knowledge and practices are responsible for this 'illusion' and 'figment of imagination' being assigned meaning? How does it happen that subjects come to be viewed as 'mad' and given therapy accordingly? How does madness become an 'illness' and the object of specialized, medical knowledge? And so on. This state of affairs may be summed up in a way that only seems paradoxical: starting from the premise of the non-existence of madness, Foucault shows its factual, historical existence: 'one has to say on the contrary that madness does not exist, but that it is not therefore nothing'.[25]

---

24. Foucault, 1984t, 'An Aesthetics of Existence' [1988], 51; see also Foucault, 1984n, 'The Concern for Truth' [1988], 256; Foucault, 1980d, *Remarks on Marx* [1991], 62–3; Lloyd, 'The (F)utility of a Feminist Turn to Foucault' (1993), 452.

25. Quoted in Veyne, 'Foucault Revolutionizes History' (1997), 170; lecture, 10 January 1979, Foucault, 2004b, *The Birth of Biopolitics* [2008], 3; Veyne, 'Foucault and Going Beyond (or the Fulfillment of) Nihilism' (1992). In other words, the hypothesis that madness does not exist means neither that there are no 'mad' subjects, nor that therapeutic success is illusory. Indeed, Foucault insists on both: 'One can show, for example, that the medicalization of madness, in other words, the organization of medical knowledge [*savoir*] around individuals designated as mad, was connected with a whole series of social and economic processes at a given time, but also with institutions and practices of power. This fact in no way impugns the scientific validity

This approach does not seek to contest that there is something like an 'object' to which 'madness' (or 'sexuality', 'illness', etc.) refers. The point is to cast doubt on claims that this 'referent' is identical with 'madness' itself. The matter does not concern the content of statements or taking a stance with respect to philosophical problems of substance so much as setting up an 'initial methodological rule' enabling one to ask about how objects are historically constituted.

> Refusing the universal of 'madness', 'delinquency', or 'sexuality' does not imply that what these terms refer to is nothing, or that they are only chimeras invented for the sake of a dubious cause. Something more is involved, however, than the simple observation that their content varies with time and circumstances: It means that one must investigate the conditions that enable people, according to the rules of true and false statements, to recognize a subject as mentally ill or to arrange that a subject recognize the most essential part of himself in the modality of his sexual desire.[26]

In offering a 'history of truth', Foucault made an important corrective to his earlier positions. In the 1976 lectures at the Collège de France, he still made positive reference to the 'warlike' viewpoint, which introduces 'perspectival discourse'[27] into history and stands *opposed* to the abstract universalism of natural law. From the standpoint of such

or the therapeutic effectiveness of psychiatry: it does not endorse psychiatry, but neither does it invalidate it'. Foucault, 1984s, 'The Ethics of the Concern for the Self as a Practice of Freedom' [1997], 296; Foucault, 1977o, 'Confinement, Psychiatry, Prison' [1988], 196–7.

26. Foucault, 1984i, '"Foucault" by Maurice Florence' [1998], 461–2. Paul Veyne has vividly described this aspect of Foucault's approach: 'To say that madness does not exist is not to claim that madmen are victims of prejudice, nor is it to deny such an assertion, for that matter. The meaning of the proposition lies elsewhere. It neither affirms nor denies that madmen should be excluded, or that madness exists because it is fabricated by society, or that madness is modified in its positivity by the attitudes various societies hold toward it, or that different societies have conceptualized madness in very different ways; the proposition does not deny, either, that madness has a behaviorist and perhaps a physiological component. But even if madness were to have such components, it would not yet be madness. A building stone becomes a keystone or a header only when it takes its place as part of a structure. The denial of madness is not situated at the level of attitudes toward the object, but at that of its objectivization'. Veyne, 'Foucault Revolutionizes History' (1997), 168–9.

27. Foucault, 1986, '21 January 1976' and '28 January 1976' [2003], 52.

*radical historicism*, truth is nothing but a weapon in battle, a means of attaining victory.[28] However, the lectures on governmentality step back from this method of investigation; now, Foucault declares that he is undertaking 'exactly the opposite of historicism'.[29]

In later works, Foucault calls this specific way of combining philosophy and history – which seeks to escape the binary of universalism and relativism – *historical nominalism*.[30] Analysing history from this perspective starts out from systematic scepticism vis-à-vis anthropological constants and natural laws; the focus changes entirely: historical nominalism does not try to ground knowledge so much as make matters cease to be self-evident; things are not shown in their generality, but in their 'singularity'. This method clarifies points of theoretical ambivalence in Foucault's past works and retroactively defines the issues. Accordingly, Foucault's books do not offer a history of madness, illness or crime so much as a history of the conditions under which it became self-evident for certain abnormalities to be classified as mental illness, sickness to be treated in terms of individual anatomy and lawbreakers to be locked up as delinquents. In this conception of history, the 'objects' do not provide the starting point so

---

28. Foucault, 1976a, *The History of Sexuality, Volume 1: An Introduction* [1978], 150; Foucault, 1986, '21 January 1976' and '28 January 1976' [2003], 52–3; as well as Foucault, 1971b, 'Nietzsche, Genealogy, History' [1984], 90.

29. Lecture, 10 January 1979, Foucault, 2004b, *The Birth of Biopolitics* [2008], 3; see also Foucault, 1982c, 'Space, Knowledge and Power' [1984], 250; Senellart, 'Michel Foucault: "gouvernementalité" et raison d'Etat' (1993), 291–3, 284; Séglard, 'Foucault et le problème du gouvernement' (1992), 119–20. In making this clarification, Foucault also does away with the inadequate conception of genealogy that had sought to emancipate 'subjugated' or 'disqualified' kinds of knowledge. The latter include discourses and experiences of individuals and groups who, inasmuch as they are marginalized or oppressed, cannot 'know the truth' within the social order – psychiatric patients, the ill, gays, women and so on. Foucault had defined his genealogy of power as 'a sort of attempt to desubjugate historical knowledges, to set them free' in opposition to the power-effects of (dominant) knowledge. Foucault, 1977e, '7 January 1976' [2003], 10. However, he came to recognize a fundamental problem: 'subjugated' knowledge does not constitute a solid mass that one might separate from dominant forms and 'emancipate'. Rather, what has been 'excluded' or 'disqualified' represents an integral component of a historico-political field that defines itself as a strategic relationship between the ruling and the ruled. Accordingly, it is impossible to 'liberate' knowledge without changing the historical field itself – and, with it, 'subjugated knowledge'.

30. Foucault, 1979m, 'Course Summary' [2008], 318; Foucault, 1980b, 'Questions of Method', 86; Foucault, 1982g, 'Des caresses d'hommes considérées comme un art', 316; Foucault, 1984e, 'Preface to the History of Sexuality, Vol. II', 334.

much as the focus of investigation, which centres on the practices that constitute objects as objects in the first place. Foucault's historiography is not a history of objects, but an analysis of the 'objectification of objectivities'.[31]

Research shifts from examining objects to looking at *practices*. Foucault inverts the primacy of objects: instead of explaining historical practices starting in terms of, for example, functionality, teleology, finality or reproduction, objects become the 'correlates' or 'projections' of practices. The philosophy of history yields to 'actual history', which reconstructs the practices combining determinate 'elements' in such a way that an 'object' appears – which now is assumed to have preceded the historical process.[32]

Nominalist historiography operates in two steps. Its first 'theoretico-political function'[33] is to call universals into question and destroy the idea that anything is obvious. The aim is to show that 'matters were not self-evident'. Thus, *History of Madness* demonstrates that determinate, but historically contingent, social practices led the mad to be classified as mentally ill; *The Birth of the Clinic* shows that there was

---

31. Foucault, 1980b, 'Questions of Method', 86; Rajchman, *Michel Foucault. The Freedom of Philosophy* (1985), 50–60; Flynn, 'Foucault's Mapping of History' (1994).

32. See once again a formulation by Paul Veyne: 'The whole difficulty arises from the illusion that allows us to "reify" objectivations as if they were natural objects. We mistake the end result for a goal; we take the place where a projectile happens to land as its intentionally chosen target. Instead of grasping the problem at its center, which is the practice, we start from the periphery, which is the object, in such a way that successive practices resemble reactions to a single object, whether "material" or rational, that is taken as the starting point, as a given. [...] We take the points of impact of successive practices to be preexisting objects that these practices were aiming for: their targets. Madness and the common good throughout the ages have been targeted differently by successive societies whose "attitudes" were not the same, so that they touched the target at different points'. Veyne, 'Foucault Revolutionizes History' (1997), 161.

In this sense, practices do not define themselves in contrast to the field of thinking, nor do they constitute its more or less permeable border. Reflection is not something secondary that joins practices in order to give them direction or animate them; rather, practices are always reflected – 'unthinkable' without the dimension of reflection. Whether the matter concerns discourse or not, power or the self, the terms always refers to the systematic interplay of thought and action: 'These are the "practices", understood as a way of acting and thinking at once, that provide the intelligibility key for the correlative constitution of the subject and the object'. Foucault, 1984i, '"Foucault" by Maurice Florence' [1998], 463; Foucault, 1984e, 'Preface to the History of Sexuality, Vol. II', 334.

33. Foucault, 1980b, 'Questions of Method', 76.

nothing obvious about seeking the causes for disease by examining
bodies individually; *Discipline and Punish* makes it clear that incarcer-
ating lawbreakers is not the only form of penal practice; *The History
of Sexuality* reveals how sexuality represents one way among others
of organizing pleasure and desire. It is especially meaningful to break
down such 'certainties' because our knowledge, habits and practices
rest on these epistemologico-political positivities.

The second step of Foucault's historical nominalism builds on the
first. Inasmuch as certain objects no longer count as 'self-understood',
it is necessary to determine the network of connections, relations of
force, points of blockage, strategies, circularities and so on, which
makes it possible to establish, at a given point in time, what counts
as universal, necessary and a matter of course. Hereby, universals no
longer provide the starting point for analysis, but appear as the effects
of historical practices. They are not monolithic entities that undergo
historical modulation so much as a system of heterogeneous elements
that cannot be boiled down to an underlying essence or an individualized species.[34]

The aim of historical nominalism is to avoid tracing singularities
back to universals. On the contrary, the task is to decipher 'universals'
as singularities. Inasmuch as the principles of determination no longer
stand outside the realm of history – ordering historical material and
lending it 'meaning' – the question no longer arises how some possibilities within a system ultimately achieve realization, how certain
structures determine forms of action, or what phenomena bring
fundamental laws to expression. Instead, the problem of historical
nominalism concerns how, when elements possess the same 'ontological value', some of them become linked to each other and yield a
whole – or are separated and stand apart.

## The Concept of Problematization

And so, the 'history of truth' also provides a 'genealogy of power'. If
it is true that 'madness', 'sexuality', 'illness', 'delinquency' and so on
are simultaneously 'real' and historically contingent, then the question
arises what has 'objectivated' them. Only when it is not (or no longer)

---

34. Ibid., 76; Foucault, 1990b, 'What Is Critique?' [2007], 62–3.

self-evident or natural for lawbreakers to be locked up, for instance, can the question arise why this – and not something else – occurs. In a seeming paradox, then, the 'question of power' does not follow from determining what is necessary; instead, it follows from a non-necessary relation: 'One needs to be nominalistic, no doubt: power is not an institution, and not a structure; neither is it a certain strength we are endowed with; it is the name that one attributes to a complex strategical situation in a particular society'.[35]

By conceptualizing power along nominalist lines, Foucault avoids the essentialism of his earlier works. Whereas *Discipline and Punish* and *The History of Sexuality, Volume 1* at least implicitly presupposed the fact of (bourgeois) domination, Foucault now recognizes 'the obscurities of [his] own discourse': 'A dominant class isn't a mere abstraction, but neither is it a pre-given entity'.[36] The task of nominalist analysis is to avoid the alternative of viewing domination either as fact or fiction – and to define it, instead, as 'a reciprocal relation of production'.[37]

To this end, Foucault introduces the concept of *problematization*. The term is meant to bring the methodological profile of his work

---

35. Foucault, 1976a, *The History of Sexuality, Volume 1: An Introduction* [1978], 93; Foucault, 1977m, 'The Confession of the Flesh' [1980], 199–200. This is why no *theory* of power should be sought. Such an endeavour would have to presuppose precisely what must be historically reconstructed: 'Since a theory assumes a prior objectification, it cannot be asserted as a basis for analytical work'. Foucault, 1982b, 'The Subject and Power', 209. However, Foucault's refusal to make objects his starting point does not mean giving up on developing concepts and theoretical designs; rather, the shift involves moving from 'theory' to the '"analytics" of power': Foucault, 1976a, *The History of Sexuality, Volume 1: An Introduction* [1978], 82, incorporating the historical conditions underlying concepts and terminology into analysis. No object can escape historicity; the same holds for words, ideas, theories and concepts. It is a matter of analysing objects and the 'descriptive terminology' that bears on them simultaneously. In consequence, the language employed should be as value-neutral as possible. This is one reason why Foucault frequently uses 'technical' terms ('mechanism', 'technology', 'dispositive', etc.).

36. Foucault, 1977m, 'The Confession of the Flesh' [1980], 203.

37. Ibid., 203. 'Since Aristotle, politics has been considered as the relation between the governed and the governing. This starting-point is one which Foucault accepts, provided that it is agreed that "the governed" and "the governing" are not, in their turn, natural objects which refer back to a trans-historical substance or condition, but, rather, the names which are given to the terms of a relation which is established within every exercise of power and which, in fact, constitutes that exercise of power'. Pasquino, 'Michel Foucault (1926–84): The Will to Knowledge' (1986b), 104; Foucault, 1977f, '14 January 1976' [2003], 31–2.

into relief by setting it apart from the history of mentalities or ideas, on the one hand, and philosophical anthropology, on the other.[38] But Foucault does not mobilize the concept of problematization only to mark a distance from other approaches; it also serves to systematize his own studies and clarify the theoretical claims they make. 'Problematization' becomes a central concept: a methodological approach that rearticulates the relations between archaeology and genealogy and incorporates both as dimensions of analysis. *Archaeology* engages with the forms of problematization themselves, analysing and describing them. *Genealogy* examines the relationships that these forms of problematization entertain with determinate practices, whether discursive or non-discursive.

> I seem to have gained a better perspective on the way I worked – gropingly, and by means of different or successive fragments – on this project, whose goal is a history of truth. It was a matter of analysing, not behaviors or ideas, nor societies and their 'ideologies', but the *problematizations* through which being offers itself to be, necessarily, thought – and the *practices* on the basis of which these problematizations are formed. The archaeological dimension of the analysis made it possible to examine the forms themselves; its genealogical dimension enabled me to analyse their formation out of the practices and the modifications undergone by the latter.[39]

Problematization aims to analyse relations between forms of thought and action. Inasmuch as historiographical work makes the arbitrariness and contingency of such connections 'visible', other practices become 'thinkable'. These spaces of freedom and potentials for resistance do not open up in spite of, but because of the close connection between practices and modes of problematization: if, on the one hand, 'thinking' is indissolubly tied to a given configuration of discursive

---

38. 'Problematization doesn't mean representation of a preexisting object, nor the creation by discourse of an object that doesn't exist. It is the totality of discursive or non-discursive practices that introduces something into the play of true and false and constitutes it as an object for thought (whether in the form of moral reflection, scientific knowledge, political analysis, etc.)'. Foucault, 1984n, 'The Concern for Truth' [1988], 257.

39. Foucault, 1984a, *The Use of Pleasure* [1990], 11–12; see also Foucault, 1984n, 'The Concern for Truth' [1988], 258.

and non-discursive practices, on the other, it provides the means for stepping back from socially routine actions and 'problematizing' them through the distance that emerges:[40]

> For when I say that I am studying the 'problematization' of madness, crime, or sexuality, it is not a way of denying the reality of such phenomena. On the contrary, I have tried to show that it was precisely some real existent in the world which was the target of social regulation at a given moment. The question I raise is this one: how and why were very different things in the world gathered together, characterized, analysed, and treated as, for example, 'mental illness'? What are the elements which are relevant for a given 'problematization'? And even if I won't say that what is characterized as 'schizophrenia' corresponds to something real in the world, this has nothing to do with idealism. For I think there is a relation between the thing which is problematized and the process of problematization. The problematization is an 'answer' to a concrete situation which is real.[41]

It is clear, then, that Foucault does not picture 'thinking' as an inward, autonomous and self-referential process. Changes to 'systems' do not simply follow from another way of thinking. Inasmuch as 'thought' represents a social practice, it is necessary for an array of social, political and economic factors to emerge, which provoke 'difficulties', 'incompatibilities' or 'problems'. In other words, for forms of thought

---

40. '[R]ecourse to history [...] is meaningful to the extent that history serves to show how that-which-is has not always been [...]. What reason perceives as *its* necessity, or rather, what different forms of rationality offer as their necessary being, can perfectly well be shown to have a history; and the network of contingencies from which it emerges can be traced. Which is not to say, however, that these forms of rationality were irrational. It means that they reside on a base of human practice and human history; and that since these things have been made, they can be unmade'. Foucault, 1983e, 'Critical Theory/Intellectual History' [1988], 37.

On 'thought': 'By thought I mean what establishes, in a variety of possible forms, the play of true and false, and which as a consequence constitutes the human being as a subject of learning (*connaissance*); in other words, it is the basis for accepting or refusing rules, and constitutes human beings as social and juridical subjects; it is what establishes the relation with oneself and with others, and constitutes the human being as ethical subject. [...] In this sense, thought is understood as the very form of action'. Ibid., 334–5; Foucault, 1984n, 'The Concern for Truth' [1988], 258.

41. Foucault, 1985b, 'Discourse and Truth: The Problematization of Parrhesia' [1983], 171–2.

to cease to be familiar and become 'problematic', there must a change of the historical and social field of which thinking itself forms a part.[42]

But all the same, 'thought' does not directly follow or express these 'problems'. Instead, it constitutes a specific (effort to) 'answer' in its own right. Any given set of 'difficulties' can receive very different – and even contradictory – answers. As such, 'problematizations' do not simply represent concrete (political, economic, etc.) problems; they refer to creative work defining the conditions under which certain possible answers may be 'constructed' or 'created'.[43]


## Fiction and Construction

From the perspective of problematization, truth is no longer something to be discovered or found so much as something that is 'invented' or 'produced'. The 'history of truth' examines phenomena as social *constructions* and historical *fictions*. Foucault's shift of accent has given rise to any number of misunderstandings and polemics about the historical truth of these 'fictions' and the methodological status of these 'constructions'.

Indeed, a central ambivalence pervades Foucault's books. On the one hand, like traditional historical works, they stick to conventional criteria: reasoned argument on the basis of documents, reference to primary material, discussion of relationships between ideas and events, proposing schemes of analysis and so on. Accordingly, Foucault's works may be compared with competing studies and other interpretations, in order to verify or disprove the historical reconstruction proposed. The author's explanations may be contested; one can criticize the line of

---

42. Foucault, 1984g, 'Polemics, Politics and Problematizations: An Interview with Michel Foucault', 388. The concept of problematization also led Foucault to reassess the political dimensions of his work. He recognized the 'great naïveté' he had demonstrated at the beginning of the 1970s, when, in studying the prison and forms of punishment, he held that theory would translate directly into politics. Foucault, 1980j, 'Discussion with Philosophers'. In the 1980s, he came to view the GIP as a project for 'problematizing' practices, rules and habits in order to prepare the ground for another penal politics. Foucault, 1984p, 'Interview with *Actes*' [2000], 394–5; see also Rajchman, 'Foucault: The Ethic and the Work' (1992).

43. Foucault, 1984g, 'Polemics, Politics and Problematizations: An Interview with Michel Foucault', 389–90; Foucault, 1985b, 'Discourse and Truth: The Problematization of Parrhesia' [1983], 171–3.

argument and evidence mustered. In a word, no room for doubt exists that the 'history of truth' is meant as 'true history'.

On the other hand, Foucault's books occupy a different terrain than standard historical works. *History of Madness* does not offer the history of European psychiatric institutions between the seventeenth and nineteenth centuries any more than *Discipline and Punish* presents a history of the prison or *The History of Sexuality* a history of sexual practices. The defining feature of these books does not lie in historical reconstruction as such. On the contrary, historical truth provides an 'indispensable means' for achieving another, more ambitious goal: the production of experiences. Foucault did not understand his works as 'truth books' (*livre-vérité*) so much as 'experience books' (*livre-expérience*); by making certain historical material 'real', they bear on an 'experience' of the present, from which we emerge changed. The works should enable readers to entertain a new relation with the object under investigation (which thereby becomes the object of adaptation and reworking). 'Experience books' do not limit themselves to taking stock of historical truths on a theoretical plane; they make these truths the starting point for analysis that pursues a practical goal: problematizing the ways we judge and think about certain things, stripping them of their 'self-evidence' or 'naturalness' and making new experiences possible.[44]

Foucault illustrates this 'truth effect' on the example of the reception of two of his books:

1. When *History of Madness* was first published at the beginning of the 1960s, academic historians paid it almost no attention. A few years later, it was read as an anti-psychiatry manifesto. According to Foucault, such a reception was simultaneously right and wrong. Evaluating the book in the context of anti-psychiatry was inaccurate inasmuch as he was not interested in writing anything of the sort: for one, the anti-psychiatry movement did not yet exist at this point, and second, the book, which stops at the beginning of the twentieth century, contains no attack on contemporary psychiatry. Still, Foucault concedes, it was correct to see something like a critique of contemporary psychiatry inasmuch as his work sought to change relations to madness, psychiatry and the 'truth' of the latter discourse.[45]

---

44. Foucault, 1980d, *Remarks on Marx* [1991], 26–36.
45. Foucault, 1978n, 'Clarifications on the Question of Power' [1996], 259–61;

2. *Discipline and Punish* neither reports on current prison conditions, nor does it appeal for a different penal politics; its scope does not extend beyond the mid-nineteenth century. Nevertheless, the book was universally read – whether disapprovingly or with appreciation – as a description of contemporary society. Yet the study's 'bearing on the present' does not lie in the object itself but the way Foucault treats the material. Demonstrating that the prison is a relatively recent 'invention' – and not the 'natural' mode of punishing – makes it possible to consider alternative penal practices. Still, the book does not formulate a programme for carrying out any change.

The project of problematization means taking distance from political pragmatics:

> it's true that certain people, such as those who work in the institutional setting of the prison – which is not quite the same as being in prison – are not likely to find advice or instruction in my books that tell them 'what is to be done'. But my project is precisely to bring it about that they 'no longer know what to do', so that the acts, gestures, discourses which up until then had seemed to go without saying become problematic, difficult, dangerous. This effect is intentional.[46]

If the books are to enable the experience of 'other truths', the facts they present must be historically accurate. As such, the 'history of truth' plays a 'double game'. On the one hand, it exposes what ties us to our present. But inasmuch as it looks into the historical conditions of constitution for present-day practices – in order to show their 'madeness' or 'singularity' – it paves the way for them to be changed; indeed, it 'contributes' to the process of transformation. Ultimately, it is necessary for 'experiences' to be tied to collective practices and social movements (as in the case of anti-psychiatry or prison reform) for changes to occur:

---

Foucault, 1980d, *Remarks on Marx* [1991], 35–6; Foucault, 1984g, 'Polemics, Politics and Problematizations: An Interview with Michel Foucault', 385.

46. Foucault, 1980b, 'Questions of Method', 84; see also Foucault, 1978n, 'Clarifications on the Question of Power' [1996], 261–2; Foucault, 1980d, *Remarks on Marx* [1991], 36–40.

What I am trying to do is provoke an interference between our reality and the knowledge of our past history. If I succeed, this will have real effects in our present history … [T]wo years ago there was turmoil, in several prisons in France, prisoners revolting. In two prisons, the prisoners in their cells read my book. They shouted the text to other prisoners. I know it's pretentious to say, but that's a proof of a truth – a political and actual truth – which started after the book was written. I hope that the truth of my books is in the future.[47]

The relationship between fiction and truth is central to Foucault's methodological approach. The history of truth is not restricted to charting standing truths; it sketches a movement that, starting from the reconstruction of historical facts, moves towards constructing 'other', future truths:

As to the problem of fiction, it seems to me to be a very important one; I am well aware that I have never written anything but fictions. I do

---

47. Foucault, 1979k, 'Conversation with Michel Foucault' [1980], 5. Foucault also specifies this aim in response to Marxist critics who accuse him of simply mirroring standing facts in his analyses and failing to denounce ideology as 'false reality': 'In reality, what I want to do, and here is the difficulty of trying to do it, is to solve this problem: to work out an interpretation, a reading of a certain reality [*un certain réel*], which might be such that, on the one hand, this interpretation could produce some of the effects of truth; and on the other hand, these effects of truth could become implements within possible struggles. *Telling the truth so that it might be acceptable.* Deciphering a layer of reality in such a way that the lines of force and the lines of fragility come forth; the points of resistance and the possible points of attack; the paths marked out and the shortcuts. It is the reality of possible struggles that I wish to bring to light'. Foucault, 1978n, 'Clarifications on the Question of Power' [1996], 261, emphasis added.

The 'production of effects of truth' corresponds to what Gramsci called the 'struggle for objectivity', which does not aim for passive recognition of standing truths but the active construction of new ones: 'In reality one can "foresee" to the extent that one act, to the extent that one applies a voluntary effort and therefore contributes concretely to creating the result "foreseen". Prediction reveals itself thus not as a scientific act of knowledge, but as the abstract expression of the effort made, the practical way of creating a collective will. And how could prediction be an act of knowledge? One knows what has been and what is, not what will be, which is something "non-existent" and therefore unknowable by definition. Prediction is therefore only a practical act'. Gramsci, *Selections from the Prison Notebooks of Antonio Gramsci* (1971), 438. On the difference between 'fiction' and 'fable', see Foucault, 1966c, 'Behind the Fable' [1998]; Bellour, 'Towards Fiction' (1992) and de Certeau, *Histoire et psychanalyse entre science et fiction* (1987).

not mean to say, however, that truth is therefore absent. It seems to me that the possibility exists for fiction to function in truth, for a fictional discourse to induce effects of truth, and for bringing it about that a true discourse engenders or 'manufactures' something that does not as yet exist, that is, 'fictions' it. One 'fictions' history on the basis of a political reality that makes it true, one 'fictions' a politics not yet in existence on the basis of a historical truth.[48]

---

48. Foucault, 1977i, 'The History of Sexuality' [1980], 193; see also Foucault, 1979k, 'Conversation with Michel Foucault' [1980], 5.

# 14

## An Answer to the Question: What Is Critique?

What is the answer to the question? The problem. How is the problem
resolved? By displacing the question. The problem escapes the logic
of the excluded third, because it is a dispersed multiplicity; it cannot
be resolved by the clear distinctions of a Cartesian idea, because as an
idea it is obscure-distinct; it seriously disobeys the Hegelian negative
because it is a multiple affirmation; it is not subjected to the contradiction of being and non-being, since it is being. We must think
problematically rather than question and answer dialectically.

Foucault[1]

Let us return to where we started. The study at hand took the problem
of critique as the point of departure. We noted the surprising fact that
the question of the relationship between theory and politics plays a
decisive role in readings of Foucault's works. By turns, this relationship
has been described as 'paradoxical', 'aporetic' and 'contradictory' – in
order to limit or discredit the critical claims the 'genealogy of power'
advances. For the most part, reasons are sought in the theoretical
shortcomings of a conception of power that supposedly fails to signal
the normative criteria justifying political critique.

In order to be able to answer the question about the critical
potential of a 'genealogy of power', I have made an extended 'detour'
through the problematic of government. In so doing, my main
concern has been to demonstrate the coherence and consistency of
a theoretico-methodological approach that, in resisting dominant

---

1. Foucault, 1970b, 'Theatrum Philosophicum' [1998], 359.

truths, 'necessarily' proves paradoxical, contradictory and aporetic. I have emphasized problematics more than specific problems because I wanted to delineate the contours of a kind of critique that 'problematizes' the traditional understanding of politics, theory, power and truth. In closing, I would like to explore, in fuller detail, the characteristics and limits of this form of critique in order to answer the question that opened the book. What is critique?

## The Genealogy of Critique

As we have seen, government refers to a form of power that operates indirectly, by way of actions performed by subjects who are 'led' by means of the truth. In this context, Foucault defines critique as a social practice that seeks to escape being led and 'dominant truths'. His thesis is that the generalization and spread of arts of government from the sixteenth century on cannot be separated from a correlative moment, which simultaneously limits them and poses the condition for their unfolding. For this reason, the genealogy of governmental technology is also a *genealogy of critique*:

> Facing them head on and as compensation, or rather, as both partner and adversary to the arts of governing, as an act of defiance, as a challenge, as a way of limiting these arts of governing and sizing them up, of finding a way to escape from them or, in any case, a way to displace them, with a basic distrust, but also and by the same token, as a line of development of the arts of governing, there would have been something born in Europe at that time, a kind of general cultural form, both a political and moral attitude, a way of thinking, etc. and which I would very simply call the art of not being governed or better, the art of not being governed like that and at any cost. I would therefore propose, as a very first definition of critique, this general characterization: the art of not being governed quite so much.[2]

As such, critique does not move in simple opposition, or reaction, to intensified practices of government. Instead, it functions as an element within them. Inasmuch as government represents a form of power that

---

2. Foucault, 1990b, 'What Is Critique?' [2007], 44–5.

structures the field of subjects' possible actions through the production of truth, it must constantly confront the question of its principles, scope and aims – the problem of 'true government':

> And if governmentalization is indeed this movement through which individuals are subjugated in the reality of a social practice through mechanisms of power that adhere to a truth, well, then I will say that critique is the movement by which the subject gives himself the right to question truth on its effects of power and question power on its discourses of truth. Well, then: Critique will be the act of voluntary insubordination, that of reflected intractability. Critique would essentially insure the desubjugation of the subject in the context of what we could call, in a word, the politics of truth.[3]

However, Foucault presents this definition of critique as 'the art of not being governed quite so much' as 'both very general and very vague or fluid' – 'empirical' and 'approximate'.[4] Still, he maintains, it approaches what Kant understood as 'enlightenment', or *Aufklärung*. Engagement with Kant shaped Foucault's conception of critique in decisive ways. Again and again, he returned to a short text entitled *Was ist Aufklärung?* where Kant discusses enlightenment in relation to an authoritarian state of immaturity (*Unmündigkeit*).[5]

Kant's point of departure is the positive relation between 'immaturity' and government (*Führung*); the project of enlightenment aims to break with this state. On this score, Kant's definition of enlightenment agrees with Foucault's definition of critique. Foucault does not diverge from Kant on the basis of his understanding of enlightenment so much as the separation between enlightenment and critique. He considers Kant's project to be marked by a 'certain ambiguity'[6] inasmuch as his forebear seeks a principle that will make the private use of

---

3. Ibid., 47.

4. Ibid., 45 and 47.

5. '*Enlightenment is man's emergence from his self-incurred immaturity. Immaturity* is the inability to use one's own understanding without the guidance of another. This immaturity is *self-incurred* if its cause is not lack of understanding, but lack of resolution and courage to use it without the guidance of another. The motto of enlightenment is therefore: *Sapere aude!* Have the courage to use your *own* understanding!'. Kant, 'An Answer to the Question: "What Is Enlightenment?"'' (1991), 54; Foucault, 1984d, 'What Is Enlightenment?', 34–7.

6. Foucault, 1984d, 'What Is Enlightenment?', 35.

reason overlap with its public use – in order to serve the purposes of 'rational rule'. For Kant, enlightenment and critique are 'situated at a distance',[7] inasmuch as critique means epistemological critique in particular ('knowledge of knowledge'). This is why Kant assigns critique the task of determining the conditions for the correct use of reason and the latter's legitimate borders.

According to Kant, enlightenment does not simply found personal freedom of opinion and conscience. It introduces a 'political problem':[8] how can the private use of freedom be made to agree with obeying public authorities? The 'solution' he proposes involves devising a 'compromise' between maturity and government – or, more precisely, he ties the maturity of subjects to their 'reasonable' insight into the need for subordination, which itself follows rational principles. According to this view, subjects experience greater freedom the more they accept their subjugation to the pressures of an order of domination. This order is not a matter of arbitrary discretion; rather, it defers to the constraints of universal reason:

> The question, in any event, is that of knowing how the use of reason can take the public form that it requires, how the audacity to know can be exercised in broad daylight, while individuals are obeying as scrupulously as possible. And Kant, in conclusion, proposes to Frederick II, in scarcely veiled terms, a sort of contract – what might be called the contract of rational despotism with free reason: the public and free use of autonomous reason will be the best guarantee of obedience, on condition, however, that the political principle that must be obeyed itself be in conformity with universal reason.[9]

Engaging with Kant holds strategic significance for Foucault's project because the 'ambivalent' tradition of enlightenment that he represents has remained dominant to this day. It still determines the form that critique assumes – as well as its limits. Following Kant, philosophical convention has sought to bind critique to 'rationality' and viewed it as a negative enterprise, above all: 'clearing up' illusion, error, repression and so on. This philosophico-juridical tradition calls for identifying

---

7. Foucault, 1990b, 'What Is Critique?' [2007], 50.
8. Foucault, 1984d, 'What Is Enlightenment?', 37.
9. Ibid., 37.

norms that will authenticate critique and ensure its rightness, justification, appropriateness and so on. As such, it forms an important
component of modern political rationality:

> [S]ince Kant, the role of philosophy has been to prevent reason going
> beyond the limits of what is given in experience; but from the same
> moment – that is, from the development of modern states and polit-
> ical management of society – the role of philosophy has also been to
> keep watch over the excessive powers of political rationality – which is
> rather a promising life expectancy.[10]

*Contra* this philosophico-juridical conception, Foucault wants to
uncover, within the tradition of Enlightenment, 'possible tracks other
than those which seemed to have been up till now most willingly
cleared'.[11] Accordingly, the question of critique cannot be separated
from another question: what is Enlightenment?

## What Is Enlightenment?

Foucault's work has largely been read as an attack on the rationalist
and humanist tradition of Enlightenment. Especially in *Discipline
and Punish*, Foucault points to the 'dark side'[12] of Enlightenment by
noting a historical parallel between rights to freedom and disciplinary techniques. That said, this observation does not amount to a
wholesale condemnation of the Enlightenment; instead, it forms part
of the search for its historical conditions of possibility. Foucault is not
interested in discrediting the Enlightenment as a whole so much as
clarifying the relationship between general, legal form and social discipline – nominal equality combined with a system of differentiated
normalization.[13]

But a major shift occurred in Foucault's assessment of Enlightenment. In shorter texts that appeared at the end of the 1970s and
beginning of the 1980s, he started to make positive reference to the

---

10. Foucault, 1981a, '"Omnes et Singulatim"', 225.
11. Foucault, 1990b, 'What Is Critique?' [2007], 58.
12. Foucault, 1975a, *Discipline and Punish* [1995], 222.
13. Ibid., 221–4.

Enlightenment, which differed markedly from his earlier efforts to counter a humanist history of progress with analysis of its social pre-conditions and political costs. Now, he no longer held a mirror up to Enlightenment; instead, he situated his own research programme in a tradition inaugurated by Kant that extends – via Hegel, Marx, Nietzsche and Weber – up to Adorno and Horkheimer.[14]

For Foucault, these different thinkers have a point in common inas-much as they define a field of problems anchored in an 'ontology of the present'.[15] Such a historico-philosophical perspective does not locate the present in the continuity of a universal history – as a step on the way from a yesterday towards a tomorrow – but analyses it in its 'dif-ference'.[16] For Foucault, the particularity of the Enlightenment is to have inaugurated a form of thinking that understands itself as an inte-gral component of the historical process. Thereby, for the first time, the question of the 'present' and belonging to a historical moment came to represent a decisive condition for philosophical reflection.[17]

Foucault distinguishes between two traditions of Enlightenment: on the one hand, the 'analytics of truth',[18] which asks about the formal conditions of true insight, and, on the other, a 'history of truth', which examines the historical conditions of rationality. The former concen-trates on the question of (right or wrong) knowledge. The latter is not concerned with determining 'whether or not [practices] conform to principles of rationality'; instead, it seeks 'to discover which kind of rationality they are using'.[19] Needless to say, the relationship between rationality and power was thematized time and again in critical movements following Kant; for all that, the line of questioning itself remained indebted to a rationalist prejudice inasmuch as the problem

---

14. Thomas Schäfer identifies three stages in which Foucault engaged with the Enlightenment: a largely negative assessment in books up to *The Archaeology of Knowledge*, an examination of its conditions of possibility in *Discipline and Punish*, and, finally, a positive view in late essays. Schäfer, 'Aufklärung und Kritik' (1990), 74–9. For a discussion of Foucault's early critique of Enlightenment, see Kögler, *Michel Foucault* (1994), 10–26.

15. Foucault, 1984o, 'The Art of Telling the Truth' [1994], 148.

16. Foucault, 1984d, 'What Is Enlightenment?', 34.

17. 'It is a question of showing how he who speaks as a thinker, as a scientist, as a philosopher, is himself part of this process and (more than that) how he has a certain role to play in this process, in which he is to find himself, therefore, both element and actor'. Foucault, 1984o, 'The Art of Telling the Truth' [1994], 140.

18. Ibid., 148.

19. Foucault, 1981a, '"Omnes et Singulatim"', 226.

continued to be cast in epistemological terms. Rationality was subjected to a 'legitimacy test': 'what false idea has knowledge gotten of itself and what excessive use has it exposed itself to, to what domination is it therefore linked?'.[20]

Stepping away from the dominant tradition of critique – which broaches the question of Enlightenment through the problem of knowledge – Foucault proposes 'a different procedure'.[21] Instead of approaching the question of critique via the problem of knowledge, he approaches it by way of the problem of power. With that, the question of what is right or false, scientific or ideological, and so on, fades into the background. Examining how power and knowledge meet and interconnect historically moves to the fore. Foucault does not take aim at the Enlightenment as such, but at a certain way of treating it that obligates it to operate with the rigid distinction of rationality and irrationality:

There is the problem raised by Habermas: if one abandons the work of Kant or Weber, for example, one runs the risk of lapsing into irrationality. I am completely in agreement with this, but at the same time, our question is quite different: I think that the central issue of philosophy and critical thought since the eighteenth century has always been, still is, and will, I hope, remain the question: *What* is this Reason that we use? What are its historical effects? What are its limits, and what are its dangers? ... One should remain as close to this question as possible, keeping in mind that it is both central and extremely difficult to resolve. In addition, if it is extremely dangerous to say that Reason is the enemy that should be eliminated, it is just as dangerous to say that any critical questioning of this rationality risks sending us into irrationality.[22]

---

20. Foucault, 1990b, 'What Is Critique?' [2007], 58–9.
21. Ibid., 59.
22. Foucault, 1982c, 'Space, Knowledge and Power' [1984], 248–9. 'But that does not mean that one has to be "for" or "against" the Enlightenment. It even means precisely that one has to refuse everything that might present itself in the form of a simplistic and authoritarian alternative: you either accept the Enlightenment and remain within the tradition of its rationalism (this is considered a positive term by some and used by others, on the contrary, as a reproach); or else you criticize the Enlightenment and then try to escape from its principles of rationality (which may be seen once again as good or bad)'. Foucault, 1984d, 'What Is Enlightenment?', 43. See also Dreyfus and Rabinow, *Michel Foucault: Beyond Structuralism and Hermeneutics*

Foucault's question about the historical form of rationality ('What is this Reason that we use?') presupposes that different rationalities are possible. Determining the defining trait of 'Reason' calls for distinguishing it from other forms of rationality. In this light, the Enlightenment notion of universal reason represents a historical effect, not an anthropological constant. And if this is so, then the Enlightenment did not 'discover' rationality so much as it 'invented' a specific and historical rationality that takes itself to be universal and eternal: 'a rationality that aspires to the universal while developing within contingency, that asserts its unity and yet proceeds only through partial modifications, that validates itself by its own supremacy but that cannot be dissociated in its history from the inertias, the dullnesses, or the coercions that subjugate it'.[23]

Foucault's critical perspective does not mean to summon rationality before the court of universal 'Reason', where it could be measured and judged. Reason as such does not stand in question – only its claim to universality. According to Foucault, what should be retained of the Enlightenment are not its universals so much as 'that event and its meaning', i.e. 'the question of the historicity of thinking about the universal'.[24] In other words, no *a priori* rejection of universals should occur. Universals themselves do not stand at issue so much as their historical significance and political status: their own necessity and the need for the constraints they imply.[25]

---

(1983), 205: 'Foucault himself has described his tactic as a "slalom" [...] between the traditional philosophy and an abandonment of all seriousness'.

23. Foucault, 1985a, 'Life: Experience and Science' [1998], 469; Foucault, 1984e, 'Preface to the History of Sexuality, Vol. II', 335–6; Foucault, 1984o, 'The Art of Telling the Truth' [1994], 145–8; Foucault, 1983e, 'Critical Theory/Intellectual History' [1988], 25–6.

24. Foucault, 1984o, 'The Art of Telling the Truth' [1994], 147.

25. Kelly, 'Foucault, Habermas, and the Self-Referentiality of Critique' (1994), 385–6; Deleuze, 'A Portrait of Foucault' (1995a), 109–10. One of Foucault's central ambitions is to combat an 'order of truth' that justifies coercion on the basis of universals: 'It is one of my targets to show people that a lot of things that are a part of their landscape – that people think are universal – are the result of some very precise historical changes. All my analyses are against the idea of universal necessities in human existence'. Foucault, 1988a, 'Truth, Power, Self', 11. '[T]his is precisely the point at issue, both in historical analysis and political critique. We aren't, nor do we have to put ourselves, under the sign of a unitary necessity'. Foucault, 1980b, 'Questions of Method', 78.

That is, Foucault does not mean to reject humanism and its principles categorically, for instance; instead, his critique bears on humanism's claim to universality and

In the context of a 'history of truth', one cannot speak of a universal process of 'rationalization' or a split into technical and communicative reason. For all that, rationality does not dissolve into relativism, either. For Foucault, forms of thought, criteria and values cannot be detached from the historical context to which they refer and belong. Accordingly, *Discipline and Punish* does not advocate public torture, nor does it declare that the forms punishment assumes are arbitrary. Likewise, *History of Madness* does not offer the apology of madness or a history of irrationalism. Instead, these books focus on rationality that has a history inasmuch as it cannot be separated from political struggles and social practices. A single way out – admittedly, a paradoxical one – remains: 'a rational critique of rationality'.[26]

This means shifting the point of application of critique: its basis no longer lies with the 'right theory' so much as a thought-out decision or 'option'.[27] If Kant undertook the 'critique of pure reason' in order to demonstrate its capacities and limitations, Foucault performs a 'critique of impure reason',[28] which understands the limits of knowledge as the borders of our historical being. Such critique is no longer negative – that is, oriented on the (theoretical) question of frontiers that knowledge must not violate. Instead, it is positive, articulating the (political) question of power by demonstrating the singular and contingent aspects of what appears universal and necessary – and thereby bringing into view the possibility of other historical forms: a 'critique of political reason'.[29]

Such critique can no longer appeal to theoretical justifications. Instead, it takes form as a matter of practical will: 'The point, in brief, is to transform the critique conducted in the form of necessary

---

the constraints that this entails: 'What I am afraid of about humanism is that it presents a certain form of our ethics as a universal model for any kind of freedom. I think there are more secrets, more possible freedoms, and more inventions in our future than we can imagine in humanism'. Foucault, 1988a, 'Truth, Power, Self', 15; Foucault, 1984d, 'What Is Enlightenment?', 43–5; on the problem of Foucault's 'anti-humanism', see Hooke, 'The Order of Others' (1987).

26. Foucault, 1983e, 'Critical Theory/Intellectual History' [1988], 27; Foucault, 1980b, 'Questions of Method', 78; Foucault, 1980d, *Remarks on Marx* [1991], 65–6; {1983} 24, 26.

27. Foucault, 1984o, 'The Art of Telling the Truth' [1994], 148.

28. Bernauer, 'Beyond Life and Death: On Foucault's Post-Auschwitz Ethic' (1992), 188.

29. Foucault, 1981a, '"Omnes et Singulatim"'.

limitation into a practical critique that takes the form of a possible transgression.[30]

## The Critical Attitude

Problematization is a specific form of critique that defines itself in contradistinction to the search for universal rules and necessary constraints. In this perspective, knowledge does not ground and legitimate critique; instead, the status of knowledge stands in question. Problematization pursues the historical critique of our social being; it does not presume to offer transcendental critique. Its defining trait is to introduce a break in the continuum between knowledge and will. For Foucault, critique cannot be derived from underlying and motivating knowledge. It does not represent neutral, theoretical knowledge so much as it embodies an ethico-political bearing: a *critical attitude*. It is not insight into the necessary limits of knowledge or the consequence of correct insight into phenomena, but a 'virtue'[31] or ethos with a foundation that does not need to legitimate itself by recourse to external knowledge: 'The critical ontology of ourselves has to be considered not, certainly, as a theory, a doctrine, nor even as a permanent body of knowledge that is accumulating; it has to be conceived as an attitude.'[32]

Although Foucault sets critique apart from knowledge and presents it as an 'attitude', not every attitude is critical. Critique means analysing the epistemologico-political limits of our historical existence – and thereby indicating how they may be surpassed. Accordingly, critique is not a matter of affirming or negating the standing order; its problematizations aim at a deeper, more basic level – the common ground of both these 'solutions': 'This philosophical ethos may be characterized as a *limit-attitude*. We are not talking about a gesture of rejection. We have to move beyond the outside-inside alternative; we have to be

---

30. Foucault, 1984d, 'What Is Enlightenment?', 45.
31. Foucault, 1990b, 'What Is Critique?' [2007], 43.
32. Foucault, 1984d, 'What Is Enlightenment?', 50. This does not mean opting for subjectivism or voluntarism: 'by "attitude", I mean a mode of relating to contemporary reality; a voluntary choice made by certain people; in the end, a way of thinking and feeling; a way, too, of acting and behaving that at one and the same time marks a relation of belonging and presents itself as a task. A bit, no doubt, like what the Greeks called an *ethos*'. Foucault, 1984d, 'What Is Enlightenment?', 39.

at the frontiers. Criticism indeed consists of analysing and reflecting upon limits.'[33]

It follows that there is no need to elaborate theoretical justifications to make normative judgements. At the same time, this does not mean that valuations are arbitrary and random; rather, the normative judgements defining the goals of struggles are founded by repressive institutions and practices, and they function in relative independence from theoretical justifications. In order to recognize that discriminating against minorities or exploiting workers is 'wrong' or 'unjust', no theory is required. (Conversely, it can be theoretically 'proven' that these practices are 'right' and 'just'.) The normative criteria according to which we evaluate social practices positively or negatively do not follow a theoretical logic that forms their basis and precondition; if anything, theory offers the means – a 'toolkit' – for 'rationalizing' certain normative orientations.[34]

---

33. Ibid., 45. The distance Foucault takes from an epistemological line of questioning is also explained by the latter's 'negativity' – that is, the fact that it denounces things in the name of 'real' or 'true' reality. 'People may ask why I've allowed myself to get involved in this – why I've agreed to ask these questions ... But, in the end, I've become rather irritated by an attitude, which for a long time was mine, too, and which I no longer subscribe to, which [...] is to denounce and to criticize; [...] That doesn't seem to me the right attitude'. Foucault, 1977o, 'Confinement, Psychiatry, Prison' [1988], 209.

Critique that is 'positive' in this sense takes distance from all forms of a morally motivated critique in order to subject the standards, with which critique is practiced, themselves to a critical reflection, since they are part of a social and historical reality to which they relate (critically): 'When I say "critical", I don't mean a demolition job, one of rejection or refusal, but a work of examination that consists of suspending as far as possible the system of values to which one refers when testing and assessing it'. Foucault, 1984x, 'On Power' [1988], 107.

34. Positing a 'non-necessary' connection between theory and politics does not mean that theory can be 'implemented' to any end at all. Like other tools, theoretical instruments have a 'materiality' making them more suited for certain purposes than others. Theory is not arbitrary, but because the 'right' politics cannot be 'derived' from theory, the nature of their relationship must provide the object for critical reflection: 'there is a very tenuous "analytic" link between a philosophical conception and the concrete political attitude of someone who is appealing to it; the "best" theories do not constitute a very effective protection against disastrous political choices; certain great themes such as "humanism" can be used to any end whatever [...]. I do not conclude from this that one may say just anything within the order of theory, but, on the contrary, that a demanding, prudent, "experimental" attitude is necessary; at every moment, step by step, one must confront what one is thinking and saying with what one is doing, with who one is'. Foucault, 1984f, 'Politics and Ethics: An Interview', 374.

Foucault goes further still. Not only is it unnecessary to base critique on scientific knowledge; doing so harbours a host of dangers and problems. Inasmuch as social movements and projects of political liberation seek to legitimate themselves by appealing to scientificity, they subjugate themselves to an imperative of knowledge – one that exercises censoring effects and rejects whatever does not fulfil established criteria as 'unfounded' and 'unjustified'. Such critique remains limited insofar as it is committed to 'truths' concerning individuals and society and seeks to affirm, against domination and exploitation, a larger truth which itself is tied up in manifold power relations. As such, change and resistance are admitted only inasmuch as they respect human 'nature' and the social 'laws'. This perspective compels individuals to recognize constraints in order to 'explain' universal patterns and laws and 'prove' that resistance must assume a certain form in order to qualify as 'resistance' at all.[35]

By defining critique as an *ethos*, Foucault rejects the view of resistance and critique that posits a necessary relationship to expert knowledge. His position refuses to 'authenticate' itself with normative criteria; indeed, such 'normality' is not the aim of criteria so much as its target. Foucauldian critique declines to 'identify' itself because what stands in question is, precisely, attachment to a 'true' identity. Critique does not occupy a scientific dimension so much as an ethical one. It stresses that we are responsible for the 'truths' that we think, say and perform – and that no theoretical justification can relieve us of such responsibility. This ethos does not show us necessary constraints to which we must submit so much as possible liberties and starting points for resistance.

It bears repeating what such a decentring of knowledge seeks to achieve. Declaring that no necessary connection holds between knowledge and critique does not mean that theory cannot perform a critical role. On the contrary: theory performs an important task in problematization because it checks claims to universality and reveals elements of arbitrariness and contingency within them. As such, theory – if it reflects on its own, historical conditions – plays the role

---

35. Gutting, *Michel Foucault's Archaeology of Scientific Reason* (1989), 282–4. At several points, Foucault rejected this form of 'blackmail' or 'trap'; rejecting 'obligatory, politico-normative authentication' is part of his critical project. Foucault, 1980b, 'Questions of Method', 84; Foucault, 1984d, 'What Is Enlightenment?', 42; Foucault, 1984t, 'An Aesthetics of Existence' [1988], 52.

of a 'counter-science' that opens the way for changing social practices by liberating us from the sovereignty of knowledge and its constraints. For all that, the fundamental, normative judgement that liberation and struggle are important does not follow from theory; instead, it defines the context in which theory operates: it is not a justification of, but an instrument for, resistance.[36]

Uncoupling knowledge and critique holds another important consequence. If critique can no longer justify itself through claims to universality and 'ultimate reason', if it never achieves 'saturation', then it can only ever be historical and '*experimental*'.[37] Problematization represents a form of critique that cannot appeal to conclusive certainty or true insight; it must always stand open to critique and admit (self-) correction. Foucault's understanding of critique implies calling his own work into question. As such, problematization itself proves to be a 'problematic' undertaking; it is necessary to examine how, and in what contexts, it operates, the 'dangers' it produces and the possibilities it affords.[38] Precisely because it can never be sure of itself, problematization must inevitably 'put itself to the test of reality, of contemporary reality, both to grasp the points where change is possible and desirable, and to determine the precise form this change should take'.[39]

---

36. The question concerning the basis for resistance presumes that it requires justification. That is precisely what Foucault contests: 'Your question is: why am I so interested in politics? But if I were to answer you very simply, I would say this: why *shouldn't* I be interested? That is to say, what blindness, what deafness, what density of ideology would have to weigh me down to prevent me from being interested in what is probably the most crucial subject to our existence, that is to say the society in which we live, the economic relations within which it functions, and the system of power which defines the regular forms and the regular permissions and prohibitions of our conduct'. Foucault, 1974a, 'Human Nature: Justice versus Power', 167–8.

37. Foucault, 1984d, 'What Is Enlightenment?', 46.

38. Castel, '"Problematization" as a Mode of Reading History' (1994); Sawicki, *Disciplining Foucault* (1991), 1–15. In this sense, every form of critique stands exposed to the counterfactual supposition of an 'ideal situation of power': 'I have an unfortunate habit. When people speak about this or that, I try to imagine what the result would be if translated into reality. When they "criticize" someone, when they "denounce" his ideas, when they "condemn" what he writes, I imagine them in the ideal situation in which they would have complete power over him. I take the words they use – *demolish, destroy, reduce to silence, bury* – and see what the effect would be if they were taken literally'. Foucault, 1980g, 'The Masked Philosopher' [1988], 324; Hacking, 'The Archaeology of Michel Foucault' (1986), 36.

39. Foucault, 1984d, 'What Is Enlightenment?', 46; Foucault, 1984f, 'Politics and Ethics: An Interview', 375–6.

To be sure: Foucault's understanding of the relationship between theory and critique contains points of difficulty and weakness. Indeed, it stresses that all critique is 'problematic' – that any idea of 'secure', or 'certain', critique is purely 'theoretical'. Conceiving critique as a 'limit-attitude' gives rise to a host of questions. If we simply accept the norms that are implied in certain struggles, what guarantees that these norms are 'more just' or 'better' than those they combat? How do conflicting norms admit comparison? Why should we prefer the normative valuations of Foucault, a figure of the left, to those presented by people on the right, who deem immigrants and unions to be the real problem? Is it not necessary, in order to defend our convictions, to appeal to the solid foundation of human nature and universal values?

These problems undoubtedly remain unresolved in Foucault's work. Moreover, genealogy is unable to offer an answer. But Foucault's conception of critique as problematization implies that this form of critique is not the only one possible: problematization does not represent the 'correct' form of critique – one that replaces universalism and inherits its claims. That would be contradictory, indeed. In this regard, he is consistent. Foucault does not opt for critique that follows the seemingly 'unconstrained constraint of argument' in order to tell us what we are supposed to do and not to do; he shows a form of critique which functions less as prescription and law than as 'suggestion' and 'invitation'. Foucault's 'alternative' to legitimating normative valuations on the basis of general, theoretical principles is to ground claims in concrete experiences of (putative) causes of domination and exploitation. In order to identify prisons and madhouses – or unions and asylum seekers – as obstacles to a 'better society', we must have experienced them as practical realities, not as theoretical principles. As such, Foucault's books are also the result of his own experience of asylums, prison revolts and social reactions to homosexuality; the analyses they present are inconceivable without this 'personal' dimension. The possibility of other ('more egalitarian', 'better', etc.) experiences animates his works.[40]

---

40. Foucault, 1988a, 'Truth, Power, Self', 11–12; Gutting, *Michel Foucault's Archaeology of Scientific Reason* (1989), 282–4. 'Every time I have tried to do a piece of theoretical work it has been on the basis of elements of my own experience: always in connection with processes I see unfolding around me'. Foucault, 1981d, 'So Is It Important to Think?' [2000], 458. On this 'autobiographical dimension' of Foucault's work, see Eribon, '... quelque fragment d'autobiographie' (1994b). James Miller's

Understanding critique as an attitude does not guarantee that power of processes will be properly assessed. Judgements from experience are prone to a host of errors. That said, every form of critique stands exposed to this problem; moreover, such mistakes admit faster correction through further experience than judgements rooted in general theories. Indeed, experience of the abstractness of theory is what made the dangerousness of such an approach plain:

> In fact we know from experience that the claim to escape from the system of contemporary reality so as to produce the overall programs of another society, of another way of thinking, another culture, another vision of the world, has led only to the return of the most dangerous traditions.[41]

A further problem is that 'experimental' critique based on practical experience does not aim for changes with a scope as radical as critique built on comprehensive theories. Still, concentrating on local practices does not mean disregarding 'global' or 'general' structures, nor does it require giving up a 'systematic' claim in favour of an arbitrary and wilful analysis.[42] Instead, it entails a shift of the 'revolutionary perspective': great revolutionary breaks are not the precondition for, so much as the result of, local changes: 'I prefer even these partial transformations that have been made in the correlation of historical analysis and the practical attitude, to the programs for a new man that the worst political systems have repeated throughout the twentieth century'.[43]

Many will find this statement unsatisfying. The critical voices mentioned at the outset of this study certainly attest to such 'disappointment'. In this regard, Foucault offers both too much and too little. He does *too little* because he offers no theoretical grounding for

---

biography suffers from making these 'elements' the sole principle of explanation. His 'blend of anecdote and exegesis' dissolves the tension between life and theory and interprets Foucault's works as the substrate of personal experience and problems; for example, the 'history of the prison' is supposed to represent the author's own sadomasochistic fantasies. Miller, *The Passion of Michel Foucault* (1993), 5.

41. Foucault, 1984d, 'What Is Enlightenment?', 46. 'But experience has taught me that the history of various forms of rationality is sometimes more effective in unsettling our certitudes and dogmatism than is abstract criticism'. Foucault, 1981a, '"Omnes et Singulatim"', 253.

42. Foucault, 1984d, 'What Is Enlightenment?', 47–9.

43. Ibid., 47.

the normative criteria of his work. He does *too much* because he calls the very connection between normativity and critique into question. Foucault does not ask whom, what, when and how to engage in critique – what reasons there are for resistance, and what prospects for reform there might be. Instead, he starts with the historical fact of resistance:

> The necessity of reform mustn't be allowed to become a form of blackmail serving to limit, reduce, or halt the exercise of criticism. Under no circumstances should one pay attention to those who tell one, 'Don't criticize, since you're not capable of carrying out a reform'. That's ministerial cabinet talk. Critique doesn't have to be the premise of a deduction which concludes: this then is what needs to be done. It should be an instrument for those who fight, those who resist and refuse what is. Its use should be in processes of conflict and confrontation, essays in refusal. It doesn't have to lay down the law for the law. It isn't a stage in a programming. It is a challenge directed to what is.[44]

For Foucault, normative questions cannot be separated from practical ones. More precisely: normative questions are not theoretical problems, but practical matters. They admit justification only within the historical context of praxis to which they belong. In this regard, Foucauldian critique is indeed 'groundless' and 'unfounded'. That said, its foundation is significantly more solid than a theoretical foundation: critique arises from the everyday functioning of power, and it is the operations of power itself that form its basis.[45]

## What Is Maturity?

One further aspect must be considered. Foucault does not view critique only in relation to knowledge and power, but also as it bears on subjectivity. Critique is both a means of struggle on the way to maturity and a 'sign' of its attainment. As such, his characterization of critique as an attitude not only points to its independence from

---

44. Foucault, 1980b, 'Questions of Method', 84.
45. Kelly, 'Foucault, Habermas, and the Self-Referentiality of Critique' (1994), 382.

knowledge that legitimates it and power that provokes it; it also defines a bearing vis-à-vis social 'circumstances': unwillingness to accept them as they stand.

Once more, Kant's definition of Enlightenment proves relevant. According to Kant, Enlightenment heralds a break with the state of immaturity vis-à-vis authority. Maturity is the capacity 'to make use of one's understanding without the guidance of another'. That said, Kant understands maturity as insight into the universal limits of knowledge and freedom that occurs in subordination to a general law. His conception of the universal subject fuses the ethical subject, the epistemological subject and the juridico-political subject: 'Kant says, "I must recognize myself as universal subject, that is, I must constitute myself in each of my actions as a universal subject by conforming to universal rules".[46]

It is precisely such congruity between knowledge, power and subjectivity that Foucault rejects: 'The search for a form of morality acceptable to everybody in the sense that everyone should submit to it, strikes me as catastrophic'.[47] For Foucault, free subjectivity does not arise from discovering universal necessities and constraints, but from rejecting them and constructing social conditions that differ from those founded on universal norms. Accordingly, he is not interested

---

46. Foucault, 1983b, 'On the Genealogy of Ethics: An Overview of Work in Progress', 252; Dreyfus and Rabinow, 'What Is Maturity? Habermas and Foucault on "What Is Enlightenment?"' (1986). Kant's conception of a universal subject responds to a problem that arose with the autonomization of knowledge in modern times. Before Descartes, knowing something had always presupposed work on the self: to have access to the truth, the subject had to possess certain capacities or undergo an ascetic procedure. Descartes replaced ascesis with experience. For the first time, a 'cognitive subject' emerged without any moral qualification. A special relationship to the truth is no longer necessary; now, it is enough to be *any subject* at all.

This epistemological break enabled not just the institutionalization of the modern sciences but also posed the problem of 'immoral knowledge', the question of the relationship between the cognitive subject and the ethical subject: 'After Descartes, we have a subject of knowledge which poses for Kant the problem of knowing the relationship between the subject of ethics and that of knowledge. There was much debate in the Enlightenment as to whether these two subjects were completely different or not. Kant's solution was to find a universal subject, which, to the extent that it was universal could be the subject of knowledge, but which demanded, nonetheless, an ethical attitude – precisely the relationship to the self which Kant proposes in *The Critique of Practical Reason*'. Foucault, 1983b, 'On the Genealogy of Ethics: An Overview of Work in Progress', 252.

47. Foucault, 1984q, 'The Return of Morality' [1988], 253–4.

in how individual or social subjects 'identify' with shared norms and come to resist on the basis of shared convictions. On the contrary, his interest bears on inventing new subjectivities with new experiences and other norms:

> But the problem is, precisely, to decide if it is actually suitable to place oneself within a 'we' in order to assert the principles one recognizes and the values one accepts; or if it is not, rather, necessary to make the future formation of a 'we' possible, by elaborating the question. Because it seems to me that the 'we' must not be previous to the question; it can only be the result – and the necessarily temporary result – of the question as it is posed in the new terms in which one formulates it.[48]

Foucault adds nuance to his conception of critique by distinguishing between universal and specific intellectuals. The universal intellectual is an Enlightenment figure embodying a juridical form of critique, opposing 'to power, despotism and the abuses and arrogance of wealth the universality of justice and the equity of an ideal law'.[49] Such critique proceeds along the lines of a 'correct representation' of the world, on the basis of which it both declares and prescribes what should be. Inasmuch as such critique knows that it already possesses the truth, it can limit itself to a polemical, negative strategy. Standing at a remove, it 'judges' and 'condemns' and denounces the 'falsehood' of social conditions against the backdrop of their 'true' lawfulness. It does not simply represent a theory that is then applied; taking the stage with a 'legislative function',[50] it makes practice possible.

The role of the *specific intellectual* is both more modest and more radical. Whereas the 'universal intellectual' generalizes his/her individual position and speaks in the name of a law or a set of historical rules to which all people must conform, the specific intellectual speaks only for himself/herself, not for others. Or, more precisely: the specific intellectual only speaks for others inasmuch as s/he speaks for, and

---

48. Foucault, 1984g, 'Polemics, Politics and Problematizations: An Interview with Michel Foucault', 385.

49. Foucault, 1977d, 'Truth and Power' [1984], 70.

50. Foucault, 1977k, 'The End of the Monarchy of Sex' [1996], 225; Foucault, 1984g, 'Polemics, Politics and Problematizations: An Interview with Michel Foucault', 381–3.

about, herself/himself – from the standpoint of his own personal experience. Thus, the effectiveness of such critique does not occur in spite of the specificity of experiences; instead, the restricted claim to validity is the precondition for its use in concrete strategies of resistance. More still: the specificity of experiences achieves general meaning through 'the specificity of the politics of truth in our societies'.[51] This intellectual is someone

> occupying a specific position – but whose specificity is linked, in a society like ours, to the general functioning of an apparatus of truth. … [And it's here that] his position can take on a general significance and that his local, specific struggle can have effects and implications which are not simply professional or sectoral. The intellectual can operate and struggle at the general level of that regime of truth which is so essential to the structure and functioning of our society. There is a battle 'for truth', or at least 'around truth'.[52]

---

51. Foucault, 1977d, 'Truth and Power' [1984], 73.

52. Ibid., 73–4. Foucault later elaborated this conception of a 'specific critique' by adding the dimension of *parrhesia*, the theme of his final lectures at the Collège de France. In Greek antiquity, parrhesia represented a form of 'veridiction' different from prophecy and wisdom. It is distinguished by political and moral virtue and embodies a practice of freedom, since it declares the truth vis-à-vis the ruler and requires the courage of exposing oneself to the dangers such 'audacious' candour entails. Its significance involves calling into question the prevailing truth and practicing, in the name of other truths, critique of political decisions and procedural forms: 'this is the *parrhesia* (free speech) of the governed, who can and must question those who govern them, in the name of the knowledge, the experience they have, by virtue of being citizens, of what those who govern do, of the meaning of their action, of the decisions they have taken'. Foucault, 1984t, 'An Aesthetics of Existence' [1988], 51–2.

Parrhesia interests Foucault in terms of the 'genealogy of the critical attitude in … Western philosophy'. Foucault, 1985b, 'Discourse and Truth: The Problematization of Parrhesia' [1983], 170–1. It names an ethos distinguished by the unity of 'theory' and 'politics', which stands apart from two other ways of treating the truth: *rhetorical strategy* on the one hand, and *performative acts*, on the other. Parrhesia is not an art of persuasion; unlike the rhetorician, the speaker must believe in himself and the truth he declares. In this context, truth does mean the external agreement of thinking and being, but demands an inner bearing. By the same token, parrhesia should not be confused with speech acts. Performative acts presuppose a concrete, institutional framework and certain speaker positions, and they elicit coded effects. In contrast, parrhesia is defined by the openness and indeterminacy of the effects that it provokes. Foucault, 1985c, *The Hermeneutics of the Subject* [2005], 381–91. On Foucault's last lectures and the concept of parrhesia, see Foucault, 1985b, 'Discourse and Truth: The Problematization of Parrhesia' [1983]; Foucault, 1985c, *The Hermeneutics of the Subject* [2005]; Flynn, 'Foucault as a Parrhesiast' (1984); Schmid, *Auf der Suche nach*

Thus, it is not universality and necessity so much as partisanship and volition that define this conception of critique. Critique does not result from an act of reasoning that rejects other solutions in favour of the only correct one; instead, it occurs as the freedom of a will that does not accept standing forms of action and thought. Readings of *Discipline and Punish* or *The History of Sexuality, Volume 1* do not tell us what we should now do. These books do not sketch concrete alternatives or announce a political programme. They are 'problematizations' – that is, 'invitations' or 'enjoinders' that launch an appeal more than they prescribe anything. They call for other practices and forms of thinking, but they do not take the place of political action. Their imperative is not categorical so much as 'conditional'.[53]

That is why problematization is not a matter of denouncing power in general. Instead, it seeks to determine how power functions concretely – by way of what constraints, restrictions, power effects, exclusionary mechanisms, inequalities, etc., it operates. In this framework, historical reconstruction offers a means of critique and an instrument of 'counter-history' that reveals the possibility of 'other histories' within the hollows of grand narratives. Foucault's works do not formulate a theory so much as they afford a *diagnostics of the present*:

> I would like to say something about the function of any diagnosis concerning the nature of the present. It does not consist in a simple characterization of what we are but, instead – by following lines of

*einer neuen Lebenskunst* (1991), 65–8, 269–79; Gradev, 'Les jeux de la vérité' (1994); Gros, *Michel Foucault* (1996), 116–23.

53. Foucault, 2004a, *Security, Territory, Population* [2007], 3. 'At this point I think we need to bring into discussion the problem of the function of the intellectual. It is absolutely true that when I write a book I refuse to take a prophetic stance, that is, the one of saying to people: here is what you must do – and also: this is good and this is not. I say to them: roughly speaking, it seems to me that things have gone this way; but I describe those things in such a way that the possible paths of attack are delineated. Yet even with this approach I do not force or compel anyone to attack. So then, it becomes a completely personal question when I choose, if I want, to take certain courses of action with reference to prisons, psychiatric asylums, this or that issue. But I say that political action belongs to a category of participation completely different from these written or bookish acts of participation. It is a problem of groups, of personal and physical commitment. One is not radical because one pronounces a few words; no, the essence of being radical is physical; the essence of being radical is the radicalness of existence itself'. Foucault, 1978n, 'Clarifications on the Question of Power' [1996], 262; Foucault, 1983e, 'Critical Theory/Intellectual History' [1988], 40.

fragility in the present – in managing to grasp why and how that which is might no longer be that-which-is. In this sense, any description must always be made in accordance with these kinds of virtual fracture which open up the space of freedom understood as a space of concrete freedom, i.e., of possible transformation.[54]

For Foucault, critique does not mean exposing unpassable borders or describing closed systems. Instead, its purpose is to make changeable singularities visible. Critique does not have the negative task of revealing what is veiled or distorted in order to separate the true from the untrue and ultimately attain complete transparency. Rather, it has the paradoxical goal of 'making visible what is already visible, that is, to make evident what is so closely, so immediately and tightly tied to us, that we fail to perceive it for precisely this reason'.[55]

In this regard, all of Foucault's books resemble journalistic writing: they seek to provoke 'scandal' and call seemingly 'unproblematic' practices into question. They have the aim of prompting individuals and groups to defend themselves against the power effects they chronicle, to practice resistance. These works do not mark the end of Enlightenment so much as they stand inscribed in the tradition it inaugurated. Their point is to 'shake up' and 'make aware' – in a word, they want to 'enlighten'.[56]

One last parallel to Kant's definition of Enlightenment. 'What Is Enlightenment?' is not a theoretical treatise, but a journal article. It does not describe a historical process obeying external logic so much as it represents an 'engagement' in this development and an integral part of the events to which it means to respond. Kant considered immaturity to be the result of excessive authority, on the one hand, and a lack of courage, on the other. His text starts at this point of intersection, offering diagnosis and therapy at the same time. 'What Is Enlightenment?' attests to the will not to be governed and enjoins readers to become 'mature' in order to free themselves from comfortable dependency on

---

54. Ibid., 36; see also Kelly, 'Foucault, Habermas, and the Self-Referentiality of Critique' (1994), 372–3.

55. Foucault, 1978j, 'La philosophie analytique de la politique', 540–1; Foucault, 1984e, 'Preface to the History of Sexuality, Vol. II', 335.

56. See Foucault, 1973d, 'Le monde est un grand asile', 434; Foucault, 1978c, 'Dialogue on Power' [1975], 20; Foucault, 1979h, 'For an Ethics of Discomfort' [2000], 443–4.

established authorities. Enlightenment, in this sense, means not just observing what is but anticipating what could yet be:

> consequently, this definition of the *Aufklärung* is not simply going to be a kind of historical and speculative definition. In this definition of the *Aufklärung*, there will be something which no doubt it may be a little ridiculous to call a sermon, and yet it is very much a call for courage.[57]

## 'By Way of Conclusion'

In sum, against the backdrop of critique as Foucault defines it, paradoxes, contradictions, aporias and so on appear in a different light. Foucault's critics claim that he becomes entangled in insoluble difficulties when he makes recourse to liberal values yet rejects them – when he simultaneously invokes civil rights and criticizes them. But in fact, this 'bottleneck'[58] does not arise from a theoretical shortcoming on Foucault's part so much as it stems from a general problem of politics: every socio-critical perspective must work with the 'material' that constitutes the historical present – and any change that occurs has an index in what is called into question. Reference to civil rights, liberal freedoms and principles of justice is not cut off or distorted when a socio-critical position is taken. That said, Foucault's critical strategy does not stop there, as an example will illustrate.

As a 'homosexual', Foucault was subject to power processes that posit 'true' (hetero)sexuality as a matter of natural fact in order to disqualify forms of desire deviating from this norm as 'sick' or 'perverse'. The strategy of resistance he practised in *The History of Sexuality* involved describing the historical process through which sexual practices came to be viewed as defining personal identity. In this context, he advanced the view that struggles for liberation calling for the personal right to one's own sexuality prove limited inasmuch as they remain fixated on the idea of 'true' sexuality – a category established by institutions seeking to effect regulation and control. Foucault sought to take distance from such a conception in order to make new and other forms of sexual experiences possible. That said, it does not follow that he

---

57. Foucault, 1990b, 'What Is Critique?' [2007], 48.
58. Foucault, 1977f, '14 January 1976' [2003], 39.

rejected the concept of identity or appeals to rights. On the contrary, he insisted that homosexuals should have civil rights as homosexuals. It is not a matter of either-or. Cultivating a homosexual way of life does not take the place of fighting for rights and self-determination. Rather, the movement should move beyond demanding rights and tolerance; for real recognition and securing gains, new modes of living must be developed: 'It is important, first, to have the possibility – and the right – to choose your own sexuality. ... Still, I think *we have to go a step further*. ... Not only do we have to defend ourselves, not only affirm ourselves, as an identity but as a creative force'.[59]

As a form of critique, problematization represents a theoretical innovation precisely by making this 'step further', which turns the will to truth against itself. In such an undertaking, it is not possible to occupy the solid ground of the truth, nor is it possible simply to reject it. As such, the only 'way out' from this 'dead end' is to combat the truth by means of the truth in order, ultimately, to change the system of producing truth itself and to 'invent' other (perhaps 'freer', 'more just', 'more egalitarian', etc.) practices:

> This is the situation that we are in and that we must combat. If intel-
> lectuals in general are to have a function, if critical thought itself has
> a function, ... it is precisely to accept this sort of spiral, this sort of
> revolving door of rationality that refers us to its necessity, to its indis-
> pensability, and at the same time to its intrinsic dangers.[60]

---

59. Foucault, 1984u, 'Sex, Power, and the Politics of Identity' [1997], 164, empha-sis added; Sawicki, *Disciplining Foucault* (1991), 100. As such, being gay does not refer to a biological disposition for Foucault; rather, it signifies the possibility of another way of living, in contrast to compulsory heterosexuality. In lieu of linking sexuality and truth – as commonly occurs – Foucault wants 'not to discover in oneself the truth of one's sex, but, rather, to use one's sexuality henceforth to arrive at a multiplicity of relationships. And, no doubt, that's the real reason why homosexuality is not a form of desire but something desirable. Therefore, we have to work at becoming homosexuals and not be obstinate in recognizing that we are'. Foucault, 1981b, 'Friendship as a Way of Life' [1997], 135–6. For an attempt to sketch a 'gay ethos', see Blasius, 'An Ethos of Lesbian and Gay Existence' (1992).

60. Foucault, 1982c, 'Space, Knowledge and Power' [1984], 249. Tom Keenan and Jana Sawicki pinpoint this problem in exemplary manner: 'We recall the futures of a right beyond right, a right without right, but only by making reference or gesturing to the "rights" we have. There is "no way out", because there is no "out" – not because the present is somehow self-enclosed or self-identical, but on the contrary precisely because it differs itself and thus makes politics necessary. The only way out is out of

Paradoxically, then, Foucault is radical because he sticks to the rules. In order to change games of truth and power, it is not enough to study the stakes and know the rules. One must also play the game. At the same time, this does not mean taking a place on a politico-epistemological 'chessboard',[61] which permits certain moves and forbids others. The rules and the game do not correspond to two different ontological realities, abstract principles applied to concrete instances, whereby generality and specificity, structure and action, stand opposed. Instead, it means the immanence of a historical present that is always playing for its very existence, because subjects make 'their' history. 'By virtue of its splintering and repetition, the present is a throw of the dice. This is not because it forms part of a game in which it insinuates small contingencies or elements of uncertainty. It is at once the chance within the game and the game itself as chance; in the same stroke, both the dice and rules are thrown.'[62]

In a piece entitled 'By Way of Conclusion' ('En guise de conclusion'), Foucault presents two ways of introducing humour to science. On the one hand, there is the 'humour of naiveté', which constantly demands that 'self-evident' matters be explained, in order to expose

---

politics'. Keenan, 'The "Paradox" of Knowledge and Power' (1987), 29. 'In the absence of alternatives to present principles and values governing political struggle, we must continue to appeal to the standards of rationality and justice that are available to us within the specific contexts in which we find ourselves'. Sawicki, *Disciplining Foucault* (1991), 100.

In contrast to early writings (see the sections 'War and Struggle: The Strategic Conception of Power' in Chapter 4 and 'The Microphysics and Macrophysics of Power' in Chapter 5), Foucault now identifies the strategic importance of law. See, for instance, his discussion of the 'Croissant Affair': 'It's a right to have a lawyer – who speaks for you and with you, who lets you be heard and keep your life, your identity, and the force of your refusal. [...] This right is neither a juridical abstraction nor some dreamer's ideal – it's part of our historical reality and shouldn't be wiped away'. Foucault, 1977p, 'Va-t-on extrader Klaus Croissant?', 365; see also Foucault, 1984r, 'Confronting Governments: Human Rights' [2000].

61. 'Political analysis and criticism have in a large measure still to be invented – so too have the strategies which will make it possible to modify the relations of force, to co-ordinate them in such a way that such a modification is possible and can be inscribed in reality. That is to say, the problem is not so much that of defining a political "position" (which is to choose from a pre-existing set of possibilities) but to imagine and to bring into being new schemas of politicisation'. Foucault, 1977i, 'The History of Sexuality' [1980], 190; see Foucault, 1984f, 'Politics and Ethics: An Interview', 375.

62. Foucault, 1970b, 'Theatrum Philosophicum' [1998], 366.

points of resistance and problems. On the other hand, there is the 'humour of betrayal': 'you make some huge declaration, something that stands everything on end, but you do it without any violence; adopting a familiar tone and pretending to live calmly in the house you've lined with explosives, you talk like everybody else'.[63]

In the context of the 'humour of betrayal', critique means playing the game while simultaneously refusing to accept it – by playing the game differently. In this sense, critique represents a search for new and different 'rules' that ultimately change the 'game' itself:

> Thus, one escaped from a domination of truth not by playing a game that was totally different from the game of truth but by playing the same game differently, or playing another game, another hand, with other trump cards. I believe that the same holds true in the order of politics; here one can criticize on the basis, for example, of the consequences of the state of domination caused by an unjustified political situation, but one can only do so by playing a certain game of truth, by showing its consequences, by pointing out that there are other reasonable options, by teaching people what they don't know about their own situation, their working conditions, and their exploitation.[64]

We must play the game because we have no other choice. Yet for the same reason, we make this fact the basis for choosing not to accept the circumstances. The matter resembles Baron Munchhausen's effort to pull himself out of the swamp by his own hair. For Foucault, critique is an ethical choice that creates itself out of nothing and opens room

---

63. Foucault, 1973b, 'En guise de conclusion', 417. Some commentators – like Foucault himself – have pointed to this ironic aspect of his work. Foucault, 1984d, 'What Is Enlightenment?', 40; Dreyfus and Rabinow, 'What Is Maturity? Habermas and Foucault on "What Is Enlightenment?"' (1986), 117; Kusch, *Foucault's Strata and Fields* (1991), 191–2.

64. Foucault, 1984s, 'The Ethics of the Concern for the Self as a Practice of Freedom' [1997], 295–6. This definition of critique calls to mind Marx's words in *Critique of Hegel's 'Philosophy of Right'*: 'Criticism dealing with this situation is criticism in hand-to-hand combat ... It is a question of permitting the Germans not a single moment of illusion or resignation. The burden must be made still more oppressive by adding to it a consciousness of it, and the shame made still more shameful by making it public. Every sphere of German society must be described as the *partie honteuse* of German society, and these petrified conditions must be made to dance by singing to them their own melody. The nation must be taught to be terrified of itself in order to give it courage'. Marx, *Critique of Hegel's 'Philosophy of Right'* (1977), 133–4.

for freedom inasmuch as it does not accept the force of 'necessity' and reveals contingency and arbitrariness in what seems to be universal and suprahistorical. Perhaps the 'rule of the game' that Foucault identified finds its most fitting expression in what he wrote about Pierre Boulez:

> What he expected from thought was precisely that it always enable him to do something different from what he was doing. He demanded that it open up, in the highly regulated very deliberate game that he played, a new space of freedom. One heard some people accuse him of technical gratuitousness, others, of too much theory. But for him the main thing was to conceive of practice strictly in terms of its internal necessities without submitting to any of them as if they were sovereign requirements. What is the role of thought, then, in what one does if it is to be neither a mere savoir-faire nor pure theory? Boulez showed what it is – to supply the strength for breaking the rules with the act that brings them into play.[65]

---

65. Foucault, 1982a, 'Pierre Boulez, Passing through the Screens' [1998], 244; see also Macherey, 'Foucault: Ethics and Subjectivity' (1998), 190–1.

# Bibliography

Although it is extensive, the bibliography makes no claim to be comprehensive. It focuses on works bearing directly on the study at hand; thus, Foucault's early writings and theoretical discussions of literature and art are not included. The arrangement of material follows the four-volume edition of Foucault's shorter texts (*Dits et Ecrits I–IV, 1954–1988*, edited by Daniel Defert and François Ewald, Paris: Gallimard, 1994), that is to say, the order of initial publication. In contrast to that edition, which reproduces only works authorized by Foucault, this bibliography includes unauthorized and unpublished lectures, interviews and so on – also ordered by year of first publication/origin. Among its contents are manuscripts, transcripts and tape recordings assembled in the 1990s in the Foucault Archive located at the Bibliothèque du Saulchoir in Paris (now part of the Institut Mémoires de l'Edition Contemporaine in Caen); the original archive reference number is noted in brackets. While I have kept the original bibliography of the German first edition, this English edition also includes an updated publication list of Foucault's lectures at the Collège de France.

## Works by Michel Foucault

1954a: *Maladie mentale et psychologie*. Paris: PUF. *Mental Illness and Psychology*. Trans. Alan Sheridan. Berkeley: University of California Press, 1987.
1954b: 'Introduction'. L. Binswanger. *Le Rêve et l'Existence*. Paris: Desclée de

Brouwer. 'Dream, Imagination, and Existence'. Trans. Forrest Williams, Ed. Keith Hoeller. *Review of Existential Psychology and Psychiatry* 19/1 (1986): 29–78 [1].

1961: *Folie et déraison: Historie de la folie à l'âge classique*. Paris: Plon. *History of Madness*. Trans. Jonathan Murphy. London: Routledge, 2006.

1963: *Naissance de la clinique: une archéologie du regard médical*. Paris: PUF. *The Birth of the Clinic: An Archaeology of Medical Perception*. Trans. Alan Sheridan. London: Routledge, 2003.

1966a: *Les mots et les choses: une archéologie des sciences humaines*. Paris: Gallimard. *The Order of Things: An Archaeology of the Human Sciences*. New York: Vintage, 1994.

1966b: 'Michel Foucault, "Les Mots et les Choses"'. (Conversation with R. Bellour.) *Les Lettres françaises* 1125 (31 March–6 April). 'The Order of Things'. *Foucault Live (Interviews, 1961–1984)*. Ed. Sylvère Lotringer. New York: Semiotexte, 1996. 13–18 [34].

1966c: 'L'arrière-fable'. *L'Arc* 29: *Jules Verne*. 'Behind the Fable'. *Essential Foucault, Volume 2: Aesthetics, Method, and Epistemology*. Ed. James D. Faubion. New York: New Press, 1998. 137–45 [36].

1966d: 'Entretien avec Madeleine Chapsal'. *La Quinzaine littéraire* 5 (16 May). I, 513–18 [37].

1967: 'Sur les façons d'écrire l'histoire'. (Conversation with R. Bellour.) *Les Lettres françaises* (15–21 June). 'The Discourse of History'. *Foucault Live (Interviews, 1961–1984)*. Ed. Sylvère Lotringer. New York: Semiotexte, 1996. 19–32 [48].

1968a: 'Foucault répond à Sartre'. (Conversation with J.-P. Elkabbach.) *La Quinzaine littéraire* 46 (1–15 March). 'Foucault Responds to Sartre'. *Foucault Live (Interviews, 1961–1984)*. Ed. Sylvère Lotringer. New York: Semiotexte, 1996. 51–6 [55].

1968b: 'Réponse à une question'. *Esprit* 371 (May). 'History, Discourse and Discontinuity'. *Salmagundi* 20: *Psychological Man: Approaches to an Emergent Social Type*. (Summer/Fall 1972): 225–48 [58].

1968c: 'Sur l'archéologie des sciences: Réponse au Cercle d'epistemologie'. *Cahiers pour l'analyse* 9. 'On the Archaeology of the Sciences: Response to the Epistemology Circle'. *Essential Foucault, Volume 2: Aesthetics, Method, and Epistemology*. Ed. James D. Faubion. New York: New Press, 1998. 297–333 [59].

1969a: *L'Archéologie du savoir*. Paris: Gallimard. *Archaeology of Knowledge*. Trans. A.M. Sheridan Smith. London: Routledge, 2002.

1969b: 'Conversazione con Michel Foucault'. (Conversation with P. Caruso from 1967.) Paolo Caruso, *Conversazioni con Lévi-Strauss, Foucault, Lacan*, Milan (Mursia). 'Who Are You, Professor Foucault?' *Religion and Culture*. Ed. Jeremy R. Carrette. Manchester: Manchester University

Press, 1999. 87–103 [50].

1969c: 'Michel Foucault explique son dernier livre'. (Conversation with J.-J. Brochier.) *Magazine littéraire* 28 (April–May). 'The Archaeology of Knowledge'. *Foucault Live (Interviews, 1961–1984)*. Ed. Sylvère Lotringer. New York: Semiotexte, 1996. 57–64 [66].

1969d: 'La naissance d'un monde'. (Conversation with J.-M. Palmier.) *Le Monde* 7558 (3 May). 'The Birth of a World'. *Foucault Live (Interviews, 1961–1984)*. Ed. Sylvère Lotringer. New York: Semiotexte, 1996. 65–7 [68].

1969e: 'Titres et travaux'. (List and description of works on the occasion of candidacy at the Collège de France), Paris. I, 842–6 [71].

1970a: 'Le piège de Vincennes'. (Conversation with P. Loriot.) *Le Nouvel Observateur* 274 (9–15 February). II, 67–73 [78].

1970b: 'Theatrum philosophicum'. (On Gilles Deleuze, *Différence et répétition* and *Logique du sens*.) *Critique* 282. 'Theatrum Philosophicum'. *Essential Foucault, Volume 2: Aesthetics, Method, and Epistemology*. Ed. James D. Faubion. New York: New Press, 1998. 343–67 [80].

1971a: *L'ordre du discours*. (Inaugural address at the Collège de France, 2 December 1970.) Paris: Gallimard. 'The Order of Discourse'. *Untying the Text: A Post-Structuralist Reader*. Ed. Robert Young. London: Routledge and Kegan Paul, 1981. 48–78.

1971b: 'Nietzsche, la généalogie, l'histoire'. *Hommage à Jean Hyppolite*. Paris: PUF. 'Nietzsche, Genealogy, History'. *The Foucault Reader*. Ed. Paul Rabinow. New York: Pantheon, 1984. 76–100 [84].

1971c: 'Entrevista com Michel Foucault'. (Conversation with J.G. Merquior and S.P. Rouanet.) J.G. Merquior and S.P. Rouanet. *O Homen e o Discurso*. Rio de Janeiro: Tempo Brasileiro, 1971. 'Entretien avec Michel Foucault'. II, 157–74 [85].

1971d: 'A Conversation with Michel Foucault'. (Conversation with J.K. Simon.) *Partisan Review* 38/2 (April–June 1971). 192–201 [89].

1971e: 'Je perçois l'intolerable'. (Conversation with G. Armleder.) *Journal de Genève* 170 (24–5 July). II, 203–5 [94].

1971f: 'Par-delà le bien et le mal'. (Discussion with Alain, Frédéric, Jean-François, Jean-Pierre, Phillipe, and Serge, compiled by M.-A. Burnier and P. Graine.) *Actuel* 14. 'Revolutionary Action: "Until Now"'. *Language, Counter-memory, Practice: Selected Essays and Interviews by Michel Foucault*. Ed. Donald F. Bouchard. Ithaca, NY: Cornell University Press, 1977. 218–33 [98].

1971g: 'Le discours de Toul'. *Le Nouvel Observateur* 372 (27 December 1971–2 January 1972). II, 236–8 [99].

1971h: 'La volonté de savoir'. *Annuaire du Collège de France, année 1970–1971*. 'The Will to Knowledge'. *Essential Foucault, Volume 1: Ethics, Subjectivity, and Truth*. Ed. Paul Rabinow. New York: New Press, 1997. 11–16 [101].

1972a: 'Die Große Einsperrung'. (Conversation with N. Meienberg.) *Tages-Anzeiger Magazin* (25 March), 15, 17, 20, and 37. 'Le grand enferment'. II, 296–306 [105].

1972b: 'Les intellectuels et le pouvoir'. (Conversation with G. Deleuze, 4 March 1972.) *L'Arc* 49. 'Intellectuals and Power'. *Language, Counter-memory, Practice: Selected Essays and Interviews by Michel Foucault*. Ed. Donald F. Bouchard. Ithaca, NY: Cornell University Press, 1977. 205–17 [106].

1972c: 'Table ronde'. (Conversation with J.-M. Domenach, J. Donzelot, J. Julliard, P. Meyer, R. Pucheu, P. Thibaud, J.-R. Tréanton and P. Virilio.) *Esprit* 413 (April–May). [Abridged] 'Confining Societies'. *Foucault Live (Interviews, 1961–1984)*. Ed. Sylvère Lotringer. New York: Semiotexte, 1996. 83–94 [107].

1972d: 'Sur la justice populaire: Débat avec les maos'. (Conversation with Gilles and Victor, 5 February 1972.) *Les Temps modernes* 310. 'On Popular Justice: A Discussion with Maoists'. *Power/Knowledge: Selected Interviews and Other Writings 1972–1977*. Ed. Colin Gordon. New York: Pantheon, 1980. 1–36 [108].

1972e: 'I problemi della cultura: Un dibattito Foucault-Preti'. (Conversation with G. Preti.) *Il Bimestre* 22/23 (September/December). 'An Historian of Culture'. *Foucault Live (Interviews, 1961–1984)*. Ed. Sylvère Lotringer. New York: Semiotexte, 1996. 95–104 [109].

1972f: 'Piéger sa propre culture'. (On Gaston Bachelard). *Le Figaro littéraire* 1376 (30 September). II, 382 [111].

1972g: 'Les deux morts de Pompidou'. *Le Nouvel Observateur* 421 (4–10 December). 'Pompidou's Two Deaths'. *Essential Foucault, Volume 3: Power*. Ed. James D. Faubion. New York: New Press, 2000. 418–22 [114].

1972h: 'Théories et institutions pénales'. *Annuaire du Collège de France, année 1971–72*. 'Penal Theories and Institutions'. *Essential Foucault, Volume 1: Ethics, Subjectivity, and Truth*. Ed. Paul Rabinow. New York: New Press, 1997. 17–21 [115].

1972i: 'Medicine et lutte des classes'. (By Foucault and members of 'Groupe d'Information sur la Santé'.) *Nef* 49: 67–73.

1973a: 'Préface'. S. Livrozet, *De la prison à la révolte*. Paris: Mercure de France. II, 394–9 [116].

1973b: 'En guise de conclusion'. *Le Nouvel Observateur* 435 (13–19 March). II, 416–19 [120].

1973c: 'Gefängnisse und Gefängnisrevolten'. (Conversation with B. Morawe.) *Dokumente: Zeitschrift für übernationale Zusammenarbeit* 2. 'Prisons et révoltes dans les prisons'. II, 425–432 [125].

1973d: 'O mundo é um grande hospício'. (Conversation with R.G. Leite.) *Revista Manchete* (16 June). 'Le monde est un grand asile'. II, 433–4 [126].

1973e: 'A propos de l'enfermement pénitentiaire'. (Conversation with A. Krywin and F. Ringelheim.) *Pro Justitia: Revue politique de droit* 3/4 (October). II, 435–45 [127].

1973f: 'Convoqués à la P.J.' (Written with A. Landau and J.Y. Petit.) *Le Nouvel Observateur* 468 (29 October–4 November). 'Summoned to Court'. *Essential Foucault, Volume 1: Ethics, Subjectivity, and Truth.* Ed. James D. Faubion. New York: New Press, 2000. 423–5 [128].

1973g: 'La société punitive'. *Annuaire du Collège de France, année 1972–73.* 'The Punitive Society'. *Essential Foucault, Volume 1: Ethics, Subjectivity, and Truth.* Ed. Paul Rabinow. New York: New Press, 1997. 23–37 [131].

1973h: 'Présentation'. *Moi, Pierre Rivière, ayant égorgé ma mère, ma soeur et mon frère: Un cas de parricide au XIXe siècle.* Paris: Gallimard-Julliard. 'I, Pierre Rivière'. *Foucault Live (Interviews, 1961–1984).* Ed. Sylvère Lotringer. New York: Semiotexte, 1996. 203–6.

1973i: 'Le Pouvoir et la norme'. (Unauthorized transcript of lecture at the Collège de France, 28 March 1973.) Gilles Deleuze and Michel Foucault, *Mélanges: Pouvoir et surface,* n.p. '28 March 1973'. *The Punitive Society: Lectures at the Collège de France, 1972–1973.* Ed. Bernard Harcourt. Trans. Graham Burchell. Basingstoke: Palgrave Macmillan, 2015. 225–47.

1974a: 'Human Nature: Justice versus Power'. (Conversation with N. Chomsky and F. Elders, November 1971.) *Reflexive Water: The Basic Concepts of Mankind.* Ed. Fons Elders. London: Souvenir Press. 133–97 [132].

1974b: 'Michel Foucault on Attica: An Interview'. (Conversation with J. K. Simon.) *Social Justice* 18/3 (1991): 26–34 [137].

1974c: 'A verdad e as formas juridicas'. (Talks and discussions at the University of Rio de Janeiro, 21–5 May 1974). *Cadernos da P.U.C.* 16 (June). 'Truth and Juridical Forms'. *Essential Foucault, Volume 3: Power.* Ed. James D. Faubion. New York: New Press, 2000. 1–89 [139].

1974d: 'Table ronde sur l'expertise psychiatrique'. (Discussion with A. Bompart, L. Cossard, F. Domenach, et al.) *Actes* 5–6 (December 1974–January 1975). 'White Magic and Black Gown (edited version)'. *Foucault Live (Interviews, 1961–1984).* Ed. Sylvère Lotringer. New York: Semiotexte, 1996. 287–91 [142].

1975a: *Surveiller et punir: Naissance de la prison.* Paris: Gallimard. *Discipline and Punish: The Birth of the Prison.* Trans. Alan Sheridan. New York: Vintage, 1995.

1975b: 'La politique est la continuation de la guerre par d'autres moyens'. (Conversation with B.-H. Lévy.) *L'imprévu* 1 (27 January). II, 702–4 [148].

1975c: 'Des supplices aux cellules'. (Conversation with R.-P. Droit.) *Le*

*Monde* 9363 (21 February). 'From Torture to Cellblock'. *Foucault Live (Interviews, 1961–1984)*. Ed. Sylvère Lotringer. New York: Semiotexte, 1996. 146–9 [151].

1975d: 'Sur la sellette'. (Conversation with J.-L. Enzine.) *Les Nouvelles littéraires* 2477 (17–23 March). 'An Interview with Michel Foucault'. *History of the Present* 1 (1985): 2–3, 14 [152].

1975e: 'La mort du père'. (Conversation with P. Daix, P. Gavi, J. Rancière and I. Yannakakis.) *Libération* 421 (30 April). II, 734–9 [155].

1975f: 'Entretien sur la prison: le livre et sa méthode'. (Conversation with J.-J. Brochier.) *Magazine littéraire* 101 (June). 'Prison Talk'. *Power/Knowledge: Selected Interviews and Other Writings 1972–1977*. Ed. Colin Gordon. New York: Pantheon, 1980. 37–54 [156].

1975g: 'Pouvoir et corps'. (Conversation with members of the journal *Quel Corps?*) *Quel corps?* 2 (September/October). 'Body/Power'. *Power/Knowledge: Selected Interviews and Other Writings 1972–1977*. Ed. Colin Gordon. New York: Pantheon, 1980. 55–62 [157].

1975h: 'Radioscopie de Michel Foucault'. (Conversation with J. Chancel, 10 March 1975.) Radio France, Paris (3 October). 'Talk Show'. *Foucault Live (Interviews, 1961–1984)*. Ed. Sylvère Lotringer. New York: Semiotexte, 1996. 133–45 [161].

1976a: *La volonté de savoir: Histoire de la sexualité, tome 1*, Paris: Gallimard. *The History of Sexuality, Volume 1: An Introduction*. Trans. Robert Hurley. New York: Pantheon, 1978.

1976b: 'La politique de la santé au XVIIIème siècle'. *Les machines à guérir: Aux origines de l'hôpital moderne; dossiers et documents*. Paris: L'institut de l'environnement. 'The Politics of Health in the Eighteenth Century'. *Essential Foucault, Volume 3: Power*. Ed. James D. Faubion. New York: New Press, 2000. 90–105 [168].

1976c: 'Questions à Michel Foucault sur la géographie'. *Hérodote* 1 (January–March). 'Questions on Geography'. *Power/Knowledge: Selected Interviews and Other Writings, 1972–1977*. Ed. Colin Gordon. New York: Pantheon, 1980. 63–77 [169].

1976d: 'Crise de un modelo en la medicina'. (First lecture in Rio de Janeiro, October 1974.) *Revista centroamericana de Ciencas de la Salud* 3 (January–April). 'The Crisis of Medicine or the Crisis of Antimedicine?' *Foucault Studies* 1 (2004): 5–19 [170].

1976f: 'Crimes et châtiments en URSS et ailleurs'. *Le Nouvel Observateur* 585 (26 January–1 February). 'The Politics of Soviet Crime'. *Foucault Live (Interviews, 1961–1984)*. Ed. Sylvère Lotringer. New York: Semiotexte, 1996. 190–5 [172].

1976g: 'L'extension sociale de la norme'. (Conversation with P. Weber on Thomas Szasz, *Fabriquer la folie*.) *Politique Hebdo* 212: *Délier la folie*

(4–10 March). 'The Social Extension of the Norm'. *Foucault Live (Interviews, 1961–1984)*. Ed. Sylvère Lotringer. New York: Semiotexte, 1996. 196–9 [173].

1976h: 'Michel Foucault, l'illegalisme et l'art de punir'. (Conversation with G. Tarrab.) *La Presse* 80 (3 April). III, 86–9 [175].

1976i: 'Sorcellerie et folie'. (Conversation with R. Jaccard on Thomas Szasz, *Fabriquer la folie*). *Le Monde* 9720 (23 April). 'Sorcery and Madness'. *Foucault Live (Interviews, 1961–1984)*. Ed. Sylvère Lotringer. New York: Semiotexte, 1996. 200–2 [175].

1976j: 'Des questions de Michel Foucault à Hérodote'. *Hérodote* 3 (July–September). 'Some Questions from Michel Foucault to Hérodote'. *Space, Knowledge and Power: Foucault and Geography*. Ed. Jeremy W. Crampton and Stuart Elden. Aldershot: Ashgate, 2007. 19–20 [178].

1976k: 'Bio-histoire et bio-politique'. (On Jacques Ruffié, *De la biologie à la culture*, Paris: Flammarion, 1976.) *Le Monde* 9869 (17–18 October). 'Bio-history and Bio-politics'. *Foucault Studies* 18 (2014): 128–30 [179].

1976l: 'L'occident le la vérité du sexe'. *Le Monde* 9885 (5 November). 'The West and the Truth of Sex'. *SubStance* 6–7/20 (1978): 5–8 [181].

1976m: 'Il faut défendre la société'. *Annuaire du Collège de France, année 1975–1976*. 'Course Summary'. *'Society Must Be Defended': Lectures at the Collège de France, 1975–1976*. Ed. Mauro Bertani and Alessandro Fontana. Trans. David Macey. New York: Picador, 2003. 265–72 [187].

1976n: 'Conférence sur les mesures alternatives à l'emprisonnement'. (Lecture in Montreal, 15 March 1976.) [D 215]. 'Alternatives to the Prison: Dissemination or Decline of Social Control'. *Theory, Culture & Society* 26/6 (2009): 12–24.

1977a: 'Preface'. Gilles Deleuze and Felix Guattari, *Anti-Oedipus: Capitalism and Schizophrenia*. New York: Viking Press [189].

1977b: 'Sexualität und Wahrheit'. (Preface to German edition of *La Volonté de savoir*.) *Der Wille zum Wissen*, Frankfurt a.M.: Suhrkamp. 7–8.

1977c: 'Préface'. M. Debard and J.L. Hennig. *Les juges kaki*, Paris: A. Moreau. III, 138–40 [191].

1977d: 'Intervista a Michel Foucault'. (Conversation with A. Fontana and P. Pasquino, June 1976.) *Microfisica del Potere: Interventi politici*. Ed. Alessandro Fontana and Pasquale Pasquino. Turin: Einaudi. 'Truth and Power'. *The Foucault Reader*. Ed. Paul Rabinow. New York: Pantheon, 1984. 51–75 [192].

1977e: 'Corso del 7 gennaio 1976'. (Lecture at the Collège de France, 7 January 1976). *Microfisica del Potere: Interventi politici*. Ed. Alessandro Fontana and Pasquale Pasquino. Turin: Einaudi. '7 January 1976'. *'Society Must Be Defended': Lectures at the Collège de France, 1975–1976*. Ed. Mauro Bertani and Alessandro Fontana. Trans. David Macey. New York:

Picador, 2003. 1–21 [193].

1977f: 'Corso del 14 gennaio 1976'. (Lecture at the Collège de France, 14 January 1976.) *Microfisica del Potere: Interventi politici.* Ed. Alessandro Fontana and Pasquale Pasquino. Turin: Einaudi. '14 January 1976'. *'Society Must Be Defended': Lectures at the Collège de France, 1975–1976.* Ed. Mauro Bertani and Alessandro Fontana. Trans. David Macey. New York: Picador, 2003. 23–41 [194].

1977g: 'L'oeil du pouvoir'. (Conversation with J.-P. Barou and M. Perrot.) Jeremy Bentham, *Le Panoptique.* Paris: Belfond. 'The Eye of Power: A Conversation with Jean-Pierre Barou and Michelle Perrot'. *The Impossible Prison: A Foucault Reader.* Nottingham: Nottingham Contemporary, 2008. 8–15 [195].

1977h: 'El nacimiento de la medicina social'. (Second lecture in Rio de Janeiro, October 1974.) *Revista centroamericana de Ciencias de la Salud* 6 (January–April). 'The Birth of Social Medicine'. *Essential Foucault, Volume 3: Power.* Ed. James D. Faubion. New York: New Press, 2000. 134–56 [196].

1977i: 'Les rapports de pouvoir passent à l'interieur des corps'. (Conversation with Lucette Finas.) *La Quinzaine littéraire* 247 (1–15 January). 'The History of Sexuality'. *Power/Knowledge: Selected Interviews and Other Writings 1972–1977.* Ed. Colin Gordon. New York: Pantheon, 1980. 183–93 [197].

1977j: 'La vie des hommes infâmes'. *Les Cahiers du chemin* 29 (15 January). 'Lives of Infamous Men'. *Essential Foucault, Volume 3: Power.* Ed. James D. Faubion. New York: New Press, 2000. 157–75 [198].

1977k: 'Non au sexe roi'. (Conversation with B.-H. Lévy.) *Le Nouvel Observateur* 644 (12–21 March). 'The End of the Monarchy of Sex'. *Foucault Live (Interviews, 1961–1984).* Ed. Sylvère Lotringer. New York: Semiotexte, 1996. 214–25 [200].

1977l: 'La grande colère des faits'. (On André Glucksmann, *Les Maîtres Penseurs,* Paris: Grasset, 1977.) *Le Nouvel Observateur* 652 (9–15 May). III, 277-81 [204].

1977m: 'Le jeu de Michel Foucault'. (Conversation with D. Colas, A. Grosrichard, G. Le Gaufey, J. Livi, G. Miller, et al.) *Ornicar? Bulletin périodique du champ freudien* 10 (July). 'The Confession of the Flesh'. *Power/Knowledge: Selected Interviews and Other Writings 1972–1977.* Ed. Colin Gordon. New York: Pantheon, 1980. 194–228 [206].

1977n: 'Une mobilisation culturelle'. (Conversation on the forum, 'La gauche, l'expérimentation et le changement social'.) *Le Nouvel Observateur* 670 (12–18 September). III, 329–31 [207].

1977o: 'Enfermement, Psychiatrie, Prison'. (Conversation between J.-P. Faye, M. Foucault, D. Cooper, M. Zecca and M.-O. Faye.) *Change* 22–3

(October): *La folie encerclée*. 'Confinement, Psychiatry, Prison'. *Politics, Philosophy, Culture: Interviews and Other Writings 1977–1984*. Ed. Lawrence D. Kritzman. New York and London: Routledge, 1988. 178–210 [209].

1977p: 'Va-t-on extrader Klaus Croissant?' *Le Nouvel Observateur* 679 (14–20 November). III, 361–5 [210].

1977q: 'Désormais la sécurité est au-dessus des lois'. *Le Matin* 225 (18 November). III, 366–8 [211].

1977r: 'El poder, una bestia magnifica'. (Conversation with M. Osorio.) *Quadernos para el dialogo* 238 (November): 19–25. 'Le pouvoir, une bête magnifique'. III, 368–82 [212].

1977s: 'La sécurité et l'Etat'. (Conversation with R. Lefort.) *Tribune socialiste* (24–30 November). III, 383–8 [213].

1977t: 'Lettre à quelques leaders de la gauche'. *Le Nouvel Observateur* 681 (28 November–4 December). 'Letter to Certain Leaders of the Left'. *Essential Foucault, Volume 3: Power*. Ed. James D. Faubion. New York: New Press, 2000. 426–8 [214].

1977u: 'Die Folter, das ist die Vernunft'. (Conversation with K. Boesers.) *Literaturmagazin* 8 (December). 'La torture, c'est la raison'. III, 390–8 [215].

1977v: 'Kenryoku to chi'. (Conversation with S. Hasumi, 13 October 1977.) *Umi* (December). 'Pouvoir et savoir'. III, 399–414 [216].

1977w: 'Pouvoirs et stratégies'. (Conversation with J. Rancière.) *Les Révoltes Logiques* 4 (Winter). 'Power and Strategies'. *Power/Knowledge: Selected Interviews and Other Writings 1972–1977*. Ed. Colin Gordon. New York: Pantheon Books, 1980. 134–45 [218].

1978a: 'Introduction by Michel Foucault'. Georges Canguilhem, *The Normal and the Pathological*. New York: Zone Books, 1991. 7–24 [219].

1978b: 'About the Concept of the "Dangerous Individual" in 19th Century Legal Psychiatry'. *International Journal of Law and Psychiatry* 1 (1978): 1–18 [220].

1978c: 'Dialogue on Power'. (Discussion with students in Los Angeles, May 1975.) *Chez Foucault*. Ed. Simeon Wade. Los Angeles: Circabook. 4–22 [221].

1978d: 'Kyôki to shakai'. (Lecture at the University of Tokyo, October 1970.) M. Foucault and M. Watanabe, *Telsugaku no butai*. Tokio: Asahi- Shuppansha. 'La folie et la société'. III, 477–99 [222].

1978e: 'Eugène Sue que j'aime'. (On E. Sue, *Les mystéres du peuple*, Paris: Régine Deforges, 1978.) *Les Nouvelles littéraires* 2618 (12–19 January). III, 500–3 [224].

1978f: 'Attention: danger'. *Libération* 1286 (22 March). III, 507–8 [228].

1978g: 'Incorporación del hospital en la tecnología moderna'. (Lecture at the University of Rio de Janeiro, October 1974.) *Revista centroamericana de*

*Ciencias de la Salud* 10 (May–August). 'The Incorporation of the Hospital into Modern Technology'. *Space, Knowledge and Power: Foucault and Geography*. Ed. Jeremy W. Crampton and Stuart Elden. Aldershot: Ashgate, 2007. 141–51 [229].

1978h: 'Sei to seiji wo Kataru'. (Conversation with C. Nemoto and M. Watanabe, 27 April 1978). *Asahi Jaanaru* (12 May). 'Sexualité et politique'. III, 522–31 [230].

1978i: 'La société disciplinaire en crise'. (Lecture at the French-Japanese Institute, Kyoto). *Asahi Jaamaru* (12 May). III, 532–4 [231].

1978j: 'Gendai no Kenryoku wo tou'. (Lecture in Tokyo, 27 April 1978.) *Asahi Jaamaru* (2 June). 'La philosophie analytique de la politique'. III, 534–51 [232].

1978k: 'Sei to Kenryoku'. (Lecture and discussion at the University of Tokyo, 20 April 1978). *Gendai-shisô* (July). 'Sexuality and Power'. *Religion and Culture*. Ed. Jeremy R. Carrette. Manchester: Manchester University Press, 1999. 115–30 [233].

1978l: 'Tetsugaku no butai'. (Conversation with M. Watanabe, 22 April 1978.) *Sekai* (July). 'La scène de la philosophie'. III, 571–95 [234].

1978m: 'Sekai-ninshiki no hôhô: Marx-shugi wo dô shimatsu suruka'. (Conversation with R. Yoschimoto, 25 April 1978.) *Umi* (July). 'Méthodologie pour la connaissance du monde: comment se débarraser du marxisme'. III, 595–617 [235].

1978n: 'Precisazioni sul potere: Riposta ad alcuni critici'. (Conversation with P. Pasquino, February 1978.) *Aut-Aut* 167–8 (September– December). 'Clarifications on the Question of Power'. *Foucault Live (Interviews, 1961–1984)*. Ed. Sylvère Lotringer. New York: Semiotexte, 1996. 255–63 [238].

1978o: 'La "governementalità"'. (Lecture at the Collège de France, 1 February 1978.) *Aut-Aut* 167–8 (September–December). 'Governmentality'. *Essential Foucault, Volume 3: Power*. Ed. James D. Faubion. New York: New Press, 2000. 201–22 [239].

1978p: 'Taccuino Persiano: L'esercito, quando la terra trema'. *Corriere della sera* 103/228 (28 September). 'The Army – When the Earth Quakes'. Janet Afary and Kevin B. Anderson, *Foucault and the Iranian Revolution: Gender and the Seductions of Islamism*. Chicago: University of Chicago Press, 2005. 189–94 [241].

1978q: 'M. Foucault: Conversazione senza complessi con il filosofo che analizza le "strutture del potere"'. (Conversation with J. Bauer). *Playmen* 10 (October). 'M. Foucault: Conversation sans complexes avec le philosophe qui analyse les "structures du pouvoir"'. III, 669–78 [242].

1978r: 'La scia ha cento anni di ritardo'. *Corriere della sera* 103/230 (1 October). 'The Shah Is a Hundred Years behind the Times'. Janet Afary and Kevin B. Anderson, *Foucault and the Iranian Revolution: Gender and the Seductions of Islamism*. Chicago: University of Chicago Press, 2005. 194–8 [243].

1978s: 'Téhéran: la fede contro la scia'. *Corriere della sera* 103/237 (8 October). 'Tehran – Faith against the Shah'. Janet Afary and Kevin B. Anderson, *Foucault and the Iranian Revolution: Gender and the Seductions of Islamism*. Chicago: University of Chicago Press, 2005. 198–203 [244].

1978t: 'A quoi rêvent les Iraniens'. *Le Nouvel Observateur* 727 (16–22 October). 'What Are the Iranians Dreaming About?' Janet Afary and Kevin B. Anderson, *Foucault and the Iranian Revolution: Gender and the Seductions of Islamism*. Chicago: University of Chicago Press, 2005. 203–9 [245].

1978u: 'Le citron et le lait'. (On Phillipe Boucher, *Le Ghetto judiciaire*, Paris: Grasset 1978.) *Le Monde* 10490 (21–2 October). 'Lemon and Milk'. *Essential Foucault, Volume 3: Power*. Ed. James D. Faubion. New York: New Press, 2000. 435–8 [246].

1978v: 'Una rivolta con le mani nude'. *Corriere della sera* 103/261 (5 November). 'A Revolt with Bare Hands'. Janet Afary and Kevin B. Anderson, *Foucault and the Iranian Revolution: Gender and the Seductions of Islamism*. Chicago: University of Chicago Press, 2005. 210–13 [248].

1978w: 'I "reportages" di idee'. *Corriere della sera* 103/267 (12 November). '"Les reportages" des idées'. III, 706–7. [250].

1978x: 'Réponse de Michel Foucault à une lectrice iranienne'. *Le Nouvel Observateur* 731 (13–19 November). 'Foucault's Response to Atoussa H.'. Janet Afary and Kevin B. Anderson, *Foucault and the Iranian Revolution: Gender and the Seductions of Islamism*. Chicago: University of Chicago Press, 2005. 210 [251].

1978y: 'Il mitico capo della rivolta dell'Iran'. *Corriere della sera* 103/279 (26 September). 'The Mythical Leader of the Iranian Revolt'. Janet Afary and Kevin B. Anderson, *Foucault and the Iranian Revolution: Gender and the Seductions of Islamism*. Chicago: University of Chicago Press, 2005. 220–3 [253].

1978z: 'Sécurité, territoire et population'. *Annuaire du Collège de France, année 1977–8*. 'Course Summary'. *Security, Territory, Population. Lectures at the Collège de France, 1977–1978*. Ed. Michel Senellart. Trans. Graham Burchell. New York: Palgrave Macmillan 2007. 363–7 [255].

1979a: 'Préface de Michel Foucault'. Peter Brückner and Alfred Krovoza, *Ennemis de l'État*. Claix: La Pensée sauvage. III, 724–5 [256].

1979b: 'La politique de la santé au XVIIIème siècle'. (Expanded version of 1976b.) *Les Machines à guérir: Aux origines de l'hôpital moderne*. Brussels: Pierre Mardaga. 'The Politics of Health in the Eighteenth Century'.

*Foucault Studies* 18 (2014): 113–27 [257].

1979c: 'L'esprit d'un monde sans esprit'. (Conversation with P. Blanchet and C. Brière.) Pierre Blanchet and Claire Brière, *Iran: la révolution au nom de Dieu*. Paris: Seuil. 'Iran: The Spirit of a World without Spirit'. *Politics, Philosophy, Culture: Interviews and Other Writings 1977–1984*. Ed. Lawrence D. Kritzman. New York and London: Routledge, 1988. 211–24 [259].

1979d: 'Manières de justice'. *Le Nouvel Observateur* 743 (5–11 February). III, 755–9 [260].

1979e: 'Una polveriera chiamata Islam'. *Corriere della sera* 104/36 (13 February). 'A Powder Keg Called Islam'. Janet Afary and Kevin B. Anderson, *Foucault and the Iranian Revolution: Gender and the Seductions of Islamism*. Chicago: University of Chicago Press, 2005. 239–41 [261].

1979f: 'La loi de la pudeur'. (Conversation with J. Danet, P. Hahn and G. Hocquenghem, 4 April 1978.) *Recherches: Fous d'enfance* 37. 'Sexual Morality and the Law'. *Politics, Philosophy, Culture: Interviews and Other Writings 1977–1984*. Ed. Lawrence D. Kritzman. New York and London: Routledge, 1988. 271–85 [263].

1979g: 'Lettre ouverte à Mehdi Bazargan'. *Le Nouvel Observateur* 753 (14–20 April). 'Open Letter to Mehdi Bazargan'. *Essential Foucault, Volume 3: Power*. Ed. James D. Faubion. New York: New Press, 2000. 439–42 [265].

1979h: 'Pour une morale de l'inconfort'. (On Jean Daniel, *L'ère des ruptures*, Paris: Grasset, 1979.) *Le Nouvel Observateur* 754 (23–9 April). 'For an Ethics of Discomfort'. *Essential Foucault, Volume 3: Power*. Ed. James D. Faubion. New York: New Press, 2000. 443–8 [266].

1979i: 'Inutile de se soulever?' *Le Monde* 10661 (11–12 May). 'Useless to Revolt?' *Essential Foucault, Volume 3: Power*. Ed. James D. Faubion. New York: New Press, 2000. 449–53 [269].

1979j: 'La stratégie du pourtour'. *Le Nouvel Observateur* 759 (28 May–3 June). 'The Catch-All Strategy'. *International Journal of the Sociology of Law* 16 (1988): 159–62 [270].

1979k: 'Foucault Examines Reason in Service of State Power'. (Conversation with M. Dillon.) *Campus Report* 12/6 (October). Reprinted as 'Conversation with Michel Foucault'. *The Threepenny Review* 1 (1980): 4–5 [272].

1979l: 'Luttes autour des prisons'. (Conversation, under the pseudonym 'Louis Appert', with F. Colcombet and A. Lazarus.) *Esprit* 11 (November): *Toujours les prisons*. III, 806–18 [273].

1979m: 'Naissance de la biopolitique'. *Annuaire du Collège de France, année 1978–9*. 'Course Summary'. *The Birth of Biopolitics: Lectures at the Collège de France 1978–1979*. Ed. Michel Senellart. Trans. Graham Burchell. New York: Palgrave Macmillan, 2008. 317–25 [274].

1979n: 'Discussion at Stanford'. (Tape recording, 11 October 1979.) Foucault Archive [C 9].

1980a: 'La poussière et le nuage'. (Response to an article by J. Léonard.) *L'impossible prison: Recherches sur le système pénitentiaire au XIXème siècle.* Ed. Michelle Perrot. Paris: Seuil. 29-39 [277].

1980b: 'Table ronde du 20 mai 1978'. (Conversation with A. Farge, A. Fontana, J. Léonard, M. Perrot, et al.) *L'impossible prison: Recherches sur le système penitentiaire au XIXème siècle.* Ed. Michelle Perrot. Paris: Seuil. 'Questions of Method'. *The Foucault Effect: Studies in Governmentality.* Ed. Graham Burchell, Colin Gordon and Peter Miller. Hemel Hempstead: Harvester Wheatsheaf, 1991. 73-86 [278].

1980c: 'Postface'. *L'impossible prison: Recherches sur le système penitentiaire au XIXème siècle.* Ed. Michelle Perrot. Paris: Seuil. IV, 35-7 [279].

1980d: 'Conversazione con Michel Foucault'. (Conversation with D. Trombadori, 1978, in Paris.) *Il Contributo* 1 (January–March). *Remarks on Marx: Conversations with Ducio Trombadori.* Trans. R. James Goldstein and James Cascaito. New York: Semiotexte, 1991 [281].

1980e: 'Toujours les prisons'. *Esprit* 1 (January). IV, 96-9 [282].

1980f: 'Le Nouvel Observateur e l'Unione della sinistra'. (Excerpt from a discussion of Jean Daniel, *L'ère des ruptures*, Paris: Grasset 1979.) *Spirali, Giornale internazionale di cultura* 15 (January). 'Le Nouvel Observateur et l'Union de la gauche'. IV, 100-2 [283].

1980g: 'Le philosophe masqué'. (Conversation with C. Delacampagne, February 1980.) *Le Monde* 10945 (6 April). 'The Masked Philosopher'. *Politics, Philosophy, Culture: Interviews and Other Writings 1977-1984.* Ed. Lawrence D. Kritzman. New York and London: Routledge, 1988. 323-30 [285].

1980h: 'Le vrai sexe'. (Complemented French version of the English-language introduction to *Herculine Barbin, Being the Recently Discovered Memoirs of a Nineteenth-Century French Hermaphrodite.* Brighton, Sussex: Harverster Press, 1980. vii-xvii). *Arcadie* 323 (November). IV, 115-23 [287].

1980i: 'Du gouvernement des vivants'. *Annuaire du Collège de France, année 1979-80.* 'Course Summary'. *On the Government of the Living: Lectures at the Collège de France, 1979-1980.* Ed. Michel Senellart. Trans. Graham Burchell. New York: Picador, 2014. 321-5 [289].

1980j: 'Discussion with Philosophers'. (Tape recording of a conversation in Berkeley, California, 23 October 1980.) Foucault Archive [C 16].

1981a: '"Omnes et Singulatim": Towards a Criticism of Political Reason'. (Lecture at Stanford University, 10 and 16 October 1979.) *The Tanner Lectures on Human Values.* Ed. Sterling M. McMurrin. Salt Lake City: University of Utah Press, 1981. 225-54 [291].

1981b: 'De l'amitié comme mode de vie'. (Conversation with R. de Ceccaty, J. Danet and J. Le Bitoux.) *Gai Pied* 25 (April). 'Friendship as a Way of Life'. *Essential Foucault, Volume 1: Ethics, Subjectivity, and Truth*. Ed. Paul Rabinow. New York: New Press, 1997. 135–40 [293].

1981c: 'Sexuality and Solitude'. (Seminar with Richard Sennett at the Institute for the Humanities in New York, 20 November 1980.) *Essential Foucault, Volume 1: Ethics, Subjectivity, and Truth*. Ed. Paul Rabinow. New York: New Press, 1997. 175–84 [295].

1981d: 'Est-il donc important de penser?' (Conversation with D. Eribon.) *Libération* 15 (30–1 May). 'So Is It Important to Think?' *Essential Foucault, Volume 3: Power*. Ed. James D. Faubion. New York: New Press, 2000. 454–8 [296].

1981e: 'As malhas do poder'. (Lecture at the University of Bahia, 1976.) *Barbarie* 4 (Summer 1981) and *Barbarie* 5 (Summer 1982). 'The Meshes of Power'. *Space, Knowledge, Power: Foucault and Geography*. Ed. Jeremy W. Crampton and Stuart Elden. Aldershot: Ashgate Press, 2007. 153–62 [297].

1981f: 'Il faut tout repenser, la loi et la prison'. *Libération* 45 (5 July). IV, 202–4 [298].

1981g: 'Contre les peines de substitution'. *Libération* 108 (18 September). 'Against Replacement Penalties'. *Essential Foucault, Volume 3: Power*. Ed. James D. Faubion. New York: New Press, 2000. 459–61 [300].

1981h: 'Subjectivité et vérité'. *Annuaire du Collège de France, année 1980–1981*. 'Subjectivity and Truth'. *Essential Foucault, Volume 1: Ethics, Subjectivity, and Truth*. Ed. Paul Rabinow. New York: New Press, 1997. 87–92 [304].

1981i: 'Entretien de Louvain avec André Berten'. (Conversation with A. Berten, May.) Typescript, 14 pp. Foucault Archive [D 200].

1982a: 'Pierre Boulez, l'écran traversé'. *Dix ans et après: Album souvenir du festival d'automne*. Ed. Marie Colin, Jean-Pierre Léonardini and Joséphine Markovits. Paris: Messidor. 'Pierre Boulez, Passing through the Screens'. *Essential Foucault, Volume 2: Aesthetics, Method, and Epistemology*. Ed. James D. Faubion. New York: New Press, 1998. 241–4 [305].

1982b: 'The Subject and Power' (Afterword). Hubert Dreyfus and Paul Rabinow, *Michel Foucault: Beyond Structuralism and Hermeneutics*, Chicago: University of Chicago Press 1982. 208–26 [306].

1982c: 'Space, Knowledge and Power'. (Conversation with P. Rabinow.) *The Foucault Reader*. Ed. Paul Rabinow. New York: Pantheon, 1984. 239–56 [310].

1982d: 'Entretien avec Michel Foucault'. (Conversation with J.P. Joecker, M. Ouerd and A. Sanzio.) *Masques* 13 (Spring). 'History and Homosexuality'. *Foucault Live (Interviews, 1961–1984)*. Ed. Sylvère Lotringer. New

York: Semiotexte, 1996. 363–70 [311].

1982e: 'Le combat de la chasteté'. *Communications: Sexualités occidentales* 35 (May). 'The Battle for Chastity'. *Essential Foucault, Volume 1: Ethics: Subjectivity and Truth*. Ed. Paul Rabinow. New York: The New Press, 1997. 185–97. [312].

1982f: 'The Social Triumph of the Sexual Will: A Conversation with Michel Foucault'. (Conversation with G. Barbedette, 20 October 1981.) *Christopher Street* 6/4: 36–41 [313].

1982g: 'Des caresses d'hommes considérées comme un art'. (On Sir Kenneth J. Dover, *Homosexualité grecque*, Grenoble: La Pensée sauvage, 1982). *Libération* 323 (1 June). IV, 315–17 [314].

1982h: 'Le terrorisme ici et là'. (Conversation with D. Eribon.) *Libération* 403 (3 September). IV, 318–19 [316].

1982i: 'Sexual Choice, Sexual Act'. (Conversation with J. O'Higgins, March 1982.) *Salmagundi* 58/59 (Fall–Winter). Reprinted in *Foucault Live (Collected Interviews, 1961–1984)*. Ed. Sylvère Lotringer. New York: Semiotexte, 1996. 322–34. [317].

1982j: 'Foucault: non aux compromis'. (Conversation with R. Surzur.) *Gai Pied* 43 (October). IV, 336–7 [318].

1982k: 'Michel Foucault: Vorlesungen zur Analyse der Machtmechanismen 1978'. (Incomplete transcript of 1978 lectures at the Collège de France). In *Der Staub und die Wolke*. Trans. Andreas Pribersky. Bremen: Impuls. 1–44. *Security, Territory, Population: Lectures at the Collège de France, 1977–1978*. Ed. Michel Senellart. Trans. Graham Burchell. New York: Palgrave Macmillan, 2007.

1982l: 'Il n'y pas de neutralité possible'. (Conversation with A. Levy-Willard and D. Eribon.) *Libération* 434 (9 October). IV, 338–40 [319].

1982m: 'En abandonnant les Polonais, nous renonçons à une part de nous-mêmes'. (Conversation with P. Blanchet, B. Kouchner and S. Signoret.) *Le Nouvel Observateur* 935 (9–15 October). IV, 340–3 [320].

1982n: 'Michel Foucault: "L'expérience morale et sociale des Polonais ne peut plus être effacée"'. *Les Nouvelles littéraires* 2857 (14–20. October). 'The Moral and Social Experience of the Poles Can No Longer Be Obliterated'. *Essential Foucault, Volume 3: Power*. Ed. James D. Faubion. New York: New Press, 2000. 465–73 [321].

1982o: 'L'âge d'or de la lettre de cachet'. (Conversation with Y. Hersant and A. Farge.) *L'Express* 1638 (26 November–3 December). IV, 351–2 [322].

1982p: 'L'herméneutique du sujet'. *Annuaire du Collège de France, année 1981–2*. 'Course Summary'. *The Hermeneutics of the Subject: Lectures at the Collège de France, 1981–1982*. Ed. Frédéric Gros. Trans. Graham Burchell. New York: Picador, 2005. 491–505 [323].

1982q: *Le désordre des familles: Lettres de cachet des Archives de la Bastille*. Ed. Arlette Farge and Michel Foucault. Paris: Gallimard. *Disorderly Families: Infamous Letters from the Bastille Archives*. Trans. Thomas Scott-Railton. Minneapolis: University of Minnesota Press, 2016.

1983a: 'Un système fini face à une demande infinie'. (Conversation with R. Bono.) *Sécurité social: l'enjeu*. Paris: Syros. 'The Risks of Security'. *Essential Foucault, Volume 3: Power*. Ed. James D. Faubion. New York: New Press, 2000. 365–81 [325].

1983b: 'On the Genealogy of Ethics: An Overview of Work in Progress'. (Conversation with H. L. Dreyfus and P. Rabinow.) *Michel Foucault: Beyond Structuralism and Hermeneutics*, 2nd edition. Ed. Hubert L. Dreyfus and Paul Rabinow. Chicago: University of Chicago Press (see 1984h). 229–52 [326].

1983c: 'A propos des faiseurs d'histoire'. (Conversation with D. Eribon.) *Libération* 521 (21 January). IV, 412–15 [328].

1983d: 'L'écriture de soi'. *Corps écrit* 5: *L'Autoportrait* (February). 'Self-Writing'. *Essential Foucault, Volume 1: Ethics, Subjectivity, and Truth*. Ed. Paul Rabinow. New York: New Press, 1997. 207–22 [329].

1983e: 'Critical Theory/Intellectual History'. (Conversation with G. Raulet, May 1982.) *Politics, Philosophy, Culture: Interviews and Other Writings 1977–1984*. Ed. Lawrence D. Kritzman. New York and London: Routledge, 1988. 17–46 [330].

1983f: 'La Pologne, et après?' (Conversation with E. Marie.) *Le Débat* 25 (May). IV, 496–522 [334].

1983g: 'Vous êtes dangereux'. *Libération* 639 (10 June). IV, 522–4 [335].

1983h: 'Michel Foucault: An Interview with Stephen Riggins'. (Conversation, 22 June 1982.) *Ethos* 1/2 (Autumn): 4–9. 'An Ethics of Pleasure'. *Foucault Live (Interviews, 1961–1984)*. Ed. Sylvère Lotringer. New York: Semiotexte, 1996. 371–81 [336].

1983i: 'Usage de plaisirs et techniques de soi'. (Draft of the foreword for volumes 2 and 3 of *The History of Sexuality*.) *Le Débat* 27 (November). IV, 539–61 [338].

1983j: 'Discussion'. (Tape recording of a discussion at Berkeley, April 1983). Foucault Archive [C 6].

1983k: 'On the Genealogy of Ethics: An Overview of Work in Progress'. (Conversation with H.L. Dreyfus and P. Rabinow, 15 April 1983.) Typescript, 40 pp. Foucault Archive [D 250(4)].

1983l: 'Discussion with Michel Foucault'. (Conversation with H. L. Dreyfus and P. Rabinow, April 1983.) Typescript, 35 pp. Foucault Archive [D 250 (5)].

1983m: 'Discussion with Michel Foucault'. (Conversation with H. L. Dreyfus, P. Rabinow, C. Taylor, R. Bellah, M. Jay and L. Löwenthal, 21 April 1983.) Typescript, 32 pp. Foucault Archive [D 250 (7)].

1983n: 'A propos de Nietzsche, Habermas, Arendt, McPherson'. (Conversation with P. Rabinow et al.) Typescript, 44 pp. Foucault Archive [D 250 (8)].

1983o: 'Conversation with Foucault'. (Conversation with P. Rabinow.) Typescript, 19 pp. Foucault Archive [D 250 (17)].

1984a: *L'usage des plaisirs: Histoire de la sexualité, tome 2*. Paris: Gallimard. *The History of Sexuality, Volume 2: The Use of Pleasure*. Trans. Robert Hurley. New York: Vintage, 1990.

1984b: *Le souci de soi: Historie de la sexualité, tome 3*. Paris: Gallimard. *The History of Sexuality, Volume 3: The Care of the Self*. Trans. Robert Hurley. New York: Pantheon Books, 1986.

1984c: *Les aveux de la chair: Historie de la sexualité, tome 4*. (Unpublished manuscript.) Foucault Archive. [The manuscript was finally edited by Frédéric Gros and published in 2018 by Gallimard.]

1984d: 'What Is Enlightenment?' *The Foucault Reader*. Ed. Paul Rabinow. New York: Pantheon, 1984. 32–50 [339].

1984e: 'Preface to the History of Sexuality, Vol. II'. (Draft for the foreword to volume 2 of *The History of Sexuality*.) *The Foucault Reader*. Ed. Paul Rabinow. New York: Pantheon. 333–9 [340].

1984f: 'Politics and Ethics: An Interview'. (Conversation with M. Jay, L. Löwenthal, P. Rabinow, R. Rorty and C. Taylor; see 1983m.) *The Foucault Reader*. Ed. Paul Rabinow. New York: Pantheon. 373–80 [341].

1984g: 'Polemics, Politics and Problematizations: An Interview with Michel Foucault'. (Conversation with P. Rabinow, May 1984.) *The Foucault Reader*. Ed. Paul Rabinow. New York: Pantheon, 1984. 381–90 [342].

1984h: 'A propos de la généalogie de l'éthique: un aperçu du travail en cours'. (Slightly abbreviated version of the conversation between M. Foucault, H. L. Dreyfus and P. Rabinow, see 1983b. *Michel Foucault: un parcours philosophique*. Ed. Hubert L. Dreyfus and Paul Rabinow. Paris: Gallimard [344].

1984i: 'Foucault'. (Encyclopedia article written by François Ewald and Michel Foucault under the pseudonym Maurice Florence.) *Dictionnaire des philosophes*. Ed. Denis Huisman. Paris: PUF. '"Foucault" by Maurice Florence'. *Essential Foucault, Volume 2: Aesthetics, Method, and Epistemology*. Ed. James D. Faubion. New York: New Press, 1998. 459–63 [345].

1984j: 'Qu'appelle-t-on punir?' (Conversation with F. Ringelheim, December 1983.) *Revue de l'université de Bruxelles: Punir, mon beau souci. Pour une raison pénale* n° 1–3. 'What Is Called "Punishing"?' *Essential Foucault, Volume 3: Power*. Ed. James D. Faubion. New York: New Press, 2000. 382–93 [346].

1984k: 'Le souci de la vérité'. *Le Nouvel Observateur* 1006 (February). IV, 646–9 [347].

1984l: 'Le style de l'histoire'. (Conversation with A. Farge, F. Dumont and J.-P.

Iommi-Amunategui.) *Le Matin* 2168 (21 February). IV, 649–55 [348].

1984m: 'Interview met Michel Foucault'. (Conversation with J. François and J. de Witt, 22 May 1981.) *Krisis, Tijdschrift voor filosofie*, March 1984. 'Michel Foucault Interview with Jean François and John De Wit'. *Wrong-Doing, Truth-Telling: The Function of Avowal in Justice*. Trans. Stephen W. Sawyer. Chicago: University of Chicago Press, 2014. 253–70 [349].

1984n: 'Le souci de la vérité'. (Conversation with F. Ewald.) *Magazine littéraire* 207 (May). 'The Concern for Truth'. *Politics, Philosophy, Culture: Interviews and Other Writings 1977–84*. Ed. Lawrence D. Kritzman. New York and London: Routledge, 1988. 255–67 [350].

1984o: 'Qu'est-ce que les Lumières?' (Excerpt from the lecture on 5 January 1983 at the Collège de France.) *Magazine littéraire* 207 (May). 'The Art of Telling the Truth'. *Critique and Power: Recasting the Foucault/Habermas Debate*. Ed. Michael Kelly. Cambridge, MA: MIT Press, 1994. 139–48 [351].

1984p: 'Interview de Michel Foucault'. (Conversation with C. Baker, April 1984.) *Actes: cahiers d'action juridique* 45–6 (June). 'Interview with *Actes*'. *Essential Foucault, Volume 3: Power*. Ed. James D. Faubion. New York: New Press, 2000. 394–402 [353].

1984q: 'Le retour de la morale'. (Conversation with G. Barbadette and A. Scala, 29 May 1984) *Les Nouvelles littéraires* 2937 (28 June–5 July). 'The Return of Morality'. *Politics, Philosophy, Culture: Interviews and Other Writings 1977–1984*. Ed. Lawrence D. Kritzman. New York and London: Routledge, 1988. 242–54 [354].

1984r: 'Face aux gouvernements, les droits de l'homme'. (Press release, June 1981, for the defence of Vietnamese boat people.) *Libération* 967 (30 June–1 July). 'Confronting Governments: Human Rights'. *Essential Foucault, Volume 3: Power*. Ed. James D. Faubion. New York: New Press, 2000. 474–5 [355].

1984s: 'L'éthique du souci de soi comme practique de liberté'. (Conversation with H. Becker, R. Fornet-Betancourt and A. Gomez-Müller, 20 January 1984.) *Concordia, Revista Internacional de Filisofia* 6 (July–December). 'The Ethics of the Concern for the Self as a Practice of Freedom'. *Essential Foucault, Volume 1: Ethics, Subjectivity, and Truth*. Ed. Paul Rabinow. New York: New Press, 1997. 281–301 [356].

1984t: 'Une esthétique de l'existence'. (Conversation with A. Fontana). *Le Monde* (15–16 July). 'An Aesthetics of Existence'. *Politics, Philosophy, Culture: Interviews and Other Writings 1977–1984*. Ed. Lawrence D. Kritzman. New York and London: Routledge, 1988. 47–53 [357].

1984u: 'Michel Foucault, an Interview: Sex, Power and the Politics of Identity'. (Conversation with B. Gallagher and A. Wilson, June 1982, Toronto.) *The Advocate* 400 (7 August). 'Sex, Power, and the Politics of

Identity'. *Essential Foucault, Volume 1: Ethics, Subjectivity, and Truth*. Ed. Paul Rabinow. New York: New Press, 1997. 163–73 [358].

1984v: 'L'intellectuel et les pouvoirs'. (Conversation with C. Panier and P. Watté, 14 May 1981.) *La Revue nouvelle: Juger ... de quel droit?* 10 (October). 'Michel Foucault Interview with Christian Panier and Pierre Watté'. *Wrong-Doing, Truth-Telling: The Function of Avowal in Justice*. Trans. Stephen W. Sawyer. Chicago: University of Chicago Press, 2014. 247–52 [359].

1984w: 'La phobie d'État'. (Excerpt from lecture at the Collège de France, 31 January 1979.) *Libération* 967 (30 June–1 July): 21. *The Birth of Biopolitics: Lectures at the Collège de France, 1978–1979*. Ed. Michel Senellart. Trans. Graham Burchell. Basingstoke: Palgrave Macmillan, 2008. 75–100.

1984x: 'Du pouvoir'. (Conversation with P. Boncenne from 1978.) *L'Express* 1722 (6–12 July): 56–68. 'On Power'. *Politics, Philosophy, Culture: Interviews and Other Writings 1977–1984*. Ed. Lawrence D. Kritzman. New York and London: Routledge, 1988. 96–109.

1985a: 'La vie: l'expérience et la science'. (Slightly modified version of 1978a.) *Revue métaphysique et de morale: Canguilhem* 1 (January–March). 'Life: Experience and Science'. *Essential Foucault, Volume 2: Aesthetics, Method, and Epistemology*. Ed. James D. Faubion. New York: New Press, 1998. 465–78 [361].

1985b: 'Discourse and Truth: The Problematization of Parrhesia'. (Transcript of six lectures at the University of California, Berkeley, October and November 1983.) *Discourse and Truth*. Ed. Joseph Pearson. Evanson: Northwestern University Press.

1985c: 'Michel Foucaults Hermeneutik des Subjekts'. (Partial transcript of 1982 lectures at Collège de France.) *Michel Foucault, Freiheit und Selbstsorge*. Ed. Helmut Becker and Lothar Wolfstetter. Frankfurt a.M.: Materialis. *The Hermeneutics of the Subject: Lectures at the Collège de France, 1981–1982*. Ed. Frédéric Gros. Trans. Graham Burchell. New York: Picador, 2005.

1986: *Vom Licht des Krieges zur Geburt der Geschichte*. (Transcript of lectures at the Collège de France, 21 and 28 January 1976.) Trans. Walter Seitter. Berlin: Merve. '21 January 1976' and '28 January 1976'. *'Society Must Be Defended': Lectures at the Collège de France, 1975–1976*. Ed. Mauro Bertani and Alessandro Fontana. Trans. David Macey. New York: Picador, 2003. 43–85.

1988a: 'Truth, Power, Self: An Interview with Michel Foucault'. (Conversation with R. Martin, 25 October 1982.) *Technologies of the Self: A Seminar with Michel Foucault*. Ed. Luther H. Martin, Huck Gutman and Patrick H. Hutton. Amherst: University of Massachusetts Press. 9–15 [362].

1988b: 'Technologies of the Self'. (Seminar with Michel Foucault at the

University of Vermont, October 1982.) *Technologies of the Self: A Seminar with Michel Foucault*. Ed. Luther H. Martin, Huck Gutman and Patrick H. Hutton. Amherst: University of Massachusetts Press. 16–49 [363].

1988c: 'The Political Technology of Individuals'. *Technologies of the Self: A Seminar with Michel Foucault*. Ed. Luther H. Martin, Huck Gutman and Patrick H. Hutton. Amherst: University of Massachusetts Press. 145–62 [364].

1988d: 'Power, Moral Values, and the Intellectual'. (Conversation with M. Bess, 3 November 1980, San Francisco.) *History of the Present* 4 (Spring): 1–2, 11–13.

1988e: 'Das Wahrsprechen des Anderen'. (Two lectures at the Collège de France, 1984.) *Das Wahrsprechen des Anderen*. Ed. Ulrike Reuter. Frankfurt a.M.: Materialis, 1988. 15–42. *The Courage of Truth: Lectures at the Collège de France, 1983-1984*. Ed. Frédéric Gros. Trans. Graham Burchell. New York: Picador, 2011.

1988f: 'Le Gai Savoir II'. (Conversation with J. Le Bitoux, 10 July 1978.) *Mec Magazine* 6/7: 30–3. 'The Gay Science'. *Critical Inquiry* 37/3 (2011): 385–403.

1990a: *Difendere la Società: Dalla guerra delle razze al razzismo di Stato*. (Transcript of 1976 lectures at the Collège de France.) Trans. Mauro Bertani and Alessandro Fontana. Florence: Ponte alle Grazie. *'Society Must Be Defended': Lectures at the Collège de France, 1975-1976*. Ed. Mauro Bertani and Alessandro Fontana. Trans. David Macey. New York: Picador 2003.

1990b: 'Qu'est-ce que la critique? Critique et Aufklärung'. (Lecture and discussion at the Société française de philosophie, 27 May 1978.) *Bulletin de la Société française de philosophie* 2 (April–June). 'What Is Critique?' *The Politics of Truth*. Ed. Sylvère Lotringer. Los Angeles: Semiotexte, 2007. 41–82.

1991: 'Faire vivre et laisser mourir: La naissance du racisme'. (Lecture excerpt, Collège de France, 17 March 1976.) *Les Temps modernes*, 535, February. *'Society Must Be Defended': Lectures at the Collège de France, 1975-1976*. Ed. Mauro Bertani and Alessandro Fontana. Trans. David Macey. New York: Picador 2003. 239–64.

1992: 'La population'. (Transcript of lecture at the Collège de France, 25 January 1978, made by Stéphane Olivesi.) *Mémoire de DEA de philosophie sous la direction de Monsieur P. Macherey, Université de Paris I, Année 1991-2*. Foucault Archive [A 271].

1993: 'About the Beginning of the Hermeneutics of the Self'. (Transcript of two lectures at Dartmouth, 17 and 24 November 1980.) *Political Theory* 21/2 (May): 198–227.

1997: Il faut Defendre la Société. Cours au Collége de France. 1976. Paris:

Seuil/Gallimard, 1997. *'Society Must Be Defended': Lectures at the Collège de France, 1975–1976.* Ed. Mauro Bertani and Alessandro Fontana. Trans. David Macey. New York: Picador, 2003 [see also 1990a].

### Foucault's Lectures at the Collège de France Published since 1997

1999: [*Les Anormaux: Cours au Collège de France 1974–1975.* Paris: Seuil, 1999.] *Abnormal: Lectures at the Collège de France, 1974–1975.* Ed. Valerio Marchetti and Antonella Salomoni. Trans. Graham Burchell. London: Verso, 2003.

2001: [*L'Herméneutique du sujet: Cours au Collège de France 1981–1982.* Paris: Seuil, 2001.] *The Hermeneutics of the Subject: Lectures at the Collège de France, 1981–1982.* Ed. Frédéric Gros. Trans. Graham Burchell. New York: Picador, 2005.

2003: [*Le Pouvoir psychiatrique: Cours au Collège de France 1973–1974.* Paris: Seuil, 2003.] *Psychiatric Power: Lectures at the Collège de France, 1973–1974.* Ed. Jacques Lagrange. Trans. Graham Burchell. New York: Picador, 2006.

2004a: [*Sécurité, Territoire, Population: Cours au Collège de France 1977–1978.* Paris: Seuil, 2004.] *Security, Territory, Population: Lectures at the Collège de France, 1977–1978.* Ed. Michel Senellart. Trans. Graham Burchell. Basingstoke: Palgrave Macmillan, 2007.

2004b: [*La Naissance de la Biopolitique: Cours au Collège de France 1978–1979.* Paris: Seuil, 2004.] *The Birth of Biopolitics: Lectures at the Collège de France, 1978–1979.* Ed. Michel Senellart. Trans. Graham Burchell. Basingstoke: Palgrave Macmillan, 2008.

2008: [*Le Gouvernement de soi et des autres: Cours au Collège de France 1982–1983.* Paris: Seuil, 2008.] *The Government of Self and Others: Lectures at the Collège de France, 1982–1983.* Ed. Frédéric Gros. Trans. Graham Burchell. New York: Picador, 2010.

2009: [*Le Courage de la vérité: Le Gouvernement de soi et des autres II, Cours au Collège de France, 1983–1984.* Paris: Seuil, 2009.] *The Courage of Truth: The Government of Self and Others II, Lectures at the Collège de France, 1983–1984.* Ed. Frédéric Gros. Trans. Graham Burchell. New York: Picador, 2011.

2011: [*Leçons sur la volonté de savoir: Cours au Collège de France 1970–1971. Suivi de Le savoir d'oedipe.* Paris: Seuil, 2011.] *Lectures on the Will to Know: Lectures at the Collège de France, 1970–1971.* Ed. Daniel Defert. Trans. Graham Burchell. Basingstoke: Palgrave Macmillan, 2013.

2012: [*Du Gouvernement des vivants: Cours au Collège de France 1979–1980.* Paris: Seuil, 2012.] *On the Government of the Living: Lectures at the Collège de France, 1979–1980.* Ed. Michel Senellart. Trans. Graham Burchell. New York: Picador, 2014.

2013: [*La Société punitive: Cours au Collège de France, 1972–1973*. Paris: Seuil, 2013.] *The Punitive Society: Lectures at the Collège de France 1972–1973*. Ed. Bernard Harcourt. Trans. Graham Burchell. Basingstoke: Palgrave Macmillan, 2015.

2014: [*Subjectivité et vérité: Cours au Collège de France 1980–1981*. Paris: Seuil, 2014.] *Subjectivity and Truth: Lectures at the Collège de France, 1980–1981*. Ed. Frédéric Gros. Trans. Graham Burchell. Basingstoke: Palgrave Macmillan, 2017.

## Other Works

Adorno, Francesco Paolo 1996: *Le style du philosophe: Foucault et le dire-vrai*. Paris: Kimé.

Allen, Barry 1991: 'Government in Foucault'. *Canadian Journal of Philosophy* 21/4: 421–40.

Althusser, Louis 1993: 'Spinoza – Machiavel'. *Lignes, Art – littérature – philosophie – politique* 1 (January): 71–119.

Althusser, Louis 2001: 'Ideology and Ideological State Apparatuses (Notes Towards an Investigation)'. *Lenin and Philosophy and Other Essays*. Trans. Ben Brewster. New York: Monthly Review Press. 127–86 [Orig. 1971].

Althusser, Louis 2006: *For Marx*. Trans. Ben Brewster. London: Verso [Orig. 1965].

Althusser, Louis et al. 2009: *Reading Capital*. Trans. Ben Brewster. London: Verso [Orig. 1965].

Althusser, Louis 2014: *On the Reproduction of Capitalism: Ideology and Ideological State Apparatuses*. Trans. G. Michael Goshgarian. London: Verso [Orig. 1995].

Balibar, Etienne 1992: 'Foucault and Marx: The Question of Nominalism'. *Michel Foucault, Philosopher*. Trans. Timothy J. Armstrong. Hemel Hempstead: Harvester Wheatsheaf. 38–56 [Orig. 1989].

Ball, Stephen J. (ed.) 1990: *Foucault and Education: Disciplines and Knowledge*. London and New York: Routledge.

Barrett, Michèle 1991: *The Politics of Truth: From Marx to Foucault*. Oxford: Polity.

Barrett-Kriegel, Blandine 1992: 'Michel Foucault and the Police State'. *Michel Foucault, Philosopher*. Trans. Timothy J. Armstrong. Hemel Hempstead: Harvester Wheatsheaf. 192–7.

Barry, Andrew, Thomas Osborne and Nikolas Rose (eds) 1996: *Foucault and Political Reason: Liberalism, Neo-liberalism and Rationalities of Government*. London: UCL Press.

Barthes, Roland 1989: *Mythologies*. New York: The Noonday Press [Orig. 1957].

Bellour, Raymond 1992: 'Towards Fiction'. *Michel Foucault, Philosopher*. Trans. Timothy J. Armstrong. Hemel Hempstead: Harvester Wheatsheaf. 148–55 [Orig. 1989].

Bernauer, James W. 1990: *Michel Foucault's Force of Flight: Toward an Ethics for Thought*. London: Humanities Press International.

Bernauer, James W. 1992: 'Beyond Life and Death: On Foucault's Post-Auschwitz Ethic'. *Michel Foucault, Philosopher*. Trans. Timothy J. Armstrong. Hemel Hempstead: Harvester Wheatsheaf. 260–75 [Orig. 1989].

Bernstein, Richard J. 1989: 'Foucault: Critique as a Philosophical Ethos'. *Zwischenbetrachtungen: Im Prozeß der Aufklärung*. Ed. Axel Honneth. Frankfurt a.M.: Suhrkamp. 395–425.

Bierich, Nora 1994: 'Foucault und Japan'. *Deutsche Zeitschrift für Philosophie* 42/4: 633–42.

Blanchot, Maurice 1989: 'Michel Foucault as I Imagine Him'. *Foucault/Blanchot*. Trans. Jeffrey Mehlman and Brian Massumi. New York: Zone [Orig. 1986].

Blasius, Mark 1992: 'An Ethos of Lesbian and Gay Existence'. *Political Theory* 20/4: 642–71.

Bomio, Giorgio 1986a: 'L'effeto Foucault'. *Actes: les cahiers d'action juridique* 54 (Summer): 30–2.

Bomio, Giorgio 1986b: 'Michel Foucault: Homenaje a un vago y maleante'. *Actes: les cahiers d'action juridique* 54 (Summer): 36–7.

Boswell, John 1980: *Christianity, Social Tolerance, and Homosexuality: Gay People in Western Europe from the Beginning of the Christian Era to the Fourteenth Century*. Chicago and London: University of Chicago Press.

Boullant, François 1986a: 'Michel Foucault à hue et à dia'. *Actes: les cahiers d'actions juridique* 54 (Summer): 50–8.

Boullant, François 1986b: 'Que faire du colloque de la CFDT? (Colloque Foucault, Paris 1985)'. *Actes: les cahiers d'actions juridique* 54 (Summer): 63–7.

Breuer, Stefan 1986: 'Sozialdisziplinierung: Probleme und Problemverlagerungen eines Konzepts bei Max Weber, Gerhard Oestreich und Michel Foucault'. *Soziale Sicherheit und soziale Disziplinierung: Beiträge zu einer historischen Theorie der Sozialpolitik*. Ed. Christoph Sachße and Florian Tennstedt. Frankfurt a.M.: Suhrkamp. 45–69.

Breuer, Stefan 1987: 'Foucaults Theorie der Disziplinargesellschaft: Eine Zwischenbilanz'. *Leviathan* 3: 319–37.

Bröckling, Ulrich, Susanne Krasmann, & Thomas Lemke (eds) 2011: *Governmentality: Current Issues and Future Challenges*, New York/London: Routledge.

Buci-Glucksmann, Christine 1982: 'Formen der Politik und Konzeptionen
    der Macht: Entformalisierung der Politik, Demokratie und Hegemonie'.
    *Argument* 78: 39–63.
Buker, Eloise A. 1990: 'Hidden Desires and Missing Persons: A Feminist
    Deconstruction of Foucault'. *Western Political Quarterly* 43/4: 811–32.
Burchell, Graham 1991: 'Peculiar Interests: Civil Society and "Governing
    the System of Natural Liberty"'. *The Foucault Effect: Studies in Govern-
    mentality*. Ed. Graham Burchell, Colin Gordon and Peter Miller. Hemel
    Hempstead: Harvester Wheatsheaf. 119–50.
Burchell, Graham 1993: 'Liberal Government and Techniques of the Self'.
    *Economy & Society* 22/3: 267–82.
Burchell, Graham, Colin Gordon and Peter Miller (eds) 1991: *The Foucault
    Effect: Studies in Governmentality*. Hemel Hempstead: Harvester Wheatsheaf.
Burke, Peter 1990: *The French Historical Revolution: The Annales School
    1929–89*. Cambridge: Polity.
Burkitt, Ian 1993: 'Overcoming Metaphysics: Elias and Foucault on Power
    and Freedom'. *Philosophy of the Social Sciences* 23/1: 50–72.
Canguilhem, Georges 1967: 'Mort de l'homme ou épuisement du cogito'.
    *Critique* 242.
Canguilhem, Georges 1989: *The Normal and the Pathological*. Trans. C.R.
    Fewcett. New York: Zone Books [Orig. 1966].
Castel, Robert 1973: *Le Psychanalysme*. Paris: Maspéro.
Castel, Robert 1986: 'Les aventures de la pratique'. *Le débat* 41.
Castel, Robert 1988: *The Regulation of Madness: The Origins of Incarcera-
    tion in France*. Trans. W.D. Halls. Berkeley: University of California Press
    [Orig. 1976].
Castel, Robert 1991: 'From Dangerousness to Risk'. *The Foucault Effect:
    Studies in Governmentality*. Ed. Graham Burchell, Colin Gordon and
    Peter Miller. Hemel Hempstead: Harvester Wheatsheaf. 281–98.
Castel, Robert 1994: '"Problematization" as a Mode of Reading History'.
    *Foucault and the Writing of History*. Ed. Jan Goldstein. Oxford: Basil
    Blackwell. 237–52.
Castel, Robert 2003: *From Manual Workers to Wage Laborers: Transforma-
    tion of the Social Question*. Trans. Richard Boyd. Somerset: Transaction
    [Orig. 1995].
Certeau, Michel de 1984: *The Practice of Everyday Life*. Trans. Steven
    Rendall. Berkeley: University of California Press [Orig. 1980].
Certeau, Michel de 1987: *Histoire et psychanalyse entre science et fiction*.
    Paris: Gallimard.
Cohen, David and Richard Saller 1994: 'Foucault on Sexuality in Greco-
    Roman Antiquity'. *Foucault and the Writing of History*. Ed. Jan Goldstein.
    Oxford: Basil Blackwell. 35–59.

Connolly, William E. 1985: 'Taylor, Foucault, and Otherness'. *Political Theory* 13/3: 365–76.

Daraki, Maria 1985: 'Le voyage en Grèce de Michel Foucault'. *Esprit* 100 (April): 55–83.

Dauk, Elke 1989a: *Denken als Ethos und Methode: Foucault lesen*. Berlin: Dietrich Reimer.

Dauk, Elke 1989b: 'Stille Post: Zum Königsweg der Foucaultrezeption'. *Lendemains* 54: 103–9.

Davidson, Arnold I. 1986: 'Archaeology, Genealogy, Ethics'. *Foucault: A Critical Reader*. Ed. David C. Hoy. Oxford: Basil Blackwell. 221–33.

Davidson, Arnold I. 1994: 'Ethics as Ascetics: Foucault, the History of Ethics, and Ancient Thought'. *Foucault and the Writing of History*. Ed. Jan Goldstein. Oxford: Basil Blackwell. 63–80.

Dean, Mitchell 1991: *The Constitution of Poverty: Toward a Genealogy of Liberal Government*. London and New York: Routledge.

Dean, Mitchell 1992: 'A Genealogy of the Government of Poverty'. *Economy & Society* 23/3: 215–51.

Dean, Mitchell 1994: *Critical and Effective Histories: Foucault's Methods and Historical Sociology*. London and New York: Routledge.

Defert, Daniel 1991: '"Popular Life" and Insurance Technology'. *The Foucault Effect: Studies in Governmentality*. Ed. Graham Burchell, Colin Gordon and Peter Miller. Hemel Hempstead: Harvester Wheatsheaf. 211–33.

Defert, Daniel and Jacques Donzelot 1976: 'La charnière des prisons'. *Magazine littéraire* 112–13 (May): 33–5.

Deleuze, Gilles 1986a: 'Die Geschichte einer Freundschaft'. (Conversation with R. Maggiori.) *Die Tageszeitung* (14 October 1986): 18–19.

Deleuze, Gilles 1986b: 'Foucault and the Prison: An Interview with Gilles Deleuze'. *History of the Present* 2 (Spring): 1–2, 20–1.

Deleuze, Gilles 1988: *Foucault*. Trans. Seán Hand. Minneapolis: University of Minnesota Press [Orig. 1986].

Deleuze, Gilles 1992: 'What Is a Dispositive?' *Michel Foucault, Philosopher*. Trans. Timothy J. Armstrong. Hemel Hempstead: Harvester Wheatsheaf. 159–66 [Orig. 1989].

Deleuze, Gilles 1994: 'Désir et plaisir'. *Magazine littéraire* 325 (October): 59–65.

Deleuze, Gilles 1995a: 'A Portrait of Foucault'. *Negotiations, 1972–1990*. Trans. Martin Joughin. New York: Columbia University Press. 102–18 [Orig. 1990].

Deleuze, Gilles 1995b: 'Control and Becoming'. *Negotiations, 1972–1990*. Trans. Martin Joughin. New York: Columbia University Press. 169–76 [Orig. 1990].

Deleuze, Gilles 1995c: 'Life as Work of Art'. *Negotiations, 1972–1990*. Trans.

Martin Joughin. New York: Columbia University Press. 94–101 [Orig. 1986].

Deleuze, Gilles 1998: 'How Do We Recognize Structuralism?' *The Two-fold Thought of Deleuze and Guattari: Intersections and Animations.* Ed. Charles J. Stivale, Trans. Melissa McMahon and Charles J. Stivale. New York: Guilford. 251–82 [Orig. 1973].

Deleuze, Gilles 2008: 'Postscript on the Societies of Control'. *The Impossible Prison: A Foucault Reader.* Nottingham: Ed. Daniel Defert, Trans. Martin Joughin. Nottingham Contemporary. 28–31 [Orig. 1990].

Deleuze, Gilles and Félix Guattari 1977: *Anti-Oedipus: Capitalism and Schizophrenia.* Trans. Robert Hurley. New York: The Viking Press [Orig. 1972].

Demirović, Alex 1995: 'Wahrheitspolitik: Zum Problem der Geschichte der Philosophie'. *Flaschenpost und Postkarte: Korrespondenzen zwischen kritischer Theorie und Poststrukturalismus.* Ed. Sigrid Weigel. Cologne, Weimar and Vienna: Böhlau. 91–116.

Descombes, Vincent 1980: *Modern French Philosophy.* Trans. Lorna Scott-Fox. New York: Cambridge University Press [Orig. 1979].

Diamond, Irene and Lee Quinby (eds) 1988: *Feminism and Foucault: Reflections on Resistance.* Boston: Northeastern University Press.

Dinges, Martin 1994: 'The Reception of Michel Foucault's Ideas on Social Discipline, Mental Asylums, Hospitals and the Medical Profession in German Historiography'. *Reassessing Foucault: Power, Medicine and the Body.* Ed. Colin Jones and Roy Porter. London and New York: Routledge. 181–212.

Donnelly, Michael 1992: 'On Foucault's Uses of the Notion "Biopower"'. *Michel Foucault, Philosopher.* Trans. Timothy J. Armstrong. Hemel Hempstead: Harvester Wheatsheaf. 199–203 [Orig. 1989].

Donzelot, Jacques 1978: 'La misère de la culture politique'. *Critique* 373/374 (June–July). 572–86.

Donzelot, Jacques 1979: *The Policing of Families.* Trans. Robert Hurley. New York: Pantheon [Orig. 1977].

Donzelot, Jacques 1982: 'The Mobilization of Society'. *The Foucault Effect: Studies in Governmentality.* Ed. Graham Burchell, Colin Gordon and Peter Miller. Hemel Hempstead: Harvester Wheatsheaf, 1991. 169–79.

Donzelot, Jacques 1984: *L'invention du social: Essai sur le déclin des passions politiques.* Paris: Seuil.

Donzelot, Jacques 1986: 'Les mésaventures de la théorie: A propos de "Surveillir et punir" de Michel Foucault'. *Le débat* 41/4. 52–62.

Donzelot, Jacques 1991: 'Pleasure in Work'. *The Foucault Effect: Studies in Governmentality.* Ed. Graham Burchell, Colin Gordon and Peter Miller. Hemel Hempstead: Harvester Wheatsheaf. 251–80 [Orig. 1980].

Donzelot, Jacques 1995: 'Wiederkehr des Sozialen – Von der passiven Sicherheit zuraktiven Solidarität'. Trans. Mathias Richter. *Tüte: Wissen und Macht. Die Krise des Regierens.* Tübingen. 54–9.

Donzelot, Jacques 1996: 'L'avenir du social'. *Esprit* 219 (March): 58–81.

Dosse, François 1997a: *History of Structuralism, Volume 1: The Rising Sign, 1945–1966.* Trans. Deborah Glassman. Minneapolis: University of Minnesota Press [Orig. 1991].

Dosse, François 1997b: *History of Structuralism, Volume 2: The Sign Sets, 1967–present.* Trans. Deborah Glassman. Minneapolis: University of Minnesota Press [Orig. 1992].

Dotzler, Bernhard and J. Villinger 1986: 'Zwei Kapitel für sich: Notizen zu Habermas' Foucault-Kritik'. *kultuRRevolution* 11: 67–9.

Dover, Kenneth J. 1978: *Greek Homosexuality.* London: Gerald Duckworth.

Dreyfus, Hubert L. and Paul Rabinow 1982: *Michel Foucault: Beyond Structuralism and Hermeneutics,* 2nd edition. Chicago: University of Chicago Press.

Dreyfus, Hubert L. and Paul Rabinow 1983: 'What Is Maturity? Habermas and Foucault on "What Is Enlightenment?"' *Foucault: A Critical Reader.* Ed. David C. Hoy. Oxford: Basil Blackwell, 109–22.

Engler, Wolfgang 1990: 'Macht, Wissen und Freiheit: Was Foucaults dreifacher Bruch mit der Ideengeschichte zu sagen hat'. *Deutsche Zeitschrift für Philosophie* 10: 874–86.

Erdmann, Eva, Rainer Forst and Axel Honneth (eds) 1990: *Ethos der Moderne: Foucaults Kritik der Aufklärung.* Frankfurt a.M. and New York: Campus.

Eribon, Didier 1991: *Michel Foucault.* Trans. Betsy Wing. Cambridge, MA: MIT Press [Orig. 1989].

Eribon, Didier 1994a: *Michel Foucault et ses contemporains.* Paris: Fayard.

Eribon, Didier 1994b: '… quelque fragment d'autobiographie'. *Michel Foucault: Les jeux de vérité et du pouvoir.* Ed. Alain Brossat. Nancy: Presses universitaires de Nancy. 127–31.

Eßbach, Wolfgang 1984: 'Michel Foucault und die deutsche Linke'. *Links* 174 (September): 28–9.

Eßbach, Wolfgang 1989: 'Zum Eigensinn deutscher Foucault-Rezeption'. *Spuren* 26/27 (February/March): 40–4.

Ewald, François 1975: 'Anatomie et corps politique'. *Critique* 31: 343–70.

Ewald, François 1977: 'Foucault, une pensée sans aveu'. *Magazine littéraire* 127/128 (September): 23–5.

Ewald, François 1986a: *Histoire De L'Etat Providence.* Paris: Grasset.

Ewald, François 1986b: 'Bio-Power'. *History of the Present* 2: 8–9.

Ewald, François 1987: 'Risk, Insurance, Society'. *History of the Present* 3: 1–2, 6–12.

Ewald, François 1989: 'Foucault verdauen'. (Interview with Wilhelm Schmid.) *Spuren* 26/27: 53–6.

Ewald, François 1991a: 'Insurance and Risk'. *The Foucault Effect: Studies in Governmentality.* Ed. Graham Burchell, Colin Gordon and Peter Miller. Hemel Hempstead: Harvester Wheatsheaf. 197–210.

Ewald, François 1992: 'Michel Foucault et la norme'. *Michel Foucault: Lire l'oeuvre.* Ed. Luce Giard. Grenoble: Jérôme Millon. 201–21.

Ferry, Luc and Alain Renaut 1990: *French Philosophy of the Sixties: An Essay on Antihumanism.* Trans. Mary H.S. Cattani. Amherst: University of Massachusetts Press [Orig. 1985].

Feyerabend, Erika 1997: 'Gentests im Vorsorgestaat'. *alaska* 211/212 (April–May): 38–40.

Fink-Eitel, Hinrich 1980: 'Michel Foucaults Analytik der Macht'. *Die Austreibung des Geistes aus den Geisteswissenschaften: Programme des Poststrukturalismus.* Ed. Friedrich A. Kittler. Paderborn: Schöningh. 38–78.

Fink-Eitel, Hinrich 1989: *Foucault zur Einführung.* Hamburg: Junius.

Fink-Eitel, Hinrich 1990: 'Zwischen Nietzsche und Heidegger: Michel Foucaults "Sexualität und Wahrheit" im Spiegel neuerer Sekundärliteratur'. *Philosophisches Jahrbuch* 97: 367–90.

Flynn, Thomas R. 1987: 'Foucault as a Parrhesiast: His Last Course at the Collège de France (1984)'. *Philosophy and Social Criticism* 2/3: 213–29.

Flynn, Thomas R. 1989: 'Foucault and the Politics of Postmodernity'. *Noûs* 23: 187–98.

Flynn, Thomas R. 1994: 'Foucault's Mapping of History'. *The Cambridge Compendium to Foucault.* Ed. Gary Gutting. Cambridge: Cambridge University Press. 28–46.

Fontana, Alessandro and Mauro Bertani 2003: 'Situating the Lectures'. *'Society Must be Defended': Lectures at the Collège de France, 1975–1976.* Ed. François Ewald and Alessandro Fontana. New York: Picador. 273–293.

Forst, Rainer 1990: 'Endlichkeit Freiheit Individualität: Die Sorge um das Selbst bei Heidegger und Foucault'. *Ethos der Moderne: Foucaults Kritik der Aufklärung.* Ed. Eva Erdmann, Rainer Forst and Axel Honneth. Frankfurt a.M.: Campus. 146–86.

Frank, Manfred 1992: *What Is Neostructuralism?* Trans. Sabine Wilke and Richard T. Gray. Minneapolis: University of Minnesota Press [Orig. 1983].

Frank, Manfred 1992: 'On Foucault's Concept of Discourse'. *Michel Foucault, Philosopher.* Trans. Timothy J. Armstrong. Hemel Hempstead: Harvester Wheatsheaf. 99–114 [Orig. 1988].

Fraser, Nancy 1981: 'Foucault on Modern Power: Empirical Insights and Normative Confusions'. *Praxis International* 1/3: 272–87.

Fraser, Nancy 1983: 'Foucault's Body-Language: A Post-Humanist Political Rhetoric?' *Samagundi* 61: 55–70.

Fraser, Nancy 1985: 'Michel Foucault: A "Young Conservative"?' *Ethics* 96/1: 165–84.

Gandal, Keith 1986: 'Intellectual Work as a Political Tool: The Example of Michel Foucault'. *History of the Present* 2/6+7: 15–18.

Gandal, Keith and Stephen Kotkin 1985: 'Governing Work and Social Life in the USA and the USSR'. *History of the Present* 1: 4–14.

Gane, Mike and Terry Johnson (eds) 1993: *Foucault's New Domains*. London and New York: Routledge.

Gaudillière, Jean-Paul 1995: 'Sequenzieren, Zählen und Vorhersehen – Praktiken einer Gen-Verwaltung'. *Tüte: Wissen und Macht. Die Krise des Regierens*. Tübingen. 34–9.

Goldstein, Jan (ed.) 1994: *Foucault and the Writing of History*. Oxford: Basil Blackwell.

Gordon, Colin 1979: 'Other Inquisitions'. *I & C* 6: 23–46.

Gordon, Colin 1980: 'Afterword'. *Power/Knowledge: Selected Interviews and Other Writings 1972–1977*. Ed. Colin Gordon. New York: Pantheon Books, 1980. 229–59.

Gordon, Colin 1986a: 'Question, Ethos, Event: Foucault on Kant'. *Economy & Society* 15/1 (February): 71–87.

Gordon, Colin 1986b: 'Foucault en Angleterre'. *Critique* 471/472: 826–39.

Gordon, Colin 1987: 'The Soul of the Citizen: Max Weber and Michel Foucault on Rationality and Government'. *Max Weber: Rationality and Modernity*. Ed. Scott Lash and Sam Whimster. London: Allen and Unwin. 293–316.

Gordon, Colin 1991: 'Governmental Rationality: An Introduction'. *The Foucault Effect: Studies in Governmentality*. Ed. Graham Burchell, Colin Gordon and Peter Miller. Hemel Hempstead: Harvester Wheatsheaf. 1–51.

Gradev, Vladimir 1994: 'Les jeux de la vérité'. *Michel Foucault: Les jeux de la vérité et du pouvoir*. Ed. Alain Brossat. Nancy: Presses universitaires de Nancy. 41–9.

Gramsci, Antonio 1971: *Selections from the Prison Notebooks of Antonio Gramsci*. Ed./Trans. Quintin Hoare and Geoffrey N. Smith. New York: International Publishers.

Gramsci, Antonio 2007: *Prison Notebooks*. Ed./Trans. Joseph A. Buttigieg. New York: Columbia University Press [Orig. 1975].

Grimm, Dieter 1987: *Recht und Staat in der bürgerlichen Gesellschaft*. Frankfurt a.M.: Suhrkamp.

Gros, Frédéric 1996: *Michel Foucault*. Paris: PUF.

Gutting, Gary 1989: *Michel Foucault's Archaeology of Scientific Reason*. Cambridge: Cambridge University Press.

Habermas, Jürgen 1981: 'Modernity versus Postmodernity'. *New German Critique* 22: 3–14.

Habermas, Jürgen 1986: 'Taking Aim at the Heart of the Present'. *Foucault: A Critical Reader*. Ed. and Trans. David C. Hoy. Oxford: Basil Blackwell. 103–8 [Orig. 1984].

Habermas, Jürgen 1990: *The Philosophical Discourse of Modernity: Twelve Lectures*. Trans. Frederick G. Lawrence. Cambridge, MA: MIT Press [Orig. 1985].

Habermas, Jürgen 2014: 'Technology and Science as "Ideology"'. *Toward a Rational Society: Student Protest, Science, and Politics*. Trans. Jeremy J. Shapiro. Oxford: Wiley. 81–122 [Orig. 1968].

Hacking, Ian 1984: *Historical Ontology*. Cambridge, MA: Harvard University Press.

Hacking, Ian 1986: 'The Archaeology of Michel Foucault'. *Foucault: A Critical Reader*. Ed. David C. Hoy. Oxford: Basil Blackwell. 27–40 [Orig. 1981].

Hacking, Ian 1990: *The Taming of Chance*. Cambridge: Cambridge University Press.

Hacking, Ian 1991: 'How Should We Do the History of Statistics?' *The Foucault Effect: Studies in Governmentality*. Ed. Graham Burchell, Colin Gordon and Peter Miller. Hemel Hempstead: Harvester Wheatsheaf. 181–95 [Orig. 1981].

Hackman, William R. 1982: 'The Foucault Conference'. (Conference at the University of Southern California, October 1981.) *Telos* 51: 191–6.

Hadot, Pierre 1981: *Exercices spirituels et philosophie antique*. Paris: Études Augustiniennes.

Hadot, Pierre 1995: 'Reflections on the Idea of the "Cultivation of the Self"'. *Philosophy as a Way of Life*. Trans. Arnold Davidson. Oxford: Blackwell. 206–14 [Orig. 1989].

Haroche, Claudine 1994: 'Le gouvernement des conduites'. *Magazine littéraire* 325 (October): 40–5.

Hegel, Georg W.F. 1967: *Hegel's Philosophy of Right*. Ed. and Trans. Thomas M. Knox. Oxford: Oxford University Press [Orig. 1820].

Hegel, Georg W.F. 2011: *Lectures on the Philosophy of World History*. Oxford: Oxford University Press [Orig. 1837].

Hesse, Heidrun 1986: 'RFA: une réception critique'. *actes: les cahiers d'action juridique* 54 (Summer): 33–5.

Hindess, Barry 1993: 'Liberalism, Socialism and Democracy: Variations on a Governmental Theme'. *Economy & Society* 22/3: 300–13.

Hindess, Barry 1996: *Discourses of Power: From Hobbes to Foucault*. Oxford: Basil Blackwell.

Hirsch, Joachim 1980: *Der Sicherheitsstaat: Das 'Modell Deutschland', seine Krise und die neuen sozialen Bewegungen*. Frankfurt a.M.: EVA.

Hirschman, Albert O. 1977: *The Passions and the Interests: Political Arguments for Capitalism before Its Triumph*. Princeton: Princeton University Press.

Honegger, Claudia (ed.) 1977: *Schrift und Materie der Geschichte: Vorschläge zur systematischen Aneignung historischer Prozesse*. Frankfurt a.M.: Suhrkamp.

Honneth, Axel 1995a: 'Eine Ergänzung zur Diskursethik'. (Conversation with Reinhard Brunner.) *Tüte: Wissen und Macht. Die Krise des Regierens*. Tübingen. 18–21.

Honneth, Axel 1995b: 'Foucault and Adorno: Two Forms of the Critique of Modernity'. *The Fragmented World of the Social: Essays in Social and Political Philosophy*. Ed. Charles W. Wright, Trans. David Roberts. Albany: SUNY. 121–34 [Orig. 1988].

Honneth, Axel 1997a: 'Afterword to the Second German Edition'. *The Critique of Power: Reflective Stages in a Critical Social Theory*. Trans. Kenneth Baynes. Cambridge, MA: MIT Press. xiii–xxxii [Orig. 1990].

Honneth, Axel 1997b: *The Critique of Power: Reflective Stages in a Critical Social Theory*. Trans. Kenneth Baynes. Cambridge, MA: MIT Press [Orig. 1985].

Hooke, Alexander E. 1987: 'The Order of Others: Is Foucault's Antihumanism against Human Action?' *Political Theory* 15/1: 38–60.

Horkheimer, Max and Theodor W. Adorno 2002: *Dialectic of Enlightenment: Philosophical Fragments*. Stanford: Stanford University Press [Orig. 1944].

Horn, David 1986: 'Conference Notes: Effetto Foucault (Milan, 31 May–1 June 1985)'. *History of the Present* 2: 19–20.

Hunt, Alan and Gary Wickham 1994: *Foucault and Law: Towards a Sociology of Law as Governance*. London: Pluto.

Hutton, Patrick H. 1981: 'Die Geschichte der Mentalitäten: Eine andere Landkarte der Kulturgeschichte'. *Vom Umschreiben der Geschichte: Neue historische Perspektiven*. Ed. Ulrich Raulff. Berlin: Wagenbach. 103–31.

Jaeggi, Urs 1970: *Ordnung und Chaos: Strukturalismus als Methode und Mode*. Frankfurt a.M.: Suhrkamp.

Jambet, Christian 1992: 'The Constitution of the Subject and Spiritual Practice'. *Michel Foucault, Philosopher*. Trans. Timothy J. Armstrong. Hemel Hempstead: Harvester Wheatsheaf, 1992. 233–47 [Orig. 1989].

Janicaud, Dominique 1992: 'Rationality, Force and Power: Foucault and Habermas's Criticisms'. *Michel Foucault, Philosopher*. Trans. Timothy J.

Armstrong. Hemel Hempstead: Harvester Wheatsheaf. 283–99 [Orig. 1989].

Jessop, Bob 1985: *Nicos Poulantzas: Marxist Theory and Political Strategy*. New York: St Martin's Press.

Jessop, Bob 1990: 'Poulantzas and Foucault on Power and Strategy'. *State Theory: Putting the Capitalist State in its Place*. Oxford: Basil Blackwell. 220–47.

Judt, Tony 1986: *Marxism and the French Left: Studies in Labour and Politics in France 1830–1981*. Oxford: Clarendon Press.

Kammler, Clemens 1986: *Michel Foucault: Eine kritische Analyse seines Werks*. Bonn: Bouvier.

Kammler, Clemens and Gerhard Plumpe 1987: 'Antikes Ethos und post-moderne Lebenskunst: Michel Foucaults Studien zur Geschichte der Sexualität'. *Philosophische Rundschau* 34: 186–94.

Kant, Immanuel 1991: 'An Answer to the Question: "What Is Enlighten-ment?"' *Political Writings*. Trans. H. B. Nisbet. Cambridge: Cambridge University Press. 54–60 [Orig. 1784].

Kantorowicz, Ernst H. 1957: *The King's Two Bodies: A Study in Medieval Political Theology*. Princeton: Princeton University Press.

Keenan, Tom 1982: 'Foucault on Government'. *Philosophy and Social Crit-icism* 1: 35–40.

Keenan, Tom 1987: 'The "Paradox" of Knowledge and Power: Reading Foucault on a Bias'. *Political Theory* 15/1 (February): 5–37.

Kelly, Michael 1994: 'Foucault, Habermas, and the Self-Referentiality of Cri-tique'. *Critique and Power: Recasting the Foucault/Habermas Debate*. Ed. Michael Kelly. Cambridge, MA: MIT Press. 365–400.

Kim, Eun-Young 1995: *Nobert Elias im Diskurs von Moderne und Postmod-erne: Ein Rekonstruktionsversuch der Eliasschen Theorie im Licht der Diskussion von Foucault und Habermas*. Marburg: Tectum.

Kocyba, Hermann 1988: 'Eine reine Beschreibung diskursiver Ereignisse'. *kultuRRevolution* 17/18: 33–6.

Kögler, Hans Herbert 1990: 'Fröhliche Subjektivität: Historische Ethik und dreifache Ontologie beim späten Foucault'. *Ethos der Moderne: Foucaults Kritik der Aufklärung*. Ed. Eva Erdmann, Rainer Forst and Axel Honneth. Frankfurt a.M.: Campus. 202–26.

Kögler, Hans Herbert 1994: *Michel Foucault*. Stuttgart and Weimar: Metzler.

Kögler, Hans Herbert 1995: 'Der hermeneutische Mangel der Machttheorie: Foucault als Gesellschaftstheoretiker'. *Tüte: Wissen und Macht. Die Krise des Regierens*. Tübingen. 12–17.

Kritzman, Lawrence D. 1988: 'Foucault and the Politics of Experience'. *Michel Foucault: Politics, Philosophy, Culture*. Ed. Lawrence D. Kritzman.

London: Routledge. 9–25.

Kusch, Martin 1991: *Foucault's Strata and Fields: An Investigation into Archaeological and Genealogical Science Studies.* Dordrecht: Kluwer Academic Publishers.

Laclau, Ernesto 1982: 'Diskurs, Hegemonie und Politik: Betrachtungen über die Krise des Marxismus'. *Argument* 78: 6–22.

Larrauri, Maite 1994: 'Vérité et mensonge des jeux de vérité'. *Rue Descartes* 11 (November): 32–49.

Lecourt, Dominique 1972: *Pour une Critique de l'Epistémologie (Bachelard, Canguilhem, Foucault).* Paris: Maspero.

Le Goff, Jacques 1997: 'Foucault et la "nouvelle histoire"'. *Au risque de Foucault.* Ed. Dominique Franche, Sabine Prokhoris and Yves Roussel. Paris: Éditions du Centre Pompidou.

Lemke, Thomas 1995: '"Der Eisberg der Politik": Foucault und das Problem der Regierung'. *kultuRRevolution* 31: 31–41.

Lemke, Thomas 1997: *Eine Kritik der politischen Vernunft: Foucault und die Analyse der modernen Gouvernementalität.* Berlin and Hamburg: Argument.

Lemke, Thomas 2001: 'The Birth of Bio-Politics: Michel Foucault's Lecture at the Collège de France on Neo-Liberal Governmentality'. *Economy & Society* 30/2: 190–207.

Lemke, Thomas 2011a: *Foucault, Governmentality, and Critique.* Boulder, CO/London: Paradigm Publishers.

Lemke, Thomas 2011b: *Biopolitics: An Advanced Introduction.* Trans. Eric F. Trump. New York/London: New York University Press.

Lenoir, Remi (ed.) 1996: *Sociétés and Représentations: Michel Foucault. Surveillir et punir: la prison vingt ans après.* Paris: CREDHESS.

Lévy, René and Harwig Zander 1996: 'Un grand livre: Peine et structure sociale'. *Sociétés and Représentations: Michel Foucault. Surveiller et punir: la prison vingt ans après.* Ed. Remi Lenoir. Paris: CREDHESS. 111–22.

Liebmann-Schaub, Ute 1989: 'Foucault, Alternative Presses, and Alternative Ideology in West Germany: A Report'. *German Studies Review* 12/1 (February): 139–53.

Link, Jürgen 1985: 'Warum Foucault aufhörte, Symbole zu analysieren: Mutmaßungen über "Ideologie" und Interdiskurs'. *Anschlüsse: Versuche nach Foucault.* Ed. Gesa Dane. Tübingen: Diskord. 105–14.

Lloyd, Moya 1993: 'The (F)utility of a Feminist Turn to Foucault'. *Economy & Society* 22/4: 437–60.

Lukes, Steven 1983: 'Macht und Herrschaft bei Weber, Marx, Foucault'. *Krise der Arbeitsgesellschaft: Verhandlungen des 21. Deutschen Soziologentages in Bamberg 1982.* Ed. Joachim Matthes. Frankfurt a.M.: Campus. 106–19.

Macdonell, Diane 1986: *Theories of Discourse: An Introduction*. Oxford: Basil Blackwell.

Macey, David 1993: *The Lives of Michel Foucault*. London: Hutchinson.

Macherey, Pierre 1992: 'Towards a Natural History of Norms'. *Michel Foucault, Philosopher*. Trans. Timothy J. Armstrong. Hemel Hempstead: Harvester Wheatsheaf. 176–91 [Orig. 1989].

Macherey, Pierre 1998: 'Foucault: Ethics and Subjectivity'. *In a Materialist Way*. Trans. Ted Stolze. London: Verso. 96–107 [Orig. 1988].

Magiros, Angelika 1995: *Foucaults Beitrag zur Rassismustheorie*. Hamburg: Argument.

Maier, Hans 1986: *Die ältere deutsche Staats- und Vewaltungslehre*. Munich: dtv.

Malagola, Hervé 1994: 'Foucault en Iran'. *Michel Foucault: Les jeux de la vérité et du pouvoir*. Ed. Alain Brossat. Nancy: Presses universitaires de Nancy. 150–62.

Maler, Henri 1994: 'Foucault et Marx: une confrontation inactuelle?' *Michel Foucault: Les jeux de la vérité et du pouvoir*. Ed. Alain Brossat. Nancy: Presses universitaires de Nancy. 87–100.

Marchetti, Valerio 1997: 'La naissance de la biopolitique'. *Au risque de Foucault*. Ed. Dominique Franche, Sabine Prokhoris and Yves Roussel. Paris: Éditions du Centre Pompidou. 239–48.

Marques, Marcelo (ed.) 1990: *Foucault und die Psychoanalyse*. Tübingen: Diskord.

Marti, Urs 1988: *Michel Foucault*. Munich: Beck.

Martin, Biddy 1982: 'Feminism, Criticism, and Foucault'. *New German Critique* 27: 3–30.

Marx, Karl 1975: 'Letter from Marx to Engels on 25 September 1857'. *Karl Marx and Frederick Engels: Collected Works, Volume 40, Marx and Engels 1856–59*. Trans. Peter and Betty Ross. New York: International Publishers. 186 [Orig. 1913].

Marx, Karl 1976: *Capital: A Critique of Political Economy*. Trans. Ben Fowkes. New York: Penguin [Orig. 1867].

Marx, Karl 1977: *Critique of Hegel's 'Philosophy of Right'*. Trans. and Ed. Joseph O'Malley. Cambridge: Cambridge University Press [Orig. 1843/44].

Marx, Karl 1979: 'The Eighteenth Brumaire of Louis Bonaparte'. *Karl Marx and Frederick Engels: Collected Works, Volume 11, Marx and Engels 1851–53*. Trans. Clemens Dutt, Rodney Linvingstone and Christopher Upward. New York: International Publishers. 99–197 [Orig. 1852].

McCarthy, Thomas 1990: 'The Critique of Impure Reason: Foucault and the Frankfurt School'. *Political Theory* 18/3 (August): 437–69.

McNay, Lois 1992: *Foucault and Feminism*. Cambridge: Polity.

McNay, Lois 1994: *Foucault: A Critical Introduction*. Cambridge: Polity.

Megill, Allan 1987: 'The Reception of Foucault by Historians'. *Journal of the History of Ideas* 48: 117–41.

Merquior, José-Guilherme 1985: *Foucault*. London: Fontana.

Meuret, Denis 1988: 'A Political Genealogy of Political Economy'. *Economy & Society* 17/2 (May): 225–50.

Miller, Jacques-Alain 1992: 'Michel Foucault and Psychoanalysis'. *Michel Foucault, Philosopher*. Trans. Timothy J. Armstrong. Hemel Hempstead: Harvester Wheatsheaf. 58–63 [Orig. 1989].

Miller, James 1993: *The Passion of Michel Foucault*. New York: Simon and Schuster.

Miller, Peter 1987: *Domination and Power*. London and New York: Routledge.

Miller, Peter and Nikolas Rose 1990: 'Governing Economic Life'. *Economy & Society* 19/1 (February): 1–31.

Minston, Jeff 1980: 'Strategies for Socialists? Foucault's Conception of Power'. *Economy & Society* 9/1 (February): 1–43.

Montag, Warren 1995: '"The Soul Is the Prison of the Body": Althusser and Foucault, 1970–1975'. *Yale French Studies. Depositions: Althusser, Balibar, Macherey, and the Labour of Reading* (88): 53–77.

Moore Jr., Robert 1993: 'Law, Normativity, and the Level Playing Field: The Production of Rights in American Labor Law'. *Foucault and the Critique of Institutions*. Ed. John Caputo and Mark Yount. University Park: Penn State Press. 165–89.

Münster, Arno 1987: 'Zur Kritik des strukturalistischen Ansatzes in den Humanwissenschaften am Beispiel von Michel Foucaults "Archäologie des Wissens"'. *Pariser philosophisches Journal: Von Sartre bis Derrida*. Frankfurt a.M.: Athenäum. 18–42.

Napoli, Paolo 1993: 'Michel Foucault et les passions de l'histoire'. *Futur antérieur* (18): 37–49.

Neuenhaus, Petra 1993: *Max Weber und Michel Foucault: Über Macht und Herrschaft in der Moderne*. Pfaffenweiler: Centaurus.

Neumann, Franz 1986a: 'Angst und Politik'. *Demokratischer und autoritärer Staat*. Ed. Herbert Marcuse. Frankfurt a.M.: Fischer. 261–91 [Orig. 1954].

Neumann, Franz 1986b: 'Der Funktionswandel des Gesetzes im Recht der bürgerlichen Gesellschaft'. *Demokratischer und autoritärer Staat*. Ed. Herbert Marcuse. Frankfurt a.M.: Fischer. 31–81 [Orig. 1937].

Neumann, Norbert 1988: 'Der Diskurs der Regierung: Michel Foucaults Begriff der "gouvernementalité"'. *kultuRRevolution* 17/18: 64–70.

Nietzsche, Friedrich 2003: 'Notebook 10, autumn 1887'. *Writings from the Late Notebooks*. Trans. Kate Sturge. Cambridge: Cambridge University

Press. 172–206 [Orig. 1887].

Nietzsche, Friedrich 2005: 'Twilight of the Idols, or How to Philosophize with a Hammer'. *The Anti-Christ, Ecce Homo, Twilight of the Idols: And Other Writings*. Trans. Judith Norman. Cambridge: Cambridge University Press. 153–230 [Orig. 1889].

Nikolinakos, Derek D. 1990: 'Foucault's Ethical Quandary'. *Telos* 83: 123–40.

Oestreich, Gerhard 1969: *Geist und Gestalt des frühmodernen Staates*. Berlin: Duncker and Humblot.

O'Farrell, Clare 1989: *Foucault: Historian or Philosopher?* London: Macmillan.

Olivier, Lawrence 1996: 'Michel Foucault, éthique et politique'. *Politique et Sociétés* 15/29 (Spring): 41–69.

Olivier, Lawrence and Sylvain Labbé 1991: 'Foucault et l'Iran: A propos du désir de révolution'. *Canadian Journal of Political Science* (24/2): 219–34.

O'Malley, Pat 1996: 'Risk and Responsibility'. *Foucault and Political Reason*. Ed. Andrew Barry, Thomas Osborne and Nikolas Rose. London: UCL Press. 189–207.

Ortega, Francisco Guerrero 1995: *Freie Formen von Sozietät als Problem einer Ethik der ästhetischen Selbstkonstitution in Foucaults historischer Anthropologie des Subjekts*. Dissertation. Bielefeld.

Palmer, Jerry and Frank Pearce 1983: 'Legal Discourse and State Power: Foucault and the Juridical Relation'. *International Journal of the Sociology of Law* 11: 361–83.

Pasquino, Pasquale 1986a: 'La problématique du "gouvernement" et de la "véridiction"'. *actes: les cahiers d'action juridique* 54 (Summer): 16–21.

Pasquino, Pasquale 1986b: 'Michel Foucault (1926–84): The Will to Knowledge'. *Economy and Society* 15/1: 97–109.

Pasquino, Pasquale 1991a: 'Criminology: The Birth of a Special Knowledge'. *The Foucault Effect: Studies in Governmentality*. Ed. Graham Burchell, Colin Gordon and Peter Miller. Hemel Hempstead: Harvester Wheatsheaf. 235–50 [Orig. 1979].

Pasquino, Pasquale 1991b: 'Theatrum Politicum: The Genealogy of Capital – Police and the State of Prosperity'. *The Foucault Effect: Studies in Governmentality*. Ed. Graham Burchell, Colin Gordon and Peter Miller. Hemel Hempstead: Harvester Wheatsheaf. 105–18 [Orig. 1978].

Pasquino, Pasquale 1993: 'Political Theory of War and Peace: Foucault and the History of Modern Political Theory'. *Economy & Society* 22/1: 77–88.

Pêcheux, Michel 1983: 'Ideology: Fortress or Paradoxical Space'. *Rethinking Ideology: A Marxist Debate*. Ed. Sakari Hänninen. Berlin: Argument. 31–5.

Pêcheux, Michel 2014: 'Dare to Think and Dare to Rebel! Ideology, Marxism,

Resistance, Class Struggle'. *Décalages* 1/4: 1–27 [Orig. 1984].

Perrot, Michelle (ed.) 1980: *L'Impossible Prison: Recherches sur le système pénitentiaire au XIXéme siècle*. Paris: Seuil.

Perrot, Michelle 1986: 'La leçon des ténèbres: Michel Foucault et la prison'. *actes: les cahiers d'action juridique* 54 (Summer): 74–9.

Petersen, Alan and Robin Bunton (ed.) 1997: *Foucault, Health and Medicine*. London and New York: Routledge.

Phelan, Shane 1990: 'Foucault and Feminism'. *American Journal of Political Science* 34/2 (May): 421–40.

Pizzorno, Alessandro 1992: 'Foucault and the Liberal View of the Individual'. *Michel Foucault, Philosopher*. Trans. Timothy J. Armstrong. Hemel Hempstead: Harvester Wheatsheaf. 204–11 [Orig. 1989].

Plumpe, Gerhard 1986: 'Postmoderne Lebenskunst'. *kultuRRevolution* 13: 13–15.

Plumpe, Gerhard and Clemens Kammler 1980: 'Wissen ist Macht'. *Philosophische Rundschau* 27: 185–218.

Polanyi, Karl 2001: *The Great Transformation: The Political and Economic Origins of Our Time*. Boston: Beacon [Orig. 1944].

Poster, Mark 1984: *Foucault, Marxism and History*. Oxford: Polity.

Poulantzas, Nicos 2000: *State, Power, Socialism*. Trans. Patrick Camiller. London: Verso [Orig. 1977].

Privitera, Walter 1990: *Stilprobleme: Zur Epistemologie Michel Foucaults*. Frankfurt a.M.: Anton Hain.

Procacci, Giovanna 1987: 'Notes on the Government of the Social'. *History of the Present* 3: 5, 12–15.

Procacci, Giovanna 1991: 'Social Economy and the Government of Poverty'. *The Foucault Effect: Studies in Governmentality*. Ed. Graham Burchell, Colin Gordon and Peter Miller. Hemel Hempstead: Harvester Wheatsheaf. 151–68 [Orig. 1978].

Procacci, Giovanna 1993: *Gouverner la misère: La question sociale en France 1789–1848*. Paris: Seuil.

Procacci, Giovanna 1994: 'Governing Poverty: Sources of the Social Question in Nineteenth-Century France'. *Foucault and the Writing of History*. Ed. Jan Goldstein. Oxford: Basil Blackwell. 206–19.

Rajchman, John 1985: *Michel Foucault: The Freedom of Philosophy*. New York: Columbia University Press.

Rajchman, John 1992: 'Foucault: The Ethic and the Work'. *Michel Foucault, Philosopher*. Trans. Timothy J. Armstrong. Hemel Hempstead: Harvester Wheatsheaf. 215–23 [Orig. 1989].

Raulff, Ulrich 1977: *Das normale Leben: Michel Foucaults Theorie der Normalisierungsmacht*. Dissertation. Marburg.

Reid, Roddey 1994: 'Foucault en Amérique: biographème et kulturkampf'.

*Futur antérieur* 23–4: 133–65.

Revel, Judith 1992: 'Scolies de Michel Foucault: de la transgression littéraire à la pratique politique'. *Futur antérieur* 14: 75–91.

Rippel, Philipp and Herfried Münkler 1982: 'Der Diskurs und die Macht: Zur Nietzsche-Rezeption des Poststrukturalismus – Foucault, Lévy, Glucksmann'. *Politische Vierteljahresschrift* 23: 115–38.

Rochlitz, Rainer 1992: 'The Aesthetics of Existence: Post-Conventional Morality and the Theory of Power in Michel Foucault'. *Michel Foucault, Philosopher*. Trans. Timothy J. Armstrong. Hemel Hempstead: Harvester Wheatsheaf. 248–58 [Orig. 1989].

Rose, Nikolas 1993: 'Government, Authority and Expertise in Advanced Liberalism'. *Economy & Society* 22/3: 283–99.

Rose, Nikolas 1996: 'Governing "Advanced" Liberal Democracies'. *Foucault and Political Reason*. Ed. Andrew Barry, Thomas Osborne and Nikolas Rose. London: UCL Press. 37–64.

Rose, Nikolas and Peter Miller 1992: 'Political Power beyond the State: Problematics of Government'. *British Journal of Sociology* 43/2 (June): 173–205.

Roth, Michael S. 1988: 'Review Essay of Recent Literature on Foucault'. *History and Theory* (1987): 70–80.

Rouse, Joseph 1994: 'Power/Knowledge'. *The Cambridge Companion to Foucault*. Ed. Gary Gutting. Cambridge: Cambridge University Press. 92–114.

Rüb, Matthias 1988: 'Von der Macht zur Lebenskunst: Foucaults letzte Werke und ihre Interpretation in der Sekundärliteratur'. *Leviathan* 1: 97–107.

Rusche, Georg and Otto Kirchheimer 1939: *Punishment and Social Structure*. New York: Columbia University Press.

Sartre, Jean-Paul 1966: 'Jean-Paul Sartre répond'. (Conversation with B. Pingaud.) *L'Arc* 30: 87–97.

Sawicki, Jana 1991: *Disciplining Foucault: Feminism, Power, and the Body*. London and New York: Routledge.

Sawicki, Jana 1997: 'Le féminisme et Foucault en Amérique du Nord: convergence, critique, possibilité'. *Au risque de Foucault*. Ed. Dominique Franche, Sabine Prokhoris and Yves Roussel. Paris: Éditions du Centre Pompidou. 87–93.

Schäfer, Thomas 1990: 'Aufklärung und Kritik: Foucaults Geschichte des Denkens als Alternative zur "Dialektik der Aufklärung"'. *Ethos der Moderne: Foucaults Kritik der Aufklärung*. Ed. Eva Erdmann, Rainer Forst and Axel Honneth. Frankfurt a.M.: Campus. 70–86.

Schäfer, Thomas 1995: *Reflektierte Vernunft: Michel Foucaults philosophisches Projekt einer antitotalitären Macht- und Wahrheitskritik*. Frankfurt a.M.: Suhrkamp.

Schenkel, Lambert and Simon Joosten de Vries 1989: *Umleitung oder: Wie heißt Bruno mit Nachnamen? Marginalien zu Althusser-Deleuze-Foucault.* Giessen: Germinal.

Schlesier, Renate 1984: 'Humaniora: Eine Kolumne'. *Merkur* 38/7 (October): 817–23.

Schmid, Wilhelm 1991: *Auf der Suche nach einer neuen Lebenskunst: die Frage nach dem Grund der Ethik bei Foucault.* Frankfurt a.M.: Suhrkamp.

Schmidt, Alfred 1969: 'Der strukturalistische Angriff auf die Geschichte'. *Beiträge zur marxistischen Erkenntnistheorie.* Frankfurt a.M.: Suhrkamp. 194–265.

Schmidt, Alfred 1971: *Geschichte und Struktur: Fragen einer marxistischen Historik.* Munich: Hanser.

Schneider, Ulrich Johannes 1988: 'Eine Philosophie der Kritik: Zur amerikanischen und deutschen Rezeption Michel Foucaults'. *Zeitschrift für philosophische Forschung* 42/2: 311–17.

Schneider, Ulrich Johannes 1991: 'Foucault in Deutschland: Ein Literaturbericht'. *Allgemeine Zeitschrift für Philosophie* 16/3: 71–86.

Schoch, Bruno 1980: *Marxismus in Frankreich seit 1945.* Frankfurt a.M.: Campus.

Schöttler, Peter 1988a: 'Mentalitäten, Ideologien, Diskurse: Zur sozialgeschichtlichen Thematisierung der "dritten Ebene"'. *Alltagsgeschichten: Diskussionen und Perspektiven.* Ed. Alf Lüdtke. Frankfurt a.M.: Campus. 85–136.

Schöttler, Peter 1988b: 'Sozialgeschichtliches Paradigma und historische Diskursanalyse'. *Diskurstheorien und Literaturwissenschaft.* Ed. Jürgen Fohrmann and Harro Müller. Frankfurt a.M.: Suhrkamp. 159–99.

Séglard, Dominique 1992: 'Foucault et le problème du gouvernement'. *La raison d'Etat.* Ed. Christian Lazzeri and Dominique Reynié. Paris: PUF. 117–40.

Seibert, Thomas 1995: 'Das Subjekt der Revolten: Michel Foucaults Ästhetik der Existenz'. *Die Beute* 4: 19–31.

Senellart, Michel 1993: 'Michel Foucault: "gouvernementalité" et raison d'Etat'. *Penseé Politique* 1 (May): 276–303.

Senellart, Michel 1995: *Les arts de gouverner: Du regimen médiéval au concept de gouvernement.* Paris: Seuil.

Senellart, Michel 2007: 'Course Context'. *Michel Foucault, Security, Territory, Population: Lectures at the Collège de France, 1977–1978.* Trans. Graham Burchell. Basingstoke: Palgrave Macmillan. 369–401.

Simon, Jonathan 1986: 'Foucault in America'. *actes: les cahiers d'actions juridique* 54 (Summer): 24–9.

Sintomer, Yves 1995: 'Zwischen Ruhm und Mumifizierung: Die französische Foucault-Rezeption'. *Tüte: Wissen und Macht. Die Krise des Regierens*. Tübingen. 2–4.

Smart, Barry 1983: *Foucault, Marxism and Critique*. London and New York: Routledge.

Smart, Barry 1986: 'The Politics of Truth'. *Foucault: A Critical Reader*. Ed. David C. Hoy. Oxford: Basil Blackwell. 157–73.

Smart, Barry 1991: 'On the Subjects of Sexuality, Ethics, and Politics in the Work of Foucault'. *Boundary Two* 18/1: 201–25.

Stauth, Georg 1991: 'Revolution in Spiritless Times: An Essay on M. Foucault's Inquiries into the Iranian Revolution'. *International Sociology* 6/3: 259–80.

Stoler, Ann L. 1995: *Race and the Education of Desire*. Durham, NC and London: Duke University Press.

Stolleis, Michael (ed.) 1996: *Policy im Europa der Frühen Neuzeit*. Frankfurt a.M.: Vittorio Klostermann.

Szakolczai, Arpád 1993: 'From Governmentality to the Genealogy of Subjectivity: On Foucault's Path in the 1980s'. *European University Institute Paper* 93/94.

Taylor, Charles 1985: 'Connolly, Foucault, and Truth'. *Political Theory* 13/3 (August): 377–85.

Taylor, Charles 1986: 'Foucault on Freedom and Truth'. *Foucault: A Critical Reader*. Ed. David C. Hoy. Oxford: Basil Blackwell. 69–102.

Tocqueville, Alexis de 2004: *Democracy in America*. Trans. Arthur Goldhammer. New York: Library of America [Orig. 1835/40].

Treusch-Dieter, Gerburg 1985: '"Cherchez la femme" bei Foucault'. *Anschlüsse: Versuche nach Foucault*. Ed. Gesa Dane. Tübingen: Diskord. 80–94.

Tribe, Kenneth 1984: 'Cameralism and the Science of Government'. *The Journal of Modern History* 56/2: 263–84.

Tsiros, Nikolaos 1993: *Die politische Theorie der Postmoderne*. Frankfurt a.M.: Peter Lang.

Tulkens, Françoise 1986: 'Généalogie de la défense sociale en Belgique (1880–1914)'. *actes: les cahiers d'action juridique* 54 (Summer): 38–41.

Tulkens, Françoise (ed.) 1988: *Généalogie de la défense sociale en Belgique (1880–1914)*. Brussels: E. Story-Scientia.

Turkel, Gerald 1990: 'Michel Foucault: Law, Power, and Knowledge'. *Journal of Law and Society* 17/2 (Summer): 170–93.

Turner, Bryan S. 1987: 'The Rationalization of the Body: Reflexions on Modernity and Discipline'. *Max Weber, Rationality and Modernity*. Ed. Scott Lash and Sam Whimster. London: Allen and Unwin. 222–41.

Vegetti, Mario 1986: 'Foucault et les anciens'. *Critique* 471/472 (August/

September): 925–32.

Veyne, Paul 1977: 'L'idéologie selon Marx et selon Nietzsche'. *Diogène* 99 (July/September): 93–115.

Veyne, Paul 1983: 'Comment on écrit Rome'. *Magazine littéraire* 199 (October): 84–9.

Veyne, Paul 1984: 'La Planète Foucault'. *Le Nouvel Observateur* (22 June): 44–6.

Veyne, Paul 1992: 'Foucault and Going Beyond (or the Fulfillment of) Nihilism'. *Michel Foucault, Philosopher*. Trans. Timothy J. Armstrong. Hemel Hempstead: Harvester Wheatsheaf. 320–43 [Orig. 1989].

Veyne, Paul 1993: 'The Final Foucault and His Ethics'. *Critical Inquiry* 20/1 (Autumn): 1–9 [Orig. 1986].

Veyne, Paul 1997: 'Foucault Revolutionizes History'. *Foucault and His Interlocutors*. Ed. Arnold Al Davidson, Trans. Catherine Porter. Chicago: University of Chicago Press. 146–82 [Orig. 1978].

Visker, Rudi 1991: *Michel Foucault: Genealogie als Kritik*. Munich: Fink.

Walzer, Michael 1986: 'The Politics of Michel Foucault'. *Foucault: A Critical Reader*. Ed. David C. Hoy. Oxford: Basil Blackwell. 51–68.

Walzer, Michael 1988: *The Company of Critics: Social Criticism and Political Commitment in the Twentieth Century*. New York: Basic Books.

Weber, Max 2002: *The Protestant Ethic and the 'Spirit' of Capitalism: And Other Writings*. Trans. Talcott Parsons. New York: Penguin [Orig. 1920].

Wickham, Gary 1983: 'Power and Power Analysis: Beyond Foucault?' *Economy & Society* 12/4 (November): 468–98.

Wolin, Richard 1986: 'Foucault's Aesthetic Decisionism'. *Telos* 67: 71–86.

Žižek, Slavoj 1988: 'The Subject before Subjectivation'. *Vestnik* 9: 85–96.

# Index

economic growth, 251n16, 258, 260
economic inequality, 200, 201, 209
economics, as conduct in marriage
and the household, 291–2
economic sovereignty, 172, 180, 181
economy
household economy, 172
market economy, 246, 247, 248,
252
political economy. *See* political
economy
power of and economy of power,
70–2
social economy and paternalism,
211–15
the economic, the social as form of,
252–6
Elias, Norbert, 185n65
enlightenment, 365–6, 365n5, 367–71,
379, 383–4
entrepreneurship, 250, 251, 252
*Entstehung* (emergence), 50n3
epidemics, handling of, 192–3
*episteme*, 92–93n19
epistemological interest
(*Erkenntnisinteresse*), 62
epistemological sovereignty, 93n24
epistemology
archaeology as differing from, 35
French epistemology, 35
political epistemology of Foucault,
6
equality, 73, 200, 201, 202, 203, 209,
210, 212, 214, 217, 257, 299, 367
Eribon, Didier, 270n15, 330n60
erotics, as love for boys, 291, 292–4
*Essay on the History of Civil Society*
(Ferguson), 185
ethics
Christian, pastoral ethics, 287
as conduct, 315–316n25
Foucault's conception of, 280, 308,
315
Foucault's interest in, 266–267n8
and freedom, 324
genealogy of, 282
Greek ethics, 290, 313n20

Hellenistic-Roman ethics, 295–300
morality and, 278–83
morality and ethics in Christianity,
300–6
politics as, 328
Eucken, Walter, 246
Ewald, François, xi, 199–200n2, 203,
203n9, 204, 205, 207–208n18, 213,
213n28, 217, 220, 221, 221n41, 222,
227
experience
subjectivity and, 274–8
use of term, 274–5
experience books (*livre-expérience*),
359
exploitation, 52, 71

**F**
family, crisis of, 241n88
Ferguson, Adam, 185–7
Ferri, Enrico, 234–235n73
Ferry, Luc, 268n9
Feuerbach, Anselm, 234–235n73
fiction, and construction, 358–62
formal equality, 73, 209, 210
Forst, Rainer, 271n18
Foucault, Michel
as aware of paradoxes, 14
contradictory and mutually
incompatible assessments of
works of, 3
disquieting contradiction in works
of, 11
early works of, 32n8
Habermas's misinterpretations of
work of, 9–10n25
as homosexual, 384
intellectual crisis of, 127–128n1
Nietzschean orientation of, 6
paradoxical nature of work of, 5
polarizing effect of, 1
political consequences and
ambivalence of work of, 3n1
political epistemology of, 6
politics of, 2, 14, 17–18n54
as rejecting discipline in every
form, 7

132–133n17
thesis of production, 130–131n10
thesis of the invisible hand (Smith),
    180
Third Estate, 210n23
Thirty Years War, 167n32, 171
Thompson, E. P., 38–39n28
torture, fight against, 81n74
*Treatise of Human Nature* (Hume),
    183
Treaty of Westphalia, 167n32
truth
    game of, 347, 347n19, 348, 349–50
    history of, 346–52, 354, 360, 371
    politics of, xi, 23, 342–6, 345–
        346n13, 365, 381
    problem of, 341–62
Tsiros, Nikolaos, 117n29
Turner, Bryan S., 315–316n25

**U**
unholy subjectivism, 309–15
universal suffrage, 210n23
university, 53n13
*The Use of Pleasure* (Foucault), 266,
    268, 278, 284, 288, 307, 310, 312
utterance (*énoncé*), 41, 44

**V**
Veyne, Paul, 351n26
Vidal-Naquet, Pierre, 58
Vietnam War, 56
vital politics (*Vitalpolitik*), 251, 252

**W**
Walzer, Michael, 6–7
war
    as politics pursued by other means,
        103–4
    Thirty Years War, 167n32, 171
warfare, 167n32
war hypothesis, 124, 133–5, 143
war paradigm, biopower and, 141–5
*Was ist Aufklärung?*(Kant), 365
*The Wealth of Nations* (Smith), 181
Weber, Max, 247, 251n16, 298n35,
    307, 315–316n25, 368

welfare, 202
welfare state, 25, 167–168n33, 168,
    200, 243n1, 244, 258, 259
wellness, duty of, 259–260n30
Wickham, Gary, 121–122n51
Williams, Raymond, 38–39n28
will of all (*volonté de tous*), 72, 334
*The Will to Knowledge* (Foucault),
    112n8, 130n8, 132–133n17, 137n31,
    164n23, 265, 278, 284, 305n51, 355,
    382
will to revolution, 338n79
will to truth, 22, 45n60, 385
women, equal rights for, 54
work, and poverty, 207–11

**Y**
Yoshimoto, Rumei, 124n62